COMMENTARIES

ON THE

CONFLICT OF LAWS,

FOREIGN AND DOMESTIC,

IN REGARD TO

CONTRACTS, RIGHTS, AND REMEDIES,

AND ESPECIALLY IN REGARD TO

MARRIAGES, DIVORCES, WILLS, SUCCESSIONS, AND JUDGMENTS.

BY

JOSEPH STORY, LL.D.

EIGHTH EDITION.

BY

MELVILLE M. BIGELOW.

BOSTON:

LITTLE, BROWN, AND COMPANY.

1883.

PREFACE TO THIS EDITION.

THE text and notes of the author, as they stood in the third edition of the present work, which edition contained the last revisions and emendations made by him, are in the present edition restored in their integrity by the removal of all matter interpolated since the author's death.

The notes and additions to the text made since that time have been used as materials for the double-column notes of this edition. In a few cases the notes of former editors stand as they appeared in the seventh edition; but most of the notes now appearing in double columns are new. The author's notes run across the page.

The notes, other than the author's, from the beginning of the work to the end of Chapter V., at page 226, and those at the end of section 473 a (page 650), and of section 514 b (page 731), were written by Mr. J. L. Thorndike, of the Boston Bar.

The editor's thanks are due to Mr. George J. Tufts for valuable assistance throughout the work.

MELVILLE M. BIGELOW.

Boston, May 1, 1883.

ADVERTISEMENT TO THE SECOND EDITION.

THE former edition of this work being exhausted, I have availed myself, in the preparation of the present edition, of the opportunity of revising, correcting, and amending the text and notes throughout, and of adding such new materials as have been furnished by the recent authorities at the common law, as well as by more diligent researches into foreign jurisprudence. For the opinions of some foreign jurists, I was obliged, in the former edition (as the reader was informed in the notes) to rely upon the citations from their works which I found in other authors, not having access to the originals. With one or two unimportant exceptions, the originals of these foreign jurists are now in my possession, and have been consulted by me; so that I have been enabled to correct some errors in those citations, and also to furnish more complete and perfect statements of their respective opinions. Perhaps it may not be useless here to add that, in every case where any authority for any position is cited at the bottom of the page, the reader may rest assured that the very citation has been perused and diligently compared by me with the original.

As the works of foreign jurists, especially of those who lived before the middle of the eighteenth century, are rarely to be found in American libraries, either public or private, and are becoming daily more scarce and difficult to be purchased abroad, I have made my extracts therefrom more copious, and often cited the words of the original, so that the reader might be spared the necessity of further researches into the originals, and also might possess the means of ascertaining the accuracy of the expositions in the text.

These explanations may account for the fact, that the work, unexpectedly to myself, has swelled to double its former size ; a fact which (as the pages and sections of the former edition are still preserved) might not readily occur to those who are not accustomed to examine the signatures at the bottom of the different sheets.

Since the publication of the former edition, Mr. Burge has published his very able and comprehensive Commentaries on Colonial and Foreign Law, mainly as applicable to the colonies of Great Britain, in which he has devoted a number of chapters to the consideration of many of the topics embraced in the present work. The plan of his work, however, essentially differs from my own in its leading objects. It exhibits great learning and research ; and, as its merits are not as yet generally known to the profession on this side of the Atlantic, I have made many references to it, and occasional quotations from it, with the view of enabling the profession to obtain many more illustrations of the doctrines than my own brief text would suggest, and also fully to appreciate his learned labors. Monsieur Foelix, also, the accomplished editor of the Revue Étrangère et Française (a highly useful and meritorious periodical published at Paris), has, in the volume of the year 1840, discussed, in a series of articles, many topics of the Conflict of Laws, and given the opinions of the leading foreign jurists on the subject. I have gladly referred to his very interesting and lucid expositions, that my own countrymen may more readily understand their great value and importance.

It is not probable that, in the course of my own life, this work will undergo any essential change from its present form. Other avocations and other pressing duties, judicial as well as professorial, will necessarily occupy all the time and attention which I may hereafter be permitted to command for any juridical pursuits. I must, therefore, dismiss these Commentaries to the indulgent consideration of the reader, not as a work which has surveyed the whole subject or exhausted the materials, but as an essay towards opening the leading doctrines and inquiries belonging to private international jurisprudence, which the genius and learning and labors of more gifted minds may hereafter mould and polish and expand into an enduring system of public law. My own wishes will be fully satisfied, if (to use the language of my Lord Coke, in the close of his first Institute) anything shall be found herein, which " may either open some windows of the law to let in more light to the student, by diligent search to see the secrets of the law, or to move him to doubt, and withal to enable him to inquire and learn of the sages, what the law, together with the true reason thereof, in these cases is."

JOSEPH STORY.

January, 1841.

TO THE

HON. JAMES KENT, LL.D.

SIR,

IT affords me very sincere satisfaction to have the opportunity of dedicating this work to you. It belongs to a branch of international jurisprudence which has been long familiar to your studies, and in which you have the honor of having been the guide and instructor of the American youth. I can trace back to your early labors in expounding the civil and the foreign law the motive and encouragement of my own far more limited researches. I wish the present work to be considered as a tribute of respect to a distinguished master from his grateful pupil.

It is now about thirty-six years since you began your judicial career on the bench of the Supreme Court of the State of New York. In the intervening period between that time and the present, you have successively occupied the offices of Chief Justice and of Chancellor of the same State. I speak but the common voice of the profession and the public when I say, that in each of these stations you have brought to its duties a maturity of judgment, a depth of learning, a fidelity of purpose, and an enthusiasm for justice, which have laid the solid foundations of an imperishable fame. In the full vigor of your intellectual powers, you left the bench only to engage in a new task, which of itself seemed to demand by its extent and magnitude a whole life of strenuous diligence. That task has been accomplished. The Commentaries on American Law have already acquired the reputation of a juridical classic, and have placed their author in the first rank of the benefactors of the profession. You have done for America what Mr. Justice Blackstone in his invaluable Commentaries has done for England. You have embodied the principles of our law in pages as attractive by the persuasive elegance of their style as they are instructive by the fulness and accuracy of their learning.

You have earned the fairest title to the repose which you now seek, and which at last seems within your reach. It is in the noblest sense, *Otium cum dignitate.* May you live many years to enjoy it! The consciousness of a life like yours, in which have been blended at every step public spirit and private virtue, the affections which cheer and the taste which adorns the domestic circle, cannot but make the recollections of the past sweet, and the hopes of the future animating.

I am, with the highest respect,

Your obliged friend,

JOSEPH STORY.

CAMBRIDGE, MASSACHUSETTS,
    January 1, 1834.

PREFACE.

I NOW submit to the indulgent consideration of the profession and the public another portion of the labors appertaining to the Dane Professorship of Law in Harvard University. The subject is one of great importance and interest; and from the increasing intercourse between foreign States as well as between the different States of the American Union, it is daily brought home more and more to the ordinary business and pursuits of human life. The difficulty of treating such a subject in a manner suited to its importance and interest can scarcely be exaggerated. The materials are loose and scattered, and are to be gathered from many sources, not only uninviting but absolutely repulsive to the mere student of the common law. There exists no treatise upon it in the English language; and not the slightest effort has been made, except by Mr. Chancellor Kent, to arrange in any general order even the more familiar maxims of the common law in regard to it. Until a comparatively recent period, neither the English lawyers nor the English judges seem to have had their attention drawn towards it as a great branch of international jurisprudence, which they were required to administer. And as far as their researches appear as yet to have gone, they are less profound and satisfactory than their admirable expositions of municipal law.

The subject has been discussed with much more fulness, learning, and ability by the foreign jurists of continental Europe. But even among them there exists no systematical treatise embracing all the general topics. For the most part, they have discussed it only with reference to some few branches of jurisprudence, peculiar to the civil law, or to the customary law (almost infinitely varied) of the neighboring States of Europe or the different prov-

inces of the same empire. And it must be confessed that their
writings are often of so controversial a character, and abound
with so many nice distinctions (not very intelligible to jurists of
the school of the common law), and with so many theories of
doubtful utility, that it is not always easy to extract from them
such principles as may afford safe guides to the judgment. Rodenburg, Boullenois, Bouhier, and Froland have written upon it
with the most clearness, comprehensiveness, and acuteness. But
they rather stimulate than satisfy inquiry ; and they are far more
elaborate in detecting the errors of others than in widening and
deepening the foundations of the practical doctrines of international jurisprudence. I am not aware that the works of these
eminent jurists have been cited at the English bar ; and I should
draw the conclusion that they are in a great measure, if not
altogether, unknown to the studies of Westminster Hall. How
it should happen that, in this age, English lawyers should be so
utterly indifferent to all foreign jurisprudence, it is not easy to
conceive. Many occasions are constantly occurring in which they
would derive essential assistance from it to illustrate the questions which are brought into contestation in all their courts.

In consulting the foreign jurists, I have felt great embarrassment, as well from my own imperfect knowledge of the jurisprudence which they profess to discuss, as from the remote analogies
which it sometimes bears to the rights, titles, and remedies recognized in the common law. To give their opinions at large upon
many topics would fill volumes ; to omit all statements whatever
of their opinions would be to withhold from the reader many
most important lights to guide his own studies and instruct his
own judgment. I have adopted an intermediate course, and have
laid before the reader such portions of the opinions and reasonings of foreign jurists as seemed to me most useful to enable him
to understand their doctrines and principles, and to assist him
with the means of making more ample researches if his leisure or
his curiosity should invite him to the pursuit. Humble as this
task may appear to many minds, it has been attended with a labor
truly discouraging and exhausting. I dare not even now indulge

the belief that my success has been at all proportionate to my wishes or my efforts. I feel, however, cheered by the reflection (is it a vain illusion ?) that other minds of more ability, leisure, and learning, may be excited to explore the paths which I have ventured only to point out. I beg, in conclusion, to address to the candor of the profession my own apology in the language of Strykius : " Crescit disputatio nostra sub manibus; unum enim si absolveris jus, plura se offerunt consideranda. At nos temporis, quod nimis breve nobis fit, rationem habentes, accuratius illa inquirere haud possumus. Hinc sufficerit, in præsens sparsisse quædam saltem adhuc jura, quidque de iis statuamus, vel obiter dixisse." [1]

JOSEPH STORY.

CAMBRIDGE, MASSACHUSETTS,
   January 1, 1834.

[1] Strykii, Disputatio 1, ch. 2, § 92, Tom. ii. p. 24.

LIST OF AUTHORS CITED.

Thε following list of some of the more important authors, whose works have been cited, may assist the student in his researches :—

D'Aguesseau, Henry Francis, Chancellor of France, born at Limoges, 1668, and died 1751. His works are collected and published in 13 vols. 4to.

Alexander ab Alexandro, a Neapolitan lawyer, born 1461, and died at Rome about the age of 62.

D'Argentre, Bertrand, President of the *Presidial* of Rennes, born in 1519, and died in 1590. His works are entitled "Commentarii in Patrias Britonum Leges, seu Consuetudines generales Ducatus Britanniæ."

Baldus, Ubaldus, born about 1324, died 1400. His works are comprised in 4 vols. folio.

[Bar on "International Law." Boston, 1883.]

Bartolo, or Bartholus, born at Sasse Ferrato, in the March of Ancona, 1313, and died in his 46th year. He was called "the star and luminary of lawyers, the master of truth, the lantern of equity, the guide of the blind," &c. His works were printed at Venice, 1499, in 4 vols. fol., according to Camus, in 1599, in 10 or 11 vols. fol., according to Watt.

Bouhier, J., President of the Parliament of Dijon, born at that place, 1673, and died 1746. His works, relating to the present subject, are published in 2 vols fol., and entitled, "Les Coutumes du Duché de Bourgogne avec les Observations du Président Bouhier."

Boullenois, Louis, advocate in the Parliament of Paris, born at Paris, 1680, and died 1762. There are two works by him on the present subject: "Traité et de la Personalité et de la Réalité des Loix, Coutumes, Statuts, par forme d'Observations," in two vols. 4to, and "Dissertations sur des Questions, qui naissent de la Contrariété des Loix et des Coutumes," 4to. This last was published first, and is the original outline of the larger work which afterwards appeared.

Bretonnier, Bartholomew Joseph, advocate of the Parliament of Paris, born at Montrotier, near Lyons, 1656, and died 1727. He is the author of a work in 2 vols. 12mo, entitled "Recueil des principales Questions de Droit qui se jugent diversement dans les différens Tribunaux du Royaume, avec des Réflexions pour concilier la Diversité de la Jurisprudence." He also edited the works of Henrys.

Burge, William, "Commentaries on Colonial and Foreign Laws generally and in their conflict with each other." 4 vols. 8vo. London, 1838.

Burgundus, Burgundius, or Bourgoigne, Nicolaus, jurisconsult, born at Enghien in Hainault, 1586. He is the author of a work entitled "Tractatus Controversiarum ad Consuetudinem Flandriæ."

Bynkershoek, Cornelius van, born at Middlebourg, 1673, and died 1737. His works are well known.

Casaregis, Joseph Laurentius de, born at Genoa, 1670, and died 1737. His works are entitled, "Discursus legales de Commercio," and are published in 2, 3, and 4 vols. folio.

CHRISTINÆUS, PAULUS, born at Malines, 1533, and died 1638. His works are, " Practicarum Quæstionum Rerumque in Supremis Belgarum Curiis actarum et observationum Decisiones ; " and " Commentarii in Leges Municipales Mechlinienses."

COCHIN, HENRY, advocate in Parliament, born at Paris, 1687, and died 1747. His works are collected in 6 vols. 4to.

COQUILLE, GUI. advocate of the Parliament of Paris, born at Decize in Nivernois, 1523, and died 1603. There is a work by him, " Des Coutumes des Nivernois."

CUJAS, JAMES, born at Toulouse, 1520, and died 1590. His voluminous works need not be particularly mentioned.

DENISART, J. B., jurisconsult, born 1712, and died 1765. He published " Collections de Décisions nouvelles relatives à la Jurisprudence."

[DICEY on " Domicil." London, 1879.]

DOMAT, JOHN, born at Clermont in Auvergne, 1625, and died 1696. His " Civil Law " in its natural order is well known through the translation of Dr. Strahan.

DUMOULIN (in Latin MOLINÆUS), CHARLES, born 1500, and died 1560. What he has written upon the present subject is to be found in his Commentary on the first book of the Code, verb. Conclusiones de Statutis, in his 53d Consilium, and in his notes on Alexander, Decius, and Chasseneuz.

DURANTON, A., Professor of Law at Paris. His works are, " Cours de Droit Français, suivant le Code Civil," in 20 vols. 8vo.

EMERIGON, BALTAZARD MARIE, advocate of the Parliament of Aix, born about 1725, and died 1784. His " Traité des Assurances," 2 vols. 4to, is referred to in the present Commentaries.

ERSKINE, JOHN, Professor of Law at Edinburgh. His principal work is entitled " Institutes of the Laws of Scotland."

EVERHARD, NICHOLAS, born in the island of Walcheren, 1462, and died 1532. His works are " Topica Juris, sive Loci Argumentorum Legales ; " and " Consilia, sive Responsa Juris."

FOELIX, M., editor of the " Revue Étrangère et Française," a learned periodical published at Paris, beginning in 1833 and still (1840) continued.

FROLAND, LOUIS, advocate of the Parliament of Rouen, died 1764. His works relating to the present subject, in two 4to vols., are entitled, " Mémoire concernant la Nature et la Qualité des Statuts."

GAILL, ANDREW, born at Cologne, 1525, and died 1587. He was called the Papinian of Germany.

GROTIUS, HUGO, born at Delft, 1583, and died 1645. His works are well known.

HEINECCIUS, JOHANNES GOTLEIB, Professor of Philosophy and Law at Halle, born at Eisenburg, 1681, and died 1741. His works need not be particularly mentioned.

HENRYS, CLAUDE, jurisconsult, born at Monthrison, 1615, and died 1662. His works are collected in 4 vols. folio.

HERTIUS, JOHANNES NICOLAUS, born near Giessen, 1651, and died 1710. His treatise " De Collisione Legum " is to be found in his select works in 2 vols. 4to.

HUBERUS ULRICUS, a lawyer, historian, and philologer, born at Dockum in the Dutch territories, 1635, and died 1694. His treatise " De Conflictu Legum " is to be found in his " Prælectiones Juris Civilis," 3 vols. 4to.

KAMES, LORD (HENRY HOME), born at Kames, in Berwickshire, 1696, and died 1782. The reader is referred to his " Principles of Equity."

LE BRUN, DENIS, advocate, died 1708, before the publication of his principal work, " Traité de Communautés."

LEEUWEN, SIMON VAN, born at Leyden, 1625, and died 1682. His work referred to, in the present Commentaries, is translated into English, with the title of " Commentaries on the Roman-Dutch Law."

[LINDLEY on " Partnership," 4th ed. London, 1878.]

LIVERMORE, SAMUEL, of New Orleans, died 1833. He is the author of " Dissertations on the Contrariety of Laws."

MASCARDUS, JOSEPHUS, an ecclesiastic and Italian jurisconsult, born at Sarzana towards the end of the 16th century, and died about 1630. He is the author of an extensive work, entitled " De Probationibus Conclusiones."

MERLIN, M. (de DOUAL). His voluminous works are entitled, " Répertoire Universel et Raisonné de Jurisprudence ; " and " Questions de Droit."

MORNAC, ANTOINE, born near Tours, first appeared before the Parliament of Paris in 1580, and died 1620. His works are comprised in 4 vols. folio.

PARDESSUS, J. M., " Cours de Droit Commercial," 5 vols. 8vo. Paris, 1831.

PECK, PETER, born at Zirckzee, in Zealand, 1529, and died 1589. His works are collected in 1 vol. folio.

POTHIER, ROBERT JOSEPH, born at Orleans, 1699, and died 1772. His works need not be particularly mentioned.

PUFFENDORF, SAMUEL, born in Upper Saxony, 1632, and died 1694. His works are well known.

RODENBURG was a judge of the Supreme Court of Utrecht, and flourished about the middle of the 17th century. His treatise, " De Jure quod oritur ex Statutorum vel Consuetudinum Diversitate," is to be found at the end of Boullenois's " Traité de la Personalité et de la Réalité des Loix."

[SAVIGNY's Private International Law, Guthrie's transl. Edinburgh, 1869.]

STOCKMANS, PETER, born at Antwerp, 1608, and died 1671. His works are comprised in 1 vol. 4to.

STRYKIUS, SAMUEL, born 1640, and died 1710. His son, JOHN SAMUEL, was born 1668, and died 1715. Their works, with those of RHETIUS, are collected in 14 vols. folio.

VOET, PAUL (the father), born at Heusden, in Brabant, 1619, and died 1677. His work on the present subject is entitled, " De Statutis et eorum Concursu."

VOET, JOHN, son of Paul, born at Utrecht, 1647, and died 1714. His " Commentary on the Pandects," contains a short chapter, " De Statutis."

[WESTLAKE on " Private International Law." London, 1880.

WHARTON, Conflict of Laws. Philadelphia, 1872.]

CONTENTS.

INDEX TO CASES CITED.

COMMENTARIES

ON THE

CONFLICT BETWEEN FOREIGN AND DOMESTIC LAWS.

CHAPTER I.

INTRODUCTORY REMARKS.

1. *Diversity of Laws in different Countries.*—The earth has long since been divided into distinct nations, inhabiting different regions, speaking different languages, engaged in different pursuits, and attached to different forms of government.[1] It is natural that, under such circumstances, there should be many variances in their institutions, customs, laws, and polity, and that these variances should result sometimes from accident, and sometimes from design, sometimes from superior skill and knowledge of local interests, and sometimes from a choice founded in ignorance and supported by the prejudices of imperfect civilization. Climate and geographical position, and the physical adaptations springing from them, must at all times have had a powerful influence in the organization of each society, and have given a peculiar complexion and character to many of its arrangements. The bold, intrepid, and hardy natives of the north of Europe, whether civilized or barbarous, would scarcely desire or tolerate the indolent inactivity and luxurious indulgences of the Asiatics. Nations inhabiting the borders of the ocean, and accustomed to maritime intercourse with other nations, would naturally require institutions and laws adapted to their pursuits and enterprises, which would be wholly unfit for those who should be placed in the interior of a continent, and should main-

[1] Upon the subject of this chapter the learned reader is referred to Burge's Commentaries on Colonial and Foreign Law, vol. 1, pt. 1, c. 1, p. 1–32.

tain very different relations with their neighbors, both in peace and war. Accordingly we find that, from the earliest records of authentic history, there has been (as far at least as we can trace them) little uniformity in the laws, usages, policy, and institutions either of contiguous or of distant nations. The Egyptians, the Medes, the Persians, the Greeks, and the Romans differed not more in their characters and employments from each other, than in their institutions and laws. They had little desire to learn or to borrow from each other; and indifference, if not contempt, was the habitual state of almost every ancient nation in regard to the internal polity of all others.

2. *Intercourse between the ancient Nations.*—Yet even under such circumstances, from their mutual intercourse with each other, questions must sometimes have arisen as to the operation of the laws of one nation upon the rights and remedies of parties in the domestic tribunals, especially when they were in any measure dependent upon, or connected with, foreign transactions. How these questions were disposed of we do not know. But it is most probable that they were left to be decided by the analogies of the municipal code, or were abandoned to their fate, as belonging to that large class of imperfect rights, which rests wholly on personal confidence, and is left without any appeal to remedial justice. It is certain that the nations of antiquity did not recognize the existence of any general or universal rights and obligations, such as among the moderns constitute what is now emphatically called the Law of Nations. Even among the Romans, whose jurisprudence has come down to us in a far more perfect and comprehensive shape than that of any other nation, there cannot be traced out any distinct system of principles applicable to international cases of mixed rights. This has been in some measure accounted for by Huberus [1] upon the supposition that, at the time to which the Roman jurisprudence relates, the Roman dominion extended over so great a portion of the habitable world, that frequent cases of contrariety or conflict of laws could scarcely occur.[2] But this is a very inadequate account of the matter; since the antecedent jurisprudence of

[1] 2 Hub. lib. 1, tit. 3, p. 24.

[2] The language of Huberus is, " In jure Romano non est mirum nihil hac de re extare, cum populi Romani per omnes orbis partes diffusum, et æquabili jure gubernatum imperium, conflictui diversarum legum non æque potuerit esse subjectum." — 2 Hub. lib. 1, tit. 3, s. 1.

Rome must have embraced many such cases at earlier periods; and if there had been any rules, even traditionally known, to govern them, they could scarcely have failed of being incorporated into the Civil Codes of Justinian. In many of the nations over which the Romans extended their dominion, the inhabitants were left in possession of the local institutions, usages, and laws, to a large extent; and commercial as well as political intercourse must have brought many diversities of laws and usages in judgment before the tribunals of justice.[1] We have the most abundant evidence on this head, in relation to the Jews, after they had submitted to the Roman yoke, who were still permitted to follow their own laws in the times of our Saviour, and down to the destruction of Jerusalem.[2]

2 a. *Barbarian Irruption into the Roman Empire.*—When the northern nations by their irruptions finally succeeded in establishing themselves in the Roman Empire, and the dependent nations subjected to its sway, they seem to have adopted, either by design, or from accident or necessity, the policy of allowing the different races to live together, and to be governed by and to preserve their own separate manners, laws, and institutions in their mutual intercourse. While the conquerors, the Goths, Burgundians, Franks, and Lombards, maintained their own laws and usages and customs over their own race, they silently or expressly allowed each of the races over whom they had obtained an absolute sovereignty, to regulate their own private rights and affairs according to their own municipal jurisprudence. It has accordingly been remarked by a most learned and eminent jurist, that from this state of society arose that condition of civil rights denominated personal rights, or personal laws, in opposition to territorial laws.[3]

---

[1] See 1 Hertii Opera, s. 4, de Collis. Leg. p. 119, s. 2; Id. p. 169, ed. 1716.

[2] There are traces to be found in the Digest of the existence and operation of the lex loci. See Dig. 50, 1, 21, 7; Dig. 50, 6, 5, 1; Dig. 50, 4, 18, 27; Dig. 50, 3, 1; Livermore, Dissert. p. 1, n. a.

[3] Savigny's History of the Roman Law in the Middle Ages. The whole passage is exceedingly interesting and curious, and therefore I quote it at large from Mr. Cathcart's translation, vol. 1, c. 3, p. 99–104. — 'When the Goths, Burgundians, Franks, and Lombards founded kingdoms in the countries formerly subject to the power of Rome, there were two different modes of treating the conquered race. They might be extirpated by destroying or enslaving the freemen, or the conquering nations for the sake of increasing their own numbers, might transform the Romans into Germans, by forcing

2 *b*. *Absence of Remedy in case of Conflict of Laws.*—Still however this was but a mere arrangement in the domestic polity of

on them their manners, constitution, and laws. Neither mode however was followed ; for although many Romans were slain, expatriated, or enslaved, this was only the lot of individuals, and not the systematic treatment of the nation. Both races on the contrary lived together and preserved their separate manners and laws. From this state of society arose that condition of civil rights denominated personal rights, or personal laws, in opposition to territorial laws. The moderns always assume that the law to which the individual owes obedience, is that of the country where he lives ; and that the property and contracts of every resident are regulated by the law of his domicil. In this theory the distinction between native and foreigner is overlooked, and national descent is entirely disregarded. Not so however in the Middle Ages, where, in the same country, and often indeed in the same city, the Lombard lived under the Lombardic, and the Roman under the Roman law. The same distinction of laws was also applicable to the different races of Germans. The Frank, Burgundian, and Goth, resided in the same place, each under his own law, as is forcibly stated by the Bishop Agobardus, in an epistle to Louis le Debonnaire. "It often happens," says he, "that five men, each under a different law, may be found walking or sitting together."

' In the East Gothic kingdom alone, this custom was not originally followed. There, an artificial and systematic plan was adopted, which belongs to the particular history of that nation, and cannot be brought within the general inquiry. All the other states followed the system of personal laws; and this universal practice could not have arisen from accidental reasons, but from common views, principles, and wants. These may be appropriately illustrated at present.

' According to the general opinion the system of personal laws prevailed among all the German nations, from the earliest times; and it is customary to explain this circumstance by the love of freedom so peculiar to these races. In the first place however it is difficult to perceive how such an institution could arise merely from regard to liberty. Such an attachment might indeed create a wish among nations or individuals, to preserve their own laws in a foreign country, or under a foreign yoke; but the question is, how were the predominant people induced to grant them this privilege? The benevolent and hospitable disposition of the victorious may have been partly the cause; but their mere love of freedom affords no satisfactory explanation. This humane treatment of foreigners was not deeply seated in the character of the old Germans. It is probable that among them every foreigner was, at first, a Wildfang, and belonged to the class of the Biesterfreien, denied the advantages arising from service in the national army or from the obligations of fealty, and living as an alien, unprotected by any power except the weak hand of the general government, who, while they excluded him from the rights of marriage, inherited his property, and exacted his composition, if slain. Further, the want of such an institution as the personal laws, could never have been felt in a country without trade, and where few foreigners resided. In these circumstances, its introduction was impossible. If only a single Goth lived in the Burgundian Empire, none of his countrymen could be found to administer Gothic law, and the Burgundians themselves were entirely ignorant of it.

each particular nation; and even then it must often have involved serious embarrassments whenever questions arose in regard to conflicting rights and claims and remedies, growing out of dealings and acts and contracts between individuals belonging to different races. But when the question assumed a more comprehensive character, and the point to be decided was, what rule should prevail, where there was a conflict of laws between different sovereignties wholly independent of each other, and there were rights to be established of a private nature between some of the subjects of each sovereignty, there was no recognized principle or practice, which was promulgated by all, or submitted to by all. Such rights were probably left without any remedy, and became either the subject of private adjustment, or were silently disregarded.

8. *The Law of Nations.*—The truth is, that the Law of Nations, strictly so called, was in a great measure unknown to an-

---

' The truth is, that the want of such an institution, and the possibility of introducing it, could occur only after the nations were blended together in considerable masses. The internal condition of each kingdom would then produce what could never have been brought about by mere benevolence toward individual foreigners. According to this account of the origin of the system of personal laws, it prevailed in all the German states, settled in countries formerly subject to Rome. At first, the validity of two laws only was admitted: e. g., the law of the victorious race, and of the vanquished Romans. Individuals belonging to other German nations did not at first enjoy the right of living under their own laws; but when our supposed kingdom had extended its conquests, and spread out its dominion over other German tribes, then the laws of the conquered German races were acknowledged in the same manner as the Roman formerly had been. Thus also every foreign law prevailing in the empire of the conqueror was admitted and considered as valid among all the vanquished. This practice ought to have produced the following results. At first, in the northern parts of France, the Frank and Roman laws must have been exclusively received; and under the Carlovingian dynasty it would become necessary to admit likewise the laws of the West Goths, Burgundians, Alemans, Bavarians, and Saxons; because these, as nations, belonged to the empire. Italy however did not form a province under the Franks, and there could not consequently be the same reason for admitting the validity of Lombardic law within the Frank empire. In Italy also under the Lombardic kings, only Lombardic and Roman law could have prevailed to the exclusion of every other; but after its conquest by the Franks, all the multifarious foreign laws existing in the territory of the conquerors must have been introduced. Now these anticipated results are supported by history; and this accordance is a strong practical confirmation of that account of the origin of personal laws already established by general reasoning.' — The same passage will be found in Mr. Guenoux's French translation of the same work, vol. 1, c. 3, p. 84–88, ed. 1830; Id. c. 3, s. 30, ed. 1839.

tiquity, and is the slow growth of modern times, under the combined influence of Christianity and commerce.[1] It is well known
that when the Roman Empire was destroyed, the Christian world
was divided into many independent sovereignties, acknowledging
no common head, and connected by no uniform civil polity. The
invasions of the barbarians of the North, the establishment of
the feudal system in the Middle Ages, and the military spirit and
enterprise cherished by the Crusades, struck down all regular
commerce, and surrendered all private rights and contracts to
mere despotic power. It was not until the revival of commerce
on the shores of the Mediterranean, and the revival of letters
and the study of the Civil Law by the discovery of the Pandects had given an increased enterprise to maritime navigation,
and a consequent importance to maritime contracts, that anything like a system of international justice began to be developed.
It first assumed the modest form of commercial usages ; it was
next promulgated under the more imposing authority of royal
ordinances ; and it finally became by silent adoption a generally
connected system, founded in the natural convenience, and asserted by the general comity of the commercial nations of Europe.
The system thus introduced for the purposes of commerce has
gradually extended itself to other objects, as the intercourse of
nations has become more free and frequent. New rules, resting
on the basis of general convenience and an enlarged sense of
national duty, have from time to time been promulgated by
jurists, and supported by courts of justice, by a course of juridical reasoning which has commanded almost universal confidence,
respect, and obedience, without the aid either of municipal statutes, or of royal ordinances, or of international treaties.

4. *Necessity for General Rules.*—Indeed, in the present times,
without some general rules of right and obligation, recognized
by civilized nations to govern their intercourse with each other,
the most serious mischiefs and most injurious conflicts would
arise. Commerce is now so absolutely universal among all countries, the inhabitants of all have such a free intercourse with
each other, contracts, sales, marriages, nuptial settlements, wills,
and successions, are so common among persons whose domicils
are in different countries, having different and even opposite laws
on the same subjects, that without some common principles

[1] See 1 Ward, Law of Nations, c. 6, p. 171–200 ; Id. c. 3, p. 120–130.

adopted by all nations in this regard, there would be an utter confusion of all rights and remedies ; and intolerable grievances would grow up to weaken all the domestic relations, as well as to destroy the sanctity of contracts and the security of property.[1]

5. *Illustrations.*—A few simple cases will sufficiently illustrate the importance of some international principles in matters of mere private right and duty. Suppose a contract, valid by the laws of the country where it is made, is sought to be enforced in another country where such a contract is positively prohibited by its laws ; or, vice versa, suppose a contract invalid by the laws of the country where it is made, but valid by that of the country where it is sought to be enforced, it is plain that unless some uniform rules are adopted to govern such cases (which are not uncommon), the grossest inequalities will arise in the administration of justice between the subjects of the different countries in regard to such contracts. Again : by the laws of some countries marriage cannot be contracted until the parties arrive at twenty-one years of age ; in other countries not until they arrive at the age of twenty-five years. Suppose a marriage to be contracted between two persons in the same country, both of whom are over twenty-one years but less than twenty-five, and one of them is a subject of the latter country. Is such a marriage valid or not? If valid in the country where it is celebrated, is it valid also in the other country? Or the question may be propounded in a still more general form : is a marriage, valid between the parties in the place where it is solemnized, equally valid in all other countries? Or is it obligatory only as a local regulation, and to be treated everywhere else as a mere nullity?

6. Questions of this sort must be of frequent occurrence, not only in different countries wholly independent of each other, but also in provinces of the same empire which are governed by different laws, as was the case in France before the Revolution ; and also in countries acknowledging a common sovereign, but yet organized as distinct communities, as is still the case in regard to

---

[1] Boullenois, in his preface (vol. 1, p. xviii), says: ' Il régnera donc toujours entre les nations une contrariété perpetuelle de loix ; peut-être régnera-t-elle perpétuellement entre nous sur bien des objets. De là la nécessité de s'instruire des règles et des principes que peuvent nous conduire dans la décision des questions, que cette variété peut faire naître.'

the communities composing the British Empire, the Germanic Confederacy, the States of Holland, and the dominions of Austria and Russia.[1] Innumerable suits must be litigated in the judicial forums of these countries and provinces and communities, in which the decision must depend upon the point whether the nature of a contract should be determined by the law of the place where it is litigated, or by the law of the domicil of one or of both of the parties, or by the law of the place where the contract is made; whether the capacity to make a testament should be regulated by the law of the testator's domicil, or that of the location (situs) of his property; whether the form of his testament should be prescribed by the law of the place of his domicil, or by that of the location of his property, or by that of the place where the testament is made; and in like manner, whether the law of the domicil, or what other law, should govern in cases of succession to intestate estates.[2]

7. *Territorial Limits of Laws.*—It is plain that the laws of one country can have no intrinsic force, proprio vigore, except within the territorial limits and jurisdiction of that country. They can bind only its own subjects, and others who are within its jurisdictional limits; and the latter only while they remain therein. No other nation, or its subjects, are bound to yield the slightest obedience to those laws. Whatever extra-territorial force they are to have, is the result, not of any original power to extend them abroad, but of that respect, which from motives of public policy other nations are disposed to yield to them, giving them effect, as the phrase is, sub mutuæ vicissitudinis obtentu, with a wise and liberal regard to common convenience and mutual benefits and necessities. Boullenois has laid down the same exposition as a part of his fundamental maxims. ' Of strict right,' says he, ' all the laws made by a sovereign have no force or authority, except within the limits of his domains. But the necessity of the public general welfare has introduced some exceptions in regard to civil commerce.' ' De droit étroit, toutes les lois, que fait un souverain, n'ont force et autorité que dans l'étendue de sa domination ; mais la nécessité du bien public et général des nations a admis quelques exceptions dans ce qui regarde le commerce civil.' [3]

---

[1] See 1 Froland, Mémoires sur les Statuts, pt. 1, c. 1, s. 5–10.
[2] Livermore, Dissert. 3, 4 ; Merlin, Répert. Statut.
[3] 1 Boullenois, Prin. Gén. 6, p. 4.

8. *Consequence of the Independence of Nations.*—This is the natural principle flowing from the equality and independence of nations. For it is an essential attribute of every sovereignty, that it has no admitted superior, and that it gives the supreme law within its own dominions on all subjects appertaining to its sovereignty. What it yields, it is its own choice to yield, and it cannot be commanded by another to yield it as matter of right. And accordingly it is laid down by all publicists and jurists, as an incontestable rule of public law, that one may with impunity disregard the law pronounced by a magistrate beyond his own territory. 'Extra territorium jus dicenti impune non paretur,' is the doctrine of the Digest;[1] and it is equally as true in relation to nations, as the Roman law held it to be in relation to magistrates. The other part of the rule is equally applicable: 'Idem est, et si supra jurisdictionem suam velit jus dicere;' for he exceeds his proper jurisdiction when he seeks to make it operate extra-territorially as a matter of power.[2] Vattel has deduced a similar conclusion from the general independence and equality of nations, very properly holding that relative strength or weakness cannot produce any difference in regard to public rights and duties; that whatever is lawful for one nation is equally lawful for another; and whatever is unjustifiable in one is equally so in another.[3] And he affirms in the most positive manner (what indeed cannot well be denied), that sovereignty, united with domain, establishes the exclusive jurisdiction of a nation within its own territories, as to controversies, to crimes, and to rights arising therein.[4]

9. *Conflict of Laws.*—The jurisprudence, then, arising from the conflict of the laws of different nations in their actual application to modern commerce and intercourse, is a most interesting and important branch of public law. To no part of the world is it of more interest and importance than to the United States, since the union of a national government with already that of twenty-six distinct states, and in some respects independent states, necessarily creates very complicated private relations and rights between the citizens of those states, which call for the

[1] Dig. 2, 1, 20; Pothier, Pand. 2, 1, n. 7.
[2] Dig. 2, 1, 20 ; Pothier, Pand. 2, 1, n. 7.
[3] Vattel, Prelim. s. 15–20; Id. bk. 2, c. 3, s. 35, 36; Le Louis, 2 Dod. 210.
[4] Vattel, bk. 2, c. 7, s. 84, 85.

constant administration of extra-municipal principles. This branch of public law may therefore be fitly denominated private international law, since it is chiefly seen and felt in its application to the common business of private persons, and rarely rises to the dignity of national negotiations, or of national controversies.[1]

10. *Treatment of the Subject by English Writers.*—The subject has never been systematically treated by writers on the common law of England, and indeed seems to be of very modern growth in that kingdom, and can hardly as yet be deemed to be there cultivated as a science, built up and defined with entire accuracy and decision of principles. More has been done to give it form and symmetry within the last fifty years than in all preceding time. But much yet remains to be done to make it what it ought to be, in a country of such vast extent in its commerce, and such universal reach in its intercourse and polity.[2]

11. *Its Discussion by Continental Jurists.*—The civilians of continental Europe have examined the subject in many of its bearings with a much more comprehensive philosophy, if not with a more enlightened spirit. Their works however abound with theoretical distinctions, which serve little other purpose than to provoke idle discussions, and with metaphysical subtilties which perplex, if they do not confound, the inquirer. They are also mainly addressed to questions intimately connected with their own provincial or municipal laws and customs, some of which are of a purely local, and others of a technical and peculiar character; and they do not always separate those considerations and doctrines which belong to the elements of the general science, from those which may be deemed founded in particular national interests and local ordinances. Precedents too have not, either in the courts of continental Europe or in the juridical discussions of its eminent jurists, the same force and authority, which we, who live under the influence of the common law, are

---

[1] The civilians are accustomed to call the questions arising from the conflict of foreign and domestic laws, mixed questions (questions mixtes). 1 Froland, Mémoires des Statuts, c. 1, s. 9, p. 13 ; Id. c. 7, s. 1, p. 155.

[2] Mr. Chancellor Kent has remarked that these topics of international law were almost unknown in the English courts prior to the time of Lord Hardwicke and Lord Mansfield, and that the English lawyers seem generally to have been strangers to the discussions on foreign law by the celebrated jurists of continental Europe. 2 Kent Comm. 455.

accustomed to attribute to them; and it is unavoidable that
many differences of opinion should exist among them, even in
relation to leading principles. But the strong sense and critical
learning of the best minds among foreign jurists, have generally
maintained those doctrines which at the present day are deemed
entirely persuasive and satisfactory with us, who live under the
common law, as well for the solid grounds on which they rest,
as for the universal approbation with which they are entertained
by courts of justice.[1]

12. *Personal, Real, and Mixed Statutes.*—In their discussions
upon this subject the civilians have divided statutes into three
classes, personal, real, and mixed. By statutes, they mean, not
the positive legislation, which in England and America is known
by the same name, namely, the acts of parliament and of other
legislative bodies, as contradistinguished from the common law,
but the whole municipal law of the particular state, from whatever source arising.[2] Sometimes the word is used by them in
contradistinction to the imperial Roman law, which they are
accustomed to style, by way of eminence, the *common law*, since
it constitutes the general basis of the jurisprudence of all continental Europe, modified and restrained by local customs and
usages, and positive legislation.[3] Paul Voet says: 'Sequitur
jus particulare, seu non commune, quod uno vocabulo usitatis-

---

[1] The late Mr. Livermore (whose lamented death occurred in July, 1833),
in his learned Dissertations on the Contrariety of Laws, printed at New Orleans in 1828, has enumerated the principal continental writers who have discussed this subject at large. I gladly refer the reader to these Dissertations,
as very able and clear. There is also a catalogue of the principal writers in
Boullenois, Traité des Statuts, Preface, vol. 1, p. 29, note 1; in Dupin's edition of Camus, Profession d'Avocat, vol. 2, tit. 7, s. 5, art. 1561-1566; in
Froland, Mémoires concernans les Qualités des Statuts, vol. 1, pt. 1, c. 2,
p. 15; in Bouhier, Coutum. de Bourg. vol. 1, c. 23, p. 450; and in Mr.
Burge's recent Commentaries on Colonial and Foreign Law, pt. 1, c. 1, p. 6-
22. In the preparation of these Commentaries I have availed myself chiefly
of the writings of Rodenburg, the Voets (father and son), Burgundus, Du
Moulin (Molinaeus), Froland, Boullenois, Bouhier, and Huberus, as embracing the most satisfactory illustrations of the leading doctrines. My object has
not been to engage in any critical examination of the comparative merits or
mistakes of the different commentators, but rather to gather from each of
them what seemed most entitled to respect and confidence.

[2] Bouhier, Coutum. de Bourg. vol. 1, p. 173-179, s. 9-32; 1 Hertii Opera,
de Collisione Legum, s. 4, art. 5, p. 121; Id. p. 172, ed. 1716.

[3] Bouhier, Coutum. de Bourg. vol. 1, p. 175, 178, s. 16, 28, 29.

simo *statutum* dicitur, quasi statum publicum tuens.[1] Appella-
tur etiam *jus municipale*. Etiam in jure nostro dicta *lex* seu *lex
municipii*, quemadmodum in genere signat jus commune.'[2] And
he defines it thus: ' Est jus particulare ab alio legislatore quam
Imperatore constitutum.[3] Dico, *jus particulare*, in quantum
opponitur juri communi, non prout est gentium et naturale, sed
prout est jus civile Romanorum, populo Romano commune, et
omnibus, qui illo populo parebant.[4] Additur, *ab alio legislatore*,
cum qui statuta condit, recte et suo modo legislator appelletur,
ut ipsa statuta leges dicuntur municipiorum. Et quidem, *ab alio*,
quia regulariter statuta non condit Imperator; excipe, nisi muni-
cipibus jura det, statuta' præscribat, secundum quæ ipsi sua
regant municipia.[5] Denique adjicitur, *quam imperatore*, quod
licet Imperator solummodo dicatur legislator, id tamen, non alio
sensu obtineat, quam quod suis legibus non hunc aut illum popu-
lum, verum omnes constringat, quos suæ clementiæ regit imperium.'[6] Merlin says: ' This term, *statute*, is generally applied
to all sorts of laws and regulations. Every provision of law is
a statute, which permits, ordains, or prohibits anything.' 'Ce
terme (*statut*), s'applique en général à toutes sortes de lois et de
règlemens. Chaque disposition d'une loi est un statut, qui
permet, ordonne, ou défend quelque chose.'[7]

13. *Definition of the three Classes of Statutes.*—The civilians
have variously defined· the different classes of statutes or laws.
The definitions of Merlin are sufficiently clear and explicit for
all the purposes of the present work, and will therefore be here
cited. The distinctions between the different classes are very
important to be observed in consulting foreign jurists, since they
have been adopted by them from a very early period, and per-
vade all their discussions. Personal statutes are held by them
to be of general obligation and force everywhere; but real statutes are held to have no extra-territorial force or obligation.[8]

---

[1] P. Voet, de Statut. s. 4, c. 1, s. 1; Id. p. 123, ed. 1661.　　[2] Ibid.
[3] P. Voet, de Statut. s. 4, c. 1, s. 2; Id. p. 124, ed. 1661.　　[4] Ibid..
[5] P. Voet, de Statut. s. 4, c. 1, s. 2; Id. p. 125, ed. 1661.
[6] P. Voet, de Statut. s. 4, c. 1, s. 2; Id. p. 125, ed. 1661; Id. s. 1, c. 4 ;
Id. p. 35, ed. 1661; Liverm. Dissert. II. p. 21, note (b), ed. 1828.
[7] Merlin, Répertoire, art. Statut. vol. 31, ed. 1828, Bruxelles; Saul *v.*
His Creditors, 5 Mart. N.S. (La.) 569, 589.
[8] Rodenburg, de Statut. Divers. c. 3, p. 7; 1 Froland, Mémoires des Statuts, c. 7, s. 1, 2.

'Personal statutes,' says Merlin, 'are those which have principally for their object the person, and treat only of property (biens [1]) incidentally (accessoirement) ; such are those which regard birth, legitimacy, freedom, the right of instituting suits, majority as to age, incapacity to contract, to make a will, to plead in proper person, &c.[2]   Real statutes are those which have principally for their object property (biens), and which do not speak of persons, except in relation to property ; such are those which concern the disposition which one may make of his property, either while he is living, or by testament.[3]   Mixed statutes are those which concern at once persons and property.' But Merlin adds, ' that in this sense almost all statutes are mixed, there being scarcely any law relative to persons, which does not at the same time relate to things.' [4]   He therefore deems the last classification unnecessary, and holds that every statute ought to receive its denomination according to its principal object.   As that object is real or personal, so ought the quality of the statute to be determined.[5]   But this distribution into three classes is usually adopted precisely as it is stated by Rodenburg: 'Aut enim statutum simpliciter disponit de personis; aut solummodo de rebus; aut conjunctim de utrisque.' [6]   And he pro-

---

[1] The term *biens*, in the sense of the civilians and continental jurists, comprehends not merely goods and chattels, as in the cômmon law, but real estate. But the distinction between movable and immovable property is nevertheless recognized by them, and gives rise in the civil law, as well as in the common law, to many important distinctions as to rights and remedies.

[2] See Pothier, Coutum. d'Orléans, c. 1, s. 1, art. 6.

[3] See Pothier, Coutum. d'Orléans, c. 1, s. 2, art. 21.

[4] Merlin, Répertoire, Statut.; Id. Autorisation Maritale, s. 10.   [5] Ibid.

[6] Rodenburg, de Statut. Diversitate, c. 2, p. 4; Le Brun, Traité de la Communauté, liv. 2, c. 3, s. 20–48; Bouhier, Coutum. de Bourg. c. 21-37; Voet, de Statut. s. 4, c. 2, p. 116–124; Id. p. 129–143, ed. 1661; Livermore, Dissert. s. 65-162 ; 1 Froland, Mémoires, Qualité des Statuts, pt. 1, c. 3, p. 25; Id. c. 4, p. 49, c. 5, p. 81, c. 6, p. 214; Boullenois, Traité des Statuts, vol. 1, preface, p. 22; Pothier, Coutum. d'Orléans, c. 1, s. 1, art. 6-8. — Boullenois distributes all statutes into three classes: ' Ou le statut dispose simplement des personnes ; ou il dispose simplement des choses; ou il dispose tout à la fois des personnes et des choses.' 1 Boullenois, Traité des Statuts réels et personnels, tit. 1, c. 2, obs. 2, p. 25; Id. Princ. Gén. p. 4, 6.   Mr. Henry, in his Dissertation on Personal, Real, and Mixed Statutes, has adopted the like distribution, without any acknowledgment of the source (Boullenois) from which he has drawn all his materials. See Henry on Personal and Real Statutes, c. 1, s. 2 to c. 3, s. 1, p. 2-83.   See also Livermore's Dissert. 2, s. 65-162, p. 62-106; Id. s. 168, p. 109.   Mr. Justice Porter in delivering the opinion of

ceeds to explain this division in the following manner: 'Quæ
ita constrictim dicta sic habentur explicatius: Aut universus
personæ status, aut conditio in dispositione statuti vertitur, citra
ullam rerum adjectionem, adeoque de personis agitur in abstracto,
absque ulla consideratione rerum, ut, verbi gratia, quoto quis
ætatis anno sui juris sit, quando exeat parentum potestate, de
quibus et consimilibus exemplis mox fusius. Aut in solas nu-
dasque res statuti dispositio dirigitur, ut nullum intervenire
necesse sit actum hominis, aut aliquam concurrere personæ
operam ; cujusmodi sunt, quibus rerum successionibus ab intestato
jus ponitur, ut bona materna cedant maternis, paterna paternis,
nothi succedant matribus, non succedant patribus, quando suc-
cedatur in stirpes, quando in capita ; quæ jura successionum ab
intestato appellaveris. Aut permittit denique, vetat, aut ordinat,
actum a personis circa res peragendum, ex utriusque complexu
constructum statutum, contra quod, ut queat committi quippiam,
personæ actum intervenire necesse est. Quo pertinent. Sine in-
dulto principis de rebus suis nemo testator ; conjuges sibi in-
vicem non leganto ; vir citra consensum uxorium res soli non
alienato.' [1]

14. *Classification.*—In the application of this classification to
particular cases, there has been no inconsiderable diversity of
opinion among the civilians. What particular statutes are to be
deemed personal, and what real ; when they may be said principally to regard persons, and when principally to regard things ;
these have been vexed questions, upon which much subtility of
discussion and much heat of controversy have been displayed.
The subject is in itself full of intrinsic difficulties ; but it has
been rendered more perplexed by metaphysical niceties and over-
curious learning.[2] Hertius admits, that these subtilities have so

the Supreme Court of Louisiana, in the case of Saul *v.* His Creditors (5 Mart.
N.S. 569, 590), said, that foreign jurists, by a personal statute, mean that
which follows and governs the party subject to it, wherever he goes; and a real
statute is that which controls things, and does not extend beyond the limits of
the country from which it derives its authority. Is not this a description of
the effect of such statutes, rather than a definition of their nature? See Id.
593.

[1] Rodenburg, de Statut. Divers. c. 2, p. 4 (2 Boullenois, Appendix, p. 4).

[2] See 1 Boullenois, tit. 1, c. 1, obs. 2, p. 16, &c. ; Id. c. 2, obs. 5, p. 114–122;
1 Froland, Mém. des Stat. c. 2, p. 15; 2 Kent Comm. 453–457; Saul *v.* His
Creditors, 5 Mart. N.S. (La.) 569–596 ; Henry on Foreign Law, c. 3, p. 23,
&c. The Supreme Court of Louisiana have made some very just remarks on

perplexed the subject, that it is difficult to venture even upon an explanation. His language is : 'De collisu legum anceps, difficilis, et late diffusa est disputatio, quam nescio, an quisquam explicare totam aggressus fuerit.'[1]   And in another place he adds : 'Cæterum junioribus plerisque placuit distinctio inter statuta, realia, personalia, et mixta. Verum in iis definiendis mirum est, quam sudant doctores.'[2] Bartolus has furnished a memorable example of these niceties. After remarking upon the distinction between personal and real statutes, and the mode of distinguishing the one from the other, and that in England the custom obtains of the eldest son's succeeding to all the property, he says : 'Mihi videtur, quod verba statuti seu consuetudinis, sunt diligenter intuenda. Aut illa disponunt circa res ; ut per hæc verba, " Bona decedentis ut veniant in primogenitum ; " et tunc de

this subject. 'We are led,' says Mr. Justice Porter, in delivering the opinion of the court, 'into an examination of the doctrine of real and personal statutes, as it is called by the continental writers of Europe, a subject the most intricate and perplexed of any that has occupied the attention of lawyers and courts, one on which scarcely any writers are found entirely to agree, and on which it is rare to find one consistent with himself throughout. We know of no matter in jurisprudence so unsettled, or none that should more teach men distrust of their own opinions and charity for those of others.' Saul v. His Creditors (5 Mart. N.S. (La.) 569, 588). Chancellor D'Aguesseau has attempted a definition, or test, of real and personal laws. He says : 'The true principle in this matter is to examine if the statute has property directly for its object, or its destination to certain persons, or its preservation in families, so that it is not the interest of the person whose rights or acts are examined, but the interests of others to whom it is intended to assure the property, or the real rights, which were the cause of the law. Or if, on the contrary, all the attention of the law is directed towards the person, to provide in general for his qualifications, or his general absolute capacity, as when it relates to the qualities of major or minor, of father or son, of legitimate or illegitimate, of ability or inability to contract, by reason of personal causes. In the first hypothesis, the statute is real; in the second, it is personal.' Cited in 5 Mart. N.S. (La.) p. 594; D'Aguesseau, Œuvres, tom. 4, p. 660, 4to ed. How unsatisfactory is this description, when applied in practice.

[1] 1 Hertii, Opera, de Collis. Legum, s. 1, n. 1, p. 91; Id. s. 4, n. 3, p. 121, 122; Id. p. 129, and p. 170, ed. 1716.

[2] 1 Hertii, Opera, s. 4, n. 3, p. 120; Id. p. 170, ed. 1716. See also 1 Froland, Mém. Qualité des Statut. c. 3–7; Bouhier, Coutum. de Bourg. c. 23, s. 58, 59. — Mr. Livermore has given a concise view of the various opinions of foreign jurists on this subject, which will well reward a diligent perusal. Liverm. Dissert. 2, s. 56–162. His own opinions, which exhibit great acuteness, will also be found in the same work from s. 163–214. The subject is very amply discussed in Froland, Boullenois, Bouhier, Le Brun, and Rodenburg.

omnibus bonis judicabo secundum usum et statutum, ubi res sunt situatæ, quia jus affecit res ipsas, sive possideantur a cive, sive ab advena. Aut verba statuti seu consuetudinis disponunt circa personas ; ut per hæc verba, " Primogenitus succedat ; " et tunc, aut ille talis decedens non erat de Anglia, sed ibi haberet possessiones ; et tunc tale statutum ad eum et ejus filios non porrigitur, quia dispositio circa personas non porrigitur ad forenses.[1] Aut talis decedens erat Anglicus, et tunc filius primogenitus succederet in bonis quæ sunt in Anglia, et in aliis succederet de jure communi.' So that, according to Bartolus, if a statute declares in words, that ' The estate of the intestate shall descend to the eldest son,' (Bona decedentis ut veniant in primogenitum), it is a real statute ; if it says in words, that ' The eldest son shall succeed to the estate ' (Primogenitus succedat), it is a personal statute.[2] This distinction has been justly exploded by other civilians, as the mere order and construction of the words of the statute, and not its objects, would otherwise decide its character.[3]

---

[1] Bartolus, ad Cod. 1, 1, De Sum. Trinit. l. 1, Cunctos populos, n. 42 ; Liverm. Dissert. s. 68, 69, p. 63, 64 ; 1 Boullenois, obs. 2, p. 16, 17. — The text of Bartolus, in the only edition to which I have access (Venet. 1602), abounds exceedingly in abbreviations, so that in some few instances I am not perfectly sure that I have given the exact word.

[2] 1 Boullenois, tit. 1, c. 1, obs. 2, p. 16, 17 ; Liverm. Dissert. s. 3, p. 22, 23 ; Id. s. 67, 68, p. 62, 63 ; Mr. Justice Porter in the case of Saul v. His Creditors, 5 Mart. N.S. (La.) 569, 590–595 ; Burgundus, tract. 1, s. 4, p. 16 ; Stockman. decis. 125, s. 8, p. 263.

[3] Ibid. p. 19 ; Liverm. Dissert. 2, s. 67, 68 ; Id. s. 69–77 ; 1 Froland Mém. Statut. pt. 1, c. 3, s. 3, 4 ; Bouhier, Coutum. de Bourg. c. 53, s. 58–99. — The opinion of the court by Mr. Justice Porter, in Saul v. His Creditors (5 Mart. N.S. (La.) 569, 590–596), illustrates this subject in a very striking manner. ' According to the jurists,' says he, ' of those countries, a personal statute is that which follows and governs the party subject to it wherever he goes. The real statute controls things, and does not extend beyond the limits of the country from which it derives its authority. The personal statute of one country controls the personal statute of another country, into which a party once governed by the former, or who may contract under it, should remove. But it is subject to a real statute of the place where the person subject to the personal should fix himself, or where the property on which the contest arises may be situated. So far the rules are plain and intelligible. But the moment we attempt to discover from these writers what statutes are real, and what are personal, the most extraordinary confusion is presented. Their definitions often differ, and when they agree on their definitions, they dispute as to their application. Bartolus, who was one of the first by whom this subject was examined, and the most distinguished jurist of his day, established as a rule that, whenever the statute commenced by treating of persons, it was a personal

15. Le Brun says that in order to ascertain whether a statute is personal or not, it is necessary to examine whether it univer-

one; but if it began by disposing of things, it was real. So that if a law, as the counsel for the appellants has stated, was written thus: "The estate of the deceased shall be inherited by the eldest son," the statute was real; but if it said: "The eldest son shall inherit the estate," it was personal. This distinction, though purely verbal and most unsatisfactory, was followed for a long time, and sanctioned by many whose names are illustrious in the annals of jurisprudence; but it was ultimately discarded by all. D'Argentré, who rejected this rule, to real and personal statutes added a third, which he called mixed. The real statute, according to this writer, is that which treats of immovables: In quo de rebus soli, id est immobilibus, agitur. And the personal, that which concerns the person abstracted from things: Statutum personale est illud quod afficit personam universaliter, abstracte ab omni materia reali. The mixed he states to be one which concerns both persons and things. D'Argentré, Comm. ad Leg. Brit. des. Donat. art. 228, n. 5 to n. 9; tom. 1, p. 648. This definition of D'Argentré of a personal statute has been adopted by every writer who has treated of this matter. A long list of them, amounting to twenty-five, is given by Froland, in his Mémoires concernans la Qualité des Statuts, among which are found Burgundus, Rodenburg, Stockmans, Voet, and Dumoulin. (Froland, Mémoires concernans la Qualité des Statuts, c. 5, no. 1.) But the definition which he has given of a real statute does not seem to have been so generally adopted. It was however followed by Burgundus, Rodenburg, and Stockmans. Boullenois, who is one of the latest writers, attacks the definitions given by D'Argentré, and, as he supposes, refutes them; he adds others, which appear to be as little satisfactory as those he rejects. He divides personal statutes into personal particular and personal universal; personal particular he subdivides again into pure personal, and personal real. (Boullenois, Traité de la Personalité et de la Réalité des Lois, tit. 1, cap. 2, obs. 4, p. 44–52.) Voet has two definitions: one, that a real statute is that which affects principally things, though it also relates to persons; and the other, that a personal statute is that which affects principally persons, although it treats also of things. It would be a painful and a useless task to follow these authors through all their refinements. President Bouhier, who wrote about the same time as Boullenois, and who has treated the subject as extensively as any other writer, after quoting the definitions just given, and others, says that they are all defective, and that he cannot venture on any until the world are more agreed what statutes are real and what are personal. While they remain so uncertain, he thinks the best way is to follow the second definition of Voet, which is, "that a real statute is that which does not extend beyond the territory within which it is passed, and a personal is that which does." (Bouhier, sur les Coutumes de Bourgogne, c. 23, no. 59.) This last mode of distinguishing statutes, which teaches us what effect a statute should have, by directing us to inquire what effect it has, is quite as unsatisfactory as the rule given by Bartolus, who judged of it by the words with which it is commenced. The rules given by Chancellor D'Aguesseau are perhaps preferable to any other. "That," says he, "which truly characterizes a real statute, and essentially distinguishes it from a personal one, is not that it should be relative to certain personal circumstances, or certain personal events; otherwise, we should be obliged to say that the statutes which relate to the paternal power,

sally governs the state of the person, independent of property.
If it does not universally govern the state of the person, but only
particular acts of the person, it is not personal.   Thus, a statute
which prohibits married persons from making donations to each
other is purely real and local, because it regulates a particular
act only.   And a statute to be personal must regulate the state
of the person without speaking of property (biens).   Thus a
statute which excludes females from inheriting fiefs, in favor of

the right of wardship, the tenancy by curtesy (droit de viduité), the prohibition of married persons to confer advantages on each other, are personal statutes; and yet it is clear, in our jurisprudence, that they are considered as real
statutes, the execution of which is regulated, not by the place of domicil, but
by that where the property is situated.   The true principle in this matter is,
to examine if the statute has property directly for its object or its destination
to certain persons, or its preservation in families, so that it is not the interest
of the person whose rights or acts are examined, but the interest of others, to
whom it is intended to assure the property, or the real rights, which were the
cause of the law.   Or if, on the contrary, all the attention of the law is directed
towards the person, to provide in general for his qualifications, or his general
and absolute capacity; as when it relates to the qualities of major or minor,
of father or of son, legitimate or illegitimate, ability or inability to contract, by
reason of personal causes.''   "In the first hypothesis the statute is real, in
the second it is personal, as is well explained in these words of D'Argentré:
' Cum statutum non simpliciter inhabilitat, sed ratione fundi aut juris realis
alterum respicientis extra personas contrahentes, totas hanc inhabilitatem non
egredi locum statuti.' "   (Œuvres D'Aguesseau, vol. 4, 660, cinquante-qua-
trième plaidoyer.)   This definition is, we think, better than any of the rest;
though even in the application of it to some cases, difficulty would exist.   If
the subject had been susceptible of clear and positive rules, we may safely believe this illustrious man would not have left it in doubt; for if anything be
more remarkable in him than his genius and his knowledge, it is the extraordinary fulness and clearness with which he expresses himself on all questions
of jurisprudence.   When he therefore, and so many other men of great talents
and learning, are thus found to fail in fixing certain principles, we are forced
to conclude that they have failed, not from want of ability, but because the
matter was not susceptible of being settled on certain principles.   They have
attempted to go too far; to define and fix that which cannot in the nature of
things be defined and fixed.   They seem to have forgotten that they wrote on
a question which touched the comity of nations, and that that comity is, and
ever must be, uncertain; that it must necessarily depend on a variety of circumstances which cannot be reduced within any certain rule; that no nation
will suffer the laws of another to interfere with her own to the injury of her
citizens; that whether they do or not must depend upon the condition of the
country in which the foreign law is sought to be enforced, the particular law
of her legislation, her policy, and the character of her institutions; that in the
conflict of laws, it must be often a matter of doubt which should prevail; and
that, whenever that doubt does exist, the court which decides will prefer the
laws of its own country to that of the stranger.'

males; or which excludes a beneficiary heir from the succession, in favor of the simple heir; or which excludes a daughter who is endowed from the succession, is real and local; for all these statutes speak of property. For the same reason, he holds the Senatus-consultum Velleianum, by which a married woman was prohibited from binding herself for the debt of another person[1] (and which was borrowed from the Roman law into the customary jurisprudence of some of the French provinces), to be a real statute, because it regulates a particular act of the person only.[2] And he adds that the definition of a real statute results from that of a personal statute. In one word, a statute is real which regulates a particular act of the person, or which speaks of property.[3] Other jurists of distinguished reputation (among whom is Boullenois) have denied this to be a sound distinction, and have specially held the Senatus-consultum Velleianum to be a personal statute."[4]

16. *Purpose of this Work.*—It is not my design to engage in the controversy as to what constitutes the true distinction between personal statutes and real statutes, or to examine the merits of the various systems propounded by foreign jurists on this subject. It would carry me too far from the immediate purpose of these commentaries, even if I felt myself possessed (which I certainly do not) of that critical skill and learning which such an examination would require, in order to treat the subject with suitable dignity. My object is rather to present the leading principles upon some of the more important topics of private international jurisprudence, and to use the works of the civilians to illustrate, confirm, and expand the doctrines of the common law, so far at least as the latter have assumed a settled form. If, in referring to the authority of the civilians I should speak of the personality of laws (personnalité des statuts), and the reality of laws (réalité des statuts), let it not be attributed to a spirit of innovation upon the received usages of our language, but rather to a desire to familiarize expressions, which in this

---

[1] Dig. 16, 1, 1; Dig. 16, 1, 16, 1.
[2] Le Brun, Traité de la Communauté, liv. 2, c. 3, s. 5, n. 20–48, p. 310–319.
[3] Ibid.
[4] 1 Boullenois, Princep. Gén. 5; Id. obs. 3, p. 40; Id. obs. 4, p. 43, 49; Id. obs. 5, p. 78, 79, 82, 101, 103, 105, 106, 118; Henry on Foreign Law, 31, 50.

peculiar sense have already found their way into our juridical
discussions, and are becoming daily more and more important to
be understood by American lawyers, since they are incorporated
into the very substance of the jurisprudence of some of the states
in the Union.[1] By the personality of laws foreign jurists generally mean all laws which concern the condition, state, and
capacity of persons; by the reality of laws, all laws which
concern property or things; quæ ad rem spectant.[2] Whenever
they wish to express that the operation of a law is universal,
they compendiously announce that it is a personal statute; and
whenever, on the other hand, they wish to express that its operation is confined to the country of its origin, they simply declare
it to be a real statute.

[1] See note to 2 Kent Comm. 456.
[2] 1 Boullenois, obs. 3, p. 41, 42. Mr. Livermore, in his Dissertations, used
the words *personality* and *reality;* Mr. Henry, in his work, the words, *personalty* and *realty.* I have preferred the former, as least likely to lead to mistakes, as *personalty* is in our law confined to personal estate, and *realty* to
real estate.

CHAPTER II.

GENERAL MAXIMS OF INTERNATIONAL JURISPRUDENCE.

17. *Subject of the Chapter.*—Before entering upon any examination of the various heads which a treatise upon the Conflict of Laws will naturally embrace, it seems necessary to advert to a few general maxims or axioms which constitute the basis upon which all reasonings on the subject must necessarily rest; and without the express or tacit admission of which it will be found impossible to arrive at any principles to govern the conduct of nations, or to regulate the due administration of justice.

18. I. *Territorial Sovereignty of every Nation.*—The first and most general maxim or proposition is that which has been already adverted to, that every nation possesses an exclusive sovereignty and jurisdiction within its own territory. The direct consequence of this rule is, that the laws of every state affect and bind directly all property, whether real or personal, within its territory, and all persons who are resident within it, whether natural-born subjects or aliens, and also all contracts made and acts done within it.[1] A state may therefore regulate the manner and circumstances under which property, whether real or personal or in action, within it, shall be held, transmitted, bequeathed, transferred, or enforced; the condition, capacity, and state of all persons within it; the validity of contracts and other acts done within it; the resulting rights and duties growing out of these contracts and acts; and the remedies and modes of administering justice in all cases calling for the interposition of its tribunals to protect and vindicate and secure the wholesome agency of its own laws within its own domains.

19. Accordingly Boullenois has laid down the following among his general principles (principes généraux). He says,

[1] Henry on Foreign Law, pt. 1, c. 1, s. 1, p. 1; Huberus, lib. 1, tit. 3, s. 2; Campbell *v.* Hall, Cowp. 208; Ruding *v.* Smith, 2 Hagg. Cons. 383.

(1) He, or those, who have the sovereign authority, have the sole right to make laws; and these laws ought to be executed in all places within the sovereignty where they are known, in the prescribed manner. (2) The sovereign has power and authority over his subjects, and over the property which they possess within his dominions. (3) The sovereign has also authority to regulate the forms and solemnities of contracts which his subjects make within the territories under his dominions, and to prescribe the rules for the administration of justice. (4) The sovereign has also a right to make laws to govern foreigners in many cases; for example, in relation to property which they possess within the reach of his sovereignty; in relation to the formalities of contracts which they make within his territories, and in relation to judiciary proceedings, if they institute suits before his tribunals. (5) The sovereign may in like manner make laws for foreigners who even pass through his territories; but these are commonly simple laws of police, made for the preservation of order within his dominions; and these laws are either permanent, or they are made only for certain particular occurrences.[1] The same doctrine is, either tacitly or expressly, conceded by every other jurist who has discussed the subject at large, whether he has written upon municipal law or upon public law.[2]

20. II. *Territorial Limits of Sovereignty.* Another maxim or proposition is, that no state or nation can by its laws directly affect or bind property out of its own territory, or bind persons not resident therein, whether they are natural-born subjects or others. This is a natural consequence of the first proposition; for it would be wholly incompatible with the equality and exclusiveness of the sovereignty of all nations, that any one nation should be at liberty to regulate either persons or things not within its own territory. It would be equivalent to a declaration that the sovereignty over a territory was never exclusive in any nation, but only concurrent with that of all nations; that each could legislate for all, and none for itself; and that all might establish rules which none were bound to obey. The absurd results of such a state of things need not be dwelt upon. Accordingly, Rodenburg has significantly said, that no sovereign

[1] 1 Boullenois, Traité des Statuts, p. 2-4.
[2] Vattel, b. 2, c. 7, s. 84, 85.

has a right to give the law beyond his own dominions; and if he attempts it, he may be lawfully refused obedience; for wherever the foundation of laws fails, there their force and jurisdiction fail also. *' Constat igitur extra territorium legem dicere licere nemini, idque si fecerit quis, impune ei non pareri; quippe ubi cesset statutorum fundamentum, robur et jurisdictio.'* [1] P. Voet speaks to the same effect: 'Nullum statutum, sive in rem, sive in personam, si de ratione juris civilis sermo instituatur, sese extendit ultra statuentis territorium.'* [2] Boullenois (as we have seen) announces the same rule: 'De droit étroit, toutes les loix, que fait un souverain, n'ont force et autorité que dans l'étendue de sa domination;'* [3] and indeed it is the common language of jurists.[4] Mr. Chief Justice Parker has recognized the doctrine in the fullest manner. 'That the laws,' says he, 'of any state cannot by any inherent authority be entitled to respect extra-territorially, or beyond the jurisdiction of the state which enacts them, is the necessary result of the independence of distinct sovereignties.'* [5]

21. *Natural Allegiance.*—Upon this rule there is often ingrafted an exception of some importance to be rightfully understood. It is that although the laws of a nation have no direct binding force or effect, except upon persons within its own territories, yet that every nation has a right to bind its own subjects by its own laws in every other place.[6] In one sense this exception may be admitted to be correct and well founded in the practice of nations; in another sense it is incorrect, or at least it requires qualification. Every nation has hitherto assumed it as clear that it possesses the right to regulate and govern its own native-born subjects everywhere; and consequently that its laws extend to and bind such subjects at all times and in all places. This is commonly adduced as a consequence of what is called natural allegiance, that is, of allegiance to the government of the territory of a man's birth. Thus Mr. Justice Blackstone says: 'Natural allegiance is such as is due from all men

---

[1] Rodenburg, de Stat. c. 3, s. 1, p. 7.

[2] Voet, de Stat. s. 4, c. 2, n. 7, p. 124; Id. 138, 139, ed. 1661.

[3] 1 Boullenois, Princ. Gén. 6, p. 4; Id. c. 3, obs. 10, p. 152.   [4] Id.

[5] Blanchard v. Russell, 13 Mass. 4. The same doctrine is reasoned out with great ability in the opinion of Mr. Chief Justice Taney in the case of the Bank of Augusta v. Earle, 13 Pet. 584–591.

[6] Henry on Real and Personal Statutes, pt. 1, c. 1, p. 1.

born within the king's dominions, immediately upon their birth.'
'Natural allegiance is therefore a debt of gratitude which cannot be forfeited, cancelled, or altered, by any change of time,
place, or circumstance. An Englishman who removes to France
or to China owes the same allegiance to the king of England
there as at home, and twenty years hence as well as now.'[1] And
he proceeds to distinguish it from local allegiance, which is
such as is due from an alien, or stranger born, for so long a time
as he continues within the dominions of a foreign prince. The former is universal and perpetual; the latter ceases the instant the
stranger transfers himself to another country;[2] and it is therefore local and temporary. Vattel on the other hand seems to
admit the right of allegiance not to be perpetual even in natives; and that they have a right to expatriate themselves, and,
under some circumstances, to dissolve their connection with the
parent country.[3]

22. *Rights of a Nation over its own Subjects.*—Without entering upon this subject (which properly belongs to a general treatise upon public law) it may be truly said that no nation is bound
to respect the laws of another nation, made in regard to the subjects of the latter, who are non-residents. The obligatory force
of such laws of any nation cannot extend beyond its own territories. And if such laws are incompatible with the laws of the
country where such subjects reside, or interfere with the duties
which they owe to the country where they reside, they will be
disregarded by the latter. Whatever may be the intrinsic or
obligatory force of such laws upon such persons if they should
return to their native country, they can have none in other nations wherein they reside. Such laws may give rise to personal
relations between the sovereign and subjects, to be enforced in
his own domains; but they do not rightfully extend to other nations. 'Statuta suo clauduntur territorio, nec ultra territorium
disponunt.' Nor indeed is there, strictly speaking, any difference in this respect, whether such laws concern the persons, or
concern the property of native subjects. A state has just as
much intrinsic right, and no more, to give to its own laws an
extra-territorial force as to the property of its subjects situated
abroad, as it has in relation to the persons of its subjects domi-

[1] 1 Black. Comm. 369, 370; Foster, C. L. 184.   [2] Ibid.
[3] Vattel, b. 1, c. 19, s. 220–228.

ciled abroad.   That is, as sovereign laws, they have no obligation on either the person or the property.   When, therefore, we speak of the right of a state to bind its own native subjects everywhere, we speak only of its own claim and exercise of sovereignty over them when they return within its own territorial jurisdiction, and not of its right to compel or require obedience to such laws on the part of other nations within their own territorial sovereignty.   On the contrary, every nation has an exclusive right to regulate persons and things within its own territory, according to its own sovereign will and public policy.

23. III. *Recognition of the Laws of one State by another.* — From these two maxims or propositions there flows a third, and that is, that whatever force and obligation the laws of one country have in another depend solely upon the laws and municipal regulations of the latter, that is to say, upon its own proper jurisprudence and polity, and upon its own express or tacit consent.[1] A state may prohibit the operation of all foreign laws, and the rights growing out of them, within its own territories. It may prohibit some foreign laws, and it may admit the operation of others. It may recognize and modify and qualify some foreign laws; it may enlarge or give universal effect to others. It may interdict the administration of some foreign laws; it may favor the introduction of others. When its own code speaks positively on the subject, it must be obeyed by all persons who are within the reach of its sovereignty. When its customary, unwritten, or common law speaks directly on the subject, it is equally to be obeyed; for it has an equal obligation with its positive code. When both are silent, then, and then only, can the question properly arise, what law is to govern in the absence of any clear declaration of the sovereign will. Is the rule to be promulgated by a legislative act of the sovereign power? Or is it to be promulgated by courts of law, according to the analogies which are furnished in the municipal jurisprudence? This question does not admit of any universal answer; or rather, it will be answered differently in different communities, according to the organization of the departments of each particular government.[2]

24. *Authority exercised by the Courts.*—Upon the continent of Europe some of the principal states have silently suffered their courts to draw this portion of their jurisprudence from the analo-

[1] Huberus, lib. 1, tit. 3, s. 2.   [2] See post, s. 38.

gies furnished by the civil law, or by their own customary or
positive code. France, for instance, composed, as it formerly was,
of a great number of provinces, governed by different laws and
customs, was early obliged to sanction such exertions of authority by its courts, in order to provide for the constantly occurring
claims of its own subjects living and owning property in different
provinces, in a conflict between the different provincial laws. In
England and America the courts of justice have hitherto exercised the same authority in the most ample manner; and the
legislatures have in no instance (it is believed) in either country
interfered to provide any positive regulations. The common law
of both countries has been expanded to meet the exigencies of
the times as they have arisen; and so far as the practice of nations, or the jus gentium privatum, has been supposed to furnish
any general principle, it has been followed out with a wise and
manly liberality.

25. *Difficulty of establishing Principles of Recognition.*—The
real difficulty is to ascertain what principles in point of public
convenience ought to regulate the conduct of nations on this subject, in regard to each other, and in what manner they can be best
applied to the infinite variety of cases arising from the complicated concerns of human society in modern times. No nation
can be justly required to yield up its own fundamental policy
and institutions in favor of those of another nation. Much less
can any nation be required to sacrifice its own interests in favor
of another, or to enforce doctrines which, in a moral or political
view, are incompatible with its own safety or happiness or conscientious regard to justice and duty. In the endless diversities
of human jurisprudence, many laws must exist in one country,
which are the result of local or accidental circumstances, and are
wholly unfit to be ingrafted upon the institutions and habits
of another. Many laws, well enough adapted to the notions of
heathen nations, would be totally repugnant to the feelings, as
well as to the justice, of those which embrace Christianity. A
heathen nation might justify polygamy, or incest, contracts of
moral turpitude, or exercises of despotic cruelty over persons,
which would be repugnant to the first principles of Christian
duty. The laws of one nation may be founded upon a narrow
selfishness, exclusively adapted to promote its own peculiar policy,
or the personal or proprietary interest of its own subjects, to the

injury or even the ruin of those of the subjects of all other countries. A particular nation may refuse all reciprocity of commerce, rights, and remedies to others. It may assume a superiority of powers and prerogatives, for the very purpose of crushing those of its neighbors who are less fortunate or less powerful. In these, and in many other cases which may easily be put without any extravagance of supposition, there would be extreme difficulty in saying that other nations were bound to enforce laws, institutions, or customs of that nation which were subversive of their own morals, justice, interest, or polity. Who, for instance (not to multiply cases), who would contend that any nation in Christendom ought to carry into effect, to its utmost range, the paternal power of the ancient Romans in their early jurisprudence, extending to the life and death of their children?[1] Or, who would now contend for that terrible power (if it ever really existed) under the law of the Twelve Tables, which enabled creditors to cut their debtor's body into pieces, and divide it among them?[2]

26. *Views of Continental Jurists.*—The jurists of continental Europe have, with uncommon skill and acuteness, endeavored to collect principles which ought to regulate this subject among all nations. But it is very questionable whether their success has been at all proportionate to their labor; and whether their principles, if universally adopted, would be found either convenient or desirable, or even just, under all circumstances. Their systems indeed have had mainly in view the juridical polity, fit for the different provinces and states of a common empire, although they are by no means limited to such cases. It is easy to see that in a nation like France before the Revolution, governed by different laws in its various provinces, some uniform rules might be adopted which would not be equally fit for the adoption of independent nations, possessing no such common interests, or such a common basis of jurisprudence. The leading positions maintained by many of the French jurists are, that the laws of a country which concern persons who reside within and are subject

---

[1] Laws of the Twelve Tables, table 4, c. 1; 1 Pothier, Pandects, and Id. s. 1, 2 (8vo. ed. Paris, 1818), p. 386, 387; 1 Black. Comm. 452; Fergusson on Marriage and Divorce, 411; Grotius, b. 2, c. 5. s. 7.

[2] Table 3, c. 4; 1 Pothier, Pandects, and Id. Comm. s. 2 (8vo. ed. Paris, 1818), p. 372, 380, 381; 2 Black. Comm. 472, 473.

to its territorial jurisdiction ought to be deemed of universal
obligation in all other countries; that the laws which concern
the property of such persons ought to be deemed purely local,
and the laws of a mixed character, concerning such persons and
property, ought to be deemed local or universal according to
their predominant character.   Thus Boullenois lays down these
rules in pointed terms: 'Les loix pures personnelles, soit personnelles universelles, soit personnelles particulières, se portent partout; c'est à dire, que l'homme est partout de l'état, soit universel, soit particulier, dont sa personne est affectée, par la loi de
son domicil.   Les loix réelles n'ont point d'extension directe, ni
indirecte, hors la jurisdiction et la domination du legislateur.
Le sujet et le matériel dominant direct et immédiat du statut en
détermine la nature et qualité; c'est à dire, que le sujet et le
matériel le font être réel, ou personnel.' [1]

27. *Difficulty of applying their Rules.*—Independent of the
almost insurmountable difficulties in which the continental jurists
admit themselves to be involved in the attempt to settle the true
character of these mixed cases of international jurisprudence, and
about which they have been engaged in endless controversies with
each other, there are certain exceptions to these rules, generally admitted, which shake the very foundation on which they
rest, and admonish us that it is far easier to give simplicity to
systems than to reconcile them with the true duties and interests
of all nations in all cases.   Take, for example, two neighboring
states, one of which admits, and the other of which prohibits, the
existence of slavery and the rights of property growing out of
it; what help would it be to either, in ascertaining its own
duties and interests in regard to the other, to say that their
laws, so far as they regard the persons of the slaves, were of
universal obligation, and, so far as they regard the property in
slaves, they were real, and of no obligation beyond the territory
of the lawgiver? [2]

28. *Remarks of Mr. Justice Porter.*—There is indeed great
truth in the remarks which have been judicially promulgated
on this subject by a learned court.   'When so many men of
great talents and learning are thus found to fail in fixing certain

---

[1] 1 Boullenois, Traité des Statuts, Princep. Gén. 18, 23, 27, p. 6, 7.
[2] See Somerset's Case (Lofft, 1; 20 How. St. Trials, 1), and Hargrave's
note to Co. Lit. 79 *b*, note 44.

principles, we are forced to conclude that they have failed, not from want of ability, but because the matter was not susceptible of being settled on certain principles. They have attempted to go too far, to define and fix that which cannot, in the nature of things, be defined and fixed. They seem to have forgotten that they wrote on a question which touched the comity of nations, and that that comity is, and ever must be, uncertain; that it must necessarily depend on a variety of circumstances which cannot be reduced to any certain rule; that no nation will suffer the laws of another to interfere with her own to the injury of her citizens; that whether they do or not must depend on the condition of the country in which the foreign law is sought to be enforced, the particular nature of her legislation, her policy, and the character of her institutions; that in the conflict of laws it must often be a matter of doubt which should prevail; and that, whenever a doubt does exist, the court, which decides, will prefer the laws of its own country to that of the stranger.' [1]

29. *Huberus.*—Huberus has laid down three axioms, which he deems sufficient to solve all the intricacies of the subject. The first is, that the laws of every empire have force only within the limits of its own government, and bind all who are subjects thereof, but not beyond those limits.[2] The second is, that all persons who are found within the limits of a government, whether their residence is permanent or temporary, are to be deemed subjects thereof.[3] The third is, that the rulers of every empire from comity admit that the laws of every people in force within its own limits ought to have the same force everywhere, so far as they do not prejudice the powers or rights of other governments, or of their citizens.[4] 'From this,' he adds, 'it appears that this matter is to be determined, not simply by the civil laws, but by the convenience and tacit consent of different people; for since the laws of one people cannot have any direct force among another people, so nothing could be more inconvenient in the commerce and general intercourse of nations than that what is valid by the laws of one place should become without effect by the diversity of laws of another; and that this is the true reason

[1] Mr. Justice Porter, in delivering the opinion of the court in the case of Saul *v.* His Creditors, 5 Mart. N.S. (La.) 569, 595, 596.
[2] Huberus, lib. 1, tit. 3; De Conflictu Legum, s. 2, p. 538.
[3] Ibid.   [4] Ibid.

of the last axiom, of which no one hitherto seems to have entertained any doubt.'[1]

30. *Hertius.*—Hertius seems to have been dissatisfied with these rules, and especially with the last; and he doubts exceedingly whether this comity of nations, founded upon the notion of mutual convenience and utility, can furnish any sufficiently solid basis of a system. 'Ob reciprocam enim utilitatem, in disciplinam juris gentium abiise, ut civitas alterius civitatis leges apud se valere patiatur, adeoque exemplum hoc, ut evidentissimi argumenti ad probandum, quod jus gentium revera a jure naturæ distinctum sit, vult observari. Verum enim nos valde dubitamus, num res hæc ex jure gentium, sive mutua earum indulgentia, possit definiri, presertim cum in una eademque civitate collisio sæpissime fiat. Norunt etiam periti ex solis exemplis jus gentium adstruere, quam sit fallax; tum si sola populorum conniventia id niti dicamus, quæ juris erit efficacia?'[2] He adds, that he is disposed to search deeper into the matter: 'Nobis paullo altius libet repetere;'[3] and he proceeds to enunciate his own views under the known distinctions of personal statutes and real statutes, and then lays down the following rules. (1) 'When a law is directed or has regard to the person, we are to look to (be governed by) the laws of the country to which he is personally subject.' 'Quando lex in personam dirigitur, respiciendum est ad leges illius civitatis, quæ personam habet subjectam.'[4] (2) 'If a law bears directly upon things, it is local, in whatever place and by whomsoever the act is done.' 'Si lex directo rei imponitur, ea locum habet, ubicunque etiam locorum et a quocunque actus celebretur.'[5] (3) 'If a law gives the form (prescribes the form)

[1] Ibid. These axioms of Huberus are so often cited, that it may be well to give them in his own words. (1) 'Leges cujusque imperii vim habent intra terminos ejusdem reipublicæ, omnesque ei subjectos obligant, nec ultra. (2) Pro subjectis imperio habendi sunt omnes, qui intra terminos ejusdem reperiuntur, sive in perpetuum, sive ad tempus ibi commorentur. (3) Rectores imperiorum id comiter agunt, ut jura cujusque populi intra terminos ejus exercita teneant ubique suam vim, quatenus nihil potestati aut juri alterius imperantis ejusque civium præjudicetur. 2 Hub. lib. 1, tit. 3; De Conflictu Legum, s. 2.

[2] Hertii, Opera, de Collis. Leg. s. 4, n. 3, 4, p. 120; Id. p. 170, 171, ed. 1716.
[3] Ibid.
[4] 1 Hertii, Opera, de Collis. s. 4, art. 8, p. 123; Id. p. 175, ed. 1716; post, s. 238.
[5] Id. s. 4, art. 9, p. 123; Id. p. 177, ed. 1716; post, s. 238.

to the act, then the place of the act, and not of the domicil of
the party, or of the situation of the thing, is to be regarded.'
'Si lex actui formam dat, inspiciendus est locus actus, non domicilii, non rei sitæ.' [1]   Now, after the admission of Hertius himself,
that the usage of nations must furnish a very fallacious guide on
such a subject, it is not a little difficult to perceive what superior
authority or value his own rules have over those of Huberus.
The latter has at least this satisfactory foundation for his most
important rule, that he is mainly guided in it by the practice of
nations; and he thus aimed, as Grotius had done before him, to
avail himself of the practice of nations, as a solid proof of the
acknowledged law of nations.[2]

31. *Authority of Huberus.*—Some attempts have been made,
but without success, to undervalue the authority of Huberus.
It is certainly true that he is not often spoken of, except by
jurists belonging to the Dutch school.   Boullenois, however, has
quoted his third and last axiom with manifest approbation.[3]
But it will require very little aid of authority to countenance his
works, if his maxims are well founded; and if they are not, no
approbation founded on foreign recognitions of them can disguise their defects.   It is not, however, a slight recommendation
of his works, that hitherto he has possessed an undisputed preference on this subject over other continental jurists, as well in
England as in America.   Indeed his first two maxims will in
the present day scarcely be disputed by any one; and the last
seems irresistibly to flow from the right and duty of every nation
to protect its own subjects against injuries resulting from the
unjust and prejudicial influence of foreign laws, and to refuse its
aid to carry into effect any foreign laws which are repugnant to
its own interests and polity.

32. *Laws prejudicial to other Nations.*—It is difficult to perceive upon what ground a claim can be rested, to give to any
municipal laws an extra-territorial effect, when those laws are
prejudicial to the rights of other nations, or to those of their sub-

[1] 1 Hertii, Opera, de Collis. Leg. s. 4, art. 10, p. 126; Id. p. 179, ed. 1716;
post, s. 238.
[2] The Scottish courts seem constantly to have held the doctrine of Huberus
in his third axiom to be entirely correct.   See Fergusson on Marr. and Div.
395, 396, 410.
[3] 1 Boullenois, Traité des Statuts, c. 3, obs. 10, p. 155.

jects. (*a*) It would at once annihilate the sovereignty and equality of every nation which should be called upon to recognize and enforce them, or compel it to desert its own proper interest and duty to its own subjects in favor of strangers, who were regardless of both. A claim so naked of any principle or just authority to support it is wholly inadmissible.

33. *Comity.*—It has been thought by some jurists that the term *comity* is not sufficiently expressive of the obligation of nations to give effect to foreign laws when they are not prejudicial to their own rights and interests. And it has been suggested that the doctrine rests on a deeper foundation; that it is not so much a matter of comity or courtesy as a matter of paramount moral duty.[1] Now assuming that such a moral duty does exist, it is clearly one of imperfect obligation, like that of beneficence, humanity, and charity. Every nation must be the final judge for itself, not only of the nature and extent of the duty, but of the occasions on which its exercise may be justly demanded. And certainly there can be no pretence to say that any foreign nation has a right to require the full recognition and execution of its own laws in other territories, when those laws are deemed oppressive or injurious to the rights or interests of the inhabitants of the latter, or when their moral character is questionable, or their provisions are impolitic or unjust.[2] Even in other cases it is difficult to perceive a clear foundation in morals or in natural law for declaring that any nation has a right (all others being equal in sovereignty) to insist that its own positive laws shall be of superior obligation in a foreign realm to the domestic laws of the latter of an equally positive character. What intrinsic right has one nation to declare that no contract shall be binding which is made by any of its subjects in a foreign country, unless they are twenty-five years of age, any more than another nation where the contract is made has a right to declare that such a contract shall be binding if made by any person of twenty-one years of age? One would suppose that if there be anything clearly within the scope of national sovereignty, it is the right to fix

[1] Liverm. Dissert. p. 26–30.
[2] See Mr. Justice Porter, in the case of Saul *v.* His Creditors, 5 Mart. N.S. (La.) 569, 596–599.

(*a*) The Halley, L. R. 2 P. C. 193, 203.

what shall be the rule to govern contracts made within its own territories.[1]

34. *Every Nation the Judge of its own Duty in this Respect.* — That a nation ought not to make its own jurisprudence an instrument of injustice to other nations, or to their subjects, may be admitted. But in a vast variety of cases which may be put, the rejection of the laws of a foreign nation may work less injustice than the enforcement of them will remedy. And here again every nation must judge for itself what is its true duty in the administration of justice in its domestic tribunals. It is not to be taken for granted that the rule of the foreign nation which complains of a grievance is right, and that its own rule is wrong.

35. *Foundation of the Administration of International Law.* — The true foundation on which the administration of international law must rest is, that the rules which are to govern are those which arise from mutual interest and utility, from a sense of the inconveniences which would result from a contrary doctrine, and from a sort of moral necessity to do justice, in order that justice may be done to us in return.[2] This is the ground upon which Rodenburg puts it. ' Quid, igitur,' says he, ' rei in causa est, quod personalia statuta territorium egrediantur? Unicum hoc ipsa rei natura ac necessitas invexit, ut cum de statu et conditione hominum quæritur, uni solummodo judici, et quidem domicilii, universum in illa jus sit attributum ; cum enim ab uno certoque loco statum hominis legem accipere necesse est, quod absurdum, earumque rerum naturaliter inter se pugna foret, ut in quot loca quis iter faciens, aut navigans, delatus fuerit, totidem ille statum mutaret aut conditionem ; ut uno eodemque tempore hic sui juris, illic alieni futurus sit ; uxor simul in potestate viri, et extra eandem sit ; alio loco habeatur quis prodigus, alio frugi.'[3] President Bouhier expounds the ground with still more distinctness : ' Mais avant toutes choses il faut se souvenir, qu'encore que la règle étroite soit pour la restriction des coutumes dans leurs limites, l'extension en a néanmoins été admise en faveur de l'utilité publique, et souvent même par une espèce de nécessité, &c. Ainsi, quand les peuples voisins ont souffert cette extension, ce

---

[1] See post, s. 75; and Mr. Justice Porter's opinion in Saul v. His Creditors, 5 Mart. N.S. (La.) 569, 596, 597, 598.

[2] Liverm. Dissert. p. 28; Blanchard v. Russell, 13 Mass. 4.

[3] Rodenburg de Stat. Diversit. tit. 1, c. 3, s. 4; 2 Boullenois, App. p. 8.

n'est point qu'ils se soient vus soumis à un statut étranger.   C'est
seulement, parce qu'ils y ont trouvé leur intérêt particulier en
ce qu'en pareil cas leurs coutumes ont le même avantage dans les
provinces voisines.   On peut donc dire, que cette extension est
sur une espèce de droit des gens, et de bienséance, en vertu duquel les différens peuples sont tacitement demeurés d'accord, de
souffrir cette extension de coutume à coutume, toutes les fois que
l' équité et l'utilité commune le demanderoient ; à moins que celle,
où l'extension seroit demandée ne contint en ce cas une disposition prohibitive.' [1]

36. *Extent of the Recognition of Foreign Laws.*—But of the
nature and extent and utility of this recognition of foreign laws
respecting the state and condition of persons, every nation must
judge for itself, and certainly is not bound to recognize them
when they would be prejudicial to its own interests.   The very
terms in which the doctrine is commonly enunciated carry along
with them this necessary qualification and limitation of it.   Mutual utility presupposes that the interest of all nations is consulted, and not that of one only.   Now this demonstrates that
the doctrine owes its origin and authority to the voluntary adoption and consent of nations.   It is therefore in the strictest
sense a matter of the comity of nations, and not of any absolute
paramount obligation superseding all discretion on the subject.[2]

37. *Opinions of Vattel and Lord Stowell.*—Vattel has with
great propriety said : ' That it belongs exclusively to each nation
to form its own judgment of what its conscience prescribes to it,
of what it can do or cannot do, of what is proper or improper for
it to do.   And of course it rests solely with it to examine and
determine whether it can perform any office for another nation,
without neglecting the duty which it owes to itself.' [3]   Lord
Stowell has pointed out the same principle in his usual felicitous
manner.   Speaking with reference to the validity of a Scotch
marriage, in controversy before him, he remarked : ' Being entertained in an English court, it [the cause] must be adjudicated
according to the principles of English law applicable to such a
case.   But the only principle applicable to such a case by the
law of England is, that the validity of Miss Gordon's [the plain-

[1] Bouhier, Cout. de Bourg. c. 23, s. 62, 63, p. 467.
[2] 2 Kent Com. 457, 458.
[3] Vattel, Prelim. Disc. p. 61, 62, s. 14, 16.

tiff's] marriage rights must be tried by reference to the law of the country where, if they exist at all, they had their origin. Having furnished this principle, the law of England withdraws altogether, and leaves the legal question to the exclusive judgment of the law of Scotland.'[1]

38. *Comity of Nations.*—There is then not only no impropriety in the use of the phrase 'comity of nations,' but it is the most appropriate phrase to express the true foundation and extent of the obligation of the laws of one nation within the territories of another.[2] It is derived altogether from the voluntary consent of the latter, and is inadmissible when it is contrary to its known policy or prejudicial to its interests. In the silence of any positive rule affirming or denying or restraining the operation of foreign laws, courts of justice presume the tacit adoption of them by their own government, unless they are repugnant to its policy or prejudicial to its interests. (a) It is not comity of the courts, but the comity of the nation, which is administered and ascertained in the same way, and guided by the same reasoning, by which all other principles of the municipal law are ascertained and guided.[3] The doctrine of Huberus would seem therefore

[1] Dalrymple *v.* Dalrymple, 2 Hagg. Cons. 58. See Scrimshire *v.* Scrimshire, 2 Hagg. Cons. 407, 416.

[2] See Robinson *v.* Bland, 2 Burr. 1077, 1079; Blanchard *v.* Russell, 13 Mass. 4.

[3] See this doctrine expressly recognized by the Supreme Court of the United States, in Bank of Augusta *v.* Earle, 13 Pet. 519, 589. Mr. Chief Justice Taney, in delivering the opinion of the court, said: ' It is needless to enumerate here the instances in which, by the general practice of civilized countries, the laws of the one will, by the comity of nations, be recognized and executed in another, where the rights of individuals are concerned. The cases of contracts made in a foreign country are familiar examples; and courts of justice have always expounded and executed them according to the laws of the place in which they were made, provided that law was not repugnant to the laws or policy of their own country. The comity thus extended to other nations is no impeachment of sovereignty. It is the voluntary act of the nation by which it is offered, and is inadmissible when contrary to its policy or prejudicial to its interests. But it contributes so largely to promote justice between individuals, and to produce a friendly intercourse between the sovereignties to which they belong, that courts of justice have continually acted upon it, as a part of the voluntary law of nations. It is truly said, in Story's Conflict of Laws, s. 38, that, " In the silence of any positive rule, affirming or denying or restraining the operation of foreign laws, courts of justice presume the tacit adoption of them by their own government, unless they are repug-

(a) Bateman *v.* Service, 6 App. Cas. 386, 389 (P. C.).

to stand upon just principles; and though, from its generality, it leaves behind many grave questions as to its application, it has much to commend it in point of truth, as well as of simplicity. It has accordingly been sanctioned both in England and America by a judicial approbation, as direct and universal as can fairly be desired for the purpose of giving sanction to it as authority, or as reasoning.[1] (a).

nant to its policy or prejudicial to its interests. It is not the comity of the courts, but the comity of the nation, which is administered and ascertained in the same way, and guided by the same reasoning, by which all other principles of municipal law are ascertained and guided.'' '

[1] Out of the great variety of authorities in which the rules of Huberus are directly or indirectly approved, the reader is referred to the following: Co. Lit. 79 b, Hargrave's note, 44; Robinson v. Bland, 2 Burr. 1077, 1078; Holman v. Johnson, Cowp. 341; 2 Kent Com. 453–463; Pearsall v. Dwight, 2 Mass. 84, 90; Desesbats v. Berquier, 1 Binn. (Pa.) 336; Holmes v. Remsen, 4 Johns. Ch. (N. Y.) 469; Mr. Cowen's note to 4 Cowen (N. Y.) 510; Saul v. His Creditors, 5 Mart. N.S. (La.) 569, 596–598; Greenwood v. Curtis, 6 Mass. 358; Bank of Augusta v. Earle, 13 Pet. 519, 588–591.

(a) *Comity and Law*. The principle upon which a foreign law is applied in dealing with a matter that is governed by it is stated by Lord Brougham in Warrender v. Warrender, 9 Bligh, 115; 2 Cl. & F. 529, as follows: 'This is sometimes expressed, and I take leave to say inaccurately expressed, by saying that there is a comitas shown by the tribunals of one country towards the laws of the other country. Such a thing as comitas or courtesy may be said to exist in certain cases, as where the French courts inquire how our law would deal with a Frenchman in similar or parallel circumstances, and, upon proof of it, so deal with an Englishman in those circumstances. This is truly a comitas, and can be explained upon no other ground; and I must be permitted to say, with all respect for the usage, it is not easily reconcilable to any sound reason. But when the courts of one country consider the laws of another in which any contract has been made, or is alleged to have been made, in construing its meaning, or ascertaining its existence, they can hardly be said to act from courtesy, ex comitate; for it is of the essence of the subject-matter to ascertain the meaning of the parties, and that they did solemnly bind themselves; and it is clear that you must presume them to have intended what the law of the country sanctions or supposes; it is equally clear that their adopting the forms and solemnities which that law prescribes, shows their intention to bind themselves, nay, more, is the only safe criterion of their having entertained such an intention. Therefore the courts of the country where the question arises, resort to the law of the country where the contract was made, not ex comitate, but ex debito justitiæ; and in order to explicate their own jurisdiction by discovering that which they are in quest of, and which alone they are in quest of, the meaning and intent of the parties.'

Mr. Redfield, in the 6th edition of this work (p. 36), said, 'The foreign law by which the contract or relation was created, and according to which, in its inception, it was expected by the parties to the relation to be performed, becomes an indispensable element, in order to translate such contract, relation, or duty into the vernacular language of the forum where the remedy is sought. And the courts, in referring to the law of the foreign state in order to give the proper force and interpretation to the contract or relation and the consequent duties and obligations, cannot be said to act from comity, any more than they could be said to refer to a dictionary of the foreign language from comity, when such reference was indispensable to the proper understanding of the terms in which the contract is expressed. The knowledge of the foreign language is not more indispensable to comprehend the natural force of the terms of the contract, than the knowledge of the foreign law is to a full comprehension of the legal effect of such terms.'

The principle upon which the courts enforce foreign judgments was considered by Blackburn, J., in Godard *v.* Gray, L. R. 6 Q. B. 148. After stating that the duty of enforcing such judgments was not an admitted principle of the law of nations, and that several of the continental nations did not enforce them except where there were reciprocal treaties to that effect, he continued, 'But in England and in those states which are governed by the common law, such judgments are enforced, not by virtue of any treaty, nor by virtue of any statute, but upon a principle very well stated by Parke, B., in Williams *v.* Jones, 13 M. & W. 633: "Where a court of competent jurisdiction has adjudicated a certain sum to be due from one person to another, a legal obligation arises to pay that sum, on which an action of debt to enforce the judgment may be maintained. It is in this way that the judgments of foreign and colonial courts are supported and enforced."' In Schibsby *v.* Westenholz, L. R. 6 Q. B. 159, Blackburn, J., stated this principle again, and added, 'And we

think that if the principle on which foreign judgments were enforced was that which is loosely called *comity*, we could hardly decline to enforce a foreign judgment given in France against a resident in Great Britain under circumstances hardly, if at all, distinguishable from those under which we, mutatis mutandis, might give judgment against a resident in France; but it is quite different if the principle be that which we have just laid down.' Referring to an English statute by which foreigners may be summoned in certain cases and judgment may be given against them if they fail to appear, he said, ' Should a foreigner be sued under the provisions of the statute referred to, and then come to the courts of this country and desire to be discharged, the only questions which our courts could entertain would be whether the acts of the British legislature, rightly construed, gave us jurisdiction over this foreigner, for we must obey them. But if, judgment being given against him in our courts, an action were brought upon it in the courts of the United States (where the law as to the enforcing of foreign judgments is the same as our own), a further question would be open, viz., not only whether the British legislature had given the English courts jurisdiction over the defendant, but whether he was under any obligation which the American courts could recognize to submit to the jurisdiction thus created. This is precisely the question which we have now to determine with regard to the jurisdiction assumed by the French jurisprudence over foreigners. . . . The question we have now to answer is, can the empire of France pass a law to bind the whole world? We admit, with perfect candor, that in the supposed case of a judgment obtained in this country against a foreigner under the provisions of the Common Law Procedure Act, being sued on in a court of the United States, the question for the court of the United States would be, can the Island of Great Britain pass a law to bind the whole world? We think in each case the answer should be, No, but every country can pass laws to bind a great many persons; and therefore the further question has to be determined, whether the defendant in the particular suit was such a person as to be bound by the judgment which it is sought to enforce.'

The notion that comity or courtesy is the foundation of the effect given to foreign laws seems to be similar to that from which the terms *conflict of laws* and *private international law* came to be applied to the subject that treats of the effect to be given to such laws. There is really neither a conflict of any laws, nor anything international in the law that is treated of.

If, in a case before an American court, the rights of the parties depend upon a transaction which took place in France, and the transaction is of a kind concerning which the French law and that of the American court are different, the question arises whether the transaction is governed by the French law or not. If the court decides that it is governed by the French law, then it is bound to apply that law in determining the rights of the parties, not from courtesy or politeness to France, but because justice requires it. The rights of the parties depend partly on the circumstances of the transaction, and partly on the law which gave the transaction its force and effect. It would be as unjust to apply a different law, as it would be to determine the rights of the parties by a different transaction. In applying the French law, the court does not allow it to operate in America, but only recognizes the fact that it did operate in France.

In such a case as this, it is evident that there is no *conflict* of laws. There is a difference between the French law and the American law, and there

is a question which of them applies to the case, but the question itself assumes that only one does apply, and there can be no conflict between a law that applies to a case and another that does not. The *question* which of the two laws is applicable cannot properly be called a conflict of the laws.

There is nothing *international* in the rules by which the court determines which law is applicable. They do not belong to that system of rules which nations observe in their conduct towards one another. There is no obligation or duty recognized between nations to deal with such cases at all, or to deal with them in any particular way. If the court takes jurisdiction of the case in which the question arises, it must establish some rules for determining which law is applicable. These rules are part of the municipal law of the country or state to which the court belongs. This was expressed by Lord Stowell in a case where the validity of a ceremony of marriage performed in Scotland was in question: 'Being entertained in an English court, it must be adjudicated according to the principles of English law applicable to such a case. But the only principle applicable to such a case by the law of England is, that the validity of Miss Gordon's marriage rights must be tried by reference to the law of the country where, if they exist at all, they had their origin. Having furnished this principle, the law of England withdraws altogether, and leaves the legal question to the exclusive judgment of the law of Scotland.' Dalrymple *v.* Dalrymple, 2 Hagg. Cons. 58; supra, s. 37. As the subject is common to the law of all nations, the opinions of foreign judges and jurists upon questions of this kind are useful in the same way as their opinions upon other subjects common to different countries. It may also be said with regard to this subject, as was said with regard to marine insurance by Brett, L.J., referring to a remark of Chancellor Kent, that 'it is most advisable that the law should, if possible, be in conformity with what it is in all countries,' (Cory *v.* Burr, 9 Q. B. D. 469; American Ins. Co. *v.* Dunham, 15 Wend. (N.Y.) 11), but it is certain that there is a difference in the laws of different countries upon this subject, especially between those of continental Europe and those of countries governed by the English common law.

It cannot be said even that the *jurisdiction* of cases involving questions of foreign law is founded upon comity or courtesy. It exists because the cases are of a kind within the general jurisdiction of the court, and the circumstance that a question of foreign law is involved is not a ground for an exception to the jurisdiction. See Mostyn *v.* Fabrigas, 1 Sm. L. C. (6th ed.) 623 ; Scott *v.* Seymour, 1 H. & C. 219. The jurisdiction of the court depends upon the policy or interest of the state, not upon courtesy to foreign states or sovereigns. Even if the jurisdiction could be rested upon courtesy when the parties were foreigners, or when the obligation or liability to be enforced was created by foreign laws, as in case of a contract made, or a tort committed, in a foreign country, still there would be cases where the jurisdiction could not rest upon that foundation. A right of dower may depend upon the validity of a marriage in a foreign country. A right of action for taking goods from a person's possession in the country where the action is brought may depend upon whether he acquired a title to them by a transaction in a foreign country. Courtesy to a foreign state could not be the ground upon which the court would take cognizance of a claim to dower in land within its jurisdiction, or of a trespass committed within its jurisdiction, although a question of foreign law be involved. If the court takes cognizance of the case, it must decide whether the foreign law applies to it or not. If it decides that the foreign law is applicable, it will give effect to it, not from comity, but because it is the law that governs the case.

CHAPTER III.

NATIONAL DOMICIL.

39. *Matters to be dealt with in this Work.*—Having disposed of these preliminary considerations, it is proposed, in the further progress of these commentaries, to examine the operation and effect of laws: first, in relation to persons, their capacity, state, and condition; secondly, in relation to contracts; thirdly, in relation to property, personal, mixed, and real; fourthly, in relation to wills, successions, and distributions; fifthly, in relation to persons acting in autre droit, such as guardians, executors, and administrators; sixthly, in relation to remedies and judicial sentences; seventhly, in relation to penal laws and offences; and eighthly, in relation to evidence and proofs.

40. *Domicil.*—As however in all the discussions upon this subject, perpetual reference will be made to the domicil of the party it may be proper to ascertain what is the true meaning of the term *domicil;* or rather, what constitutes the national or local domicil of a party, according to the understanding of publicists and jurists.[1]

41. *Definition.*—By the term *domicil*, in its ordinary acceptation, is meant the place where a person lives or has his home. In this sense the place where a person has his actual residence, inhabitancy, or commorancy, is sometimes called his domicil. In a strict and legal sense that is properly the domicil of a person where he has his true, fixed, permanent home and principal establishment, and to which, whenever he is absent, he has the intention of returning (animus revertendi).[2] (a)

[1] Upon the subject of this chapter the learned reader is referred to Burge's Col. & For. Law, vol. 1, p. 1, c. 2, p. 32–57.
[2] Dr. Lieber's Encyc. Americ. art. Domicil.

(a) The term *domicil* in its technical sense, in which it is used in the Conflict of Laws, always signifies a country or territory subject to one

42. *Roman Law.*—In the Roman law it is said: 'There is no doubt that every person has his domicil in that place which he makes his family residence and principal place of his business; from which he is not about to depart, unless some business requires; when he leaves it, he deems himself a wanderer; and when he returns to it, he deems himself no longer abroad.' 'In eodem loco singulos habere domicilium, non ambigitur, ubi quis larem rerumque ac fortunarum summam constituit; unde rursus non sit discessurus, si nihil avocet; unde cum profectus est,

system of law. It does not signify any particular place within such country. The object of the branch of law treated of in this work is to determine by what system of law a case is governed. When it is governed by the law of domicil, the law which governs is that of the country in which the person is domiciled. The purpose of an inquiry as to his domicil is accomplished as soon as it is ascertained in what country he has his domicil. It is to that country that the term *domicil* is applied. All the facts which make it his domicil may also exist in respect of some particular place in that country, but this is immaterial and it is not always the case. Mr. Dicey shows how a person may be domiciled in a country without being domiciled at any particular place in it; e. g. a Frenchman might come to England and live at Manchester, with the intention of residing permanently in England, but intending to live at Manchester for a limited time only; or, a person domiciled in England might live in a house which he had taken on a lease for three years and intended to live in no longer; or, a person, without having a more permanent residence, might go from hotel to hotel and from watering-place to watering-place (see Dicey on Domicil, 55–59).

Lord Westbury said, in Udny v. Udny, L. R. 1 H. L. Sc. 457, 'The law of England, and of almost all civilized countries, ascribes to each individual at his birth two distinct legal states or conditions; one by virtue of which he becomes the subject of some particular country, binding him by the tie of natural allegiance, and which may be called his political status; another, by virtue of which he has ascribed to him the character of a citizen of some particular country, and as such is possessed of certain municipal rights, and subject to certain obligations, which latter character is the civil status or condition of the individual, and may be quite different from his political status. The political status may depend on different laws in different countries; whereas the civil status is governed universally by one single principle, namely, that of domicil, which is the criterion established by law for the purpose of determining civil status. For it is on this basis that the personal rights of the party, that is to say, the law which determines his majority or minority, his marriage, succession, testacy, or intestacy, must depend.'

Commercial or *trade domicil* is a term used to designate the residence which in time of war determines whether a person's property embarked in trade is to be regarded as of a belligerent or neutral character. This subject belongs to public international law, and is not within the scope of this work. See Westlake (ed. 1880) 285; Dicey on Domicil, 341.

peregrinari videtur; quod si rediit, peregrinari jam destitit.'[1] And in another place it is said: 'If any one always carries on his business, not in a colony, but in a municipality or city where he buys, sells, and contracts, where he makes use of and attends the forum, the public baths and public shows, where he celebrates the holidays and enjoys all municipal privileges, and none in colony, he is deemed there to have his domicil, rather than in the place (colony) in which he sojourns for purposes of agriculture.' 'Si quis negotia sua non in colonia, sed in municipio, semper agit, in illo vendit, emit, contrahit, eo in foro, balneo, spectaculis utitur, ibi festos dies celebrat, omnibus denique municipii commodis, nullis coloniarum, fruitur, ibi magis habere domicilium, quam ubi colendi causa diversatur.'[2] And again: 'He is deemed an inhabitant who has his domicil in any place, and whom the Greeks call πάροικον, that is to say, a neighbor or person inhabiting near to a village. For those are not alone to be deemed inhabitants who dwell in a town, but those also who cultivate grounds near its limits so that they conduct themselves as if their place of abode were there.' 'Incola est, qui aliqua regione domicilium suum contulit; quem Græci πάροικον (id est, juxta habitantem) appellant. Nec tantum hi, qui in oppido morantur, incolæ sunt; sed etiam, qui alicujus oppidi finibus ita agrum habent, ut in eum se quasi in aliquam sedem, recipiant.'[3] Some at least of these are more properly descriptions than definitions of domicil. Pothier has generalized them in his own introduction to this title of the Pandects, and says: 'The seat of the fortune or property which any person possesses in any place constitutes his chief domicil.' 'Domicilium facit potissimum sedes fortunarum suarum, quas quis in aliquo loco habet.'[4] Voet says: 'Proprie dictum domicilium est, quod quis sibi constituet animo inde non decedendi, si non aliud avocet.'[5]

48. *Definitions by French Jurists.*—The French jurists have defined domicil to be the place where a person has his principal establishment. Thus Denizart says: 'The domicil of a person

---

[1] Cod. 10, 39, 7; Pothier, Pand. 50, n. 15; 1 Voet, ad Pand. 5, 1, n. 92, p. 344; Id. n. 94, p. 345.

[2] Dig. 50, 1, 27; Pothier, Pand. 50, 1, n. 18; 2 Domat, Public Law, b. 1, tit. 16, s. 3, art. 4.

[3] Dig. 50, 16, 239, s. 2; Id. 50, 16, 203; Pothier, Pand. 50, n. 16.

[4] Pothier, Pand. 50, 1, introd. art. 2, n. 18.

[5] Voet, ad Pand. 5, 1, n. 94.

is the place where a person enjoys his rights, and establishes his
abode, and makes the seat of his property.' 'Le domicile est le
lieu, où une personne, jouissant de ses droits, établit sa demeure
et le siége de sa fortune.'[1] The Encyclopedists say: 'That it is,
properly speaking, the place where one has fixed the centre of
his business.' 'C'est, à proprement parler, l'endroit, où l'on a
placé le centre de ses affaires.'[2] Pothier says: 'It is the place
where a person has established the principal seat of his residence
and of his business.' 'C'est le lieu, où une personne a établi le
siége principal de sa demeure et de ses affaires.'[3] And the modern French Code declares that the domicil of every Frenchman,
as to the exercise of civil rights, is at the place where he has his
principal establishment (est au lieu, où il a son principal établissement).'[4] Vattel has defined domicil to be a fixed residence
in any place with an intention of always staying there.[5] But
this is not an accurate statement. It would be more correct to
say that that place is properly the domicil of a person in which
his habitation is fixed without any present intention of removing
therefrom.[6]

44. *What constitutes Domicil.*—Two things then must concur
to constitute domicil: first, residence; and secondly, the intention of making it the home of the party. There must be the fact
and the intent; for, as Pothier has truly observed, a person cannot establish a domicil in a place, except it be animo et facto.[7] (a)

[1] Denizart, art. Domicil.
[2] Encyclop. Moderne, art. Domicil.
[3] Pothier, Introd. Gén. Cout. d'Orléans, c. 1, s. 1, art. 8.
[4] Cod. Civ. art. 102. See also Merlin, Répert. art. Domicil.
[5] Vattel, b. 1, c. 19, s. 22.
[6] Dr. Lieber's Encyc. Amer. Domicil; Putnam v. Johnson, 10 Mass. 488;
Tanner v. King, 11 La. 175.
[7] Pothier, Cout. d'Orléans, c. 1, s. 1, art. 9. See Scrimshire v. Scrimshire,
2 Hagg. Cons. 405, 406.

(1) Munro v. Munro, 7 Cl. & F. 842, 877, 891; Bell v. Kennedy, L. R. 1 H. L. Sc. 307; Udny v. Udny, L. R. 1 H. L. Sc. 441; Hodgson v. Beauchesne, 12 Moore P. C. 285; Craigie v. Lewin, 3 Curteis, 435; Burton v. Fisher, 1 Milw. Ecc. 183, 188; Colber v. Rivaz. 2 Curteis, 855, 857; Mitchell v. United States, 21 Wall. 350; Catlin v. Gladding, 4 Mason, 308; The Ann Green, 1 Gall. 274, 285; Burnham v. Rangeley, 1 Woodb. & M. 7; White v. Brown, 1 Wall. jun. 217; Harvard College v. Gore, 5 Pick. (Mass.) 370; Ross v. Ross, 103 Mass. 575; Leach v. Pillsbury, 15 N.H. 137; Dupuy v. Wurtz, 53 N. Y. 556; Isham v. Gibbons, 1 Bradf. (N. Y.) 69; Foster v. Hall, 4 Humph. (Tenn.) 346; Williams v. Saunders, 5 Cold.

Voet emphatically says: 'Illud certum est, neque solo animo atque destinatione patris familias, aut contestatione sola, sine re et pacto, domicilium constitui; neque sola domus comparatione in aliqua regione; neque sola habitatione, sine proposito illic perpetuo morandi.'[1] So D'Argentré says: 'Quamobrem, qui figendi ejus animum non habent, sed usus, necessitatis, aut negotiationis causa alicubi sint, protinus a negotio discessuri, domicilium nullo temporis spatio constituent; cum neque animus sine facto neque factum sine animo ad id sufficiat.'[2] However in many cases actual residence is not indispensable to retain a domicil after it is once acquired; but it is retained, animo solo, by the mere intention not to change it or to adopt another. If, therefore, a person leaves his home for temporary purposes, but with an intention to return to it, this change of place is not in law a change of domicil. (a)   Thus, if a person should go on a voyage to sea, or to a foreign country, for health, (b) or for pleasure, or for business of a temporary nature, with an intention to return, such a transitory residence would not constitute a new domicil, or amount to an abandonment of the old one; for it is not the mere act of inhabitancy in a place which makes it the domicil, but it is the fact coupled with the intention of remaining there, animo manendi.[3]

45. *Ascertainment of Domicil.*—It is sometimes a matter of no small difficulty to decide in what place a person has his true

[1] 1 Voet, ad Pand. 5, 1, n. 98, p. 346.
[2] D'Argentré, ad Leg. Britonum, art. 9, n. 4, p. 26.
[3] Pothier, Cout. d'Orléans, c. 1, s. 1, art. 9; Encyclop. Amer. art. Domicil; Cochin, Œuvres, tom. 5, p. 4–6, 4to ed.

(Tenn.) 60; Horne v. Horne, 9 Ired. (N. C.) 99; Hairston v. Hairston, 27 Miss. 704; State v. Hallett, 8 Ala. 159; Sanderson v. Ralston, 20 La. An. 312; Smith v. People, 44 Ill. 16; Carey's Appeal, 75 Pa. St. 201; Adams v. Evans, 19 Kans. 174; Ex parte Blumer, 27 Tex. 734.

(a) Sears v. Boston, 1 Met. (Mass.) 250.

(b) Udny v. Udny, L. R. 1 H. L. Sc. 458; Moorhouse v. Lord, 10 H. L. C. 283, 285; Still v. Woodville, 38 Miss. 646. Even if the person expected to die in the foreign country, it would not become his domicil, for the animus manendi would not exist. Johnstone v. Beattie, 10 Cl. & F. 139; Dupuy v. Wurtz, 53 N. Y. 556. But if a person resides in a foreign country animo manendi, a change of domicil will not be prevented by the circumstance that he chose that country as his residence because he thought it suitable to his health. Hoskins v. Matthews, 8 D. M. & G. 13, 28; Hegeman v. Fox, 31 Barb. (N. Y. 475. See Dicey on Domicil, 133–137.

or proper domicil. (*a*) His residence is often of a very equivocal nature; and his intention as to that residence is often still
more obscure.[1] Both are sometimes to be gathered from slight
circumstances of mere presumption, and from equivocal and conflicting acts. (*b*) An intention of permanent residence may often
be ingrafted upon an inhabitancy originally taken for a special
or fugitive purpose.[2] (*c*) And, on the other hand, an intention
to change the domicil may be fully announced, and yet no correspondent change of inhabitancy may be actually made.[3] (*d*)

[1] Pothier, Cout. d'Orléans, c. 1, art. 20; Merlin, Répert, Domicil, s. 2, 6;
Bouhier, Cout. de Bourg. c. 22, s. 196–206.

[2] The Harmony, 2 C. Rob. 322, 324; Pothier, Cout. d'Orléans, c. 1, art. 15.

[3] See Harvard College *v.* Gore, 5 Pick. (Mass.) 370.

(*a*) No one can be without a domicil, and no one can have more than one domicil at the same time. Udny *v.* Udny, L. R. 1 H. L. Sc. 441; Abington *v.* North Bridgewater, 23 Pick. (Mass.) 170, 177; Thorndike *v.* Boston, 1 Met. (Mass.) 242; Dupuy *v.* Wurtz, 53 N. Y. 556; Cross *v.* Everts, 28 Tex. 523. It is sometimes said that a person cannot have more than one domicil at the same time *for the same purpose*. This qualification was probably suggested by the use of the term *domicil* to designate different kinds of residence, to which the term is not applicable in its technical sense stated above (s. 41, note). For instances of this use of the term see s. 49, note. See also Dicey on Domicil, 61–64. It has never been held that a person can have a domicil, in its technical sense, in more than one country at one time. The rules for ascertaining domicil admit of only one domicil at a time. In order to give any effect to the suggestion that a man may have different domicils for different purposes, the purpose for which reference is made to domicil in cases of a conflict of laws, must be regarded as a single purpose. For this purpose he cannot have more than one domicil at the same time.

(*b*) See Whicker *v.* Hume, 7 H.L. C.

124; Cockrell *v.* Cockrell, 25 L. J. Ch. 730; 2 Jur. N.S. 727; Drevon *v.* Drevon, 34 L. J. Ch. 129; 10 Jur. N.S. 717; Stevenson *v.* Masson, L. R. 17 Eq. 78; Thorndike *v.* Boston, 1 Met. (Mass.) 245, 246; Sears *v.* Boston, 1 Met. (Mass.) 250.

(*c*) Udny *v.* Udny, L. R. 1 H. L. Sc. 458; Platt *v.* Att.-Gen., 3 App. Cas. 336 (P. C.); Haldane *v.* Eckford, L. R. 8 Eq. 631.

(*d*) A change of domicil from one country or state to another under the same sovereign or government, as from Scotland to England, or from one of the United States to another, is more easily inferred than a change to a foreign country. Whicker *v.* Hume, 7 H. L. C. 159; Moorhouse *v.* Lord, 10 H. L. C. 286, 287; Att.-Gen. *v.* Pottinger, 6 H. & N. 733.

Little evidence is required to show that a man desires to resign his domicil of origin, where the probability of such a desire is great; as where a man had a Portuguese domicil of origin, but his family was English and he had been brought up in England and always expressed a dislike of Portugal and a desire to leave it. Sharpe *v.* Crispin, L. R. 1 P. & M. 620.

Length of residence raises the presumption of intention to acquire domicil. Hodgson *v.* Beauchesne, 12

'Domicilium re et facto transfertur, non nuda contestatione.'[1]
The Roman lawyers were themselves greatly puzzled upon this

[1] Dig. 50, 1, 20; Pothier, Pand. 50, 1, n. 26.

Moore P. C. 329; King v. Foxwell, 3 Ch. D. 518; Doucet v. Geoghegan, 9 Ch. D. 456 ; President of the United States v. Drummond, 33 Beav. 449; Shelton v. Tiffin, 6 How. 185.

The declarations, oral or written, of a person whose domicil is in question, are admissible evidence of his intention in residing at any place, if they are made before the controversy has arisen, but their weight depends much upon the circumstances. Hodgson v. Beauchesne, 12 Moore P. C. 325 ; Forbes v. Forbes, Kay, 341; In re Steer, 3 H. & N. 594; Crookenden v. Fuller, 1 Sw. & T. 441; Drevon v. Drevon, 34 L. J. Ch. 129; Jopp v. Wood, 4 D. J. & S. 616; Haldane v. Eckford, L. R. 8 Eq. 631, 642; Doucet v. Geoghegan, 9 Ch. D. 441; Dupuy v. Wurtz, 53 N. Y. 556; Thorndike v. Boston, 1 Met. (Mass.) 242; Kilburn v. Bennett, 3 Met. (Mass.) 199; Monson v. Palmer, 8 Allen (Mass.) 551; Wilson v. Terry, 9 Allen (Mass.) 214; Reeder v. Holcomb, 105 Mass. 93; Baptiste v. Volunbrun, 5 Harr. & J. (Md.) 97; Smith v. Croom, 7 Fla. 161; Beason v. State, 34 Miss. 602. His descriptions of himself in legal instruments are treated as declarations, but in some cases it has been said that by themselves they are entitled to but little weight. Forbes v. Forbes, Kay, 341; Whicker v. Hume, 13 Beav. 366, 400; Att.-Gen. v. Pottinger, 6 H. & N. 733; Ennis v. Smith, 14 How. 422; In re Stover, 4 Redf. (N. Y.) 82; Wilson v. Terry, 9 Allen (Mass.) 214; Wright v. Boston, 126 Mass. 161; Weld v. Boston, 126 Mass. 166; Smith v. Croom, 7 Fla. 81, 161; Gilman v. Gilman, 52 Me. 177. In Massachusetts such declarations were rejected in Wright v. Boston, 126 Mass. 161, and Weld v. Boston, 126

Mass. 166, on the ground that declarations were not admissible in favor of the party making them except when they accompanied acts of which evidence was admissible, and the reception of such declarations in evidence in Wilson v. Terry, 9 Allen, 214, was disapproved; but it would seem that although the declarations might be of little value, yet, according to the rule laid down in the case where they were rejected, they ought to have been deemed competent, because they accompanied the act of residing, and might show the person's intention in doing that act. See Bangor v. Brewer, 47 Me. at p. 102.

A person may himself testify as to his intention. Wilson v. Wilson, L. R. 2 P. & M. 435; Reeder v. Holcomb, 105 Mass. 93.

A Frenchman's marrying in England without taking the steps necessary to perfect the marriage by French law has been treated as evidence of his intention to abandon his French domicil of origin. Doucet v. Geoghegan, 9 Ch. D. 441 (C.A.); Drevon v. Drevon, 34 L. J. Ch. 129.

So has the making of a will the provisions of which would not be valid if the testator retained his former domicil. Doucet v. Geoghegan, 9 Ch. D. 441 (C.A.); Drevon v. Drevon, 34 L. J. Ch. 129; Haldane v. Eckford, L. R. 8 Eq. 631; Hood's Estate, 21 Pa. St. 106.

A person's removing the remains of his deceased children from a cemetery in another country to the place where he was residing, and his burying them there, has been considered important evidence of his intention to make that place his permanent residence. Haldane v. Eckford, L. R. 8 Eq. 631. But where an Englishman who had married a Frenchwoman

subject by cases of an equivocal nature ; and Ulpian and Labeo and others held different opinions respecting them.[1] Thus, to the question where a person had his domicil, who did his business equally in two places, Labeo answered that he had no domicil in either place.[2] But other jurists, and among them was Ulpian, were of opinion that a man might in such a case have two domicils, one in each place.[3] Celsus seems to have thought that, in such a case, which place was the domicil of the party depended upon his own choice and intention.[4] And Julian doubted whether, if he had no fixed choice and intention, he could have two domicils.[5]

46. *Acquisition and Change of Domicil.* — Without speculating upon all the various cases which may be started upon this subject, it may be useful to collect together some of the more important rules which have been generally adopted as guides in the cases which are of most familiar occurrence. *First*, the place of birth of a person is considered as his domicil if it is at the time of his birth the domicil of his parents. ' Patris originem unusquis-

[1] Dig. 50, 1, 5; Id. 50, 1, 27, s. 1–3; Pothier, Pand. 50, 1, n. 16; Id. n. 18, 21, 22.
[2] Dig. 50, 1, 5; Pothier, Pand. 50, 1, n. 18; post, s. 47.
[3] Dig. 50, 1, 6, 2; Pothier, Pand. 50, 1, n. 18.
[4] Dig. 50, 1, 27, 2; Pothier, Pand. 50, 1, n. 18.
[5] Dig. 50, 1, 27, 2; Pothier, Pand. 50, 1, n. 18; Somerville v. Somerville, 5 Ves. 750, 786, 790; 2 Domat, Public Law, b. 1, tit. 16, s. 3, p. 462; Id. art. 6; post, s. 47.

and resided at Paris, purchased on her death there a burial place in Paris for her interment, and expressed his purpose to be buried there himself, the purchase was not considered as any cogent evidence of an intention to acquire a French domicil. Hodgson v. Beauchesne, 12 Moore P. C. 285, 323. The expression of a wish to be buried at a particular place is not regarded as an important circumstance in questions of domicil. Platt v. Att.-Gen., 3 App. Cas. 336, 344 (P. C.); Hood's Estate, 21 Pa. St. 106.

There is a strong presumption against a person who is in the military service of the country of his domicil, abandoning that domicil and acquiring a foreign domicil, but it seems that this presumption may be overcome by evidence of intention. Hodgson v. Beauchesne, 12 Moore P. C. 319; Craigie v. Lewin, 3 Curteis, 435; Att.-Gen. v. Pottinger, 6 H. & N. 733. There has however been an opinion that a man, by entering the military service of a foreign country, acquires a domicil in that country. See Somerville v. Somerville, 5 Ves. 759, in argument; President of the United States v. Drummond, 33 Beav. 451; Dicey on Domicil, 139.

An English peer is not incapacitated by his political duties from acquiring a foreign domicil of choice. Hamilton v. Dallas, 1 Ch. D. 257.

que sequatur.'[1] This is usually denominated the domicil of birth or nativity, *domicilium originis.* But if the parents are then on a visit, or on a journey (*in itinere*), the home of the parents (at least if it is in the same country) will be deemed the domicil of birth or nativity.[2] If he is an illegitimate child, he follows the domicil of his mother. (*a*) 'Ejus, qui justum patrem non habet, prima origo a matre.'[3] *Secondly,* the domicil of birth of minors continues until they have obtained a new domicil. (*b*) *Thirdly,* minors are generally deemed incapable, *proprio marte,* of changing their domicil during their minority, and therefore they retain the domicil of their parents; and if the parents change their domicil, that of the infant children follows it; and if the father dies, his last domicil is that of the infant children.[4] (*c*) 'Placet

---

[1] Cod. 10, 31, 36; 2 Domat, Public Law, b. 1, tit. 16, s. 3, art. 10; 1 Boullenois, obs. 4, p. 53; Voet, ad Pand. 5, 1, n. 91, 92, 100. See Scrimshire *v.* Scrimshire, 2 Hagg. Cons. 405, 406; Cochin, Œuvres, tom. 5, p. 5, 6; Id. 698, 4to ed.

[2] Dr. Lieber's Encyc. Amer. art. Domicil; Pothier, Cout. d'Orléans, c. 1, art. 10, 12; Somerville *v.* Somerville, 5 Ves. 750, 787; 1 Boullenois, obs. 4, p. 53.

[3] Dig. 50, 1, 9; Pothier, Pand. 50, 1, n. 3.

[4] Id.; Pothier, Cout. d'Orléans, c. 1, art. 12, 16; 2 Domat, Public Law, b. 16, tit. 16, s. 3, art. 10; Guier *v.* O'Daniel, 1 Binn. (Pa.) 349, 351; Voet, ad Pand. 5, 1, n. 91, 92, 100.

(*a*) The law attributes to every individual, as soon as he is born, the domicil of his father if the child be legitimate, and the domicil of the mother if illegitimate. Udny *v.* Udny, L. R. 1 H. L. Sc. 441; Douglas *v.* Douglas, L. R. 12 Eq. 617.

(*b*) Bell *v.* Kennedy, L. R. 1 H. L. Sc. 307.

(*c*) The domicil of a *minor* changes with that of his father. Sharpe *v.* Crispin, L. R. 1 P. & M. 611, 617; Jopp *v.* Wood, 34 Beav. 88; 4 D. J. & S. 616; Guier *v.* O'Daniel, 1 Binn. (Pa.) 352, n.; School Directors *v.* James, 2 Watts & S. (Pa.) 570; Kennedy *v.* Ryall, 67 N. Y. 379; 8 Jones & Sp. (N. Y.) 347; In re Hubbard, 82 N. Y. 90; Wheeler *v.* Burrow, 18 Ind. 14; Johnson *v.* Copeland, 35 Ala. 521; Metcalf *v.* Lowther, 56 Ala. 312; Blumenthal *v.* Tannenholz, 31 N. J. Eq. 194; Mears *v.* Sinclair, 1 W. Va. 185. After the father's death the domicil of the minor changes with that of his mother. Potinger *v.* Wightman, 3 Mer. 67; Johnstone *v.* Beattie, 10 Cl. & F. 138; Sharpe *v.* Crispin, L. R. 1 P. & M. 617; Brown *v.* Lynch, 2 Bradf. (N. Y.) 214; School Directors *v.* James, 2 Watts & S. (Pa.) 570; Carlisle *v.* Tuttle, 30 Ala. 613. Upon the mother's marrying again, the minor child does not necessarily acquire the domicil of the husband without any actual change. Brown *v.* Lynch, 2 Bradf. (N. Y.) 214; School Directors *v.* James, 2 Watts & S. (Pa.) 568. In Mears *v.* Sinclair, 1 W. Va. 185, it was held that the mother, after marrying again, could not change the domicil of her minor children. It is not easy to see a reason for the rule asserted in this

etiam filium-familias domicilium habere posse; non utique ibi, ubi pater habuit, sed ubicunque ipse constituit.'[1] *Fourthly*, a married woman follows the domicil of her husband.[2] (*a*) This

[1] Dig. 50, 1, l. 1, 3, 4; Pothier, Pand. 50, 1, n. 25. Whether a guardian or father can change the domicil of a minor, or idiot, or insane person, under his charge, has been matter of doubt, upon which different opinions have been expressed by jurists. In the affirmative there may be found among others, Bynkershoek, Boullenois, Bretaunier. In the negative, Pothier and Mornac. See Pothier, Cout. d'Orléans, c. 1, art. 17; Bynker. Quæst. Privat. Juris. lib. 1, c. 16; Merlin, Répert. Domicil, s. 5, art. 2, 3; Boullenois, Quest. de la Contrariété des Lois, quest. 2, p. 40, ed. 1732. See also Guier v. O'Daniel, 1 Binn. (Pa.) 349, n.; Somerville v. Somerville, 5 Ves. 750, 787; Potinger v. Wightman, 3 Mer. 67; Cutts v. Haskins, 9 Mass. 543; Holyoke v. Haskins, 5 Pick. (Mass.) 20.

[2] Voet, ad Pand. 5, 1, n. 101; Warrender v. Warrender, 9 Bligh, 89, 103, 104.

decision. See Dicey on Domicil, 103.

The domicil of a *lunatic* does not change with that of his guardian or committee. Westlake (ed. 1880) 273; Dicey on Domicil, 132. See Bempde v. Johnstone, 3 Ves. 198; Sharpe v. Crispin, L. R. 1 P. & M. 611; Hepburn v. Skirving, 9 W. R. 764. A similar rule applies to the domicil of a *minor*. School Directors v. James, 2 Watts & S. (Pa.) 571; Daniel v. Hill, 52 Ala. 430; Mears v. Sinclair, 1 W. Va. 185. But the guardian or committee may change the *residence* of a lunatic from one place to another within the same state or country. This has been held in cases where the jurisdiction of a probate court to grant administration depended upon the lunatic's residence in a particular county or place. Holyoke v. Haskins, 5 Pick. (Mass.) 20; Anderson v. Anderson, 42 Vt. 350. It would probably be so in a question of residence arising under the English poor-laws. Reg. v. Whitby, L. R. 5 Q. B. p. 331. A similar rule has been applied in the case of a minor whose father and mother were dead, where the question was in what town the minor should be taxed (Kirkland v. Whately, 4 Allen (Mass.) 462), and where the

question was one of jurisdiction (Ex parte Bartlett, 4 Bradf. (N. Y.) 221; see Marheineke v. Grothaus, 72 Mo. 204). If a lunatic has been of unsound mind continuously from the time he attained his majority, his domicil continues to change with that of his father, as during minority. Sharpe v. Crispin, L. R. 1 P. & M. 611.

(*a*) Dolphin v. Robins, 7 H. L. C. 390; Yelverton v. Yelverton, 1 Sw. & T. 574; Pennsylvania v. Ravenel, 21 How. 103; Greene v. Greene, 11 Pick. (Mass.) 410; Johnson v. Johnson, 12 Bush (Ky.) 485; Hick v. Hick, 5 Bush (Ky.) 670; Williams v. Saunders, 5 Cold. (Tenn.) 60, 79; Sanderson v. Ralston, 20 La. An. 312; Succession of McKenna, 23 La. An. 369; Lacey v. Clements, 36 Tex. 661.

It has been held that after a divorce a mensa et thoro a wife may have a separate domicil from that of her husband. Barber v Barber, 21 How. 582. See Dolphin v. Robins, 7 H. L. C. 390.

As to the power of a wife to acquire a separate domicil that will give jurisdiction to grant a divorce, see s. 229 *a*, post.

results from the general principle that a person who is under the power and authority of another possesses no right to choose a domicil.[1] 'Mulierem, quamdiu nupta est, incolam ejusdem civitatis videri, cujus maritus ejus est.'[2] *Fifthly*, a widow retains the domicil of her deceased husband until she obtains another domicil. 'Vidua mulier amissi mariti domicilium retinet.'[3] *Sixthly*, prima facie, the place where a person lives is taken to be his domicil, until other facts establish the contrary.[4] (a) *Seventhly*, every person of full age having a right to change his domicil, it follows, that if he removes to another place with an intention to make it his permanent residence (animo manendi), it becomes instantaneously his place of domicil.[5] *Eighthly*, if a person has actually removed to another place, with an intention of remaining there for an indefinite time, and as a place of fixed present domicil, it is to be deemed his place of domicil, notwithstanding he may entertain a floating intention to return at some future period.[6] (b)   *Ninthly*, the place where a married man's

<hr/>

[1] Dr. Lieber's Encyc. Amer. Domicil; Pothier, Cout. d'Orléans, c. 1, art. 10; 2 Domat, Public Law, b. 1, tit. 16, s. 3, art. 11, 13; Merlin, Répert. Domicil, s. 5.

[2] Dig. 50, 1, 38, 3; Id. 5, 1, 65; Pothier, Pand. 50, 1, n. 24; 2 Domat, Public Law, b. 1, tit. 16, s. 3, art. 12; Voet, ad Pand. 5, 1, n. 101.

[3] Dig. 50, 1, 22, 1; Pothier, Pand. 50, 1, n. 28.

[4] Bruce v. Bruce, 2 B. & P. 229, n.; Id. 230; Bempde v. Johnstone, 3 Ves. 198, 201; Stanley v. Bernes, 3 Hagg. Ecc. 373, 437.

[5] Pothier, Cout. d'Orléans, c. 1, art. 13.

[6] Bruce v. Bruce, 2 B. & P. 229, n.; Id. 230; Stanley v. Bernes, 3 Hagg. Ecc. 373.

(a) Sears v. Boston, 1 Met. (Mass.) 251; Mitchell v. United States, 21 Wall. 352; Dicey on Domicil, 116.

(b) 'Domicil of choice is a conclusion or inference which the law derives from the fact of a man fixing voluntarily his sole or chief residence in a particular place, with an intention of continuing to reside there for an unlimited time.' Udny v. Udny, L. R. 1 H. L. Sc. 458 (by Lord Westbury); Haldane v. Eckford, L. R. 8 Eq. 631; King v. Foxwell, 3 Ch. D. 518; Platt v. Att.-Gen., 3 App. Cas. 336 (P. C.); Doucet v. Geoghegan, 9 Ch. D. 441 (C. A.); Mitchell v. United States, 21 Wall. 350; Guier v. O'Daniel, 1 Binn. (Pa.) 352, n.; White v. Brown, 1 Wall. jun. 217; Hegeman v. Fox, 31 Barb. (N. Y.) 475; Thorndike v. Boston, 1 Met. (Mass.) 242; Ringgold v. Barley, 5 Md. 186. See Gilman v. Gilman, 52 Me. 165; State v. Groome, 10 Iowa, 308.

In Moorhouse v. Lord, 10 H. L. C. 283, Lord Cranworth said, 'In order to acquire a new domicil, according to an expression which I believe I used on a former occasion (Whicker v. Hume, 7 H. L. C. 159), and which I shall not shrink on that account from repeating, because I think it is a correct statement of the law, a man

family resides is generally to be deemed his domicil.[1] (a)　But the presumption from this circumstance may be controlled by

[1] Pothier, Cout. d'Orléans, c. 1, art. 20; Bempde v. Johnstone, 3 Ves. 198, 201.

(a) Platt v. Att.-Gen., 3 App. Cas. 336 (P. C.); Forbes v. Forbes, Kay, 341; Aitchison v. Dixon, L. R. 10 Eq. 589; Roberti v. Methodist Book Concern, 1 Daly (N. Y.) 3; Smith v. Croom, 7 Fla. 81, 156.

"must intend quatenus in illo exuere patriam." It is not enough that you merely mean to take another house in some other place, and that on account of your health, or for some other reason, you think it tolerably certain that you had better remain there all the days of your life. That does not signify; you do not lose your domicil of origin, or your resumed domicil, merely because you go to some other place that suits your health better, unless, indeed, you mean either on account of your health, or for some other motive, to cease to be a Scotchman and become an Englishman, or a Frenchman, or a German.' Lord Kingsdown said (p. 292), 'A man must intend to become a Frenchman instead of an Englishman.' The rule thus laid down cannot now be considered as a correct statement of the law. It was followed in In re Capdevielle, 2 H. & C. 985, and Att.-Gen. v. Wahlstatt, 3 H. & C. 374, but in the former Bramwell, B., said, ' The expressions used appear to me, with great deference, far too extensive. To say that a man cannot abandon his domicil of origin without doing all that in him lies to divest himself of his country, is a proposition which, with great submission, I think cannot be maintained.' Lord Hatherley said in Udny v. Udny, L. R. 1 H. L. Sc. 452, ' I think some of the expressions used in former cases as to the intent " exuere patriam," or to become " a Frenchman instead of an Englishman," go beyond the question of domicil. The question of naturalization and of allegiance is distinct from that of domicil. A man may continue to be an Englishman, and yet his contracts and the succession to his estate may have to be determined by the law of the country in which he has chosen to settle himself.' Lord Westbury, in the same case (p. 460), referring to the expressions of Lord Kingsdown above quoted, said, ' These words are likely to mislead, if they were intended to signify that for a change of domicil there must be a change of nationality, that is, of national allegiance. That would be to confound the political and civil states of an individual, and to destroy the difference between patria and domicilium.' In Haldane v. Eckford, L. R. 8 Eq. 640, James, V.C., said that the rule as laid down by Lord Westbury in Udny v. Udny differed from the rule as laid down in Moorhouse v. Lord, and the cases following it, ' in which, if I may use the expression, that unfortunate term exuere patriam was introduced, as if it were a question of nationality, and not of more or less permanence of residence. It does differ from those cases, but it differs in bringing back the law to that which (in my opinion) was always, before those cases, considered to have been the law, and evidently is the law as laid down by the treatise writers, viz., that domicil was to be considered as changed whenever there was a change of residence of a permanent character voluntarily assumed.' Wickens, V.C., in Douglas v. Douglas, L. R. 12 Eq. 644, expressed his concurrence in this view of the law.

In Aikman v. Aikman, 3 Macq.

other circumstances; (a) for if it is a place of temporary establishment only for his family, or for transient objects, it will not be deemed his domicil.[1] *Tenthly*, if a married man has his family fixed in one place, and he does his business in another, the former is considered the place of his domicil.[2]

47. *Eleventhly*, if a married man has two places of residence at different times of the year, that will be esteemed his domicil which he himself selects, or describes, or deems to be his home, or which appears to be the centre of his affairs, or where he votes,

---

[1] Pothier, Cout. d'Orléans, c. 1, art. 15.   [2] Ante, s. 42-44.

(a) Douglas *v.* Douglas, L. R. 12 Eq. 617; Burnham *v.* Rangely, 1 Woodb. & M. 7.

858, Lord Campbell said, ' If a man is settled in a foreign country, engaged in some permanent pursuit requiring his residence there, a mere intention to return to his native country on a doubtful contingency will not prevent such a residence in a foreign country from putting an end to his domicil of origin.' This is probably what Story meant by ' a floating intention to return.' A refusal by a Frenchman to be naturalized in England on the ground that he might return to reside in France, and that he would not give up his French citizenship, is not enough to prevent the acquisition of an English domicil. Brunel *v.* Brunel, L. R. 12 Eq. 298. See also Anderson *v.* Laneuville, 9 Moore P. C. 325, 334. In Doucet *v.* Geoghegan, 9 Ch. D. 441, declarations of a testator that he would go back to France when he had made his fortune were relied on to prove that he never meant to acquire an English domicil. Jessel M.R. and James, L.J., said that the declarations were too indefinite for that purpose, and that they were not sufficient to outweigh actions which showed an intention of permanent residence. Brett, L.J., said, ' I think such a condition [making a fortune] is not sufficient; it ought to be a condition which limits the residence to a definite time; and when the condition refers only to a time as indefinite as it can possibly be, it cannot be said to confine the residence to a definite time. There can be nothing so indefinite as the time at which a man expects to make his fortune.' It seems doubtful whether these expressions of Brett, L.J., can be supported. In Jopp *v.* Wood, 4 D. J. & S. 616, it was held that a residence in India for the mere purpose of business did not change a Scotch domicil of origin, where it appeared that there was an intention of returning finally to Scotland. See Allardice *v.* Onslow, 33 L. J. Ch. 434; 10 Jur. N.S. 352.

In an early case it was established that a domicil in India, commonly called an Anglo-Indian domicil, was acquired by residence in India in the service of the East India Company. Bruce *v.* Bruce, 2 B. & P. 229, n.; Munroe *v.* Douglas, 5 Mad. 379, 401; Forbes *v.* Forbes, Kay, 341, 356; Moorhouse *v.* Lord, 10 H. L. C. 281; Allardice *v.* Onslow, 33 L. J. Ch. 434; 10 Jur. N.S. 352. But in Jopp *v.* Wood, 4 D. J. & S. 616, it was held that such a residence did not change the domicil of a person who was not in the service of the East India Company and who did not intend to abandon his previous domicil. See Dicey on Domicil, 140; Westlake (ed. 1880) 277, 282.

or exercises the rights and duties of a citizen.[1] *Twelfthly*, if a man is unmarried, that is generally deemed the place of his domicil where he transacts his business, exercises his profession, or assumes and exercises municipal duties or privileges.[2] But this rule is of course subject to some qualifications in its application.[3] *Thirteenthly*, residence in a place, to produce a change of domicil, must be voluntary. If therefore it be by constraint or involuntary, as by banishment, arrest, or imprisonment, the antecedent domicil of the party remains.[4] (a) *Fourteenthly*, the mere intention to acquire a new domicil, without the fact of an actual removal, avails nothing; neither does the fact of removal without the intention.[5] *Fifteenthly*, presumptions from mere circumstances will not prevail against positive facts, which fix or determine the domicil.[6] *Sixteenthly*, a domicil once acquired remains until a new one is acquired.[7] (b) It is sometimes laid down that a person may be without any domicil; as, if he quits a place with an intent to fix in another place, it has been said that while he is in transitu he has no domicil. Julian, in the Roman law, has so affirmed. 'Si quis domicilio relicto naviget, vel iter faciat, quærens quo se conferat, atque ubi constituat; hunc puto sine domicilio esse.'[8] But the more correct principle would seem to

---

[1] Pothier, Cout. d'Orléans, c. 1, art. 20; Somerville v. Somerville, 5 Ves. 750, 788–790; Harvard College v. Gore, 5 Pick. (Mass.) 370; Cochin, Œuvres, tom. 3, p. 702, 4to ed.

[2] Somerville v. Somerville, 5 Ves. 750, 788, 789.   [3] Idem.

[4] 2 Domat, Public Law, b. 1, tit. 16, s. 3, art. 14; Merlin, Répertoire, Domicil, s. 4, art. 3; Bempde v. Johnstone, 3 Ves. 198, 202.

[5] Ante, s. 44.

[6] Dr. Lieber, Encyc. Amer., Domicil; ante, s. 42–44.

[7] Somerville v. Somerville, 5 Ves. 750, 787; Merlin, Répertoire, Domicil, s. 2; Harvard College v. Gore, 5 Pick. (Mass.) 370; Cochin, Œuvres, tom. 5, p. 6, 4to ed.

[8] Dig. 50, 1, 27, 2; Pothier, Pand. 30, 1, n. 18; 2 Domat, Public Law, b. 1, tit. 16, s. 3, art. 9; ante, s. 45.

(a) De Bonneval v. De Bonneval, 1 Curtis, 856; White v. Brown, 1 Wall. jun. 217.

(b) The onus probandi lies upon those who assert a change of domicil. Bell v. Kennedy, L. R. 1 H. L. Sc. 307; Aikman v. Aikman, 3 Macq. 877; Hodgson v. Beauchesne, 12 Moore P. C. 285; Crookenden v.

Fuller, 1 Sw. & T. 441; Mitchell v. United States, 21 Wall. 350; White v. Brown, 1 Wall. jun. 217; Dupuy v. Wurtz, 53 N. Y. 562.

In Hicks v. Skinner, 72 N. C. 1, it was held that a man might abandon his domicil of origin, and, until he acquired another, be without domicil, except that of actual residence.

be, that the original domicil is not gone until a new one has been actually acquired, facto et animo.[1] (a)   *Seventeenthly*, if a man has acquired a new domicil different from that of his birth, and he removes from it with an intention to resume his native domicil, the latter is reacquired, even while he is on his way, in itinere, (b) for it reverts from the moment the other is given up.[2] (c)

[1] See Jennison *v.* Hapgood, 10 Pick. (Mass.) 77; Bruce *v.* Bruce, 2 B. & P. 229, n.; Cochin, Œuvres, tom. 5, p. 5, 6, 4to ed.; ante, s. 44.

[2] The Indian Chief, 3 C. Rob. 12; La Virginie, 5 C. Rob. 98. On the subject of domicil, the learned reader is referred to Fergusson on Marriage and Divorce, ˉAppendix, p. 277–362; and Henry on Foreign Law, Appendix A, p. 181, &c.; Cochin, Œuvres, tom. 5, p. 4–6, 4to ed.; In re Wrigley, 8 Wend. (N. Y.) 134.

(a) Bell *v.* Kennedy, L. R. 1 H. L. Sc. 307; Shaw *v.* Shaw, 98 Mass. 158.

In Forbes *v.* Forbes, Kay, 353, Lord Hatherley, when vice-chancellor, stated as one of the propositions he considered settled, ' That a new domicil cannot be acquired except by intention and act, "animo et facto;" and apparently, if a man be in itinere, it is a sufficient act for this purpose. (See Sir John Leach's judgment in Munroe *v.* Douglas, 5 Mad. 379).' Sir J. Leach's words were, ' A domicil cannot be lost by mere abandonment. It is not to be defeated animo merely, but animo et facto, and necessarily remains until a subsequent domicil be acquired, unless the party die in itinere toward an intended domicil.' These last words were designated by Lord Hatherley in Udny *v.* Udny, L. R. 1 H. L. Sc. 449, as ' a remarkable qualification,' and he suggested that it was founded upon a decision that a domicil of origin had revived although the person died in itinere; Lord Chelmsford said, ' There is an apparent inconsistency in this passage, for the vice-chancellor having said that a domicil necessarily remains until a subsequent domicil be acquired animo et facto, added, " unless the party die in itinere towards

an intended domicil; " that is, at a time when the acquisition of the subsequent domicil is incomplete and rests in intention only.' See also Lyall *v.* Paton, 25 L. J. Ch. 746; Dicey on Domicil, 84. Westlake however (ed. 1880, p. 276) states as a rule for the change from one domicil of choice to another, that ' In the event of death in itinere, the last domicil is the one towards which the person is journeying,' and says, ' this part of Leach's doctrine does not seem to have been censured in Udny *v.* Udny.'

(b) In bonis Bianchi, 3 Sw. & T. 16. 18. The abandonment of the acquired domicil is not complete until the person has left the country. In bonis Raffenel, 3 Sw. & T. 49.

(c) Udny *v.* Udny, L. R. 1 H. L. Sc. 441; King *v.* Foxwell, 3 Ch. D. 518; In re Wrigley, 8 Wend. (N. Y.) 134, 140; Reed's Appeal, 71 Pa. St. 378. See White *v.* Brown, 1 Wall. jun. 217, 265; Kellar *v.* Baird, 5 Heisk. (Tenn.) 39.

In Udny *v.* Udny, Lord Hatherley said (L. R. 1 H. L. Sc. p. 450), ' It seems reasonable to say that if the choice of a new abode and actual settlement there constitute a change of the original domicil, then the exact converse of such a procedure, viz. the intention to abandon the new domicil,

48. The foregoing rules principally relate to changes of domicil from one place to another within the same country or terri-

and an actual abandonment of it, ought to be equally effective to destroy the new domicil. That which may be acquired may surely be abandoned, and though a man cannot, for civil reasons, be left without a domicil, no such difficulty arises if it be simply held that the original domicil revives,' Referring to the last part of s. 47 (supra), he said, (p. 451), 'The qualification that he must abandon the new domicil with the special intent to resume that of origin is not, I think, a reasonable deduction from the rules already laid down by decision, because intent not followed by a definitive act is not sufficient. The more consistent theory is, that the abandonment of the new domicil is complete animo et facto, because the *factum* is the abandonment, the *animus* is that of never returning.' Lord Chelmsford said (p. 454), ' I do not think that the circumstances mentioned by Story in the above passage, viz., that the person has removed from his acquired domicil with an intention to resume his native domicil, and that he is in itinere for the purpose, are at all necessary to restore the domicil of origin. The true doctrine appears to me to be expressed in the last words of the passage: " It (the domicil of origin) reverts from the moment the other is given up." This is a necessary conclusion if it be true that an acquired domicil ceases entirely whenever it is intentionally abandoned, and that a man can never be without a domicil. The domicil of origin always remains, as it were, in reserve, to be resorted to in case no other domicil is found to exist. This appears to me to be the true principle upon this subject, and it will govern my opinion upon the present appeal.' Lord Westbury said (p. 458), ' Domicil of choice, as it is gained animo et facto, so it

may be put an end in the same manner. Expressions are found in some of the books, and in one or two cases, that the first or existing domicil remains until another is acquired. This is true if applied to the domicil of origin, but cannot be true if such general words were intended (which is not probable) to convey the conclusion that a domicil of choice, though unequivocally relinquished and abandoned, clings, in despite of his will and acts, to the party, until another domicil has animo et facto been acquired. . . . A natural-born Englishman may, if he domicils himself in Holland, acquire and have the status civilis of a Dutchman, which is of course ascribed to him in respect of his settled abode in the land, but if he breaks up his establishment, sells his house and furniture, discharges his servants, and quits Holland, declaring that he will never return to it again, and taking with him his wife and children, for the purpose of travelling in France or Italy in search of another place of residence, is it meant to be said that he carries his Dutch domicil, that is, his Dutch citizenship, at his back, and that it clings to him pertinaciously until he finally sets up his tabernacle in another country? Such a conclusion would be absurd; but there is no absurdity, and on the contrary much reason, in holding that an acquired domicil may be effectually abandoned by unequivocal intention and act; and that when it is so determined the domicil of origin revives until a new domicil of choice be acquired. . . . In Mr. Justice Story's Conflict of Laws ' (s. 48) 'it is stated that " the moment the foreign domicil (that is, the domicil of choice) is abandoned, the native domicil or domicil of origin is reacquired." And such appears to be the just conclusion from

torial sovereignty, although many of them are applicable to
residence in different countries or sovereignties.   In respect
to the latter there are certain principles which have been generally recognized by tribunals administering public law, or the law
of nations, as of unquestionable authority.   *First*, persons who
are born in a country, are generally deemed to be citizens and
subjects of that country.[1]   A reasonable qualification of the rule
would seem to be, that it should not apply to the children of
parents who were in itinere in the country, or who were abiding
there for temporary purposes, as for health, or curiosity, or occasional business.   It would be difficult however to assert that in
the present state of public law such a qualification is universally
established.   *Secondly*, foreigners who reside in a country for
permanent or indefinite purposes, animo manendi, are treated
universally as inhabitants of that country.[2]   *Thirdly*, a national
character acquired in a foreign country by residence changes
when the party has left the country animo non revertendi, and
is on his return to the country where he had his antecedent
domicil.   And especially if he be in itinere to his native country with that intent, his native domicil revives while he is yet
in transitu ; for the native domicil easily reverts.[3]   The moment

[1] 1 Black. Com. 366, 369.   [2] Vattel, b. 1, c. 19, s. 213.
[3] The Venus, 8 Cranch, 278, 281; The Frances, 8 Cranch, 335; The Indian
Chief, 3 C. Rob. 12; Bempde v. Johnstone, 3 Ves. 198, 202; The Friendschaft,
3 Wheat. 14; Ommaney v. Bingham, cited 5 Ves. 757, 765.

several decided cases, as well as from
the principles of the law of domicil.'
In Connecticut it has been held that
this rule does not apply where the
domicil of origin and the domicil of
choice are both under the same national jurisdiction, as in the case of
two of the United States, and that
therefore a domicil of origin in the
state of New York did not revive
upon the abandonment of an acquired
domicil in Connecticut.   First National Bank v. Balcom, 35 Conn. 351.
It is stated in the judgment that the
rule grew out of native allegiance or
citizenship; but this, to use the words
of Lord Westbury, is ' to confound the
political and civil states of an individual, and to destroy the difference
between patria and domicilium'
(Udny v. Udny, L. R. 1 H. L. Sc.
460; see also ante, s. 41, note).   The
case was decided in 1868, the year
before Udny v. Udny, and reliance
was placed upon Munroe v. Douglas,
5 Mad. 379, in which Sir John Leach
held that the original domicil did not
revive upon an abandonment of an
acquired domicil, and which was overruled in Udny v. Udny.   In this last-
mentioned case the domicil of origin
was Scotland, and it revived upon the
abandonment of the domicil of choice,
which was England; this is quite as
strong an instance of both being under the same national jurisdiction, as
if one were New York and the other
Connecticut.

a foreign domicil is abandoned, the native domicil is reacquired. (a) But a mere return to his native country, without
an intent to abandon his foreign domicil, does not work any
change of his domicil.[1] *Fourthly*, ambassadors and other foreign
ministers retain their domicil in the country which they repre-
sent, and to which they belong.[2] But a different rule generally
applies to consuls and to other commercial agents, who are presumed to remain in a country for purposes of trade, and who
therefore acquire a domicil where they reside.[3] (b) *Fifthly*,
children born upon the sea are deemed to belong, and to have
their domicil in, the country to which their parents belong.[4]

49. *Kinds of Domicil.*—From these considerations and rules
the general conclusion may be deduced, that domicil is of three
sorts; domicil by birth, domicil by choice, and domicil by operation of law. The first is the common case of the place of birth,
domicilium originis; the second is that which is voluntarily
acquired by a party, proprio marte. The last is consequential,
as that of the wife arising from marriage.[5] (c)

[1] Ibid.
[2] Vattel, b. 1, c. 19, s. 217; The Indian Chief, 3 C. Rob. 12, 27; The
Josephine, 4 C. Rob. 25.
[3] Ibid.
[4] Vattel, b. 1, c. 19, s. 216; Dr. Lieber's Encyc. Amer. art. Domicil.
[5] Pothier, Cout. d'Orléans, c. 1, art. 12. Whoever wishes to make more
extensive researches upon this subject may consult Denizart's Dictionary, art.
Domicil; Encyclopédie Moderne, tom. 10, art. Domicil; Merlin, Répertoire,
Domicil; 2 Domat (by Strahan), p. 484; lib. 1, tit. 16, s. 3, of Public Law;

(a) Udny v. Udny, L. R. 1 H. L.
Sc. 441, 453, 459.

(b) It cannot be inferred from a
person's residing in a country as an
ambassador or attaché, that he intends
to make that country his home. On
the other hand, if he has already acquired a domicil there, he does not
lose it by accepting such an office.
Heath v. Samson, 14 Beav. 441; Att.-
Gen. v. Kent, 1 H. & C. 12. The
rule is the same as regards consuls.
Udny v. Udny, L. R. 1 H. L. Sc. 441;
Sharpe v. Crispin, L. R. 1 P. & M.
611. The expressions in The Indian
Chief, 3 C. Rob. at p. 27, related, not
to domicil, but to the national character of property of a consul employed
in trade in time of war, which is a
question of public international law.
Ante, s. 41, note.

It is not presumed that a man intends to change his domicil when he
resides in another country in the service, military, naval, or civil, of his
sovereign. Att.-Gen. v. Napier, 6
Ex. 217; Brown v. Smith, 15 Beav.
444; Yelverton v. Yelverton, 1 Sw. &
T. 574; Att.-Gen. v. Rowe, 1 H. & C.
31; Dennis v. State, 17 Fla. 389. But
he may change his domicil under such
circumstances if he has the intention
of doing so. Mooar v. Harvey, 128
Mass. 219; Ames v. Duryea, 6 Lans.
(N. Y.) 155.

(c) *Interpretation of ' Residence,' ' In-*

Dig. 50, 1, per tot.; Cod. 10, 30, 2, 7; Voet, ad Pand. 5, 1, 90–92; Bynkershoek, Quæst. Priv. Juris. lib. 1, c. 11, and the authorities cited in Dr. Lieber's Encyclopedia Americana, Domicil; Henry on Foreign Law, Appendix A, on Domicil, 181–209.

habitant,' &c., in Statutes. — It often becomes necessary to determine the place in which a person *resides*, or of which he is an *inhabitant*, in the sense in which the word is used in some statute. Sometimes the question is whether he resides in a particular country or state, at others it is in what part of a country or state he resides, as, for example, in what town. As instances of such statutes may be mentioned those which provide that an inhabitant of a state shall be taxed, or shall be entitled to vote, in the town where he resides, or that a pauper shall have a right to support in the town where he resides, and those which limit the time for bringing an action against a person who resides out of the state, or provide a special mode of procedure in such cases. *Residence* is used in these statutes in different senses. When it is used in reference to a country, e.g., one of the American states, it may or may not have the meaning of *domicil* according to the purpose of the statute. When it is applied to a town or other part of a country or state, it has not the technical meaning of domicil, because in its technical sense *domicil* is applicable only to a country (ante, s. 41, note), but in such cases it may in some respects resemble domicil. It does not belong to the subject of this work to ascertain the residence intended by these statutes, except when the word has the technical meaning of domicil. But in some American cases, the term *domicil* has been applied to such *residence* when the latter word did not have that technical meaning. It is important that the rules laid down in these cases for ascertaining such residence should not be confused with the rules for ascertaining domicil. It will be useful therefore to point out some of the differences, as well as some of the resemblances, which exist between *domicil* and the different meanings of *residence*.

In some of the United States the *statute of limitations* contains a provision that the time during which a person is absent from and resides out of the state shall not be taken as part of the time limited for the commencement of an action against him. A state being a country, in the sense of a territory subject to one system of law (Dicey on Domicil, 1; ante, s. 41, note), the term *domicil* is one that may properly be applied to it, but, in construing the statute, the question is whether *residence* or *domicil* is referred to by the expression ' Resides out of the state.' In Maine it has been declared that *residence* in the statute does not mean *domicil*, but ' is synonymous' with *dwelling-place* or *home.*' ' The absence of the debtor must be something more than a transient departure from his home on business or pleasure, and a temporary sojourn out of the state.' Drew *v.* Drew, 37 Me. 389; Bucknam *v.* Thompson, 38 Me. 171. In Vermont a similar construction has been given to the statute. Hackett *v.* Kendall, 23 Vt. 275; Hall *v.* Nasmith, 28 Vt. 791. The word *domicil* is sometimes used in the decisions as the equivalent of *residence*, but it is clear that it is not so used in its technical sense. Thus the court says, in Hackett *v.* Kendall, 23 Vt. 278, ' This question of domicil may possibly be viewed differently with reference to different subjects. But the consideration which must have operated upon the legislature in so framing the statute in this case seems to us to have been what is suggested by counsel, — whether the defendant's domicil in this state was so broken up that it would not have been competent to serve process upon him by leaving a copy there. And for that purpose, it seems to us, there must be some place of abode, which his family or his effects exclusively maintain in his absence, and to which he may be expected soon, or in some convenient time, to return, so that, a copy being left there and notice in fact proved, the plaintiff may take a valid judgment.' By the statutes of Vermont, process might be served on the defendant personally or by leaving a copy ' at the house of his usual abode ' (Rev. Sts. c. 28, s. 12; Comp. Sts. c. 31, s. 16). In this case the defendant, who lived at Granville, Vermont, went to Massachusetts in April or May, intending to remain there and work during the season, and then to return to Granville, and not intending to change his residence from Granville to Massachusetts. He took his wife and child with him, and left his furniture and effects at Granville, but apparently he kept no place of abode there to which he might return. The intention of his wife in accompanying him was to visit some friends. He remained in Massachusetts at work till the following January, and then returned to Granville. During the last three or four months of his stay in Massachusetts he kept house there, and about the time he began to keep house he made arrangements for returning to Granville in pursuance of his original intention. It was held that he did not reside in Vermont within the meaning of the statute during his absence in Massachusetts. A similar effect is given to the provision in New Hampshire. Gilman v. Cutts, 23 N. H. 376; 27 N. H. 348. In New York the provision was declared to refer to residence out of the state as distinguished from merely temporary absence, excursions for pleasure or business, with a return to the state as the residence of the debtor. Wheeler v. Webster, 1 E. D. Smith, 1; Harden v. Palmer, 2 E. D. Smith, 172; Hickok v. Bliss, 34 Barb. 321; Ford v. Babcock, 2 Sandf.

518, 529. The exception from the time limited was afterwards extended by the St. 1867, c. 781, s. 6, so as to include continuous absence for a year or more. In Iowa the provision was that ' the time during which a defendant is a non-resident of the state shall not be included ' in the period of limitation; and in Savage v. Scott, 45 Iowa, 130, 133, the court says, ' We need not inquire in what state he holds a domicil; he had a residence here of the character that would subject him to the process of the courts of this state. While he held this residence, the statute of limitations ran against the note and mortgage. . . . That residence in the state, and not citizenship or domicil, determines the fact of the meaning of the statute, cannot be doubted. The distinction which the law draws between the place of residence and that of domicil or citizenship, is plain.' In Massachusetts the provision was taken from the New York statute, and was first enacted in the Rev. Sts. of 1836 (Commissioners' Report. pt. 3, p. 275). The commissioners, who suggested it, stated its object to be that ' the debtor must remain within the state during the whole period prescribed for the limitation, in order to avail himself of its provisions.' In Collester v. Hailey, 6 Gray, 517, it was held that the absence shown was not to be excluded from the period, Shaw, C.J., saying, ' The facts disclosed temporary absences only, or visits, leaving his family here, effecting no change of domicil or residence.' In Langdon v. Doud, 6 Allen, 423, the court said, ' In the case of Collester v. Hailey, it was decided that . . . the time of a debtor's absence from the state without losing his domicil is not to be excluded in computing the period of limitation of an action against him; in other words, that temporary absences, although extending over consecutive periods of several months, but effecting no change in the legal domicil of the debtor, do not operate to extend the period of limitation;' and, 'A residence out of the state, as applied to the subject-matter, may well mean the acquisition of a domicil without its limits.' In subsequent cases the question has been dealt with as one of domicil. Hallet *v.* Bassett, 100 Mass. 167; Whitton *v.* Wass, 109 Mass. 40; Perkins *v.* Davis, 109 Mass. 239. The following reason for attributing this signification to the statute was given in Langdon *v.* Doud, 6 Allen, 425, ' A creditor can at any time commence a suit to enforce a claim against a debtor domiciled within the state. A writ can be served by leaving a summons at his last and usual place of abode, and, in case of his absence from the state, actual notice of the pendency of the action can be given to him, so that a valid and binding judgment can be obtained.' But it is also held in Massachusetts that a defendant *not* domiciled in the state may, if he has ever been an inhabitant, be proceeded against in precisely the same way. Lawrence *v.* Bassett, 5 Allen, 140, 142; Wright *v.* Oakley, 5 Met. 400. It would seem reasonable that the time within which a creditor should have a right to sue should depend upon the debtor's having his residence in the state (*factum*), rather than upon his intention (*animus*) in residing elsewhere, upon which his domicil would depend. By another provision of the statute, the time limited does not begin to run until the defendant comes into the state, if, when the action accrues, he is simply *out of the state.* The subsequent provision, suspending the running of the statute when he afterwards is absent from and resides out of the state, might reasonably not have been intended to be limited to cases where he resides out of the state with the intention necessary to constitute a domicil in another state or country. It may be doubted however whether, in the Massachusetts cases upon this subject, the word *domicil* has been used in its technical sense. In the case where

the rule was first laid down (Langdon *v.* Dowd, 6 Allen, 423) the court said that the construction adopted was the same as in other states where there was a similar provision, citing cases in Vermont, New York, Maine, and New Hampshire, which are mentioned above, and in which *residence* was held to have a signification different from *domicil.* The *residence*, which in Massachusetts is called *domicil,* is held to be changed, notwithstanding an intention to return, which would prevent a change of *domicil,* in its technical sense. Sleeper *v.* Paige, 15 Gray, 349, 350; Hallet *v.* Bassett, 100 Mass. 171. In Ware *v.* Gowen, 111 Mass. 526, the defendant, an inhabitant of Massachusetts, went to Russia to perform a contract with the Russian government, and was absent eight years; he always intended to return; while he was absent, his wife went back and forth between Europe and America; some of his children remained in Massachusetts; and his furniture was stored there; the court declared this to be sufficient evidence that he ' was absent from and resided out of the state within the meaning of the statute.' In Minnesota, in Venable *v.* Paulding, 19 Minn. 488, 492, the court says, ' To depart from and reside out of the state means a change of residence from this state to some other state, not a temporary or occasional absence. Hickok *v.* Bliss, supra;' and it seems to have adopted as a rule, ' that such residence out of the state must be, not merely temporary and occasional, but of such a character, and with such intent, as to constitute a change of domicil (Hallet *v.* Bassett, 100 Mass. 167), understanding *domicil,* as the Massachusetts court understands it, to mean, in this connection, the debtor's home or place of abode. Langdon *v.* Doud, 6 Allen, 423.'

In states where the statutes authorize an *attachment* of property when the defendant is not a resident of the state, it has been generally held that residence, and not domicil, determines the operation of the statute, and *residence* is defined as a permanent abode for the time being. Haggart *v.* Morgan, 5 N. Y. 422; Hurlbut *v.* Seeley, 11 How. Pr. (N. Y.) 507; Mayor *v.* Genet, 4 Hun, 487; 63 N. Y. 646; Long *v.* Ryan, 30 Grat. (Va.) 718; Morgan *v.* Nunes, 54 Miss. 308; Alston *v.* Newcomer, 42 Miss. 186.

The liability of a person to *taxation* in a particular state or country, as well as the place within such state or country where he shall be taxed, often depends upon the meaning of the words *inhabitant* and *resident* in the statute. When the statute says that every inhabitant of the state shall be taxed, his liability to taxation generally depends upon domicil, in its technical sense. Thorndike *v.* Boston, 1 Met. (Mass.) 242; Sears *v.* Boston, 1 Met. (Mass.) 250; Borland *v.* Boston, 132 Mass. 89; Church *v.* Rowell, 49 Me. 367; Parsons *v.* Bangor, 61 Me. 457; State *v.* Ross, 23 N. J. L. 517; Culbertson *v.* Floyd, 52 Ind. 361; Kellogg *v.* Winnebago, 42 Wis. 97. This construction is consistent with the probable intention that all persons domiciled in the state should be taxed. It is also somewhat analogous to the construction given to the English statutes imposing legacy or succession duties upon the personal estate of deceased persons; these statutes contain no express limitation of their application, but they have been held to apply only to persons domiciled in the country. Thomson *v.* Adv.-Gen., 12 Cl. & F. 1; Wallace *v.* Att.-Gen., L. R. 1 Ch. 1. In Briggs *v.* Rochester, 16 Gray (Mass.) 337, which was followed in Colton *v.* Longmeadow, 12 Allen (Mass.) 598, it was held that a person domiciled in Massachusetts, who was on his way to a place in another state, which he intended to make his permanent residence, and had actually passed the limits of Massachusetts on his way to that place, had

ceased to be an inhabitant of Massachusetts, and was therefore not taxable, although he had not lost his domicil there. But in Borland *v.* Boston, 132 Mass. 89, it was decided that domicil, in its technical sense, was the test of liability to taxation, and the doctrine of those cases was disapproved, and they should be considered as overruled, though in terms it is left for future litigation to determine whether they will be followed ' in cases presenting precisely similar circumstances.' It should be observed however that, even by the test of domicil, Briggs *v.* Rochester (16 Gray, 337), was rightly decided, for the person whose liability to taxation was in question had actually acquired a new domicil in the state of New York, though the fact does not seem to have been noticed; he had left Massachusetts intending to reside at Motthaven in New York, and he was staying at another place in New York, with the intention of remaining permanently in that state, though not at that place; he had thereby acquired a domicil in New York, and lost his domicil in Massachusetts (Dicey on Domicil, 56–59; ante, s. 41, note). In Parsons *v.* Bangor, 61 Me. 457, the cases of Briggs *v.* Rochester, and Colton *v.* Longmeadow, were approved, but perhaps unnecessarily, for the decision seems to have been placed upon the ground (p. 460) that there was an actual change of domicil. In Illinois, where a statute provided that certain personal property of persons residing in the state should be taxed, it was held that *residence* meant, not *domicil*, but a settled fixed abode with an intention to remain permanently, at least for a time, and that a person having such a residence in that state was subject to taxation, although his domicil was in another state. Tazewell *v.* Davenport, 40 Ill. 197.

When the right of *voting* at elections is limited to such citizens as reside in the state, it is held that domicil is the criterion of the right to vote, as it is of the liability to taxation. Borland v. Boston, 132 Mass. 89; Fry's Case, 71 Pa. St. 302. But in Holmes v. Greene, 7 Gray (Mass.) 299, a rule is laid down as to domicil for this purpose, which might properly be applied to the residence intended by the statute of limitations, but cannot be considered applicable to domicil in its technical sense, and it is doubtful whether the case can be supported since the decision in Borland v. Boston (supra). A citizen of Massachusetts, residing at Fall River in that state, being obliged to give up the house he occupied, and not being able to find such a house as he desired in Fall River, removed temporarily, across the state line, to a place in Rhode Island, a short distance from his former residence, intending to return to Fall River, and retaining his place of business there; he actually returned in thirteen months. It was held that he was not entitled to vote at an election in Fall River six months after his removal to Rhode Island, because he had changed his domicil. In the judgment it is said, ' where the domicil of a party is in issue, evidence of his intent may have an important and decisive bearing on the question, but it must be in connection with other facts, to which the intent of the party gives efficacy and significance. . . . But no case can be found where the domicil of a party has been made to depend on a bald intent, unaided by other proof. The *factum* and the *animus* must concur in order to establish a domicil.' They must undoubtedly concur in order to establish a *new* domicil, but until they do concur, the old domicil remains. If there be residence (factum), the domicil must depend entirely upon the intention (animus), for until they concur, there is no change (ante, s. 44). In this case, the intention of remaining did not concur with the act of residing in Rhode Island, and so no domicil there

was established. The plaintiff would have found it difficult to escape taxation in Massachusetts, according to Borland v. Boston, 132 Mass. 89, and it is there stated that the test of the right to vote is the same as that of liability to taxation. In the latter case the plaintiff, who was held liable to taxation, had left Massachusetts with the intention of not returning, and had gone to Europe with his family, intending to reside there for an indefinite time, and had formed the intention of residing, upon his return to America, at a place in Connecticut.

The ' *residence* ' or ' *habitancy* ' *in a town*, which by statute determines where a person liable to taxation shall be taxed, resembles domicil in some respects, while in others it differs from it. It has already been mentioned that the term *domicil*, in its technical sense, is not properly applicable to a town or part of a state. As every person domiciled in the state is liable to taxation, and the place of taxation is the town where he resides, a residence, actual or constructive, in some town in the state, is attributed to him, in order that the purpose of the statute may be carried out. Otis v. Boston, 12 Cush. (Mass.) 44, 48; Littlefield v. Brooks, 50 Me. 475, 476. The place for voting is fixed by the same residence as the place of taxation (Opinion of Justices, 5 Met. (Mass.) 590; Borland v. Boston, 132 Mass. 89: Otis v. Boston, 12 Cush. (Mass.) 44, 49; State v. Casper, 36 N. J. L. 367), except in New York in one instance mentioned below. *Residence* or *habitancy* for these purposes is commonly defined in the words of the Massachusetts constitution) as the place ' where he dwelleth or hath his home; the term *domicil* is often applied to it, and it has been said that it ' must be practically equivalent to that legal residence which establishes the domicil.' Otis v. Boston, 12 Cush. (Mass.) 44, 49; Thayer v. Boston,124 Mass. 144; Stockton v. Staples, 66 Me. 197; Cadwalader *v.* Howell, 18 N. J. L. 138. When a person has his home in a town, he retains his residence there, if his domicil in the state continues, until he acquires another residence in the state. Otis *v.* Boston, 12 Cush. (Mass.) 44; Bulkley *v.* Williamstown, 3 Gray (Mass.) 493; Sears *v.* Boston, 1 Met. (Mass.) 250; Littlefield *v.* Brooks, 50 Me. 475, 477. He does not lose his residence by temporary absence. Lee *v.* Boston, 2 Gray (Mass.) 484, 492; Lincoln *v.* Hapgood, 11 Mass. 350. But if he removes to another town for an indefinite time with the intention of not returning, his residence is changed, although he intends not to remain in that town permanently, but to remove again after a limited time. Mead *v.* Boxborough, 11 Cush. (Mass.) 362; Whitney *v.* Sherborn, 12 Allen (Mass.) 111. If he retained no place of abode in the former town, his residence would probably be deemed to be changed, even if he did intend to return; as between two towns in the same state, Holmes *v.* Greene, 7 Gray (Mass.) 299, which is mentioned above, seems rightly decided. It is also probable that, if an inhabitant of one town should remove to another without retaining any dwelling-place in the former to return to, an intention of returning after a *definite* time would not prevent a change of residence, unless his absence under the circumstances could be considered as temporary. (See Wellington *v.* Whitchurch, 4 B. & S. 100.) A person who has come into the state with the intention of making it his home, and has thus acquired a domicil in the state, may never have resided in any place in the state, except temporarily, as at a hotel, and without any intention of making his home there. His domicil in the state would make him liable to taxation somewhere, and he must therefore be deemed to reside in some town in the state. Yet if the rules of domicil were applied to ascertain what we will in this instance call the town of his do-

micil, his domicil would not be in any town in the state. When a person has two or more places of residence in different towns, in which he resides at different times in the year, it is held in New York that he is taxable at the one where he is actually residing at the time when the tax is assessed, though he would vote at the place of his principal residence (Bell *v.* Pierce, 51 N.Y. 12), but in Massachusetts it is held that he should be taxed at the place which under all the circumstances of the case should be considered his home (Thayer *v.* Boston, 124 Mass. 132).

A settlement or *right to support under the poor-laws* is often acquired by residence in a place for a certain length of time. The residence by which this right is gained has much less resemblance to domicil than the residence which fixes the place of taxation. Laws imposing taxes create an obligation which an inhabitant of the state is not permitted to throw off at will, and for the purposes of such laws he must therefore have a residence somewhere. North Yarmouth *v.* West Gardiner, 58 Me. 211. But there is not a similar necessity for attributing to every person a residence by which he may in course of time acquire a right to support. A person cannot, for this purpose of the poor-laws, be resident in two places at the same time (Reg. *v.* Worcester, L. R. 9 Q. B. 344, 345), but he may be without any residence, and a residence may be abandoned or lost without another being acquired. (Jefferson *v.* Washington, 19 Me. 293; North Yarmouth *v.* West Gardiner, 58 Me. 207; Barton *v.* Irasburgh, 33 Vt. 159.) In North Yarmouth *v.* West Gardiner, 58 Me. 212, the court says, ' Upon the party alleging a five years' residence is the burden of proof, and he must show it to have continued all the five years. But if the abandonment of a home, " with bag and baggage," with no intention of returning, is not an end of that home, then, in many cases, the jury would be obliged to find a five years' *residence* upon the proof of one month, or a day even.' A residence may be retained during an absence for a temporary purpose, if there is an intention to return when the purpose is accomplished. Jamaica v. Townshend, 19 Vt. 267; Warren v. Thomaston, 43 Me. 406; Corinth v. Bradley, 51 Me. 540; Ripley v. Hebron, 60 Me. 379; Granby v. Amherst, 7 Mass. 1; Cambridge v. Charlestown, 13 Mass. 501; Lee v. Lenox, 15 Gray (Mass.) 496, 498; Reg. r. Brighton, 4 E. & B. 236; Reg. r. St. Leonard, L. R. 1 Q. B. 21; Reg. v. St. Ives, L. R. 7 Q. B. 467; Guildford v. St. Olave's, 25 L. T. 803. But it will be lost notwithstanding an intention to return, if the absence is too long to be considered temporary. Reg. v. Stapleton, 1 E. & B. 766; Wellington v. Whitchurch, 4 B. & S. 100; Barton v. Irasburgh, 33 Vt. 159. In determining whether residence is retained during absence, an important element to be considered is whether the person has any dwelling-place to return to. Reg. v. St. Ives, L. R. 7 Q. B. 467, 470; Guildford v. St. Olave's, 25 L. T. 803, 804; Jamaica v. Townshend, 19 Vt. 267; Barton v. Irasburgh, 33 Vt. 159. In Warren v. Thomaston, 43 Me. 418, the court says, ' In the discussions in our books upon the pauper laws the term *domicil* is frequently used. . . . Its introduction has, at times, it is feared, tended to confuse and mislead, rather than to simplify and aid in the trial of this class of causes. In its ordinary sense, as used by legal writers, it has not the same restricted meaning as the words *residence*, *dwelling-place*, and *home* have in the statute under consideration.' In Jefferson v. Washington, 19 Me. 300, the same court says, '.The counsel . . . treats the words *dwelling-place* and *home* as if synonymous with *domicil*, and proceeds to argue that one domicil continues till another is gained;

and that to have a domicil a man need not have any particular place of dwelling, or for his home; and he cites numerous authorities to support his position. But the answer to them all is, that domicil, though in familiar language used very properly to signify a man's dwelling-house, has, in cases arising under international law, and kindred cases thereto, a sort of technical meaning. And the authorities cited all apply to it in this sense.' See also Reg. v. Stapleton, 1 E. & B. 766, 771; Littlefield v. Brooks, 50 Me. 477–479. Residence is broken by a departure without an intention to return, however short the absence may be. Detroit v. Palmyra, 72 Me. 256; Hampden v. Levant, 59 Me. 557; Billerica v. Chelmsford, 10 Mass. 394; Reg. v. Worcester, L. R. 9 Q. B. 340; Newark v. Glanford Brigg, 2 Q. B. D. 522. The residence by which a settlement is gained must be voluntary and not by legal constraint. Woodstock v. Hartland, 21 Vt. 563; Brownington v. Charlestown, 32 Vt. 411. Under a statute requiring seven years' residence to gain a settlement, it has been held that the residence is not broken by imprisonment for two years for a criminal offence, where the man has a home to which he intends to return. Baltimore v. Chester, 53 Vt. 315. Where a statute provided that a pauper should not be removed from a parish in which he had resided for a certain time next before the application to remove him, it was held, in the case of a woman who had resided in a parish during that period, that she did not lose her residence by being afterwards taken from the parish by her relations when she had become insane and was incapable of exercising any choice. Reg. v. Whitby, L. R. 5 Q. B. 325. In Massachusetts the word *domicil* has been applied, as it has elsewhere, to the residence mentioned in the poor-laws, but it appears from Wilbraham v. Ludlow, 99 Mass. p. 592, that it has not been so used in its technical sense. In Abington *v.* North Bridgewater, 23 Pick. 170, the court, after saying that in these laws, the terms *being an inhabitant, residing,* &c., were used to designate the place of a person's domicil, stated some of the general rules of domicil, and among them, that 'every one has a domicil of origin, which he retains until he acquires another; and the one thus acquired is in like manner retained.' The point decided in this case was that, where a man lived in a house upon the line between two towns, and the part in one town was not sufficient for a habitation, his residence was in the other town. No case decides that a residence continues for the purpose of gaining a settlement, till another residence is acquired, though there are expressions in Worcester *v.* Wilbraham, 13 Gray, p. 590, which have a tendency that way. The question there decided was, whether, upon proof of a short absence followed by a return, the presumption was that the person had an intention of returning or not. In Chicopee *v.* Whately, 6 Allen, 508, it was held that insanity occurring after a change of residence did not prevent the gaining of a settlement by a continuance of the residence; and the rule applied was, not that a residence continues till another is acquired, but that 'a state of things once shown to exist is presumed to continue till a change is proved.' In Lee *v.* Lenox, 15 Gray, 498, where it is decided that residence is not broken by a temporary absence with an intention to return, the court refers with approval to the discussion of the question of residence in Warren *v.* Thomaston, 43 Me. 406, which is quoted from above. In Wilbraham *v.* Ludlow, 99 Mass. 587, it was decided that a man who left his home without any intention of returning, and worked as a day-laborer in different towns, did not retain a constructive residence in the town where his

former home was. It is said in the judgment, 'Such a man, so situated, when he is laboring in one town with no other intention as to residence except to have a home wherever he works, may well be deemed to live there with the purpose of remaining for an indefinite period of time, and thus to have all the home he has anywhere, as much of a domicil as a wanderer can have.' This case practically decides, as Jefferson *v.* Washington, 19 Me. 293, and Barton *v.* Irasburgh, 33 Vt. 159, expressly did under similar circumstances, that a residence does not necessarily continue until another is acquired. In cases arising under other statutes, so little weight has been given to a mere intention of returning (Holmes *v.* Greene, 7 Gray, 299; Sleeper *v.* Paige, 15 Gray, 349, 350; Hallet *v.* Bassett, 100 Mass. 171), that such an intention would probably not be considered sufficient to retain a constructive residence under the poor-laws in a place where the person had ceased to reside, unless his absence was a temporary one. The consequence of a different rule would be (as pointed out in North Yarmouth *v.* West Gardiner, 58 Me. 212) that a settlement might be acquired as if by a five years' residence, where there had really been a residence of only a month or a day.

By the 2 Will. 4. c. 45, s. 27, a person is not entitled, by reason of certain qualifications, to be registered as a *voter* in a borough, unless he has resided for the six months previous to the last day of July within the borough or within seven miles of it. Although absence will not prevent a constructive residence within the meaning of the act, so long as the person possesses a house to return to, and retains the liberty of returning and the intention of returning, yet he ceases to be a resident if he deprives himself of the liberty of returning, as by letting his house or giving another the right of occupying it for a time however short (Ford *v.* Pye, L. R. 9 C. P. 269; Durant *v.* Carter, L. R. 9 C. P. 261), or by entering the army (Ford *v.* Hart, L. R. 9 C. P. 273), or by committing a criminal offence for which he is imprisoned for a part of the period (Powell *v.* Guest, 18 C. B. N.S. 72). By the 30 & 31 Vict. c. 102, s. 4, it is a part of the qualification for the lodger franchise in boroughs, that the person shall have resided in the lodgings during the twelve months preceding the last day of July. A man was held to be qualified, who possessed during the twelve months lodgings in London, and resided in them when he was in London, which had been, at intervals, for two months out of the twelve, although he had a house in the country where he kept an establishment of servants through the year, and where he resided when not in London (Bond *v.* St. George, L. R. 6 C. P. 312). So a man was held to be qualified in respect of lodgings in which his wife and family resided, and in which he could sleep at any time and did sleep once or twice a week during the twelve months, although he also resided in lodgings which had been taken for him in the same house with a gentleman whom he had been employed to attend, and in which he slept when he did not sleep at the former place (Taylor *v.* St. Mary Abbott, L. R. 6 C. P. 309). In these cases the persons had two residences.

From the cases that have been mentioned, it will be seen that a man may be *domiciled* in a state, and be deemed to *reside* in it and in a particular town in it for the purposes of taxation, and at the same time he may *reside* out of the state within the meaning of the provision in the statute of limitations that has been referred to. He may reside in a particular town so as to be taxable there, and may at the same time not reside there so as to acquire a settlement under the poor-laws. For the purposes of the poor-laws he can reside in but one place at the same time, while under the English election laws he may reside in several places at the same time.

CHAPTER IV.

CAPACITY OF PERSONS.

50. WE now come to the consideration of the operation and
effect of foreign laws in relation to persons and their capacity,
state, and condition.[1] (a)

51. *Obligation of Personal Laws.* — All laws which have for
their principal object the regulation of the capacity, state, and
condition of persons, have been treated by foreign jurists generally as personal laws.[2]   They are by them divided into

[1] Upon the subject of this chapter the learned reader is referred to Burge's
Commentaries on Colonial and Foreign Law, vol. 1, pt. 1, c. 3, s. 1, p. 52, &c.;
Id. s. 2, p. 92, &c.; Id. s. 3, p. 101; and to Id. c. 4, p. 113-135. Cujacius defines the condition of a party thus: Conditio pro statu accipitur; puta, paterfamilias sit, an filius-familias, servus, an liber. Ætatem, valitudinem, facul-
tates, mores non significat. Liverm. Dissert. s. 26, p. 38, cites Cujacii, Obs.
lib. 7, cap. 36.

[2] See Saul v. His Creditors, 5 Mart. N.S. (La.) 569, 596. Boullenois
enumerates as personal all laws which regard majority or minority, emancipation, interdiction for lunacy or prodigality, subjection of married women to
the marital power, subjection of minors to the power of their parents and
guardians, legitimacy and illegitimacy, excommunication, civil death, infamy, nobility, foreigners and strangers, and naturalization. 1 Boullenois,
obs. 4, p. 46, 51; Id. 78; Id. 800. See also Merlin, Répert. Statut. Pothier
enumerates among personal laws those respecting the paternal power, the
guardianship of minors and their emancipation, the age required to make a
will, and the marital authority.   Pothier, Cout. d'Orléans, introd. c. 1, art. 6.
See, also, Rodenburg, de Div. Stat. tit. 2, c. 5, s. 16; 2 Boullenois, App. 48.
Le Brun enumerates among personal statutes those respecting majority, legitimacy, guardianship, and the paternal power. Le Brun, Traité de la Communauté, liv. 2, c. 3, s. 5, n. 25. See also Bouhier, Cout. de Bourg. c. 23,
s. 64; 1 Boullenois, c. 2, obs. 5, p. 74-122; 1 Burge, Col. & For. Law, c. 3,
s. 1, p. 57, &c.

(a) Questions of *personal status* depend on the law of the domicil. Shaw
v. Gould, L. R. 3 H. L. 55, 83; Udny
v. Udny, L. R. 1 H. L. Sc. 441, 457;
Harvey v. Farnie, 8 App. Cas. 43;
Ross v. Ross, 129 Mass. 243; Keegan
v. Geraghty, 101 Ill. 26. ' The status
of an individual, used as a legal term,
means the legal position of the individual in or with regard to the rest
of a community.' Niboyet v. Niboyet, 4 P. D. p. 11, by Brett, L.J.

two sorts; those which are universal, and those which are special. The former (universal laws) regulate universally the capacity, state, and condition of persons, such as their minority, majority, emancipation, and power of administration of their own affairs. The latter (special laws) create an ability or a disability to do certain acts, leaving the party in all other respects with his general capacity or incapacity.[1] But whether laws purely personal belong to the one class or to the other, they are for the most part held by foreign jurists to be of absolute obligation everywhere, when they have once attached upon the person by the law of his domicil.[2] Boullenois has stated the doctrine among his general principles. Personal laws, says he, affect the person with a quality which is inherent in him, and his person is the same everywhere. Laws purely personal, whether universal or particular, extend themselves everywhere; that is to say, a man is everywhere deemed in the same state, whether universal or particular, by which he is affected by the law of his domicil. 'Ces loix personnelles affectent la personne d'une qualité qui lui est inhérente, et la personne est telle partout.'[3] And again, 'Les loix pures personnelles, soit personelles universelles, soit personelles particulières, se portent partout; c'est à dire, que l'homme est partout de l'état, soit universel, soit particulier, dont sa personne est affectée par la loi de son domicile.[4] L'état personnel du domicile se porte partout. Habilis vel inhabilis in loco domicilii, est habilis vel inhabilis in omni loco.'[5] Rodenburg says: 'Whenever inquiry is made as to the state and condition of a person, there is

[1] See Henry on For. Law, 2, 3; 1 Froland, Mem. c. 5, p. 81.

[2] How extensively this rule may operate, may be readily understood by simply referring to the different ages at which majority is attained in different countries. By the civil law full age was not attained until twenty-four. By the old law of France the age of majority was twenty-five. By the custom of Normandy the age of majority was twenty; by the law of Spain, the age of twenty-four; by that of Holland, twenty-five. In some parts of Germany the majority is attained at twenty-one; in others, at eighteen; in others, at twenty-five; in Saxony, at twenty-one; and so in England, Scotland, Ireland, and the United States of America. The present law of France, for all purposes except marriage, adopts the same age; but for marriage the rule is still twenty-five. 1 Burge, Col. & For. Law, pt. 1, c. 4, p. 113, 114, 115; post, s. 66, note, s. 90.

[3] 1 Boullenois, Prin. Gén. p. 4.

[4] 1 Boullenois, Prin. Gén. 10, 18, p. 4, 6; obs. 4, 10, 12, 14, 46.

[5] Boullenois, Dissert. sur Quest. de Contrarieté des Loix, ed. 1732, Disc. Prél. p. 20, règle, 10.

but one judge, that of his domicil, to whom the right appertains to settle the matter.'   'Cum de statu et conditione hominum quæritur, uno solummodo judici, et quidem domicilii, universum in illa jus sit attributum.'[1]   Hence, says Hertius, the state and quality of a person are governed by the law of the place to which he is by his domicil subjected.   Whenever a law is directed to the person, we are to refer to the law of the place to which he is personally subject.   'Hinc status et qualitas personæ regitur a legibus loci, cui ipsa sese per domicilium subjecit.[2]   Quando lex in personam dirigitur, respiciendum est ad leges illius civitatis, quæ personam habet subjectam.'[3]

51 a. *Foreign Jurists.* — Froland, Bouhier, Rodenburg, Paul Voet, Pothier, and others lay down a similar rule.[4]   Froland lays down the doctrine in the following broad terms. A personal statute not only exerts its authority in the place of the domicil of the party; but its provisions follow the party, and accompany his person, in every place where he goes to contract; and it extends over all his property (biens) under whatever customs it may be situated: 'Et qu'elle influe sur tous ses biens sous quelques coutumes, qu'ils soient assis.'[5]   Bouhier adopts the very rule of Boullenois: 'Quand le statut personnel du domicile est en concurrence avec le statut personnel de la situation des biens, celui du domicile doit l'emporter sur celui de la situation des biens.'[6]   And again he says: It is necessary constantly to hold that the capacity or incapacity which the law of the domicil has impressed upon the person should follow the person into all places; so that it shall become utterly impossible that a person, being incapable in the place of his residence, should go to contract in another place

[1] Rodenburg, de Div. Stat. tit. 1, c. 3, s. 4–10; 1 Boullenois, p. 145, 146; Id. obs. 14, p. 196; 2 Boull. App. 789.

[2] 1 Hertius, de Collis. Leg. s. 4, n. 5, p. 122; Id. p. 173, 174, ed. 1716.

[3] Id.; Id. n. 8, p. 123; Id. n. 12, p. 128; Id. p. 175; Id. p. 182, ed. 1716.

[4] 1 Froland, Mém. de Statut. c. 7, s. 2, p. 156; Id. vol. 2. c. 33, s. 8, 9, 10, p. 157; Bouhier, Cout. de Bourg. c. 23, s. 92, p. 461; Id. c. 24, s. 11, p. 463; Id. c. 22, s. 5–11. p. 418; Voet, de Statut. s. 4, c. 2, n. 6, p. 137, 138; Henry on For. Law, c. 4, p. 34; Pothier, Introd. Gén. Cout. d'Orléans, c. 1, art. 7; 1 Hert. Opera, de Coll. s. 4, n. 5, p. 121, n. 8, p. 123; Id. p. 172, 173, 175, ed. 1716. See also Foelix, Revue Etrangère et Française, &c., 1840, vol. 7, p. 200–216. Since the present work was in the press I have for the first time seen these Dissertations of Mr. Foelix, and I shall gladly avail myself of his learned labors.

[5] 1 Froland, Mém. c. 7, s. 2, p. 156; Id. c. 5, s. 4, p. 89; post, s. 84.

[6] Bouhier, Cout. de Bourg. c. 23, s. 91–96, p. 461; Id. c. 22, s. 4–14, s. 19.

where he would have been capable if he had been domiciled there. 'Il faut donc tenir pour constant, que la capacité ou l'incapacité, que la loi du domicile a imprimée sur la personne la suit en tous lieux. En sorte que ce seroit inutilement, que étant incapable au lieu de sa résidence, elle voudroit aller contracter dans un endroit, où il auroit été capable, si elle y avoit été domiciliée.'[1] Abraham à Wesel uses language equally strong: 'Quotiescunque enim de habilitate atque inhabilitate personæ quæritur, toties domicilii leges et statuta spectanda, ut quocumque persona abeat, id jus sit, quod judex domicilii statuerit;'[2] and he applies the rule to movable and immovable property.[3] Pothier says that personal statutes exert their power upon the persons in relation to their property (biens) wherever it may be situated: 'Au reste, ces statuts personnels exercent leur empire sur les personnes par rapport a tous leur biens, quelque part qu'ils soient situés.'[4] Rodenburg says: 'Quocumque modo se cassus habuerit, contrahentium erit respicere ad suum cujusque domicilii locum, impressam ibidem personæ qualitatem, aut adeptam domi conditionem cujus ignarus non sit oportet, qui cum alio volet contrahere. Quare Hollandiæ incola major Ultrajecti, minor apud suos, contrahit apud nostrates invalide. Contra Ultrajectinus lege domicilii major contrahit in Hollandiæ efficaciter; ut maxime ex more regionis istius rerum suarum necdum habentur compos.'[5] Stockmannus holds equally strong language; 'Unde recte, eum, qui inhabilis est in uno loco, etiam in alio inhabilem censeri; et si aliter statuamus, incertus et varius erit personarum status; cum tamen uti personam ubique eandem, ita qualitatem personæ inhærentem, velut ejus accidens, ubique uniformem esse conveniat.'[6] Merlin has expressed it in equally comprehensive terms,[7] saying that the law of the domicil

[1] Bouhier, Cout. de Bourg. c. 24, s. 11, p. 463.
[2] Wesel, Com. ad Novell. Constit. Ultraj. art. 18, s. 23, p. 169, 170.
[3] Id. s. 25, 27, p. 170, 173; Liverm. Diss. s. 55, p. 56.
[4] Pothier, Introd. Gén. aux Cout. d'Orléans, c. 1, art. 7; post, s. 69.
[5] Rodenburg, de Diversit. Statut. tit. 2, c. 1, s, 2; 2 Boullenois, App. p. 11.
[6] Stockmann. Decis. 125, s. 6, p. 262, cited also 1 Boullenois, obs. 6, p. 131; Liverm. Dissert. s. 22, p. 35. See also Abraham à Wesel, Comment. ad Nov. Constit. Ultraject. art. 13, n. 24, 25, p. 170–172; Liverm. Dissert. s. 55, p. 56.
[7] Merlin, Répert. Stat.; Id. Majorité, s. 5; Id. Autorisation Maritale, s. 10. The like rule is maintained by Burgundus, Stockmans, and D'Argentré, as to personal property and covenants. See Liverm. Diss. p. 34, 35, 50; Merlin, Répert. Majorité, s. 5; Id. Autorisation Maritale, s. 10.

as to majority or minority governs in respect even to property (biens) situate in another territory.[1]

51 *b*. Paul Voet, on the other hand, speaks in far more qualified language, and lays down several rules on the subject. (1) That a personal statute only affects the subjects of the state or territory wherein it is promulgated, and not foreigners, although doing some business there. 'Statutum personale tantum afficit subditos territorii, ubi statutum conditum est; non autem forenses, licet ibidem aliquid agentes.'[2] (2) That as a personal statute does not affect a person out of the territory, it cannot therefore be reputed to be the same without the territory as it is within. 'Statutum personale non afficit personam extra territorium; sic ut pro tali non reputetur extra territorium, qualis erat intra.'[3] (3) That a personal quality cannot be added out of the territory to a person not a subject. 'Personalis qualitas non potest extra territorium addi personæ non subjectæ.'[4] (4) A personal statute accompanies the person everywhere in respect to property (biens) situate within the territory of the state where the person affected by it has his domicil. 'Statutum personale ubique locorum personam comitatur, in ordine ad bona intra territorium statuentis sita, ubi persona affecta domicilium habet.'[5] We shall also presently see that he distinguishes between the effect of a personal statute upon movable, and its effect upon immovable property.[6]

52. The result of the doctrine maintained by the jurists above named, except Paul Voet, is, that a person who has attained the age of majority by the law of his native domicil, is to be deemed everywhere the same, of age; and, on the other hand, that a person who is in his minority by the law of his native domicil, is to be deemed everywhere in the same state or condition.[7] Thus, for example, if, by the law of the place of his original domicil, a person cannot make a will of his property before he is twenty-one years of age, he cannot, if under that age, make a valid will, even of such property as is situate in a place where the law allows persons of the age of fourteen years to make a will of the like pro-

---

[1] Merlin, Répert. Majorité, s. 5, edit. Brux. 1827, p. 189.
[2] Voet, de Stat. s. 4, c. 2, p. 137, ed. 1661.
[3] Id.   [4] Id. p. 138.
[5] Id. p. 138.   [6] Post, s. 52.
[7] 1 Boullenois, p. 108, &c., 1 Burge, Col. & For. Law, pt. 1, c. 4, p. 118–135.

perty.[1] So, if by the law of her original domicil a married
woman cannot dispose of her property except with the consent
of her husband, she is equally prohibited from disposing of her
property situate in another place, where no such consent is requisite.[2] Many jurists apply this doctrine indiscriminately to movable, as well as to immovable property. Thus, Boullenois says:
" If a man has immovable property, situate in a place where the
age of majority is fixed at twenty-five, and by the law of his own
domicil he is of age at twenty, he may at twenty sell or alienate
such immovable property. On the other hand, if by the law of
the place where the immovable property is situate he is of age at
twenty, but by the law of his domicil not until twenty-five, he
cannot sell or alienate such property until the age of twenty-
five.'[3] But other jurists distinguish between movable and immovable property, applying the law of situs to the latter, and the
law of the domicil to the former.[4] Paul Voet insists throughout
upon this distinction, and holds that no personal statute extends
to immovable property situate elsewhere. ' Non tamen statutum
personale sese regulariter extendet ad bona immobilia alibi sita.'[5]
But he admits that such a statute will apply to movable property,
upon the ground that, wherever it may be situate, it follows the
domicil of the owner. ' Quin tamen ratione mobilium ubicunque
sitorum, domicilium seu personam domini sequamur, ut tamen
spectentur loca, quo destinata, nullus iverit inficias; idque propter
expressos textus juris civilis, quibus mobilia certo loco non alli-
gantur, verum secundum juris intellectum personam comitari,
eique adhærere judicantur ; id quod etiam mores ubique locorum
sequuntur."[6] Burgundus holds the same opinion: " Consequenter ea, quæ sunt personalia, una cum persona circumferun-

[1] Pothier, Cout. d'Orléans, c. 1, art. 7; 1 Boullenois, Prin. Gén. 19, p. 7;
Id. obs. 16, p. 205; 1 Froland, Mém. c. 7, p. 156; Bouhier, Cout. de Bourg.
c. 22, s. 5-11; c. 24, s. 7-13; Mer. Répert. Majorité, s. 5; Id. Autorisation
Maritale, s. 10; Rodenburg, de Divers. Statut. tit. 2, c. 1, s. 1; 2 Boullenois,
App. p. 11.
[2] Ibid. Henry on Foreign Law, s. 1, p. 31.
[3] Boullenois, Dissert. sur des Quest. de la Contrar. des Loix, Quest. 1, p. 19,
20; Basnage, Coutum. de Normand. tom. 2, art. 431, p. 243. See also Merlin, Répert. Majorité, s. 4, 5.
[4] Voet, Burgundus, Stockmans, and Peckius, cited in Merlin, Répert. Majorité, s. 5, p. 189, ed. 1827; ante, s. 52 a.
[5] P. Voet, ad Statut. s. 4, c. 2, n. 6, p. 138, ed. 1661; Id. c. 3, n. 4, p. 148.
[6] P. Voet, ad Statut. s. 4, c. 2, n. 9, p. 139, 148, ed. 1661.

. tur, quocumque loco se transtulerit, et per universa territoria, viresque et effectum porrigunt. Realia situm rerum sic spectant, ut territorii limites non excedant; quia rebus ipsis sunt affixa.'[1] Many other jurists maintain the same distinction;[2] but it needs not be here further insisted on, as it will hereafter come more fully under our consideration.

53. The doctrine as to the nature and operation of personal statutes, thus asserted by foreign jurists, even with the distinction in its application between movable property and immovable property, is found attended with many difficulties; and many of these jurists are compelled to make exceptions in its application which go far to limit, if not to impair, its real force and efficiency.[3] Indeed the language held by some of them on this subject has not always such a precision, as to its actual extent and operation, as to free the mind from all doubt in regard to the true meaning. Merlin says :[4] ' The law of the domicil governs the state of the person and his personal capacity or incapacity. It also governs personal actions, movables, and movable effects, in whatever place they may in fact be situated. The power of the law of the domicil extends everywhere to everything within its reach or jurisdiction, so that he who is of a majority by the law of his domicil, is of the age of majority everywhere. The law of the place where the property (biens) is situate regulates the quality and disposition of it. When the law of the domicil and that of the situation (situs) are in conflict with each other, if the question is respecting the state and condition of the person, the law of the domicil ought to prevail; if it is respecting the disposition of property (biens), the law of the place where they are situate is to be followed.'[5] ' If several real statutes are found in conflict with each other, each one has its own effect upon the property (biens) which it governs.'[6] Now, this language of Merlin is in some parts sufficiently broad to cover movable property, as well as immovable property, and yet it is very clear that the disposition of movable property and the capacity to dispose of it are by many

---

[1] Burgundus, tract. 1, s. 3, p. 15.

[2] See J. Voet, Stockmannus, and Peckius, cited post, s. 54, and 1 Boullenois, obs. 4, p. 57; Id. obs. 6, p. 131; Sandius, lib. 4, tit. 8, definit. 7, p. 104.

[3] See Livermore, Diss. p. 62–106.

[4] Merlin, Répert. Statut. See also Id. Majorité, s. 5; Id. Autorisation Maritale, s. 10.

[5] Ibid.　　　　　　　　　[6] Ibid.

foreign jurists and by Merlin himself held to be governed by the law of the domicil of the owner, according to the maxim that movables follow the person: 'Mobilia sequuntur personam.'[1] What perhaps Merlin intends here to assert may be, that where a person is incapable by the law of his domicil, he cannot dispose of any of his property situate elsewhere, the incapacity extending even to places where he is not domiciled, and where, by the local law, he would otherwise have capacity to dispose of it; but that, where a person is capable by the law of his domicil, and the question does not respect his personal capacity to dispose of property, but only the extent to which it may be exercised by persons who are capable, there the law of the place where it is situate will govern.[2] Yet he would seem also to intimate that there is or may be some distinction between personal property and real property (between movables and immovables), as to the effect of the operation of the lex domicilii.[3]

54. In another place Merlin lays down the rule that a law which declares a person a major or a minor who is born within its reach of jurisdiction, is personal, and extends to property (biens) situate out of the territory; or in other words, that a statute respecting majority full and entire is personal, and extends to property (biens) situate out of the territory. 'Le statut de la majorité pleine et entière est personnel, et s'étend aux biens situés hors de son territoire.'[4] Thus if, by the law of the place where a person has his domicil, he is of majority at the age of twenty, and has the faculty of disposing of his property situate there, the same faculty will extend to his property situate in another country, where he would not be capable of alienating until he was twenty-five years of age. And he applies this doctrine equally to movables and immovables.[5] He admits that the Voets, Burgundus, Stockmans, and Peckius, while they deem such a law to be personal, insist that it does not extend to the disposal of immovables situate in a foreign country, where a different rule as to capacity

[1] Ibid.
[2] Pothier, Cout. d'Orléans, c. 1, art. 7; 1 Boullenois, Prin. Gén. 16, p. 7; Id. obs. 19, p. 338, &c.; Rodenburg, c. 3, s. 4, 9, 10, p. 7–9; Id. c. 2, p. 6; Voet, de Stat. s. 7, c. 2, p. 125, s. 8; Pothier, de Choses, pt. 2, s. 3; Livermore, Dissert. 82.
[3] See Merlin, Répert. Majorité, s. 5, p. 188, 189, ed. Brux. 1827.
[4] Ibid.
[5] See Merlin, Répert. Majorité, s. 5, p. 188, 189, ed. Brux. 1827.

or majority prevails.[1] Merlin in another place says: 'If the law of the domicil declares a person incapable to sell, alien, contract, or to bind himself in any manner to another, it is impossible that his immovables, in whatever country they may be situated, can be aliened, bound, or hypothecated by him. Who has ever doubted that the interdiction pronounced against a prodigal, or a madman, by the judge of his domicil, was an obstacle to the alienation of his property (biens) which is situate within the reach of another jurisdiction? Who has ever doubted that the tutor (guardian) named by the judge of the domicil has the right to administer the property (biens) which is within the territory of another judge?'[2] This is very bold and uncompromising language, but it will be very difficult to sustain it without many qualifications. It may be added that the modern Civil Code of France expressly declares that the laws concerning the condition and capacity of persons govern Frenchmen even if residing in a foreign country.[3] In the progress of our inquiries it will be found that many exceptions are admitted to exist as to the operation of personal laws, and that the practice of nations by no means justifies the doctrine in the extent to which it is ordinarily laid down by many foreign jurists.

54 a. John Voet, on the other hand, is one of the few jurists who insist that personal statutes of all sorts respecting capacity or incapacity, majority or minority, legitimacy or illegitimacy, have no extra-territorial operation, either directly or consequentially. 'Verius est,' says he, 'personalia non magis quam realia territorium statuentis posse excedere, sive directo, sive per consequentiam.'[4] And he goes on to add: 'Ita nec ratio ulla est, cur

---

[1] See Merlin, Répert. Majorité, s. 5, ed. Brux. 1827, p. 188; Id. Autorisation Maritale, s. 10. I do not find the citations from some of these authors accurately given by Merlin. But I believe that the following will be found to verify his statement : J. Voet, ad Pand. 4, 4, n. 8; ad Pand. 23, 2, n. 60, n. 136; P. Voet, ad Statut. s. 4, c. 3, n. 10, p. 153; Burgundus, Tract. 1, n. 5, 6, 7, 8; Peck. de Testam. Conjug. lib. 4, c. 28, introd. n. 5, 6, 7; Stockmans, decis. 125, s. 6, 9, p. 262, 263; Christin. tom. 2, decis. 56, s. 12; Livermore, Dissert. s. 47–52, p. 50–54. Immobilia .(says P. Voet) statutis loci, ubi sita; mobilia loci statutis, ubi testator habuit domicilium. P. Voet, de Statut. s. 4, c. 3, n. 10, p. 153, ed. 1661. Again, he adds: Quid circa successionem. Spectabitur loci statuta ubi immobilium sita, non ubi testator moritur. Id. s. 9, c. 1, n. 3, p. 305. See 1 Burge's Col. & For. Law, pt. 1, c. 3, s. 3, p. 118–129.
[2] Merlin, Répert. Autorisation Maritale, s. 10, art. 2.
[3] Code Civil of France, art. 3; post, s. 68.
[4] Voet, ad Pand. 1, 4, 7, p. 40.

magis qualitas et habilitas privato per statutum data vel denegata,
vires extenderet per ea loca, in quibus diversum quid aut contrarium circa personarum qualitatem lege cautum est. Quod, si
hæc cuiquam minus videantur sufficere, is velim mihi rationem
modumve expediat, per quem legislator personam, domicilii intuitu
sibi suppositam, habilem quem inhabilemve ad actus gerendos
declarans, alterius loci legislatorem, potestate parem cogeret, ut
is alienis decretis statutisve pareret, aut rata irritave haberet, quæ
judex domicilii talia esse jussit in persona domicilium, illic fovente;
maxime, si fateatur (ut fateri necesse est) pari in parem nullam
competere cogendi potestatem. Exponat, obsecro, prodigo declarato, vel infamia notato, vel legitimato, vel in ipso pubertatis tempore habili ad testamentum condendum declarato per magistratum
Hollandum, ac Ultrajectum se conferente vel immobilia possidente;
exponat, inquam, qua juris via magistratus Ultrajectinus adstringi
posset, ut istum ratione bonorum, in Ultrajectino solo sitorum, pro
tali agnosceret; adeoque contractus prodigi Hollandici haberet
irritos; dignitates Hollando infamato denegaret; successionem in
bona Trajectina ad spurium Hollandum legitimatum pertinentia,
tanquam in legitime nati patrimonium, pateretur proximis deferri;
testamentum masculi, ante annum ætatis octavum decimentum
conditum, juberet ratum esse.' [1]

55. Hitherto we have been considering cases of the capacity
or incapacity of persons arising from the domicil of origin, where
there has been no subsequent change of domicil; as to which, as
we have seen, the doctrine of foreign jurists is, that the law of the
original domicil is to prevail, as to such capacity or incapacity,
some of them holding that it applies to all personal acts whatever,
and to all alienation of property, whether movable or immovable,
and others apply it only to personal acts and movable property,
where there is a conflict of personal laws. But suppose that a
person has had different domicils, a domicil by birth and a subsequent domicil by choice, when he is sui juris, which is to prevail,
as to his capacity or incapacity? [2] Hertius does not hesitate to
say that the law of the new domicil is to prevail. 'Hinc status
et qualitas personæ regitur a legibus loci,' says he, 'cui ipsa sese
per domicilium subjecit. Atque inde etiam fit, ut quis major hic,

---

[1] Ibid.

[2] See, on this subject, 1 Burge, Col. & For. Law, pt. 1, c. 3, s. 3, p. 102–
106; Id. c. 4, p. 113–125.

alibi, mutato scilicet domicilio, incipiat fieri minor.'[1]　The like opinion appears to be held both by Paul Voet and by John Voet.[2] The former says: 'Nullum statutum, sive in rem, sive in perso- nam, si de ratione juris civilis sermo instituatur, sese extendit ultra statuentis territorium.'[3]　The latter holds that the change of domicil of a person gives him the capacity or incapacity of his new domicil, so that if he is of majority by the law of the place of his birth, and he removes to another country, by whose laws he would, according to his age, be a minor, he will acquire the character of his new domicil.　'Si quis ex lege domicilii derelicti anno forte vicesimo completo major factus fuerit, translato domi- cilio ad locum illum, ubi non nisi absoluto viginti quinque anno- rum curriculo quisque major habetur, non dubitem quin ex novi domicilii jura incipiat iterum minorennis esse.'[4]

55 a. Froland thinks this question cannot be answered univer- sally, and he puts a distinction.　'If,' says he, 'the question is purely as to the state of the person, abstracted from all consid- eration of property or subject-matter (abstracte ab omni materia reali), in this case the law which first commenced to fix his con- dition (that is, the law of the domicil of his birth) will preserve its force and authority, and follow him wherever he may go. Thus if by the law of the domicil of his origin a person attains his majority at twenty years, and he goes to reside in another place where the age of majority is twenty-five years, he is held to be of the age of majority everywhere ; and, notwithstanding he is under twenty-five years, he may in his new domicil sell, alien, hypothe- cate, and contract as he pleases, and vice versa.'[5]　'But,' he adds, ' when the question is as to the ability or disability of a person who has changed his domicil, to do a certain thing (à faire une certaine chose), then that which had governed his power (that is, the law of his original domicil) falls, and fails entirely in this respect, and yields its authority to the law of his new domicil.

---

[1] 2 Hertii, Opera, s. 4, n. 5, p. 122; Id. n. 8, p. 123; Id. p. 173, 175, ed. 1716.

[2] 1 Boullenois, App. p. 57; Merlin, Répert. Majorité, s. 4, ed. Brux. 1827, p. 186; Merlin, Rép. Effet Rétroactif, s. 3, art. 9, n. 3; P. Voet, de Stat. s. 4, c. 2, n. 6, p. 137, 138; Rodenburg, de Div. Stat. p. 2, c. 1, s. 5, 6; J. Voet. ad Pand. 4, 4, n. 10; 1 Boullenois, obs. 4, p. 58.

[3] P. Voet. ad Statut. s. 4, c. 2, n. 7, p. 138, ed. 1661.

[4] 1 J. Voet, ad Pand. 4, 4, n. 10; ad Pand. 5, 1, n. 101.

[5] Froland, Mém. c. 7, s. 13, 14, p. 171; post, s. 138, note.　See 2 Boulle- nois, obs. 32, p. 7–11; Bouhier, Cout. de Bourg. c. 22, s. 4–10.

Thus, if a married woman, by the law of the country of her birth, is not allowed to pass property by will without the consent of her husband, and she acquires a new domicil in another country where no such restriction exists, she has full liberty to dispose of her property in the latter country by will, without the consent of her husband, and vice versa.'[1] This is a very nice, if it be not in many cases an evanescent, distinction; and Froland admits that a different doctrine is held by many jurists.[2] But he is not singular in his opinion of the value and importance of this distinction.[3] Boullenois has given to it a qualified sanction.[4] Bouhier also cites the same distinction with approbation, declaring it to be judicious; and he insists that, in case of a transfer of the domicil, the law of the original domicil ought in all cases to regulate the personal capacity, and he enlarges on the subject with much ability.[5]

56. On the other hand, Burgundus does not hesitate to hold that the law of the new or actual domicil ought to prevail. After citing the opinion of Baldus and Gail and Imbertus, that the state of the person is to be decided by the place of his domicil : ' Ideo, si status personæ inspici debeat, dumtaxat rationem haberi Baldus existimat, cujus opinionem Andreas Gail et Imbertus amplectuntur ; adeo ego,' he adds, ' nisi ex privilegio vel longissimo usu aliud sit introductum. Proinde ut sciamus uxor in potestate sit mariti necne, qua ætate minor contrahere posset, et ejusmodi, respicere oportet ad legem cujusque domicilii. Hæc enim imprimit qualitatem personæ, atque adeo naturam ejus afficit, ut quocumque terrarum sit transitura, incapacitatem domi adeptam non aliter quam cicatricam in corpore foras circumferat. Consequenter dicemus ; si mutaverit domicilium persona, novi domicilii conditionem induere.'[6] Rodenburg is of the same opinion upon the

[1] 1 Froland, Mém. c. 7, s. 15, p. 172; post, s. 138, note.
[2] Ibid. Boullenois remarks on this distinction of Froland, that it contains some truth mixed up with much obscurity, and embarrassed with ideas liable to contradiction without being answered. 2 Boullenois, obs. 32, p. 8, 9.
[3] See Rodenburg, de Div. Stat. tit. 2, c. 1–4; tit. 3, c. 1–4; tit. 4, c. 1–4; 2 Boullenois, App. p. 1–33; Id. p. 71–79; Id. p. 84–95; 2 Boullenois, c. 1, obs. 32, p. 1–53; Merlin, Répert. Effet Rétroactif, s. 3, p. 2, art. 5, n. 3, ed. Brux. 1827, p. 15–18; Id. Majorité, s. 4, p. 186, 187.
[4] 2 Boullenois, obs. 32, p. 7–11.
[5] Bouhier, Cout. de Bourg. c. 22, s. 4–10; Id. s. 22, cited Merlin, Répert., Autorisation Maritale, s. 10, art. 4, ed. Brux. 1827, p. 243.
[6] Burgundus, Tract. 2, n. 5–7; post, s. 140 a. Cited also in Merlin, Répert. Effet Rétroactif, s. 3, p. 2, art. 5, p. 14, Brux. ed. 1827.

ground that the state and condition of the person is wholly governed by the law of his actual domicil, and when that is changed his state and condition change with it: ' Personæ enim status et conditio cum tota regatur a legibus loci, cui illa sese per domicilium subdiderit, utique mutato domicilio, mutari et necesse est personæ conditionem.' [1] And he applies the rule indiscriminately to the case of minors and to the case of married women.[2] D'Argentré is also of the same opinion, and says: ' Quotiescunque de habilitate aut inhabilitate personæ quæratur, toties domicilii leges et statuta spectanda. Ratio est, quia hic abstracta de habilitate personæ et universali ejus statu quæratur, ideoque personæ a foro domicilii afficiatur. Nam originis locus nusquam in foro considerationem habet, cum aliud domicilium proponitur.' [3]

57. Boullenois (whose opinions will be stated more fully hereafter) [4] admits the general principle to be as Rodenburg states it, and asserts that the whole world acknowledges that the state of the person depends on his actual domicil, and that the natural consequence is that if a person changes his domicil, and the law of the new domicil is contrary to that of the old one, the state and condition of the person change accordingly.[5] But then he insists that it is necessary to make a distinction between the states and conditions of persons which arise from laws (droits) founded in public reasons admitted by all nations, and which have a cause absolutely unconnected with domicil, so that the moment a man is affected with these states and conditions, the original domicil not having any influence upon them, the new domicil ought not to have any, but merely the public reasons, superior to those of domicil, to which all nations pay respect, and other subordinate states and conditions which are in truth founded in public laws (droits

---

[1] Rodenburg, de Div. Stat. tit. 2, pt. 2, c. 1, n. 3; 2 Boullenois, obs. 32, p. 2, 5, 7; Id. Appx. p. 56, 57; post, s. 71.

[2] Rodenburg, de Div. Stat. tit. 2, pt. 2, c. 1; Id. n. 5, 6; 2 Boullenois, obs. 32, p. 2, 5, 7, 8; Id. Appx. p. 56, 57; post, s. 71.

[3] D'Argentré, de Leg. Briton. art. 218, n. 47, 49; 1 Boullenois, obs. 4, p. 53; post, s. 84. Yet, though the language of D'Argentré is thus explicit, Bouhier seems to suppose that he aided his own opinion, because he has added in another place, "Affecta quocunque modo persona domicilii lege, aut jure, eo perpetuo sic tenetur, ut ne ulla mutatione loci sese possit exercere.' Bouhier, Cout. de Bourg. c. 22, s. 9. But it is plain that D'Argentré is here speaking of a mere change of place without a change of domicil. D'Argentré, de Leg. Briton. art. 218, s. 13, p. 603.

[4] Post, s. 71.   [5] 2 Boullenois, obs. 32, p. 10, 13.

publics), but for one nation only, or for certain provinces of that nation.[1]   Among the former class he enumerates interdiction, or prohibition to do acts by reason of insanity, or of prodigality, emancipation by royal authority, legitimacy of birth, nobility, infamy, &c.   These, he contends, are never altered by any change of domicil, but that, having at first fixed the condition of the person, the change of domicil does not cause them to cease.[2] Among the latter class he enumerates the community of property between husband and wife, the state of the husband as to the marital power, the state of the father as to real rights of the paternal power, and other subordinate states.   These, he contends, sometimes are affected by a change of domicil, and sometimes are not.[3]   Some of this last class, he adds, affect the person at least in vim conventionis tacitæ ; and this, according to the opinion of a great number of jurists, is the case in respect to the law of the community of property between husband and wife.[4]   Others of the same class affect the person in vim solius legis ; such is the statute or law, Senatus consultum Velleianum, which prohibits married women from making obligatory personal contracts with others.[5]   Boullenois himself holds that the capacity of married women is governed by the law of the actual or new domicil ;[6] but that the capacity of minors is governed by the law of their domicil of birth.[7]   He also holds that the paternal power is regulated by the domicil of birth.[8]   But here again he distinguishes between movable property and immovable property, holding that the law of the domicil of birth governs as to the former, and the law of the situation (situs) as to the latter.[9]

58. Merlin, after citing the opinions of other jurists, formerly came to the conclusion that the law of the place of birth, and not that of the new domicil, ought to govern equally in all these cases of minority, of paternal power, and of marital power after

[1] 2 Boullenois, obs. 32, p. 10, 11, 13, 19; post, s. 71.
[2] 2 Boullenois, obs. 32, p. 11; post, s. 71; 1 Boullenois, obs. 4, p. 50, 64.
[3] 2 Boullenois, obs. 32, p. 11, 12, 13; post, s. 71.
[4] 2 Boullenois, obs. 32, p. 11; post, s. 143–171.
[5] 2 Boullenois, obs. 32, p. 11, 13; ante, s. 15; post, s. 71, 425.
[6] 2 Boullenois, obs. 32, p. 13–19; 1 Boull. obs. 4, p. 61, post, s. 71.
[7] 2 Boullenois, obs. 32, p. 19–31; 1 Boull. obs. 4, p. 53, 54; Id. Dissert. Mixtes, quest. 2, p. 40–62; Id. quest. 20, p. 406–447.
[8] 2 Boullenois, obs. 32, p. 31–53; 1 Boull. obs. 32, p. 68; post, s. 71.
[9] 1 Boullenois, obs. 32, p. 32, 33–53; Id. Dissert. Mixtes. quest. 20, p. 406–447.

marriage ; and he expressed surprise, and not without reason, that Boullenois should have attempted to distinguish between them.[1] It is certainly not for me to interfere in such grave controversies between these learned jurists, differing from each other, sometimes in leading principles, and sometimes in deductions and distinctions applicable to principles in which they agree. 'Non nostrum inter vos tantas componere lites.' Yet Merlin himself, after having advocated this doctrine, as best founded in principle, although involving some inconveniences, still insisted that upon such a removal to a new domicil, the capacity of a person to dispose of his movable property by a testament is to be governed by the law of the new domicil, because the state of a person has no influence as to the distribution of his movable property after his death; and the capacity to make a will, resulting from age, has nothing in common with what is properly called the state of the person; which is so true, that his state is governed by the domicil, and the situation decides solely concerning the age at which a person may dispose of movable property upon his death.[2] It seems however that Merlin has since, upon further reflection, come to a different conclusion; and he may be now numbered among those who support the doctrine that the law of the new domicil ought to govern in all cases, whether they respect capacity, or minority, or the paternal power, or the marital power after marriage.[3]

59. Pothier holds the doctrine in the most unqualified terms, that the law of the new or actual domicil ought in all cases to govern; and that the change of domicil discharges the party from the law of his former domicil, and subjects him to that of his new domicil. "Le changement de domicile delivre les personnes de l'empire des lois du lieu du domicile qu'elles quittent, et les assujettit à celles du lieu du nouveau domicile qu'elles acquièrent."[4] Whatever doubts may be suggested of the correct-

[1] Merlin, Répert. Autorisation Maritale, s. 10, art. 4, ed. Brux. 1827, p. 243, 244; post, s. 139.
[2] Merlin, Répert. Majorité, s. 4; Id. Effet Rétroactif, s. 3, n. 2, art. 5, n. 3; Id. Autorisation Maritale, s. 10, art. 4, ed. Brux. 1827.
[3] See Merlin, Répert. Effet Rétroactif, s. 3, n. 2, art. 5, p. 13, &c., ed. Brux. 1827; Id. Autorisation Maritale, s. 10, art. 4, p. 243, 244; Id. Majorité, s. 4, p. 187, 188. See also Id. Testament, s. 1, n. 5, art. 1, art. 2, p. 309–324; post, s. 139.
[4] Pothier, Cout. d'Orléans, c. 1, art. 1, n. 13. We shall presently see that

6

ness of his opinion in a juridical sense, it must be admitted to
possess the strong recommendation of general convenience and
certainty of application.[1]

60. Huberus, instead of relying upon the mere quality of laws,
as personal, or real, or mixed, lays down the following doctrine.
Personal qualities, impressed by the laws of any place, surround
and accompany the person wherever he goes, with this effect,
that in every place he enjoys and is subject to the same law
which such persons elsewhere enjoy or are subject to. 'Qualitates personales certo loco alicui jure impressas, ubique circumferri et personam comitari, cum hoc effectu, ut ubique locorum eo
jure, quo tales personæ alibi gaudent vel subjectae sunt, fruantur
et subjiciantur.' [2]   Therefore, he adds, those who with us are
under tutelage or guardianship, such as minors, prodigals, and
married women, are everywhere deemed to be persons subject to
such guardianship, and possess and enjoy the rights which the
law of the place attributes to persons under guardianship.[3]
Hence, he who in Friesland has obtained the privilege of age
(veniam ætatis), contracting in Holland, will not there be entitled to restitution in integrum, as if he were a minor.[4] In
other words, he who in Friesland has obtained the privilege of an
exemption from the disabilities of his minority, will not, if he
afterwards contracts in Holland, be deemed entitled to the privilege of being there held a minor, so as to exempt him from liability on his contract. (Ibi non restituitur in integrum.)[5] He

---

Lord Stowell holds the opinion that a change of domicil may change the state
and condition of the party; as, for example, if he be a slave. See The Slave
Grace, 2 Hagg. Adm. 94, 113; post, s. 96, 96 a.

[1] See 1 Burge, Col. & For. Law, pt. 1, c. 3, s. 3, p. 118, 119.

[2] Huberus, de Conflict. Leg. lib. 1, tit. 3, s. 12.   [3] Ibid.

[4] Ibid. Under the Roman Law the prætor by his edict declared that he
would grant redress in regard to transactions with minors under twenty-five
years of age. 'Quod cum minore quam viginti-quinque annos natu, gestum
esse dicetur, uti quæque res erit, animadvertam.' Dig. 4, 4, 1; Pothier, Pand.
4, 4, n. 1. But those persons who had obtained the privilege of age were not
entitled to any such relief. 'Eos, qui veniam ætatis a principali clementia
impetraverunt, etiamsi minus idonee rem suam administrare videantur, in integrum restitutionis auxilium impetrare non posse, manifestissimum est, ne
hi, qui cum eis contrahunt, principali auctoritate circumscripti esse videantur.'
Cod. 2, 45, 1; Pothier, Pand, 4, 4, n. 4. The action thus given to minors was
often called Restitutio in integrum. Vicat. Vocab. Voce, Restitutio.

[5] The Veniam Ætatis is a privilege granted by the prince or sovereign,
whereby the party is entitled to act, and to have all the powers to act sui juris,
as if he were of full age. See Vicat. Vocabul. Voce, ' Veniam Ætatis.' Cal-

who is declared a prodigal here, cannot enter into a valid contract or be sued in another place. ' Hinc qui apud nos in tutela curave sunt ut adolescentes, filii-familias, prodigi, mulieres, nuptæ, ubique pro personis curæ subjectis habentur, et jure, quod cura singulis in locis tribuit, utuntur [et] fruuntur. Hinc, qui in Frisia veniam ætatis impetravit, in Hollandia contrahens, ibi non restituitur in integrum. Qui prodigus hic est declaratus, alibi contrahens valide non obligatur, neque convenitur.' [1] Again, in some provinces, those who are over twenty-one years of age are deemed of majority, and may alienate their immovable property, and exercise other rights less important, even in those places where no one is deemed of majority until he has attained twenty-five years; because all other governments give effect by comity to the laws and adjudications of other cities in regard to their subjects, so always that there be no prejudice to their own subjects, or their own law.[2]

61. He goes on to remark, ' There are some persons who thus interpret the effect of laws respecting the quality of persons, that he who in a certain place is a major or a minor, in puberty or beyond it, a son subject to paternal power or a father of a family, under or out of guardianship, everywhere enjoys and is subject to the same law which he enjoys, and to which he is subject, in that place where he first becomes or is deemed such; so that whatever he could do or could not do in his own country, the same is allowed and prohibited to him to do.[3] This seems to me unreasonable, and would occasion too great a confusion of laws, and a burden upon neighboring nations, arising from the laws of others.[4] The importance of this thing will be made plain by a few examples. Thus, an unemancipated son (filius-familias) who cannot in Friesland make a testament, goes into Holland, and there makes a testament; it is asked whether it has any validity. I suppose it is valid in Holland according to my first and second rule;[5] because the laws bind all those who are within any territory; neither is it proper (civile sit) that Hollanders, in respect to business done among themselves, should,

vias, Lex. Jurid. c. 5; Cod. 2, 45, 1; Rodenburg, de Diversit. Statut. tit. 1, c. 2, s. 9; 2 Boullenois, App. 9; 1 Burge, Col. and For. Law, pt. 1, c. 3, s. 3, p. 116.

[1] Huberus, de Conflict. Leg. lib. 1, tit. 3, s. 12.
[2] Huberus, lib. 1, tit. 3, s. 12; ante, s. 29; post, s. 139, 145.
[3] Huberus, lib. 1, tit. 3, s. 12.   [4] Ibid.   [5] Ante, s. 29.

neglecting their own laws, be governed by foreign laws.[1] But it is true that this testament would not have effect in Friesland according to the third rule;[2] because in that way nothing would be more easy than for our citizens to elude our laws, as they might be evaded every day.[3] But such a testament would be of validity elsewhere, even where an unemancipated son could not make a will; for there the reason of evading the laws of a country by its own citizens ceases; for in such a case the fact (of evasion) would not be committed.'[4]

62. This doctrine of Huberus is not in its full extent maintainable, and, especially in relation to immovable property, it is universally repudiated by the common law, and in many cases is also denied by foreign jurists.[5] Lord Stowell has expressly said that he does not mean to affirm that Huberus is correct in laying down as universally true, that, being of age in one country, a man is of age in every other country, be the law of majority of the latter what it may.[6]

63. Without venturing further into the particular opinions maintained by foreign jurists on this subject under all its various aspects (a task, considering the great diversity of judgment among them, which would be almost endless), it may perhaps be useful to place before the reader some of the doctrines maintained by foreign jurists, which appear best established, or, at least, which seem to have the sanction of such authority as has given them a superior weight and recommendation in the jurisprudence of continental Europe.[7]

64. In the first place, the acts of a person done in the place of his domicil in regard to property situated therein are to be judged of by the laws of that place, and will not be permitted to have any other legal effect elsewhere than they have in that place.[8] There are exceptions to this rule; but they result from some direct or implied provisions of law in the customary or positive code of the

---

[1] Huberus, lib. 1, tit. 3, s. 13.   [2] Ante, s. 29.
[3] Huberus, lib. 1, tit. 3, s. 13.   [4] Ibid.
[5] See the authors cited by Merlin, Répert. Majorité, s. 5; post, s. 363–373, s. 474–479.
[6] Ruding v. Smith, 2 Hagg. Cons. 391, 392.
[7] See 1 Burge, Col. and For. Law, pt. 1, c. 4, p. 118–129.
[8] 'Statutum personale,' says Paul Voet, 'ubique locorum personam comitatur, in ordine ad bona intra territorium statuentis sita, ubi persona affecta domicilium habet.' P. Voet, de Statut, s. 4, c. 2, s. 6, p. 138, ed. 1661. See 1 Burge, Col. & For. Law, pt. 1, c. 4, p. 113.

country in which the act comes in judgment, applying to the very
case; for it is competent for a country, if it pleases, to prescribe
its own rule for all cases arising out of transactions in foreign
countries, whenever any rights under them are brought into controversy, or are sought to be enforced in its own tribunals. If
therefore a person has a capacity to do any act, or is under an incapacity to do any act, by the law of the place of his domicil, the
act, when done there, will be governed by the same law, whenever its validity may come into contestation in any other country.
Thus, an act done by a minor, in regard to his property, situate in
the place of domicil, without the consent of his guardian, if valid
by the law of the place of his domicil, where it is done, will be
recognized as valid in every other place; if invalid there, it will
be held invalid in every other place. So, if a married woman, who
is disabled by the law of the place of her domicil from entering
into a contract or from transferring any property therein without
the consent of her husband, should make a contract, or transfer
any property situated therein, the transaction will be held invalid
and a nullity in every other country.[1] This seems to be a principle
generally recognized by all nations in the absence of any positive
or implied municipal regulations to the contrary; according to the
maxim ' quando lex in personam dirigitur, respiciendum est ad
leges illius civitatis, quæ personam habet subjectam.' [2]

65. In the next place, another rule directly connected with the
former, is, that the personal capacity or incapacity attached to a
party by the law of the place of his domicil, is deemed to exist in
every other country (qualitas personam, sicut umbra sequitur), so
long as his domicil remains unchanged, even in relation to transactions in any foreign country where they might otherwise be
obligatory.[3] Thus, a minor, a married woman, a prodigal, or a

---

[1] 1 Boullenois, Prin. Gén. 6; 1 Froland, Mém. des Statuts, c. 7, p. 156.

[2] 1 Hertii, Opera, de Collis. Leg. s. 4, art. 8, p. 123, ed. 1737; Id. p. 175,
ed. 1716. The learned reader is referred for proofs to Huberus, de Conflict.
Leg. lib. 1, tit. 3, s. 12, 13, 15; 1 Boullenois, Prin. Gén. 10, 12, 16, 17; Id.
rea. 5, tit. 1, c. 3, p. 145, &c.; 2 Boullenois, obs. 32, tit. 2, c. 1, p. 1–53;
Rodenburg, de Divers. Statut. c. 3; 2 Boull. Appx. p. 7; Id. tit. 2, c. 1; 2
Boull. Appx. p. 10; P. Voet, de Statut, s. 4, c. 2; Id. c. 3, p. 128, 143, ed.
1661: 1 Hertii Opera, de Collis. Leg. s. 4, 8, p. 123, ed. 1737; Id. p. 175, ed.
1716; Froland Mém. des Statuts, pt. 1, c. 5, 7; Id. pt. 2, c. 33; Bouhier,
Cout. de Bourg. c. 22–24.

[3] · Ergo conditio personæ a causa domicilii tota regitur. Nam ut consentiunt doctores, idem sunt forum sortiri et statutis subjici; et unusquisque talis

spendthrift, a person non compos mentis, or any other person who is deemed incapable of transacting business (sui juris) in the place of his or her domicil, will be deemed incapable everywhere, not only as to transactions in the place of his or her domicil, but as to transactions in every other place.[1]

66. Thus, according to this rule, if an American citizen domiciled in an American state, as, for instance, in Massachusetts, where he would be of age at twenty-one years, should order a purchase of goods to be made for him in a foreign country where he would not be of age until twenty-five years old, the contract will nevertheless be obligatory upon him.[2] On the other hand, a person domiciled in such foreign country of twenty-one years of age only, who should order a like purchase to be made of goods in Massachusetts, will not be bound by his contract; for he will be deemed a minor and incapable of making such a contract.[3] The same rule will govern in relation to the disposition of personal or movable property by any person who is a minor or a major in the place of his domicil; for it will be valid or not, according

esse præsumitur, qualis est dispositio statuti suæ patriæ. Proinde, ut sciamus, uxor in potestate sit mariti necne, qua ætate minor contrahere possit, et ejusmodi respicere oportet ad legem cujusque domicilii.' Burgundus, Tract. 2, n. 6; 1 Boullenois, obs. 4, p. 53. 'C'est ainsi,' says Boullenois, 'que la majorité et la minorité du domicile ont lieu partout, même pour les biens situés ailleurs.' 1 Boullenois, Prin. Gén. art. 6; Id. obs. 10, 12, and 46. 'Celui qui est majeur,' says Froland, 'suivant la coutume où il a pris naissance et sous laquelle il réside, est majeur partout, et peut comme tel, aligner, hypothéquer, vendre ses biens, sans considérer si, suivant la loi de leur situation, il seroit mineur.' 1 Froland, Mém. des Statuts, c. 7, p. 156. Rodenburg holds the same doctrine. Rodenburg, de Divers. Stat. tit. 2, c. 1. So D'Argentré: 'Quotiescunque de habilitate aut de inhabilitate personarum quæratur, toties domicilii leges et statuta spectanda.' D'Argentré, de Briton. Leg. des Donations, art. 218,. gloss. 7, n. 48, 49. 1 Livermore, Diss. 34. So John Voet: 'Potius domicilii leges observandas existimem; quoties in quæstione, an quis minor vel majorennis, sit, obtinuit, id dijudicandum esse ex lege domicilii; sit ut in loco domicilii minorennis, ubique terrarum pro tali habendus sit, et contra.' J. Voet, ad Pand, 4, 1, 29. See also, Foelix, Conflit des Lois, Revue Étrang. et Fran. tom. 7, 1840, p. 200–216.

[1] 1 Boullenois, Prin. Gén. 10, 19, et obs. 4, 12, 16, p. 5; 1 Froland, Mém. des Stat. c. 7, p. 155, 156; Rodenburg, de Divers. Stat. tit. 2, c. 1; 2 Boullenois, Appx. p. 10.

[2] By the law of some commercial countries, the age of twenty-five years is that of majority. This was the old law of France; but the modern code has changed the age of majority to twenty-one, except as to marriage without the consent of parents. Code Civil of France, art. 488; Id. art. 148. See also, Rodenburg, de Statut. tit. 2, c. 1; 2 Boullenois, Appx. 10.

[3] Huberus, de Conflictu Legum, lib. 1, tit. 3, s. 12.

to the law of the place of his domicil, wherever such property may be situate.[1] There are exceptions also made to this rule ; but they stand upon peculiar grounds, as expounded by foreign jurists.

66 *a*. The like rule will apply to the capacity and incapacity of married women. If by the law of the place of the domicil of the husband a married woman has a capacity to sue, or to make a contract, or to ratify an act, her acts so done will be held valid everywhere. On the contrary, if she is deprived of such capacity by the law of the domicil of her husband, that incapacity exists in relation to all the like acts and contracts, even when done in a foreign country, or with reference to property in a foreign country.[2]

67. The ground upon which this rule has been generally adopted by many eminent Continental jurists doubtless is that suggested by Rodenburg, namely, the extreme inconvenience which would otherwise result to all nations from a perpetual fluctuation of capacity, state, and condition upon every accidental change of place of the person, or of his movable property.[3] The language of Rodenburg is: ' Quid igitur rei in causa est, quod personalia statuta territorium egrediantur? Unicum hoc ipsa rei natura ac necessitas invexit, ut, cum de statu ac conditione hominum quæritur, uni solummodo judici, et quidem domicilii, universum in illa jus sit attributum: cum enim ab uno certoque loco statum hominis legem accipere necesse esset, quod absurdum, earumque rerum naturaliter inter se pugna foret, ut in quot loca quis ita faciens, aut navigans delatus fuerit, totidem ille statum mutaret aut conditionem; ut uno eodemque tempore hic sui juris, illic alieni futurus sit; uxor simul in potestate viri, et extra eandem sit; alio loco habeatur quis prodigus, alio frugi; ac præterea quod persona certo loco non affigeretur, cum res soli loco fixæ citra, incommodum ejusdem legibus subjaceant, summa providentia constitutum est, ut a loco domicilii, cui quis larem fovendo se subdiderit, statum ac conditionem induat: illis legislatoribus, pro soli sui genio, optime omnium compertum habentibus, qua judicii maturi-

---

[1] 1 Froland, des Stat. Mém. c. 7, p. 157, 158; 1 Boullenois, Princ. Gén. c. 19; Id. obs. 4, 12; Rodenburg, de Divers. Stat. tit. 2, c. 1; 2 Boullenois, Appx. p. 10.

[2] Garnier v. Poydras, 13 La. 177.

[3] Rodenburg, de Divers. Stat. tit. 1, c. 3, n. 4; 2 Boullenois, Appx. p. 8. See also 1 Boullenois, obs. 4, p. 48, 49.

tate polleant subditi, ut possint constituere, qui eorum, ac quando ad sua tuenda negotia indigeant auctoritate. Hæc igitur personarum qualitas ac conditio, ubi venerit applicanda ad res aut actus alterius territorii, jam indirecte, ac per consequentiam vis illius personalis statuti extra statuentis, pertinget locum : cum et alias non insolitum sit multa indirecte permitti et per consequentiam, quæ directe et expressim non valerent. Nec est, quod quemquam turbet, quod et illa statuta extra territorii limites diximus excurrere, quibus nominatim status hominum in universum non discutitur, quæ in incertos personales actus a persona exercendos, prohibendo eos aut permittendo, concepta sunt.' [1]

68. *French Law.* — The modern law of France, as it is laid down by Pardessus, is to the same effect.[2] ' No act, whatsoever may be its nature,' says he, ' can be stipulated, except by persons capable of binding themselves ; and the general consent of civilized nations has allowed that whatever concerns the capacity of a person should be regulated by the laws of the country to which he belongs. A person declared incapable by the law of the country of which he is a subject cannot be relieved of that incapacity, except by the law of that country, as well in regard to the acts which it permits him to do, as to the conditions which it prescribes in doing them. Thus, French minors, incapable of binding themselves by engagements of commerce, unless they are emancipated or authorized, cannot bind themselves in commercial transactions in a foreign country, even when the law of that country does not require the like conditions. So French married women who are not public traders are not deemed to have contracted valid engagements, even in commerce, unless they should be authorized by their husbands. Their personal incapacity follows them everywhere. For the same reason, the French tribunals will not consider as valid any commercial engagements entered into in France by minors, or persons of either sex, who, by the law of their own country, are rendered incapable, even though the law to which they are subject should require other conditions than those prescribed by the law of France. For it is the interest of one government to respect in favor of the subject of another government,

---

[1] 2 Boullenois, Appx. p. 8 ; Foelix, Conflit des Lois, Revue Etrang. et Fran. tom. 7, 1840, p. 200–216.

[2] Pardessus, de Droit Commercial, vol. 5, art. 1482, p. 248.

when he is cited before its tribunals, the laws upon the faith of which that foreigner has contracted, and not to tolerate him in withdrawing himself, by a mere change of jurisdiction, from the laws which regulate his capacity, and to which he is bound by his allegiance, wherever he may inhabit. Without this, the government would expose its own subject to be treated with a like injustice by what is denominated the right of retaliation or reprisals.[1] So also a foreigner, born under a legislation which does not require certain formalities like those of France, by which a minor, or other person of either sex, may be authorized to engage in commerce, cannot avail himself of our laws to escape from his engagement. One has no right to invoke for the same object two different legislations; the law which regulates the capacity of the foreigner, regulates it everywhere. It would be unjust that he should derive from our legislation, to which he is not subjected, an advantage which is not granted to him by his own proper legislation.' Yet Pardessus is compelled to admit that there may be exceptions to the doctrine. Thus, for example, he says, that certain particular prohibitions, such as the prohibition of persons who are nobles, or possessing a certain dignity, to sign bills of exchange or other engagements, which carry with them a right to arrest the body, ought not to govern transactions of that sort in foreign countries. However the modern Civil Code of France[2] lays down the general rule in the broadest terms, and declares that the laws concerning the state and capacity of persons govern Frenchmen even if resident in a foreign country: ' Les loix concernant l'état et la capacité des personnes régissent les François même résidant en pais étranger.'[3]

69. In the third place another rule is, that upon a change of domicil the capacity or incapacity of the person is regulated by the law of the new domicil.[4] Pothier lays down this rule, as we have seen, in emphatic terms. ' The change of domicil,' says he, ' delivers persons from the empire of the laws of the place of the domicil they have quitted, and subjects them to those of the new domicil they have acquired.' ' Le changement de domicile

[1] 5 Pardessus, pt. 6, tit. 7, c. 2, s. 1, art. 1482; Henry on Foreign Law, Appx. p. 221, 222. See Cochin, Œuvres, tom. 1, p. 154, 4to ed.
[2] Pardessus, de Droit Commercial, vol. 5, art. 1483, p. 250; post, s. 74.
[3] Code Civil of France, art. 3; ante, s. 54.
[4] Consult 1 Burge, Col. & For. Law, pt. 1, c. 3, s. 3, p. 102, 103; Id. pt. 1, c. 4, p. 118–128, where the principal authorities are collected.

délivre les personnes de l'empire des lois du lieu du domicile qu'elles quittent, et les assujettit à celles du lieu du nouveau domicile qu'elles acquièrent.'[1]   Burgundus adopts the same rule: 'Consequenter dicemus, si mutaverit domicilium persona, novi domicilii conditionem induere.'[2]   So Rodenburg: 'Personæ enim status et conditio cum tota regatur a legibus loci, cui illa sese per domicilium subdiderit, utique mutato domicilio mutari et necesse est personæ conditionem.'[3]   Froland indeed, as we have already seen, mentions a different doctrine, in which to some extent he is followed by Bouhier and others.[4]   The doctrine however which is most generally approved is that which has been maintained by Pothier, although it is contradicted by the modern Code of France.[5]

70. Having stated these rules it may be proper to notice a distinction which in many cases may have a material operation. So far as respects the capacity or incapacity of the person, the law of the new domicil would probably prevail in the tribunals of the country of that domicil as to all rights, contracts, and acts, done or litigated there.   The same law would probably have a like recognition in every other country, except that of the original or native domicil.   The principal difficulty which would arise would be, how far any rights, contracts, and acts would be recognized by the latter where they were dependent upon the law of the new domicil, which should be in conflict with its own law on the same subject.   It is precisely under circumstances of this sort that the third axiom of Huberus may be presumed to have a material influence, namely, that a nation is not under any obligation to recognize rights, contracts, or acts, which are to its own prejudice, or in opposition to its own settled policy.[6]

[1] Pothier, Coutum. d'Orléans, c. 1, art. 1, n. 13; ante, s. 51.

[2] 1 Boullenois, obs. 4, p. 53; ante, s. 51 a, 56; Burgundus, Tract. 2, n. 7, p. 61.

[3] Rodenburg, de Divers. Stat. tit. 2, p. 2, c. 1, n. 3; 2 Boullenois, Appx. p. 56; 2 Boullenois, c. 1, and obs. 32; ante, s. 51 a.

[4] 1 Froland, Mém. c. 7, s. 13–15, p. 171, 172; Id. c. 33, s. 4–7, p. 1575–1582; ante, s. 55 a; Bouhier, Coutum. de Bourg. c. 22, s. 17–20, 31, p. 419–421.   See also, Henry on Foreign Law, Appendix A, p. 196.   See 2 Boullenois, p. 1–53; Merlin: Répertoire, Majorité, s. 5; Autorisation Maritale, s. 10; Effet Rétroactif, s. 2, art. 5; ante, s. 55, 55 a, 56.

[5] Code Civil of France, art. 3.   See also Cochin, Œuvres, tom. 1, p. 154, 4to ed.; ante, s. 51 a, 68.

[6] See, on this subject, 1 Burge, Col. & For. Law, pt. 1, c. 4, p. 129–134.

71. Boullenois was sensible of this distinction, as we have already seen,[1] and says : ' On this point it is necessary to distinguish from others the states and conditions of persons which arise from laws (qui sont des droits) founded upon public reasons, admitted among all nations, and which have a foundation or cause absolutely foreign from the domicil; so that the domicil, from the moment a man is affected with these states or conditions, not influencing it in any manner, the new domicil ought not to influence it, but merely the public reasons, superior to those of the domicil, to which all nations pay respect. Such are interdiction or incapacity from insanity or from prodigality, emancipation from the paternal power by royal authority, legitimacy of birth, nobility, infamy, &c. These states do not change with the change of domicil; and of these it is properly said that, having at first fixed the condition of the person, the change of domicil does not put an end to them.'[2] And he adds: ' But there are states and conditions more subordinate, and which in truth arise from public laws (qui sont à la vérité, des droits publics), but are for one nation only, or for some provinces of the same nation. Such are the state of community or non-community (of property) among married persons (conjoints) ; the state of the husband as to his marital power; the state of the father as to the rights of property from the paternal power; and these subordinate states are almost infinitely various.'[3] In regard to these latter states, he admits the embarrassment of laying down any general rules as to the effect of a change of domicil.[4] And he concludes his remarks by saying: ' In the occurrence of so great a number of laws (having enumerated several), which have so different an effect, what ought one to do in the decision of the questions which may be presented by them ? For myself I do not see any other means than these.'[5] He then proceeds to lay down these rules: (1) First, to follow the general principles, which declare that the person should be affected by the state and condition which his domicil gives him. (2) Secondly, not to derogate from these principles, except when the spirit of justice and necessity of not injuring the rights of parties requires that it should be departed from. (3) Thirdly, not to impair these principles,

[1] Ante, s. 57; 2 Boullenois, obs. 32, p. 10, 11, 13, 19.
[2] 2 Boullenois, obs. 32, p. 10, 11, 19.
[3] Id. p. 11.   [4] Ibid.   [5] Id. p. 12.

when otherwise the law furnishes the means of remedying any wrong which the change of domicil might cause.[1] Or, in other words, he affirms: first, that the law of the domicil ought generally to be followed as to the state and condition of the persons; secondly, that it ought not to be derogated from, except so far as the spirit of justice, and the necessity of not injuring the rights of parties, require a departure; thirdly, that the general rule ought not to be impaired, when the law will otherwise furnish means to remedy any injury which the change of domicil may occasion.[2] He goes on to declare what he supposes to be perfectly consistent with this doctrine, that when a person in the domicil of his birth (domicilium originis) has arrived at the age of majority, and he afterwards removes to another place, where, at the same years he would still be a minor, the law of the domicil of his birth ought to prevail.[3] For instance, if a person who by the law of the domicil of his birth is of age at twenty removes to another place after that age, where the minority extends to twenty-five years, he does not lose his majority, and become a minor, in his new domicil.[4] And on the other hand, if the same person is a minor by the law of the place of his birth, and not so by that of his new domicil, his state of minority continues notwithstanding his removal.[5] He deduces the former from the injustice which he supposes would follow from reducing a person of majority in the domicil of his birth to a state of minority upon a change of domicil, so that thereby he is not of an age sufficiently mature to contract, or to sell, or to alienate property. The latter he seems to ground upon a like inconvenience of allowing a man thus to escape from the disabilities of a minority in the place of his birth by a mere change of domicil.[6] This however is but changing the postures of the case. For Boullenois himself does not hesitate to declare the general principle to be incontestable that the law of the actual domicil decides the state and condition of the person; so that a person by changing his domicil changes at the same time his condition.[7] And he is compelled to admit that while he has Froland and Maillaud in support of his opinion, Lauterback and Burgundus and Rodenburg are against him.[8] Perhaps a better illustration of the

[1] Id. p. 12, 13.   [2] 2 Boullenois, obs. 32, p. 11–13, 19; ante, s. 57.
[3] Id. p. 12.   [4] Id. p. 12, 19, 20.   [5] Id.   [6] Id.
[7] 2 Boullenois, obs. 32, p. 13; ante, s. 57.   [8] Id. p. 19, 20.

intrinsic difficulties of laying down any general rules for all cases could not well be imagined; for Boullenois himself, as we have seen, holds laws respecting the majority and minority of age to be laws affecting the state and condition of persons, and, as such, governed by the law of the domicil; and yet, in this instance, he rejects the natural inference from this doctrine.[1]

72. The reason given by those civilians who hold the opinion that the law of the domicil of birth ought in all cases to prevail over the law of the place of the actual domicil in fixing the age of majority, and that it remains unalterable by any change of domicil, is, that each state or nation is presumed to be the best capable of judging from the physical circumstances of climate or otherwise, when the faculties of its citizens are morally or civilly perfect, for the purposes of society. And with respect to cases of lunacy, idiocy, and prodigality, it is supported by them upon the general argument from inconvenience, and the great confusion and mischief which would arise from the same person being considered as capable to contract in one place, and incapable in another; so that he might change his civil character and capacity with every change of his domicil.[2] There may perhaps be a solid ground of argument in favor of giving a universal operation in all other countries to certain classes of personal incapacities, created by the law of the domicil of the party; but it will be difficult to maintain that the same reasoning does or can apply with equal force in favor of all personal incapacities, or that the law of the domicil of birth ought to prevail over the law of the actual domicil. And even in relation to those personal incapacities which are supposed most easily to admit of a general application, it is by no means so clear that the argument from inconvenience is not equally strong on the other side.[3]

73. The truth however seems to be that there are, properly speaking, no universal rules by which nations are or ought to be morally or politically bound to each other on this subject. Each nation may well adopt for itself such modifications of the

---

[1] 1 Boullenois, Princ. Gén. 8, 10, 11, 17, 18; Id. obs. 4, p. 51, 52.

[2] Henry on Foreign Law, p. 5, 6; Rodenburg, tit. 1, c. 3, n. 4; 2 Boullenois, Appx. p. 8.

[3] See 1 Burge, Col. & For. Law, pt. 1, c. 4, p. 129–134.

general doctrine as it deems most convenient, and most in harmony with its own institutions and interests and policy. It may suffer the same rule as to the capacity, state, and condition of foreigners to prevail within its own territory, as does prevail in the place of their own native or acquired domicil; and it may at the same time refuse to allow any other rule than its own law to prevail within its own territory in respect to the capacity, state, and condition of its own subjects, wherever they may reside, at home or abroad. It may adopt a more limited doctrine, and recognize the law of the domicil both as to foreigners and as to its own subjects, in respect to transactions and property in that domicil, whether native or acquired, and at the same time exclude any operation except of its own law, as to the transactions and property either of foreigners or of its own subjects within its own territory. It may adopt the more general doctrine, and allow the rule of the actual domicil, as to capacity, state, and condition, to prevail under every variety of change of domicil; or, on the other hand, it may adhere to the stricter doctrine that the domicil of birth shall exclusively furnish the rule to govern in all such matters. But whatever rules it may adopt, or whatever it may repudiate, will be alike the dictate of its own policy and sense of justice; and whatever it may allow or withhold will always be measured by its own opinion of the public convenience and benefit, or of the public prejudice and injury resulting therefrom. Probably the law of the actual domicil (domicilium habitationis) will be found in most cases to furnish the most safe, convenient, and least prejudicial rule, at least in regard to transactions and property out of the country of the birth of the party (domicilium originis).[1] As to transactions and property within the country of his birth, the policy of most nations will naturally incline them to hold their own laws conclusive over their own subjects, wherever they may be domiciled, so far as regards their minority and majority, and their other capacity or incapacity to do acts.

74. Illustrations may be easily found to confirm these remarks in the actual jurisprudence of many countries. Thus, as we have seen,[2] Pardessus, while he contends that the law of France as to personal capacity and incapacity generally, ought to

---

[1] See 1 Burge, Col. & For. Law, pt. 1, c. 4, p. 129–134.
[2] Ante, s. 68.

prevail as to French subjects, wherever they reside, abroad or at home, at the same time admits that it ought not to govern in relation to certain particular disabilities. Thus he thinks that the law of France, which forbids nobles or persons of official dignity to sign bills of exchange or other engagements, by which the bodies of the parties are liable to an arrest for a breach of the contract, ought not to extend to the like acts of the same persons done in other countries.[1] For although it may be urged that it is a personal law, which follows the person everywhere, as in the case of a minor, or of a married woman under the marital power, and every person is bound to know the state and condition of the person with whom he contracts, yet he contends that the rule ought not to be applied except to the universal state of the person, such as that of a minor or a major, or of a woman subject to, or free from, the marital power. For, he adds, all nations agreed in fixing the capacity to contract to a certain age, and in placing women in dependence upon their husbands.[2] Every one will at once perceive how exceedingly loose the distinction is for which Pardessus contends, and how unsatisfactory his reasoning by which this exception is attempted to be maintained. The objection to the reasoning is, that, if well founded, the argument from inconvenience would carry it much further; and persons dealing with others may require proof of their majority, or of their special authority to contract if they are minors, or whether they are married or not; and in both cases may guard against false statements by requiring a guaranty. On the contrary, these special prohibitions, on account of a certain quality or dignity, are more arbitrary. They are founded less in general public utility, and ought not, therefore, to be invoked in aid of the party. At least, the exception ought not to be admitted, except between subjects of the same state, or unless the incapacity of the person, and the nullity of the obligation by the law, were known at the time of the contract by the other party.[3]

75. *Rule in Louisiana.*—Now it so happens that what Pardessus (and many other jurists are certainly of the same opinion) supposed to be very clear doctrine, has been directly overturned, and the contrary doctrine has been held by the Supreme Court of

---

[1] Pardessus, de Droit Commercial, vol. 5, art. 1483, p. 250.

[2] Pardessus, vol. 5, pt. 6, tit. 7, c. 2, s. 1, art. 1483, p. 250; Henry on Foreign Law, Appx. 222.   [3] Ibid.

Louisiana.   That court, in a very learned opinion, have said:
'The writers on this subject, with scarcely an exception, agree
that the laws or statutes which regulate minority and majority,
and those which fix the state or condition of man, are personal
statutes, and follow and govern him in every country.   Now,
supposing the case of our law fixing the age of majority at twenty-five, and the country in which a man was born and lived
previous to his coming here, placing it at twenty-one, no objection could perhaps be made to the rule just stated.   And it may
be, and, we believe, would be true that a contract, made here at
any time between the two periods already mentioned, would bind
him.   But, reverse the facts of this case; and suppose, as is the
truth, that our law placed the age of majority at twenty-one;
that twenty-five was the period at which a man ceased to be a
minor in the country where he resided; and that, at the age of
twenty-four, he came into this state, and entered into contracts;
would it be permitted that he should in our courts, and to the
demand of one of our citizens, plead, as to protection against his
engagements, the laws of a foreign country, of which the people
of Louisiana had no knowledge?   And would we tell them that
ignorance of foreign laws in relation to a contract made here was
to prevent him from enforcing it, though the agreement was binding by those of their own state?   Most assuredly we would
not.'[1]

76.   The case first put seems founded upon a principle entirely repugnant to that upon which the second rests.   In the
former case, the law of the place of the domicil of the party is
allowed to prevail, in respect to a contract made in another country; in the latter case, the law of the place where the contract
is made, is allowed to govern, without any reference whatsoever

[1] Saul v. His Creditors, 5 Mart. N.S. (La.) 596–598.   The opinion of the
court was delivered by Mr. Justice Porter.   See also Andrews v. His Creditors, 11 La. 464, 476.   A like doctrine was held by the same court in another
case.   The court on that occasion said: ' A foreigner coming into Louisiana,
who was twenty-three years old, could not escape from a contract with one of
our citizens, by averring that, according to the laws of the country he left, he
was not a major until he reached the age of twenty-five.' Baldwin v. Gray,
4 Mart. N.S. (La.) 192, 193.   See also Fergusson on Divorce, Appx. p. 276-
363; post, s. 82.   Hertius, de Collisione, tom. 1, s. 4, n. 5, p. 120, 121; Id.
p. 173, 174, ed. 1716.   Grotius seems to have been of opinion that the lex
loci contractus ought to govern in cases of minority.   Grotius, b. 2, c. 11,
s. 5.

to the law of the domicil of the party.   Such a course of decision certainly may be adopted by a government if it shall so choose. But then it would seem to stand upon mere arbitrary legislation and positive law, and not upon principle.   The difficulty is in seeing how a court, without any such positive legislation, could arrive at both conclusions.   General reasoning would lead us to the opinion that both cases ought to be decided in the same way, that is, either by the law of the domicil of the party, or by that of the place where the contract is actually made.   Many foreign jurists maintain the former opinion,[1] some the latter.[2]   Perhaps

[1] See Livermore, Dissert. s. 17, p. 32, to s. 56, p. 57.   Mr. Livermore denies this doctrine of the Supreme Court of Louisiana to be correct, and has collected in the place cited the leading authorities in favor of the doctrine, which he contends is the true one, that the law of the domicil of the person ought universally to prevail, as to his personal capacity or incapacity.   Among the authorities in its favor, he enumerates D'Argentré, Bartolus, Rodenburg, Jason, and Paolo da Castro, Livermore, Dissert. s. 21, p. 34.   D'Argentré, Comm. Leg. Briton. art. 218 (gloss. 6, n. 47, 48), says: ' Quotiescunque de habilitate aut inhabilitate personarum quæratur, toties domicilii leges et statuta spectanda.   Nam de omni personali negotio, judicis ejus cognitionem esse, cui persona subsit, ut quocunque persona abeat, ad jus sit, quod ille statuerit.'   Bartolus put: the case, whether, if a filius-familias (an unemancipated son) is allowed by the local law to make a testament, a foreign filius-familias can in the same place make a valid testament; and he answers in the negative.   ' Dico quod non; quia statuta non possunt legitimare personam sibi non subditam, nec circa ipsam personam aliquid disponere.'   Bartolus, ad Cod. 1, 1, 1, n. 25, 26.   Da Castro (as cited in D'Argentré, ubi supra) says, that a statute of Modena, permitting minors to contract at fourteen years of age, will not make valid a contract at Modena by a minor of that age belonging to Bologna.   ' Ratio est, quia hic abstracte de habilitate personæ, et universali ejus statu quæratur, ideoque persona a statuto domicilii efficiatur.' Livermore, Dissert. s. 21, p. 34, 35, s. 25, p. 37.   Burgundus, Christinæus, Grotius, and De Wesel appear to hold the same opinion.   See Voet, ad Pand. 1, 4, pt. 2, n. 7; Burgundus, Tract. 1, n. 8, 34.   Rodenburg is still more full to the same point.   Rodenb. de Diversit. Statut. tit. 2, c. 1, n. 1; 2 Boullenois, Appx. p. 11, cited also Livermore, Dissert. s. 31, p. 40, 41.   See also Hertii, Opera, tom. 1, De Collis. s. 4, n. 8.

[2] Mr. Livermore says that Huberus alone is in favor of the latter opinion. I draw the conclusion that P. Voet (Voet, de Statut. s. 4, c. 2, n. 6, p. 137, 138, ed. 1661) and J. Voet (Voet, ad Pand. 1, 4, pt. 2, n. 7) entertain the same opinion.   There are probably many other jurists who are on the same side.   It is very certain that the rule, that either the law of the domicil of origin, or the law of the actual domicil, or even the law of the lex loci contractus, is to govern in all cases, has never been adopted in the English courts. The rule of the actual domicil or the place of the contract has been admitted generally; but does not, as we shall presently see, universally govern. Mr. Burge has propounded the same doctrine as the Supreme Court of Louisiana, and said: " In a conflict between the personal law of the domicil and

7

it is not very easy to decide which rule would, on the whole, be most convenient for any nation to adopt. It may be said that he who contracts with another ought not to be ignorant of his condition: 'Qui cum alio contrahit, vel est, vel esse debet, non ignarus conditionis ejus.'[1] But this rule, however reasonable in its application to the condition of a person as fixed by the law of the country where he is domiciled, is not so clear in point of convenience or equity when applied to the condition of a person as fixed by the law of a foreign country. How are the inhabitants of any country to ascertain the condition of a stranger dwelling among them, as fixed by the law of a foreign country where he was born or had acquired a new domicil? Even courts of justice do not assume to know what the laws of a foreign country are, but require them to be proved. How then shall private persons be presumed to have better means of knowledge? On the other hand, it may be said with great force that contracts ought to be governed by the law of the country where they are made, as to the competence of the parties to make them, and as to their validity; because the parties may well be presumed to contract with reference to the laws of the place where the contract is made and is to be executed. Such a rule has certainty and simplicity in its application. It ought not therefore to be matter of surprise if the country of the party's birth should hold such a contract valid or void, according to its own law, and that nevertheless the country where it is made and to be executed should

the personal law of another place at variance with it, that of the domicil prevails. But the preceding rule admits of some qualification. It is not to be applied when it would enable a person to avoid a contract which he was competent to make by the personal law of the place in which he made it, although he was incompetent by the personal law of his domicil. Thus, if a person whose domicil of origin was in Spain, where he does not attain his majority until his twenty-fifth year, should, at the age of twenty-three, enter into a contract in England, or any other place where his minority ceases at twenty-one, he would not be permitted to avoid his contract by alleging that he was a minor, and incompetent to contract, according to the law of Spain. The maxim, that every man is bound to know the laws of a country in which he enters into a contract is of universal application, and is perfectly just and reasonable because it is in his power to obtain that knowledge; but the maxim, 'Qui cum alio contrahit, vel est, vel debet esse non ignarus conditionis ejus,' cannot be applied to those cases in which the condition depends on facts and law to which he is a perfect stranger. 1 Burge, Col. & For. Law, pt. 1, c. 4, p. 27, 28. See post, s. 79–82.

[1] Dig. 50, 17, 19. See Livermore, Dissert. p. 38.

hold it valid or void, according to its own law. It has been well observed by an eminent judge, that 'with respect to any ignorance arising from foreign birth and education, it is an indispensable rule of law, as exercised in all civilized countries, that a man who contracts in a country engages for a competent knowledge of the law of contracts in that country. If he rashly presumes to contract without such knowledge, he must take the inconveniences resulting from such ignorance upon himself, and not attempt to throw them upon the other party, who has engaged under a proper knowledge and sense of the obligation which the law would impose upon him by virtue of that engagement.'[1]

77. In another case, decided at an earlier period, the Supreme Court of Louisiana adopted the doctrine that the laws of the domicil of origin ought to govern the state and condition of the party, whether as major or as minor, into whatever country the party removes. But the decision may perhaps be thought to rest on its own peculiar circumstances. The case was this. The plaintiff in the suit (a female) was born in Louisiana in 1802, and the laws of the state at that time fixed the age of majority at twenty-five years. In the year 1808 the period of majority in the state was altered to twenty-one years. The plaintiff in 1827 (when the suit was brought) was, and for several years before had been, a Spanish subject and a resident in Spain, where minority does not cease until twenty-five years. The suit having been brought by her to recover her share in the succession to her grandmother, in the courts of Louisiana, before she was twenty-five, the question arose whether she was competent to maintain the suit; and that turned upon another question, whether she was to be deemed a minor or not. The court upon that occasion decided that she was to be deemed a major, as she was then over twenty-one years of age, although not twenty-five. Mr. Justice Porter, in delivering the opinion of the court, said: 'The general rule is, that the laws of the domicil of origin govern the state and condition of the minor into whatever country he removes. The laws of Louisiana therefore must determine at what period the plaintiff became of age; and by them she was a major at twenty-five. Admitting that her removal into another country, before the alteration of our law,

[1] Lord Stowell, in Dalrymple v. Dalrymple, 2 Hagg. Cons. 61; ante, s. 75; post, s. 82.

would exempt her from its operation, and that her state and condition were fixed by the rules prevailing in the place where she was born at the time she left it, a point by no means free from difficulty, no proof has been given that the plaintiff was taken out of Louisiana before the change made in 1808. And as the defendant, by pleading the minority, assumed the affirmative, it was her duty to establish the fact on which the exception could be sustained.'[1] The question therefore did not here arise as to the effect of any contract made in Louisiana (as in the preceding case), but the simple question of the state of minority or majority, or the competency of the party to maintain a suit in her own name, as being sui juris. The court seem to have acted upon the general doctrine that the capacity of the party did not depend upon her actual domicil, but upon the law of her domicil of origin. But it is difficult to perceive why the same rule should not apply to a case of contract, arising under the like circumstances ; since the capacity or incapacity to contract would depend upon the very point, whether the law of the actual domicil, or that of the domicil of origin, or that of the place of the contract, ought to govern in respect to capacity or incapacity. And if the same rule would apply, it is not easy to reconcile this with the preceding doctrine, unless upon the ground that the courts of the native domicil ought to follow their own law as to minority and majority in all cases, in preference to any other.

78. There is an earlier case in the same court, in which it seems to have been incidentally stated that, according to the law of nations, 'personal incapacities, communicated by the laws of any particular place, accompany the person wherever he goes. Thus he who is excused from the consequences of contracts for want of age in his country cannot make binding contracts in another.'[2] (a) This doctrine is certainly at variance with that maintained by the same court at other and later periods.[3] It is somewhat curious that it was avowed in the case of what is called a runaway marriage, celebrated at Natchez in Mississippi, between a young man and a young woman, a minor of thirteen years of age,

---

[1] Barrera r. Alpuente, 6 Mart. N.S. (La.) 69.
[2] Le Breton v. Fouchet, 3 Mart. (La.) 60, 70; post, s. 180.
[3] Saul v. His Creditors, 5 Mart. N.S. (La.) 597, 598; Baldwin v. Gray, 4 Mart. N.S. (La.) 192, 193.

(a) See also Kelly v. Davis, 28 La. An. 773.

both of them being at the time domiciled in Louisiana, without the consent of her parents; and which marriage would seem to have been void without such consent, by the law of Louisiana, if celebrated in that state. It was not however the main point in the case; and the decision itself was placed, as we shall hereafter see, upon a far broader foundation.[1]

79. English Decisions. — Marriage. — In respect to contracts of marriage, the English decisions have established the rule that a foreign marriage valid according to the law of the place where celebrated, is good everywhere else.[2] (a) But these decisions have not, e converso, established that marriages of British subjects, not good according to the law of the place where celebrated, are universally, and under all possible circumstances, to be regarded as invalid in England.[3] On the contrary, Lord Stowell has decided that a marriage had under peculiar circumstances at the Cape of Good Hope, during British occupation, was valid, although not in conformity to the Dutch law, which was then in force there.[4] In that case, the husband (an Englishman) was a person entitled by the laws of his own country to marry without the consent of parents or guardians, he being of the age of twenty-one; but by the Dutch law he could not marry without such consent until he was thirty years of age. The lady (an Englishwoman) was under the age of nineteen, her father was dead, her mother had

---

[1] Post, s. 180.
[2] Ryan v. Ryan, 2 Phillim. Ecc. 332; Herbert v. Herbert, 3 Phillim. Ecc. 56; 2 Hagg. Cons. 263, 271; Lacon v. Higgins, 3 Stark. 178; D. & R. N. P. C. 3a. See Smith v. Maxwell, Ry. & M. 80.
[3] Ruding v. Smith, 2 Hagg. Cons. 390, 391; Hartford v. Morris, 2 Hagg. Cons. 432; post, s. 79, note 1; s. 118, 119.
[4] Ruding v. Smith, 2 Hagg. Cons. 371.

(a) The word *marriage* signifies sometimes the ceremony of marriage, sometimes the union in matrimony which the ceremony is intended to effect. See Harvey v. Farnie, 6 P. D. p. 47; Campbell v. Crampton, 2 Fed. R. p. 424. The English decisions referred to in this and the succeeding sections of the text relate only to the ceremony of marriage. They establish that if the ceremony is in accordance with the law of the place where it is performed, it is deemed valid everywhere. It does not follow however that it is lawful for a man and woman to be united in matrimony because it is lawful in the place where the ceremony is performed. The union involves a change of status, and status generally depends on the law of the domicil. Other English decisions establish that the lawfulness of their being united is to be determined by the law of the domicil. See note, s. 124 a, post.

married a second husband, and she had no guardian. (*a*)   Upon that occasion Lord Stowell said: ' Suppose the Dutch law had thought fit to fix the age of majority at a still more advanced period than thirty, at which it then stood — at forty — it might surely be a question in an English court, whether a Dutch marriage of two British subjects, not absolutely domiciled in Holland, should be invalidated in England upon that account; or, in other words, whether a protection, intended for the rights of Dutch parents, given to them by the Dutch law, should operate to the annulling a marriage of British subjects, upon the ground of protecting rights which do not belong in any such extent to parents living in England, and of which the law of England could take no notice, but for the severe purpose of this disqualification.   The Dutch jurists, *as represented in this libel*, would have no doubt whatever that this law would clearly govern a British court.   But a British court might think that a question not unworthy of further consideration before it adopted such a rule for the subjects of this country. . . .   In deciding for Great Britain upon the marriages of British subjects, they [the Dutch jurists] are certainly the best and only authority upon the question, whether the marriage is conformable to the general Dutch law of Holland; and they can decide that question definitely for themselves and for other countries.   But questions of a wider extent may lie beyond this: whether the marriage be not good in England, although not conformable to the general Dutch law, and whether there are not principles leading to such a conclusion?   Of this question, and of those principles, they are not the authorized judges; for this question and those principles belong either to the law of England, of which they are not the authorized expositors at all, or to the jus gentium, upon which the courts of this country may be supposed as competent as themselves, and certainly, in the case of British subjects, much more appropriate judges.' [1]

[1] Ruding *v.* Smith, 2 Hagg. Cons. 389, 390; post, s. 118, 119.   That there are other cases excepted from the operation of foreign law seems to have been directly held by Sir George Hay, in Harford *v.* Morris, 2 Hagg. Cons. 423. He there said: " I do not mean that every domicil is to give jurisdiction to a foreign country, so that the laws of that country are necessarily to obtain and

(*a*) The marriage in this case (Ruding *v.* Smith, 2 Hagg. Cons. 371, 391, 394) was held valid on account of the insuperable difficulties of obtaining any marriage conformable to the Dutch law.   See Dicey on Domicil, 201, 209–211; Westlake (ed. 1880), 57.

80. *Scrimshire* v. *Scrimshire.* — In another case, where two British subjects, being minors, and in France, solely for purposes of education, intermarried, it was held by the court that the marriage, being void by the law of France, was a mere nullity.[1] (a) The court (Sir Edward Simpson) said: 'The question before me is not, whether English subjects are to be bound by the law of France; for undoubtedly no law or statute in France can bind subjects of England who are not under its authority; nor is the consequence of pronouncing for or against the marriage, with respect to civil rights in England, to be considered in determining this case. The only question before me is, whether this be a good or bad marriage by the law of England? and I am inclined to think that it is not good. On this point I apprehend that it is the law of this country to take notice of the laws of France, or of any foreign country, in determining upon marriages of this kind. The question being in substance this, whether, by the law of this country, marriage contracts are not to be deemed good or bad according to the laws of the country in which they are formed; and whether they are not to be construed by that law? If such be the law of this country, the rights of English subjects cannot be said to be determined by the laws of France, but by those of their own country, which sanction and adopt this rule of decision. By the general law, all parties contracting gain a forum in the place where the contract is entered into. All our books lay this down for law; it is needless at present to mention more than one. Gayll, lib. 2, obs. 123, says, "In contractibus locus contractus considerandus sit. Quoties enim statutum principaliter habilitat, vel inhabilitat contractum, quoad solemnitates, semper attenditur locus, in quo talis contractus celebratur, et obligat etiam non subditum." And again, lib. 2, obs. 86, "Quis forum in loco contractus sortitur, si ibi loci, ubi contraxit, reperiatur; non tamen ratione contractus, aut ratione rei, quis subditus dicitur illius loci,

attach upon a marriage solemnized there. For what would become of our factories abroad, at Leghorn or elsewhere, where the marriage is only by the law of England, and might be void by the law of that country? Nothing will be admitted in this court to affect such marriages, so celebrated, even where the parties are so domiciled." Id. 432.

[1] Scrimshire *v.* Scrimshire, 2 Hagg. Cons. 395.

(a) This marriage was declared void because the ceremony was not according to the French laws. Scrim- shire *v.* Scrimshire, 2 Hagg. Cons. 395.

ubi contraxit, aut res sita est; quia aliud est forum sortiri, et aliud subditum esse. Constat unumquemque subjici jurisdictioni judicis, in eo loco in quo contraxit." This is according to the text law, and the opinion of Donellus and other commentators. There can be no doubt, then, but that both the parties in this cause, though they were English subjects, obtained a forum, by virtue of the contract, in France. By entering into the marriage there, they subjected themselves to have the validity of it determined by the laws of that country.'[1] And he afterwards proceeded to add: ' This doctrine of trying contracts, especially those of marriage, according to the laws of the country where they were made, is conformable to what is laid down in our books, and what is practised in all civilized countries, and what is agreeable to the law of nations, which is the law of every particular country, and taken notice of as such.'[2]

80 a. The learned judge proceeded to cite the opinions of civilians to the same precise effect; and he afterwards concluded with these remarks: ' Why may not this court then take notice of foreign laws, there being nothing illegal in doing it? From the doctrine laid down in our books — the practice of nations — and the mischief and confusion that would arise to the subjects of every country from a contrary doctrine, I may infer that it is the consent of all nations, that it is the jus gentium, that the solemnities of the different nations with respect to marriages should be observed, and that contracts of this kind are to be determined by the laws of the country where they are made. If that principle is not to govern such cases, what is to be the rule where one party is domiciled and the other not? The jus gentium is the law of every country, and is obligatory on the subjects of every country. Every country takes notice of it; and this court observing that law in determining upon this case cannot be said to determine English rights by the laws of France, but by the law of England, of which the jus gentium is part. All nations allow marriage contracts; they are "juris gentium," and the subjects of all nations are concerned in them ; and from the infinite mischief and confusion that must necessarily arise to the subjects of all nations with respect to legitimacy, successions, and other rights,

[1] Scrimshire v. Scrimshire, 2 Hagg. Cons. 407, 408. See Kent v. Burgess, 11 Sim. 361.
[2] Scrimshire v. Scrimshire, 2 Hagg. Cons. 412.

if the respective laws of different countries were only to be observed, as to marriages contracted by the subjects of those countries abroad, all nations have consented, or must be presumed to consent, for the common benefit and advantage, that such marriages should be good or not, according to the laws of the country where they are made. It is of equal consequence to all that one rule in all these cases should be observed by all countries — that is, the law where the contract is made. By observing this law no inconvenience can arise; but infinite mischief will ensue if it is not.'[1] 'Again — If countries do not take notice of the laws of each other with respect to marriages, what would be the consequence if two English persons should marry clandestinely in England, and that should not be deemed a marriage in France? Might not either of them, or both, go into France and marry again, because by the French law such a marriage is not good? And what would be the confusion in such a case? Or again — Suppose two French subjects, not domiciled here, should clandestinely marry, and there should be a sentence for the marriage; undoubtedly the wife, though French, would be entitled to all the rights of a wife by our law. But if no faith should be given to that sentence in France, and the marriage should be declared null, because the man was not domiciled, he might take a second wife in France, and that wife would be entitled to legal rights there, and the children would be bastards in one country, and legitimate in the other. So that, in cases of this kind, the matter of domicil makes no sort of difference in determining them, because the inconvenience to society and the public in general is the same, whether the parties contracting are domiciled or not. Neither does it make any difference whether the cause be that of contract or marriage; for if both countries do not observe the same law, the inconveniences to society must be the same in both cases. And as it is of consequence to the subjects of both countries, and to all nations, that there should be one rule of determining in all nations on contracts of this kind, it is to be presumed that all nations do consent to determine on these contracts, by the laws of the country where they are made; as such a rule would prevent all the inconveniences that must necessarily arise from judging by different laws, and is attended by no manner of

---

[1] Scrimshire v. Scrimshire, 2 Hagg. Cons. 416, 417.

inconvenience, but is for the advantage of the subjects of all nations.'[1]

81. *Dalrymple* v. *Dalrymple*. — Here then we have a doctrine laid down as the rule of the jus gentium, at least, as it is understood and recognized in England, in regard to contracts generally, and especially in regard to contracts of marriage, very different from the rule which we have seen laid down by many foreign jurists, that the law of the domicil of origin, or the law of the actual domicil, is of universal obligation as to the capacity, state, and condition of persons.[2] The same doctrine has been formally promulgated upon other occasions by the English courts.[3] In a grave case of extraordinary interest,[4] which turned upon the validity of a Scotch marriage, where one of the parties was an English minor, Lord Stowell said : ' Being entertained in an English court, it [the case then before him] must be adjudicated according to the principles of English law applicable to such a case. But the only principle applicable to such a case by the law of England is, that the validity of Miss Gordon's [the plaintiff's] marriage rights must be tried by reference to the law of the country where, if they exist at all, they had their origin.'[5] (a)

82. *Contracts of Minors.* — *Male* v. *Roberts.* — In regard to other contracts made by minors, a similar rule has prevailed. In a case where money had been advanced for a minor during his stay in Scotland, who seems to have had his general domicil in England, it was held by Lord Eldon that the question, whether in an English court a recovery could be had for the money so advanced, depended upon the law of Scotland ; for the general rule was that the law of the place where the contract is made must govern the contract.[6] This also seems to be a just inference from the doc-

[1] Scrimshire v. Scrimshire, 2 Hagg. Cons. 418, 419. See Lord Meadowbank's Opinion, Fergusson on Mar. and Divorce, Appx. p. 361, 362.

[2] Ante, s. 51–68.

[3] Birtwhistle v. Vardill, 5 B. & C. 438, 452, 453.

[4] Dalrymple v. Dalrymple, 2 Hagg. Cons. 54.

[5] Id. 58, 59; Kent v. Burgess, 11 Sim. 361. See also Conway v. Beazley, 3 Hagg. Ecc. 639; Middleton v. Janverin, 2 Hagg. Cons. 437, 446.

[6] Male v. Roberts, 3 Esp. 163. See also, Thompson v. Ketcham, 8 Johns.

(a) In this case the marriage was contracted in Scotland according to the law of Scotland, without any religious celebration. The only question was whether the form of contracting marriage was valid. Dalrymple v. Dalrymple, 2 Hagg. Cons. 54.

trine maintained by Lord Stowell in the case of a contract of marriage.[1] (a)

82 a. Foreign Jurists. — Upon this point there is a diversity of opinion among foreign jurists.[2] Some of them are strongly inclined to act upon the doctrine of the Roman law as applicable to this subject. 'Aut si non appareat, quid actum est, erit consequens, ut id sequamur, quod in regione in qua actum est frequentatur.'[3] Dumoulin is supposed to have adopted this doctrine; but it is far from being certain that he intended by his language to embrace this case. 'In concernentibus contractibus et emergentibus tempore contractus inspici debet locus, in quo contrahitur.'[4] Paul Voet puts the doctrine thus: 'Quid, si de contractibus proprie dictis, et quidem eorum solemnibus contentio; quis locus spectabitur? An domicilii contrahentis, an loci, ubi quis contrahit. Respondeo affirmate. Posterius. Quia censetur quis semet contrahendo, legibus istius loci, ubi contrahit etiam ratione solemnium subjicere voluisse. Ut quemadmodum loci consuetudo subintrat contractum, ejusque est declarativa; ita etiam loci statutum.'[5] From the other known doctrine of Paul Voet, that personal laws have no extra-territorial operation,[6] we see at once that he meant to apply his statement to laws of personal capacity and incapacity. It has been supposed that Christinæus and Bartolus entertain a similar opinion. But their language does not necessarily lead to that conclusion, since the place of the contract, spoken of by them, may mean the place also of the domicil of origin of the minor.[7] Grotius however is

(N. Y.) 189; Grotius, lib. 2, c. 11, s. 5. See also, Dalrymple *v.* Dalrymple, 2 Hagg. Cons. 60, 61; ante, s. 21, 25, p. 34, s. 75, note (1) 37.

[1] Dalrymple *v.* Dalrymple, 2 Hagg. Cons. 61; ante, s. 80.
[2] Post, s. 368.   [3] Dig. 50, 17, 34; post, s. 270.
[4] Molin, tom. 1, tit. 1, De feud. s. 12, gloss. 7, s. 37. In another place, Dumoulin says, after adverting to the fact, that personal laws affect subjects and not foreigners: 'Quamvis is, qui datus est tutor vel curator a suo competenti judice sit inhabilitatus propter tutelam et curam, ubique locorum pro bonis ubicumque sitis. Quia non est in vim statuti solius, sed in vim juris communis, et per passivam interpretationem legis, quæ locum habet ubique.' Molin, in Cod. 1, 1, tom. 3, p. 556. See 1 Burge, Col. & For. Law, pt. 1, c, 3, s. 3, p. 129, 130; post, s. 294; 1 Boullenois, obs. 23, p. 463, 464.
[5] P. Voet, de Statut., s. 9, c. 2, n. 9, p. 323, ed. 1661; post, s. 261.
[6] P. Voet, de Statut., s. 4, c. 2, n. 6, p. 137, ed. 1661.
[7] See the passages cited from these authors in 1 Burge, pt. 1, c. 4, p. 130;

(a) See note, s. 102, post.

more explicit to the purpose. 'Leges civiles,' says he, 'justa
ratione motæ, quasdam promissiones pupillorum ac minorum
irritas pronunciant. Sed hi effectus sunt proprii legis civilis, ac
proinde cum jure naturæ ac gentium nihil habent commune ; nisi
quod quibus locis obtinent, ibi eas servare naturale est. Quæ
etiam si peregrinus cum cive paciscatur, tenebitur illis legibus;
quia qui in loco aliquo contrahit, tanquam subditus temporarius
legibus loci subjicitur.' [1]

83. On the other hand, many foreign jurists, as we have seen,
entertain a very different opinion on this very point of the capacity of a person to contract in another country, when he is disabled, as a minor, by the law of his own country and domicil.[2]
Thus it has been said by Da Castro, and approved by D'Argentré,
that where the law of Modena enabled a minor of fourteen years
of age to contract,·that would not enable a minor of Bologna of
the same age to make a valid contract at Modena.[3] And Rodenburg asserts the same doctrine in the most emphatic terms, in
which he is followed by Boullenois.[4]

Christin. Decis. vol. 1, Decis. 183, p. 155 ; Bartolus, ad Cod. 1, 1, 1, n. 13, 20;
2 Boullenois, obs. 46, p. 455, 456; post, s. 299.
    [1] Grotius, de Jure Belli, lib. 2, c. 11, s. 5.   [2] Ante, s. 51–68.
    [3] D'Argentré, Comm. ad Leges Britonum. art. 218, gloss. 6, n. 47, 48,
cited ante, s. 76, note, and also in Liverm. Dissert. p. 42, s. 33–56; 1 Froland,
Mém. des Statuts, 112, 156, 159.
    [4] Rodenburg, de Div. Stat. tit. 2, c. 1, s. 1; 2 Boullenois, Appx. p. 11; 1 Id.
obs. 16, p. 200, 201, 204, 205; Bouhier, c. 23, n. 92; 1 Froland, Mém. p. 112,
159; 2 Froland, Mém. p. 1576–1582. The language of Rodenburg is: 'De
quibus et consimilibus id juris est, ut quocunque se transtulerit persona
statuto loci domicilii ita affecta, habilitatem aut inhabilitatem ademptam
domi, circumferat ubique, ut in universa territoria suum statutum exerceat
effectum. Apertius rem intuebimur in exemplis. Ultrajecti sui juris effici-
untur qui vigesimum ætatis annum impleverint, apud Hollandos contra, ante
vigesimum quintum rebus suis nemo intervenit. Apud utrumque populorum
nupta citra viri consensum a rebus gerendis arcetur. In regionibus, quæ
jure Romanorum hic utuntur, commerciis gaudet uxor liberrime, potestati
virili non supposita. Fac autem Ultrajactinum, qui vigesimum quintum
ætatis annum necdum habuerit, contrahere in Hollandia: aut e contra Hollandiæ incolam vigesimum jam annum egressum. Ultrajecti: aut nuptam
nostratem contrahere in regione juris scripti, aut e contra. Quocumque modo
se casus habuerit, contrahentium erit respicere ad suum cujusque domicilii
locum, impressamque ibidem personæ qualitatem, aut ademptam domi conditionem, cujus ignarus non sit oportet, qui cum alio volet contrahere. Quare
Hollandiæ incola major Ultrajecti, minor apud suos, contrahit apud nostrates
invalide. Contra, Ultrajectinus lege domicilii major contrahit in Hollandia
efficaciter, ut maxime ex more regionis istius rerum suarum necdum haberetur
compos. Uxores domi sub maritorum potestate ita constitutæ, ut sine iis nec

84. Bouhier, as we have seen,[1] holds to the doctrine that the capacity and incapacity by the law of the domicil extends to every other place,[2] but yet he is manifestly startled when it is applied to the case of marriages. He admits that in such cases it is commonly held that the law of the place where the marriage is celebrated ought to prevail.[3] But he insists that such a rule ought not to be adopted in regard to persons who are both subjects of the same country, who designedly go to a foreign country and contract marriage there in order to evade the law of the country of their own domicil.[4] He applies also similar considerations to the case of an unemancipated son or minor belonging to one country, who, finding a woman of his own country in a foreign country, marries her there, without the knowledge of his parents, holding that under such circumstance the marriage ought not to be held valid.[5] But he propounds as a case of more difficulty, where such a person going into a foreign country, without any intention of marrying, finds there a woman of his own country to his liking, whom he seeks in marriage and espouses. For if such a marriage is celebrated according to the usual formalities in that country, he deems it valid as being done in good faith, and affirms that the parties are not bound to follow the laws of their own country.[6] D'Argentré states the general doctrine in the following manner : ' When the question is as to the right or capacity of any person to do civil acts generally, it is to be referred to the judge who exercises judicial functions in the place of his domicil ; that is to say, to whom his person is subject, and who has authority so to pronounce respecting him, so that whatever he shall promulgate, adjudge, or ordain respecting the rights of persons, ought to obtain and be of force in every place to which he may transfer himself,

---

alimmet nec contrahant, nullibi locorum hanc incapacitatem exuunt. Cum mulieris contra juri scripto obnoxiæ contractus, apud nos celebratus, consistat omnimodo. Et quidem si ad personales actus, contractus puta, personæ appli-ortur habilitas, Argentrei, Burgundique (quos jure præcipui hic semper nomino). cæterorumque scribentium placita sat consentiunt.' See ante, s. 51. See also. Liverm. Dissert. s. 21, p. 34, to s. 34, p. 43; 2 Boull. Appx. 11. See also, Foelix, Conflit des Lois, Revue Étrangère et Française, tom. 7, s. 24, p. 204, to s. 26. p. 216.

[1] Ante, s. 57 a.
[2] Bouhier, Cout. de Bourg. c. 24, s. 11, p. 463; post, s. 123.
[3] Id. c. 28, s. 50, 60, p. 556, 557.
[4] Id. c. 28, s. 61. p. 537.   [5] Id. c. 28, s. 62, p. 557.
[6] Id. c. 28, s, 59-67, p. 556, 557; Id. c. 24, s. 11, p. 463.

on account of this authority over the person.' 'Quare cum de personæ jure aut habilitate quæritur ad actus civiles, in universum ea judicis ejus potestas est, qui domicilio judicat, id est, cui persona subjicitur, qui sic de eo statuere potest, ut quod edixerit, judicarit, ordinarit de personarum jure, ubicumque obtineat, cocumque se persona contulerit, propter afficentium personæ.'[1] Froland asserts the same doctrine and expressly extends it to cases of contract. 'Le statut personnel n'exerce pas seulement son autorité dans le lieu du domicile de la personne, qui sa dispensation la suit, et l'accompagne en quelque lieu qu'elle aille contracter; et qu'elle influe sur tous les biens sous quelques coutumes qu'ils soient assis.'[2] Mr. Henry, in his judicial capacity, has given the doctrine a like extent in the English colony of Demerara; for he declares that, in cases of prodigals, minors, idiots, and lunatics, the law of the domicil accompanies the party everywhere.[3] Cochin lays down the doctrine with great boldness, that a marriage contracted in a foreign country by French subjects, although contracted in the form prescribed by the foreign law, is void if it violates the laws of France.[4] The subjects of the king of France, says he, are always his subjects. And the parties contracting at a place in Brabant have only that capacity to contract which is given by the laws of their own country. It is a personal statute which follows them everywhere.[5]

85. Huberus seems in some places to affirm a doctrine in some respects quite as extensive, although it is liable to be modified in some measure by the local law, while in other places he deems it too broad and indiscriminate, and introduces several exceptions. Thus, as we have seen, he lays it down as a general rule: 'Qualitates personales certo loco alicui jure impressas, ubique circumferri et personam comitari, cum hoc effectu, ut ubivis locorum eo jure, quo tales personæ alibi gaudent vel subjecti sunt, fruuntur, et subjiciantur.'[6] So that, according to Huberus, the state or

---

[1] D'Argentré, de Leg. Briton, art. 218, gloss. 6, n. 4, p. 647; ante, s. 56; 1 Froland, Mém. des Statuts, 112; Liverm. Dissert. s. 21, p. 34.

[2] 1 Froland, Mém. des Statuts, 156–160; Id. 112; ante, s. 51 a. See also 1 Hertii, Opera, s. 4, n. 8, p. 123; Id. n. 5, p. 122, ed. 1737; Id. p. 171, 172, ed. 1715.

[3] Henry on Foreign Law, p. 38, 39; Odwin v. Forbes, Id. p. 95–97.

[4] Cochin, Œuvres, tom. 1, p. 153, 154, 4to ed.; Id. tom. 3, p. 36, 8vo ed. 1821. [5] Ibid.

[6] Huberus, de Conflictu Legum, lib. 1, tit. 3, s. 12, 13.

condition of the party as to capacity or incapacity in the place of his original domicil accompanies him everywhere, so far and so far only, that the law of the place where he happens to be attaches to him so far as it touches rights or powers growing out of such capacity or incapacity. A minor, for example, in his own country, is subject in every other country to the laws of minority of the latter country. In regard to the contract of matrimony he holds that it is to be governed by the law of the place where the marriage is celebrated, with the exception however of cases of incest. ' If,' says he, ' the marriage is lawful in the place where it is contracted and celebrated, it will be held valid and have effect everywhere, with this exception, that it does not create a prejudice to others. To which it may be added, if it is not of an evil example, as if it should be a case of incest within the second degree according to the law of nations.' ' Si licitum est eo loco, ubi contractum et celebratum est, ubique validum erit, affectumque habebit sub eadem exceptione, prejudicii aliis non creandi. Cui licet addere, si exempli nimis sit abominandi, ut si incestum juris gentium in secundo gradu contingeret, alicubi esse permissum; quod vix est, ut usu venire possit.' [1] Huberus also puts another exception, where persons belonging to one country go into another to be married, merely to evade the law of their own country, in which case he holds the marriage to be void, although it is good by the law of the place where it is celebrated.[2] ' Sæpe fit, ut adolescentes sub curatoribus agentes, furtivos amores nuptiis conglutinare cupientes, abeant in Frisiam Orientalem, aliave loca, in quibus curatorum consensus ad matrimonium non requiretur, juxta leges Romanos, quæ apud nos hac parte cessant. Celebrant ibi matrimonium, et mox redeant in patriam. Ego ita existimo, hanc rem manifesto pertinere ad eversionem juris nostri; et ideo non esse magistratus heic obligatos, e jure gentium, ejusmodi nuptias agnoscere et ratas habere. Multoque magis statuendum est eos contra jus gentium facere videri, qui civibus alieni imperii sua facilitate, jus patriis legibus contrarium, scientes, volentes, impertiuntur.' [3]

86. *English law. — Marriage.* — This latter doctrine has, upon the most solemn consideration, been overturned in England, as we shall hereafter see,[4] and such a marriage in evasion of the domestic

---

[1] Huberus, lib. 1, tit. 3, s. 8; post, s. 122.   [2] Ibid.
[3] Ibid.; post, s. 123.   [4] Post, s.123, 124. See Kent, Com. 91, 92.

laws has been held valid. But we are not therefore to conclude
that every marriage by and between British subjects in foreign
countries will be held valid, because it is celebrated according to
the laws of such countries. On the contrary, where the laws of
England create a personal incapacity to contract marriage, that
incapacity has, in some cases, been held to have a universal operation, so as to·make a subsequent marriage in a foreign country
a mere nullity when litigated in a British court.[1]

87. *Legitimation per Subsequens Matrimonium.* — Indeed the
general principle adopted in England in regard to cases of this
sort appears to be, that the lex loci contractus shall be permitted
to prevail, unless when it works some manifest injustice, or is
contra bonos mores, or is repugnant to the settled principles and
policy of its own laws. An illustration of the general principle,
and of the exception, may be found in the known difference between the Scottish law and the English law on the subject of
legitimation of antenuptial offspring. By the law of Scotland,
illegitimate children become, by the subsequent marriage of the
parents, legitimate, and may inherit as heirs. But the law of
England is otherwise, and a subsequent marriage between the
parents will not take away the character of illegitimacy. Upon a
recent occasion the question arose in an English court (the Court
of King's Bench), whether a person, born in Scotland of Scottish
parents, who afterwards intermarried there, and thereby became
legitimate in Scotland, could inherit real estate as a legitimate
heir in England. It was held by the court that he could not.[2]
On that occasion it was admitted by the court that a foreign marriage, however solemnized, if good by the foreign local law, ought
to be held valid everywhere; but that it did not follow from this,
that all the consequences of such a marriage by such foreign
local law were to be adopted. On the other hand, that it was sufficient that all such consequences as follow from a lawful marriage solemnized in England were admitted to govern in such
cases.[3] One of the learned judges on that occasion said: 'The

[1] Conway *v.* Beazley, 3 Hagg. Ecc. 639, 647, 652; Lolley's Case, Russ. &
Ry. 237. It will probably be found very difficult to maintain the doctrine in
Lolley's Case, and in subsequent discussions its authority has certainly been a
good deal shaken. See Warrender *v.* Warrender, 9 Bligh, 89; and post, s.
117, 124, 221–231.

[2] Birtwhistle *v.* Vardill, 5 B. & C. 438; 9 Bligh, 32–88.

[3] Birtwhistle *v.* Vardill, 5 B. & C. 438; 9 Bligh. 32–88. This case was

very rule, that a personal status accompanies a man everywhere, is admitted to have this qualification, that it does not militate against the law of the country where the consequences of that status are sought to be enforced.'[1]

87 *a*. Yet the law of foreign countries as to legitimacy is so far respected in England, that a person illegitimate by the law of his domicil of birth will be held illegitimate in England.[2] Thus, it has been decided by the House of Lords, as a general doctrine, that the courts of the country where the lands lie, in a question respecting the heirship to these lands, ought to govern themselves as to the question of legitimacy, not by the law of the country where the lands lie, but by that of the country where the marriage of the parents was contracted and the child born ; and if he is not the legitimate heir by that foreign law, his claim to the inheritance ought to be rejected.[3] The natural conclusion from this doctrine would seem to be, that if he was the legitimate heir by that foreign law, his claim to the inheritance ought to be firmly established. Yet this conclusion has been pointedly repelled by the learned judges in the case already alluded to,[4] and which we shall have occasion to consider more fully hereafter.[5]

88. *Dissolution of English Marriages.* — Another illustration, touching the capacity of persons to contract marriage, may be stated from English jurisprudence. By the law of England marriage is an indissoluble contract, except by the transcendent power of parliament. Hence it has been held that a marriage once

carried to the House of Lords by a writ of error, and there the question was propounded to the judges, who returned an answer affirming the decision of the King's Bench. But the question has since been reargued, and the case has not as yet been finally decided by the House of Lords. See post, s. 93.

[1] Per Littledale, J., 5 B. & C. 455.

[2] See Munro *v.* Saunders, 6 Bligh, 468; Shedden *v.* Patrick, and the Strathmore Peerage, cited in 5 B. & C. 444; in 3 Hagg. Ecc. 652; in 6 Bligh, 474, 475, 487; and in 9 Bligh, 51, 52, 75, 76, 80, and reported in 4 Wils. & Shaw, Appx. 89–95.

[3] See Shedden *v.* Patrick, and the case of the Strathmore Peerage, as cited in 9 Bligh, 51, 52, 75, 76, 80, 81.

[4] Birtwhistle *v.* Vardill, 9 Bligh, 52, 53. I confess myself wholly unable to reconcile these latter decisions with the former. The attempt to reconcile them seems to me more ingenious than satisfactory. Lord Brougham's comments on the subject, in Birtwhistle *v.* Vardill, 9 Bligh, 75, 80, 81, appear to me exceedingly forcible and difficult to be answered. Post, s. 93.

[5] Post, 93, n.

8

celebrated between British subjects in an English domicil cannot be dissolved by a divorce obtained under the laws of a foreign country, to which the parties may temporarily remove.[1] (*a*) Thus, for example, that an English marriage cannot be dissolved, under such circumstances, by a Scotch divorce, regularly obtained according to the law of Scotland by persons going thither for that purpose, who have their domicil in England.[2] And a second marriage in Scotland after such divorce will be unlawful, and will subject the parties to the charge of bigamy.[3] This doctrine however seems open to much controversy, and can scarcely now be held firmly established, if indeed it has not been overthrown by recent adjudications.[4] Perhaps it yet remains an undecided question in the English law, as we shall hereafter see, whether bona fide change of domicil, and a divorce subsequently obtained, would change the legal predicament of the parties in an English tribunal.[5] But it has been directly decided that the mere fact that the marriage takes place in England between British subjects will not, if the husband at that time has his domicil in Scotland, take away the right of the courts in Scotland to entertain jurisdiction to decree a divorce founded on such domicil.[6] But this subject will presently come more fully under consideration.[7]

89. *American Decisions.* — *Marriage.* — In the American courts the doctrine as to capacity or incapacity to marry has been held to depend generally on the law of the place where the marriage is celebrated, and not on that of the place of domicil of the parties. (*b*) An exception would doubtless be applied to cases of incest and polygamy.[8] But, in affirmation of the general principle, it has been held that if a person, divorced from his first wife, is rendered by the law of the place of the divorce incapable of contracting a second marriage, still, if he contracts marriage in another state, where the same disability does not exist, the marriage

---

[1] Lolley's Case, Russ. & Ry. 237. But see Warrender *v.* Warrender, 9 Bligh, 89; post, s. 219 *a*.

[2] See Rex *v.* Lolley, Russ. & Ry. 237; Tovey *v.* Lindsay, 1 Dow, 124; Conway *v.* Beazley, 3 Hagg. Ecc. 639. See also, Fergusson on Marr. and Div. App. 269; Warrender *v.* Warrender, 9 Bligh, 89; post, s. 319 *a*.

[3] Ante, s. 88, n. 6.   [4] Ibid.   [5] Ibid.
[6] Ibid.   [7] Post, c. 7, s. 200–231.   [8] Post, s. 113, 114.

(*a*) See post, s. 218–226.   tion see the note to s. 102, and the note
(*b*) Upon the subjects of this sec-   at the end of s. 124 *a*, post.

will be held valid.[1] (a)　And a marriage, celebrated in a foreign
state, to evade the law of the place of domicil, is on the same account held valid.[2]　Mr. Chancellor Kent formerly laid down the
doctrine in regard to contracts generally in terms which might
admit of a different interpretation.　He said : ' The personal incompetency of individuals to contract, as in the case of infancy,
and the general capacity of parties to contract, depend, as a general rule, upon the law of the domicil.'[3]　But he was then to be
understood as referring to the law of the domicil only when it is
the place where the contract is made ; for in the same paragraph
he stated that the lex loci contractus governs in relation to the
validity of contracts, and he applied it especially to nuptial
contracts.[4]

90. *Disabilities imposed by Foreign Laws.* — The difficulty of
applying any other rule, as to the capacity and incapacity of the
person, in respect to the class of nuptial contracts, will become
still more clear by attending to the great extent of the parental

[1] 2 Kent Com. 91–93, 458, 459, 3d ed. ; Putnam v. Putnam, 8 Pick. (Mass.)
433; West Cambridge v. Lexington, 1 Pick. (Mass.) 506; Decouche v. Savetier, 3 Johns. Ch. (N. Y.) 190; post, s. 123.

[2] Ibid.　　　[3] 2 Kent Com. 458, 2d ed. ; post, s. 123.

[4] 2 Kent Com. 458, 2d ed. ; and Decouche v. Savetier, 3 Johns. Ch. (N. Y.)
190.　The English authorities, cited by Mr. Chancellor Kent, justify this conclusion.　One is Male v. Roberts, in 3 Esp. 163, which was a case of a contract by a minor in Scotland during his temporary residence there, and it was
held to be governed by the law of Scotland.　Another is Ex parte Otto Lewis,
1 Ves. 298, where a lunatic heir of a mortgagee, who had been declared a non
compos in Hamburg, and no commission of lunacy had been taken out in England, was ordered to convey the estate in payment of the mortgage in Hamburg,
under statute 4 Geo. 2, c. 10.　Here Lord Hardwicke manifestly acted upon the
ground that the mortgage-money was personal property; and the lunatic being
domiciled in Hamburg, the court would take notice of his disability to convey
there by the law of that place.　The remaining authority is Pardessus.　His
doctrine is certainly more broad.　But it could not have been intended by Mr.
Chancellor Kent to overrule the English doctrine, and his own prior statement, upon the authority of a foreign jurist.　The ambiguity is corrected in
the third edition; and the words ' the law of the place of contract ' are substituted for the words ' the law of the domicil.'　2 Kent Com. 458, 3d ed.
Pardessus is an authority in favor of the limited doctrine that a person incapacitated by the law of his domicil cannot contract with validity there; but he
carries his doctrine much further.　The cases of Saul v. His Creditors, 5 Mart.
N.S. (La.) 596, 598, and Baldwin v. Gray, 4 Mart. N.S. (La.) 192, 193, already
cited, establish a like limited doctrine, and decide that a contract by a minor
is to be governed by the lex loci contractus; ante, s. 75.

(a) See note, s. 92, post.

power recognized by the continental nations of Europe, and derived by them from the civil law. Parental restraints upon the marriage of minors exist to a very great extent in Germany, Holland, France, and other civil law countries; to so great an extent, indeed, that the marriage of minors without the consent of their parents, or at least of their father, is absolutely void; and the disability of minority is in these countries carried to a much greater age than it is by the common law.[1] In some of these countries majority is not attained until thirty, and until a very recent period, even in France, the age of majority of males was fixed at twenty-five and of females at twenty-one. It is now fixed at twenty-one in all other cases, except for the purpose of contracting marriage, and a marriage cannot even now be contracted in France by a man until twenty-five years of age, and by a woman until twenty-one, without the consent of their parents, or at least of their fathers, if the parents differ in opinion.[2] Yet France has ventured upon the bold doctrine that the marriages of Frenchmen in foreign countries shall not be deemed valid if the parties are not by its own law competent to contract by reason of their being under the parental power.[3] There can be little doubt that foreign countries where such marriages are celebrated, will follow their own law and disregard that of France.[4]

91. *Penal Disabilities.* — If we pass from cases of minority to other disabilities, enforced by the law of the native domicil, or that of an after-acquired domicil, there will be still more reason to doubt whether any rule of such law, respecting personal capacity and incapacity, ought to be declared to be of universal obligation and efficacy. Let us take the case of a person declared infamous by the law of the place of his domicil. It is said that under such circumstances he ought to be deemed everywhere infamous. 'Hinc,' says Hertius, 'in uno loco infamis, ubique infamis habetur.' Surely it will not be contended that if a Protestant should be declared a heretic in a Catholic country, and there rendered infamous, and inhabilitated thereby, he is to be deemed under the like infamy and disability in all Protestant

---

[1] 2 Kent Com. 86, 3d ed.; 1 Black. Com. 437; Ruding v. Smith, 2 Hagg. Con. 372, 389; Id. 395; 1 Brown, Civ. & Adm. Law, 59.

[2] Code Civil of France, art. 148, 488.

[3] 2 Kent Com. 93, note, 3d ed.; Code Civil of France, art. 170; Id. art. 148; 1 Toullier, Droit Civil, art. 576, 577.   [4] See post, s. 123, 124.

countries. That surely would be pressing the doctrine to a wanton extravagance.[1] Yet certainly many foreign jurists do press it to that extent.[2]

92. In like manner let us consider the civil disabilities imposed by the English laws in cases of outlawry, excommunication, civil death, and popish recusancy.[3] It would be difficult to maintain that these accompanied the person to America, where no like disabilities exist, and where they are foreign to the whole genius of our institutions. Yet many foreign jurists strenuously maintain the doctrine.[4] We have no positive laws declaring that such foreign disabilities shall not be recognized. But an American court would deem them purely local, and incapable of being enforced here. (a) Even the conviction of a crime in a foreign country, which makes the party infamous there and incapable of being a witness in their courts, has been held not to produce a like effect here.[5] (b) The capacity or incapacity of any persons to do acts in their own country would undoubtedly, under such circumstances, be judged by their own laws, but not their capacity or incapacity to do the like acts in any foreign territory where different laws prevail.

93. *Legitimacy.* — Foreign jurists also generally, although not

[1] See 1 Hertii Opera, s. 4, n. 8, p. 124, ed. 1737; Id. 178, ed. 1716; Liverm. Diss. p. 30, 31.

[2] See Henry on Foreign Law, p. 30; 1 Boullenois, obs. 4, p. 52–67; 1 Voet, ad Pand. 1, 4, n. 7, p. 40.

[3] See 3 Black. Comm. 101, 102, 283; 1 Black. Comm. 132; 4 Black. Comm. 54, 319, 320.

[4] 1 Boullenois, obs. p. 59–67; 2 Boullenois, p. 9, 10, 19. But see *contra*, J. Voet, de Statut. s. 4, c. 3, n. 17, 18, p. 130, ed. 1737.

[5] Commonwealth *v.* Green, 17 Mass. 515, 540, 541.

(a) The prohibition which exists in some states against the marriage of a person from whom a divorce has been obtained by reason of his or her fault, is a penal disability imposed for the offence, and therefore has no effect beyond the limits of the state. Dickson *r.* Dickson, 1 Yerg. (Tenn.) 110; Ponsford *v.* Johnson, 2 Blatch. C. C. 51, 59; Van Voorhis *v.* Brintnall, 86 N.Y. 18, 28; Commonwealth *v.* Lane, 113 Mass. 458, 471; West Cambridge *v.* Lexington, 1 Pick. (Mass.) 506. But see Williams *v.* Oates, 5 Ired. (N.C.) 535. See also note, s. 124 a, post.

Upon the point that effect will not be given to foreign penal laws, see Dicey on Domicil, 161, 162; Lynch *v.* Government of Paraguay, L.R. 2 P. & M. 268, 272; Jackson *v.* Rose, 2 Va. Cas. 34.

(b) Sims *v.* Sims, 75 N.Y. 466; Campbell *v.* State, 23 Ala. 44; 1 Greenl. Ev. s. 376. The contrary was held in Chase *v.* Blodgett, 10 N.H. 22; State *v.* Candler, 3 Hawks. (N.C.) 393.

universally, maintain that the question of legitimacy or illegitimacy is to be decided exclusively by the law of the domicil of origin.   They assert the general maxim to be of universal obligation, pater est, quem justæ nuptiæ demonstrant, applying it in its broadest sense.[1]   They therefore hold that if by the law of a country (as, for example, of Scotland), a man born a bastard becomes legitimate by a subsequent marriage of his parents there, he ought to be deemed legitimate everywhere.   And so, on the contrary, if a man would, by the law of the country of his birth, be deemed illegitimate (as, for example, in England), he ought to be deemed illegitimate everywhere, even in another country, where he would by its law otherwise be deemed legitimate.[2]

93 *a. Doctrines to be considered.* — It has been above stated that foreign jurists generally, although not universally, hold this opinion ; for there is some diversity of opinion among them, if not as to the application of the rule ex directo to the persons, at least as to its application to property situate in a foreign country. Considering therefore the importance of the subject, and that it has already undergone a most elaborate discussion in England, in the case already adverted to, and which we shall have occasion to consider more fully hereafter,[3] it is desirable that doctrines maintained by foreign jurists, as well as the reasoning of the English courts on the subject, should be here brought under review.

93 *b. Foreign Jurists.* — It seems, then, generally admitted by foreign jurists that, as the validity of the marriage must depend upon the law of the country where it is celebrated, the status, or state, or condition of their offspring, as to legitimacy or illegitimacy, ought to depend upon the same law.   So that, if by the law of the place of the marriage, at all events if the parents were then

---

[1] Post, s. 93 *a*–93 *m*.

[2] 1 Boull. obs. 4, p. 62–64.   But see Voet, de Statut. s. 4, c. 3, n. 15. p. 138, ed. 1712; 1 Hertii Opera, s. 4, n. 14, 15, p. 129, ed. 1737.   Legitimation by a subsequent marriage is admitted with different modifications by the law of Scotland, France, Spain, Portugal, Germany, and most of the continental nations of Europe.   The rule was imported into their jurisprudence from the Roman law. 1 Burge, Col. & For. Law, pt. 1, c. 3, s. 2, p. 92, 93; Cod. 5, 27, 5; Novell. 78, c. 4; Id. 89, c. 8.   In some of the American States the same rule prevails. 1 Burge, Col. & For. Law, c. 3, s. 3, p. 101; Griffith's Law Register.

[3] Birtwhistle *v.* Vardill, 5 B. & C. 438; 9 Bligh, 32; ante, s. 87 *a.*

domiciled there, the offspring, although born before the marriage, would be legitimated, they ought to be deemed legitimate in every other country, for all purposes whatsoever, including heirship of immovable property.[1]

93 c. This is certainly the doctrine maintained by many, perhaps by a large majority of foreign jurists.[2] Vinnius says: 'Item, jus personæ hic esse quod statum et conditionem personæ sequitur. Nam status ipse est personæ conditio aut qualitas, quæ efficit, ut hoc vel illo jure utatur, ut esse liberum, esse servum, esse ingenuum, esse libertinum, esse alieni, esse sui juris.'[3] Huberus also extends the rule not only to the marriage itself, but also to all rights and effects flowing therefrom. 'Porro, non tantum ipsi contractus ipsæque nuptiæ, certis locis rite celebratæ, ubique pro justis et validis habentur, sed etiam jura et effecta contractuum et nuptiarum, in iis locis recepta, ubique vim suam obtinebunt.'[4] Stockmannus says: 'Statuta, in personas directa, quæ certam iis qualitatem affigunt, transeunt quidem cum personis extra territorium statuentum, ut personæ ubique sit uniformis, ejusque unus status.'[5]

93 d. Bouhier adopts the doctrine in its fullest extent, and applies it to the very case of legitimacy. He says that the state of the child, whether legitimate or illegitimate, must be decided by the law of the domicil of his parents, and that this is an inviolable rule upon every question of his state or condition. And hence he holds that if he is at his birth illegitimate, and he is legitimated by a subsequent marriage in the same country between his parents, he is in all respects to be treated as legitimate everywhere.[6] Hertius holds a similar opinion.[7] Froland is of the same opinion.[8] Boullenois is very full on the same point.

---

[1] See 1 Burge, Col. & For. Law, pt. 1, c. 3, p. 101–106.

[2] See 1 Burge, Col. & For. Law, pt. 1, c. 3, s. 3, p. 101–106.

[3] Vinnius, ad Inst. lib. 1, tit. 3, introd.

[4] Huberus, de Conn. Leg. lib. 1, tit. 3, s. 9.

[5] Stockman. Decis. 125, s. 6, p. 262; also cited 1 Boullenois, obs. 6, p. 131; Livermore, Dissert. s. 50, p. 52. John Voet in the most explicit terms admits that this rule is held to apply to questions of legitimacy by many jurists, and especially by D'Argentré, Grotius, Christinæus, and Rodenburg. J. Voet, ad Pand. 1, 4, n. 7, p. 40.

[6] Bouhier, Cout. de Bourg. c. 24, s. 122, 123, p. 481.

[7] Hertii, de Collis. Leg. tom. 1, s. 4, n. 15, p. 184, ed. 1716; Id. p. 129, ed. 1737.

[8] 1 Froland, Mém. c. 5, s. 4, p. 89; Id. c. 7, s. 2, p. 156, ed. 1716; ante, s. 51 a.

He holds that the general rule is, pater est, quem justæ nuptiæ demonstrant; and that if a person is legitimate or illegitimate by the law of the place of the marriage, he is to be held of the same state and condition wherever he may go, and whatever change of domicil may take place.[1] Hence he declares that if by the law of a country a man born a bastard is legitimated by the subsequent marriage of his parents, or, e contra, if by the law of the country such subsequent marriage does not legitimate him, he is in every other country affected by his original state or condition; that is to say, if legitimated by the subsequent marriage, he is legitimate everywhere; if not so legitimated, he is illegitimate everywhere.[2] Even Burgundus and Stockmannus and Christinæus, whose systems are founded upon a different theory, namely, that personal statutes have no extra-territorial effect, admit that, so far as the person is concerned, though not as to immovable property, as we shall presently see,[3] the original state or condition ought to govern everywhere.[4] The opinion of Paul Voet and John Voet on the same subject is far more limited and qualified, and will come under our review hereafter.[5]

93 *e. English Rule as to Legitimacy.* — The same general doctrine is avowedly adopted by the courts of England. Lord Stowell on one occasion in effect maintained that by the law of England the status or condition of a claimant must be tried by reference to the law of the country where that status originated.[6] The same doctrine was adopted by the judges of England in giving their opinion to the House of Lords. They admitted in the most solemn form, that the legitimacy or illegitimacy of a person must be decided by the law of the place where the marriage was celebrated; and that if by the law of that place (for example, Scotland) a son, born before the marriage of his parents, would by a subsequent marriage between them, be legitimated, that status of legitimacy must be deemed equally true and valid everywhere else, where the question might arise.[7]

[1] 1 Boullenois, obs. 4, p. 62, 63; post, s. 93 *i*.
[2] Ibid.   [3] Post, s. 93 *k*.
[4] Ante, s. 52; Burgundus, Tract. 1, s. 3, p. 15; Christinæus, tom. 2, decis. 3, s. 3, p. 4; Id. decis. 56, s. 12, p. 55; Stockmann. decis. 125, s. 6, 9, p. 262, 263; 1 Boullenois, obs. 4, p. 130, 131.
[5] Post, s. 93 *l*.
[6] Dalrymple v. Dalrymple, 2 Hagg. Cons. 54, 59; 9 Bligh, 45, 46.
[7] Birtwhistle v. Vardill, 9 Bligh, 45, 46, 48; Id. 71; post, s. 93 *n*, 93 *q*.

93 *f. Extent of its Application.* Still, however, although the general doctrine is thus extensively admitted, there is some diversity of opinion as to the true nature and extent of its application in regard to different kinds of property, and also in regard to the circumstances of particular cases.[1] Thus, for example, although its positive application in regard to movable property is generally admitted ; yet in regard to immovable property in a foreign country there has been some contrariety of judgment. The circumstances, also, under which the question of legitimacy or illegitimacy may arise, may be very various and admit of important distinctions in the application of the general doctrine. The birth may be in one country, the marriage be in another, and the domicil of the parents be in a third.[2]

93 *g. Illustrations.*—Several cases may easily be put to illustrate this suggestion. The question of legitimacy or illegitimacy may arise among others in the following cases. (1) Where a child is born before marriage in the domicil of his parents, who afterwards intermarry there, and by the law of that domicil the child is thereby legitimated. (2) Where a child is born before marriage in the domicil of his parents, and by the law thereof a subsequent marriage would legitimate the child, and the parents are afterwards married in another country, by whose law no such legitimation would follow. (3) Where a child is born before marriage in the domicil of his parents, by whose law no legitimation would follow on their subsequent marriage, and they remove to a new domicil, where the law would, upon such marriage, legitimate the child, and they are there married. (4) Where the child is born before marriage in the domicil of his parents, by whose law no legitimation would follow from a subsequent marriage, and they are there married, and subsequently remove to a new domicil, by the law whereof such subsequent marriage would legitimate the child. It is plain that these several cases may admit of, if they do not absolutely require, the application of different principles to resolve them, and different questions may be put in respect to them. Ought the law of the place of birth, or that of the place of the marriage, or that of the actual domicil of the parents, or that of the actual domicil of the child, to govern?[3]

---

[1] See 1 Burge, Col. & For. Law, pt. 1, c. 3, s. 3, p. 105, 106, 109, 110.

[2] See Lord Brougham's remarks in Birtwhistle v. Vardill, 9 Bligh, 79.

[3] A case still more complicated is said to be now pending before the House

93 *h. Inheritance of Land as affected by Legitimation.* — The most simple case, and that which has most frequently arisen for discussion, is the first stated ; where the birth, domicil, and marriage of the parties took place in the country, by the laws whereof a subsequent marriage would legitimate the child. Suppose then the question to arise, whether in such a case the child so legitimated by such marriage could inherit lands in another country by the laws whereof no such legitimation would follow upon such marriage. Or, in other words, let us put the very case as it actually occurred in the courts of England, in the case above alluded to,[1] the case of an illegitimate son born in Scotland, whose parents afterwards intermarried there, and, dying, held lands in England; would such son be entitled to inherit the land as lawful heir under the law of England ? We have already seen how this question has been decided by the English courts ;[2] but as the question is still supposed to be unsettled there, and is also of very general application and importance, it may be well to give it a fuller consideration.

93 *i. Foreign Jurists.* — It is plain from what has been already stated, and indeed is directly established by their positive declarations, that those of the foreign jurists already mentioned, who affirm the general doctrine of the universality of the rule that capacity and incapacity depend upon the law of the domicil of birth, and that it equally applies to movable property and immovable property situate in foreign countries, would hold the same rule applicable to the question of legitimacy and illegitimacy, in regard to the inheritance of real property in all foreign countries. This is certainly maintained by Vinnius, Huberus, Wesel, Froland, Rodenburg, Bouhier, Boullenois, Pothier, and Merlin,[3]

---

of Lords on an appeal from Scotland. In effect it is this: A, a Scotchman, domiciled in Scotland, had an illicit connection with B, an Englishwoman, domiciled in England, by whom he had a son born in England. The parents afterwards intermarried in England, the father retaining his Scotch domicil. They then returned to Scotland; and the question before the court was, whether, under these circumstances, the son was legitimated by the subsequent marriage. The Court of Session of Scotland held that he was. From this decision appeal is taken. (*a*)

[1] Birtwhistle *v.* Vardill, 5 B. & C. 438; 9 Bligh, 51, 52; ante, s. 93 *a*, 93 *e*; post, 93 *n.*

[2] Ante, s. 87 *a.*   [3] Ante, s. 51 *a*, 52, 53, 54, 93, 93 *d.*

(*a*) Affirmed: Munro *v.* Munro, 7 Cl. & F. 842.

and probably by Baldus and Grotius.[1] Hertius puts the converse
case: 'An filius, quem pater ante legitimum connubium in
Anglia genuerat, succedere possit patri huic naturali in bonis
ex Anglia sitis?' And he holds that he could not; because the
son, being illegitimate in England, would be held illegitimate
everywhere.[2] And this naturally flows from one of his rules:
'Quando lex in personam dirigitur, respiciendum est ad leges
illius civitatis, quæ personam habet subjectam.'[3] Bouhier states
this as the universal rule, as we have seen;[4] but he admits
that if the law of a particular nation should allow the inheritance only to a child born in lawful matrimony (only in loyal
marriage), then, as to land there situate, it ought to prevail, upon
the ground that the law in such a case designated the condition of
heirship. And this seems to have been also Dumoulin's opinion.[5]
Boullenois, as we have seen,[6] holds the doctrine without any qualification whatever. He presses the doctrine further, and insists
that if a child is born before marriage in England, and his parents
are afterwards naturalized in France, and subsequently intermarry
there, the child becomes legitimate to all intents and purposes.[7]
He adds, that if a child is so born illegitimately in England, and his
parents marry there, and then die, and he then takes up his domicil in France and is naturalized there, he will be entitled to succeed to their property in France, to the exclusion of collaterals.[8]

93 k. Burgundus, Christinæus, and Stockmannus may be thought
to hold the contrary doctrine, upon the general foundation of their
system, that personal laws have no operation as to immovable property situate elsewhere.[9] But I am not aware that they have ever
directly discussed this question. And it may be, that while they
hold that immovable property must, as to heirship, be decided by
the lex loci status, they may deem the capacity of legitimacy, as
to that heirship, as conclusively established by the law of the

---

[1] J. Voet, ad Pand. 1, 4, n. 7, p. 40; Liverm. Dissert. s. 56, p. 57, s. 109–
114, p. 84–87.

[2] 1 Hertii Opera, de Collis. Leg. s. 4, n. 15, p. 183, ed. 1716; Id. p. 129, ed. 1737.

[3] Id. s. 4, n. 8, p. 175; Id. p. 123, ed. 1837.   [4] Ante, s. 93 d.

[5] Bouhier, Cout. de Bourg. c. 24, s. 124, p. 481.

[6] Ante, s. 93 d; 1 Boullenois, obs. 4, p. 62, 63; Id. obs. 6, p. 129, 130, 134–137.

[7] 1 Boullenois, obs. 4, p. 62, 63; ante, s. 93 d.

[8] 1 Boullenois, obs. 4, p. 63.

[9] See Burgundus, tract. 1, n. 8, 10, 25, 26; Christinæus, vol. 2, lib. 1, decis.
56; Stockmann. decis. 125, n. 10; Livermore, Dissert. s. 47, p. 50; Id. s. 106,
p. 81; ante, s. 93 d.

birth and domicil of the party.   The one doctrine is certainly not necessarily inconsistent with the other.[1]

93 *l.* Paul Voet and John Voet are, as far as my researches have gone, the only jurists who contend that the law of legitimacy of the domicil of the party, although a personal statute, is exclusively, like all other personal statutes, confined to the territory, and has no operation directly or indirectly beyond it. 'Verius est,' says John Voet, 'personalia, non magis quam realia, territorium statuentis posse excedere, sive directo, sive per consequentiam;' and he goes on, as we have seen,[2] to deny that a bastard who is legitimated by the law of his domicil can inherit by succession property situate in another country where no such legitimation would take place.   Paul Voet holds the same opinion. 'Quid autem statuendum erit de legitimato in uno territorio; censebitur, ne, ratione bonorum alibi jacentium, ubi legitimatus, non erat statutum vires suos excercere; vel, an illa qualitas, seu habilitas, eum ubique locorum comitabitur, quoad effectum consequendæ dignitatis, vel succedendi ab intestato?   Respondeo, etsi per legitimationem habilitetur persona, ut velient D. D., qualitatem eam comitari ubique locorum, etiam ex comitate id servari possit; quia tamen potissimum illa legitimatio fit ad effectum vel honoris vel hereditatis consequendæ; in quam nihil juris habet is, quia in suo territorio legitimavit; existimarem illum legitimationem ad honores subeundos et hereditatem extra territorium capiendam non sufficere.'[3]

93 *m. Weight of Foreign Authority.* — The weight of foreign authority would therefore, on the whole, seem decidedly to preponderate in favor of the rule that an illegitimate person, who by the subsequent marriage of his parents becomes legitimated as heir by the law of his domicil, ought to be deemed such as to the inheritance of land in all other countries, at least where it is not expressly prohibited by the terms of the local law that such a person, born before marriage, should inherit.[4]   Indeed, the opinion of the Voets is perhaps less fairly maintainable, because it proceeds upon the

---

[1] John Voet seems to have understood that those jurists who hold that legitimacy by the law of domicil extended the same capacity everywhere, gave the effect to it here supposed.   J. Voet, ad Pand. 1, 4, n. 7, p. 40.

[2] Ante, s. 54 *a;* Livermore, Dissert. s. 51, 52, p. 54.

[3] Paul Voet, de Statut. s. 4, c. 3, s. 15, p. 156, ed. 1661; Livermore, Dissert. s. 51, 52, p. 54.

[4] Livermore, Dissert. s. 57–59, p. 58, 59.

ground that the status or condition of the person by the law of his domicil has no operation beyond the territory, either directly or consequentially. To this extent the doctrine has certainly never been carried in England.[1]

93 n. *Birtwhistle* v. *Vardill.*— In the case already alluded to (a) in the English courts, where the question was, whether a son, born of Scottish parents in Scotland before marriage, but who afterwards intermarried there, could inherit lands in England, as heir, there was much learned discussion on the point. The Court of King's Bench decided in the negative, and that opinion was afterwards, upon a writ of error to the House of Lords, held by all the judges of England to be correct. But it not being satisfactory, the case has since been ordered to be reargued, and is still pending. (b) Lord Brougham upon this occasion expressed an opinion directly opposed to that of the learned judges. It may therefore be well to present a summary of the reasoning on each side of the question, and thus to exhibit the grounds of difference.

93 o. It was conceded on all sides that the right to inherit lands in England must depend upon the laws of England; in other words, that the right of inheritance follows the law of the rei sitæ, and not that of the domicil of the parties. In every case therefore in which an inheritance is sought in England, the question is, whether the claimant is the heritable heir according to the law of England. The learned Chief Baron Alexander, who delivered the opinion of the judges against the Scottish claimant, though legitimate in Scotland, reasoned to this effect. He admitted that the status or condition of the claimant must be tried by the law of Scotland, where that status originated; that by the law of Scotland the claimant was clearly legitimate, and must be held so everywhere. But he insisted that the question was not whether the claimant was legitimate or not, but whether he was heir in England; that he might be legitimate, and yet might not be heir. By the law of England no person could inherit lands there unless he was born within lawful wedlock. This was so expressly affirmed by the statute of Merton, which declared that 'he is a bastard that is born before the marriage of his parents.' In order therefore to see whether the claimant was entitled, it was not sufficient to ascer-

[1] Ante, s. 93 e.

(a) Ante, s. 87 a.   (b) See note at end of s. 93 r, post.

tain whether he was legitimate, but also to ascertain whether he
was born in lawful wedlock ; for that circumstance is essential to
heirship in England.   Lord Coke has indeed said, ' Hæres, in the
legal understanding of the common law, implieth that he is ex
justis nuptiis procreatus ; for, Hæres legitimus est, quem nuptiæ
demonstrant.'   But his expression would have been more accurate if, instead of saying ' ex justis nuptiis procreatus,' he had said,
' ex justis nuptiis natus.'   As to the argument used for the claimant,
that he is deemed born in lawful wedlock, because by a presumption of the Scottish law, a presumption juris et de jure, there was
a marriage anterior to the procreation, it is a mere fiction of that
law, and cannot govern in England, where the actual fact of birth
after marriage decides the right.   The cases alluded to, where
illegitimacy in the place of birth settled the question against the
heirship,[1] are perfectly consistent with this doctrine ; for both
facts must concur to establish heirship in England, legitimacy
and birth after marriage.   In these cases the first fact was entirely wanting, and in the first step therefore in the claimant's
title, the ground sunk under him.[2]

---

[1] Ante, s. 87.

[2] His lordship's opinion deserves here to be cited at large. ' As to the
first of these questions, I believe I express the opinion of the judges, when
I say, in the well-considered language of Lord Stowell, in the case of Dalrymple *v.* Dalrymple, " The cause, being entertained in an English court, must be
adjudicated according to the principle of the English law applicable to such a
case; but the only principle applicable to such a case by the law of England
is, that the status or condition of the claimant must be tried by reference to
the law of the country where the status originated; having furnished this principle, the law of England withdraws altogether, and leaves the question of
status in the case put to the law of Scotland."   Such is the sentiment of that
great judge, and such is his language, varied only so far as to apply to a question of legitimacy what was said of a question respecting the validity of marriage.   When the question of personal status has been settled upon these
principles, when it has been ascertained what the claimant's character and
situation are, it becomes then necessary to inquire what are the rules and
maxims of inheritance, which the law of that country where the inheritance is
placed, and whose tribunals are to decide upon it, has stamped and impressed
upon the land in debate.   In order the more distinctly to explain what is
meant, I will suppose a case in many circumstances resembling the present.
In addition to the circumstances stated in the question, let it be further supposed that the father and mother of the claimant had, after their marriage,
one or more sons born to them.   Suppose then the present claim to be made.
The first inquiry having been satisfied, and it being upon that inquiry perfectly ascertained that the claimant is the eldest legitimate son of his deceased
parent, for the purpose of taking land, and for every other purpose, by the law

93 *p.* On the other hand, the reasoning of Lord Brougham was to this effect. The reasoning of the judges admitted the

of Scotland, it will next be requisite to inquire what are the rules and maxims of inheritance which the law of England has impressed upon that land which is the subject of the claim. Let it further be supposed that upon this inquiry it shall turn out that the land claimed is of that description which is called borough-English. This being proved, we think it clear that the claimant's legitimacy by the law of Scotland, his right to inherit by that law, will give the claimant no right whatever to the land in England held in borough-English. The comity between nations is conclusive to give to the claimant the character of the eldest legitimate son of his father, and to give him all the rights which are necessarily consequent upon that character; but what these rights are respecting English land must be left to the law of England, and the comity is totally ineffectual to alter in the slightest degree the rules of inheritance and descent which the law of England has attached to this English land. It would unquestionably descend upon the youngest son. I am anxious to mark clearly the distinction which I have pointed out, because it is upon that distinction that our opinion turns. I will therefore illustrate it by another example. Take the case of Ilderton *v.* Ilderton (2 H. Bl. 145); that is the case of a claim to dower by a foreign widow; whether she is a widow or not, that is, whether she was the lawful wife of the man who was, during the coverture, seized of the land, is a question which the law of England permits, upon a claim to English land, to be determined by the foreign law, the law of the country where the contract of marriage was made; there the comity stops. When her character of widow shall have been fixed according to these foreign rules, the law of England comes into action, and, proceeding inexorably by its own provisions and regulations, decides what are the interests in the English land which her character of widow has conferred upon her. It inquires what are the rules which attach upon the particular land in favor of a widow. If, upon that inquiry, it appears that the land is subject to the common law, it will give her a third; if it appears to be gavel-kind, one half, while she remains casta et sola. If the and be customary land of any manor, the custom must be looked into; and she can have only what that custom shall bestow, however strange and capricious that custom may be. The distinction to which I am directing your lordship's attention is very familiar to foreign jurists, and is noticed by them as the difference between real and personal status; the last being those which respect the person, and follow it everywhere; the first being those which are connected with the land, and adhere to it, and are as immovable as the subject to which they are applied. My lords, it appears to us that the answer to the question which your lordships have put, must be founded upon this distinction: while we assume that B is the eldest legitimate son of his father, in England as well as in Scotland, we think that we have also to consider whether that status, that character, entitles him to the land in dispute as the heir of that father; and we think that this question, inasmuch as it regards real property situated in England, must be decided according to those rules which govern the descent of real property in that country, without the least regard to the rules which govern the descent of real property in Scotland. We have therefore considered whether, by the law of England, a man is the heir of English land merely because he is the eldest legitimate son of his father. We are of opinion that these circumstances are

validity of the marriage, and the status of legitimacy of the claimant.   But it was said that the question was of heirship.

not sufficient of themselves, but that we must look further, and ascertain whether he was born within the state of lawful matrimony; because, by the law of England, that circumstance is essential to heirship; and that this is a rule not of a personal nature, but of that class which, if I may use the expression, is sown in the land, springs out of it, and cannot, according to the law of England, be abrogated or destroyed by any foreign rule or law whatsoever. It is this circumstance which, in my judgment, dictates the answer we must give to your lordship's question, viz., that in selecting the heir for English inheritance, we must inquire only who is that heir by the local law.   It has appeared to us that the vice of the appellant's argument consists in treating the question of who shall be heir to English land, as a question of personal status.   So it is, no doubt, up to a certain point, but beyond that point it becomes a question to be decided entirely by the local rules relating to real property in the realm of England.   That the rule of the English law is what I have represented can hardly require proof.   If the argument from the comity of nations be shaken off, no man will doubt that a person legitimated per subsequens matrimonium is not the heir of English land.   What my Lord Coke says, in page 7 of the first Institute, affords the rule: " *Hæres*, in the legal understanding of the common law, implieth that he is ex justis nuptiis procreatus, for Hæres legitimus est, quem nuptiæ demonstrant."   Perhaps my Lord Coke's expression would have been more precise and accurate, if instead of saying " ex justis nuptiis procreatus," he had said " ex justis nuptiis natus." But this is what is meant, as all experience shows.   It would be useless to follow this further, but it will be material to recollect that this maxim, which pervades all our books, and which is confirmed by all our practice, though it is in form a description of the person who shall be heir, is in substance, in our opinion, a maxim regarding the land, describes one of its most important qualities, traces out the course in which it shall descend, and is no more liable to be broken in upon by any foreign constitution than are the degree of interest which the heir shall take in the land, the conditions on which he shall hold it, the proportion which a woman shall obtain as a widow, or the limitations and conditions attached to her estate.   I have endeavored to state the principles and to show the course of reasoning which has conducted my learned brothers and myself to the conclusion that B, the person designated by your lordships, is not entitled to the property in question as the heir of A.   Before I finish I will notice two arguments used on behalf of the appellant, which merit particular attention.   It is said for the appellant that, according to the rule we adopt, if he is born in lawful wedlock, he fulfils every condition required of him.   Now they say he is born in lawful wedlock because, by a presumption of the Scottish law, a presumption juris et de jure, there was a marriage anterior to his procreation.   It is by force of this presumption that he is legitimate; by this fiction he is born within the pale of lawful matrimony.   We know that this fiction is, by many respectable writers on the Scottish law, represented as accompanying the legitimation per subsequens matrimonium. But we do not concede the consequence deduced from it as applicable to the present question.   The question is, what the law of England requires, and as we are advised the law of England requires that the claimant should *actually*, and *in fact*, be born within the pale of lawful matrimony, we cannot agree

That was true. But then who was the heir? Why, according
to the law of England, the eldest legitimate son. Now, the

that the presumption of a foreign jurisprudence, contrary to the acknowledged
fact, should abrogate the law of England, and that by such a fiction a principle should be introduced which, upon a great and memorable occasion, the
legislature of the kingdom distinctly rejected; your lordships will perceive
that I allude to the statute of Merton. It would seem strange to introduce
indirectly, and from comity to a foreign nation, a rule of inheritance which
may affect every honor and all the real property of the realm; which rule,
when proposed directly and positively to the legislature, they directly and
positively negatived and refused; a refusal that, in England, has obtained the
approbation of every succeeding age. Again, my lords, it is said that two
cases have been decided in this House which are nearly in point, and will
prove that the claim of B should be supported. These cases are the cases of
Shedden v. Patrick, and the case of Lord Strathmore. These two cases are
alike in principle, and establish the same proposition. In the one case the
parents lived in a state of concubinage in America, and the other in England.
In both children were born to them. Afterwards the parties married in their
respective countries; by force of their marriages the American issue claimed
Scottish land, and the English issue claimed Scottish honors; in both, your
lordships decided against the claimants. Now it is said these authorities are
exactly the converse of the present case. They establish the principle that the
courts of the country where the lands lie, in a question respecting the heirship
to these lands or honors, inform themselves whether the claimant is heir, not
by the law of the country where the lands lie, but in the country of the domicil
where the marriage of the parents was contracted; and if he is not heir by
that foreign law, his claim is rejected; from which they deduce this consequence, that if he is heir, his claim should be sustained. This argument presents itself in a very plausible shape, and was pressed at the bar, as it seemed
to me, with striking ingenuity and force. But if I have the good fortune sufficiently to explain the principles which have conducted my learned brothers
and myself to the opinion I have stated, you will soon perceive that these principles afford a conclusive answer to it. The first step to be taken in every case
of this kind, as I have already explained, is to inquire into the status of the
claimant. The status, it is argued, is to be determined by the law of the foreign
country; with this the lex rei sitæ does not intermeddle, and intermeddles no
more when that foreign law establishes the claimant's bastardy than when it
proves his legitimacy. In both the cases the claimants were bastards; the laws
of their own country, the laws of their domicil, the laws of the spot where
the matrimonial contract was entered into, declared them to be illegitimate;
the law which by the acknowledged principles ascertained their personal status fixed upon these persons a character of illegitimacy fatal to their claims;
on the first step the ground sunk under them, and it became impossible for
them to advance. It is obvious that if, in the cases to which I am now referring, the claimants had been declared heirs by the Scottish law, the Scottish law,
admitting of no heirship without legitimacy, must have been called in aid to
bestow upon them that personal character of legitimacy refused to them by
their own law; in other words, a law foreign to their birth, to their domicil,
and to the marriage of their parents, would have been held to bestow upon
them their personal status and character, — a decision certainly contrary to

9

claimant answered to this very character. He was the eldest son,
and he was legitimate. In truth, legitimate son means lawful
son, and the rule of inheritance is, that the eldest lawful son shall
succeed the father. But *lawful or not* depends upon the law
which is to govern; and no other definition can be given of what
is lawful than this, that he is the lawful son whom the law declares such. What law? There are two, it is said, in this case:
the law of the place of the party's birth and of his parents'
marriage, and the law of place where the land lies. Then, which
law is to prevail? The law of the birth-place. Any other rule
would involve great inconvenience, and be inconsistent with
principle; for then a man would be legitimate in one place, and
illegitimate in another; legitimate as to personal property, and
illegitimate as to real property in the same country. And this
would not only affect him, but all persons who after his death
should claim through him, even purchasers claiming from him or
them.

93 *q*. Then as to the argument that *heir* means he who is
born in lawful wedlock, ex justis nuptiis. It is true. But what
is lawful wedlock? It is that which is so by the law of the place
of marriage; and there is no greater reason for being bound by
that law as to marriage, than there is as to legitimacy as consequent upon the marriage. Why may not the court look behind
the marriage, and ascertain whether the parties were competent
to marry by the law of England? It is not correct to say that
the law of the place of marriage governs as to that alone, it must
govern as to all the effects consequent thereon. So it was held
by Huberus. So it was held in the cases of Crawford *v*. Patrick,
and Strathmore *v*. Bowes, already alluded to.[1] In Scotland, the
child born before the marriage · ceremony has been performed is
legitimate, not because of the subsequent act of his parents, but
because he is considered as born in lawful wedlock. The mar-

the acknowledged principles upon this subject. The character of illegitimacy
attached to the persons of the English and American claimants by their own
law, accompanied them everywhere, and would prevent their being received as
heirs anywhere within the limits of the Christian world. This view in our
judgment renders these decisions entirely consistent with the principles I have
unfolded, and prevents our considering them as objections to the opinion I
entertain, that B is not entitled to the property in question as the heir of A.'
Birtwhistle *v*. Vardill, 9 Bligh, 45–53.

[1] Ante, s. 87.

riage is held to have preceded his birth, and so he is deemed non
legitimatus, sed legitimus ab initio. This is not a mere refinement
or fiction, because in Scotland marriage is a consensual contract ;
and such consent and marriage before the birth are deemed to be
evidenced by the subsequent open ceremony and celebration of
the marriage. This is no more a fiction than the English law as to
this very point. If, in England, a child is born the day after the
marriage, he is deemed legitimate, although procreated long
before. The law will not inquire into the fact.

93 *r.* As to the statute of Merton, it has no bearing on the
subject. That statute applies only to children born in England.
It is no authority for saying that he only can inherit English
lands whom that statute declares legitimate. That statute can
in no just sense apply to persons born out of England. Their
status, as to legitimacy, depends not on that statute, but on the
laws of the country of their birth.[1] He is legitimate whom the

---

[1] It may be far more satisfactory to the learned reader to have his lordship's reasoning at large in his own words : ' In approaching this question
there are some things not disputed. It is admitted that the validity of a marriage must depend on the law of the country where it is had, and that consequently the parents of this party were validly married. It seems also to be
agreed that, generally speaking, legitimacy is a status, and must be determined
by the law of the country to which the party belongs. But it is said by those
who support this judgment, that whether the party here is legitimate or not, is
no question before us; the only question being, it is alleged, whether or not he
is the heir to an English real estate. This distinction, I confess, appears to
me founded on an inaccurate view of the subject. It is true that the question
here arises upon the claim of an heir as such, and that therefore the only question may be said to be, whether he is heir or not. But it is also very possible
that this question may turn wholly upon another, namely, whether or not the
claimant is eldest legitimate son of his father, the person last seised? Nor do
I well see how legitimacy can ever come in question in any other way than as
connected with the claim to succession, either real or personal, in England, or
in Scotland either, unless in the single case of a declarator of bastardy or of
legitimacy, — a proceeding unknown in the English law. It is therefore by no
means sufficient for deciding this case to say that the question touches not
legitimacy, but inheritance; not the personal status of the party, but his right
to real property. It may touch both those matters, and the latter may wholly
depend upon the former. In truth, legitimate son means lawful son; and the
rule of inheritance is, that the eldest lawful son shall succeed to the father;
but *lawful or not* depends upon the law which is to govern; and no other
definition can be given of what is lawful than this, that he is lawful son whom
the law declares to be such. What law? There are two, it is said, in this
case, — the law of the place of the party's birth and of his parents' marriage,
and the law of the place where the land lies. Then which of these two laws
shall prevail? The whole inclination of every one's mind must be towards

law of his birth declares to be so.   He is lawful heir whom
the law of his birth declares to be born in lawful wedlock.   We

that law which prevails where each person is born, and where his parents were
married, supposing the countries to be one and the same; and if they differ, I
should then say certainly the law of the birthplace.   Nor can anything be
more inconvenient or more inconsistent with principle, than the inevitable consequence of taking the lex loci rei sitæ for the rule; because this makes a man
legitimate or illegitimate, according to the place where his property lies, or
rights come in question; legitimate, when he sues for distribution of personal
estate; a bastard, when he sues for succession to real; nay, legitimate in one
country, where part of his land may lie, and a bastard in some other, where he
has the residue.   So, in like manner, all who claim through him must have
their rights determined by the same vague and uncertain canon, — a circumstance which I nowhere find adverted to below.   All the learned judges proceed upon the case being one of an inheritance claimed by the party himself.
But what if he were dead years ago, and another claimed an estate in England,
to which he, the alleged bastard, never had been, and never could have been
entitled; an estate, for example, descending from a collateral, who took it by
purchase after the death of the alleged bastard?   Then the pedigree of the
claimant must be made out through legitimate persons; and the question of
legitimacy is raised as to one who is not himself claiming any land, who never
did or could claim any land, and it is not raised in respect of any right in him
to inherit, any right to be called the heir to any land.   I apprehend this shows
strongly the necessity of taking another view than the learned judges seemed
to have deemed sufficient for getting over the difficulty of the case, and of admitting that there is a status of legitimacy which is personal, and, travelling
about with the individual, must be determined by the law of his country.   In
the argument for the judgment below, it is thought enough to say that heir
means he who is born in lawful wedlock — ex justis nuptiis.   Then what is
lawful wedlock?   Is there any greater reason for being bound by the law of
the country where the marriage contract was made, in deciding whether or not
the wedlock was lawful, than there is for being governed in ascertaining the
legitimacy of the issue of the marriage by the law of the country where that
issue was born, more especially when it was also the country where the marriage was had?   But can the court stop short according to its own principle, at
the mere fact of the marriage being according to the lex loci contractus?   Do
not the principles on which their decision proceeds demand this further inquiry: Were the parties able to marry by the lex loci rei sitæ? and thus a door
is opened to the further examination of how far a preceding divorce of one of
the parties was sufficient to dissolve a previous English marriage.   All such
difficulties are got rid of by holding the lex loci contractus and nativitatis as
governing the validity of the contract and legitimacy of its issue; but they are
not to be got over in this way by any argument which does not with equal
force apply to holding that the legitimacy of the issue is a question equally to
be governed by the lex loci contractus and the law of the birthplace.   Nor is
it correct to say, as the judges below assumed, that the lex loci only influences
the validity of the contract, and extends not to its effects.   The highest authorities have held expressly the reverse.   Huber, in the treatise De Conflictu
Legum, which forms part of his larger work, and is constantly cited as the
greatest authority on this question, says: " Non solum ipsi contractus ipsæque

are necessarily driven to this conclusion ; and we must resort to the foreign law to solve all such questions.   If it is said that he

nuptiæ certis locis rite celebratæ ubique pro justis et validis habentur, *sed etiam jura et effectus* contractuum nuptiarumque in iis locis recepta *ubique* vim suam obtinebunt." I. 3, 9.   It would be difficult to state anything more clearly and properly the effect of the matrimonial contract, than the legitimacy of the issue; it is, in fact, the main object, and therefore the principal effect of that contract.   But to remove all doubt on this subject, and to extend the same rule also to the lex loci nativitatis, he adds, " Qualitates personales certo loco alicui impressas ubique circumferri et personam comitari, cum hoc effectu ut *ubiris locorum* eo jure quo tales personæ *alibi* gaudent vel subjecti sunt, gaudeantur et subjiciantur."   This principle was adopted and acted on in two very remarkable cases by your lordships then proceeding under the advice of Lord Eldon; I mean Crawford v. Patrick, and Strathmore v. Bowes.   In the former, a child having been born before marriage in America, where the English law prevails, claimed a Scotch estate in respect of the subsequent marriage of his parents there, *of whom the father was Scotch*.   He contended that, the question having arisen upon a real estate in Scotland, the Court of Session was bound to administer the law loci rei sitæ, and that law declared him legitimate.   But the court below and your lordships held that legitimacy is a status to be determined by the law of the party's birthplace, or, at any rate, by that of the country where the marriage of his parents was had, as well as himself born; and they held him bastard in Scotland, where the land lay, because he was bastard in America, where his birth and his parents' marriage took place.   In Strathmore v. Bowes, a marriage, had in London after the birth of the child, was held not to legitimate the issue either as to Scotch honors or estate on the same grounds; and in both these cases one of the points made for the judgment was the absurdity of holding the same person to be bastard in one country and legitimate in another.   It is plain that legitimacy has but one meaning, namely, born in lawful wedlock.   Now in Scotland the child born before the marriage ceremony has been performed is legitimate, not because of a subsequent act of his parents, but because he is considered as born in lawful wedlock.   The marriage is held to have preceded his birth, and according to the doctrine and language of the civil law, from which Scotland and other countries have borrowed this principle, he is considered as non legitimatus, sed legitimus ab initio.   Nor is this a mere fiction of law and a technical refinement.   Marriage in Scotland is a *consensual* contract, and perfected by consent alone.   But this may be given, and the contract made in two ways, either per verba de præsenti, or by a promise subsequente copula.   Now in the latter case, the copula makes the previous promise a consent; it turns the promise concerning the future into a present consent.   A child, then, born in the interval between the promise and the copula would be legitimate, for the copula would show that consent, and therefore a marriage had preceded his birth. But so does a marriage after the birth, for that raises the legal presumption, that there was a consent before the birth and at the cohabitation.   The cohabitation is held to have been a consent and a marriage; the ceremony is only held as evidence of that previous consent and contract.   So much is this the case, that if either party was married to another at the time of the child's birth, or during the interval between that birth and the ceremony, no legitimation takes place, because no room exists for the presumption of law that the consent or

is the lawful heir in England, who is the eldest son born within
lawful wedlock, it is but changing the position of the point; for

marriage took place before the birth. All this is certain and clear, but the
learned judges in the court below appear not to have taken it into their consideration.   The judgment is rested entirely upon the statute of Merton, and
it is contended that, by that famous act, he is declared a bastard who is born
before the marriage of his parents; no doubt so he is in England; and no doubt
bastardy, the status of bastardy, is what the English law is there dealing with.
But is this an authority for saying that he only shall inherit English lands
whom that statute declares legitimate?   It is said that the lex loci rei sitæ
must govern the succession to real estate; undoubtedly it must; and if that
law gives it in Kent to all the sons, and in Brentford to the youngest, and elsewhere to the eldest, these several sons are the heirs in those several places.
But when it is said the lawful issue shall take, I agree; I, too, say only the
legitimate son or sons shall inherit; but to find who are the legitimate sons, I
must ask the law of the birthplace, which fixes the status of legitimacy; of the
personal quality, according to Huber, that travels round everywhere with the
party.   But the argument assumes a narrower and apparently closer form still,
for it is said that the statute declares those only inheritable who are born in
marriage, and that Lord Coke accordingly defines the heir to be him who is
ex justis nuptiis procreatus.   There is in this however a great fallacy: " Born
in marriage " or not, " ex justis nuptiis procreatus " or not, is to be determined
by some law or other; it is not a question that answers itself and in one way
only.   Then what law shall determine?   Certainly either the law of the country where the party was born, or where the marriage was had; the law either
of the country where the nuptiæ were had, or where the procreatio took place.
A question might arise, where the events happened in different countries; it
might then be doubted which law should govern, which should be resorted to
for answer to the question.   But where both events happened in the same
country, as here, there seems no doubt at all in the matter.   Now the law of
the country where both the marriage and the birth took place declares that
the party was born in lawful wedlock; that he was ex justis nuptiis procreatus,
and wholly denies that he was born before marriage or out of wedlock.   But
it is said that this is a fiction, and that our law cannot import the fictions of
a foreign system, though its principles we are allowed to import.   This distinction I do not profess to comprehend; what is a fiction but a principle? It
is only one particular view which the law takes, and one doctrine which it lays
down.   Suppose a Scotch court were to deny the legitimacy of a child who was
born on the day after his parents married in England, should we not say that
a gross absurdity was committed?   Should we not say the child was born in
lawful wedlock, and hold the doctrine absurd which should question his being
lawfully begotten?   Nay, suppose a gift, in the usual terms, to the heirs of
the body lawfully begotten; we should let the child born the day after marriage
take under such a gift, although it was clearly not lawfully begotten in point
of fact.   This is a fiction exactly analogous to the Scotch fiction.   The Scotch
law presumes, against the fact, the marriage to have been had before the birth
of the child; our law presumes, against the fact, the marriage to have been
had before the cohabitation of the parents.   The fiction, or rather presumption, is parcel of the legal principle in both, and there can be no reason for importing the residue of the doctrine, and rejecting the presumption; there can

we may just as well say that he who is the eldest son born in lawful wedlock (and so the claimant is) is the lawful heir in Eng-

be no reason for importing the English law presumption into Scotland, which does not justify and require us to import the Scotch law presumption into England. It must be recollected, too, that the special verdict finds as a fact the legitimacy of the party, and not his legitimation; it finds as a fact, that he is legitimate; that is to say, lawfully born. Now we know this to mean by the Scotch law, born in lawful wedlock; but the finding in the verdict is sufficient; for legitimate, as contradistinguished from legitimated, means born in lawful wedlock, and can mean nothing else. So in the civil law, from whence this doctrine is wholly taken, both in Scotland and Holland and other countries, the child is legitimus, not legitimatus, as in the same system of jurisprudence, liber is a free man, libertinus, one of the condition of a freed man, ingenuus, one free born. If any person were found to be ingenuus by an inquisition, we should contend that he never had been a slave, though a finding of liber might leave it equivocal. In like manner, and by parity of reason, a person being found legitimate, or legitimus, and not legitimated or legitimatus, excludes the supposition of his ever having been a bastard, and shows him to be lawfully born and begotten. Suppose a Scotch estate devolved to one born before marriage, as it might by devise, or rather Scotch conveyance in the nature of devise, to the first son of A, I apprehend that, A marrying the mother the day after the devisor's death, the estate would be vested in the son, because he would become legitimate, though born before the death. But it is unnecessary to argue this, though it illustrates the principle; the fact found is, that the lessor of the plaintiff was born in Scotland legitimate, or in lawful wedlock. The cases of Crawford v. Patrick, and Strathmore v. Bowes, have been already referred to, but they require another remark. They were decided in this House, by appeal, it is true, from Scotland, and respecting the Scotch real estate, but still by this House, and upon general principles of law. Those cases were the precise converse of this; they decided the bastardy of parties, and on the distinct ground that, as Lord Redesdale said, they were 'bastard by the law of their birthplace, and therefore bastard in Scotland, where the rights claimed respected real estate.' It is not more the rule of the English law, that children born out of wedlock shall not inherit, though their parents intermarry, than it is the rule of the Scotch law that such children shall inherit, if their parents do intermarry. It is not more alien to the English law to adopt the fiction that such children are born in wedlock, than it is alien to the Scotch law to exclude this principle. The English rule being statutory can make no difference. A fixed and known principle of common law has exactly the same force with statutory provision. How then can the opposite principle be adopted in two cases identically the same? The court below says that the English law gives not an estate to the bastard eigne, and that it treats him as bastard, although by the law of his birthplace he was legitimate. The Scotch law gives the estate to the bastard eigne, regarding him as legitimate, and this House adjudged, that he should not take that estate, only because he was illegitimate by the law of his birthplace. Your lordships decided that the lex loci rei sitæ should not be regarded when it differed from the lex loci contractus et nativitatis; you decided that, when the former law declared for legitimacy, it should yield to the latter, which declared for bastardy. How can you be called upon here to decide that the lex loci rei

land. The real point in difficulty was not met nor considered by the learned judges. The very question was, whether the law of

sitæ shall not overrule the other law, and that again in favor of bastardy? I profess my inability to understand how these two decisions of the same question can in any way stand together; nor am I able to perceive that the least attention was paid by the court below to those important decisions of your lordships. I perceive that the whole argument in that court turned upon a question not in dispute here. The learned judges suppose that they decide the question when they prove that the English law is to govern the case, because the question relates to real property situated in England. Now undeniably the English law is to govern the case in one sense; the eldest lawful son is to succeed; but who that son is must be determined by the law of his birthplace, and by the fact found that, under that law, the lessor of the plaintiff is eldest lawful son. Nay, even if we take the English law to be that the lawful son or heir is he who was born in wedlock, then we have here the fact found, and found as a fact, that in the country where he was born, the party was born in wedlock. No one, it must be always borne in mind, pretends to say that the English law can in any way dispose of the whole question. Admitting that the rule cited from Lord Coke in reference to the statute of Merton is to govern us, hæres, qui ex justis nuptiis procreatus est, no one contends that the question, what are justæ nuptiæ, can be determined otherwise than by a reference to the lex loci contractus, or, it may be, loci nativitatis. To that foreign law, then, we must resort; and the only question is, at what period of our inquiry this recourse shall be had. No more need be said to show how very far from decisive of the present question that position is, which alone is argued or defended by the learned judges, namely, that the law of England must govern. It does govern, but with the aid, through the ministry, of the foreign law. The reference made to the dictum of the Master of the Rolls, in Brodie v. Barry, (2 V. & B. p. 127) does not touch the case. All that his honor there said was, that questions on real rights must follow the law of the country where the land lies. This is not denied; nor was it denied by this House, when it refused to consider W. Sheddon or J. Bowes as legitimate in respect to Scotch estates, although the law of Scotland, where those estates lay, held them both to be so; or rather would so have held, had they been born in Scotland. But while this House and the Court of Session admitted that the Scotch law must decide, they also held that the Scotch law refused estate to bastards, and that it regarded one as a bastard who was so by the law of his birthplace. That was the same case in principle with this, in every material respect. It is not easy in such a question, a question raised on the conflictus legum, to omit all considerations of convenience; inasmuch as it is principally on views of convenience that the whole doctrine of what is generally called comitas turns. One should say that nothing can be more pregnant with inconvenience, nay, that nothing can lead to consequences more strange in statement, than a doctrine which sets out with assuming legitimacy to be not a personal status, but a relation to the several countries in which rights are claimed, and indeed to the nature of different rights. That a man may be bastard in one country, and legitimate in another, seems of itself a strong position to affirm, but more staggering when it is followed up by this other, that in one and the same country he is to be regarded as bastard when he comes into one court to claim an estate in land, and legitimate when he resorts

England did not take the rule as to legitimacy, the eldest son
born within lawful wedlock, from the very status as to the points

to another to obtain personal succession; nay, that the same court of equity,
when the real estate happens to be impressed with a trust, must view him as
both bastard and legitimate, in respect of a succession to the same intestate.
Further still, should he happen to be next of kin to his uncle, who had a mortgage upon the estate, he must be denied his succession to the land of the
mortgagor in his quality of bastard, and be allowed to come in as an incum-
brancer upon the self-same estate in his capacity of legitimate son to the same
mortgagor.　All this is assumed to be the law by the learned judges, who
have decided below, and advised your lordships here.　They have not assumed,
what however they cannot deny, that it is another consequence of their doctrine, to enable a descendant of the same bastard to claim through him as if
he were legitimate, while the alleged force of the statute of Merton, and of
Lord Coke's commentary thereupon, excludes him from taking it himself.　In
the same country, in the same courts, in respect to the same land, he is both
bastard and legitimate; bastard for the purpose of his own succession, legitimate when the succession of others is concerned.　May I be permitted most
respectfully to express a doubt, whether or not this question has received all
the consideration which it deserves at the hands of those learned judges?　I
know not that it carries the argument much further, but there is a proceeding,
well known to your lordships sitting here as a court of general jurisdiction
over the whole United Kingdom, though unknown to the courts of England,
— the process of declarator.　Suppose a declarator of legitimacy had been
brought in the Scotch courts by the lessor of this plaintiff, the judgment
would have been, and quite as a matter of course, that he was lawful son of
Wm. Birtwhistle; and the present defendant being made a party to this suit,
the judgment could be given in evidence before the court where the ejectment
now before us was brought.　I agree that such a judgment does not conclusively bind; yet it would place the conflict of the two laws in a somewhat
stronger light, if the English court should pronounce him bastard whom the
Scotch court, sitting in the country of his birth, had pronounced lawful
son.　But if both judgments were brought here by appeal and writ of error,
as might easily happen, your lordships would be compelled to affirm the sentence of the Scotch court, and yet you are now asked to affirm the opposite
judgment of the King's Bench.　Let it be observed, too, that all this anomaly
is in England; it begins and ends here; for the Scotch judges have decided in
such cases with perfect consistency, as well as entire uniformity.　Those
learned persons, whose familiarity with legal principle, in its enlarged sense, is
derived from a deep study of the feudal and of the civil law, as well as of the
modern jurisprudence of Scotland, have been guided in all their determina-
tions of such questions by simple, rational, and intelligible principles.　If a
declarator of legitimacy were brought before them by one born in England
before marriage, and whose parents afterwards intermarried, their sentence
would be that he was illegitimate; and even were he to claim a Scotch estate
the law would be the same.　This has been ruled in Scotland in the cases
more than once referred to, and affirmed upon appeal here.　But you are
now advised to take a different course when the same question arises in
another part of the United Kingdom.　It may be observed that, in referring
to those Scotch cases, the learned chief justice says, without discussing them,

recognized and held by the law of Scotland. The whole constituted his personal status; and that personal status travelled with him into England. (*a*)

that it is satisfactory to him that the form of the proceeding, a special verdict, was such as to carry the question before the same tribunal which pronounced those decisions. In the advice, however, which has been given to this tribunal by the same learned judges, I do not find that those decisions have been much considered.' Birtwhistle *v.* Vardill, 9 Bligh, 71–86.

(*a*) The well-known case of *Birtwhistle* v. *Vardill*, referred to in the text, was decided in the King's Bench in 1826 (5 B. & C. 438; 8 D. & R. 185). The point determined was that a child born in Scotland before the marriage of his parents, who were domiciled in that country and afterwards intermarried there, could not inherit land in England as the heir of his father, because by the law of England the heir must be a person ex justis nuptiis procreatus, although by the law of Scotland a child born of unmarried parents is rendered legitimate by their subsequent marriage. The case was an action of ejectment brought by John Birtwhistle, claiming to inherit land in England as the eldest son of the brother of the person last seised. His parents, who were domiciled in Scotland, were not married at the time of his birth, but were married afterwards. Judgment having been given for the defendant, a writ of error was brought in the House of Lords, and in 1830, Alexander, C.B., delivered the opinion of all the judges, which was against the plaintiff's claim, and is above quoted by the author (ante, s. 93 *o*.). The further consideration of the case was then adjourned. In 1835, Lord Brougham, who had argued before the House in 1830 in support of the judgment (2 Cl. & F. at p. 582), expressed the doubts concerning its correctness which have been mentioned by the author. It was then ordered that the case be re-argued. 9 Bligh, 32; 2 Cl. & F. 571. The second argument took place in 1839, and the judges again attended, and their unanimous opinion was that the claimant was not entitled as heir to land in England. Their opinion was delivered by Tindal, C.J., who in 1826 had argued as counsel for the plaintiff in the King's Bench (5 B. & C. at p. 440; 8 D. & R. at p. 186). The further consideration of the case was again postponed, and in 1840 Lord Brougham, after acknowledging that the last opinion of the judges had made very valuable additions to the former opinion, and after mentioning some doubts which he still felt, declared that he should offer no opposition to judgment for the defendant. The Lord Chancellor (Lord Cottenham) expressed his concurrence in the opinion of the judges, and his satisfaction with the ground upon which they put it. Judgment was accordingly given for the defendant. 7 Cl. & F. 895; West H. L. 500; 6 Bing. N.C. 385; 1 Scott N. R. 828; 1 Robinson App. Cas. 627. The grounds of the opinion delivered by Tindal, C.J., upon which the final decision of the case rests, are substantially these: That it is a rule or maxim of the law of England with respect to the descent of land in England from father to son, that the son must be born after actual marriage between his father and mother; that this is a rule juris positivi, as are all the laws which regulate succession to real property, this particular rule having been framed for the direct purpose of excluding, in the descent of land in England, the application of the rule of the civil and canon law, by which the sub-

93 s. Subsequent Marriage in a different Country from that of the Birth. — Another question also has arisen in England, whether a

sequent marriage between the father and mother was held to make the son born before marriage legitimate; and that this rule of descent being a rule of positive law annexed to the land itself, cannot be allowed to be broken in upon or disturbed by the law of the country where the claimant was born, and which may be allowed to govern his personal status as to legitimacy, upon the supposed ground of the comity of nations. To understand the nature and force of this rule, 'that the heir must be a person born in actual matrimony in order to enable him to take land in England by descent,' and to perceive the positive and inflexible quality of this rule, and how closely it is annexed to the land itself, it is necessary to consider the earlier authorities both before and subsequently to the statute of Merton, and more particularly the legal construction and operation of that statute. If we take the definition of heir, which Lord Coke adopts from the ancient text-writers, and which is borrowed originally from the Roman law (Co. Lit. 7 b.) viz., that he is 'ex justis nuptiis procreatus,' the very description points at a marriage celebrated according to the rules, requisites, and ritual of the civil or Roman law. But to refer to the Mirror of Justices, perhaps the very earliest of our text-books, — it is there laid down (p. 70) as an admitted principle, 'that the common law only taketh him to be a son whom the marriage proveth to be so.' Glanville, who wrote in the reign of Henry II. (probably about half a century before the statute of Merton) states (b. 7, c. 13) that 'neither a bastard nor any person not born in lawful wedlock can be, in the legal sense of the word, an heir; but if any one claims an inheritance in the character of heir, and the other party object to him that he cannot be heir because he was not born

in lawful wedlock, then indeed the plea shall cease in the King's Court, and the archbishop, or bishop of the place, shall be commanded to inquire concerning such marriage, and to make known his decision either to the King or his justices.' In chapter 14 he gives the form of the writ, viz., ' The King to the Archbishop: Health. W. appearing before me in my Court, has demanded against R., his brother, certain land, and in which the said R. has no right, as W. says, because he is a bastard born before the marriage of their mother; and since it does not belong to my Court to inquire concerning bastardy, I send these unto you, commanding you that you do, in the Court Christian, that which belongs to you; and when the suit is brought to its proper end before you, inform me by your letter what has been done before you concerning it. Witness,' &c. This writ puts the objection against the heir's title upon the very rule of the English law, ' that he was born before the marriage of his mother.' If the question had been put generally on the fact whether any marriage had taken place, or upon the legality of such marriage as had taken place, to such a question of general bastardy, as it is called, the bishop would have found no difficulty in answering. But as the canon law, on the one hand, held that the subsequent marriage of the parents made the antenatus legitimate, and as the common law of England, on the other hand, held that such antenatus was not legitimate for the purpose of inheriting land in England, if the question had gone in the general form, the answer of the bishop would have certified such antenatus to have been legitimate. The law therefore framed the question in the precise form contained in the writ, namely, a question of special bastardy. The bishops being placed in the difficulty

child born before marriage in one country, of parents domiciled in that country, by whose laws a subsequent marriage would not

of this conflictus legum, at length the statute of Merton was framed in the 20th of Henry III. That statute has not upon the original roll the title prefixed thereto, [viz. 'He is a bastard who is born before the marriage of his parents.' 7 Cl. & F. 945], upon which observations were made at the bar, that it showed the intention of the law to have been no more than to declare the personal status of those who are described in such statute. In the edition of the statutes published under the commission from the crown, there is no other than the general title 'Provisiones de Merton;' and no more argument can justly be built upon the title prefixed in some editions of the statutes, than upon the marginal notes against its different sections. That statute or provision of Merton runs thus, viz., 'To the King's writ of bastardy, whether any one being born before matrimony may inherit in like manner as he that is born after matrimony, all the bishops answered that they would not nor could not make answer to that writ, because it was directly against the common order of the church, and all the bishops instanted the lords that they would consent that all such as were born afore matrimony should be legitimate, as well as they that be born within matrimony, as to the succession to inheritance, forasmuch as the church accepteth such as legitimate. And all the earls and barons, with one voice, answered that they would not change the laws of the realm which hitherto had been used and approved.' It is manifest from Bracton, who lived and wrote in the time of Henry III., that shortly after the statute of Merton this question of special bastardy ceased to be sent to the bishop, and became the subject of inquiry and determination in the King's Court (b. 5, c. 19). At the time of the passing of the sta-

tute of Merton, the dominions of the crown included Normandy, Aquitaine, and Anjou, where the rule of the civil and canon law prevailed, by which the subsequent marriage makes the antenatus legitimate for all purposes and to all intents. Yet there is not the slightest allusion to any exception as to those born in the foreign dominions of the crown. There seems no reasonable or probable ground for the surmise of any intention in the lawmakers of that day, that, with the general refusal and repudiation of this rule of the civil and canon law as to the hereditary succession to land in England, there should be a tacit exception in favor of a claimant born beyond the seas. And it would be singular indeed, if any such exception existed, that neither Bracton, who wrote with so much diffuseness on this very question at the time of this notable refusal of parliament to alter the law, nor the authority of Fleta, nor of any of the other early writers, should have left the slightest vestige of an allusion to such exception in the rule. It therefore appears to be the just conclusion from these premises that the rule of descent to English land is, that the heir must be born after actual marriage of his father and mother, in order to enable him to inherit; and that this is a rule of a positive inflexible nature, applying to and inherent in the land itself, which is the subject of descent, of the same nature and character as that rule which prohibited the descent of land to any but those who were of the whole blood to the last taker, or like the custom of gavelkind or borough-English, which causes the land to descend, in the one case, to all the sons together, in the other, to the younger son alone. The broad proposition contended for on the part of the plaintiff is, that legitimacy is a personal status to be determined by

legitimate him, would, by a marriage of his parents in another country, by whose laws such subsequent marriage would legitimate him, become legitimate, so as to inherit lands in the latter country. It has been held by the House of Lords that the mere fact of marriage in such country, where there was no change of the domicil of the parents, would not give him such a capacity to inherit land, and that the stain of illegitimacy by his birth was not wiped away by such a marriage.[1] And it was intimated that,

[1] Munro v. Saunders, 6 Bligh, 468; Rose v. Ross, 4 Wils. & Shaw, 289. See Id. App. p. 33–89, where the opinions of the Scotch judges are also given at large.

the law of the country which gives the party birth, and that, when the law of that country has once pronounced him to be legitimate, he is, by the comity of international law, to be considered as legitimate in every other country also, and for every purpose. Now there can be no doubt but that the marriage, which is a personal contract, when entered into according to the rites of the country where the parties are domiciled and the marriage celebrated, would be considered and treated as a perfect and complete marriage throughout the whole of Christendom. But it does not therefore follow that, with the adoption of the marriage contract, the foreign law adopts also all the conclusions and consequences which hold good in the country where the marriage was celebrated. But admitting, for the sake of argument, that B, legitimate in Scotland, is to be taken to be legitimate all over the world, the question still recurs, whether, for the purpose of constituting an heir to land in England, something more is not necessary to be proved on his part than such legitimacy; and, if the grounds are right upon which the first point was rested, one other step is necessary, namely, to prove that he was born after an actual marriage between his parents; and if this be so, then, upon the distinction admitted by all the writers on international law, the lex loci rei sitæ must prevail, not the law of the place of birth. In the course of the discussion some stress appears to have been placed on the argument that, if the claimant had died before the intestate, leaving a child, such child might have inherited to the intestate, tracing through his legitimate parent; and then it was asked, if the child might inherit, why might not the parent himself inherit? But the answer to the supposed case appears to be, that if the parent be not capable of inheriting himself, he has no heritable blood which he can transmit to his child; so that the child could not, under the assumed facts, have inherited, and the question therefore becomes, in truth, the same as that before us. 7 Cl. & F. 925-938.

In Re Don's Estate, 4 Drew. 194, it was held that the provision of the Inheritance Act (3 & 4 Will. 4, c. 106, s. 6), that the lineal ancestor should be heir to his issue, in preference to certain collaterals, made the ancestor heir only to such of his issue as were capable of inheriting from him; consequently a domiciled Scotchman could not inherit land in England from his son who was born in Scotland before the marriage of his parents, and was legitimated by their subsequent marriage.

See note on *Legitimation and Adoption* at the end of s. 93 s, post.

under the like circumstances in other respects, the change of
domicil of the parents to the country where the marriage was
celebrated, would not have given any better title to inherit, as
the stain of the illegitimacy would be indelible.[1]   The converse
case has been decided in France, where it has been held that if
a child is born in a country (France) where he would become
legitimate by a subsequent marriage, he will become legitimate
by such subsequent marriage, although the marriage should take
place in a country (England) where a different law prevails,
and where a subsequent marriage would not have the effect of
rendering him legitimate.[2]   The result of these two cases seems to
be, that the law of the place of birth of the child, and not the law
of the place of the marriage of the parents, is to decide whether
a subsequent marriage will legitimate the child or not.[3] (a)

[1] Munro v. Saunders, 6 Bligh, 468; Rose v. Ross, 4 Wils. & Shaw, 289; Id.
Appx. p. 33–89.   See 1 Burge, Col. & For. Law, pt. 1, c. 3, s. 2, p. 108–110.

[2] The case of De Conty, 1668, cited by Lord Brougham in Munro v. Saunders, 6 Bligh, 478, and in Rose v. Ross, 4 Wils. & Shaw, 299.   The same case
is reported in Merlin, Quest. de Droit, art. Légitimation, s. 2, note (1), p. 151,
4to ed., Paris, 1828, who corrects the error into which Boullenois had fallen
in stating the facts of the same case.   See also 1 Burge, Col. & For. Law,
pt. 1, c. 1, s. 2, p. 102, 106, 107.   May there not be room for a distinction in
such a case, as to the state of the party or property in the country of his birth,
and that of the party or the property in the country of the marriage, each
country adhering to its own laws in regard to the property situate there?

[3] But see the elaborate opinions of the Scottish judges on the same questions,
in Rose v. Ross, 4 Wils. & Shaw, Appx. p. 33–89.   The House of Lords reversed their judgment.

(a) *Legitimation and Adoption.* —
When a person claims a right of succession to property in a character acquired
by a foreign law, it is necessary to ascertain that the character thus acquired
is, not only in name, but in fact, the
one which gives him that right according to the law which governs the succession.   It makes no difference whether
the property is movable or immovable.
Succession to the former depends on
the law of the owner's domicil (s. 481,
post).   The latter devolves according
to the law of the situs (s. 483, post).
For example, if the owner be a person
domiciled in England, both his immovable property in England and the
whole of his movable property, where-
ever it may be, devolve at his death
upon the persons designated by the
law of England to succeed to it.
Whoever claims to succeed to either
must answer the description contained
in the common law or the statute law
of England.   When the common law
declares that the real estate shall descend to the *eldest son*, or when the
statute provides that the personal estate shall be distributed among *children*, the heir must be the *son*, and
the persons entitled to share in the
distribution must be *children*, in the
sense in which those words are used in
the English law.   This is not merely
a question of status; it is a question of
description.   With regard to persons

93 t. *Foreign Jurists.* — We have already seen that the same doctrine upon these very points is maintained by Hertius, by

whose personal status is governed by English law, the word *son* or *child* always means a son or child born in wedlock. Legitimation per subsequens matrimonium and adoption do not exist by that law. Consequently no one whose status is governed by English law answers the description of a *son* or *child* unless he was born in wedlock. But the right of succession may be claimed by a person whose status is governed by the law of a foreign country, and by that law he may have the status of a child, although not born in wedlock. He may have been legitimated by the subsequent marriage of his parents, or by an act of the legislature without any such marriage, or he may have been adopted as the child of a person not related to him by blood. The question still remains whether he is what is meant in the English law by *child*. When the word is used in a law regulating the succession to real estate in England, or the personal estate of a person domiciled in England at his decease, does it mean what it does when it is applied to an English child, or has it whatever meaning may be given to it by the law of any foreign country where the claimant may be domiciled? If the latter be its meaning, then a word used in the English law cannot be defined except as meaning whatever may in any country be called by that name. It is difficult to believe that words are used in that way in the laws of any country. Before mentioning the cases upon the subject, it may be remarked that the presumption which seems the natural one is, that the words of an English law are used in the English sense, and that when the word *child* is used, it always has the meaning which it has when it is applied to English people. If this be so, a person cannot succeed to pro-

perty by virtue of an English law as the *son* or *child* of another, unless he is a child of that person born in wedlock, notwithstanding he may be his son or child by the law of the domicil. It is upon a similar principle that a marriage contracted in a polygamous country between parties belonging to it is not in other countries considered as a marriage. Hyde *v.* Hyde, L. R. 1 P. & M. 130; Harvey *v.* Farnie, 6 P. D. p. 53; Ross *v.* Ross, 129 Mass. p. 247. The reason is that the union of a man and a woman in a polygamous country is in its nature a different relation from that which is called marriage in other countries. The latter is defined as the 'union for life of one man and one woman, to the exclusion of all others.' The very terms of the former allow a plurality of wives. And ' the use of a common term to express these two separate relations will not make them one and the same, though it may tend to confuse them to a superficial observer.' Hyde *v.* Hyde, L. R. 1 P. & M. 130.

In a country where legitimation per subsequens matrimonium is allowed by law, a child legitimated in another country by such a marriage would be a child in the sense in which the term is used in the former. So a child by adoption would be recognized as a child in a country where adoption exists, and gives to an adopted child the status of a child. But it is necessary that legitimation per subsequens matrimonium in the one case, and adoption in the other, should be allowed by the laws of both countries. If it is not allowed in the country of the domicil, by the law of which his status is governed, the subsequent marriage does not legitimate him, and he does not by the adoption acquire the status of a child of the person who adopts him. If it is not allowed in the coun-

Bouhier, and by Boullenois.[1] The latter puts the very case of a child born in England in concubinage, and whose parents after-

[1] Ante, s. 93 d, 93 i.

try by the law of which he claims the right of succession, he is not, as it would seem, what is called a child in that country, although in the country of his domicil he may have the status to which that term is there applied.

None of the difficulties that have been mentioned arise when the right of succession to movables is claimed by virtue of a status acquired in a foreign country in which the owner was domiciled at his decease. The succession is governed by the law of the owner's domicil, and the only inquiry open is whether that law gives the claimant the right he asserts.

In Birtwhistle v. Vardill (supra, s. 93 r, note; 7 Cl. & F. 895) the plaintiff was a Scotchman who was born before the marriage of his parents, but was legitimated according to the law of Scotland by their subsequent marriage. His father's brother died seised of land in England, and the plaintiff claimed it as his heir. It was contended in his behalf that his legitimacy was a question of status to be determined by the law of Scotland, and by that law he was the eldest legitimate son of his father. This was not disputed; but it was answered, and the decision was put upon the ground, that it was a rule of English law with respect to the descent of land, that a person claiming to inherit land in England as the son of another must be a son born after actual marriage between his father and mother. Although this rule was laid down in respect only of the descent of land, which was the subject of the case, yet it is difficult not to think that the real foundation of the rule was in the meaning which the law of England attaches to the word *son*, and that the reason of the rule is that a person is not what is called a *son* in English law unless he was born in wedlock.

It is to be noticed that the Mirror of Justices, p. 70, the earliest authority cited by Tindal, C.J., in the opinion delivered to the House of Lords (7 Cl. & F. 926) states the principle in these words: '*that the common law only taketh him to be a son whom the marriage proveth to be so.*' The rule applied in Birtwhistle v. Vardill seems to be nothing else than this principle stated solely with reference to the descent of land. The decision is sometimes supposed to have depended upon the statute of Merton, which related only to inheritance of land. But Tindal, C.J., showed, by authorities before that statute, that the rule had an earlier existence. The statute was in terms nothing but a refusal by the barons to change an existing rule of law. Lord Brougham, who alone opposed the decision in Birtwhistle v. Vardill, said in Fenton v. Livingstone, 3 Macq. p. 532, that the former case, ' in some of the opinions of the learned judges below is supposed to have been decided in consequence of a statutory provision; but the statute of Merton is only declaratory of the common law, or rather it is a refusal to alter that law.'

In Pennsylvania and Alabama, Birtwhistle v. Vardill was followed, in Smith v. Derr, 34 Pa. St. 126; Lingen v. Lingen, 45 Ala. 410; and was cited with approval in Maryland, in Barnum v. Barnum, 42 Md. 251, 307.

In Boyes v. Bedale, 1 H. & M. 798, an illegitimate daughter, who was born in France, and whose parents were domiciled there, was legitimated according to the French law upon their subsequent marriage. Her father's uncle, a domiciled Englishman, had bequeathed a sum of money to her father's 'children.' Wood, V.C., held that she could not take under the will

wards become residents in France and there intermarry without being naturalized, and says that the child is not legitimated by

as a child. He said: 'When the testator speaks of the children of his nephew, he does so simpliciter, and he must mean such persons as the law of England would regard as the nephew's children. The testator cannot be assumed to know that there is any other kind of child extant.' He added: 'I take it that the language of the statute of distributions would be dealt with in the same way. If an intestate dies domiciled in England, the division of his property is governed throughout by English law, and no person could take by representation under that statute unless legitimate by the law of England.'

In In re Wilson's Trusts, L. R. 1 Eq. 247, 263, Kindersley, V.C., stated the rule in these words: 'Now, the will, being a will made in England by an Englishman domiciled in England, must be construed according to the law of England. Every term in it must receive that interpretation which belongs to it according to English law. What is the interpretation which the law of England gives to the word *children*. Undoubtedly children lawfully begotten, ex justis nuptiis procreatos; unless indeed there be something in the context which satisfies the court that the testator meant to use the expression in a different sense.'

The case of In re Goodman's Trusts, 14 Ch. D. 619; 17 Ch. D. 266, raised the same question under the statute of distributions. A daughter of unmarried parents domiciled in Holland, who was legitimated according to the Dutch law upon their subsequent marriage, claimed a share of the personal estate of her father's sister, who had died intestate domiciled in England. The words of the statute under which she claimed were *brothers' and sisters' children.* Jessel, M.R., held that the word *children* in the statute meant

exactly what Wood, V.C., said it meant in the will of a domiciled Englishman (Boyes *v.* Bedale, supra), that is, children according to the English law, and he therefore decided that she was not entitled to a share. He referred to the dictum of Wood, V.C., with regard to the statute of distributions, and said: 'If I had any doubt upon the subject in this case, I should follow the dictum; but in fact I feel no doubt whatever.' He also quoted with approval the remarks of Kindersley, V.C., in In re Wilson's Trusts (supra).

This decision of Jessel, M.R., in In re Goodman's Trusts, was reversed on appeal by James and Cotton, L.JJ., Lush, L.J., dissenting (17 Ch. D. 266). Cotton, L.J., said in delivering judgment: 'It was urged in support of the decision of the Master of the Rolls that the law of England recognizes as legitimate those children only who are born in wedlock. This is correct as regards the children of persons who at the time of the children's birth are domiciled in England. But the question as to legitimacy is one of status, and in my opinion by the law of England questions of status depend on the law of domicil.' Further on he said: 'I am of opinion that, if a child is legitimate by the law of the country where at the time of its birth its parents were domiciled, the law of England, except in the case of succession to real estate in England, recognizes and acts on the status thus declared by the law of the domicil. In fact the respondents wish to use the proposition, that "in an English act of parliament those only are next of kin or children of a deceased brother whom the law of England recognizes as legitimate," as if it were "whom the law of England would recognize as legitimate if, at the time of their birth, their domicil, that is,

10

such subsequent marriage, but remains illegitimate, as he was by the law of the country of his birth. The converse case of a

the domicil of their parents, had been English."' James, L.J., concurred in the judgment of Cotton, L.J., ' both in the conclusion and reasoning.' The above extracts show that it placed the decision upon the question of legitimacy. *Legitimacy* means lawfulness; and the law which it suggests is the law that governs the status, that is, the law of their domicil. By that law it must be determined whether the status was lawfully established or not. But it is clear that one may be the lawful child of another by the law of their domicil, and yet not be his child at all in the sense attached to the word in another country. It would be so if in an act of the legislature of the latter, in which the word *child* was used, an interpretation clause should provide, ' the word *child* in this act means a son or daughter born in wedlock.' And, without any statutory definition, this may be its meaning in both the common and statute law of a country. Wood, V.C., Kindersley, V.C., Jessel, M.R., and Lush, L.J., decided that it had that meaning in the law of England. Jessel, M.R., decided this case upon the word *child*. The judgment of Cotton, L.J., places the decision upon the word *legitimate*. Its effect however is, that whenever a person is the legitimate child of another by the law of the country where he was domiciled at his birth, he will be deemed a child of that person in the sense attached to the word in the law of England, except in cases of succession to real estate. According to this decision, the word *child* as used in the English law cannot be defined more precisely than as meaning whoever may be called a child according to the law of the country of the domicil. If legitimated children are entitled as children to share

in a distribution under the English statute, it seems to follow that the offspring of a connection that would not be treated as a marriage — for example, a polygamous marriage — would also be entitled as children, and that adopted children would have the same right. It will thus be in the power of any country, by adoption or decree or otherwise, to confer on any one domiciled there at his birth the status of a child, which will give him the right to succeed to property under the law of England, although that kind of children is unknown to English law.

Although Cotton, L.J., says that the question as to legitimacy is one of status, and that questions of status depend on the law of the domicil, yet it will be noticed that he afterwards says that the question whether a person is legitimate depends on the law of the place where his domicil was at the time of his birth. As a child born out of wedlock is not legitimate at the time of his birth, it is difficult to see why the law of the place where he was domiciled then should determine whether he is legitimated by an act done after his status has become subject to a different law. This point is discussed in the latter part of this note.

The decision of the Court of Appeal in In re Goodman's Trusts must be taken as the expression of the law of England until questioned before the House of Lords, but it leaves that law in a most unsatisfactory state. It is the decision of two Lords Justices opposed to the opinion of the other Lord Justice and the Master of the Rolls. The four judges, who heard the case in the first instance and on appeal were thus equally divided. The two whose opinion did not prevail were supported in their opinion by the previous decisions of Wood, V.C., and Kindersley, V.C.

child born in France, and the parents subsequently intermarrying in England, he holds equally clear, and that thereby the child

In a previous case of Goodman *v.* Goodman, 3 Giff. 643, the same legitimated daughter was held to be entitled, as one of her father's children, to a share of her grandfather's estate. But the only question raised in this case was whether her father was domiciled in Holland at the time of her birth. It was assumed that if he was domiciled there, she would be entitled as a child, but the question was not raised or decided. This was pointed out by Kindersley, V.C., in In re Wilson's Trusts, L. R. 1 Eq. 265, and by Jessel, M.R., in In re Goodman's Trusts, 14 Ch. D. 622.

Skottowe *v.* Young, L. R. 11 Eq. 474, was a case of legacy duty. An Englishman domiciled in France devised his real estate in England to trustees to sell and to divide the proceeds among his daughters. They were born in France and had been legitimated according to the French law upon the subsequent marriage of their parents. The question was whether they were to be considered, in fixing the amount of legacy duty, as his *children* or as *strangers in blood*. It was admitted that the subject of the gift was liable to legacy duty, presumably because it was the proceeds of land in England, as the personal estate of a person domiciled in a foreign country is not liable to legacy duty or succession duty. Thomson *v.* Adv.-Gen., 12 Cl. & F. 1; Wallace *v.* Att.-Gen., L. R. 1 Ch. 1. Stuart, V.C., held that they were to be considered as *children*. He said, 'If, as seems clear, the daughters of the testator are legitimate by the law of France, and must therefore in this country be considered as having the status of children, it is difficult to see how, in any sense, they can be *strangers in blood*.' This decision is right if that of the Court of Appeal

in In re Goodman's Trusts is right, but not otherwise. The words *children* and *strangers in blood*, were those of an English statute, and unless they had any meaning that might be given to them in a foreign country, the daughters were strangers in blood and not children. It has since been held that natural children whose parents were never married, were strangers in blood to their father, although their parents were domiciled in Italy when the children were born, and afterwards recognized them as their children, and by the law of Italy natural children who have been recognized are entitled as such to a right of succession. Atkinson *v.* Anderson, 21 Ch. D. 100.

In Maryland, in Barnum *v.* Barnum, 42 Md. 251, 306, an illegitimate child of a son of a testator domiciled in Maryland claimed a share of property which the testator had given by his will, after the decease of his children, to their children or descendants. The child was born in Arkansas, and by an act of the legislature of that state it was enacted that he was thereby constituted the heir of his father. The Maryland court held that this act had no operation out of Arkansas, and added that, even if it had professed to legitimate the child without reference to previous marriage, no rights under the testator's will could be affected by it, and that this seemed clear both upon reason and authority.

In Illinois, where the laws provide for the adoption of children, a child adopted in another state is treated, for the purpose of inheritance, as a child of his parents by adoption so far only as a child adopted in Illinois would be so treated, whatever may be the law of the state where he was adopted. A child adopted in Illinois is, for the purpose of inheritance from his parents by adoption, their child. But the

will become legitimate.[1] Boullenois has, as we have also seen, pushed his doctrine much further, further indeed than seems

[1] Ibid.; 1 Boullenois, obs. 4, p. 62, 63.

adoption creates no relation between him and their kindred. Accordingly a daughter adopted in another state cannot succeed to real estate in Illinois as the sister of a daughter born in wedlock to the father by adoption. Keegan v. Geraghty, 101 Ill. 26. This is strictly in accordance with what is above suggested as the true principle. If adoption did not exist in Illinois, a child adopted in another state would not be a child at all within the meaning of the laws of Illinois concerning the succession to property. So if legitimation per subsequens matrimonium did not exist there, a child legitimated elsewhere by a subsequent marriage would not be a child within the meaning of such laws.

In Louisiana a different principle was acted upon in Scott v. Key, 11 La. An. 232. A child, whose parents were never married, had been legitimated by an act of the legislature of Arkansas, where he and his putative father resided. A majority of the court held that the personal status thus acquired gave him the right to inherit real estate in Louisiana, although legitimate children only could inherit, and that mode of legitimation was unknown in Louisiana. Merrick, C.J., dissented, and expressed the opinion that if they allowed such an act to have extraterritorial effect, they would allow another state to provide a new class of heirs for immovables and successions in Louisiana; but he thought that they ought to give effect to a foreign legitimation 'where our own statute recognizes a mode of legitimation by acknowledgment by notarial act and subsequent marriage, although the form in which it has been done in another state differs from our own.' See Succession of Caballero, 24 La. An. 573.

In the cases that have thus far been mentioned, a child who has been legitimated or adopted according to the law of his domicil, has claimed to succeed to property in the character of a child, under the laws of a country where legitimation or adoption does not prevail or does not confer the same rights as in the place of his domicil. There is another class of cases in which legitimation per subsequens matrimonium prevails in the country where the right of succession is claimed, but not in the country of the domicil. In these cases a subsequent marriage does not legitimate a child born before marriage, for the law of his domicil governs his status. Therefore he cannot claim to be recognized as a child even where legitimated children answer the description of children. Shedden v. Patrick, Morison Dict. Dec. Foreign, Appx. no. 6; 5 Paton, 194; Strathmore Peerage Case, 4 Wils. & S. Appx. 89; 6 Paton, 645; Rose v. Ross or Munro v. Saunders, 4 Wils. & S. 289; 6 Bligh, 468; Smith v. Kelly, 23 Miss. 167. It is sometimes contended that it follows from this class of cases, that if a child is legitimated according to the law of the domicil, he must be recognized as a child in every country. He will be recognized as a child wherever legitimation per subsequens matrimonium prevails. But it by no means follows that in a country where such legitimation is unknown to the law, a legitimated child will answer the description of *child* in the laws giving a right of succession to children.

The Indiana case of Harvey v. Ball, 32 Ind. 98, should be mentioned, though it does not touch the general question under consideration, since it turned entirely on the construction of a statute. The court held that by the Indiana statute of descent an illegitimate

consistent with any just principle, especially in giving a retro-
active effect to a subsequent naturalization in another country.[1]

[1] Ibid.; Merlin, in his Quest. de Droit, art. Légitimation, s. 2, n. 1, com-
bats this doctrine of Boullenois.

child, acknowledged by his father after marriage with the mother, inherited land in Indiana as heir to his father, although by the law of his own state he was not legitimated. The interpretation of the statute is alone open to criticism.

When adoption prevails in the country of the domicil and in the country where a right of succession is claimed by virtue of it, and the adoption has a similar effect in both, the status of an adopted child acquired in the former is recognized in the latter. It was accordingly held in Massachusetts, that a child adopted in Pennsylvania was entitled to inherit land in Massachusetts as a *child* of his father by adoption. Ross v. Ross, 129 Mass. 243. Gray, C.J., in delivering judgment says, ' It is a general principle that the status or condition of a person, the relation in which he stands to another person, and by which he is qualified or made capable to take certain rights in that other's property, is fixed by the law of the domicil; and that this status and capacity are to be recognized and upheld in every other state, so far as they are not inconsistent with its own laws and policy.' In Keegan v. Geraghty, 101 Ill. 26, which is mentioned above, the court said that they were not disposed to question the general principle, so announced, with its limitation, but held that, according to this principle, a child adopted in the place of the domicil could not take under the Illinois statute of descent if a child adopted in Illinois could not have taken under similar circumstances.

When the law of a country recognizes as children those who have been legitimated according to the law of a foreign country, there is a question whether their legitimation depends upon the law of the domicil at the time of their birth, or upon that of the domicil at the time of the act constituting the legitimation, or upon both. The opinion of Savigny and of Bar is that legitimation depends on the law of the domicil at the time of the act constituting the legitimation. Savigny, Priv. Int. Law, s. 380 (Guthrie's trans.) 250, 260. See also In re Goodman's Trusts, 14 Ch. D. p. 623; Ross v. Ross, 129 Mass. p. 256. But Wood, V.C., held, in In re Wright's Trusts, 2 K. & J. 595, that there could be no legitimation except when it could be effected in the country where the father was domiciled at the time of the child's birth. The same judge, in Udny v. Udny, L. R. 1 H. L. Sc. p. 447, said that he saw no reason to retract that opinion. The judgments of James and Cotton, L.JJ., in In re Goodman's Trusts, 17 Ch. D. 266, contain dicta to the same effect. The reasons for this doctrine are not clear. The principle stated by Cotton, L. J., in the case last mentioned seems to be opposed to it. He says (p. 291) that the question as to legitimacy is one of status, and that questions of status depend on the law of the domicil. He states (p. 292), as the opinion of Lord Stowell, that ' the status, or condition of a claimant must be tried by reference to the law of the country where that status originated.' In cases of legitimation by a subsequent marriage, the status of legitimacy originates at the time of the marriage, and does not relate back to the birth. Shedden v. Patrick, 1 Macq. 535, 623, 641. It would seem to follow that the status should be ascertained by a reference to the law of the domicil at the time of the marriage, and that the

93 u. Merlin supports the same general doctrine, holding that it is impossible to consider as legitimate in France a natural

law of England should withdraw altogether and leave the question of status to that law. Jessel, M.R., said in In re Goodman's Trusts, 14 Ch. D. p. 623, that if the daughter who was born after her parents had become domiciled in Holland, and who was legitimated according to the Dutch law upon their subsequent marriage, was entitled to share in the distribution, he did not see on what ground the other children were excluded, who were born when their parents had an English domicil, and who were also legitimated by the Dutch law upon the marriage of their parents, which took place after the domicil in Holland had been acquired.

The decision of Wood, V.C., in In re Wright's Trusts, 2 K. & J. 595, seems to have proceeded upon the theory that the law of the father's domicil fastened on the child, and could not be shaken off upon a change of domicil. In other cases where the law of the domicil determines the validity or effect of an act, the domicil referred to is that which exists at the time of the act, and it is not easy to see why it should not be so in questions of legitimation. Wood, V.C., considered that Munro v. Munro (infra) was a conclusive authority for his decision.

In Munro v. Munro, 7 Cl. & F. 842; 1 Rob. App. 492; 16 Shaw, 18; and Dalhousie v. M'Douall, 7 Cl. & F. 817; 1 Rob. App. 475; 16 Shaw, 6, it was held that an illegitimate child of a Scotchman whose domicil was Scotch at the time of the birth, and continued to be so at the time of his subsequent marriage with the mother, was legitimated by the marriage, and so was entitled to succeed to Scotch estates as heir to the father, although the child was born in England, and the marriage was celebrated in England, and the

mother had an English domicil. Lord Cottenham, L.C., said that, ' as the laws of every country generally affect all those who have their domicil in such country, it would appear that, in order to bring any particular case within this rule of the law of Scotland [as to legitimation], it could only be necessary to show that the domicil of the parties was Scotch. . . . It can hardly be contended that the country in which the marriage takes place is material. . . . But if the place of the marriage be not material, still less can the place of the birth be so considered. The law of Scotland assumes that what in that country is considered as equivalent to a marriage took place before the birth or conception of the child. If that be assumed, how can it be material in what country the child was born? . . . It has been assumed in argument that any of such children born in a country which allowed legitimation per subsequens matrimonium would be legitimate in Scotland, but not if born in England, or in any other country which did not recognize such legitimation. This argument is founded upon the supposed indelibility of bastardy, and seems to have its origin in the circumstance of some very learned persons having used expressions applicable to English law upon a question of purely Scotch law. If English parents have a child born in another country, could the legitimacy of such child in England be affected by any law of such country? The effect of a Scotch marriage must be judged of with reference to Scotch law, and that law not only does not admit the doctrine of the indelibility of bastardy, but, on the contrary, holds that no bastardy is indelible, unless the parents were at the time of the birth incapable of marrying. If there-

child, born in England of English parents who afterwards intermarry in England;[1] but that a natural child, born in France of
French parents who should afterwards remove to England and
there intermarry without being naturalized, would by such subsequent marriage be made legitimate.[2] In each case he holds that

[1] Merlin, Quest. de Droit, art. Légitimation, s. 1, n. 1.
[2] Ibid. s. 2, n. 1, 2.

fore the law of England be imported
into the consideration, the effect of
the Scotch marriage is judged of, not
by the law of Scotland, but by the law
of England.' He came to the conclusion (p. 874) 'that the child of a
Scotchman, though born in England,
would become legitimate for all civil
purposes in Scotland by a subsequent
marriage of the parents in England,
if the domicil of the father was and
continued throughout to be Scotch.'
At the end of his judgment he said
that the claimant, ' being the child
of a domiciled Scotchman, had, at the
moment of her birth, a capacity for
being legitimated by the subsequent
marriage,' and that she accordingly
by the subsequent marriage became
legitimate and capable of succeeding
to the property. Lord Cottenham's
opinion was that the child became
legitimate if the domicil of the father
was at the birth, and continued to be
till the marriage, Scotch. He did not
say or imply that it would not be so
if the domicil was English at the time
of the birth and Scotch at the time of
the marriage. The principles stated
by him seem to lead to the conclusion
that the result would be the same in
both cases. As the domicil of the
father at the time of the marriage was
Scotch, the marriage was a Scotch
marriage, and the effects of it must be
judged of with reference to Scotch
law. Lord Brougham, who delivered
the only other judgment in the case,
placed the decision entirely upon the
domicil at the time of the marriage.
He stated the question to be (p. 882),
' whether, supposing the domicil of
the parties at the time of the marriage

to have been in Scotland, that marriage had the effect of legitimatizing
issue born in England before the marriage.'
It should be noticed that in this
case, although the father was throughout domiciled in Scotland, the domicil
of the mother at the birth and until
the marriage was English. As the
child was illegitimate until the marriage, its domicil was the same as the
mother's. Ante, s. 46; Dicey on Domicil, 69, 97. At the time of the marriage therefore, the status of the child
was governed by the English law.
The Scotch law could not affect the
status of the child, unless its domicil,
following that of the mother, became
Scotch upon the marriage. The marriage then must have had the effect of
changing the domicil of the child, and
of giving it a status which it could
not have acquired by the law of its
former domicil. The child was five
years old at the time of the marriage.
If the child had attained her majority
at that time, so that her domicil would
not have been affected by a change of
her mother's domicil, perhaps the result might have been different. There
was no such difficulty as this in In re
Wright's Trusts, supra. The mother
and child were domiciled in France
until the marriage. The father was
domiciled in England at the birth, but
had become domiciled in France at
the time of the marriage. The parties
were consequently all domiciled in
France, and it would seem that the
effect of the marriage upon their
status should have depended on the
French law.

the law of the place of the birth of the child gives the rule as to legitimacy by a subsequent marriage.

93 *v*. Merlin supposes that Hertius holds a different doctrine, and affirms that the law of the place of marriage gives the rule as to legitimacy, and not that of the place of the birth of the child. I do not so understand Hertius. To me it seems clear that Hertius was only contemplating the case of a marriage and birth both in England. ' In Anglia,' says he, ' legitimationi per subsequens matrimonium locus non est. Quæstio est igitur, An filius, quem pater ante legitimum connubium in Anglia genuerat, succedere possit patri huic naturali in bonis extra Anglia sitis? Affirmatum hoc in Auditorio Parisiensi.[1] Rectius negatur, nisi lex alterius populi etiam illegitimos ad successionem admittat; neque enim lex illa Anglorum pugnat cum æquitate naturali.'[2] It is highly probable that Hertius understood the case referred to, as Boullenois had, by mistake, as a case where the child was born in England, whereas he was born in France.[3]

94. *Marriages of Priests and Nuns.* — These cases may suffice in relation to the question of legitimacy or illegitimacy. We may now pass to another class of disabilities imposed by foreign laws, in order to illustrate the difficulty of maintaining the doctrine as a universal rule obligatory upon all countries under all circumstances, that the capacity or incapacity of a person is to be governed solely by the laws of his birth and domicil, and that is the class of persons whose marriages are void or voidable by reason of their profession. Thus, by the law of England, until after the Reformation, monks and nuns were deemed incapable of contracting marriage (as they still are in many parts of the continent of Europe), and their contracts for this purpose were held nullities. The marriages of priests are also in some countries voidable in law, as contrary to their office, at any time during their lives.[4] And to this very day in Catholic countries marriages are prohibited to the priesthood and to persons in monastic orders. Yet it would be extremely difficult to maintain that the

[1] Ante, s. 39 *s*. The case of De Conty, in 1668.

[2] Hertii Opera, de Collis. Leg. s. 4, n. 15, p. 129; Id. p. 183, 184, ed. 1716.

[3] Merlin, Quest. de Droit, s. 2, n. 2, p. 151, 4to ed., Paris, 1828; ante, s. 93 *s*, note 2.

[4] 2 Inst. 686, 687; Com. Dig. Baron and Feme, B. 2; 1 Wooddes. Lect. 16, p. 422.

marriage of a nun, or a monk, or a priest, celebrated in America, where no such prohibition exists, ought, causa professionis, to be held a mere nullity on account of such foreign prohibitions, especially where the other party is at the time of the marriage domiciled here, and as such is entitled to the protection of our laws. (*a*)

95. *Other Prohibited Marriages.*—By the laws of some countries the subjects thereof are prohibited from intermarrying with foreigners, or with persons of another religious sect; and some civilians have held that such laws are of universal obligation, and accompany the person everywhere.[1] But it can hardly be supposed that any other nation would suffer a marriage celebrated in its own dominions, according to its own laws, between such persons, and especially where one of them was a citizen or subject thereof, to be deemed a nullity in its own courts. Such a narrow prohibition would justly be deemed odious and be rejected.

96. *Status of Slaves.* — Another case may be put of even a more striking character. Suppose a person to be a slave in his own country, having no personal capacity to contract there, is he, upon his removal to a foreign country, where slavery is not tolerated, to be still deemed a slave? If so, then a Greek or Asiatic held in slavery in Turkey would, upon his arrival in England or in Massachusetts, be deemed a slave, and be there subject to be treated as mere property, and be under the uncontrollable despotic power of his master. The same rule would exist as to Africans and others held in slavery in foreign countries. But we know that no such general effect has in practice ever been attributed to the state of slavery. There is a uniformity of opinion among foreign jurists and foreign tribunals in giving no effect to the state of slavery of a party, whatever it might have been in the country of his birth or of that in which he had been pre-

[1] See P. Voet, de Statut, s. 5, c. 2, n. 1, p. 178, 179, ed. 1661; Vattel, b. 2, c. 8, s. 115.

(*a*) Westlake says in the last edition (1880) of his book (p. 55), 'Although there is no decided case on the point, I think it may be stated with confidence that an incapacity to marry imposed by the personal law in virtue of religious vows or orders would equally be disregarded, in the case of a person subject to it seeking to marry in England. The reservation in favor of any stringent domestic policy, with which all rules for giving effect to foreign laws must be understood, would there operate. No principle of English policy can be deemed to be more stringent than that which would refuse to exclude a whole class of the population from the possibility of marriage.'

viously domiciled, unless it is also recognized by the laws of the country of his actual domicil, and where he is found, and it is sought to be enforced. Christinæus states this is a clear rule, affirmed by judicial decisions, 'propter libertatis personarum usum hic per aliquot sæcula continue observatum.'[1] Groenewegen, speaking of slavery, says : 'Ejusque nomen hodie apud nos exolevit. Adeo quidem, ut servi, qui aliunde huc adducuntur, simul ac imperii nostri fines intrarunt, *invitis ipsis dominis*, ad libertatem proclamare possint. Id, quod et aliorum Christianorum gentium moribus receptum est.'[2] In Scotland the like doctrine has been solemnly adjudged.[3] The tribunals of France have adopted the same rule, even in relation to slaves coming from and belonging to their own colonies. This is also the undisputed law of England.[4] It has been solemnly decided that the law of England abhors, and will not endure, the existence of slavery within the nation ; and consequently, as soon as a slave lands in England, he becomes ipso facto a freeman, and discharged from the state of servitude.[5] Independent of the provisions of the constitution of the United States for the protection of the rights of masters in regard to domestic fugitive slaves, there is no doubt that the same principle pervades the common law of the non-slaveholding states in America ; that is to say, foreign slaves would no longer be deemed such after their removal thither.[6] (a)

[1] Christinæus, vol. 4, decis. 80, p. 114, 115, n. 4; 1 Burge, Col. & For. Law, c. 10, p. 739.

[2] Groenewegen ad Instit. lib. 1, tit. 8, n. 3, p. 5; cited also in 1 Burge, Col. & For. Law, c. 10, p. 739. Groenewegen cites many authorities in support of his opinion.

[3] Knight *v.* Wedderbern, 1778, 20 Howell, State Trials, 1–15, note.

[4] See cases cited 20 Howell, State Trials, 12–14, note; and Causes Célèbres, vol. 13, p. 492, ed. 1747; 1 Burge, Col. & For. Law, c. 10, p. 739, 740.

[5] Somerset's Case, Lofft, 1; 11 State Trials (Hargrave ed.) 339; 20 Howell, State Trials, 1–79; Co. Lit. 79, Harg. note 44; 1 Black. Com. 424, 425, Christian's note, and Coleridge's note; Forbes *v.* Cochrane, 2 B. & C. 448; The Amedie, Acton, 240; 1 Dodson, 84; Id. 91, 95; Le Louis, 2 Dodson, 210; The Slave Grace, 2 Hagg. Adm. 94, 104–107, 109–111, 118; 1 Burge, Col. & For. Law, pt. 1, c. 10. p. 734–752.

[6] See the opinion of the court delivered by Mr. Justice Porter, in Saul *v.* His Creditors, 5 Mart. N.S. (La.) 598; In re Francisco, 9 Amer. Jurist, 490; Butler *v.* Hopper, 1 Wash. C. C. 499; Ex parte Simmons, 4 Wash. C. C. 390.

(a) Lemmon *v.* People, 20 N. Y. 562; 5 Sandf. 681; 26 Barb. 270; Poly- dore *v.* Prince, 1 Ware, 402; Jackson *v.* Bulloch, 12 Conn. 38.

96 *a*. It is quite a different question, how far rights acquired and wrongs done to slave property, or contracts made respecting

See also Butler *v*. Delaplaine, 7 Serg. & R. (Pa.) 378; Commonwealth *v*. Holloway, 6 Binn. (Pa.) 213; 2 Serg. & R. 305; Lunsford *v*. Coquillon, 2 Mart. N.S. (La.) 401; Louis *v*. Cabarrus, 7 La. 170, 172; 1 Burge, Col. & For. Law, pt. 1, c. 10, p. 744–749; Prigg *v*. Commonwealth, 16 Pet. 541, 611, 612. In the recent case of Commonwealth *v*. Aves (1836), 18 Pick. 193, before Mr. Chief Justice Shaw, in Massachusetts, it was expressly held that a slave brought into Massachusetts voluntarily by his master from a slave state of the United States, was free here, and could not be recovered or carried back as a slave. Upon that occasion the learned judge said: ' The question now before the court arises upon a return to a habeas corpus, originally issued in vacation by Mr. Justice Wilde, for the purpose of bringing up the person of a colored child named Med, and instituting a legal inquiry into the fact of her detention, and the causes for which she was detained. By the provisions of the revised code, the practice upon habeas corpus is somewhat altered. In case the party complaining, or in behalf of whom complaint is made, on the ground of unlawful imprisonment, is not in the custody of an officer, as of a sheriff or deputy, or corresponding officer of the United States, the writ is directed to the sheriff, requiring him or his deputy to take the body of the person thus complaining, or in behalf of whom complaint is thus made, and have him before the court or magistrate issuing the writ, and to summon the party alleged to have or claim the custody of such person, to appear at the same time, and show the cause of the detention. The person thus summoned is to make a statement under oath, setting forth all the facts fully and particularly; and in case he claims the custody of such party, the ground of such claim must be fully set forth. The statement is in the nature of a return to the writ, as made under the former practice, and will usually present the material facts upon which the questions arise. Such return, however, is not conclusive of the facts stated in it, but the court is to proceed and inquire into all the alleged causes of detention, and decide upon them in a summary manner. But the court may, if occasion require it, adjourn the examination, and in the meantime bail the party, or commit him to a general or special custody, as the age, health, sex, and other circumstances of the case may require. It is further provided that, when the writ is issued by one judge of the court in vacation, and in the meantime, before a final decision, the court shall meet in the same county, the proceedings may be adjourned into the court, and there be conducted to a final issue, in the same manner as if they had been originally commenced by a writ issued from the court. I have stated these provisions the more minutely because there have been as yet but few proceedings under the Revised Statutes, and the practice is yet to be established. Upon the return of this writ before Mr. Justice Wilde, a statement was made by Aves, the respondent; the case was then postponed. It has since been fully and very ably argued before all the judges, and is now transferred to and entered in court, and stands here for judgment, in the same manner as if the writ had been originally returnable in court. The statement on oath is now to be considered in the same aspect as if made by Mr. Slater. It is made, in fact, by Aves, claiming the custody of the slave in right of Slater, and that claim is sanctioned by Slater, who appears by his attorney to maintain and enforce it. He claims to have the child as master, and carry her back to New Orleans, and whether the claim

such property in countries where slavery is permitted, may be
allowed to be redressed or recognized in the judicial tribunals of

has been made in terms or not, to hold and return her as a slave, that intent
is manifest, and the argument has very properly placed the claim upon that
ground.   The case presents an extremely interesting question, not so much on
account of any doubt or difficulty attending it, as on account of its important
consequences to those who may be affected by it, either as masters or slaves.
The precise question presented by the claim of the respondent is, whether a
citizen of any one of the United States where negro slavery is established by
law, coming into this state .for any temporary purpose of business or pleasure,
staying some time, but not acquiring a domicil here, who brings a slave with
him as a personal attendant, may restrain such slave of his liberty during his
continuance here, and convey him out of this state on his return, against his
consent.   It is not contended that a master can exercise here any other of the
rights of a slave-owner than such as may be necessary to retain the custody of
the slave during his residence, and to remove him on his return.   Until this
discussion, I had supposed that there had been adjudged cases on this subject
in this commonwealth; and it is believed to have been a prevalent opinion
among lawyers, that if a slave is brought voluntarily and unnecessarily within
the limits of this state, he becomes free, if he chooses to avail himself of the
provisions of our laws; not so much, because his coming within our territorial
limits, breathing our air, or treading on our soil, works any alteration in his
status or condition, as settled by the law of his domicil, as because, by the
operation of our laws, there is no authority on the part of the master, either to
restrain the slave of his liberty whilst here, or forcibly to take him into custody in order to his removal.   There seems however to be no decided case on
the subject reported.   It is now to be considered as an established rule, that
by the constitution and laws of this commonwealth, before the adoption of the
constitution of the United States in 1789, slavery was abolished, as being
contrary to the principles of justice and of nature, and repugnant to the provisions of the Declaration of Rights, which is a component part of the constitution of the state.   It is not easy, without more time for historical research
than I now have, to show the course of slavery in Massachusetts.   By a very
early colonial ordinance (1641) it was ordered that there should be no bond
slavery, villenage, or captivity amongst us, with the exception of lawful captives
taken in just wars, or those judicially sentenced to servitude as a punishment
for crime.   And by an act a few years after (1646), manifestly alluding to
some transaction then recent, the General Court, conceiving themselves bound
to bear witness against the heinous and crying sin of man-stealing, &c.,
ordered that certain negroes be sent back to their native country (Guinea) at
the charge of the country, with a letter from the governor expressive of the
indignation of the court thereabouts.   See Ancient Charters, &c., 52, c. 12,
s. 2, 3.   But notwithstanding these strong expressions in the acts of the colonial government, slavery to a certain extent seems to have crept in; not probably by force of any law, for none such is found or known to exist; but rather,
it may be presumed, from that universal custom, prevailing through the Euro-
pean colonies, in the West Indies, and on the continent of America, and which
was fostered and encouraged by the commercial policy of the parent state.
That it was so established is shortly shown by this, that by several provincial
acts, passed at various times in the early part of the last century, slavery was

governments which prohibit slavery.[1]   And it is also a very different question, how far the original state of slavery might reattach

[1] Madrazo *v.* Willes, 3 B. & A. 353; Forbes *v.* Cochrane, 2 B. & C. 448; Le Louis, 2 Dodson, 210: The Antelope, 10 Wheat. 66; Wharton, Digest, Servants and Slaves, A. D.   See 1 Burge, Col. & For. Law, pt. 1, c. 10, p. 735–752.

recognized as existing in fact, and various regulations were prescribed in reference to it.   The act passed June, 1703, imposed certain restrictions upon manumission, and subjected the master to the relief and support of the slaves, notwithstanding such manumission, if the regulations were not complied with.   The act of October, 1705, Anc. Charters, &c., 748, 749, levied a duty and imposed various restrictions upon the importation of negroes, and allowed a drawback upon any negro, thus imported, and for whom the duty had been paid, if exported within the space of twelve months, and bona fide sold in any other plantation.   How, or by what act particularly, slavery was abolished in Massachusetts, whether by the adoption of an opinion in Somerset's Case, as a declaration and modification of the common law, or by the Declaration of Independence, or by the constitution of 1780, it is not now very easy to determine, and it is rather a matter of curiosity than of utility; it being agreed on all hands that, if not abolished before, it was so by the Declaration of Rights.   In the case of Winchendon *v.* Hatfield, 4 Mass. 123, which was a case between two towns respecting the support of a pauper, Chief Justice Parsons, in giving the opinion of the court, states that in the first action which came before the court after the establishment of the constitution, the judges declared that, by virtue of the Declaration of Rights, slavery in this state was no more.   And he mentions another case, Littleton *v.* Tuttle, 4 Mass. 128, note, in which it was stated, as the unanimous opinion of the court, that a negro born within the state before the constitution, was born free, though born of a female slave.   The chief justice however states that the general practice and common usage have been opposed to this opinion.   It has recently been stated as a fact, that there were judicial decisions in this state, prior to the adoption of the present constitution, holding that negroes, born here of slave parents, were free.   A fact is stated in the above opinion of Chief Justice Parsons which may account for this suggestion.   He states that several negroes, born in this country of imported slaves, had demanded their freedom of their masters by suits of law, and obtained it by a judgment of court.   The defence of the master, he says, was faintly made, for such was the temper of the times that a restless, discontented slave was worth little, and when his freedom was obtained in a course of legal proceedings, his master was not holden for his support if he became poor.   It is very probable therefore that this surmise is correct, and that records of judgments to this effect may be found; but they would throw very little light on the subject. Without pursuing this inquiry farther, it is sufficient for the purposes of the case before us, that, by the constitution adopted in 1780, slavery was abolished in Massachusetts, upon the ground that it is contrary to natural right and the plain principles of justice.   The terms of the first article of the declaration of rights are plain and explicit.   " All men are born free and equal, and have certain natural, essential, and unalienable rights, among which are the right of enjoying and defending their lives and liberties, that of acquiring, possessing,

upon the party, if he should return to the country by whose laws he was declared to be, and was held as, a slave. Lord Stowell,

and protecting property." It would be difficult to select words more precisely adapted to the abolition of negro slavery. According to the laws prevailing in all the states where slavery is upheld, the child of a slave is not deemed to be born free, a slave has no right to enjoy and defend his own liberty, or to acquire, possess, or protect property. That the description was broad enough in its terms to embrace negroes, and that it was intended by the framers of the constitution to embrace them, is proved by the earliest contemporaneous construction, by an unbroken series of judicial decisions, and by a uniform practice from the adoption of the constitution to the present time. The whole tenor of our policy, of our legislation and jurisprudence, from that time to the present, has been consistent with this construction, and with no other. Such being the general rule of law, it becomes necessary to inquire how far it is modified or controlled in its operation either, (1) By the law of other nations and states, as admitted by the comity of nations to have a limited operation within a particular state; or, (2) By the constitution and laws of the United States. In considering the first, we may assume that the law of this state is analogous to the law of England in this respect; that, while slavery is considered as unlawful and inadmissible in both, and this because contrary to natural right and to laws designed for the security of personal liberty, yet in both the existence of slavery in other countries is recognized, and the claims of foreigners growing out of that condition are to a certain extent respected. Almost the only reason assigned by Lord Mansfield in Somerset's case was, that slavery is of such a nature that it is incapable of being introduced on any reasons moral or political, but only by positive law; and it is so odious that nothing can be suffered to support it but positive law. The same doctrine is clearly stated in the full and able opinion of Marshall, C. J., in the case of The Antelope, 10 Wheat. 120. He is speaking of the slave-trade, but the remark itself shows that it applies to the state of slavery. "That it is contrary to the law of nature will scarcely be denied. That every man has a natural right to the fruits of his own labor is generally admitted, and that no other person can rightly deprive him of those fruits, and appropriate them against his will, seems to be the necessary result of the admission." But although slavery and the slave-trade are deemed contrary to natural right, yet it is settled by the judicial decisions of this country and of England that it is not contrary to the law of nations. The authorities are cited in the case of The Antelope, and that case is itself an authority directly in point. The consequence is, that each independent community, in its intercourse with every other, is bound to act on the principle that such other country has a full and perfect authority to make such laws for the government of its own subjects as its own judgment shall dictate and its own conscience approve, provided the same are consistent with the law of nations; and no independent community has any right to interfere with the acts or conduct of another state, within the territories of such state, or on the high seas, which each has an equal right to use and occupy; and that each sovereign state governed by its own laws, although competent and well authorized to make such laws as it may think most expedient to the extent of its own territorial limits, and for the government of its own subjects, yet beyond those limits, and over those who are not its own subjects, has no authority to enforce its own laws, or to treat the laws

in a case of this sort, held that, upon such a return of the slave
to his original domicil, the state of slavery would reattach upon

of other states as void, although contrary to its own views of morality. This
view seems consistent with most of the leading cases on the subject. Somerset's Case, 20 Howell's State Trials, 1, as already cited, decides that slavery,
being odious and against natural right, cannot exist except by force of positive
law. But it clearly admits that it may exist by force of positive law. And it
may be remarked that by positive law, in this connection, may be as well
understood customary law, as the enactment of a statute; and the word is
used to designate rules established by tacit acquiescence, or by the legislative
act of any state, and which derive their force and authority from acquiescence
or enactment, and not because they are the dictates of natural justice, and as
such of universal obligation. Le Louis, 2 Dodson, 236. This was an elaborate opinion of Sir William Scott. It was the case of a French vessel seized
by an English vessel in time of peace, whilst engaged in the slave-trade.
It proceeded upon the ground that a right of visitation by the vessels of one
nation of the vessels of another, could only be exercised in time of war, or
against pirates, and that the slave-trade was not piracy by the laws of nations,
except against those by whose governments it has been so declared by law or
by treaty. And the vessel was delivered up. The Amedie, 1 Acton, 240. The
judgment of Sir William Grant in this case upon the point on which the case
was decided, that of the burden of proof, has been doubted. But upon the
point now under discussion he says: "But we do now lay down as a principle
that this is a trade which cannot, abstractedly speaking, be said to have a legitimate existence; I say, abstractedly speaking, because we cannot legislate
for other countries; nor has this country a right to control any foreign legislature that may give permission to its subjects to prosecute this trade." He
however considered, in consequence of the principles declared by the British government, that he was bound to hold prima facie that the traffic was unlawful,
and threw on the claimant the burden of proof that the traffic was permitted
by the law of his own country. The Diana, 1 Dodson, 95. This case strongly
corroborates the general principle that, though the slave-trade is contrary to
the principles of justice and humanity, it cannot with truth be said that it is
contrary to the laws of all civilized nations; and that courts will respect the
property of persons engaged in it under the sanction of the laws of their own
country. Two cases are cited from the decisions of courts of common law
which throw much light upon the subject. Madrazo v. Willes, 3 B. & A. 353.
It was an action brought by a Spaniard against a British subject who had
unlawfully, and without justifiable cause, captured a ship with three hundred
slaves on board. The only question was, the amount of damages. Abbott,
C. J., who tried the cause, in reference to the very strong language of the acts
of parliament declaring the traffic in slaves a violation of right, and contrary
to the first principles of justice and humanity, doubted whether the owner
could recover damages in an English court of justice for the value of the slaves
as property, and directed the ship and the slaves to be separately valued. On
further consideration he and the whole court were of opinion that the plaintiff
was entitled to recover for the value of the slaves. That opinion went upon
the ground that the traffic in slaves, however wrong in itself, if prosecuted by
a Spaniard between Spain and the coast of Africa, and if permitted by the
laws of Spain, and not restrained by treaty, could not be lawfully interrupted

him. (a) On that occasion he said: ' The entire change of the legal character of individuals, produced by the change of local

by a British subject on the high seas, the common highway of nations. And Mr. Justice Bayley in his opinion, after stating the general rule, that a foreigner is entitled in a British court of justice to compensation for a wrongful act, added, that, although the language used by the statutes was very strong, yet it could only apply to British subjects. It is true, he further says, that if this were a trade contrary to the laws of nations, a foreigner could not maintain this action. And Best, J., spoke strongly to the same effect, adding that the statutes " speak in just terms of indignation of the horrible traffic in human beings, but they speak only in the name of the British nation. If a ship be acting contrary to the general law of nations, she is thereby subject to confiscation; but it is impossible to say that the slave-trade is contrary to what may be called the common law of nations." Forbes v. Cochrane, 2 B. & C. 448; 3 D. & R. 679. This case has been supposed to conflict with the one last cited; but I apprehend, in considering the principles upon which they were decided, they will be found to be perfectly reconcilable. The plaintiff, a British subject domiciled in East Florida, where slavery was established by law, was the owner of a plantation and of certain slaves, who escaped thence and got on board a British ship of war on the high seas. It was held that he could not maintain an action against the master of the ship for harboring the slaves after notice and demand of them. Some of the opinions given in this case are extremely instructive and applicable to the present. Holroyd, J., in giving his opinion, said that the plaintiff could not found his claim to the slaves upon any general right, because by the English law such a right cannot be considered as warranted by the general law of nature; that if the plaintiff could claim at all, it must be in virtue of some right which he had acquired by the law of the country where he was domiciled; that where such rights are recognized by law, they must be considered as founded, not upon a law of nature, but upon the particular law of that country, and must be co-extensive with the territories of that state; that if such right were violated by a British subject within such territory, the party grieved would be entitled to a remedy; but that the law of slavery is a law in invitum, and when a party gets out of the territory where it prevails, and under the protection of another power, without any wrongful act done by the party giving that protection, the right of the master, which is founded on the municipal law of the place only, does not continue. So, in speaking of the effect of bringing a slave into England, he says, he ceases to be a slave in England only because there is no law which sanctions his detention in slavery. Best, J., declared his opinion to the same effect. " Slavery is a local law, and therefore if a man wishes to preserve his slaves, let him attach them to him by affection, or make fast the bars of their prison, or rivet well their chains, for the instant they get beyond the limits where slavery is recognized by the local law, they have broken their chains, they have escaped from their prison, and are free." That slavery is a relation founded in force, not in right, existing, where it does exist, by force of positive law, and not recognized as founded in natural right, is intimated by a definition of slavery in the civil law: " Servitus est constitutio juris gentium, qua

(a) Liza v. Puissant, 7 La. An. 80; Lewis v. Fullerton, 1 Rand. (Va.) 15; Maria v. Kirby, 12 B. Mon. (Ky.) 542; Hunter v. Fulcher, 1 Leigh (Va.) 172.

situation, is far from being a novelty in the law. A residence in
a new country often introduces a change of legal condition, which

quis dominio alieno contra naturam subjicitur." Upon a general review of the
authorities, and upon an application of the well-established principles upon
this subject, we think they fully maintain the point stated, that though slavery
is contrary to natural right, and to the principles of justice, humanity, and
sound policy, as we adopt them and found our own laws upon them, yet not
being contrary to the laws of nations, if any other state or community see fit
to establish and continue slavery by law, so far as the legislative power of that
country extends, we are bound to take notice of the existence of those laws, and
we are not at liberty to declare and hold an act done within those limits unlawful and void, upon our views of morality and policy, which the sovereign and
legislative power of the place has pronounced to be lawful. If therefore an
unwarranted interference and wrong is done by our citizens to a foreigner acting under the sanction of such laws, and within their proper limits, that is,
within the local limits of the power by whom they are thus established, or on
the high seas, which each and every nation has a right in common with all
others to occupy, our laws would no doubt afford a remedy against the wrong
done. So in pursuance of a well-known maxim, that, in the construction of
contracts, the lex loci contractus shall govern, if a person, having in other
respects a right to sue in our courts, shall bring an action against another,
liable in other respects to be sued in our courts, upon a contract made upon
the subject of slavery in a state where slavery is allowed by law, the law would
here give it effect. As if a note of hand made in New Orleans were sued on
here, and the defence should be that it was a bad consideration, or without
consideration, because given for the price of a slave sold, it may well be admitted that such a defence could not prevail, because the contract was a legal one
by the law of the place where it was made.[1] This view of the law applicable
to slavery marks strongly the distinction between the relation of master and
slave as established by the local law of particular states, and in virtue of that
sovereign power and independent authority which each independent state concedes to every other, and those natural and social relations which are everywhere and by all people recognized, and which, though they may be modified
and regulated by municipal law, are not founded upon it, such as the relation
of parent and child, and husband and wife. Such also is the principle upon
which the general right of property is founded, being in some form universally recognized as a natural right, independently of municipal law. This
affords an answer to the argument drawn from the maxim that the right of
personal property follows the person, and therefore, where by the law of a
place a person there domiciled acquires personal property, by the comity of
nations the same must be deemed his property everywhere. It is obvious that
if this were true, in the extent in which the argument employs it, if slavery
exists anywhere, and if by the laws of any place a property can be acquired in
slaves, the law of slavery must extend to every place where such slaves may
be carried. The maxim therefore, and the argument, can apply only to those
commodities which are everywhere and by all nations treated and deemed
subjects of property. But it is not speaking with strict accuracy to say that a
property can be acquired in human beings by local laws. Each state may, for

----

[1] But see post, s. 259.

11

imposes rights and obligations totally inconsistent with the former rights and obligations of the same persons. Persons bound by

its own convenience, declare that slaves shall be deemed property, and that the relations and laws of personal chattels shall be deemed to apply to them; as, for instance, that they may be bought and sold, delivered, attached, levied upon, that trespass will lie for an injury done to them, or trover for converting them. But it would be a perversion of terms to say that such local laws do in fact make them personal property generally; they can only determine that the same rules of law shall apply to them as are applicable to property, and this effect will follow only so far as such laws proprio vigore can operate. The same doctrine is recognized in Louisiana. In the case of Lunsford v. Coquillon, 2 Mart. N.S. (La.) 404, it is thus stated: "The relation of owner and slave is, in the states of this union in which it has a legal existence, a creature of the municipal law." See Story's Conflict of Laws, 92, 97 [1st ed. s. 96, 104]. The same principle is declared by the court in Kentucky, in the case of Rankin v. Lydia, 2 A. K. Marsh. 470. They say, slavery is sanctioned by the laws of this state; but we consider this as a right existing by positive law of a municipal character, without foundation in the law of nature. The conclusion to which we come with this view of the law, is this: That by the general and now well-established law of this commonwealth bond slavery cannot exist, because it is contrary to natural right, and repugnant to numerous provisions of the constitution and laws, designed to secure the liberty and personal rights of all persons within its limits, and entitled to the protection of its laws. That though by the laws of a foreign state, meaning by *foreign*, in this connection, a state governed by its own laws, and between which and our own there is no dependence one upon the other, but which in this respect are as independent as foreign states, a person may acquire a property in a slave, such acquisition, being contrary to natural right and affected by local law, is dependent upon such local law for its existence and efficacy, and being contrary to the fundamental law of the state, such general right of property cannot be exercised or recognized here. That, as a general rule, all persons coming within the limits of a state become subject to all its municipal laws, civil and criminal, and entitled to the privileges which those laws confer; that this rule applies as well to blacks as whites, except the case of fugitives to be afterwards considered; that if such persons have been slaves they become free, not so much because any alteration is made in their status, or condition, as because there is no law which will warrant. but there are laws, if they choose to avail themselves of them, which prohibit, their forcible detention or forcible removal. That the law arising from the comity of nations cannot apply, because if it did it would follow as a necessary consequence that all those persons who, by force of local laws and within all foreign places where slavery is permitted, have acquired slaves as property, might bring their slaves here and exercise over them the rights and power which an owner of property might exercise, and for any length of time, short of acquiring a domicil; that such an application of the law would be wholly repugnant to our laws, entirely inconsistent with our policy and our fundamental principles, and is therefore inadmissible. Whether if a slave voluntarily brought here, and with his own consent returning with his master, would resume his condition as a slave, is a question which was incidentally raised in the argument, but is one on which we are not called on to give an opinion in this case, and we give none. From particular contracts which restrain their liberty, debtors, apprentices, and others, lose their character and condition for the time,

the principle above stated, on which a slave brought here becomes free, to wit, that he becomes entitled to the protection of our laws, and there is no law to warrant his forcible arrest and removal, it would seem to follow, as a necessary conclusion, that if the slave waives the protection of those laws, and returns to the state where he is held as a slave, his condition is not changed. In the case of The Slave Grace, 2 Hagg. Adm. 94, this question was fully considered by Sir William Scott in the case of a slave brought from the West Indies to England, and afterwards voluntarily returning to the West Indies; and he held that she was reinstated in her condition of slavery. A different decision I believe has been made of the question in some of the United States; but for the reasons already given it is not necessary to consider it further here. The question has thus far been considered as a general one, and applicable to cases of slaves brought from any foreign state or country; and it now becomes necessary to consider how far this result differs, where the person is claimed as a slave by a citizen of another state of this Union. As the several states, in all matters of local and domestic jurisdiction, are sovereign and independent of each other, and regulate their policy by their own laws, the same rule of comity applies to them on these subjects as to foreign states, except so far as the respective rights and duties of the several states and their respective citizens are affected and modified by the constitution and laws of the United States. In art. 4, s. 2, the constitution declares that no person held to service or labor in one state under the laws thereof, escaping into another, shall in consequence of any law or regulation therein be discharged from such service or labor, but shall be delivered up on claim of the party to whom such service or labor may be due. The law of congress made in pursuance of this article provides that when any person held to labor in any of the United States, &c., shall escape into any other of the said states or territories, the person entitled, &c., is empowered to arrest the fugitive, and upon proof made that the person so seized, under the law of the state from which he or she fled, owes service, &c. Act of February 12, 1793, c. 7, s. 3. In regard to these provisions the court are of opinion that as, by the general law of this commonwealth, slavery cannot exist, and the rights and powers of slave-owners cannot be exercised therein, the effect of this provision in the constitution and laws of the United States is to limit and restrain the operation of this general rule, so far as it is done by the plain meaning and obvious intent and import of the language used, and no further. The constitution and law manifestly refer to the case of a slave escaping from a state, where he owes service or labor, into another state or territory. He is termed a fugitive from labor; the proof to be made is, that he owed service or labor under the laws of the state or territory *from which he fled*, and the authority given is to remove such fugitive to the State *from which he fled*. This language can by no reasonable construction be applied to the case of a slave who has not fled from the state, but who has been brought into this state by his master. The same conclusion will result from a consideration of the well-known circumstances under which this constitution was formed. Before the adoption of the constitution the states were to a certain extent sovereign and independent, and were in a condition to settle the terms upon which they would form a more perfect union. It has been contended by some over-zealous philanthropists that such an article in the

when they reside in another country, and are entitled as persons totally free, although they return to their original servitude and

constitution could be of no binding force or validity because it was a stipulation contrary to natural right. But it is difficult to perceive the force of this objection. It has already been shown that slavery is not contrary to the laws of nations. It would then be the proper subject of treaties among sovereign and independent powers. Suppose, instead of forming the present constitution or any other confederation, the several states had become in all respects sovereign and independent, would it not have been competent for them to stipulate that fugitive slaves should be mutually restored, and to frame suitable regulations under which such a stipulation should be carried into effect? Such a stipulation would be highly important and necessary to secure peace and harmony between adjoining nations, and to prevent perpetual collisions and border wars. It would be no encroachment on the rights of the fugitive; for no stranger has a just claim to the protection of a foreign state against its will, especially where a claim to such protection would be likely to involve the state in war; and each independent state has a right to determine by its own laws and treaties who may come to reside or seek shelter within its limits, and to prescribe the terms. Now the constitution of the United States partakes both of the nature of a treaty and of a form of government. It regards the states to a certain extent as sovereign and independent communities, with full power to make their own laws and regulate their own domestic policy, and fixes the terms upon which their intercourse with each other shall be conducted. In respect to foreign relations it regards the people of the states as one community, and constitutes a form of government for them. It is well known that, when this constitution was formed, some of the states permitted slavery and the slave-trade, and considered them highly essential to their interest, and that some other states had abolished slavery within their own limits, and, from the principles deduced and policy avowed by them, might be presumed to desire to extend such abolition further. It was therefore manifestly the intent and the object of one party to this compact to enlarge, extend, and secure as far as possible, the rights and powers of the owners of slaves within their own limits, as well as in other states, and of the other party to limit and restrain them. Under these circumstances the clause in question was agreed on and introduced into the constitution; and, as it was well considered, as it was intended to secure peace and harmony, and to fix as precisely as language could do it, the limit to which the rights of one party should be exercised within the territory of the other, it is to be presumed that they selected terms intended to express their exact and their whole meaning; and it would be a departure from the purpose and spirit of the compact to put any other construction upon it than that to be derived from the plain and natural import of the language used. Besides, this construction of the provision in the constitution gives to it a latitude sufficient to afford effectual security to the owners of slaves. The states have a plenary power to make all laws necessary for the regulation of slavery and the rights of the slave-owners whilst the slaves remain within their territorial limits; and it is only when they escape without the consent of their owners into other states that they require the aid of other states to enable them to regain their dominion over the fugitives. But this point is supported by most respectable and unexceptionable authorities. In the case of Butler r. Hopper, 1 Wash. C.C. 499, it was held by Mr. Justice Washington, in terms,

obligations upon coming back to the country they had quitted; and even in the case of slavery, slaves themselves possess rights

that the provision in the constitution which we are now considering does not "extend to the case of a slave voluntarily carried by his master into another state, and there leaving him under the protection of some law declaring him free." In this case however the master claimed to hold the slave in virtue of a law of Pennsylvania which permitted members of congress and sojourners to retain their domestic slaves, and it was held that he did not bring himself within either branch of the exception, because he had for two years of the period ceased to be a member of congress, and so lost the privilege; and by having become a resident could not claim as a sojourner. The case is an authority to this point, that the claimant of a slave, to avail himself of the provisions of the constitution and laws of the United States, must bring himself within their plain and obvious meaning, and they will not be extended by construction; and that the clause in the constitution is confined to the case of a slave escaping from one state and fleeing to another. But in a more recent case the point was decided by the same eminent judge. Ex parte Simmons, 4 Wash. C.C. 396. It was an application for a certificate under s. 3 of the act of Feb. 12, 1793. He held that both the constitution and the laws of the United States apply only to fugitives escaping from one state and fleeing to another, and not to the case of a slave voluntarily brought by his master. Another question was made in that case whether the slave was free by the laws of Pennsylvania, which, like our own in effect, liberate slaves voluntarily brought within the state; but there is an exception in favor of members of Congress, foreign ministers and consuls, and *sojourners;* but this provision is qualified as to sojourners and persons passing through the state in such manner as to exclude them from the benefit of the exception, if the slave was retained in the state longer than six months. The slave in that case having been detained in the state more than six months was therefore held free. This case is an authority to this point, — the general rule being that, if a slave is brought into a state where the laws do not admit slavery, he will be held free, the person who claims him as a slave under any exception or limitation of the general rule must show clearly that the case was within such exception. The same principle was substantially decided by the state court of the same state in the case of Commonwealth *v.* Holloway, 2 Serg. & R. 305. It was the case of a child of a fugitive slave born in Pennsylvania. It was held that the constitution of the United States was not inconsistent with the law of Pennsylvania; that as the law and constitution of the United States did not include the issue of fugitive slaves in terms, it did not embrace them by construction or implication. The court considers the law as applying only to those who *escape.* Yet by the operation of the maxim which obtains in all the states wherein slavery is permitted by law, partus sequitur ventrem, the offspring would follow the condition of the mother, if either the rule of comity contended for applied, or if the law of the United States could be extended by construction. The same decision has been made in Indiana, 3 Amer. Jurist, 404. In Louisiana it had been held, that if a person with a slave goes into a state to reside where it is declared that slavery shall not exist, for ever so short a time, the slave ipso facto becomes free, and will be so adjudged and considered afterwards in all other states; and a person moving from Kentucky to Ohio to reside, his slaves thereby became free, and were so held in Louisiana. This

and privileges in one character which they are not entitled to in
another. The domestic slave may, in that character, by law ac-

case also fully recognizes the authority of states to make laws dissolving the
relation of master and slave; and considers the special limitation of the general
power by the federal constitution as a forcible implication in proof of the existence of such general powers. Lunsford v. Coquillon, 2 Mart. N.S. 401.
And in the above-cited case from Louisiana it is very significantly remarked
that such a construction of the constitution and law of the United States can
work injury to no one, for the principle acts only on the willing, and volenti
non fit injuria. The same rule of construction is adopted in analogous cases
in other countries, that is, where an institution is forbidden, but where, for
special reasons and to a limited extent, such prohibition is relaxed, the exemption is to be construed strictly, and whoever claims the exemption must show
himself clearly within it, and where the facts do not bring the case within the
exemption, the general rule has its effect. By a general law of France, all
persons inhabiting or being within the territorial limits of France are free.
An edict was passed by Louis XIV. called Le Code Noir, respecting slavery
in the colonies. In 1716 an edict was published by Louis XV. concerning
slavery in the colonies, and reciting, among other things, that many of the
colonists were desirous of bringing their slaves into France to have them confirmed in the principles of religion, and to be instructed in various arts and
handicrafts, from which the colonists would derive much benefit on the return
of the slaves, but that many of the colonists feared that their slaves would pretend to be free on their arrival in France, from which their owners would sustain considerable loss, and be deterred from pursuing an object at once so
pious and useful. The edict then provides a series of minute regulations, to
be observed both before their departure from the West Indies and on their
arrival in France, and if all these regulations are strictly complied with, the
negroes so brought over to France shall not thereby acquire any right to their
freedom, but shall be compellable to return; but if the owners shall neglect to
comply with the prescribed regulations, the negroes shall become free, and the
owners shall lose all property in them. 20 Howell's State Trials, 15, note. The
constitution and laws of the United States, then, are confined to cases of slaves
escaping from other states and coming within the limits of this state without
the consent and against the will of their masters, and cannot by any sound
construction extend to a case where the slave does not escape and does not
come within the limits of this state against the will of the master, but by his
own act and permission. This provision is to be construed according to its
plain terms and import, and cannot be extended beyond this, and where the
case is not that of an escape, the general rule shall have its effect. It is upon
these grounds we are of opinion that an owner of a slave in another state
where slavery is warranted by law, voluntarily bringing such slave into this
state, has no authority to detain him against his will, or to carry him out of
the state against his consent, for the purpose of being held in slavery. This
opinion is not to be considered as extending to a case where the owner of a
fugitive slave, having produced a certificate according to the law of the United
States, is bona fide removing such slave to his own domicil, and in so doing
passes through a free state; where the law confers a right or favor, by necessary implication it gives the means of enjoying it. Nor do we give any
opinion upon the case where an owner of a slave in one state is bona fide re-

company his master or mistress to any part of the world. But
that privilege exists no longer than his character of domestic slave
attaches to him; for should the owner deprive him of the character of being a domestic slave by employing him as a field slave,
he would be deprived of the right of accompanying his master
out of the colony.'[1]

97. *Scotch Law as to Capacity.*—Struck with the inconveniences
of the doctrine of the ubiquity of the law of the domicil, as to the
capacity, state, and condition of persons, as an absolute and general doctrine, a learned judge in the Scottish courts[2] has not hesi-
tated to hold that no such doctrine is recognized as of universal
obligation in Scotland. 'Would a marriage here,' says he, 'be
declared void because the parties were domiciled in England and
were minors when they married here, and of course incapable, by
the law of that country, of contracting marriage? This category
of law does not affect the contracting individuals only, but the
public, and that in various ways. And the consequences would
prove not a little inconvenient, embarrassing, and probably even
inextricable, if the personal incapacities of individuals, as of majors
and minors, the competency to contract marriages, and infringe
matrimonial engagements, the rights of domestic authority and
service, and the like, were to be qualified and regulated by foreign
laws and customs, with which the mass of the population must be

moving to another state where slavery is allowed, and in so doing necessarily
passes through a free state, or, arriving by accident or necessity, he is compelled to touch or land therein, remaining no longer than necessary. Our
geographical position exempts us from the probable necessity of considering
such a case, and we give no opinion respecting it. The child who is the
subject of this habeas corpus, being of too tender years to have any will
or give any consent to be removed, and her mother being a slave and
having no will of her own and no power to act for her child, she is necessarily left in the custody of the law. The respondent having claimed the
custody of the child, in behalf of Mr. and Mrs. Slater, who claim the right to
carry her back to Louisiana, to be held in a state of slavery, we are of opinion
that his custody is not to be deemed by the court a proper and lawful
custody. Under a suggestion made in the outset of this inquiry, that a probate guardian would probably be appointed, we shall for the present order the
child into a temporary custody, to give time for an application to be made to
the judge of probate.'
[1] The Slave Grace, 2 Hagg. Adm. 94, 113, 114. It seems that Christinæus
and Godelin held the same opinion as Lord Stowell. See Christinæus, vol. 4,
dec. 80, n. 4, p. 115; cited also, 1 Burge, Col. & For. Law, pt. 1, c. 10,
p 749.
[2] Lord Meadowbank: Fergusson on Mar. and Divorce, Appx. 361, 362.

utterly unacquainted.   Accordingly, the laws of this description
seem nowhere to yield to those of foreign countries; and accordingly, it is believed, no nation has hitherto thought of conferring
powers and forms on its courts of justice, adequate for enabling
them to execute over foreigners regular authority for enforcing
the observance by them of the laws of their own country when
expatriated.   In fact, the very same principles which prescribe to
nations the administration of their own criminal law appear to
require a like exclusive administration of law relative to the domestic relations.   Hence, both in England and Scotland, the most
regular constitution abroad of domestic slavery was held to afford
no claim to domestic service in this country, though restricted for
only such service, and under such domestic authority, as our laws
recognized.   The whole order of society would be disjointed, were
the positive institutions of foreign nations concerning the domestic
relations, and the capacities of persons regarding them, admitted
to operate universally, and form privileged castes, living each under separate laws, like the barbarous nations during many cen-
turies after their settlement in the Roman empire.'[1]

98. *Conclusions.*—These diversities in the practical jurisprudence
of different countries, as to the effect of personal ability and disability, and personal capacity or incapacity, abundantly establish,
in the first place, that there is no general rule on the subject,
which is admitted by all nations; and, in the next place, that the
very exceptions introduced or conceded by those who most strenuously contend for the universal operation of the law of the domicil
of the party, either native or acquired, in cases of this nature, as
satisfactorily establish that no general rules have been or can be
established, which may not work serious inconvenience to the
interests or institutions of some particular countries, or to some
particular classes of capacities or incapacities.   The proper conclusion, then, to be drawn from this review of the subject is, that
the rule of Huberus is correct, that no nation is under any obligation to give effect to the laws of any other nation which are
prejudicial to itself or to its own citizens; that in all cases every
nation must judge for itself what foreign laws are so prejudicial
or not; and that, in cases not so prejudicial, a spirit of comity and
a sense of mutual utility ought to induce every nation to allow full
force and effect to the laws of every other nation.   This is the doc-

[1] Lord Meadowbank: Fergusson on Mar. and Divorce, Appx. 861, 362.

trine asserted by Mr. Chancellor Kent; and it certainly has a most
solid foundation in the actual practice of nations. 'There is no
doubt,' says he, 'of the truth of the general proposition that the
laws of a country have no binding force beyond its own territorial
limits; and their authority is admitted in other states, not ex
proprio vigore, but ex comitate; or, in the language of Huberus,
"quatenus sine præjudicio indulgentium fieri potest." Every independent community will judge for itself how far the comitas
inter communitates is to be permitted to interfere with its domestic interests and policy, &c; the maxim is, that locus contractus
regit actum, unless the intention of the parties to the contrary be
clearly shown. . . . It is however a necessary exception to the
universality of the rule, that no people are bound or ought to enforce or hold valid in their courts of justice, any contract which is
injurious to their public rights, or offends their morals, or contra-
venes their policy, or violates a public law.'[1]

99. *Recognition of Foreign Incapacities.* — In discussing this
subject, our attention has been more particularly drawn to the
common cases of incapacity resulting from minority, and marriage, and legitimacy. But the principles which apply to them are
not materially different from those which apply to cases of idiocy,
insanity, and prodigality. The extent of the rights and authorities of guardians, curators, parents, and masters over persons
subjected to their control, or committed to their charge, may, in
a general sense, be said to depend, so far as they are to be recognized or enforced by and in foreign nations, upon the same
common ground of international jurisprudence, that is to say,
upon a general comity, founded in the sense of mutual interests,
mutual benefits, and mutual obligations to cultivate peace and
harmony. It was said on a recent occasion, with great force and
propriety, by Mr. Chief Justice Taney, in delivering the opinion
of the Supreme Court: 'The comity thus extended to other
nations is no impeachment of sovereignty. It is the voluntary
act of the nation by which it is offered, and is inadmissible when

<hr>

[1] 2 Kent Com. 457. 458; post, s. 244–259. See also Greenwood v. Curtis,
4 Mass. 378, 379. This subject is a good deal discussed in the able work of
Mr. Fergusson on Marriage and Divorce; and the opinions of the judges in the
case of Gordon v. Pye, in 1815, and that of Edmonstone and others in 1816,
before the Scottish courts, are particularly worthy of examination, from their
comprehensive learning and ability. Fergusson, Appx. p. 276–363. See also
Id. p. 384–422.

contrary to its policy or prejudicial to its interests.   But it contributes so largely to promote justice between individuals, and to produce a friendly intercourse between the sovereignties to which they belong, that courts of justice have constantly acted upon it as a part of the voluntary law of nations.[1]

100. *Rules.* — In concluding this discussion as to the operation of foreign laws on questions relating to the capacity, state, and condition of persons, it may be useful to bring together some of those rules which seem best established in the jurisprudence of England and America, leaving others of a more doubtful character and extent to be decided, as they may arise, in the proper forum.

101. *Acts in the Country of Domicil.* — First : The capacity, state, and condition of persons according to the law of their domicil will generally be regarded as to acts done, rights acquired, and contracts made in the place of their domicil, touching property situate therein.   If these acts, rights, and contracts have validity there, they will be held equally valid everywhere.   If invalid there, they will be held invalid everywhere.[2]

102. *Acts in other Countries.* — Secondly : As to acts done, and rights acquired, and contracts made in other countries, touching property therein, the law of the country where the acts are done, the rights are acquired, or the contracts are made, will generally govern in respect to the capacity, state, and condition of persons.[3] (*a*)   In affirmance of this doctrine the Supreme Court of

---

[1] Bank of Augusta v. Earle, 13 Pet. 589.

[2] See Male v. Roberts, 3 Esp. 163; Thompson v. Ketcham, 8 Johns. (N. Y.) 189; ante, s. 64–68; s. 87.   See Foelix, Conflit des Lois Revue Étrang. et Franç. tom. 7, 1840, s. 38, p. 342–344.

[3] Ante, s. 69, 70–74; s. 80–82, 87.

(*a*) *Capacity to contract.* — There is a remarkable absence of decisions upon the question by what law capacity to contract is to be determined. The only English case is Male v. Roberts, 3 Esp. 163, a decision of Lord Eldon's at nisi prius in 1790.   The action was brought to recover money advanced in Scotland to pay a debt of the defendant's when both parties were in Scotland.   The defence was infancy.   Lord Eldon said that, as the cause of action arose in Scotland, the contract must be governed by the law of that country, and that if, by the law of Scotland, such a contract could not be enforced against the infant, that should have been given in evidence.   See Dicey on Domicil, 177. The same rule was laid down in New York in 1811 in Thompson v. Ketcham, 8 Johns. 189, in which the judgment was delivered by Kent, C.J.   In more recent American cases, it has been held that the capacity of a married woman to contract depends on the law of the place where the contract is made. Pearl v. Hansborough, 9 Humph.

Louisiana, in a case where the direct question came before them, expressly stated that they had no difficulty in assenting to the proposition that contracts entered into in other states, as it relates to their validity and the capacity of the contracting parties, are to be tried in Louisiana by the lex loci celebrati contractus. And that if a contract was entered into in another state in conformity to the local law to have its effects and execution there, the courts of Louisiana cannot declare it a nullity on the ground that it would not be valid according to the system of jurisprudence of that state, even if one or both the contracting parties were not citizens of such foreign state.[1]

---

[1] Mr. Justice Bullard, in Andrews v. His Creditors, 11 La. 464; ante, s. 95, note 3, s. 96 a.

(Tenn.) 426; Milliken v. Pratt, 125 Mass. 874; Bell v. Packard, 69 Me. 105. See Dicey on Domicil, 193. In none of these cases was any place specially appointed for the performance of the contract. The decisions were placed upon the ground that the validity of the contract depended on the law of the place where it was made. This is the principle which determines the validity of a contract when the place for its performance is not specified. But when it is to be performed in a particular place, the contract is not valid if it is prohibited by the law of the place of performance. Post, s. 242, 280, 299, 299 a. If therefore capacity depends upon the principle which governs the validity of contracts in other matters of substance, as the cases seem to indicate, a contract is not valid unless the parties have capacity by the law of the place of performance. Story says that, in transfers of immovables, the lex situs, which governs the transfer in other respects, determines also capacity. Post, s. 430, 431. It may be that capacity to contract will be regarded as a matter to be governed by the law of the place to which the contract is deemed to belong. See Westlake (ed. 1880), 234-237; Foote, Priv. Int. Law, 297; Akers v. Demond, 103 Mass. 318, 323.

The case of Sottomayor v. De Barros, 3 P. D. 1, 5, contains this dictum by Cotton, L.J., viz., 'But it is a well-recognized principle of law that the question of personal capacity to enter into any contract is to be decided by the law of domicil,' and, 'as in other contracts, so in that of marriage, personal capacity must depend on the law of domicil.' The point decided was that the law of Portugal which prohibited marriages between first cousins as incestuous, made persons so related and domiciled in Portugal incapable of marrying one another, wherever the marriage might be solemnized. No authority is referred to for the general proposition that capacity to enter into any contract depends on the law of the domicil, but if the proposition had been limited to contracts of marriage, there would have been authority for it. Brook v. Brook, 9 H. L. C. 193. Marriage creates a status, and questions of status depend upon the law of the domicil. Ante, s. 50, note. In contracts of marriage, too, the matrimonial domicil is the place with reference to which the contract is made and in which its obligations are to be performed; consequently, if the principle that governs other contracts be applied, the contract is not valid unless it is lawful by the law of the matrimonial domicil. See note, s. 124 a, post.

102 *a.* It has been well remarked by Mr. Burge: ' This doctrine promotes, whilst that to which it is opposed is inconsistent with, those principles of mutual convenience which induce the recognition of foreign laws. The obstacles to commercial intercourse between the subjects of foreign states would be almost insurmountable, if a party must pause to ascertain, not by the means within his reach, but by recourse to the law of the domicil of the person with whom he is dealing, whether the latter has attained the age of majority, and, consequently, whether he is competent to enter into a valid and binding contract. If the country in which the contract was litigated was also that in which it had been entered into, and if the party enforcing it were the subject of that country, it would be unjust, as well as unreasonable, to invoke the law of a foreign state for the benefit of the foreigner, and to deprive its own subject of the benefit of the law of his own state.' [1]

102 *b.* He adds: ' It has been hitherto assumed that, according to the law of the domicil, the person was a minor, and incapable of contracting, although he had attained the age which, in loco contractus, constituted majority, and where, according to that law, he was competent to contract. In such a case it has been submitted that the lex loci contractus ought to be followed. It ought also to be followed if the converse of that case occurred, and he had attained majority according to the law of his domicil, but was a minor according to that which prevailed in loco contractus. It is true, in the latter case, the party was subject to no greater liability than he would have incurred in the place of his domicil. But if the principle be correct, that the lex loci contractus ought to determine the validity of a contract when that validity depends on the capacity of the contracting party, it must be uniformly applied, whether the law prevailing in the domicil be that which capacitates or incapacitates. For it would not be reasonable that two different laws should be applied to one and the same contract, and that the liability of one of the parties should be decided by the lex loci contractus, and that of the other by the lex loci domicilii.' [2]

103. *Lex Loci Actus.* — Thirdly: Hence we may deduce, as a corollary, that in regard to questions of minority or majority,

[1] 1 Burge, Col. & For. Law, pt. 1, ch. 4, p. 132.
[2] Id. p. 133.

competency or incompetency to marry, incapacities incident to
coverture, guardianship, emancipation, and other personal qualities and disabilities, the law of the domicil of birth, or the law of
any other acquired and fixed domicil, is not generally to govern,
but the lex loci contractus aut actus, the law of the place where
the contract is made or the act done.(a)   Therefore a person who
is a minor until he is of the age of twenty-five years by the law
of his domicil, and incapable, as such, of making a valid contract
there, may nevertheless, in another country where he would be of
age at twenty-one years, generally make a valid contract at that
age, even a contract of marriage.[1]

104. *Penal Disabilities.* — Fourthly : Personal disqualifications,
not arising from the law of nature, but from the principles of the
customary or positive law of a foreign country, and especially
such as are of a penal nature, are not generally regarded in other
countries, where the like disqualifications do not exist.[2]   Hence,
the disqualifications resulting from heresy, excommunication, popish recusancy, infamy, and other penal disabilities, are not enforced in any other country, except that in which they originate.
They are strictly territorial.[3]   So, the state of slavery will not be
recognized in any country whose institutions and policy prohibit
slavery.[4]

105. *Legitimacy.* — Fifthly : In questions of legitimacy or illegitimacy, the law of the place of the marriage will generally
govern as to the issue subsequently born.   If the marriage is
valid by the law of that place, it will generally be held valid in
every other country, for the purpose of ascertaining legitimacy
and heirship.   If invalid there, it will generally (if not universally)
be held invalid in every other country.[5]

105 a. *Legitimation per Subsequens Matrimonium.* — Sixthly :
As to issue born before the marriage, if, by the law of the country
where they are born, they would be legitimated by the subse-

[1] Ante, s. 75, 79, 80, 81, 82.   [2] Ante, s. 91-96.
[3] Ante, s. 91, 92, 94, 95.   [4] Co. Lit. 79 *b*, Harg. n. 44; ante, s. 96.
[5] Ante, s. 79, 80, 81, 86.

(a) In re Hellmann's Will, L. R.   of their domicil, whichever first hap-
2 Eq. 363, it was held that legacies   pened.   The legatees were domiciled
bequeathed by an English will might   at Hamburg, where girls became of
be paid to legatees domiciled abroad   age at eighteen, and boys at twenty-
when they became of age according to   two.
English law or according to the law

quent marriage of their parents, they will by such subsequent marriage (perhaps in any country, but at all events in the same country) become legitimate, so that this character of legitimacy will be recognized in every other country. If ·illegitimate there, the same character will belong to them in every other country.[1]

106. *Evasion of Laws of the Domicil.* — Seventhly: No nation being under any obligation to yield up its own laws in regard to its own subjects, to the laws of other nations, it will not suffer its own subjects to evade the operation of its own fundamental policy or laws, or to commit frauds in violation of them, by any acts or contracts made with that design in a foreign country; and it will judge for itself how far it will adopt, and how far it will reject, any such acts or contracts. Hence the acts of prodigals, of minors, of idiots, of lunatics, and of married women, escaping into foreign countries, are not to be deemed as of course absolutely obligatory, even if sanctioned by the foreign law, unless the laws of their own country adopt such foreign law as a rule to govern in such cases.[2] Hence, too, a person born before wedlock, who in the country of his birth is deemed illegitimate, may not, by a subsequent marriage of his parents in another country, by whose laws such a marriage would make him legitimate, cease to be illegitimate in the country of his birth.[3] Hence, also, if a marriage is by the laws of a country indissoluble when

[1] Ante, s. 87, 87 *a*; Munro *v.* Saunders, 6 Bligh, 468.

[2] An apt illustration of this rule may be found in the present law of France. By that law, a marriage contracted in a foreign country between Frenchmen, or a Frenchman and a stranger, is valid if celebrated according to the forms used in that country, provided it is preceded by a proper publication of banns, and the Frenchman does not contravene the other provisions of the French law. Upon this law Toullier remarks that the conditions required to be complied with are those of the code respecting the contract of marriage; for, as the laws respecting a person follow a Frenchman everywhere, it results that even in a foreign country he is held to conform to the French laws relative to the age of the contracting parties, their family, and the impediments to marriage. 1 Toullier, Droit Civil Français, art. 575, p. 484. So that French minors, who are incapable of contracting a marriage in France, are disabled everywhere, even though the marriage would be good by the law of the place where the marriage is celebrated. The English and American courts would hold such a marriage good. Code Civil, art 144, 148, 170; Merlin Répert. tit. Loi, s. 6, n. 1. See also 2 Kent Com. 93, note. The doctrine of France, in this respect, is but an illustration of the general rule prescribed by the Civil Code of France (art. 3), that the laws respecting the state and condition of Frenchmen govern them, even when resident in a foreign country. Ante, s. 54.

[3] Ante, s. 79, 87, 87 *a*, 105 *a*.

once contracted between its own subjects, they may not, by a
mere removal into another country, at least without a change of
domicil, be deemed capable of contracting a new marriage after
a divorce, lawful by the law of the place to which they have removed.[1] In short, every nation, in these and the like cases, will
govern itself by such rules and principles as are best adapted in
its own judgment to subserve its own substantial interests and
fixed policy, and to uphold its own institutions, as well as to
promote a liberal intercourse, and a spirit of confidence and reciprocal comity with all other nations.   But this subject will be
more fully considered in the succeeding chapters. (a)

[1] See Rex v. Lolley, Russ. & Ry. 237; Tovey v. Lindsay, 1 Dow, 124;
Conway v. Beazley, 3 Hagg. Ecc. 639; M'Carthy v. Decaix, 1831, 2 Russ. &
My. 620. But see Warrender v. Warrender, 9 Bligh, 89; post, s. 215–
231.

(a) *Corporations.* — A corporation
created under the laws of one country
is recognized as such in other countries. The powers vested in it by its
incorporation, when there is no restriction as to the place where it
may act, may be exercised in any
place the laws of which do not prohibit its acting there.   Bateman v.
Service, 6 App. Cas. 386 (P. C.);
Bank of Augusta v. Earle, 13 Pet.
519; Merrick v. Van Santvoord, 34
N. Y. 208; Dicey on Domicil, 198;
2 Lindley, Partn. (4th ed.) 1484. It
has long been settled that a corporation may sue and be sued in other countries than that in which it originated.
Dutch West India Co. v. Moses, 1
Str. 612; Henriques v. Dutch West
India Co., 2 Ld. Raym. 1532; Newby
r Colt's Firearms Co., L. R. 7 Q. B.
253: British American Land Co. v.
Ames, 6 Met. (Mass.) 391; Smith v.
Weed Sewing-Machine Co., 26 Ohio
St. 562; Farnsworth v. Terre Haute
Rld. Co., 29 Mo. 75; St. Louis v.
Wiggins Ferry Co., 40 Mo. 580. It is
now generally established that it may
also transact business and enter into
contracts. Bank of Augusta v. Earle,
13 Pet. 519; Cowell v. Springs Co.,
100 U. S. 55; Bateman v. Service, 6
App. Cas. 386 (P. C.); Kennebec Co.
v. Augusta Ins. Co., 6 Gray (Mass.)
204; Newburg Petroleum Co. v.
Weare, 27 Ohio St. 343; Bank of Cincinnati v. Hall, 35 Ohio St. 158;
Howe Machine Co. v. Walker, 35
U. C. Q. B. 37. It may hold land.
Runyan v. Coster, 14 Pet. 122; Christian Union v. Yount, 101 U. S. 352.
It may take real or personal estate by
will. White v. Howard, 38 Conn.
342; Thompson v. Swoope, 24 Pa. St.
474; American Bible Society v. Marshall, 15 Ohio St. 537; Sherwood v.
American Bible Society, 4 Abb. App.
Dec. (N. Y.) 227.

The power of a corporation to act
in a foreign country depends both on
the law of the country where it was
created, and on the law of the country
where it assumes to act. It has only
such powers as were given to it by the
authority which created it. It cannot
do any act by virtue of those powers in
any country where the laws forbid it so
to act. It follows that every country
may impose conditions and restrictions upon foreign corporations which
transact business within its limits.
Liverpool Ins. Co. v. Massachusetts,
10 Wall. 566; Att.-Gen. v. Bay State
Mining Co., 99 Mass. 148; Bard v.

Poole, 12 N. Y. 495; Phœnix Ins. Co. v. Commonwealth, 5 Bush (Ky.) 68.

In Canada, it was intimated in some early cases that, although a foreign corporation might sue, yet it could not transact business or enter into a valid contract out of its own country. Bank of Montreal v. Bethune, 4 U. C. K. B., O.S. 341; Genesee Ins. Co. v. Westman, 8 U. C. Q. B. 487. The point actually decided in these cases was, that the foreign corporation had not, by its charter, authority to transact business in other countries than its own. See 2 Lindley, Partn. (4th ed.) 1484. In the later case of Howe Machine Co. v. Walker, 35 U. C. Q. B. 37, it was held that a foreign corporation could enforce a promissory note payable to it, made and delivered in Canada, and it was strongly intimated that such corporations could carry on their business and make contracts in Canada.

In Kansas it was held that a corporation, constituted in Pennsylvania with power to do business anywhere except in Pennsylvania, could not act in Kansas, though it could have acted there if it had not been excluded from Pennsylvania. Land Grant Ry. v. Coffey County, 6 Kans. 245. The reasoning by which this result was reached is not satisfactory. It was not suggested that any law of Kansas prohibited such a corporation from acting there. As it was conceded that Pennsylvania might give it general power to act anywhere, it is difficult to see why that state might not limit the operations of the corporation to any place within or without Pennsylvania.

It is sometimes a question of difficulty whether a foreign association is to be deemed a corporation or not. It is considered a corporation if the shareholders are not individually liable in respect of causes of action against the association. General Steam Navigation Co. v. Guillou, 11 M. & W. 877, 895. In Liverpool Ins. Co. v. Massachusetts, 10 Wall. 566, the Supreme Court of the United States held that an association might be a corporation, although the members were individually liable, and the statutes from which its powers were derived expressly provided that it should not be deemed to be incorporated. The question in this case was whether the association was an 'insurance company incorporated or associated under the laws of' a foreign state, in the sense of a statute which imposed a tax upon every such company. It was held to be a corporation, because it had these qualities of a corporation, viz., a distinctive name, the power to sue and be sued in the name of one of its officers as the representative of the whole body, perpetual succession of members by transfer and transmission of its shares, and an existence apart from its shareholders which enabled it to sue them and be sued by them. Bradley, J. agreed with the rest of the court in holding that the company was liable to the tax; he thought however that it was not a corporation, and could not maintain an action or be sued as a corporation in this country; but that it was a company associated under the laws of a foreign country, and so came within the scope of the statute. The Massachusetts court had decided in the same case (nom. Oliver v. Liverpool Ins. Co., 100 Mass. 531) that the company was liable to the tax on the ground that although it was not a corporation in the full sense of the term as defined by the common law, yet it was an association formed by legislative authority, and so far clothed with corporate powers that it might be treated, for the purposes of taxation, as an artificial body. In other cases it has been held that a company is a mere partnership, and not a corporation, where the members are individually liable, although the statutes under which the company was formed provide that it may sue and be sued in the name of its president or treasurer, and that no action shall be brought against the members until after execution against the company shall have been returned unsatisfied, and the interests of the members are held in shares assignable like those of a corporation; the provisions concerning actions have been deemed to have no operation beyond the limits of the state that enacted them, and actions were maintained in other states directly against the members. Taft v. Ward, 106 Mass. 518; Gott v. Dinsmore, 111 Mass. 45; Boston & Albany Rld. Co. v. Pearson, 128 Mass. 445; Frost v. Walker, 60 Me. 468. The question whether an association, formed under foreign law, not strictly a corporation, may be regarded as an artificial body or quasi corporation so far as to enable it to sue and be sued as such, seems not to have been directly decided. See Alivon v. Furnival, 1 C. M. & R. 277, 296; Westcott v. Fargo, 61 N. Y. 542.

Residence of a Corporation. — As a corporation is an artificial and incorporeal being, it cannot strictly have any locality. Carron Iron Co. v. Maclaren, 5 H. L. C. p. 441. It cannot be said to reside or to be present anywhere in the sense in which a natural person resides at place or is present there. But as the rights and obligations of natural persons often depend upon their residence, and corporations frequently have the same rights and obligations, it becomes necessary to attribute to a corporation a residence by analogy to a natural person. The only way in which a corporation can manifest its presence in a place is by transacting its business there. The place where the business of the corporation is carried on is therefore deemed the residence of the corporation. But the business which determines its residence is not the trading or manufacturing which the corporation does, but the management and direction of the affairs of the corporation. Cesena Sulphur Co. v. Nicholson, 1 Ex. D. 428. As a cor-

poration can carry on its business in a foreign country as well in that where it was constituted, subject to the limitation that it is not prohibited by either country, there seems to be no reason why a corporation may not be said to reside in a different country from that by which it was incorporated. In Cesena Sulphur Co. v. Nicholson, 1 Ex. D. 428, 453, in which a company incorporated in England under the Companies' Acts, was held to reside in England and consequently to be liable to income tax, because the real business was carried on there, although the trading and the property were in Italy, Huddleston, B., said, 'The attorney-general advanced a proposition to which I cannot assent. He suggested that the registration of a company was conclusive of its residence, that if a company was registered in England, it must be held to reside in England. I think the answer which was given during the argument is a good one. It is this: Registration, like the birth of an individual, is a fact which must be taken into consideration in determining the question of residence. It may be a strong circumstance, but it is only a circumstance. It would be idle to say that in the case of an individual the birth was conclusive of the residence. So, drawing an analogy between a natural and an artificial person, you may say that in the case of a corporation the place of its registration is the place of its birth, and is a fact to be considered with all the others. If you find that a company which is registered in a particular country, acts in that country, has its office and receives dividends in that country, you may say that those facts, coupled with the registration, lead you to the conclusion that its residence is in that country.'

The case of the Bank of Augusta v. Earle, 13 Pet. 519, 588, contains a dictum by Taney, C.J., to the effect that

12

a corporation can have no existence out of the state by which it was created. The point decided in this case was that a corporation could make contracts in other states. It was urged in the argument that a corporation was incapable of making a contract out of the state, because it was the mere creature of the law of the state, and could have no existence beyond the limits in which that law operated. Taney C.J., referred to this argument and said, ' It is very true that a corporation can have no legal existence out of the boundaries of the sovereignty by which it is created. It exists only in contemplation of law, and by force of the law; and where that law ceases to operate, and is no longer obligatory, the corporation can have no existence. It must dwell in the place of its creation, and cannot migrate to another sovereignty. But although it must live and have its being in that state only, yet it does not by any means follow that its existence there will not be recognized in other places; and its residence in one state creates no insuperable objection to its power of contracting in another.' These dicta are open to this further observation, which always weakens the force of any judicial dicta, that they were made in the way of concession to the party against whom they were about to decide. James, L.J., in Occleston v. Fullalove, L. R. 9 Ch. p. 160. The dicta have often been quoted as if they were the expression of a self-evident truth, yet it is difficult to find any sufficient ground for the proposition contained in them. Why cannot a corporation exist in a place where the laws of the state that created it do not operate? The status of marriage created by the laws of one state does not cease to exist when the husband and wife go into another state. A contract continues to bind the parties although they depart from the state the laws of which created the obligation of the contract. Rights of property in a chat-

tel, which have been created by the laws of one state, do not cease to exist upon the removal of the chattel into another state. In these cases the law that created the status, the obligation, and the rights of property, does not operate in the other state, yet that furnishes no reason why the effect produced by that law in the state where it did operate should not be recognized in other states as a fact. There seems also to be no reason why the existence of a corporation should be necessarily confined within the state where it originated. The court decided in the case before it that a corporation could exercise its powers in another state through agents. But the powers of the corporation were derived entirely from the laws of the state where it was created, and the court, in deciding that the powers might be exercised elsewhere, admitted that the effect of the laws which granted the powers was not confined to that state. In fact the decision that a corporation could sue in another state established the principle that the corporation was not incapable of exercising its powers there by reason that the laws of the state which created it had no force or effect in the other state. That reason could not afterwards be alleged as a valid reason why the corporation could not transact business, or make contracts, or establish its place of business or ' residence ' out of the state of its origin.

Jurisdiction. — A court may exercise jurisdiction over a defendant who is present, when process is served upon him, within the country to which the court belongs, although he is not domiciled there, nor in any way subject to the jurisdiction except by reason of his presence. Schibsby v. Westenholz, L. R. 6 Q. B. 155, 161; Peabody v. Hamilton, 106 Mass. 217; post, s. 541, 554. A corporation may, by its presence or residence in a foreign country, make itself subject to the jurisdiction of its courts. Newby v. Colt's

Firearms Co., L. R. 7 Q. B. 293; Carron Iron Co. v. Maclaren, 5 H. L. C.
p. 449, 450, 459; Bank of Commerce
v. Huntington, 129 Mass. 444; March
v. Eastern Rld. Co., 40 N. H. 548, 577;
St. Louis v. Wiggins Ferry Co., 40
Mo. 580; McNichol v. United States
Reporting Agency, 74 Mo. 457; Han-
nibal & St. Joseph Rld. Co. v. Crane,
102 Ill. 249; Fithian v. New York &
Erie Rld. Co., 31 Pa. St. 114; Brauser
v. New England Ins. Co., 21 Wis. 506;
Moulin v. Insurance Co., 24 N. J. L.
222; Moch v. Virginia Ins. Co., 10
Fed. R. 696. If the corporation merely employs an agent in the foreign
country, or transacts only a subordinate part of its business there, it will
not therefore be considered as resident
in that country. Newby v. Colt's Firearms Co., L. R. 7 Q. B. 293, 295; Mac-
kereth v. Glasgow & South-Western
Ry. Co., L. R. 8 Ex. 149. But it will
be held to reside in the foreign country, and to be subject to the jurisdiction of the courts, if it has a principal
place of business or head office there,
from which the business of the corporation or a branch of it is managed
and directed. See the two cases last
cited, and Bank of Commerce v. Huntington, 129 Mass. 444; Cesena Sulphur Co. v. Nicholson, 1 Ex. D. 428.
A corporation may thus reside in several countries.

The same point has been decided
under the statutes of the United States
regulating the jurisdiction of the federal courts. These statutes provide
that no civil suit shall be brought
against an inhabitant of the United
States except in the district ' of which
he is an inhabitant or in which he is
found at the time of serving the writ.'
The Supreme Court has held that a
corporation of one state is *found* in
another, when it has appointed an
agent there to receive service of process in accordance with the laws of
the latter state making such appoint-
ment a condition of its doing business
there, or when it has exercised its

powers in another state with the express consent of the legislature of that
state, it being considered an implied
condition of the consent that the corporation may be sued there. Ex parte
Schollenberger, 96 U. S. 369; Railroad
Co. v. Harris, 12 Wall. 65. See also
Mohr v. Insurance Cos., 12 Fed. R.
474; M'Coy v. Cincinnati Rld. Co.,
13 Fed. R. 3; Wilson Packing Co. v.
Hunter, 7 Reporter, 455; 8 Cent. L. J.
383. In Hayden v. Androscoggin Mills
1 Fed. R. 93; 9 Reporter, 270, a manufacturing corporation chartered in
Maine had a principal place of business in Massachusetts, where most of
the business except the actual manufacture was done, and from which the
manufacture itself was controlled and
directed; and it was held that the corporation was *found* in Massachusetts.
Lowell, J., said, ' I think a trading
corporation may be said to be personally present for the purposes of an
action wherever it has an established
place of trade.' These decisions seem
seriously to impair the metaphysical
doctrine that a corporation cannot exist out of the state where it originated.

Westlake says (ed. 1880, p. 296) ' The
English court will not interfere in the
internal disputes of foreign corporations.' It did interfere in Pickering
v. Stephenson, L. R. 14 Eq. 322, where
a shareholder of a Turkish railway
corporation filed a bill, on behalf of
himself and the other shareholders,
against the directors and the corporation, to prevent the misapplication of
the funds of the corporation. Westlake says that ' it does not seem to
have been strenuously argued that the
Turkish courts had exclusive jurisdiction,' and that ' for the credit of the
company it may not have been desirable to take such a line.' The point
however does seem from the report to
have been strongly urged (L. R. 14 Eq.
p. 334), and the report gives no indi-
cation that the defendants omitted,
out of regard to the credit of the com-

pany, to avail themselves of any point in their favor. See also Lewis v. Baldwin, 11 Beav. 153. In Sudlow v. Dutch Rhenish Ry. Co., 21 Beav. 43, the case cited by Westlake in support of his proposition, a shareholder of a Dutch corporation filed a bill against the corporation, the directors, and the secretary at the London office, to prevent the forfeiture of his shares. The governing body was in Holland, and there was a secretary and office in London, where a copy of the register of shares was kept, the original register being in Holland. The plaintiff insisted that by the company's articles his shares were not forfeited, but the defendants proved that, according to the decision of the Dutch courts in a similar case, the shares were forfeited. Romilly, M.R., said, during the argument, that he felt great difficulty in seeing how the plaintiff could have any decree, as the case was that of a Dutch contract, and the Dutch courts had given to it a construction opposite to that insisted on by the plaintiff. It was admitted, he said, that all the plaintiff could have would be 'a declaration in favor of the plaintiff (which, in point of fact, would be opposite to the decision of the Dutch courts), and then to make a declaration that the register of shareholders here shall not be varied by the omission of the name of the plaintiff; although it is admitted that the register of shareholders here is only a copy of the original register in Holland, and that it is the duty of the secretary here to keep the copy conformable with the original register.' The counsel for the plaintiff declining to argue the point further, the bill was dismissed. The case therefore appears to have gone off on the point that the Dutch law which controlled the case was against the plaintiff. It is difficult, too, to see how the court had any jurisdiction of the corporation, or of any of the directors except one who resided in England. Lindley (Partn. (4th ed.)

1486) cites the case simply as an authority for the proposition that, if disputes between the members have arisen and been adjudicated upon by a foreign court of competent jurisdiction, its decision will not be reviewed in England at the instance of a shareholder resident there, and not a party to the proceedings abroad.

In Smith v. Mutual Ins. Co., 14 Allen (Mass.) 336, the Massachusetts court declined to entertain a bill in equity by a non-resident against a mutual life insurance company, incorporated in another state, to prevent the forfeiture of his policy. Process had been served upon an agent in Massachusetts appointed by the company, in compliance with a statute, to receive service of process against it. The court expressed the opinion that jurisdiction of the defendant obtained by service of process did not warrant it in assuming authority over the subject-matter. It doubted whether jurisdiction could be acquired by service upon the agent, when the residence of the plaintiff, the place of the contract, and the property or life insured were out of the state; but this doubt has since been overruled in Johnston v. Trade Ins. Co., 132 Mass. 432. The court, too, appears to have been influenced by the opinion that jurisdiction of a foreign corporation could not be obtained except by an attachment of its property, which was afterwards more distinctly stated in Andrews v. Michigan Rld. Co., 99 Mass. 534, but was disapproved in Bank of Commerce v. Huntington, 129 Mass. 446, 450. The decision seems really to have been placed upon the ground that, aside from the question of jurisdiction, it was within the province of the court in its discretion to decline to exercise jurisdiction in such cases. It was expressly said that the court did not define the jurisdiction of the court in a case where the contract was made within the state, with a citizen thereof, and insuring a *life* or property therein. It can hardly be said that the court committed itself to anything except that under the particular circumstances of that case it would not exercise jurisdiction. In *the* earlier case of Williston *v.* Michigan Rld. Co., 13 Allen (Mass.) 400, the court refused to allow the owner of guaranteed shares to change an action at law for not declaring and paying dividends, into a suit in equity, under a statute authorizing such changes. In this case the court had acquired no jurisdiction of the corporation, except to the extent of certain property in the state which had been attached, and that was the ground of the decision.

It is difficult to understand how the jurisdiction of the court over a foreign corporation can be limited to any particular classes of cases, if it has acquired jurisdiction over the corporation itself. See Handy *v.* Insurance Co., 37 Ohio St. 366; Johnston *v.* Trade Ins. Co., 132 Mass. 432. There seems to be no practical difficulty in the exercise of the jurisdiction. The objection that the corporation may, before judgment or decree, withdraw from the jurisdiction, and that it may be impossible to enforce the decision, may be alleged in any case where security has not been taken for the defendants abiding the decision of the court. There is no reason why a corporation may not be subject to the bankruptcy or insolvency laws of a foreign state. In re Commercial Bank, L. R. 6 Eq. 517; Smith *v.* St. Louis Ins. Co., 6 Lea (Tenn.) 564. Proceedings under such laws are only a mode of execution given to the creditor against a corporation unable to pay its debts. In re General Land Credit Co., L. R. 5 Ch. at p. 380. But the courts of one country can have no power to dissolve a corporation created by the laws of another country. See 2 Lindley, Partn. (4th ed.) 1486.

A penal liability imposed by statute upon the officers or shareholders of a corporation will not be enforced in another state. Halsey *v.* McLean, 12 Allen (Mass.) 438; Derrickson *v.* Smith, 27 N. J. L. 166; First National Bank *v.* Price, 33 Md. 487; Woods *v.* Wicks, 7 Lea (Tenn.) 40. See ante, s. 92; post, s. 620. Where the laws make shareholders individually liable in certain cases for the debts of the corporation, the liability will not be enforced in another state, if it is impracticable to proceed in the manner prescribed by the laws creating the liability. Erickson *v.* Nesmith, 4 Allen (Mass.) 233.

A corporation is not considered a citizen or subject of a state or country in the sense of the provisions of the constitution and laws of the United States which define the jurisdiction of the federal courts. The jurisdiction depends upon the citizenship of the members of the corporation. But, by a fiction of law for the purposes of jurisdiction, the members are presumed to be citizens or subjects of the state or country where the corporation originated, and no averment to the contrary is admitted. Ohio & Mississippi Rld. Co. *v.* Wheeler, 1 Black, 286, 296; Steamship Co. *v.* Tugman, 106 U. S. 118.

Statute of Limitations. — In New York it is held that a corporation created in another state is necessarily a non-resident, and therefore cannot avail itself of the statute of limitations. Olcott *v.* Tioga Rld. Co., 20 N. Y. 210. This decision has been followed in Nevada. Robinson *v.* Imperial Silver Mining Co., 5 Nev. 44, 74. It was also followed by the Supreme Court of the United States in a case depending upon the New York statute of limitations, the court considering itself bound by the construction put upon the statute by the state courts. Tioga Rld. *v.* Blossburg & Corning Rld., 20 Wall. 137. Bradley, J., in delivering the judgment of the court, intimates that the decision of the state court was unsound, and Miller and Strong, JJ., who dissented, denied its authority and correctness. In M'Cabe v. Illinois Central Rld. Co., 13 Fed. R. 827, and Lawrence v. Ballou, 50 Cal. 258, it was held the statute of limitations was a defence to a foreign corporation that was subject to the jurisdiction of the courts.

Meetings of Shareholders and Directors. — An important question is, whether the members of a corporation, or the directors, may meet out of the state where the corporation was created. There would seem to be no doubt that they could do so were it not for the decisions of some of the American state courts. In Princess of Reuss v. Bos, L. R. 5 H. L. 176, the question was whether a company, the objects of which were principally foreign, was properly incorporated under the Companies Acts; the articles of association provided, among other things, that the first general meeting should be held at a time and place on the continent of Europe, or at London, to be appointed by the directors, and subsequent general meetings were to be held at such time and place as might be appointed by the directors. Lord Hatherley noticed this provision, and said that, although London was pointed at in this clause, the meetings might be held in London or in any other place the directors might think fit. Lord Cairns said that the articles of association were regular in all respects but one, which was that certain shares might be made payable to bearer. The company was held to be regularly incorporated. In Att.-Gen. v. Alexander, L. R. 10 Ex. 20, the question was whether a banking corporation created by Turkish law was a 'person residing within the United Kingdom' so as to be liable to income tax upon its whole profits; the circumstance that the annual general meetings of shareholders had always been held in London was mentioned by one of the judges as pointing in the direction that the whole business was carried on in London, and

that the corporation resided there. Its residence was held to be at Constantinople, because by its charter its 'seat' was fixed there. No doubt whatever was suggested as to the propriety of the meetings being held in London. In Connecticut, Vermont, Missouri, and Indiana it has been held that directors may meet out of the state in which the corporation originated. McCall v. Byram Mfg. Co., 6 Conn. 428; .Ohio & Mississippi Rld. Co. v. McPherson, 35 Mo. 13; Arms v. Conant, 36 Vt. 744; Wright v. Bundy, 11 Ind. 404. See also Coe v. Midland Ry. Co., 31 N. J. Eq. 105, 117. In Maine it has been held that, though the directors can meet out of the state, the shareholders cannot. Miller v. Ewer, 27 Me. 509. There is a similar decision iu Indiana (Aspinwall v. Ohio & Mississippi Rld. Co., 20 Ind. 492, 497), and a dictum to the same effect in New Jersey (Hilles v. Parrish, 14 N. J. Eq. 383). In New York it has been held that neither the directors nor the shareholders can meet out of the state. Ormsby v. Vermont Copper Co., 56 N. Y. 623, 625. In the case last mentioned no judgment is reported. The report states only that it was 'held that, according to the settled law of corporations, neither stockholders nor directors can do a corporate act out of the jurisdiction creating the corporation, which shall have any force to bind those who do not participate in it.' This seems to be the first case in which it has been held that directors cannot meet out of the state. The case however seems right in putting directors' meetings upon the same ground as shareholders' meetings, for any reason why shareholders cannot meet out of the state would seem to apply equally to directors. But if the shareholders and directors cannot do 'a corporate act' out of the state, it is difficult to understand how any one else can; yet it probably was not intended that a corporation could not contract and transact business in another state. The doctrine that the shareholders cannot meet out of the state was first asserted in Miller *v.* Ewer, 27 Me. 509, both as to a first meeting to organize the corporation under its charter, and as to a subsequent meeting. The court held that the charter only conferred upon the persons named in it an authority to bring the corporation into existence, and that an authority conferred by law cannot be exercised beyond the bounds of the sovereignty which confers it. It was also held that if the corporation could be considered as having existence, a subsequent meeting could not be held out of the state, because the corporation could not have any existence or presence without its limits. Neither of these reasons will bear examination. An authority conferred by law is exercised beyond the bounds of the sovereignty every time that a corporation makes a contract or transacts business out of the state. Admitting that a corporation cannot exist or be present in another state, that does not apply to the shareholders. The shareholders are not the artificial being which exists only in contemplation of law; and there is no principle upon which it can be said that the artificial being must be present in order that there may be a valid meeting of the shareholders. As this decision was based upon the impossibility of the existence of a corporation or of the exercise of an authority conferred by law beyond the limits of the state, a meeting of shareholders out of the state would not be valid, according to the decision, even if the charter gave express authority for holding meetings out of the state. In Bridge Co. *v.* Mayer, 31 Ohio St. 317, it was held that where a corporation was chartered in two states, the shareholders might meet in either state, and that the acts done at such a meeting in one would be valid in both. Yet, according to the decisions of the Supreme Court of the United States (Railway Co. *v.* Whitton, 13 Wall. 270, 283; Muller *v.* Dows, 94 U. S. 444, 447), a corporation created by the laws of two or more states is in each state a corporation existing under the laws of that state alone.

CHAPTER V.

MARRIAGE.

107. *Subject of the Chapter.* — Having treated of the capacity and incapacity of persons, as affected by foreign law, and especially in relation to their capacity or incapacity to contract marriage in a foreign country,[1] we shall next proceed to consider more fully the nature and effect of the relation of marriage contracted by and between persons who are admitted to be sui juris, and to possess competent capacity everywhere.[2] We shall then discuss the manner in which that relation may be dissolved, and the effect of such dissolution.

108. *Legal Aspect of Marriage.* — Marriage is treated by all civilized nations as a peculiar and favored contract. (a)   It is in its origin a contract of natural law.[3]   It may exist between two

[1] Ante, s. 79–90.

[2] On this subject consult 1 Burge, Col. & For. Law, pt. 1, c. 5; s. 1–3, p. 135–201.

[3] I have throughout treated marriage as a contract in the common sense of the word, because this is the light in which it is ordinarily viewed by jurists,

(a) *Marriage*, as understood in Christendom, means 'the voluntary union for life of one man and one woman, to the exclusion of all others.' The term is therefore not applicable to the union of a man and a woman as practised among the Mormons, by whose faith polygamy is lawful. Persons so united will not be considered husband and wife, although both were single at the time of their union, and they are not entitled to the benefit of the laws providing for the dissolution of marriage or the enforcement of its duties in a country where polygamy is not lawful. Hyde v. Hyde, L. R. 1 P. & M. 130; Harvey v. Farnie, 6 P. D. p. 53; Warrender v. Warrender, 2 Cl. & F. p. 531, 532; Ross v. Ross, 129 Mass. p. 247. See Wall v. Williamson, 8 Ala. 51. 'It may be, and probably is, the case that the women [in polygamous countries] there pass by some word or name which corresponds to our word *wife*. But there is no magic in a name; and if the relation there existing between men and women is not the relation which in Christendom we recognize and intend by the words *husband* or *wife*, but another and altogether different relation, the use of a common term to express these two separate relations will not make them one and the same, though it may tend to confuse them to a superficial observer.' Hyde v. Hyde, L. R. 1 P. & M. p. 134.

individuals of different sexes, although no third person existed in the world, as happened in the case of the common ancestors of mankind. It is the parent and not the child of society; principium urbis et quasi seminarium reipublicæ. In civil society it becomes a civil contract regulated and prescribed by law, and endowed with civil consequences. In many civilized countries, acting under a sense of the force of sacred obligations, it has had the sanctions of religion superadded. It then becomes a religious, as well as a natural and civil, contract; for it is a great mistake to suppose that, because it is the one, therefore it may not likewise be the other.[1] The common law of England (and the like law exists in America) considers marriage in no other light than as a civil contract. The holiness of the matrimonial state is left entirely to ecclesiastical and religious scrutiny.[2] In the Catholic countries, and in some of the Protestant countries, of Europe, it is treated as a sacrament.[3]

109. There are some remarks on this subject, made by a distinguished Scottish judge, so striking that they deserve to be quoted at large.[4] ' Marriage being entirely a personal, consensual contract, it may be thought that the lex loci must be resorted to in expounding every question that arises relative to it. But it will be observed that marriage is a contract sui generis, and differing in some respects from all other contracts; so that the rules of law which are applicable in expounding and enforcing other contracts may not apply to this. The contract of marriage is the most important of all human transactions. It is the very basis of the whole fabric of civilized society. The status of marriage is juris gentium, and the foundation of it, like that of all other contracts, rests on the consent of parties. But it differs from other contracts in this, that the rights, obligations, or duties arising from it are not left entirely to be regulated by the agreements of parties, but

domestic as well as foreign. But it appears to me to be something more than a mere contract. It is rather to be deemed an institution of society, founded upon the consent and contract of the parties; and in this view it has some peculiarities in its nature, character, operation, and extent of obligation different from what belong to ordinary contracts.

[1] Dalrymple v. Dalrymple, 2 Hagg. Cons. 63; Lindo v. Belisario, 1 Hagg. Cons. 231.

[2] 1 Black. Com. 433.

[3] Dalrymple v. Dalrymple, 2 Hagg. Cons. 63–65.

[4] Lord Robertson, in Fergusson on Mar. and Divorce, 397–399.

are, to a certain extent, matters of municipal regulation, over which the parties have no control by any declaration of their will. It confers the status of legitimacy on children born in wedlock, with all the consequential rights, duties, and privileges thence arising; it gives rise to the relations of consanguinity and affinity; in short, it pervades the whole system of civil society. Unlike other contracts, it cannot, in general, amongst civilized nations, be dissolved by mutual consent, and it subsists in full force, even although one of the parties should be forever rendered incapable, as in the case of incurable insanity, or the like, from performing his part of the mutual contract.

110. 'No wonder that the rights, duties, and obligations, arising from so important a contract, should not be left to the discretion or caprice of the contracting parties, but should be regulated in many important particulars by the laws of every civilized country. And such laws must be considered as forming a most essential part of the public law of the country. As to the constitution of the marriage, as it is merely a personal, consensual contract, it must be valid everywhere, if celebrated according to the lex loci; but, with regard to the rights, duties, and obligations thence arising, the law of the domicil must be looked to. It must be admitted that in every country the laws relative to divorce are considered as of the utmost importance, as public laws affecting the dearest interest of society.

111. 'It is said that in every contract the parties bind themselves, not only to what is expressly stipulated, but also to what is implied in the nature of the contract, and that these stipulations, whether express or implied, are not affected by any subsequent change of domicil. This may be true in the general case, but, as already noticed, marriage is a contract sui generis, and the rights, duties, and obligations which arise out of it, are matters of so much importance to the well-being of the state, that they are regulated, not by the private contract, but by the public laws of the state, which are imperative on all who are domiciled within its territory. If a man in this country were to confine his wife in an iron cage, or to beat her with a rod of the thickness of the judge's finger, would it be a justification in any court, to allege that these were powers which the law of England conferred on a husband, and that he was entitled to the exer-

cise of them, because his marriage had been celebrated in that country?

112. 'In short, although a marriage which is contracted according to the lex loci will be valid all the world over, and although many of the obligations incident to it are left to be regulated solely by the agreement of the parties, yet many of the rights, duties, and obligations arising from it are so important to the best interests of morality and good government that the parties have no control over them, but they are regulated and enforced by the public law, which is imperative on all who are domiciled within its jurisdiction, and which cannot be controlled or affected by the circumstance that the marriage was celebrated in a country where the law is different. In expounding or enforcing a contract entered into in a foreign country, and executed according to the laws of that country, regard will be paid to the lex loci, as the contract is evidence that the parties had in view the law of the country, and meant to be bound by it. But a party who is domiciled here cannot be permitted to import into this country a law peculiar to his own case, and which is in opposition to those great and important public laws which our legislature has held to be essentially connected with the best interests of society.'[1]

113. *Validity of Marriage.* — The general principle certainly is, as we have already seen, that between persons sui juris, marriage is to be decided by the law of the place where it is celebrated.[2] If valid there, it is valid everywhere. It has a legal ubiquity of obligation. If invalid there, it is equally invalid everywhere.[3] The grounds of this doctrine we shall have occasion presently to consider.[4] It is only necessary here to state

[1] Lord Robertson, in Fergusson on Mar. and Divorce, 397–399.

[2] Ante, s. 80, 81. See Kent v. Burgess, 11 Sim. 361; Patterson v. Gaines, 6 How. 550.

[3] Ryan v. Ryan, 2 Phillim. Ecc. 332; Herbert v. Herbert, 3 Phillim. Ecc. 58; Dalrymple v. Dalrymple, 2 Hagg. Cons. 54; Ruding v. Smith, 2 Hagg. Cons. 390, 391; Scrimshire v. Scrimshire, 2 Hagg. Cons. 395; Munro v. Saunders, 6 Bligh, 473, 474; Ilderton v. Ilderton, 2 H. Bl. 145; Middleton v. Janverin, 2 Hagg. Cons. 437; Lacon v. Higgins, 3 Stark. 178; 2 Kent Com. 91–93; Medway v. Needham, 16 Mass. 157; Putnam v. Putnam, 8 Pick. 433; West Cambridge v. Lexington, 1 Pick. 506; 1 Burge, Col. & For. Law, c. 5, s. 3, p. 184–201; 2 Kames on Eq. b. 3, c. 8, s. 1; Kent v. Burgess, 11 Sim. 361.

[4] Post, s. 121. See also ante, s. 80.

that it has received the most deliberate sanction of the English
and American courts.[1] (a)

113 a. *Polygamous, Incestuous, and Prohibited Marriages.* —
The most prominent, if not the only known exceptions to the
rule, are those marriages involving polygamy and incest, those
positively prohibited by the public law of a country from motives
of policy, and those celebrated in foreign countries by subjects,
entitling themselves, under special circumstances, to the benefit
of the laws of their own country.[2] Cases illustrative of each of
these exceptions have been already alluded to.[3]

114. *Polygamy and Incest.* — In respect to the first exception,
that of marriages involving polygamy and incest, Christianity is
understood to prohibit polygamy and incest, and therefore no
Christian country would recognize polygamy or incestuous marriages.[4] (b) But when we speak of incestuous marriages, care
must be taken to confine the doctrine to such cases as by the
general consent of all Christendom are deemed incestuous. (c)

[1] See cases cited supra, s. 113, note 1; post, s. 122–124.
[2] 1 Burge, Col. & For. Law, c. 5, s. 3, p. 188.   [3] Ante, s. 89.
[4] Paley on Moral Phil. b. 3, c. 6; 2 Kent Com. 81; 1 Black. Com. 436.
See Grotius, b. 2, c. 5, s. 9; Greenwood v. Curtis, 6 Mass. 378; 1 Burge, Col.
& For. Law, pt. 1, c. 5, s. 3, p. 188, 189, 190; Huberus, lib. 1, tit. 3, s. 8.
See Swift v. Kelly, 3 Knapp, 257, 279.

(a) The principle is established
that the validity of a marriage, the
word *marriage* being used in the
sense of *ceremony of marriage*, depends upon the law of the place where
the ceremony is performed. When
the question is whether it is lawful for
the two persons to be united in wedlock, there is a difference of opinion
as to the law by which the validity of
the marriage (the word being used to
designate the union in wedlock which
the ceremony is intended to effect) is
to be determined. See note, s. 124 a,
post.

(b) Sneed v. Ewing, 5 J. J. Marsh.
(Ky.) 460, 489. See Wall v. Williamson, 8 Ala. 48, 50, 51.

(c) In Brook v. Brook, 9 H. L. C.
p. 227, Lord Cranworth said, ' I cannot however refrain from expressing
my dissent from that part of Sir Cress-

well Cresswell's able opinion, in which
he repudiates a part of what is said
by Mr. Justice Story as to marriages
which are to be held void on the ground
of incest. That very learned writer
after stating (s. 113) that marriages
valid where they are contracted are,
in general, to be held valid everywhere,
proceeds thus: "The most prominent,
if not the only known exceptions to
the rule, are marriages involving polygamy or incest; those positively prohibited by the public law of a country
from motives of policy, and those celebrated in foreign countries by subjects
entitling themselves, under special circumstances, to the laws of their own
country." And then he adds that,
" as to the first exception, Christianity
is understood to prohibit polygamy
and incest, and therefore no Christian
country would recognize polygamy or

It is difficult to ascertain exactly the point at which the law of nature or the authority of Christianity ceases to prohibit marriages between kindred, and Christian nations are by no means generally agreed on this subject.[1] In most of the countries of Europe in which the canon law has had any authority or influence, marriages are prohibited between near relations by blood or by marriage, or, in other words, by consanguinity or by affinity; and the canon and the common law seem to have made no distinction on this point between consanguinity or relation by blood, and affinity or relation by marriage, although there certainly is a very material difference in the cases.[2] Marriages between relations by blood in the lineal ascending or descending line are universally held by the common law, the canon law, and the civil law, to be unnatural and unlawful.[3] So are marriages between

---

[1] Grotius, b. 2, c. 5, s. 12-14. See 1 Brown, Civ. Law, 61-65; 1 Burge, Col. & For. Law, c. 5, s. 3, p. 188.

[2] 2 Kent Com. 81, 82; 1 Black. Com. 434. See, on this subject, The London Quarterly Law Magazine for May, 1839, vol. 21, p. 371-382; The London Monthly Law Magazine for May, 1840, vol. 7, p. 330, 332, and the London Legal Observer for January, 1840.

[3] Wightman v. Wightman, 4 Johns. Ch. (N. Y.) 343; 2 Kent Com. 81-84; Harrison v. Burwell, Vaughan, 206; 2 Vent. 9; Grotius, b. 2, c. 5, s. 12, n. 1, incestuous marriages; but when we speak of incestuous marriages, care must be taken to confine the doctrine to such cases as, by the general consent of all Christendom, are deemed incestuous." With the latter portion of the doctrine of Mr. Justice Story, Sir Cresswell Cresswell does not agree. But I believe that this passage, when correctly interpreted, is strictly consonant to the law of nations. Story, there, is not speaking of marriages prohibited as incestuous by the municipal law of the country. If so prohibited, they would be void under his second class of exceptional cases; no inquiry would be open as to the general opinion of Christendom. But suppose the case of a Christian country, in which there are no laws prohibiting marriages within any specified degrees of consanguinity or affinity, or declaring or defining what is incest; still, even there, incestuous marriages would be held void, as polygamy would be held void, being forbidden by the Christian religion. But then, to ascertain what marriages are, within that rule, incestuous, a rule not depending on municipal laws, but extending generally to all Christian countries, recourse must be had to what is deemed incestuous by the general consent of Christendom. It could never be held that the subjects of such a country were guilty of incest in contracting a marriage allowed and approved by a large portion of Christendom, merely because, in the contemplation of other Christian countries, it would be considered to be against God's laws. I have thought it right to enter into this explanation, because it is important that a writer so highly and justly respected as Mr. Justice Story should not be misunderstood, as, with all deference, I think he has been in the passage under consideration.'

brother and sister in the collateral line, whether of the whole
blood or of the half-blood ; [1] and, indeed, such marriages seem
repugnant to the first principles of social order and morality. It
has been well remarked by Mr. Chancellor Kent that it will be
found difficult to carry the prohibition further in the collateral
line than the first degree (that is, beyond brother and sister), unless where the legislature have expressly provided such a prohibition.[2] Grotius has expressed an equally strong opinion upon the

2; Id. s. 13, n. 4; Id. s. 14, n. 1; 2 Heinecc. Elem. Juris. Natur. b. 2, c. 2,
s. 40, by Turnbull; 1 Burge, Col. & For. Law, pt. 1, c. 5, s. 1, p. 137, 146,
147; Com. Dig. Baron and Feme, B. 4 ; 2 Inst. 693. Lord Brougham, in
Warrender v. Warrender, 9 Bligh, 112, 113, speaking on this subject, said:
' But this rule extends, I apprehend, no further than to the ascertaining of the
validity of the contract and the meaning of the parties, that is, the existence
of the contract and its construction. If, indeed, there go two things under one
and the same name in different countries, if that which is called marriage is of
a different nature in each, there may be some room for holding that we are to
consider the thing to which the parties have bound themselves, according to
its legal acceptation in the country where the obligation was contracted. But
marriage is one and the same thing substantially all the Christian world over.
Our whole law of marriage assumes this; and it is important to observe that
we regard it as a wholly different thing, a different status, from Turkish or
other marriages among infidel nations, because we clearly never should recognize the plurality of wives, and consequent validity of second marriages, standing the first, which second marriages the laws of those countries authorize and
validate. This cannot be put upon any rational ground, except our holding
the infidel marriage to be something different from the Christian, and our also
holding the Christian marriage to be the same everywhere. Therefore, all
that the courts of one country have to determine, is, whether or not the thing
called marriage, that known relation of persons, that relation which those
courts are acquainted with, and know how to deal with, has been validly contracted in the other country where the parties professed to bind themselves.
If the question is answered in the affirmative, a marriage has been had; the
relation has been constituted; and those courts will deal with the rights of the
parties under it, according to the principles of the municipal law which they
administer.' See also Id. 114.
    [1] 2 Kent Com. 83, 84. See also Butler v. Gastrill, Gilb. Eq. 156; 1
Burge, Col. & For. Law, pt. 1, c. 6, s. 1, p. 127; Id. s. 3, p. 188; Grotius, de
Jure Belli, lib. 2, c. 5, s. 12, n. 2; Id. s. 13, n. 3–7.
    [2] Wightman v. Wightman, 4 Johns. Ch. (N. Y.) 343. The whole remarks
of the learned Chancellor on this occasion deserve to be cited at large. ' Besides the case of lunacy now before me, I have hypothetically mentioned the
case of a marriage between persons in the direct lineal line of consanguinity as
clearly unlawful by the law of the land, independent of any church canon, or
of any statute prohibition. That such a marriage is criminal and void by the
law of nature is a point universally conceded. And by the law of nature I
understand those fit and just rules of conduct which the Creator has prescribed
to man as a dependent and social being, and which are to be ascertained from

intrinsic difficulty of the subject. 'De conjugiis eorum qui san-
guine aut affinitate satis gravis est quæstio, et non raro magnis

the deductions of right reason, though they may be more precisely known, and
more explicitly declared by divine revelation. There is one other case in
which the marriage would be equally void, causa consanguinitatis, and that is
the case of brother and sister; and since it naturally arises in the consideration
of this subject, I will venture to add a few incidental observations. I am
aware that, when we leave the lineal line, and come to the relation by blood or
affinity in the collateral line, it is not so easy to ascertain the exact point at
which the natural law has ceased to discountenance the union. Though there
may be some difference in the theories of different writers on the law of nature,
in regard to this subject, yet the general current of authority and the practice
of civilized nations, and certainly of the whole Christian world, have condemned the connection in the second case which has been supposed, as grossly
indecent, immoral, and incestuous, and inimical to the purity and happiness
of families, and as forbidden by the law of nature.' Grotius, de Jure, &c.
lib. 2, c. 5, s. 13; Puffend. de Jure Gent. lib. 6, c. 1, s. 34; Id. de Off. Hom.
lib. 2, c. 2, s. 8; Heinecc. Oper. tom. 8, pars 2, p. 203; Taylor's Elem. Civ.
Law, 326; Montesq. Esp. des Lois, liv. 26, c. 14; Paley's Moral Philosophy, b. 3,
p. 3, c. 5. We accordingly find such connections expressly prohibited in different codes. Dig. 23, 2, 18; 23, 2, 14, 2; 45, 1, 35, 1; Just. Inst. 1, 10; De Nuptiis, Vinnius, h. t.; Heinecc. ubi supra; Code Civil de France, n. 161–164; Inst.
of Menu, by Sir William Jones, c. 3, s. 5; Staunton, Ta-Tsing-Leu-Lee, s. 107,
108; Sale's Koran, c. 4; Marsden's Sumatra, p. 194, 221. And whatever may
have been the practice of some ancient nations, originating, as Montesquieu
observes, in the madness of superstition, the objection to such marriages is,
undoubtedly, founded in reason and nature. It grows out of the institutions
of families, and the rights and duties, habits and affections, flowing from that
relation, and which may justly be considered as part of the law of our nature
as rational and social beings. Marriages among such near relations would not
only lead to domestic licentiousness; but, by blending in one object duties and
feelings incompatible with each other, would perplex and confound the duties,
habits, and affections proceeding from the family state, impair the perception,
and corrupt the purity of moral taste, and do violence to the moral sentiments
of mankind. Indeed we might infer the sense of mankind, and the dictates
of reason and nature, from the language of horror and detestation in which
such incestuous connections have been reprobated and condemned in all ages.
Plato de Leg. lib. 8; Cic. Orat. pro Mil. 27; Hermion. in Eurip. Androm. v.
175; Byblis. Ovid. Met. lib. 9; Tacit. Ann. lib. 12, c. 4; Vel. Paterc. Hist.
lib. 2, c. 45; Corn. Nep. Excel. Imp. Prefat. The general usage of mankind
is sufficient to settle the question, if it were possible to have any doubt on the
subject; and it must have proceeded from some strong uniform and natural
principle. Prohibitions of the natural law are of absolute, uniform, and universal obligation. They become rules of common law, which is founded in
the common reason and acknowledged duty of mankind, sanctioned by imme-
morial usage, and, as such, are clearly binding. To this extent, then, I apprehend it to be within the power and within the duty of this court to enforce the
prohibition. Such marriages should be declared void, as contra bonos mores.
But as to the other collateral degrees beyond brother and sister, I should incline to the intimation of the judges in Harrison v. Buswell, Vaugh. 206; 2

motibus agitata. Nam causas certas ac naturales, cur talia con-
jugia, ita ut legibus aut moribus vetantur, illicitata sint, assignare,
qui voluerit, experiendo discet, quam, id sit difficile, imo præstari
non possit." [1]

114 a. At all events, in other cases of consanguinity not in
the lineal line, or in the first degree of the collateral line, there
is much room for diversity of opinion and judgment among
jurists, and of practice among nations. Grotius has taken notice
of this distinction, and says: 'Quæ manifesta expressio ostendere
videtur discrimen, quod est inter hos et alios remotiores gradus.'[2]
Thus, he says that it is forbidden to marry an aunt on the father's
side, but not the daughter of a brother, who is of the same degree. ' Nam ducere amitam agnatam vetitum est. At filiam fratris, qui par est gradus, ducere vetitum non est.'[3] In England it
has been declared by statute that all persons may lawfully marry
but such as are prohibited by God's law, that is, such as are
within the Levitical degrees.[4] Under this general provision it

Vent. 9, already cited, that as we have no statute on the subject, and no train
of common-law decisions independent of any statute authority, the Levitical
degrees are not binding as a rule of municipal obedience. Marriages out of
the lineal line, and in the collateral line, beyond the degree of brothers and
sisters, could not well be declared void as against the first principles of society.
The laws or usages of all the nations to whom I have referred do, indeed, extend the prohibition to remoter degrees; but this is stepping out of the family
circle; and I cannot put the prohibition on any other ground than positive institution. There is a great diversity of usage on this subject. Neque teneo,
neque dicta refello. The limitation must be left, until the legislature thinks
proper to make some provision in the case, to the injunctions of religion, and
to the control of manners and opinion.' See also, 2 Kent Com. 83, 84; 1
Burge, Col. & For. Law, pt. 1, c. 5, s. 1, p. 188.

[1] Grotius, de Jure Belli, lib. 2, c. 5, s. 12.
[2] Grotius, de Jure Belli, lib. 2, c. 5, s. 14, n. 1.   [3] Ibid.
[4] Com. Dig. Baron and Feme, B 2, B 4; 1 Black. Com. 435; Leviticus,
c. 18. Mr. Burge states the prohibitions in England arising from the Levitical
law in the following terms: ' Cognatio, consanguinity, or relationship by blood,
and affinitas, affinity, or relationship by marriage, constitute impediments to a
lawful marriage. Marriages between parties related by blood or by affinity in
the direct ascending or descending line, in infinitum, are prohibited by the
civil and canon law. This prohibition prevents that confusion of civil duties
which would be the necessary results of such marriages. The codes of Europe
concur in this prohibition. In the collateral line the prohibition is confined to
those who stand in certain degrees of consanguinity or affinity to each other.
In the computation of these degrees there is a difference between the civil and
canon law. Thus, those who according to the civil law are in the second degree, are placed by the canon law in the first degree; and those who are placed
by the civil law in the fourth degree, are by the canon law placed in the second

has been held that a marriage between an uncle and a niece by
blood is incestuous (it being in the third degree), upon the
ground that it is against the law of God and sound morals, that
it would tend to endless confusion, and that the sanctity of pri- .
vate life would be polluted, and the proper freedom of intercourse
in families would be destroyed, if such practices were not dis-
couraged in the strongest manner.[1]   Yet Grotius not only deems
such a marriage perfectly unexceptionable, but adds that there
are examples of it among the Hebrews.[2] (a)   But marriages
between first cousins by blood, or cousins-german, being in the
fourth degree, are, according to English jurisprudence, lawful;
so that the prohibitions in the collateral line stop at the third
degree.[3]   The same rule, as to the marriage of first cousins, has
been adopted by the Protestant countries of Europe.   But the
canon law prohibited such marriages, although a dispensation
might be obtained thereof.[4]   Incestuous marriages by the English
law are not however deemed by the common law absolutely

degree. The degrees prohibited by the Levitical law are all within the fourth
degree of consanguinity, according to the computation of the civil law; all
collaterals therefore in that degree, or beyond it, may marry. First cousins
are in the fourth degree by the civil law, and therefore may marry. Nephew
and great-aunt, or niece and great-uncle, are also in the fourth degree, and
may intermarry; and though a man may not marry his grandmother, it is certainly true that he may marry her sister. All these fourth degrees in the civil
law are second degrees in the canon law. By the civil law, persons in the
fourth degree might intermarry with each other. Such is the law of England,
Scotland, Ireland, and the colonies.' 1 Burge, Col. & For. Law, pt. 1, c. 5,
s. 1, p. 146, 147. There seems to be a mistake of the press in one part of the
passage of Mr. Burge's remarks, as to the difference between the civil law and
the canon law. The latter counted the degrees only up to the common ancestor; the former also down to the propositus. So that the first degree in the
canon law was the second in the civil law, and the second in the canon law
was the fourth in the civil law. 2 Black. Com. 224; Ersk. Inst. b. 1, tit. 6,
s. 8; 2 Burn, Eccles. Law, tit. Marriage,.I. See also the London Monthly Law
Magazine for Feb. 1840, vol. 7, p. 44–46. Mr. Burge's text reverses the statement. 1 Burge, Col. & For. Law, pt. 1, c. 5, s. 1, p. 147.

   [1] Burgess v. Burgess, 1 Hagg. Cons. 384, 386; 1 Bl. Com. 435; Butler v.
Gastrill, Gilb. Eq. 156, 158; 2 Kent Com. 84; Com. Dig. Baron and Feme,
B 4.
   [2] Grotius, de Jure Belli, lib. 2, c. 5, s. 14, n. 1.   ·
   [3] 1 Black. Com. 435; Burn, Eccles. Law, tit. Marriage, I.; Harrison v.
Burwell, Vaughan, 219; 2 Vent. 9; 2 Inst. 684.
   [4] Burn, Eccles. Law, tit. Marriage, I.; 1 Burge, Col. & For. Law, pt. 1,
c. 5, s. 1, p. 147, 148.

        (a) See Bonham v. Badgley, 2 Gilman (Ill.) 622.
                              13

void ; but they are voidable only during the lives of the parties; and if not so avoided during their lives, they are deemed valid to all intents and purposes.[1] (a)

115. *Affinity.* — Hitherto we have been speaking of cases of relation by consanguinity, between which and cases of relation by affinity there seems to be a clear and just moral difference. The English law however has treated both classes of cases as falling within the same predicament of prohibition by the Levitical law. Hence it has been there held that a marriage between a father-in-law and the daughter of his first wife by a former marriage is incestuous and unlawful ;[2] and, indeed, there seems something repugnant to social feelings in such marriages. The prohibition has also been extended in England to the marriages between a man and the sister of his former deceased wife, but upon what ground of Scriptural authority it has been thought very difficult to affirm.[3] (b) In many, and indeed in most, of the American states, a different rule prevails, and marriages

[1] 1 Black. Com. 434, 435. By a recent act of Parliament, Act of 5 & 6 Will. 4, c. 54 (1835), all future incestuous marriages are declared to be utterly void, and not merely voidable.

[2] Blackmore v. Brider, 1 Hagg. Cons. 393, note; 2 Phillim. Ecc. 359.

[3] Burn, Eccles. Law, tit. Marriage, I.; 1 Black. Com. 434, 435, Christian's note (2), citing Gibson's Codex, 412; Harris v. Hicks, Salk. 548; Hill v. Good, Vaughan, 302, 312; Faremouth v. Watson, 1 Phillim. Ecc. 355; Chick v. Ramsdale, 1 Curteis, 34; Com. Dig. Baron and Feme, B 2, B 4; 2 Inst. 683; Bac. Abridg. Marriage, A. Lord Chief Justice Vaughan, in delivering the opinion of the court in Harrison v. Burwell, Vaughan, 206; 2 Vent. 9, says that a man is prohibited by the statute 32 Hen. 8, c. 38, to marry his wife's sister. But within the meaning of Leviticus (c. 18, v. 14), and the constant practice of the commonwealth of the Jews, a man was prohibited to marry his wife's sister only during her life; after he might. So the text is. Vaughan, 241; 2 Vent. 17. There seems a discrepancy between what is here said, and his judgment in the subsequent case of Hill v. Good, Vaughan, 302, 312, 320. The opinion of Lord Chief Justice Vaughan, in both cases, and the case of Butler v. Gastrill, Gilb. Eq. 156, are full of learning and instruction on the subject of the canonical and ecclesiastical prohibitions of marriage. Dr. John H. Livingston, of New Jersey, has written an elaborate dissertation upon the subject of the marriage of a man with his sister-in-law (wife's sister), which was printed at New Brunswick, N. J., in 1816. It holds the doctrine that such marriages are scripturally incestuous. The opposite doctrine has been maintained by many able writers. See also 2 Kent Com.

(a) See Fenton v. Livingstone, 3 Macq. 497.

(b.) Illegitimacy makes no difference in the application of the rules prohibiting marriages on the ground of consanguinity or affinity. Reg. v. Brighton, 1 B. & S. 447; Reg. v. St. Giles-in-the-Fields, 11 Q. B. 173.

between a man and the sister of his former deceased wife are
not only deemed in a civil sense lawful, but are deemed in
a moral, religious, and Christian sense lawful, and exceedingly praiseworthy.   In some few of the states the English
rule is adopted.   Upon the continent of Europe most of the
Protestant countries adopt the doctrine that such marriages are
lawful.[1]

116. It would be a strong point to put, that a marriage, perfectly valid between a man and the sister of his former deceased
wife in New England, should be held invalid in Virginia, or in
England, even though the parties originally belonged to or were
born in the latter country or state.   But as to persons not so born
or belonging, it would be of the most dangerous consequence
to suppose that the courts of either of them would assume the
liberty to hold such marriages a nullity, merely because their
own jurisprudence would not, in a local celebration of marriage
therein, uphold it.   This distinction between marriages incestuous by the law of nature, and such as are incestuous by the positive code or customary law of a state, has been fully recognized
by one of our most learned American courts.   ' If,' say the court,
' a foreign state allows of marriages incestuous by the law of
nature, as between parent and child, such marriage would not
be allowed to have any validity here.   But marriages not naturally unlawful, but prohibited by the law of one state and not

85, note.   There are some very able articles on this subject in the London
Quarterly Law Magazine for May, 1839, vol. 21, p. 371; in the London Legal
Observer for January, 1840; and in the London Monthly Law Magazine for
May, 1840.   All these articles are designed to show that the most learned
writers have differed upon this subject, and to establish that the doctrine is ill
founded, and ought to be abolished.   Grotius maintains in strong terms that
there is no foundation for the prohibition.   ' Certe canonibus antiquissimis,
qui apostolici dicuntur, qui duas· sorores alteram post alteram duxisset aut
ἀδελφιδἑς, id est, fratris aut sororis filiam, tantum a clero arcetur.'   Grotius,
de Jure Belli, lib. 2, c. 5, s. 14, n. 2.

[1] This is certainly the law in all the New England States and in New York.
Greenwood v. Curtis, 6 Mass. 378, 379.   In Virginia the English rule prevails.
Commonwealth v. Perryman, 2 Leigh, 717; 2 Kent Com. 85, note (a.)   Dr.
Jeremy Taylor and Sir William Jones both contend that the Levitical degrees
do not by any law of God bind Christians to their observation.   See London
Quart. Law Magazine, vol. 21, p. 373, 374.   In Prussia, Saxony, Hanover,
Baden, Mecklenburg, Hamburg, Denmark, and in most other of the Protes-
tant states of Europe, the rule prevails that a man may lawfully marry the
sister of his former wife.   Id. p. 376.   It is otherwise in Scotland.   Ersk. Inst.
b. 1, tit. 6, s. 9.

of another, if celebrated where they are not prohibited, would be holden valid in a state where they are not allowed. As in this state, a marriage between a man and his deceased wife's sister is lawful; but it is not so in some states. Such a marriage celebrated here would be held valid in any other state, and the parties entitled to the benefits of the matrimonial contract.'[1](a) Indeed, in the diversity of religious opinions in Christian countries, a large space must be allowed for interpretation, as to religious duties, rights, and solemnities.[2] In the Catholic countries of continental Europe there are many prohibitions of marriage which are connected with religious canons and establishments; and in most countries there are some positive or customary prohibitions which involve peculiarities of religious opinion or of conscientious doubt. It would be most inconvenient to hold all marriages celebrated elsewhere void, which are not in scrupulous accordance with the local institutions of a particular country.

116 a. In the cases of incest hitherto discussed, it has been supposed that the parties marrying were either natives of, or actually and bona fide domiciled in, the country where the marriage was celebrated. But suppose the case of a marriage incestuous by the law of the country where the parties are born or are bona fide domiciled, and, without changing their domicil, for the purpose of evading that law, they go to a foreign country where a different rule prevails, and the marriage, which would not be incestuous by its laws, is there celebrated, and the parties afterwards return to their own country. Ought such a marriage to be held valid in such country? Huberus has put the very case, and held that it ought not there to be held valid. 'If,' says he, 'a Brabanter, who should marry within the prohibited degrees under a dispensation from the pope, should remove here (into Holland), the marriage would be considered valid. Yet if a

---

[1] Greenwood v. Curtis, 6 Mass. 378, 379; Medway v. Needham, 16 Mass. 157, 161; Sutton v. Warren, 10 Met. (Mass.) 451. But see Huberus, lib. 1, tit. 3, s. 8; Wightman v. Wightman, 4 Johns. Ch. (N. Y.) 343.

[2] See on this point, 2 Kent Com. 85; Harrison v. Burwell, Vaugh. 206; 2 Vent. 9; Co. Litt. 149; Grotius, lib. 2, c. 5, s. 12, 13, 14; Rutherf. Inst. b. 1, c. 15, s. 10; Wightman v. Wightman, 4 Johns. Ch. (N. Y.) 343.

(a) See the remarks of Lords Campbell and Cranworth upon these cases in Brook v. Brook, 9 H. L. C. 218, 229; also Kinney's Case, 30 Grat. (Va.) 858, 867; State v. Kennedy, 76 N. C. 251; Commonwealth v. Lane, 113 Mass. 458. See also note, s. 124 a, post.

Frisian should marry the daughter of his brother in Brabant, and celebrate the nuptials there, returning here, he would not be acknowledged as a married man, because in this way our laws might be evaded by the worst examples.' 'Brabantus uxore ducta dispensatione Pontificis, in gradu prohibito, si huc migret tolerabitur. Attamen, si Frisius cum fratris filia se conferat in Brabantiam, ibique nuptias celebret, huc reversus non videtur tolerandus ; quia sic jus nostrum pessimis exemplis eluderetur." [1]

117. *Other Prohibitions.* — In respect to the second exception, that of prohibitions depending upon positive law of a particular country,[2] they of course can apply strictly only to the subjects of that country. An illustration of this nature may be found in the Civil Code of France, which annuls marriages by Frenchmen in foreign countries who are under an incapacity by the laws of France.[3] A law of a similar nature may be found in the act of 12 Geo. 3, c. 11, respecting the royal family, by which they are prohibited from contracting marriage unless under special circumstances pointed out in the act ; [4] and the provisions of that act have been actually applied to the case of a foreign marriage contracted by one of the royal princes. The doctrine of the English courts, already alluded to,[5] in regard to the indissolubility of English

---

[1] Huberus, lib. 1, tit. 3, s. 8; post, s. 123; 1 Burge, Col. & For. Law, pt. 1, c. 5, s. 1, p. 147; Id. s. 3, p. 188–291. Mr. Burge maintains this to be the true doctrine, and says: ' The law which prohibits persons related to each other in a certain degree from intermarrying, and declares their intermarriage to be null, imposes on them a personal incapacity quoad that act; and that incapacity must continue to affect them so long as they retain their domicil in the country in which that law prevails. The resort to another country where there was no such prohibitory law for the mere purpose of evading the law of their own country, and with the intention of returning thither when their marriage had taken place, cannot be considered a change of their former domicil or the acquisition of a domicil in the country to which they had resorted. They must therefore be regarded as still subject to the personal incapacity imposed by the law of their real domicil.' See post, s. 123, 124. There are certain parts of the opinion of Sir George Hay, in Harford *v.* Morris, 2 Hagg. Cons. 431, 432, 435, from which it may fairly be deduced as his opinion that the law of the place of marriage was the rule only when the parties were domiciled there; and that if they went from their own country merely to celebrate the marriage in a foreign country, and immediately to return home, the law of such country would not govern, but the law of the country of their domicil. Post, s. 124, note.

[2] Ante, s. 113 *a.*

[3] 2 Kent Com. 93; Code Civil of France, art. 170; Merlin, Répert. Loi, s. 6, n. 1.

[4] 1 Black. Com. 226. [5] Ante, s. 88.

marriages celebrated in England, notwithstanding a subsequent divorce in a foreign country, affords a still more striking illustration, as, in its practical effects, it may render the issue of a second marriage illegitimate, so that a son, the issue of the second marriage in Scotland, may be legitimate there and illegitimate in England; he may be a lawful Scotch peer, and yet lose the English estates which support his peerage.[1]

118. *Other Cases.* — In respect to the third exception, that of marriages contracted and celebrated in foreign countries by subjects under peculiar circumstances,[2] it has been deemed to arise in cases of a sort of moral necessity, and it has been held to apply to persons residing in foreign factories, in conquered places, and in desert or barbarous countries, or in countries of an opposite religion, who are therefore permitted from necessity to contract marriage there according to the laws of their own country. In short, wherever there is a local necessity from the absence of laws, or from the presence of prohibitions or obstructions in a foreign country, not binding upon other countries, or from peculiarities of religious opinion and conscientious scruples, or from circumstances of exemption from the local jurisdiction, marriages will be allowed to be valid according to the law of the native or of fixed actual domicile.[3] (*a*)

119. The doctrine upon which this exception from necessity is founded will be best explained by a quotation from the opinion of Lord Stowell in a case already referred to, in which the question of the validity of a marriage celebrated at the Cape of Good Hope between English subjects, by a chaplain of the British forces then occupying that settlement under a capitulation recently made, came before him for decision.[4] After citing

---

[1] See Conway *v.* Beazley, 3 Hagg. Ecc. 639; Rex *v.* Lolley, Russ. & Ry. 237; Tovey *v.* Lindsay, 1 Dow, 117; M'Carthy *v.* Decaix, cited 3 Hagg. Ecc. 642, note; 2 Russ. & M. 620.

[2] Ante, s. 113 *a*.

[3] See Ruding *v.* Smith, 2 Hagg. Cons. 371, 384–386; ante, s. 79; Lautour *v.* Teesdale, 8 Taunt. 830; 2 Marsh. 243; Rex *v.* Brampton, 10 East, 282. See also Harford *v.* Morris, 2 Hagg. Cons. 432, where Sir George Hay, in delivering judgment, spoke of this exception of foreign English factories. Ante, s. 79, and Id. p. 79, note 1.

[4] Ante, s. 79,

(*a*) See Hynes *v.* McDermott, 82 N. Y. 41, in which there was no evidence of the law of the country where the acts constituting the marriage were done.

the rule that the law and legislative government of every dominion equally affected all persons and all property within the limits
thereof, and remarking that to such a proposition expressed in
very general terms only general truth can be ascribed (for it is
undoubtedly subject to exceptions), he proceeded to say that
even the native and resident inhabitants are not all brought
strictly within the pale of the general law. And in illustration of
this remark he referred to the fact that even in England there
is a numerous and respectable body (referring to the Jews) distinguished by great singularity of usages, who, though native
subjects under the protection of the general law, are in many respects governed by institutions of their own, and particularly in
their marriages. For it being the practice of mankind to conse-
crate their marriages by religious ceremonies, the differences of
religion in all countries that admit residents professing religions
essentially different, unavoidably introduce exceptions in that
matter to the universality of the rule which makes mere domicil
the constituent of an unlimited subjection to the ordinary law
of the country. He then added: ' What is the law of marriage
in all foreign establishments settled in countries professing a religion essentially different? in the English factories at Lisbon,
Leghorn, Oporto, Cadiz, and in the factories in the East, Smyrna,
Aleppo, and others? in all of which (some of these establishments existing by authority under treaties, and others under indulgence and toleration) marriages are regulated by the law of
the original country to which they are still considered to belong.
An English resident at St. Petersburg does not look to the ritual
of the Greek Church, but to the rubric of the Church of England, when he contracts a marriage with an English woman.
Nobody can suppose that, whilst the Mogul empire existed, an
Englishman was bound to consult the Koran for the celebration of his marriage. Even where no foreign connection can be
ascribed, a respect is shown to the opinions and practice of a distinct people. The validity of a Greek marriage in the extensive
dominions of Turkey is left to depend, I presume, upon their
own canons, without any reference to Mahometan ceremonies.
There is a jus gentium upon this matter, a comity which treats
with tenderness, or at least with toleration, the opinion and
usages of a distinct people in this transaction of marriage. It
may be difficult to say, a priori, how far the general law should

circumscribe its own authority in this matter. But practice has established the principle in several instances, and where the practice is admitted it is entitled to acceptance and respect. It has sanctioned the marriages of foreign subjects in the houses of the ambassadors of the foreign country to which they belong.[1] I am not aware of any judicial regulation upon this point. But the reputation which the validity of such marriages has acquired makes such a recognition by no means improbable if such a question was brought to judgment.'[2]   And again : 'It is true indeed that English decisions have established this rule, that a foreign marriage, valid according to the law of the place where celebrated, is good everywhere else. But they have not, e converso, established that marriages of British subjects, not good according to the law of the place where celebrated, are universally and under all possible circumstances to be regarded as invalid in England. It is therefore certainly to be advised that the safest course is always to be married according to the law of the country, for then no question can be stirred. But if this cannot be done on account of legal or religious difficulties, the law of this country does not say that its subjects shall not marry abroad.'[3] And he accordingly held the marriage valid, on the distinct British character of the parties, on their independence of the Dutch law in their own British transactions, on the insuperable obstacles of obtaining any marriage conformable to the Dutch law, on the countenance given by British authority and British administration to this transaction, and upon the whole country being under British dominion.[4]

120. In regard to marriages by British subjects in their own foreign settlements, the general rule is, that marriages good by the laws of England will be valid there ; for they carry those laws with them into such settlements, and are not to be governed by the laws or customs of the natives. Thus it has been held that a marriage between British subjects at Madras is good, if conformable to the British laws, and not to the laws of the natives of India.[5]

121. The ground however upon which the general rule of

[1] See Pertreis v. Tondear, 1 Hagg. Cons. 136.
[2] Ruding v. Smith, 2 Hagg. Cons. 385, 386.   [3] Ibid.
[4] Id. p. 371; ante, s. 79.
[5] Lautour v. Teesdale, 8 Taunt. 830; 2 Marsh. 243.

the validity of marriages, according to the lex loci contractus, is maintained, is easily vindicated. It cannot be better expressed than in the language of Sir Edward Simpson, already cited.[1] All civilized nations allow marriage contracts. They are juris gentium, and the subjects of all nations are equally concerned in them. Infinite mischief and confusion must necessarily arise to the subjects of all nations with respect to legitimacy, successions, and other rights, if the respective laws of different countries were only to be observed as to marriages contracted by the subjects of those countries abroad ; and therefore all nations have consented, or are presumed to consent, for the common benefit and advantage, that such marriages shall be good or not according to the laws of the country where they are celebrated. By observing this rule few, if any, inconveniences can arise. By disregarding it infinite mischiefs must ensue.[2] Suppose, for instance, a marriage celebrated in France according to the law of that country, should be held void in England, what would be the consequences? Each party might marry anew in the other country. In one country the issue would be deemed legitimate, in the other illegitimate. The French wife would in France be held the only wife, and entitled as such to all the rights of property appertaining to that relation. In England the English wife would hold the same exclusive rights and character. What then would be the confusion in regard to the personal property of the parties, in its own nature transitory, passing alternately from one country to the other! Suppose there should be issue of both marriages, and then all the parties should become domiciled in England or France, what confusion of rights, what embarrassments of personal and conjugal relations must necessarily be created![3]

122. *Foreign Jurists.* — Foreign jurists in general as strenuously support the general rule, as the tribunals sitting to administer the common law, and undoubtedly from a common sense of the pernicious consequences which would flow from a different doctrine.[4] This subject is much discussed by Sanchez to the following effect. As to the maxim or general rule, ' ut non teneantur

[1] Ante, s. 80 a.
[2] Scrimshire v. Scrimshire, 2 Hagg. Cons. 417, 418, and ante, s. 79, 80, 80 a.
[3] Scrimshire v. Scrimshire, 2 Hagg. Cons. 417, 418; ante, s. 80 a.
[4] 1 Burge, Col. & For. Law, pt. 1, c. 5, s. 3, p. 184–188.

peregrini legibus et consuetudinibus loci per quem transeunt,'
this rule has exceptions: (1) 'Quoad contractuum solemnitatem; nam quicunque forenses, et peregrini tenentur servare
solemnitates in contractu requisitas legibus et consuetudinibus
oppidi in quo contrahunt. Ratione enim contractus quilibet
forum sortitur in loco contractus, hinc est contractum absolute
initum, censeri celebratum juxta consuetudines et statuta loci,
in quo initur. Quod ita provenit, quia contractus sequitur consuetudines et statuta loci in quo celebratur.'[1] And a case is
put as to inhabitants of a place where the decree of the Council
of Trent for avoiding clandestine marriages is not received.
Suppose they go from England to places per modum transitus,
ubi obligat decretum, and marry there according to the laws of
their own domicil. Some think that such marriage is good in
the case of strangers, as agreeable to their own laws, to the law
of their country in which they are domiciled, though not to the
law of the place where they are married. But Sanchez holds
that a marriage is void where it wants the solemnities prescribed
by the local law. 'What,' says he, 'the law of the place requires
where the contract is made, and what are to be followed in contracts, are to be decided solely by the laws of the place in
which the contract is celebrated:' 'Quæ petunt leges loci, ubi
contractus initur, et quoad solemnitatem adhibendam in contractibus, solæ leges loci in quo contractus celebratur inspiciuntur.[2] Locus autem, ubi hoc matrimonium initur, non petit
eam parochi et testium solemnitatem ad matrimonii valorem,
cum ibi decretum Tridentini non obliget.[3] Ea solemnitas adhibenda est quam petunt leges loci, ubi contractus initur; cum
ergo locus, ubi celebratur matrimonium, ab his peregrinis exegat solemnitatem Tridentini in eo vigentis; aliter contractum
nullum erit.'[4]

122 a. John Voet seems to affirm the same doctrine to be
generally, but not universally, true, and liable to exceptions. He
puts the case of the marriage of an inhabitant of Holland with a
female of Flanders or Brabant, in Flanders or Brabant, accord-

---

[1] Post, s. 260.

[2] I cite this whole passage from the case of Scrimshire v. Scrimshire, 2
Hagg. Cons. 412, 413. See also 1 Burge, Col. & For. Law, pt. 1, c. 5, s. 3,
p. 185, 186; Sanchez De Matrim. lib. 3, disput. 18, s. 10, n. 26, 28.

[3] Cited in Burge, ubi supra, p. 185, 186.   [4] Cited ibid.

ing to the laws of the latter, but not according to the laws of
Holland, and asks if it would be valid in Holland.   To which
he answers that prima facie it should seem that such marriages
ought in Holland to be held valid, ' because,' says he, ' it is sufficient in contracts to follow the solemnities of the place ih which
the contract is celebrated, although the solemnities are not
observed which are prescribed in the place of the domicil of the
parties, or of the situation of the property in executing the act.'
' Prima quidem specie videri posset, nuptias tales etiam in ipsa
Hollandia ratas habendas esse.   Eo quod sufficit in contrahendo
adhiberi solemnia loci illius, in quo contractus celebratur, etsi
non inveniantur observata solemnia quæ in loco domicilii contrahentium, aut rei sitæ, actui gerendo prescripta sunt.' [1]   He adds
that there had been different opinions given in Holland on this
point.   But he expresses his own opinion to be that such marriage, so celebrated out of Holland, ought to be pronounced invalid in Holland, upon the very terms of the edict of Holland,
by which marriages by Hollanders, without proper notifications
thereof published in the place of their domicil, are declared to
be void : that the general rule, that it is sufficient in negotiations
and contracts to follow the solemnities required by the law of the
place where the business is transacted, does not apply in such a
case ; for that rule has its proper place only where the business
is not so transacted in fraud of the law, or where no statute has
positively declared that the act shall be void when done by a
subject according to the foreign solemnities.   'Sed, eo non obstante, magis est, ut matrimonia, eo modo extra Hollandiam ab
Hollando celebrata, infirma per judicem Hollandicum pronun-
ciari debeant, propter edicti verba, quibus nuptiæ, per Hollandum
sine denunciationibus publicis in domicilii loco interpositis contractæ, irritæ esse jussæ sunt.   Nihil in contrarium faciente illo
axiomate, quod sufficiat in negotiis contrahendis adhiberi solemnia loci, in quo actus geritur : cum ista regula locum inveniat si
non in fraudem statuti quis alio se contulerit ad actum celebran-
dum, aut statutum nominatim irritum declaraverit actum, a suo
subjecto peregrina solemnitate gestum.' [2]

    122 b. Paul Voet holds an opinion decidedly in favor of the

----

[1] J. Voet, ad Pand. 23, 2, 4, tom. 2, p. 20; cited also in Scrimshire v.
Scrimshire, 2 Hagg. Cons. 415. See also Voet, ad Pand. 23, 2, 85, p. 55.
    [2] J. Voet, ad Pand. 23, 2, 4, p. 20.

general rule. 'Quid si de contractibus proprie dictis, et quidem eorum solemnibus contentio ; Quis locus spectabitur ; an domicilii contrahentis, an loci, ubi quis contrahit ? Respondeo affirmanter. Posterius. Quia, censetur quis semet contrahendo, legibus istius loci, ubi contrahit, etiam ratione solemnium subjicere voluisse.'[1] Huberus admits that a marriage, valid by the law of the place where it is celebrated, is binding everywhere, under the exception, which he generally applies, that it is not prejudicial to others, or that it is not incestuous. 'Matrimonium pertinet etiam ad has regulas. Si licitum est eo loco, ubi contractum et celebratum est, ubique validum erit, effectumque habebit, sub eadem exceptione prejudicii aliis non creandi ; cui licet addere, si exempli nimis sit abominandi ; ut si incestum juris gentium in secundo gradu contigerit alicubi esse permissum.'[2] Bouhier adopts the general rule, hesitating as to the nature and extent of the exceptions.[3] Hertius lays down the following axiom : If the law prescribes a form for the act, the place of the act, and not of the domicil of the parties, or of the situation of the property, is to be considered. 'Si lex actui formam dat, inspiciendus est locus actus, non domicilii, non rei sitæ.'[4] And he puts the following as an example. A marriage contracted according to the solemnities of any place where the married couple are commorant, cannot be rescinded upon the pretext that, in the domicil or country of the husband, other solemnities are required. 'Matrimonium juxta solennitates loci alicujus, ubi sponsus et sponsa commorabantur, contractum non potest prætextu illo rescindi, quod in domicilio aut patria mariti aliæ solennitates observentur.'[5] He afterwards puts exceptions to this general axiom ; one of which is, that a contract between foreigners, both belonging to a foreign country, is to be governed by the law of their own country, and not by that of the lex loci contractus.[6] In this exception he has to encounter many distinguished adver-

---

[1] Voet, de Statut. s. 9, c. 2, n. 9, p. 267, ed. 1715 ; Id. 323, ed. 1661 ; post, s. 261.

[2] Huberus, lib. 1, tit. 3, s. 8 ; ante, s. 85.

[3] Bouhier, Cout. de Bourg. c. 27, s. 59–66.

[4] Post, s. 242, 260 ; Hertii Opera, tom. 1, de Collis. Leg. s. 4, art. 10, p. 126, ed. 1737 ; Id. p. 179, ed. 1716.

[5] 1 Hertii Opera, de Collis. Leg. s. 4, art. 10, ed. 1837, p. 126 ; Id. p. 179, ed. 1716. Id. art. 10, p. 128, ed. 1737 ; Id. p. 182, ed. 1716.

[6] Id. p. 128, s. 10, ed. 1737 ; Non Valet (6).

saries.[1] The French jurists seem generally to support the doctrine that marriage is to be held valid or not, according to the
law of the place of celebration, except in cases postively prohibited by their own laws to their own subjects, or where it is in
fraud of those laws.[2] And Merlin says that it is a contract so
completely of natural and moral law that, when celebrated by
savages in places where there are no established laws, it will be
recognized as good in other countries.[3]

123. A question has been much discussed, how far a marriage
regularly celebrated in a foreign country between persons belonging to another country, who have gone thither from their own
country for that purpose, is to be deemed valid, if it is not celebrated according to the law of their own country. Huberus, as
we have seen,[4] has put the very question, and has applied it as
well to cases of minority as of incest; and he does not hesitate
to pronounce such marriages invalid, because they are an invasion
or fraud upon the law of the country to which the parties belong,
and in which they are domiciled.[5] Bouhier has advocated the
same opinion;[6] and it is also maintained by Paul Voet. He states
it as an exception to the general rule, that the law of the place of
the contract ought to govern. 'Nisi quis, quo in loco domicilii
evitaret molestam aliquam vel sumptuosam solemnitatem; adeoque
in fraudem sui statuti nulla necessitate cogente alio proficiscatur,
et mox ad eorum domicilium, gesto alibi negotio, revertatur.'[7]
John Voet, as we have seen, holds the same opinion.[8] Pothier
puts the very case in the strongest terms. He says that the conditions and ceremonies prescribed by the French laws for the validity
of marriages between French subjects, are obligatory, even when
the marriage has been celebrated between them in a foreign country, whenever it appears that they have gone thither in fraud of
those laws, and that the marriage, under such circumstances, will

[1] Ibid.   [2] Post, s. 123.
[3] Merlin, Répert. Mariage, s. 1, p. 343. See also 2 Boullenois, obs. 46,
p. 458; 1 Froland, Mém. p. 177, c. 1; Pardessus, vol. 5, pt. 6, tit. 7, c. 2, art.
1481-1495; Pothier, Traité du Mariage, n. 263; Journal des Audiences, tom.
1, c. 24; s. c. cited Scrimshire v. Scrimshire, 2 Hagg. Cons. 413, 414.
[4] Ante, s. 85, 116 a.
[5] Huberus, lib. 1, tit. 3, s. 9. See ante, s. 85, 116 a, where the passages
are cited at large.
[6] Bouhier, Cout. de Bourg. c. 28, s. 60-62, p. 557; ante, s. 84.
[7] P. Voet, de Statut. s. 9, c. 2, p. 268, ed. 1715; Id. p. 323, 324, ed. 1661.
[8] Ante, s. 122 a; 1 Burge, Col. & For. Law, pt. 1, c. 5, s. 3, p. 196.

be a nullity.[1] This doctrine turns upon the general principle that an act done designedly in fraud or evasion of the law, by a mere change of locality, is utterly void.

123 a. *English and American Rule.*— In opposition to this doctrine it has however been settled after some struggle, both in England and America, that such a marriage is good. The question in England was first solemnly decided by the High Court of Delegates in 1768;[2] and having been subsequently recognized, notwithstanding the doubts of Lord Mansfield, it may now be deemed settled there beyond controversy.[3] Lord Mansfield, on the occasion alluded to, arguendo, said : ' It has been laid down at the bar, that a marriage in a foreign country must be governed by the law of the country where the marriage was had, which in general is true. But the marriages in Scotland of persons going from hence for that purpose were instanced by way of example. They may come under a very different consideration, according to the opinion of Huberus and other writers.'[4] This is manifestly no more than the expression of a doubt upon a point not directly before the court.

123 b. In Massachusetts, upon full discussion, the doctrine has been firmly established.[5] It was admitted on that occasion by the court that the doctrine is repugnant to the general principles of law relating to contracts ; for a fraudulent evasion of or fraud upon the laws of the country where the parties have their domicil

[1] Pothier, Traité du Mariage, n. 263.

[2] Compton v. Bearcroft, cited in Bull. N. P. 114, and in Harford v. Morris, 2 Hagg. Cons. 429, 430, 443, 444. It has been said that this decision may be explained upon the ground that the English marriage act, under which that question arose, contained an express exception of marriages in Scotland; and that the marriage of the parties in that case, who were English, and had gone from England for the express purpose of celebrating the marriage in Scotland, was therefore good, as it was according to the law of Scotland. Admitting this to be the true construction of the English marriage act, yet the question directly raised by the libel was, whether a marriage in a foreign country by British subjects domiciled in England, and not changing their domicil, who had gone there expressly to avoid and evade the laws of England, was good or not; and there is strong reason to believe that this point was deemed a material ingredient in the ultimate judgment of the case. See the case of Compton v. Bearcroft, as commented on in 2 Hagg. Cons. 443, 444, and the reporter's note in p. 444.

[3] See Harford v. Morris, 2 Hagg. Cons. 423; Robinson v. Bland, 2 Burr. 1077–1080; Fergusson on Marr. & Divorce, 63–65.

[4] Robinson v. Bland, 2 Burr. 1079, 1080; Huber. lib. 1, tit. 3, s. 8.

[5] Medway v. Needham, 16 Mass. 157, 161; Putnam v. Putnam, 8 Pick. 433.

would not, except in the contract of marriage, be protected under the general principle.[1] But the exception in favor of marriages is maintained upon principles of public policy, with a view to prevent the disastrous consequences to the issue of such a marriage, which would result from the loose state in which persons so situated would live.[2] The doctrine has been carried even further, so as to admit the legitimacy of the issue of a person who had been divorced a vinculo for adultery, and had been declared by the local law incompetent to marry again, but who had gone into a neighboring state, and there contracted a new marriage, and had issue by that marriage.[3] The like rule has been applied in favor of the widow by such second marriage, so as to entitle her to dower in the real estate of her deceased husband, situate in Massachusetts.[4]

124. The English doctrine in relation to Scotch marriages by parties domiciled in England and going to Scotland to marry, though a plain violation of the real object and intent, even if not of the words, of the English marriage act, seems to have proceeded mainly upon the ground of public policy.[5] It is the least

[1] Ibid. The court put the following case: Thus, parties intending to make an usurious bargain, cannot give validity to a contract in which more than the lawful interest of their country is secured, by passing into another territory where there may be no restriction of interest, or where it is established at a higher rate, and there executing a contract before agreed on. Medway v. Needham, 16 Mass. 160.

[2] Medway v. Needham, 16 Mass. 160, 161.

[3] West Cambridge v. Lexington, 1 Pick. (Mass.) 506; 2 Kent Com. 92, 93, 3d ed. See Fergusson on Marr. & Divorce, note R, p. 469 ; ante, s. 89.

[4] Putnam v. Putnam, 8 Pick. 433.

[5] Mr. Burge does not deem it to be in fraud of the English laws, because the English marriage act does not in fact prohibit such Scottish marriages. This is true in terms; and if it did prohibit, the question of the conflict of laws in relation to such marriages would never have arisen in England; for the statute would have directly decided the matter. Nevertheless, the whole object of the parties in this class of marriages plainly is to evade the law of their own country by a marriage valid by the law of the country where it is celebrated, without changing their own domicil, and thus getting rid of all the anxious provisions of the statute against ill-advised and clandestine marriages. In short, all the Gretna Green marriages in Scotland, as they are called, are intended by the parties to get rid of the solemnities of the English law. Mr. Burge says: ' The decisions of the courts in England, which have declared valid a marriage contracted in Scotland by English persons who had resorted thither for the sole purpose of evading the prohibitions of the English marriage act, are perfectly consistent with the admission of this exception. Such a marriage is valid because it is not prohibited by the English marriage

of two evils, in a political sense, a civil sense, and a moral sense.
We have already seen that the positive code of France has pro-

act. It is a misapplication of terms to describe it as an evasion, or in fraud of
the act; for, in fact, it is not prohibited. There is an express provision that
nothing in that act shall extend to marriages in Scotland, or to any marriages
beyond sea. The act therefore left English subjects at perfect liberty to resort
to any country for the purpose of contracting and celebrating their marriage.
So far from the act containing a general and absolute prohibition, and a
declaration of the nullity of all marriages contracted otherwise than in conformity to its provisions, it confines such prohibition and declaration to marriages contracted in England. These decisions therefore are founded upon
the right of the parties, consistently with the marriage act, to resort to the foreign country for the purpose of contracting their marriage, and upon the act
itself containing no provision which renders void a marriage so contracted.
It is upon this ground, and to this extent, that the argument of Sanchez must
be understood, when he contends that a marriage is not void because the
parties have resorted to a country in which they have contracted it for the
purpose of avoiding ceremonies which are required in their own country.
" Displicet mihi hæc limitatio, et credo, licet adirent eo fine, ut possent libere
absque parocho et testibus contrahere, esse ratum matrimonium. Nam qui
jure suo utitur non potest dici fraudem committere, ut ea ratione effectus im-
pediatur." " Nullus videtur dolo facere, qui jure suo utitur." " Est enim
fraus licita, cum contrahentes utantur jure suo; ergo cum adeuntes locum, ubi
non viget Trident, animo contrahendi absque parocho et testibus, utuntur jure
suo, habet enim jus sic ibi contrahendi, erit fraus licita, nec ea ratione effectus ac valor matrimonii impedietur." The same jurist, in a subsequent passage, admits the distinction between a personal incapacity imposed by the law
of the domicil, which would accompany the party in whatever country he contracted, and a law which attached to the act only in respect of its taking
place in the country in which that law prevailed. " Dic quando inhabilitas
est constituta absolute et simpliciter, sequi personam quocumque euntem;
secus quando est constituta per modum legis, sicut enim lex illa non obligat
in illis locis, ita inhabilitas, et annullatio actus non obligat ibi, nec sequitur
personam, nisi dum est in locis, in quibus ea lex vim obligandi habet . . .
non enim ligatur lege ecclesiastica in loco, ubi ex voluntate ac dispositione
ejusdem ecclesiæ non habet robur eadem lex; ut contingit in locis, ubi aut
non recepta aut non publicata fuit." 1 Burge, Col. & For. Law, pt. 1, c. 5,
s. 3, p. 192, 193. The decisions in the Supreme Court of Massachusetts, as
they are stated in the commentaries on American Law, carry the doctrine
much further, and reject any exception founded on the purpose for which the
parties resorted to the country where they contracted the marriage. The parties in the case referred to had left the state on purpose to evade its statute
law, and to marry in opposition to it, and, being married, they returned again;
yet their marriage was held valid, if it were valid according to the laws of the
place where it was contracted, notwithstanding the parties went into the other
state with an intention to evade the laws of their own.' Ibid. In these remarks Mr. Burge is mainly borne out as to the effect of the English marriage
act, by the language of Sir George Hay, in Harford v. Morris, 2 Hagg. Cons.
p. 428-432. He there said: ' The next question is, whether by the law of
England this marriage is valid ? It is stated throughout that it is a marriage

mulgated an opposite doctrine with unrelenting severity.[1] The
wisdom of such a course remains to be established ; and it will

without the consent of the natural mother of the party, and of the testamentary
guardians and the Lord Chancellor; and that the parties went into a foreign
country to evade the laws of this realm. Whether upon that account, or any
of the accounts already mentioned, it is void by the law of England, is the first
question. Parties may go out of England and marry by necessity or choice:
in either way a foreign marriage is not void upon that account by the laws of
England. But it is said they go in violation of the order of the Chancellor
and without the consent of parents and guardians. What is the law of England that requires the consent of parents and guardians? It is the marriage
act. One of the greatest magistrates that ever appeared in this country
explains it, that the view of that act was to restrain the abuse that was so
scandalous in this country from clandestine marriages, and to get proof of
marriages which otherwise might become uncertain; as it is wherever you
cannot have evidence of the fact of the marriage being rightly performed, the
legitimacy becomes uncertain. The principal view of that law was to affect
such marriages. The law does indeed, in one respect, put a restraint which
was not known to the common law upon the marriage of minors without the
consent of parents: but it does not make all the marriages of minors even in
England void. Marriages by licence only are void for want of consent of
parents and guardians. If this marriage had been in England, and if instead
of going abroad the parties had been married in any great parish of this town
or country by banns, would that marriage have been good or not by the laws
of England? No law says that it shall be void. It is a marriage by licence
only, that is void by the law of England for want of consent of the parents or
guardians. It is observed also that the act makes particular exceptions
without which the purpose of the marriage act, though an exceeding good
act, might have been questioned before this time if there had not been so
many ways to avoid the restraint put upon the marriage of minors. It is provided that nothing in this act shall extend to marriages in Scotland, nor to
any marriages solemnized beyond sea. Then marriages in Scotland and
beyond sea by the law of England remain in the same state as if the statute
had not passed. Marriage in Scotland, if not contrary to the law of England, is
good, and it has been so determined. That determination passed, not on the
ground that the marriage was valid in Scotland, and that therefore it was
good, — nothing was laid before the court to show that the marriage was valid
in Scotland, — but because the act of parliament did not put any restraint
upon English subjects being married in Scotland, with respect to the consent
of parents. On that ground it is that those marriages are held good, not being
contrary to the law of England. The same holds as to marriages beyond
sea. For English subjects going abroad or to Scotland to marry English subjects have an exemption from that restraint in the act. What was the case
before the marriage act? Will anybody say that before the act a marriage
solemnized by persons going over to Calais, or happening to be there, was void
in this country, because such a marriage might be void by the laws of France,
as perhaps it was, if solemnized by a Protestant priest, whom they do not
acknowledge, or if any way clandestine, or without consent; and that there-

---

[1] Ante, s. 84, 90, 123, and note.

14

be no matter of surprise if hereafter we shall find a Frenchman
with two lawful wives, one according to the law of the place of

fore it should be set aside by a court in England upon account of its
being void by the law of France? No. The laws of the state to which
the parties are subject must determine the marriage, unless you can show
that the law of the other country is that by which its validity is to be
decided. That brings me to the other great consideration in this case, whether
the validity of these marriages, being solemnized in Ypres and Denmark, are
to be tried by the laws of those countries. If they are, the laws of those
countries must be laid before the court, and proved in the best manner possible; not by the opinions of lawyers, which is the most uncertain way in
the world, but by certificates, laying the ordinances of those countries before the
court. Without considering how far that law is capable of being proved in the
present case, the previous question arises with respect to jurisdiction, whether
the laws of that country in which the marriage is celebrated should operate
merely because it was celebrated there. I conceive the law to be clear that it
is not the transient residence, by coming one morning and going away the
next day, which constitutes a residence to which the lex loci can be applied, so
as to give a jurisdiction to the law, and cause it to take cognizance of a marriage celebrated there. It is certain that domicil, or established residence, that
is, such a kind of residence as makes the party subject to the laws of that
country, may have that effect; and, with respect to persons so domiciled, the
laws of the country must be adhered to in contracts made there. This was
the case of Scrimshire. All the proceedings of the court of France were laid
before the court. I remember it, though it was a long time ago; and I was
counsel for the lady. The mother of the young man was at Boulogne, where
they had gone animo morandi. It was stated in all the proceedings that they
were domiciled in France; he went there to reside for purposes of education,
and did reside there; and the mother continued to reside there till she obtained
the sentence that was pleaded in the Consistory Court. I do not in the least
call in question that determination in the Consistory Court. Every man has
allowed the great and extensive knowledge of the judge; but he founded his
judgment upon the sentence given in that court which had assumed jurisdiction, and had a right to assume it; he paid all respect to the judgment; and
upon that he gave his opinion, that the party suing should be dismissed.' A
somewhat different account of the case of Compton v. Bearcroft, here referred
to, is given by Sir W. Wynne, in Middleton v. Janverin, 2 Hagg. Cons. 443,
444. On that occasion he said: 'It is however contended that admitting the
law to invalidate the marriage in those countries, yet that is not the law by
which this case is to be decided in this court. It is not the lex loci where the
marriage ceremony is performed which is to determine the question; but you
must find out some other law, and that is declared by the counsel for Mrs.
Janverin to be the law of England. Now, in respect to the lex loci having
been adopted as a rule, I think the case of Compton v. Bearcroft proves it
very strongly. In that case the Court of Delegates affirmed the rejection of
the libel which was given in against the marriage, on different grounds, as I
have understood, from those which were taken in the Court of Arches, and
because the marriage was a good marriage in Scotland, and if all the facts
pleaded in the libel were proved, the marriage could not be pronounced void
under the marriage act, in which it is expressly declared that it shall not

the marriage, and the other according to that of his domicil of origin.[1] The doctrine in England has indeed stopped short

extend to Scotland. On those grounds it was, as I have understood, that the delegates rejected the libel. The case of that marriage was therefore determined by the lex loci. Those persons having gone to Scotland, and been married in a way not good in England, but good in Scotland, and not affected by the marriage act, were considered to have contracted a valid marriage.' The learned reporter has added a very important note to 2 Hagg. Cons. 444, note (*), on this point. It is certain that foreign jurists do not take any distinctions between a violation of the positive prohibition by the words of the laws, and the case of a mere evasion or fraud upon the known policy of the laws by a marriage in another country, without any change of domicil by the parties. See also Fergusson on Marr. & Divorce, 417; Id. 223, 461. It has always appeared to me that the true doctrine of international policy is, that a foreign marriage, valid by the law of the place of marriage is valid everywhere, notwithstanding the parties may be domiciled in another country, where the marriage, if celebrated there, would, by the laws thereof, be void, and the parties have gone thither for the express purpose of evading the requisitions of the law of their domicil. A learned writer in the London Legal Observer for January, 1840, has commented on this subject with great acuteness and ability. The following extract may be gratifying to the learned reader, as it constitutes an opposite view to that of Mr. Burge: 'The idea of fraud on the law of a country is rather a favorite one with jurists. When examined however we think it will be found to have a very narrow foundation for the supposed countenance afforded to it by our law. By the courts of several American states it has been repeatedly overruled. It is principally grounded on an opinion of the jurist Huber (Hub. de Confl. Leg. lib. 1, tit. 3, s. 8), supported by a dictum of Lord Mansfield, in Robinson v. Bland, 1 W. Bl. 234, 256; 2 Burr. 1077. In the first place it is at once met by the difficulty that it has been over and over again decided that Scotch and foreign marriages (between minors and others who could not have contracted marriage here) undertaken, expressly and admittedly, to evade our law, are good, if good per legem loci, and vice versa. But then, say the advocates of the in fraudem legis doctrine, these decisions are consistent; because the marriage act in terms excepts Scotch and foreign marriages. In this view however they at once throw over Lord Mansfield's authority, because, as Sir W. Blackstone, who was counsel in the case, notes it in the margin of his report, he threw out a " quære, whether stolen marriages in Scotland are valid.'' However, as this case is really the only one in which, as far as we are aware, the idea of evasion of our law is set up, we must go more fully into it. The case was argued in 1760. The question was whether a bill of exchange given in France by one English subject to another, but made payable in England, the consideration of which was a gambling debt, should be held recoverable in an English court. It was found not to be recoverable in France; but Lord Mansfield (though, on this plain ground, he afterwards said the case had after all come to nothing) had it argued twice as bearing on international law. In his judgment he touched on the rules applicable to foreign personal contracts. He lays down the general rule as to the

---

[1] 1 Toullier, Droit Civil, art. 576; Code Civil, art. 144, 148, 170; Merlin, Répert. tit. Loi, s. 6, n. 1; and ante, note, s. 84, 117.

of the moral mischief, if the decision promulgated in its courts can be maintained (of which doubts may justly be entertained),

lex loci prevailing. But then he says: "This rule admits of an exception, where the parties had a view to a different kingdom. Contracts are to be considered according to the place where they are to be executed." And Mr. Justice Wilmot said: "The place where the money is to be paid must govern the law. This was determined as to usury on contracts in Ireland." From this it is evident that there is no ground in the decision for the wide principle contended for. The quære thrown out, merely in answer to an illustrative argument used by counsel, comes more to the point, but is plainly overruled. Burrows, in his report, says that Lord Mansfield referred to a case before Lord Hardwicke of a minor's stolen marriage at Ostend; the validity of which Lord Hardwicke doubted, and ordered to be tried before an ecclesiastical court; but the trial was stopped by the minor's marrying again on coming of age. We have looked carefully for this case, and have no doubt Butler and Freeman, Ambl. 302, is the one referred to. It had been decided in 1756, four years before. It was the case of a ward married at Antwerp. Lord Hardwicke said: "This is the first case under the late marriage act. As to such a marriage — I was going to call it a robbery — there is a door open in the statute as to marriages beyond seas and in Scotland." He afterwards goes on to question the validity of the marriage: "It is said by a witness that he saw them married according to the rites and ceremonies of the Church of England. But it will not be valid here, unless it was so by the laws of the country where it was had." The father, it appears, instituted a suit in the ecclesiastical court to try the validity according to the foreign law. This case therefore, so far from supporting Lord Mansfield's doubt, as stated in the margin of Blackstone's report, expressly overrules it. It is more material for our present purpose, as being the first case under the marriage act. The marriage act was passed in 1753. If Lord Hardwicke had thought that before that act there was a principle of law in operation that a party going abroad to evade our laws could not set up the lex loci contractus, but that the new act had altered this, he could hardly have failed to have said so. He treats it that the new statute, by leaving the old principle of lex loci contractus untouched, had left the door open to evade its new provisions of banns, rites, consent for minors, &c.: not had opened a new door. We find but one other case before Lord Hardwicke bearing on the subject. It is Roach v. Garvan, decided in 1748 (1 Ves. 159). It is material as showing the principles of law as to foreign marriages clearly laid down before the marriage act passed. It was the case of a ward of court, aged only eleven, married in France to a boy of seventeen, the son of a Frenchman. Lord Hardwicke laid down that the infant, being a natural-born subject, could not renounce her allegiance. He said: "The most material consideration is the validity of the marriage. It has been argued to be valid from being established by the sentence of a court in France having proper jurisdiction. And it is true that, if so, it is conclusive, whether a foreign court or not, from the laws of nations in such cases; otherwise the rights of mankind would be very precarious and uncertain." Now here, if Mr. Burge is right, Lord Hardwicke was called upon to fall back on the general principle Mr. Burge contends for, that the subject, though abroad, unless bona fide domiciled there (which, in Mr. Burge's sense of domicil, was not the case), could not avail himself of the lex loci to avoid the

that a second marriage, after a divorce in Scotland from a marriage originally celebrated in England between English subjects,

operation of our law. The girl here was only eleven years old. By our common law, as stated by Mr. Burge, a female under twelve could not contract matrimony. Indeed, according to Sir Matthew Hale, the attempt would have subjected the party to a conviction for rape. 1 Hale P. C. 630, and 4 Black. Com. 212. So far from doing this, in committing unreservedly the jurisdiction as to validity to a foreign court, he lays down a principle quite destructive of all Mr. Burge's doctrines as to bona fide domicil; because, as we shall presently remark further, if that principle only means bona fide, so far as required by the foreign law, it amounts to nothing, and there is nobody who doubts it. It would then be, by common consent, one of the incidents bearing on the validity of the marriage according to the lex loci contractus. There are few opinions which command higher respect than Mr. Jacob's. In his very learned notes appended to his edition of Roper's Husband and Wife he takes the same view. He says, as to the objection that an intention to evade our law may affect the validity of the foreign contract, that, "though apparently sanctioned by Lord Mansfield, it has not prevailed, either with respect to marriages in Scotland, or with respect to marriages in other places out of England, and there does not appear any exception to the rule that a foreign marriage, valid according to the law of the place where celebrated, is good everywhere else." 2 Roper, Husb. & Wife, ed. by Jacob, p. 495. It must be observed that Mr. Jacob does not specifically advert to objections arising from affinity or from any prohibitory rules not being in the marriage act. The rule however is evidently older than the marriage act, and is always found without a limitation from the first. Except the case of legal personal disqualification against marrying at all, such as Lolley's, to which we shall soon advert, we know but of one country (France) where the validity of a foreign marriage between its own subjects is tried by its own, and not the foreign law. French subjects who are required at home to obtain the consent of parents, &c., are required so equally, if they marry out of France. Did such a broad personal rule obtain here, there would have been no room for the present article; and it is to such a result that we are addressing ourselves, unless the rules of restriction can be so narrowed as to approve themselves to the moral approbation of all the community, minority as well as majority; i. e., to those cases of affinity which, by the common consent of the country, would be discountenanced, namely, affinities in one degree, as step-father and step-daughter. We will now go on to examine the supposed second rule, as to a foreign bona fide domicil being required. Our English supposed limitation of the general rule is not, as we have seen, treated by such of the civilians as have espoused these views as an absolute personal rule, but one merely in fraudem legis; and they therefore attach to the limitation this sub-limitation, that the qualification will be removed by a sufficient domicil abroad. But sufficient by what law? The sufficiency according to the requirements of the foreign law is admitted on all sides. Our law as to domicil proceeds on quite different grounds. But supposing our law required a year's residence to make a domicil in any place, and the law of that place required two years, and also required domicil to ratify the contract of marriage within it, it is evident that we here, trying the validity of such a marriage, should require the two years' residence to be proved. These civilians admit this, and require us to fulfil the foreign law in all cases. But

is void, although such divorce and second marriage would be
unquestionably good by the law of Scotland.[1] So that here
there may be two lawful wives of the party living at the same
time in different countries, and two families of children, one of
which may be deemed legitimate by the law of the one country,
and illegitimate by the law of the other.[2] It is easy to see what
various difficulties may grow out of such a state of things. A
son by the second marriage may be entitled to the whole real and
personal estate of the father in Scotland, and incapable of touching either in England. The Massachusetts doctrine escapes from

then they require a sufficient domicil by our law as well. They would split the
unity of the contract, and determine it partly by one law and partly by the
other. They require two sorts of domicil to make up the marriage contract,
— the one by the law abroad, to get over the lex loci; the one by our law, not
as essential to the contract, but as evidence of the bona fides of the contract,
and to get over the quasi personal disability they suppose; i. e., the suspicion
of intention to evade our supposed prohibitory law. It is clear the bona fide
domicil they would exact must be by way of evidence, and evidence only.
But if so, how can it be an essential? Parties may marry without any intended
fraud on their own law, where not domiciled to the satisfaction of the civilians;
or, what is more likely, may become so domiciled with a positive intention to
evade their own law. They may get naturalized abroad, move their property
there, do everything which would show a domicil with regard to the laws
about personal estate, and yet all the while it may be capable of clear proof
that they did this only because they chose to be married, and were not permitted to be married here, and that they intended and did all for evasion.
They may intend a permanent residence also, and merely because they do not
like the English law as to affinity. What would the civilians, who countenance these refinements, say to this case? Their notion seems to have arisen
from viewing the law as an individual whose honor is to be vindicated, and
who is to be treated with at least outward show of observance and respect.
They make it, let it be observed, not a principle of English law merely, but of
general law; though they can find no instance in any one country to support
it, except Lord Mansfield's manifestly erroneous dictum in a bill of exchange
case. To us the whole scheme seems altogether insupportable. A law, we
should think, is either local or it is personal, and anything between we cannot comprehend. If it were the case of a foreigner's marriage here, would
they ask if he came here in evasion of his own law? or would they not rather
say with Fergusson, " A party domiciled here cannot be permitted to import
a law peculiar to his own case." Ferg. on Mar. & Div. 399.' See also
Huberus, lib. 1, tit. 3, de Confl. Leg. s. 13; Paul Voet, de Statut. s. 9, c. 2,
n. 4, p. 263, ed. 1715; Id. p. 319, ed. 1661. Lord Brougham, in Warrender
v. Warrender, 9 Bligh, 129, 130, manifestly considered that the doctrine that
a marriage in a foreign country was void, if it was a fraud upon the law of the
domicil of the parties, was not maintainable in point of law.

[1] Lolley's Case, Russ. & R. 237. See Warrender v. Warrender, 9 Bligh,
89; ante, s. 86, 88; post, s. 215–226.
[2] Conway v. Beazley, 3 Hagg. Ecc. 639; Rex v. Lolley, Russ. & Ry. 237.

these incongruities ; and appears to be founded upon a liberal basis
of international policy, which deems it far better to support marriages celebrated in a foreign country as valid, when in conformity with the laws of that country, although the rule may
produce some minor inconveniences, than, by introducing distinctions as to the designs and objects and motives of the parties, to
shake the general confidence in such marriages, to subject the
innocent issue to constant doubts as to their own legitimacy, and
to leave the parents themselves to cut adrift from their solemn
obligations when they may become discontented with their lot.

124 a. It is no answer to this reasoning to say that every
nation has a right, at its pleasure, to impose any restraints and
prohibitions upon the marriages of its own subjects whether they
marry within or without its own territory.   Admitting this to be
true in the fullest extent to which it can justly be claimed in
virtue of national sovereignty, it must be quite as true, and quite
as obvious, that no other nation is bound to recognize those restraints and those prohibitions as obligatory upon such subjects
while they are domiciled within its own territory, or when they
have contracted marriages there according to the laws thereof.
All such local municipal restraints and prohibitions must, under
such circumstances, necessarily tend to mutual embarrassment
and confusion in the intercourse between such nations.   The very
object of the rule, arising from the comity of nations, and a sense
of the importance and public policy of giving to marriages everywhere the most solemn and binding obligation, is to secure all
nations against such a conflict of laws.   If France has chosen to
declare that all marriages celebrated by its subjects in foreign
countries, in conformity with their laws, but not according to its
own laws, shall be utterly void, every other country has an equal
right to declare that such marriages shall be deemed valid, and
refuse to submit to the dictation of France.   France may at home
enforce such laws upon her own subjects and their property when
found within its territory.   But every other nation, by whose laws
the marriages celebrated therein would be valid, would sustain
such marriages, and treat the claims of France as an usurpation,
founded in injustice and a disregard of the true duty and policy
of all civilized nations in their intercourse with each other. (a)

(a) *Validity of Marriages.* — In con-   marriages, it is important to keep
sidering the cases upon the validity of   in mind that the word *marriage* has

two meanings : one is, the ceremony by which the parties are united in wedlock; the other is, the union in wedlock which the ceremony is intended to effect. Much confusion has arisen from the distinction between the two not having been observed; and the rules that have been laid down for determining the validity of a marriage, where the ceremony was alone in question, have sometimes been used in determining whether it was lawful for the parties to intermarry, as if the subject was the same in both cases, instead of there being two different subjects, to each of which the term *marriage* was properly applied. See Harvey *v.* Farnie, 6 P. D. p. 47; Campbell *v.* Crampton, 2 Fed. R. p. 424.

It is an established rule in England and America that the ceremony by which the parties are joined in wedlock, including all the forms to be observed, depends upon the law of the country where the ceremony is performed. Scrimshire *v.* Scrimshire, 2 Hagg. Cons. 395; Dalrymple *v.* Dalrymple, Id. 54; Herbert *v.* Herbert, Id. 263, 271; 3 Phillim. Ecc. 58; Middleton *v.* Janverin, 2 Hagg. Cons. 437; Swift *v.* Kelly, 3 Knapp, 257; Kent *v.* Burgess, 11 Sim. 361; Lacon *v.* Higgins, 3 Stark. 178; D. & R. N. P. C. 38; Butler *v.* Freeman, Amb. p. 303 (by Lord Hardwicke); Patterson *v.* Gaines, 6 How. 550, 587–589; Phillips *v.* Gregg, 10 Watts (Pa.) 158; Hutchins *v.* Kimmell, 31 Mich. 126; Morgan *v.* McGhee, 5 Humph. (Tenn.) 13; Dumaresly *v.* Fishly, 3 A. K. Marsh. (Ky.) 368; Wall *v.* Williamson, 8 Ala. 48; Loring *v.* Thorndike, 5 Allen (Mass.) 257, 269; Johnson *v.* Johnson, 30 Mo. 72. The formalities of contracting marriage are thus governed by the same rule as the formalities of other contracts (s. 260, post).

When a certain consent (as that of a father or guardian) is required to make a marriage valid, the consent is considered one of the formalities if it appears upon the interpretation of the law that its intention was, not to render the person incapable of marrying without the consent, but only to make the consent essential to a valid ceremony. In every case the question is one of construction. Brook *v.* Brook, 9 H. L. C. 215–218, 228–229; Compton *v.* Bearcroft, Bull. N. P. 114; 2 Hagg. Cons. 444; Steele *v.* Braddell, Milw. (Ir.) 1, 19; Simonin *v.* Mallac, 2 Sw. & Tr. 67; Sottomayor *v.* De Barros, 3 P. D. 7.

Compton *v.* Bearcroft (Bull. N. P. 114; 2 Hagg. Cons. 444) was the case which established the validity of the Gretna Green marriages, notwithstanding Lord Hardwicke's Marriage Act (26 Geo. 2, c. 33). By this act a marriage without publication of banns or licence was void, and a marriage by licence without the consent of the father or guardian, where either party, not being a widower or widow, was under twenty-one, was also void. The consent was necessary only in cases of marriage by licence, and a marriage by banns was valid without consent. It was accordingly held that the provision as to consent applied only to such marriages as must be celebrated either by banns or by licence, that is, to marriages solemnized in England. Therefore persons married out of England were not affected by the provision, even if they left England for the purpose of being married where they could do so without complying with its requirements. In Steele *v.* Braddell, Milw. 1, the question arose upon the Irish act of 9 Geo. 2, c. 11, which enacted that all marriages, when either party was under twenty-one, and entitled to a certain fortune, had without the consent of the father or guardian in writing first obtained, should be void, provided that the father or guardian should within one year commence a suit to annul the marriage, and if no such suit were commenced within that time, the marriage should be good and valid. Dr. Radcliff held that the effect of the statute was only to make certain marriages voidable by suit under conditions, and not to create a personal incapacity, and that it applied only to marriages celebrated in Ireland. In Simonin v. Mallac, 2 Sw. & Tr. 67, the consent was one of the formalities required by the French code, which did not absolutely prohibit marriage without consent, but only postponed it, and allowed the celebration of the marriage after a certain time had elapsed, if the consent were asked for and refused. A marriage solemnized in England between persons domiciled in France was held valid, notwithstanding the consent was not obtained or asked for. These cases were referred to and explained by Lord Campbell in Brook v. Brook, 9 H. L. C. 214-218.

On the other hand, in the Sussex Peerage Case, 11 Cl. & F. 85, 142, it was held that a personal incapacity to contract marriage anywhere was created by the Royal Marriage Act (12 Geo. 3, c. 11), which enacted that no descendant of George II. (other than the issue of princesses married into foreign families) should be capable of contracting matrimony without the previous consent of the sovereign in council, and that every marriage of any such descendant without such consent should be null and void. Lord Brougham said in this case (p. 151) that if Lord Hardwicke's Marriage Act ' had used the same phraseology as this, and had rendered the parties incapable of contracting matrimony, we should never have heard of Compton v. Bearcroft (supra) and Ilderton v. Ilderton (2 H. Bl. 145).' In Sottomayor v. De Barros, 3 P. D. 1, it appeared that by the law of Portugal a marriage between first cousins was deemed incestuous, and therefore null and void, but this impediment could be removed by a papal dispensation. It was held that the dispensation could not be regarded as a matter of form affecting only the sufficiency of the ceremony, and that a marriage without dispensation between parties so related and domiciled in Portugal was illegal and void wherever it was contracted.

When the question is, not whether the ceremony or form was sufficient, but whether it was lawful for the parties to intermarry, the rule to be deduced from the English authorities seems to be that the validity of their union must be determined by the law of the matrimonial domicil. Brook v. Brook, 9 H. L. C. 193; Sottomayor v. De Barros, 3 P. D. 1 (C. A.); Mette v. Mette, 1 Sw. & Tr. 416. And in Virginia, North Carolina, and Louisiana, a marriage between parties domiciled there is void, although it be solemnized out of the state, if the law of the state prohibits their intermarriage. Kinney's Case, 30 Grat. (Va.) 858; State v. Kennedy, 76 N. C. 251; Dupre v. Boulard, 10 La. An. 411.

In Massachusetts and Kentucky a marriage is valid, although it is forbidden by the laws of the state and the parties are domiciled there, if it is solemnized in a place where it is lawful. Medway v. Needham, 16 Mass. 157; Dannelli v. Dannelli, 4 Bush (Ky.) 51. See also Commonwealth v. Lane, 113 Mass. p. 462-471; Ross v. Ross, 129 Mass. p. 247-248; Stevenson v. Gray, 17 B. Mon. (Ky.) 193. Dicta to the same effect are to be found in Ponsford v. Johnson, 2 Blatch. C. C. 51; Van Voorhis v. Brintnall, 86 N. Y. 18 (ante, s. 92, note).

The principle that questions of personal status depend upon the law of the domicil is generally established. Udny v. Udny, L. R. 1 H. L. Sc. p. 457; Shaw v. Gould, L. R. 3 H. L. p. 83; Ross v. Ross, 129 Mass. p. 246, 248; ante, s. 50, note. It seems to follow from this principle that the lawfulness of the union of two persons in wedlock, that is, the validity of a marriage in essentials or matters of substance as distinguished from the formalities of contracting it, should be determined by the law of the matrimonial domicil. Lord Westbury said in Udny v. Udny, L. R. 1 H. L. Sc. p. 457, ' The civil status is governed universally by one single principle, namely, that of domicil, which is the criterion established by law for the purpose of determining civil status. For it is on this basis that the personal rights of the party, that is to say, the law which determines his majority or minority, his marriage, succession, testacy or intestacy, must depend.' Marriage creates a status or relation between the parties. Niboyet v. Niboyet, 4 P. D. p. 11. If they have different domicils before the marriage, the domicil of the husband becomes upon the marriage the domicil of both. This is the matrimonial domicil, by the law of which the effects and incidents of the marriage and its dissolution are governed. The same principle seems properly to govern the formation of the relation. This is also Savigny's opinion. Priv. Int. Law, Guthrie's trans., s. 379, p. 240, 241. See also Id. 248, note A.

In support of the theory that the validity of the union should be determined by the law of the place where the marriage is solemnized, it is said that the status of marriage is based upon the contract of the parties, and that the validity of the contract is governed by the law of the place where the contract is made. This rule governs contracts when no particular place is appointed for their fulfilment. But when a contract is made in one place to be performed in another, its obligations and effects are governed by the law of the place of performance. Post, s. 280, 299, 299 a, 301 a. See Westlake (ed. 1880) p. 234, 237. The obligations of the contract of marriage are to be performed in the place where the parties are domiciled as husband and wife, and its effect is to create a status which is governed by the law of that place. The law of the matrimonial domicil consequently should determine the va-

lidity of the contract of marriage. Thus the principle that governs the validity of contracts would lead to the same result as the principle that governs personal status. See Warrender v. Warrender, 2 Cl. & F. at p. 535, 536; Shreck v. Shreck, 32 Tex. at p. 587; Campbell v. Crampton, 2 Fed. R. at p. 425. In the last-mentioned case, an agreement to marry, which was made between relations whose marriage was forbidden by the law of the man's domicil, and by which the marriage was to be solemnized in a state where it was not forbidden, was held void, on the ground that the place where the parties were to be domiciled, that is, the man's domicil, and not the place where the marriage was to be solemnized, was the place of performance.

It seems to be a matter of doubt whether a marriage is valid when the union is one which is lawful by the law of the domicil of the parties and unlawful by the law of the country where the marriage is celebrated. Mr. Westlake thinks that the marriage would be invalid, and that it is indispensable that each party have capacity to contract the marriage both by the law of his or her domicil and by the law of the place where it is celebrated. Westlake (ed. 1880) p. 52-54. Mr. Dicey however thinks that the invalidity of the marriage is not free from doubt, and adds that recent decisions (Sottomayor v. De Barros, 3 P. D. 1 (C. A.); Brook v. Brook, 9 H. L. C. 193) suggest the conclusion that its validity is governed by the law of the domicil (Dicey on Domicil, p. 216). The principle that questions of status depend upon the law of the domicil seems certainly to lead to that conclusion. The law of any country may of course make it unlawful to solemnize certain marriages in that country. But the natural construction of a law which creates an incapacity to marry or forbids marriage between certain races or between persons related in certain degrees, seems to be that which limits its application to persons whose status of marriage is governed by the laws of that country.

In Brook v. Brook, which was decided in the House of Lords in 1861 (9 H. L. C. 193; 7 Jur. N.S. 422; 9 W. R. 461; 4 L. T. 93), a widower and the sister of his deceased wife were married in Denmark, where such a marriage was lawful. They were both domiciled in England, and, by an act of parliament, marriage between a widower and his wife's sister was prohibited and declared void on the ground of its being contrary to God's law. The House of Lords, affirming the decision (3 Sm. & G. 481) of Stuart, V. C., and Cresswell, J., held that the marriage was void. Lord Campbell, the Lord Chancellor, in delivering his opinion, said, ' There can be no doubt of the general rule that " a foreign marriage, valid according to the law of a country where it is celebrated, is good everywhere." But while the forms of entering into the contract of marriage are to be regulated by the lex loci contractus, the law of the country in which it is celebrated, the essentials of the contract depend upon the lex domicilii, the law of the country in which the parties are domiciled at the time of the marriage, and in which the matrimonial residence is contemplated. Although the forms of celebrating the foreign marriage may be different from those required by the law of the country of domicil, the marriage may be good everywhere. But if the contract of marriage is such in essentials as to be contrary to the law of the country of domicil, and it is declared void by that law, it is to be regarded as void in the country of domicil, though not contrary to the law of the country in which it was celebrated. This qualification upon the rule that " a marriage valid where celebrated is good everywhere " is to be found in the writings of many eminent jurists who have discussed the subject.' Lord Campbell referred to Warrender

v. Warrender, 2 Cl. & F. 488, and added, ' The doctrine being established that the incidents of the contract of marriage celebrated in a foreign country are to be determined according to the law of the country in which the parties are domiciled and mean to reside, the consequence seems to follow that by this law must its validity or invalidity be determined.' Lord Cranworth said, ' The conclusion at which I have arrived is the same as that which my noble and learned friend on the woolsack has come to, namely, that though in the case of marriages celebrated abroad, the lex loci contractus must, quoad solennitates, determine the validity of the contract, yet no law but our own can decide whether the contract is or is not one which the parties to it, being subjects of her majesty domiciled in this country, might lawfully make.'

In Mette v. Mette, 1 Sw. & Tr. 416, which was decided while the appeal in Brook v. Brook was pending, a German, who had been naturalized and was domiciled in England, married the sister of his deceased wife in Germany, where she was domiciled, and where marriage between a widower and his deceased wife's sister was lawful. Cresswell, J., held that the marriage was void on the same ground as the marriage in Brook v. Brook, and that the husband, being domiciled and naturalized in England, could not contract a marriage contrary to the act of parliament, although he was not a natural-born subject; and as he was incapacitated from contracting such a marriage, the fact that the wife was a native of Germany and, until the marriage, was domiciled there, could not have any effect.

In Sottomayor v. De Barros, 2 P. D. 81; 3 P. D. 1 (C.A.), a marriage was contracted in England between two first cousins, both of whom, as it appeared, were domiciled in Portugal. By the law of Portugal first cousins were incapable of contracting marriage on account of consanguinity, and such marriage would be considered incestuous; but this impediment could be removed by papal dispensation. Sir R. Phillimore said that, although it was established that when parties were by the law of their domicil incapable of contracting marriage, the court of the domicil recognized the incapacity as invalidating their marriage, even if it was contracted in a place where no such incapacity existed, and although it might appear to be a consequence of that doctrine that the court of the place of the contract was also bound to recognize the incapacity, yet having regard to some decisions which he mentioned, especially Simonin *v.* Mallac, 2 Sw. & Tr. 67, he did not think that sitting as a single judge he ought to pronounce the marriage void on that ground. 2 P. D. 81.   On appeal, the court (James, Baggallay, and Cotton, L.JJ.) held that the marriage was null and void on the ground that the law of Portugal imposed on its subjects an incapacity which affected them so long as they were domiciled there, and rendered invalid a marriage between persons within the prohibited degrees domiciled in that country at the time of the marriage, wherever such marriage might be solemnized. 3 P. D. 1.   Cotton, L.J., in delivering the judgment of the court, said, ' If the parties had been subjects of her majesty domiciled in England, the marriage would undoubtedly have been valid.   But it is a well-recognized principle of law that the question of personal capacity to enter into any contract is to be decided by the law of domicil. . . . The law of a country where a marriage is solemnized must alone decide all questions relating to the validity of the ceremony by which the marriage is alleged to have been constituted; but, as in other contracts, so in that of marriage, personal capacity must depend on the law of domicil; and if the

laws of any country prohibit its subjects within certain degrees of consanguinity from contracting marriage, and stamp a marriage between persons within the prohibited degrees as incestuous, this, in our opinion, imposes on the subjects of that country a personal incapacity which continues to affect them so long as they are domiciled in the country where this law prevails, and renders invalid a marriage between persons both at the time of their marriage subjects of and domiciled in the country which imposes this restriction, wherever such marriage may have been solemnized. . . . Our opinion on this appeal is confined to the case where both the contracting parties are, at the time of their marriage, domiciled in a country the laws of which prohibit their marriage.   All persons are legally bound to take notice of the laws of the country where they are domiciled. No country is bound to recognize the laws of a foreign state when they work injustice to its own subjects, and this principle would prevent the judgment in the present case being relied on as an authority for setting aside a marriage between a foreigner and an English subject domiciled in England, on the ground of any personal incapacity not recognized by the law of this country.'   As regards Simonin *v.* Mallac, 2 Sw. & Tr. 67, by which Sir R. Phillimore had considered himself bound, and in which the marriage was held to be valid, he said, ' The objection to the validity of the marriage in that case, which was solemnized in England, was the want of the consent of parents required by the law of France, but not under the circumstances by that of this country.   In our opinion, this consent must be considered a part of the ceremony of marriage, and not a matter affecting the personal capacity of the parties to contract marriage.' 3 P. D. 5–7.

Sottomayor *v.* De Barros was tried

again before Sir J. Hannen (5 P. D. 94), and upon this trial the judge found that at the time of the marriage the husband was domiciled in England and the wife in Portugal. He referred to the statement in the judgment of the Court of Appeal that their opinion was confined to the case where both parties were domiciled in a country the laws of which prohibited their marriage, and said, ' This passage leaves me free to consider whether the marriage of a domiciled Englishman in England, with a woman subject by the law of her domicil to a personal incapacity not recognized by English law, must be declared invalid by the tribunals of this country. Before entering upon this inquiry I must observe that the Lords Justices appear to have laid down, as a principle of law, a proposition which was much wider in its terms than was necessary for the determination of the case before them. It is thus expressed: " It is a well-recognized principle of law that the question of personal capacity to enter into any contract is to be decided by the law of domicil;" and again, " As in other contracts, so in that of marriage, personal capacity must depend on the law of domicil." It is of course competent for the Court of Appeal to lay down a principle which, if it formed the basis of a judgment of that court, must, unless it should be disclaimed by the House of Lords, be binding in all future cases. But I trust that I may be permitted without disrespect to say that the doctrine thus laid down has not hitherto been " well-recognized." On the contrary, it appears to me to be a novel principle, for which up to the present time there has been no English authority. What authority there is seems to me to be the other way.' He then referred to Male v. Roberts, 3 Esp. 163; Scrimshire v. Scrimshire, 2 Hagg. Cons. at p. 412, 413; 1 Burge, Col. & For. Law, 132; Story, Conflict of Laws,

s. 103; Simonin v. Mallac, 2 Sw. & Tr. at p. 77, as authorities for the proposition that the validity of a contract of marriage as well as of other contracts, depends upon the law of the place where the contract is entered into. He considered that the effect of the decision of the Court of Appeal was only to declare a further condition imposed by English law, namely, that the parties do not both belong by domicil to a country the laws of which prohibit their marriage. But as the decision expressly left altogether untouched the case of the marriage of a British subject in England, where the marriage was lawful, with a person domiciled in a country where the marriage was prohibited, he held that in such a case the marriage, being good by the law of the country where solemnized, must be deemed by the tribunals of that country to be valid, irrespective of the law of the domicil of the parties.

It will thus be seen that, although the decision of the Court of Appeal did not extend to the case as it appeared at the second trial, the reasons given by Sir J. Hannen for his decision directly contradict the principle of law laid down by the Court of Appeal. Simonin v. Mallac, 2 Sw. & Tr. 67, to which he attached so much weight, and which was explained by the Court of Appeal as relating only to the ceremony of marriage, had received the same explanation in the House of Lords in Brook v. Brook, 9 H. L. C. 193. Scrimshire v. Scrimshire, 2 Hagg. Cons. 395, from which he quoted, was clearly a case involving only the forms of marriage. He quoted this language from the judgment of Sir E. Simpson in this case: ' This doctrine of trying contracts, especially those of marriage, according to the laws of the country where they are made, is conformable to what is laid down in our books, and what is practised in all civilized countries,' and ' These authorities fully show that all contracts are to be considered according to the laws of the country where they are made. And the practice of civilized countries has been conformable to this doctrine, and by the common consent of nations has been so received.' (2 Hagg. Cons. 412, 413). The context and the authorities cited, as well as the facts of the case before him, show that Sir E. Simpson was speaking of the validity of contracts as regards forms and solemnities only. The passage in his judgment in which the above remarks occur is as follows (the original is not italicized): 'This doctrine of trying contracts, especially those of marriage, according to the laws of the country where they were made, is conformable to what is laid down in our books, and what is practised in all civilized countries, and what is agreeable to the law of nations, which is the law of every particular country, and taken notice of as such. This subject is much discussed by Sanchez, to the following effect, that as to the maxim or general rule, "Ut non teneantur peregrini legibus et consuetudinibus loci per quem transeunt," this rule has exceptions; "1st. Quoad contractuum *solemnitatem;* nam quicunque forenses et peregrini tenentur servare *solemnitates* in contractu requisitas legibus et consuetudinibus oppidi in quo contrahunt; ratione enim contractus quilibet forum sortitur in loco contractus; hinc est contractum absolute initum, censeri celebratum, juxta consuetudines et statuta loci in quo initur. Quod ita provenit, quia contractus sequitur consuetudines et statuta loci in quo celebratur." And a case is put, as to inhabitants of a place where the decree of the Council of Trent, for avoiding clandestine marriages, is not received; suppose from England they go " per modum transitus, ubi obligat decretum," and marry there according to the laws of their own domicil. Some think that such marriage is good in the case of strangers, as agreeable

to their own laws, to the law of the country in which they are domiciled, though not to the law of the place where they are married. But Sanchez thinks the marriage void, because it wants the *solemnities,* " quæ petunt leges loci ubi contractus initur; et quoad *solemnitatem* adhibendam in contractibus, solæ leges loci in quo contractus celebratur inspiciuntur." These authorities fully show that all contracts are to be considered according to the laws of the country where they are made. And the practice of civilized countries has been conformable to this doctrine, and by the common consent of nations has been so received.' See also his citations from Gayll and Voet at p. 408, 414, 415. Further on (p. 416) Sir E. Simpson said: 'From the doctrine laid down in our books — the practice of nations — and the mischief and confusion that would arise to the subjects of every country, from a contrary doctrine, I may infer that it is the consent of all nations, that it is the jus gentium, that the *solemnities* of the different nations with respect to marriages should be observed, and that contracts of this kind are to be determined by the laws of the country where they are made.' The case of Male v. Roberts, 3 Esp. 163, which was also referred to by Sir J. Hannen, did not relate to marriage; the question was, whether a debt incurred in Scotland could be enforced against an infant, and it was held that, 'the law of the country where the contract arose must govern the contract ' (see note, s. 102, ante). Sir J. Hannen's reasoning that marriage, like other contracts, should be governed by the law of the place where the contract was made, is answered by this passage from his own judgment, 'In truth, very many and serious difficulties arise if marriage be regarded only in the light of a contract. It is indeed based upon the contract of the parties, but it is a status arising out of a contract to which each country is entitled to attach its own conditions, both as to its creation and duration ' (p. 101). Although, as the same judge says, there was no previous English authority for the principle that personal capacity to enter into any contract is to be decided by the law of domicil, there was sufficient authority in the opinions of Lords Campbell and Cranworth in Brook v. Brook (supra), for the principle that the lawfulness of contracts of marriage was to be decided by the law of the domicil. As to Mette v. Mette (supra), where a marriage in Germany was held to be void because it was contrary to the law of the man's domicil, which was England, Sir J. Hannen distinguished the case on the ground that it was not a controversy arising in the country where the marriage was celebrated. According to this doctrine, if a foreigner is married in England, the validity of his marriage depends upon the law of the place where it is celebrated; but if a person domiciled in England is married in another country, the validity of the marriage is governed by the law of his domicil. With regard to the decision of the Court of Appeal that the dispensation of the pope could not be considered a matter of form affecting only the sufficiency of the ceremony, Sir J. Hannen says (p. 106), ' I would ask what is the distinction between the prohibition of a marriage unless the consent of a parent be obtained as in Simonin v. Mallac [supra], and the prohibition of a marriage unless the dispensation of the pope be granted, as in this case? And if there be a distinction, which I am unable to perceive, why is greater value to be attached by the tribunals of this country to the permission of the pope than to that of a father?' The distinction is, that in Simonin v. Mallac, marriage without the consent of the parent was not absolutely prohibited by the French code, but was permitted

if certain other formalities were observed, while by the law of Portugal, marriage between first cousins, as in Sottomayor v. De Barros, was held to be incestuous, and therefore null and void, though the impediment might be removed by papal dispensation. 2 P. D, 84; 3 P. D. 4. It seems to be a right interpretation of the Portuguese law, that, when it declares a marriage null and void because incestuous, it makes the parties incapable of contracting that marriage, even though it admit the power of the pope to remove the impediment by a dispensation. The reason why greater value is attached by the English tribunals to the dispensation of the pope than to the consent of the father is, that the Portuguese law attaches greater value to the former than the French law does to the latter, and the English tribunals are dealing in one case with Portuguese law and in the other with French law.

Although the opinions of the Court of Appeal and of Sir J. Hannen in Sottomayor v. De Barros, 3 P. D. 1; 5 P. D. 94, are directly opposed to one another, yet the actual decisions of both are in accordance with the principle that, as marriage is a status, its validity depends upon the law of the matrimonial domicil, and they are likewise consistent with the decisions in Brook v. Brook, 9 H. L. C. 193, and Mette v. Mette, 1 Sw. & Tr. 416. The marriage of the parties was absolutely forbidden by the law of the domicil of both parties in Brook v. Brook, and in Sottomayor v. De Barros, as the facts appeared in the Court of Appeal, and by the law of the man's domicil in Mette v. Mette; but the marriage was lawful by the law of the man's domicil, which was the matrimonial domicil, in Sottomayor v. De Barros, as the facts appeared before Sir J. Hannen.

The Court of Appeal said in Sottomayor v. De Barros, 3 P. D. 1, 6, ' Our opinion on this appeal is confined to the case where both the contracting parties are, at the time of their marriage, domiciled in a country the laws of which prohibit their marriage.' Mr. Dicey (Domicil, p. 221) says: 'The suggested limitation, however, to the application of the principle that capacity to marry depends upon a person's lex domicilii, cannot, it is conceived, be permanently maintained. The introduction of the proposed limitation is not necessitated by any decided cases, is illogical, and does away with the great advantage derived from basing the validity of a marriage on a broad and clear ground.'

Mr. Dicey however states the following as an exception (p. 223): 'A marriage celebrated in England is not invalid on account of any incapacity of either of the parties which, though imposed by the law of his or her domicil, is of a kind to which our courts refuse recognition.' One example which he mentions is a marriage celebrated in England between a black man and a white woman, who are both domiciled in a country where marriages between blacks and whites are prohibited. The reason he gives for this exception in this case, is, 'that the incapacity constitutes a penal or privative status, to which our courts will not give extra-territorial effect,' and he refers to the rule that a status unknown to English law, like slavery, is not recognized in England. It seems however to be incorrect to say that a prohibition of a marriage on account of a difference of race is penal or privative in its nature. It is no more so than a prohibition on account of consanguinity or affinity. It bears no resemblance to slavery. It applies to both races alike. It is difficult to perceive on what ground the English courts should not recognize this kind of prohibition. It cannot be on the ground that the English law does not prohibit such marriages, for the English courts recognize the prohibition imposed by

Portuguese law upon the marriage of first cousins, which the English law permits. The exceptions in the cases of penal disabilities and of incapacities imposed upon monks and nuns have been mentioned (s. 91, 92, 94, ante), and depend upon different principles.

In Medway v. Needham, 16 Mass. 157, which was decided in 1819, a marriage between a mulatto and a white woman, celebrated in Rhode Island, where such marriages were lawful, was held valid in Massachusetts, although the parties were domiciled in Massachusetts, by the laws of which the marriage was forbidden, and had gone to Rhode Island to be married in evasion of the laws of their domicil. Parker, C. J., in delivering judgment said, 'The celebrated jurist and civilian Huberus strongly contests this doctrine, as may be seen in the passage cited by Hargrave in the note referred to by the counsel for the defendants; and he puts strong cases, to show the grounds of his opinion. But his objections have been overcome in England by the consideration of the extreme inconveniences and cruelty of applying the principle he contends for. . . According to the case settled in England by the ecclesiastical court, and recognized by the courts of common law, the marriage is to be held valid or otherwise, according to the laws of the place where it is contracted, although the parties went to the foreign country with an intention to evade the laws of their own. This doctrine is repugnant to the general principles of law relating to contracts; for a fraudulent evasion of the laws of the country where the parties have their domicil could not, except in the contract of marriage, be protected under the general principle. . . . The exception in favor of marriages so contracted must be founded on principles of policy, with a view to prevent the disastrous consequences to the issue of such marriages, as well as to avoid the public mischief which would result from the loose state in which people so situated would live.' The case in the ecclesiastical court referred to in this judgment was Compton v. Bearcroft, which is mentioned above. The consequences of the decision in Medway v. Needham were in part averted by a subsequent statute (Rev. Sts. 1836, c. 75, s. 6 ; Pub. Sts. c. 145, s. 10), which provided that a marriage should be deemed void when persons resident in the state, in order to evade the provisions of law prohibiting their marriage, and with an intention of returning to reside, go into another state or country and there have their marriage solemnized, and afterwards return and reside in the state. The Revised Statutes Commissioners, one of whom was Judge Jackson, in recommending this provision in 1834, said (Report, pt. 2, p. 113), 'There have been different opinions on the subject of this section; and it is desirable that the law should be settled. . . . It will be observed that the provisions referred to in this section, and which it is proposed to extend to marriages solemnized without this commonwealth, are of a personal nature, founded on the relation subsisting between the parties, or on some other disqualification; and these personal disqualifications exist with equal force in whatever place, or in whatever form, the marriage is solemnized. These provisions do not include the publication of the banns, or any of the *forms* of proceeding ; all which are left to be regulated by the laws of the place where the ceremony is performed. But an incestuous marriage, for example, or one between a white person and a negro, is not rendered innoxious here, merely because the parties go to celebrate it a few miles beyond our boundary.' Thus the principle upon which Brook v. Brook was decided by the House of Lords in 1861 (9 H. L. C. 193), was stated twenty-seven years previously

in this report to the governor of Massachusetts. See the remarks of Parker, C.J., in Putnam v. Putnam, 8 Pick. at p. 435, upon the question whether the rule he had laid down in Medway v. Needham should be changed. In Brook v. Brook, 9 H. L. C. p. 219, Lord Campbell mentioned the case of Medway v. Needham, and said, 'But I cannot think that it is entitled to much weight, for the learned judge admitted that he was overruling the doctrine of Huberus and other eminent jurists; he relied on decisions in which the forms only of celebrating the marriage in the country of celebration and in the country of domicil were different ; and he took a distinction between cases where the absolute prohibition of the marriage is forbidden [founded ?] on mere motives of policy, and where the marriage is prohibited as being contrary to religion on the ground of incest. I myself must deny the distinction. If a marriage is absolutely prohibited in any country as being contrary to public policy and leading to social evils, I think that the domiciled inhabitants of that country cannot be permitted, by passing the frontier and entering another state in which this marriage is not prohibited, to celebrate a marriage forbidden by their own state, and, immediately returning to their own state, to insist on their marriage being recognized as lawful.' Lord Cranworth said (p. 229): 'I also concur entirely with my noble and learned friend that the American decision of Medway v. Needham cannot be treated as proceeding on sound principles of law. The state or province of Massachusetts positively prohibited by its laws, as contrary to public policy, the marriage of a mulatto with a white woman; and on one of the grounds of distinction pointed out by Mr. Justice Story [s. 113 *a*, supra], such a marriage certainly ought to have been held void in Massachusetts, though celebrated in another province where such marriages were lawful.' In Commonwealth v. Lane, 113 Mass. 458, the point decided in which has already been mentioned (ante s. 92, note), the decision of the House of Lords in Brook v. Brook was examined and disapproved by Gray, C.J. In the still more recent decision of Kinney's Case, 30 Grat. (Va.) 858, in which the point was the same as in Medway v. Needham, 16 Mass. 157, Christian, J., in delivering the judgment of the Virginia Court of Appeals, quoted the above remarks of Lords Campbell and Cranworth, and then added with regard to the case of Medway v. Needham, ' With such condemnation, from so high a source, of this decision as authority, and when it is opposed by the decisions of our sister southern states above referred to, and contrary to sound principles of law, I think, though a case exactly in point upon its facts, it can have but little weight in forming our judicial determination of the question before us in this case.' See also State v. Kennedy, 76 N. C. 251.

CHAPTER VI.

INCIDENTS TO MARRIAGES.

125. *Subject to be considered.* — Having considered how far the validity of marriages is to be decided by the law of the place where they are celebrated, we are next led to consider the operation of foreign law upon the incidents of marriage. These may respect either the personal capacity and powers of the husband and wife, or the rights of each in regard to the property, personal or real, acquired or held by both or either of them during the coverture.[1]

126. *Diversities of Law.* — The jurisprudence of different nations contains almost infinitely diversified regulations upon the subject of the mutual obligations and duties of husband and wife, their personal capacities and powers, and their mutual rights and interests in the property belonging to or acquired by each during the existence of the marriage; and the task of enumerating all of them would be as hopeless as it would be useless. Before the Revolution there were in France a multitude of such diversities in the local and customary law of her own provinces, and in Germany and the states of Holland and Italy and the vast domains of Austria and Russia, the like diversities existed, and probably still continue to exist. Froland has enumerated a few of these diversities, by way of illustrating the endless embarrassments arising from the conflict of laws of different provinces and nations;[2] and his ample work is mainly devoted to a consideration of the mixed questions arising from the conjugal relation, as affected by different laws in different provinces and nations. In some of the French provinces before the Revolution a married woman had a separate power to contract; in others she had not.[3]

---

[1] See on the subject of this chapter, 1 Burge, Col. & For. Law, pt. 1, c. 6, s. 1, 2, p. 201-262; Id. c. 7, s. 1, p. 262-276.

[2] Froland, Mémoires, c. 1, s. 7, 8.

[3] Ibid.; Henry on Foreign Law, 31. See also 1 Boullenois, c. 1, p. 421; Id. p. 467, 468; Merlin, Répert. Autoris. Maritale, s. 10.

In Holland, under the old laws thereof (for it is unnecessary to consider whether they have undergone any substantial alteration in more recent times), the husband had the sole power to dispose of all the property of his wife; and she was entirely deprived of any power over it.[1]   In Utrecht her consent was necessary if there were not children by the marriage; and in some other places whether there were or were not children.   In Utrecht the husband and wife were disabled from making donations to each other; in Holland they may, or might, make them.[2]   In some states there is a community of property between husband and wife; in others none; and in others again, mixed rights and qualified claims.[3]

127. *Foreign Law.*—Boullenois has put several cases showing the practical difficulties of this conflict of laws.   Suppose a husband domiciled in a place where he cannot bind his wife, if he contracts alone and without her, although she is under his marital power and authority, and the husband should go to and contract in a place where, by reason of this authority, he can bind his wife by binding himself, will the latter contract bind her?   He answers in the negative, because the obligation of the wife does not spring from the nature of the contract, nor from the place of the contract, but from the marital authority, which has no such effect in the place of his domicil.[4]   In Brittany, formerly, when a husband and wife were each bound in solido for the same contract or debt, payment was to be first sought out of the effects of the husband.   But in Paris, upon a like contract, the effects of the

[1] 1 Burge, Col. & For. Law, pt. 1, c. 7, s. 2, p. 276, 302.

[2] Rodenburg, de Divers. Stat. tit. 2, c. 5, s. 9; 2 Boullenois, Appx. p. 39. It may be useful here to state, once for all, that in referring to the laws of different countries, I generally state them as they formerly were, without any attention to the changes which they may actually have undergone.   The reasoning of the foreign jurists upon this subject would be rendered exceedingly obscure, and sometimes incorrect, in any other way; and the object of this work is not so much to show what particular conflicts of laws may now arise from the present jurisprudence of a particular country, as to illustrate the principles which different jurists have adopted in solving questions relating to the conflicts of laws generally.   See 1 Burge, Col. & For. Law, pt. 1, c. 7, s. 2, p. 276–332, where there will be found a summary of the laws of Holland on the subject of this chapter.

[3] 1 Burge, Col. & For. Law, c. 7, s. 1–8, p. 262–561; Henry on For. Law, c. 1, s. 3, p. 10, 36, note; Id. 95; 1 Boullenois, obs. 15, p. 198; Id. Princ. Gén. 8, p. 8.

[4] 1 Boullenois, obs. 46, p. 467.

husband and wife were formerly indiscriminately bound. Suppose then that at that period married persons domiciled in Brittany had gone to Paris and there contracted, or that married persons domiciled in Paris had gone to Brittany and there contracted, in what manner should the creditor seek payment? Boullenois seems to have held that in such a case the laws were to be followed which regulate the estate and condition of the wife; that is to say, the laws of her domicil.[1]

128. It is hardly possible to enumerate the different rules adopted in the customary law or in the positive law of different provinces of the same empire, upon the subject of the rights of husband and wife. In some places the laws which place the wife under the authority of her husband, extend to all her acts, as well to acts inter vivos as to acts testamentary; in others the former only are prohibited. In some places the consent of the husband is necessary to give effect to the contracts of the wife; in others the contract is valid, but is suspended in its execution during the life of the husband. In some places the wife has no power over the administration of her own property; in others the prohibition is confined to property merely *dotal*, and she has the free disposal of her own property, which is called *paraphernal*.[2]

129. But not to perplex ourselves with cases of a provincial and unusual nature, let us attend to the differences on this subject in the existing jurisprudence of two of the most polished and commercial states of Europe, in order to realize the variety of questions which may spring up and embarrass the administration of justice in the tribunals of those countries.

130. The present code of France does not undertake to regulate the conjugal association as to property, except in the absence of any special contract, which special contract the husband and wife may under certain limitations make as they shall judge proper. When no special stipulations exist, the case is governed by what is denominated the rule of community, le régime de la communauté. This community, or nuptial partnership, generally extends to all the movable property of the husband and wife, and

---

[1] 1 Boullenois, p. 468, 469.

[2] 2 Boullenois. obs. 32, p. 11; 1 Domat, b. 1, tit. 9, p. 166, 167; Id. s. 4, p. 179, 180, &c. See also 1 Froland, Mém. per tot; Merlin, Répert, Autoris. Maritale, s. 10; 1 Burge, Col. & For. Law, pt. 1, c. 6, s. 1, p. 201–244; Id. c. 7, s. 1–7, p. 262–561.

to the fruits, income, and revenues thereof, whether it is in possession or in action at the time of the marriage, or is subsequently acquired. It extends also to all immovable property of the husband and wife acquired during the marriage, but not to such immovable property as either was possessed at the time of marriage, or came to them afterwards by title of succession, or by gift.[1] The property thus acquired by this nuptial partnership is liable to the debts of the parties existing at the time of the marriage, to the debts contracted by the husband during the community, or by the wife during the community with the consent of the husband, and to debts contracted for the maintenance of the family, and other charges of the marriage. As in common cases of partnership, recompense may be claimed and had for any charges which ought to be borne exclusively by either party. The husband alone is entitled to administer the property of the community, and he may alien, sell, and mortgage it without the concurrence of the wife. He cannot however dispose inter vivos by gratuitous title of the immovables of the community, or of the movables, except under particular circumstances, and testamentary dispositions made by him cannot exceed his share in the community.[2] The community is dissolved by natural death, by civil death, by divorce, by separation of body, or by separation of property. Upon separation of body or of property, the wife resumes her free administration of her movable property, and may alien it. But she cannot alien her immovable property without the consent of her husband, or without being authorized by law upon his refusal. Dissolution of the marriage by divorce gives no right of survivorship to the wife, but that right may occur on the civil death or the natural death of the husband. Upon the death of either party, the community being dissolved, the property belongs equally to the surviving party, and to the heirs of the deceased, in equal moieties, after the due adjustment of all debts, and the payment of all charges and claims on the fund.[3]

131. Such is a very brief outline of some of the more important particulars of the French Code, in regard to the property of married persons in cases of community. The parties may vary these rights by special contract, or they may marry under what is called the dotal rule, le régime dotal. But it would carry us

---

[1] Code Civil of France, art. 1387–1408; Id. art. 1497–1541.
[2] Id. art. 1409–1440.   [3] Code Civil of France, art. 1441–1496.

too far to enter upon the consideration of these peculiarities, as our object is only to point out some of the broader distinctions between the English and the French law as to the effects of marriage.

132. In regard to the personal rights, and capacities, and disabilities of the parties, it may be stated that, independently of the ordinary rights and duties of conjugal fidelity, succor, and assistance, the husband becomes the head of the family, and the wife can do no act in law without the authority of her husband. She cannot therefore, without his consent, give, alien, sell, mortgage, or acquire property. No general authority, even though stipulated by a marriage contract, is valid, except as to the administration of the property of the wife. But the wife may make a will without the authority of her husband. If the wife is a public trader, she may, without the authority of her husband, bind herself in whatever concerns her business ; and in such case she also binds her husband if there is a community between them.[1]

133. *Contrast between English and Foreign Law.* — If we compare this nuptial jurisprudence, brief and imperfect as the outline necessarily is, with that of England, it presents, upon the most superficial examination, very striking differences. In the first place, as to personal rights, capacities, and disabilities, the law of England, with few exceptions (which it is unnecessary here to mention), places the wife completely under the guardianship and coverture of the husband. The husband and wife are, in contemplation of law, one person. He possesses the sole power and authority over the person and acts of the wife ; so that, as Mr. Justice Blackstone has well observed, the very being or legal existence of the wife is suspended during the marriage, or, at least, is incorporated and consolidated into that of the husband.[2] For this reason a man cannot grant anything to his wife, or enter into a covenant with her during his life, though he may devise to her by will. She is incapable of entering into any contract, executing any deed, or doing any other valid act in her own name. All suits, even for personal injuries to her, must be brought in the name of her husband and herself, and with his

---

[1] Code Civil of France, art. 212–226, art. 1426; 2 Toullier, Droit Civ. art. 618–655.

[2] 1 Black. Com. 441; 2 Story, Eq. Jur. s. 1366–1429.

concurrence.   Upon the marriage the husband becomes liable to all her debts, but neither the wife nor her property is liable for any of his debts.   In the Roman law, and (as we have seen) in the French law, the husband and wife are for many purposes considered as distinct persons, and may have separate estates, contracts, rights, and injuries.[1]

134. In respect to property, in England the husband, by the marriage, independently of any marriage settlement, becomes ipso facto entitled to all her personal or movable property of every description, in posesssion and in action, and may dispose of it at his pleasure.   He has also a freehold in her real estate during their joint lives ; and if he has issue by her, and survives her, he has a freehold also during his own life in her real estate, and an exclusive right to the whole profits of it during the same period. There is not any community between them in regard to property, as in the French law.   Upon his death she is simply entitled to dower of one third of his real estate during her life, and he may, at his pleasure, by a testamentary disposition, deprive her of all right and interest in his personal or movable estate, although the whole of it came to him from her by the marriage.   During the coverture she is also incapable of changing, transferring, or in any manner disposing of her real estate, except with his concurrence ; and she is incapable of making an effectual will or testament.[2]

135. Now these differences (which are by no means all that exist), exemplified in the French laws and in the English laws, are, for the most part, the very same as exist in America between the states settled under the common law, and those settled under the civil law ; between those deriving their origin from Spain or France, and those deriving their origin from England.[3]   We may see at once then upon a change of domicil, or even of temporary residence, from a State or country governed by the one law to another governed by the other law, what various questions of an interesting and practical nature may — nay, must — grow up from this conflict of local and municipal jurisprudence.

[1] 1 Black. Com. 441; 2 Story, Eq. Jur. s. 1366–1429; 1 Brown, Civ. Law, 82; 2 Kent Com. 129, &c.

[2] 2 Kent Com. 129, &c.; 2 Black. Com. 433.

[3] 2 Kent Com. 183, and note. See 1 Domat, b. 1, tit. 9; Id. tit. 10. See Christy, Louisiana Digest, art. Husband and Wife, and Louisiana Code, art. 121–133.

185 a. *Division of Subject.* — The subject naturally divides itself into two heads : first, the effect of the marriage upon the personal capacities and incapacities of the wife, or, in other words, her disabilities and her powers, consequent upon the marriage ; and secondly, the effect of the marriage upon the rights and interests of the husband or wife, or of both of them, in the property belonging to them at the time of the marriage, or subsequently acquired by them.   We will examine them under these two separate heads, although (as we shall presently see) some of the considerations applicable to them mutually run into each other.

136. *Capacity and Disability of Wife.* — And in the first place as to the capacities and disabilities of the wife.   It is extremely difficult upon the subject of the personal capacities and disabilities of the wife to lay down any satisfactory rule as to the extent to which they are or ought to be recognized by foreign nations. In general she is deemed to have the same domicil as her husband ; and she can during the coverture acquire none other, suo jure.[1]   Her acts done in the place of her domicil will have validity or not, as they are or are not valid there.   But as to her acts done elsewhere there is much room for diversity of opinion and practice among nations.   We have seen that many of the civilians and jurists of continental Europe hold that the capacity and incapacity of married women, as in other cases of the personality of laws, accompany them everywhere and govern their acts.[2]   And Mr. Chancellor Kent has said that as personal qualities and civil relations of a universal nature, such as infancy and coverture, are fixed by the law of the domicil, it becomes the interest of all nations mutually to respect and sustain that law.[3] This is true in a general sense.   But every nation will judge for itself what its own interest requires, and in framing its own jurisprudence will often hold acts valid within its own territories which the laws of a foreign domicil might prohibit or might disable the parties from doing.

137. *Change of Domicil.* — In considering this subject it is

[1] Ante, s. 46.   See, on this subject, 1 Burge, Col. & For. Law, pt. 1, c. 6, s. 2, p. 244–262.

[2] See ante, s. 51, 55, 56, 57, 58, 60; Henry on Foreign Law, p. 50; Fergusson on Marr. and Div. 334–336; Merlin, Répert. Autoris. Maritale, s. 10.

[3] 2 Kent Com. 419.

material, at least so far as foreign jurists are concerned, to distinguish between cases where there has been a change of domicil of the parties, and where there has not been any such change of domicil. Where the domicil of marriage remains unchanged, the acts of the wife and her power over her property in a foreign country are held by many foreign jurists to be exclusively governed by the law of her domicil; in other words, her acts are valid or not, as the law of her domicil gives her capacity or incapacity to do them.[1] And the rule is applied to her immovable property, as well as to her movable property. Thus if by the law of her domicil she cannot alien property or cannot contract, except with the consent of her husband, she cannot alien her property, and cannot contract without such consent, in a foreign country where no such restriction exists.[2] But suppose that the parties afterwards remove to a new domicil where the consent of the husband is not necessary, is the law of the new domicil, as to the capacity of the wife, to prevail, or that of the matrimonial domicil? This is a question upon which foreign jurists have been greatly divided in opinion.[3]

138. We may illustrate this distinction by a few examples. Thus, for example, the law of England disables a married woman from making a will in favor of her husband or any other person; the law of France allows it. Suppose a husband and wife, married in and subjects of England, should temporarily or permanently become domiciled in France, would a will of the wife in France, in regard to her property in England, made in favor of her husband or others, be held valid in England?[4] Many foreign jurists, among whom may be enumerated Hertius, Paul Voet, John Voet, Burgundus, Rodenburg, Pothier, and Merlin, hold the opinion that the law of the new domicil must, in all cases of a change of domicil, govern the capacities and rights of property of married women, as well as their obligations, acts, and duties.[5]

---

[1] Ante, s. 51–55, 57, 64, 65; post, s. 141.

[2] Merlin, Répert. Autoris. Maritale, s. 10, art. 2; Pothier, Cout. d'Orléans, c. 1, n. 7, 15; ante, s. 51–54, 64, 65, 69; Le Breton v. Miles, 8 Paige, 261.

[3] See Merlin, Répert. Effet Rétroactif, s. 2, 3, art. 5; Autoris. Maritale, s. 10; ante, s. 55–62. See also 1 Burge, Col. & For. Law, pt. 1, c. 5, s. 2, p. 244–262.

[4] See Merlin, Répert. Testament, s. 1, 5, art. 1, 2, p. 309–319.

[5] Ante, s. 55–62; post, s. 140, 141. See also 1 Burge, Col. & For. Law, pt. 1, c. 6, s. 2, p. 253–261.

Froland, it should seem, would answer this particular question upon principle in the affirmative, as a mere question of capacity or incapacity or status of the wife; for he holds that the capacity or incapacity of married women to do things changes with their domicil, and that acts, valid by the law of their original domicil, if done in a new domicil by whose laws they are void, are to be deemed nullities.[1] Thus he says that a married woman, who is incapable by the law of her domicil, where the Roman law (Droit Ecrit) prevails, of entering into a suretyship for another, by the Senatus consultum Velleianum, or of contracting with her husband, as in Normandy, if she goes to reside at Paris, where no such law exists, is there deprived of that exception. And, on the other hand, a woman married and living at Paris, and afterwards going to reside in Normandy, or in any other country where the Roman law prevails (Droit Ecrit), loses her capacity to enter into any such contract, which she previously possessed.[2] Yet Froland has in some other places made distinctions, and insisted on a different rule as applicable to the rights of married women in the property of their husbands, holding that those rights are governed by the law of the place of the marriage, rather than by that of the subsequent actual domicil.[3]

139. *Foreign Jurists.* — Other foreign jurists however have given a different response to the general question; for we have already seen that, in regard to personal laws, there is much conflict of opinion among them, how far these laws are affected by any change of domicil.[4] Huberus (as we have seen) holds a

---

[1] 1 Froland, Mém. 172; ante, s. 55.

[2] 1 Froland, Mém. 172; 1 Boullenois, obs. 4, p. 61; 2 Boullenois, obs. 32, p. 7, 13. Froland has some subtile distinctions on this subject, which, to say the least of them, are not in a practical sense very clear. Lest I should misstate the purport of his remarks, I will quote them in the original, having already referred to them in another place. ' Quand il s'agit de l'état universel de la personne, abstraction faite de toute matière réelle, abstracte ab omni materia reali, en ce cas le statut, qui a commencé à fixer sa condition, conserve sa force et son autorité, et la suit partout en quelque endroit qu'elle aille. Mais quand il est question de l'habilité ou inhabilité de la personne, qui a changé de domicile, à *faire une certaine chose*, alors le statut, qui avait réglé son pouvoir, tombe entièrement à son égard, et cède tout son empire à celui dans le territoire duquel elle va demeurer.' 1 Froland, Mém. 171, 172; ante, s. 55. See 2 Boullenois, obs. 32, p. 7–10; Bouhier, Cout. de Bourg. c. 22, s. 6–14; Id. s. 30–38; Id. s. 148, 149.

[3] 1 Froland, Mém. pt. 2, c. 4, p. 340–408; 2 Boullenois, obs. 32, p. 22, 23, 29.

[4] See ante, s. 55–62; 1 Boullenois, obs. 13, p. 187–196; Id. p. 200; 2

somewhat modified opinion.[1] Bouhier maintains the opinion in the broadest terms, that, in respect to the rights derived from the marital power (puissance maritale), the law of the matrimonial domicil determines the state or condition of the wife, and by consequence the extent of the marital authority; and this state or condition of the wife being once fixed, cannot be afterwards changed by any change of domicil.[2] Dumoulin seems to have entertained the same opinion.[3] Merlin also at one time bent the whole strength of his acknowledged ability to establish the doctrine that the law of the matrimonial domicil, and not of the new domicil, as to the capacity and incapacity of the wife, ought to prevail. He reasoned it out principally in his examination of the subject of the marital power, or the incapacity of the wife, according to certain local laws, to do any valid act, make any conveyance, or engage in any contract, without the consent and authorization of her husband. And he then held that this incapacity is not changed by a change of domicil to a place in whose laws it has no existence.[4] After maintaining this opinion, as he himself says, for forty years, he has recently changed it, and adhered to the doctrine that the law of the new domicil ought to govern.[5] In discussing the nature and extent of the parental authority conferred by the domicil of birth, in regard to foreign property he seems to have been aware of the difficulties of his early doctrine, and he has said, with great truth, that to put an end to all the difficulties of such cases, it is necessary to make a uniform law, not for France only, but for the world; for the settlement of a foreigner in France, or of a Frenchman in a foreign country, would at once raise them anew, notwithstanding

Boullenois, obs. 32, p. 2; Id. obs. 32, p. 14, 15, 17, 19 to id. obs. 37, p. 204; Rodenburg, de Div. Stat. tit. 2, c. 1, s. 3; Id. pt. 2, c. 1, s. 1, 2 Boullenois, Appx. p. 12; Id. 55, 56, and 2 Boullenois, obs. 32, p. 22–28; Henry on For. Law, p. 50, 51; Merlin, Répert. Autoris. Maritale, s. 10; Id. Effet Rétroactif, s. 3, n. 2, art. 3; Bouhier, Cout. de Bourg. c. 22, s. 4–108, and especially s. 67 and 68; 1 Burge, Col. & For. Law, pt. 1, c. 6, s. 2, p. 253–262.

[1] Ante, s. 60, 61; post, s. 145; Huberus, lib. 1, tit. 3, de Conflict. Leg. s. 12, 13; Id. s. 9.

[2] Bouhier, Cout. de Bourg. c. 22, s. 22–27; Id. s. 45–47; Id. s. 48–66; Id. s. 69, 70; Id. s. 79, 80, 82, 83; Id. s. 89, 90; Id. s. 147.

[3] Molin. Oper. Comment. ad Cod. lib. 1, tit. 1, l. 1; Conclus. de Statutis, tom. 3, p. 555, ed. 1681.

[4] Bouhier, Cout. de Bourg. c. 22, s. 22–32, s. 45.

[5] Merlin, Répert. Effet Rétroactif, s. 3, n. 2, art. 5, p. 15; Id. Autorisation Maritale, s. 10, art. 4, p. 243, 244; Id. Majorité, s. 5; ante, s. 58, 59.

all the regulations of the present Civil Code of France.[1] His reasoning upon the testamentary power, and the manner in which it is affected by the situs of the property, also affords very strong proof of the intrinsic infirmity of all general speculations on this subject.[2]

140. It has been already intimated that the opposite opinion has been maintained by many jurists. Let us briefly refer to the opinions of a few of them. Hertius has put the following case. By the law of Utrecht married persons are incapable of making a will of property in favor of each other ; not so in Holland. Is such a will of property in Utrecht, made by married persons in Holland, valid? Or e contra is such a will, made by married persons in Utrecht of property in Holland, valid? He answers the former question in the negative, and the latter in the affirmative.[3]

140 a. The language of Burgundus is still more direct, he affirming in every case of this sort as to the rights and powers of the husband and wife, that they are regulated by the law of the new domicil. 'Proinde, ut sciamus, uxor in potestate sit mariti, necne, qua ætate minor contrahere possit, et ejusmodi, respicere oportet ad legem cujusque domicilii. Hæc enim imprimit qualitatem personæ, atque adeo naturam ejus afficit, ut quocunque terrarum sit transitura, incapacitatem domi adeptam, non aliter quam cicatricem in corpore foras circumferat. Consequenter dicemus, si mutaverit domicilium persona, novi domicilii conditionem induere.'[4]

141. Rodenburg has distinguished the cases on this subject into two sorts: (1) those in which there is no change of domicil of the married parties ; (2) and those in which there is a change of domicil. In the former case he holds that the capacity and incapacity by the law of the domicil extends everywhere. In the latter case, that the capacity and incapacity of the new domicil attach.[5] So that, according to him, the disabilities of a wife by the law of her domicil attach to all her acts, wherever done, at

[1] Merlin, Répert. Puissance Paternelle, s. 7, art. 1, 2, 3.

[2] Id. Testament, s. 1, s. v. art. 1, 2, p. 309–319.

[3] Hertii Opera, de Collis. Leg. s. 4, p. 142, s. 42, 43, ed. 1737; Id. p. 201, ed. 1716.

[4] Burgundus, tract. 2, n. 7, p. 61.

[5] Rodenburg, de Div. Stat. tit. 2, c. 1, s. 1; Id. pt. 2, c. 1, s. 1; Id. c. 4, s. 1; 2 Boullenois, Appx. p. 10, 11; Id. p. 55, 56; Id. p. 63.

home or abroad, as long as the domicil exists.[1] But upon a bona fide change of domicil by her husband, she loses all disabilities not existing by the law of the new domicil, and acquires all the capacities allowed by the latter.[2] Hence if a husband, who by the law of his domicil has his wife subject to his marital authority, changes his domicil to a place where no such law exists, or e contra if he changes his domicil from a place where the wife is exempt from the marital power to one where it exists; in each case the wife has the capacity or incapacity of the new domicil. 'Fac igitur virum, qui per leges loci, ubi degit, uxorem habeat in potestate, collocare domicilium alio, ubi in potestate virorum uxores non sunt; vel vice versa. Dicendumne erit, induere uxorem potestatem qua prius liberata, et exuere, cui alligata est? In affirmationem sententiam deduci videmur per tradita Burgundi. Et recte; personæ enim status et conditio, cum tota regatur a legibus loci, cui illa sese per domicilium subdiderit, utique mutato domicilio, mutari necesse est personæ conditionem.'[3] Boullenois holds on this point the same opinion.[4] Rodenburg puts another case. By the law of Holland married persons may make a will in favor of each other; by the law of Utrecht, not. Suppose a man and wife who are married in Holland move to Utrecht, is the will between them, previously made, good? And he decides in the negative.[5]

142. Boullenois however has himself put a case which he seems to decide upon a ground which breaks in, in some measure, upon the general doctrine. He supposes the case of a woman domiciled and married in a country using the Roman law (Droit Ecrit) to a man belonging to the same country. She has the right and capacity by that law to enjoy her *paraphernal* property there, and to alienate it independently of her husband,[6] and without his being entitled to intermeddle in the administration of it in any manner. He then puts the question whether, if her husband goes to reside at Paris, where no such law exists,

---

[1] Ibid.   [2] Ibid.
[3] Rodenburg, de Divers. Stat. tit. 2, pt. 2, c. 1, s. 1; 2 Boullenois, Appx. p. 55, 56; Burgund. tract. 2, n. 7.
[4] 1 Boullenois, obs. 4, p. 61, 62; Id. obs. 16, p. 205; 2 Boullenois, obs. 32, p. 7-54; Id. p. 81, 82; Id. obs. 35, p. 93-112.
[5] Rodenburg, de Div. Stat. tit. 2, pt. 2, c. 4, s. 1; 2 Boullenois, Appx. p. 63; Id. p. 81; Id. obs. 35, p. 93-112.
[6] 1 Domat, b. 1, tit. 9, p. 167; Id. s. 4, p. 179, 180.

she then falls under his marital authority, so as to lose from that period the administration and alienation of her *paraphernal* property ? Boullenois admits that she falls under the marital authority; but at the same time he contends that she has, notwithstanding, the right of administering and alienating her *paraphernal* property, because it was given to her by the contract of marriage, supported by the law of her matrimonial domicil : and that her husband cannot by a change of domicil extinguish her right, founded upon such authentic titles. And though she cannot act without the consent of her husband in such administration and alienation, yet he is bound to give such consent.[1] But Boullenois is compelled to admit other exceptions to the doctrine, where other considerations are mixed up in the case. Thus he says : Suppose a woman is married at Paris, and has a community of property with her husband there, and she has property at Aix or Toulouse, and her husband goes to reside at either of these places ; the question is whether she is at liberty to sell her property there without the authority or consent of her husband ; and he holds that she cannot sell her property there without the consent of her husband, although she was married at Paris. The reason he assigns is, because, in the countries governed by their own customary law, the property of a married woman in community is deemed *dotal* property, and is presumed to have been brought there by the parties, as such ; and that such property, as *dotal* property, is less alienable at Aix and Toulouse than in countries governed by their customary law ; and that in those provinces, as well as in Paris, the husband has the right of the administration of *dotal* property during the marriage, so that the change of domicil does not make the right of the husband to cease. But, he adds, if the woman married at Paris had no community of property, and, having the administration thereof, came to reside at Aix or Toulouse, then she might sell her property without the authority of her husband, even if situate in Paris, because she is no longer under the authority of her husband, who has no interest in the sale. But if there were no such community, then he holds that she might sell.[2]

---

[1] 2 Boullenois, obs. 32, p. 20, 21; Id. p. 22–28. See Bouhier, Cout. de Bourg. c. 22, s. 28–30; Id. s. 40–45.

[2] 2 Boullenois, obs. 32, p. 22–24. See 2 Froland, Mém. 1007–1064; Bouhier, Cout. de Bourg. c. 22, s. 5–10; Id. s. 28–32; J. Voet, ad Pand. 5, 1, 101; 1 Burge, Col. & For. Law, pt. 1, c. 6, s. 2, p. 244–262.

143. *Common Property of Husband and Wife.* — Passing from the consideration of the personal capacities, disabilities, and powers of the wife, and of the examination of the different opinions of foreign jurists respecting them in cases where there has been no change of domicil, and in cases where there has been such a change, let us in the next place examine into the effect of marriage upon the mutual property of the husband and wife, and their respective rights in and over it.[1] The marriage may have taken place with an express nuptial contract or arrangement as to the property of the parties, or it may have taken place without any such contract or arrangement. The principal difficulty is not so much to ascertain what rule ought to govern in cases of an express nuptial contract, at least, where there is no change of domicil, as what rule ought to govern in cases where there is no such contract, or no contract which provides for the emergency. Where there is an express nuptial contract, that, if it speaks fully to the very point, will generally be admitted to govern all the property of the parties, not only in the matrimonial domicil, but in every other place, under the same limitations and restrictions as apply to other cases of contract.[2] But where there is no express nuptial contract at all, or none speaking to the very point, the question, what rule ought to govern, is surrounded with more difficulty. Is the law of the matrimonal domicil to govern? Or is the law of the local situation of the property? Or is the law of the actual or new domicil of the parties? Does the same rule apply to movable property as to immovable property when it is situated in different countries?[3] Boullenois has remarked that, even on the subject of marriage contracts, the law of the place of the contract will not always decide all the questions arising from it.[4] Many of the questions touching it must be decided by the

---

[1] See 1 Burge, Col. & For. Law, pt. 1, c. 7, s. 8, p. 599-640.

[2] See Le Brun, Traité de la Communauté, liv. 1, c. 2, s. 2; Murphy *v.* Murphy, 5 Mart. (La.) 83; Lashley *v.* Hogg, 4 Paton App. Cas. 581; Feaubert *v.* Turst, Prec. Ch. 207, 208. This doctrine has been fully recognized in England in the case of Anstruther *v.* Adair, 2 Mylne & K. 513; post, s. 184; Le Breton *v.* Miles, 8 Paige (N. Y.) 261.

[3] In some foreign codes there are express provisions that marriage contracts shall not fix the rights of the couple according to the law of foreign countries. In France there is an effective prohibition of contracts regulating marriage rights by the old customs of the provinces, which it has abolished. Code Civil, art. 1390. See also Bourcier *v.* Lanusse, 3 Mart. (La.) 581.

[4] 1 Boullenois, Prin. Gén. 48, p. 11. See also Dig. 5, 1, 65.

law of the domicil of the parties, and sometimes by the law of the domicil of one of them.[1]

144. Two classes of cases naturally present themselves in considering this subject. First, those where during the marriage there is no change of domicil; secondly, those where there is such a change.[2]

145. *No Change of Domicil. — Foreign Jurists.* — And first, in cases where there is no change of domicil and no express nuptial contract. Huberus lays down the doctrine in broad terms, that not only the contract of the marriage itself, properly celebrated in a place according to its laws, is valid in all other places; but that the rights and effects of the marriage contract, according to the laws of the place, are to be held equally in force everywhere.[3] Thus, he says, in Holland married persons have a community of all their property, unless it is otherwise agreed in their nuptial contract; and that this will have effect in respect to property situate in Friesland, although in that province there is only a community of the losses and gains, and not of the property itself. Therefore, he adds, a Frisian married couple remain after their marriage the separate owners, each of their own property situated in Holland. But whenever a married couple remove from the one province (Holland) into the other (Friesland) the property which afterwards comes to either of them ceases to be in community, and is held in distinct proprietary rights. But their antecedent property held in community remains in the state or right in which they originally possessed it. 'Porro, non tantum ipsi contractus ipsæque nuptiæ certis locis rite celebratæ, ubique pro justis et validis habentur; sed etiam jura et effecta contractuum nuptiarumque, in iis locis recepta, ubique vim suam obtinebunt. In Hollandia conjuges habent omnium bonorum communionem, quatenus aliter pactis dotalibus non convenit. Hoc etiam locum habebit in bonis sitis in Frisia, licet ibi tantum sit communio quæstus et damni, non ipsorum bonorum. Ergo et Frisii conjuges manent singuli rerum suarum, etiam in Hollandia sitarum, domini; cum primum vero conjuges migrant ex una provincia in aliam, bona deinceps quæ, alteri

---

[1] Ibid.

[2] See 1 Burge, Col. & For. Law, pt. 1, c. 7, s. 8, p. 599–640.

[3] Huberus, lib. 1, tit. 3, s. 9; post, s. 169; 1 Burge, Col. & For. Law, pt. 1, c. 6, s. 2, p. 244–262.

adveniunt, cessant esse communia, manentque distinctis proprietatibus ; sic ut res antea communes factæ, manent in eo statu
juris, quem induerunt.'[1] The example he thus puts obviously
shows that his doctrine is applied to cases where there is no express contract.

145 *a.* Mr. Chancellor Kent has applied the doctrine of Huberus in the case of an express antenuptial contract between the
parties ; and has laid down the rule that the rights dependent
upon nuptial contracts are to be determined by the lex loci contractus.[2] This may be generally correct in regard to cases of express or of implied nuptial contracts ; and it is probable that none
other were at the time in the mind of the learned judge. But
we shall presently see that, as a general question, in regard to
the universal operation of the lex loci matrimonii, there is much
controversy upon the subject among foreign jurists.

146. There are many distinguished jurists who, in common
with Huberus, maintain the opinion that the incidents and
effects of the marriage upon the property of the parties, wherever it is situate, are to be governed by the law of the matrimonial domicil, in the absence of all other positive arrangements
between the parties.[3] Thus, if English subjects are married in
England without any nuptial contract, the husband being entitled
by the law of England to all the personal or movable property
of his wife, will be entitled to it wherever it may be situated,
whether in England or in any foreign country. (*a*) And his rights,
it would seem, in her immovable property, wherever it may be
situated, would, in the opinion of many of the foreign jurists, be
exclusively regulated by the law of England.[4] So, on the other

[1] Huberus, lib. 1, tit. 3, de Conflict. Leg. s. 9; post, s. 169.
[2] See Decouche *v.* Savetier, 3 Johns. Ch. 211; 2 Kent Com. 458, 459. See
also Feaubert *v.* Turst, cited in Robertson App. Cas. 1, and Lashley *v.* Hogg,
1804, cited Id. 4; Le Breton *v.* Miles, 8 Paige (N. Y.), 261.
[3] Merlin, Répert. Commun. de Biens, s. 1, art. 3; 1 Boullenois, p. 660-673;
Id. obs. 29, p. 732-818; Rodenburg, de Div. Stat. tit. 2, c. 5, s. 12-15; 2 Boullenois, Appx, p. 41-46; 1 Burge, Col. & For. Law, pt. 1, c. 6, s. 2, p. 244-
253; Id. c. 7, s. 8, p. 599-609.
[4] Hertii Opera, de Collis. Leg. s. 47, p. 143, ed. 1737; Id. p. 204, ed. 1716.
Many jurists make no distinction in the application of the doctrine of the tacit
contract of marriage between movable and immovable property, and consider

(*a*) On the other hand, an Englishman marrying in England a lady of
Jersey becomes liable for her debts by the law of England, and not by the
law of Jersey. De Greuchy *v.* Wills,
4 C. P. D. 362.

hand, French subjects married in France, without any contract whatever, would hold, as we have seen,[1] certain kinds of their property in community generally ; and this rule would apply as well to the like property situated in foreign countries, as to that situated in France.

147. The grounds upon which this opinion has been maintained are various. Some foreign jurists hold that the law of the matrimonial domicil attaches all the rights and incidents of marriage to it, proprio vigore, and independently of any supposed consent of the parties.[2] Others hold that there is in such cases an implied consent of the parties to adopt the law of the matrimonial domicil by way of tacit contract ; and then the same rule applies as is applied to express nuptial contracts. Dumoulin was the author, or at least the most distinguished advocate, of this latter doctrine.[3] ' Quia per prædicta inest tacitum pactum, quod maritus lucrabitur dotem conventam, in casu, et pro proportione statuti illius domicilii, quod prævidetur, et intelligitur ; et istud tacitum pactum, nisi conventum fuerit, intrat in actionem ex stipulatu rei uxoriæ, et illam informat. Itaque semper remanet forma ab initio impressa.'[4] And he adds that it applies to all property, wherever situate, and whether movable or immovable: ' Non solum inspiciatur statutum vel consuetudo primi illius domicilii pro bonis sub illo sitis. Sed locum habebit ubique etiam extra fines et territorium dicti statuti, etiam interim correpti ; et hoc indistincte, sive bona dotalia sint mobilia, sive

both to be governed by the law of the domicil of marriage. Others again distinguish between them. Foreign jurists commonly in the term ' biens ' include all sorts of property, movable and immovable, in their discussions on this subject. See Merlin, Répert. Autoris. Maritale, s. 10, art. 2; Id. Majorité, s. 5; Id. Communauté de Biens, s. 1, art. 3; Voet, de Statut. s. 4, c. 2, n. 16; Rodenburg, de Div. Stat. pt. 1, tit. 2, c. 5, s. 13–15; Id. pt. 2, tit. 2, c. 4, s. 1; 2 Boullenois, Appx. p. 41–46; Id. p. 63; 1 Boullenois, p. 673, 683, 767; 2 Boullenois, p. 81, 88; obs. 35, p. 93, 94; Id. obs. 37, p. 266, 277: 1 Hertii Opera, de Collis. Leg. s. 46, 47, p. 143, 144, ed. 1737; Id. p. 203; 204, ed. 1716; Livermore, Dissert. s. 89, p. 73, 74; Huberus, lib. 1, tit. 3, s. 9; Bouhier, c. 22, s. 79, p. 429. See also 1 Burge, Col. & For. Law, pt. 1, c. 7, s. 8, p. 599–609.

[1] Ante, s. 130.

[2] See 1 Boullenois, obs. 29, p. 741, 750, 757, 758; Huberus, lib. 1, tit. 3, de Confl. Leg. s. 9.

[3] 1 Boullenois, obs. 29, p. 757.

[4] Molin. Com. ad Cod. lib. 1, tit. 1, l. 1; Opera, tom. 3, p. 555, ed. 1681; 1 Froland, Mém. 62, 218; Livermore, Dissert. s. 89, p. 73, 74; 1 Boullenois, obs. 29, p. 756, 758.

immobilia, ubicunque sita, sive nomina. Ratio punctualis specifica procedat in vim taciti pacti ad formam statuti ; veluti, quod tacitum pactum pro expresso habetur.'[1]

148. The opinion of Dumoulin, that the law of the place of the marriage constitutes the rule by which the rights of married persons are regulated, by a tacit contract of the parties in the absence of any express contract, according to the maxim, In contractibus tacite veniunt ea, quæ sunt moris et consuetudinis, has been adopted by Bouhier, Hertius, Pothier, Merlin, and other distinguished jurists.[2] It is opposed however by others of no small celebrity ; and the doctrine of tacit contract in the case of marriage (as we shall see) is treated by some of them as a mere indefensible and visionary theory.[3] D'Argentré, and Froland, and Vander Muelen are at the head of those who maintain that the law of the situs of the property constitutes the rule to decide the rights of the married couple at all times and under all circumstances.[4] D'Argentré says: ' Primum, quod Molinæus a simplici consuetudinis dispositione elicet partium conventionem et pactum, citra ullam conventionem partium adjectam consuetudini, rationem non habet. Alia enim vis et ratio, aliud et principium et causa obligationis, quæ a lege inducitur, alia ejus, quæ ab pacto et conventione partium proficiscitur.'[5]

[1] Molin. Com. ad Cod. lib. 1, tit. 1, l. 1; Conclus. de Statutis, Opera, tom. 3, p. 555, ed. 1681; 1 Froland, Mém. 61–63, 218; Livermore, Dissert. s. 89, p. 73, 74; 1 Boullenois, obs. 29, p. 757, 758.

[2] Bouhier, Cout. de Bourg. c. 23, s. 69–75, p. 458, 459; Id. c. 26, p. 462–490; 1 Froland, Mém. 61–63; Id. 178–211; Id. 214–222; Id. 274; Merlin, Répert. Communauté de Biens, s. 1, art. 3; Pothier, Traité de la Communauté, art. 1, n. 10; 1 Hertii Opera, de Collis. Leg. s. 47, p. 143, ed. 1737; Id. p. 204, ed. 1716; post, s. 150–152; 1 Burge, Col. & For. Law, pt. 1, c. 7, s. 8, p. 509–614.

[3] Froland, in opposing the doctrine of tacit contracts, derived from the supposed operation of the lex loci matrimonii, says: Ce ne sont là que des paroles, et rien au-delà. Mirificum illud Molinæi acumen; des subtilités d'esprit; des idèes; des chimères; enfin des moyens. que la seule imagination échauffée produit. Hac grandiloquentia etiamsi Molinæus personat, tamen aperte non est verum, quod dicit. 1 Froland, Mém. 316; post, s. 167.

[4] D'Argentré, in Briton. Leges des Donations, art. 218, glos. 6, n. 33, tom. 1, p. 655–657; Livermore, Dissert. s. 95, p. 77; 1 Froland, Mém. 192–200; Id. 220, 222; Id. 316; 1 Boullenois, p. 673–699; Id. obs. 29, p. 732–736; Id. p. 740–750; Id. p. 757, 792; 2 Boullenois, obs. 35, p. 110; Merlin, Répert. Communauté de Biens, s. 1, art. 3, p. 110, 111; Livermore, Dissert. s. 92–106, p. 75–82; 1 Froland, Mém. 61–64; post, s. 152 a, note 2, s. 167, 168; 1 Burge, Col. & For. Law, pt. 1, c. 7, s. 8, p. 609.

[5] D'Argentré, in Briton. Leg. des Donations, art. 218, glos. 6, n. 33, tom. 1,

149. It may be useful to bring together in this place, in a more exact form, the opinions of some other jurists of the highest reputation on this subject, for the purpose of exhibiting some of the differences as well as some of the coincidences in the doctrines respectively maintained by them.

150. Cochin holds the doctrine that, if the contract of marriage contains no stipulation for community of property, the law of the place where the parties are domiciled, and to which they submit by the contract of marriage, must govern, not only as to property (biens) situate in that place, but as to property situate in all other places.[1] The rights of married persons, he adds, over the property which they then have, as well as over that which they afterwards acquire, ought to be regulated by an uniform rule. If they have established an express rule by the contract of marriage, that ought to decide their rights as to all their property. If they have made no stipulation, then the law of the place of their common domicil establishes a rule for them ; since they are presumed to submit themselves to it, when they have not stipulated anything to the contrary.

151. Le Brun is quite as explicit. After stating that the community of property may be formed by an express contract, or by a tacit contract, he gives as a reason for the latter, that if the married couple have not made any express stipulation, and are domiciled in a place where the law of community exists when they are married, the conclusion is that they have referred themselves to that law. And this presumption has its foundation in law, which often decides that, as to things omitted in the contract, the parties have referred themselves to the usage or law of the place.[2] And he adds that as, in cases of express contracts for community of property, the contracts reach all the property of the parties, even in other countries, so in cases of tacit contracts, such as those resulting by operation of law, the same rule applies. If the law of the place of domicil and marriage of the parties creates such a community, it applies to all property, wherever it is situate. It has, in short, all the character and

p. 656; Livermore, Dissert. s. 92, p. 75, s. 95, p. 77, s. 106, p. 81. See also 1 Burge, Col. & For. Law, pt. 1, c. 7, s. 8, p. 609–614; 1 Boullenois, obs. 29, p. 761–767.

[1] Cochin, Œuvres, tom. 3, p. 703, 4to ed.
[2] Le Brun, Traité de la Communauté, liv. 1, c. 2, s. 2–4.

effect of a personal law or statute, although it regulates property.[1]

152. Hertius has put a number of cases to illustrate the general principle. At Liége, by law, the husband by marriage acquires the ownership of all the property of his wife of every nature. At Utrecht it is otherwise. Is an inhabitant of Utrecht entitled, jure connubii, to take all the property of his deceased wife situate in Liége? He answers in the negative; because the law of the place of marriage, Utrecht, does not confer it.[2] Again: a person, in whose domicil there is no community of property between married persons, possesses property in another territory where such community of all property exists, and he contracts marriage in another country where a qualified community only exists (ubi societas bonorum tantum, sive simpliciter, ita dicta, obtinet). What law is to prevail? Some jurists hold that the law of the domicil shall prevail. Others are of a different opinion. Hertius himself holds that, as the case supposes the place of the marriage to be foreign to both parties, the law of the husband's domicil ought to prevail as an implied contract between the parties.[3] Again: in the domicil of the husband, a community of property exists between married persons; will that community apply to immovable property, bought by either party in a territory where such a law does not exist? Many jurists decide in the negative. Hertius holds the affirmative, upon the ground of an implied contract resulting from the marriage.[4]

152 a. Froland puts the case of a man domiciled at Paris, who goes and marries a woman in a country governed by the Roman law, as in Rheims, Auvergne, or Normandy, or e contra; and the marriage is without any express contract; and he then asks, in such a case, what law is to prevail as to future acquisitions (conquests)? the law of the domicil of the husband, or that of the wife? or that of the place of marriage? or of the

[1] Id. liv. 1, c. 2, s. 6, 36–42.
[2] Hertii Opera, de Collis. Leg. s. 44, p. 142, 143, ed. 1737; Id. p. 201, ed. 1716.
[3] Id. s. 46, p. 143, ed. 1737; Id. p. 202, ed. 1716.
[4] Id. p. 144, s. 47, ed. 1737; Id. p. 204, ed. 1716. The decision of Mr. Chancellor Kent in Decouche v. Savetier, 3 Johns. Ch. (N. Y.) 190, 211, treating it as a case of an express or an implied contract, would lead to the same conclusion.

location of the property? And he decides in favor of the latter.[1]

153. Froland has stated the question in a more general shape: whether, if a community of property exists by the law of the place of domicil and marriage of the parties, it extends to all property situate elsewhere, where no such law prevails?[2] He gives the reasoning of different jurists, maintaining opposite opinions on the point, and concludes by stating that the opinion of Dumoulin in the affirmative has finally prevailed, in cases where there is an express contract for such community; and Dumoulin equally contends for it in cases of tacit contract, resulting from the lex loci contractus.[3] From this latter point however Froland dissents in a qualified manner.[4] He deems the law of community, independently of an express contract, to be a real law, and therefore confined to the territory. As to acquests or acquisitions, whether of movable or of immovable property, made in foreign countries where the law of community exists, he agrees that, in cases of an express contract, the law of the matrimonial domicil ought to prevail. But as to foreign countries where the law of community does not exist, he thinks the right does not extend, aut in vim consuetudinis, or, in vim contractus; for it is in vain to presume a tacit contract; and that therefore it ought to be governed by the law rei sitæ.[5] It would seem

---

[1] 1 Froland, Mém. 321. See also Voet, de Stat. s. 4, c. 3, s. 9, p. 134, 135, ed. 1715; Id. p. 151, 152, ed. 1861.

[2] 1 Froland, Mém. p. 178–200; Id. p. 211–271; Id. p. 272–340. See also 1 Boullenois, p. 660–683; Id. obs. 29, p. 732–818. Dumoulin's words are: 'Nullum habet dubium quin societas, semel contracta, complectatur bona ubicumque sita, sine ulla differentia territorii, quemadmodum quilibet contractus, sive tacitus, sive expressus, ligat personam, et res disponentis ubique. Non obstat, quod hujusmodi societas non est expressa, sed tacita; nec oritur ex contractu expresso partium, sed ex tacito vel præsumpto contractu a consuetudine locali introducto.' 1 Froland, Mém. 274. See also Livermore, Dissert. s. 78–90, p. 69, 71–74; Saul v. His Creditors, 5 Mart. N.S. 569, 599. The same doctrine is maintained by Bouhier. 'Tout statut,' says he, 'qui est fondé sur une convention tacite et presumée, des contractans, est, personnel.' Bouhier, Cout. de Bourg. c. 32, s. 69–74. And he expressly applies it to the case of tacit contracts of marriage, following out the reasoning of Dumoulin. Id. c. 26, s. 1–20. On the other hand, D'Argentré and Vander Muelen hold that all laws respecting community are real, and not personal, and therefore that they are governed by the law rei sitæ. 1 Boullenois, obs. 39, p. 758–765.

[3] Ibid.   [4] 1 Froland, Mém. 315–317.

[5] 1 Froland, Mém. 315–317, 321–323, 338, 341; 1 Boullenois, obs. 29, p. 758, 759.

however from subsequent passages, that he applied his doctrine to the case of immovables only, admitting that movables should be governed by the law of the domicil of the parties.[1]

154. Rodenburg seems to apply the same principle to cases where there is a nuptial contract as to cases where there is none, holding that in the latter cases the law of the matrimonial domicil is adopted by a tacit contract. At the same time he asserts that the law of community is not personal, but is real, and hence that, although it does not, or may not, directly act upon property aliunde, where no community exists, yet it will give a right of action, founded in the tacit contract, which may be enforced everywhere. And therefore the law of matrimonial domicil in such a case acts indirectly, and obtains universality of application by reason of the tacit contract.[2] And he applies it equally to present and future acquisitions.[3]

155. Boullenois holds an opinion somewhat different. After having stated that jurists have entertained different views as to the operation of the law of the matrimonial domicil upon the real property then possessed by the parties, and upon that afterwards acquired by them, he says that they seem generally agreed in one point, that so far as respects their property at the time of the marriage, of strict right the law of the situs ought to be followed. But as to their property acquired after the marriage they differed, some holding that it was governed by the law of the situs, others that it was not, and that the law of the place of the marriage, as to community or non-community, ought to govern. Boullenois holds that this latter doctrine is not correct, because all laws respecting property are real, and that those who adhere to this doctrine are obliged to resort to a supposed tacit contract of the parties, to be governed by the law of the matrimonial domicil. He goes on to state that, without aiming a blow against this system of tacit contract, which on account of its equity he highly approves, his own opinion is that there is no necessity for deeming the law of community to be a personal law, in order to give full effect to the doctrine as to property acquired after the marriage, upon another distinction. This distinction is that the

[1] Ibid.
[2] Rodenburg, de Div. Stat. tit. 2, c. 5, s. 12–15; 2 Boullenois, Appx. p. 41–47; 1 Boullenois, p. 673–683; Id. obs. 29, p. 732–735; Id. p. 754–757.
[3] Ibid.

law of community or non-community is one merely fixing the
state or condition of the married couple, and therefore not a
real but a personal law.[1] Hence he holds that the law of community or of non-community, existing in the matrimonial domicil,
extends to all property of the parties, wherever it is situated, not
upon the ground of any tacit contract, but proprio vigore, as a
law binding both as to their present property and as to their
future acquisitions. But if by the law of the situs the law of
community is prohibited, as to their present property, or as to
their future acquisitions, or as to both, then he admits that the
law of the situs ought to prevail ; for in all cases of this sort the
personal law yields to the real law of the situs. 'Le statut personnel cède en cette occasion au statut réel de la situation.'[2]

156. Pothier has adopted the doctrine of tacit contracts maintained by Dumoulin ; and therefore, in case there is no express
nuptial contract, if the law of the matrimonial domicil creates a
community, he holds that it applies to all property, present and
future, wherever situated, and even in provinces which do not
admit of a community.[3] Grotius is also stated to have held the
same opinion in a case where he was consulted.[4]

157. It has been remarked by the Supreme Court of Louisiana,
that the greater number of the jurists of France and Holland are
of opinion that, in settling the rights of the husband and wife,
on the dissolution of the marriage, to the property acquired by
them, the law of the place where the marriage was contracted,
and not of that where it was dissolved by death, must be the
guide ; and that this opinion is, by most of them, founded on the
idea first promulgated by Dumoulin, that, where the parties marry
without an express nuptial contract, they must be presumed to
contract with reference to the law of the country where the
marriage took place, and that this tacit contract follows them
wherever they go.[5] But that court are of opinion that the
ground is unsatisfactory, especially when it is applied to cases

---

[1] 1 Boullenois, obs. 29, p. 736, 741, 751-770.
[2] 1 Boullenois, obs. 29. p. 736, 741, 750-754; Id. p. 754-757, 759, 760, 766,
769. 770; 2 Boullenois, obs. 37, p. 277; post, s. 166.
[3] Pothier, Traité de la Communauté, art. Prélim. n. 10-18; post. s. 166.
[4] See Henry on Foreign Law, c. 5, p. 36, 37, note; 1 Burge, Col. & For.
Law, pt. 1. c. 7, s. 8, p. 605.
[5] Mr Justice Porter, in delivering the opinion of the court in Saul v. His
Creditors, 5 Mart. N.S. (La.) 599; post, s. 170.

of property acquired after a subsequent change of domicil of the parties. Their view of the subject is, that, if the doctrine of a tacit contract be admissible at all, the contract is to be construed in the same way as if the laws of the country of the marriage were inserted in it; and that, so far as they are to be deemed real laws, and not to be personal laws, they are necessarily territorial, and can be construed to apply only to acquests or acquisitions within that particular country. The extent of the tacit agreement depends upon the extent of that law. If it has no force beyond the jurisdiction of the sovereign by which it is enacted; if it is real, and not personal; then the tacit consent of the parties cannot turn it into a personal statute. The parties have not said so; and they are presumed to have contracted in reference to the law, such as it was; to have known its limitations as well as its nature; and to have had the one as much in view as the other. In one word, the parties have agreed that the law shall bind them, as far as that law extends, but no further.[1]

158. *Result.* — The result of this reasoning (and it certainly has very great force) would seem to be, that in the case of a marriage without any express nuptial contract, the lex loci contractus (assuming that it furnishes any just basis to imply a tacit contract) will govern as to all movable property, and as to all immovable property within that country, (a) and as to property in other countries, it will govern movables, but not immovables, the former having no situs, and the latter being governed by the lex rei sitæ.

159. Perhaps the most simple and satisfactory exposition of the subject, or, at least, that which best harmonizes with the analogies of the common law, is, that in the case of a marriage where there is no special nuptial contract, and there has been no change of domicil, the law of the place of celebration of the marriage

---

[1] Mr. Justice Porter, in the case of Saul v. His Creditors, 5 Mart. N.S. (La.) 569, 603–605; post, s. 187.

(a) See Bonati v. Welsch, 24 N. Y. 157; Kendall v. Coons, 1 Bush (Ky.) 530; Townes v. Durbin, 3 Met. (Ky.) 352; Keyser v. Pilgrim, 25 Tex. 217; Parrott v. Nimmo, 28 Ark. 351; Bond v. Cummings, 70 Me. 125; Smith v. McAtee, 27 Md. 420, Newcomer v. Orem, 2 Md. 297; Vertner v. Humphreys, 14 Smedes & M. 130; Bank of Louisiana v. Williams, 46 Miss. 618; Hicks v. Skinner, 71 N. Car. 539; Craycoff v. Morehead, 67 N. Car. 422. So of lands sold after the change of domicil, against purchasers with notice. Parrott v. Nimmo, supra.

ought to govern the rights of the parties in respect to all personal
or movable property, wherever that is acquired, and wherever it
may be situate; but real or immovable property ought to be left
to be adjudged by the lex rei sitæ, as not within the reach of any
extra-territorial law.[1] Where there is any special nuptial contract between the parties, that will furnish a rule for the case,
and, as a matter of contract, ought to be carried into effect everywhere, under the general limitations and exceptions belonging to
all other classes of contracts.[2]

160. In the next place, what is the principle to be adopted in
cases where there has been a change of domicil? And this admits of a double aspect: first, in relation to property acquired by
the parties before the removal; and secondly, in relation to property acquired by the parties afterwards in the new domicil. In
each instance however we are to be understood to speak of the
mere operation of law, where there is no express nuptial contract
between them.[3]

---

[1] See Henry on Foreign Law, c. 7, p. 48, 49; post, s. 454; Le Breton v.
Miles, 8 Paige (N.Y.) 261.

[2] Post, s. 454. Paul Voet lays down the following doctrine. 'Si statuto
hujus loci inter conjuges *bona sint communia*, vel *pactis antenuptialibus* ita conventum sit, ut omnia, ubique locorum sita, communia forent, etiam ad illa,
quæ in Frisia jacent, ubi non nisi quæsitorum est communio, dabitur actio, ut
communicentur.' Voet, de Stat. s. 4, c. 2, s. 16, p. 127, ed. 1716; Id. p. 142,
ed. 1661; Id. c. 3, s. 9, p. 134, ed. 1716; Id. p. 140, 141. Yet he deems laws
establishing a community of property to be real and not personal laws. Id.
s. 4, c. 3, s. 9, p. 134, 135, ed. 1716. See 1 Froland, Mém. 199, 200. This
apparent discrepancy may be reconciled by considering that, though the law
of community be real, yet it may found a right of action for property situate
elsewhere. See also Rodenburg, de Divers. Stat. tit. 2, c. 5, s. 12–15; 2 Boullenois, Appx. p. 41–46. A distinction of this sort seems not unknown to the
Scottish law. 1 Rose, Cas. in Bank. 481. Lord Meadowbank, in a Scottish
case of great importance, laid down the following doctrine as unquestionable.
'In the ordinary case of transference by contract of marriage, when a lady of
fortune, having a great deal of money in Scotland, or stock in the bank, or
public companies there, marries in London, the whole property is *ipso jure* her
husband's. It is assigned to him. The legal assignment of a marriage operates, *without regard to territory*, all the world over.' Royal Bank of Scotland
r. Smith, 1 Rose, Cas. Bank. Appx. 491. Lord Eldon has affirmed this doctrine to be correct in relation to personal property, but not in relation to real
property. In the cases of bankruptcy to which he applied it, he added that
there was no legal obligation on a bankrupt to convey his real estate, situate
in a foreign country, to the assignees. Selkrig v. Davies, 2 Rose, Bank. Cas.
99; 2 Dow, 230, 250.

[3] See 1 Burge, Col. & For. Law, pt. 1, c. 7, s. 7, p. 609–640; ante, s. 155;
post, s. 449–454; Ordronaux v. Rey, 2 Sandf. Ch. 33.

161. *Change of Domicil. — Foreign Jurists.* Upon this subject there is, as we have already seen, no small diversity of opinion among foreign jurists as well in regard to the rights to property acquired after the change of domicil, as in regard to the rights to property antecedently acquired.[1] Bouhier lays down the rule in general terms, that in relation to the beneficial and pecuniary rights (les droits utiles et pécuniaires) of the wife which result from the matrimonial contract, either express or tacit, the husband has no power by a change of domicil to alter or change them, according to the rule, nemo potest mutare consilium suum in alterius injuriam ; and he insists that this is the opinion of jurists generally.[2] Thus if by the law of the matrimonial domicil there exists a community of property between the husband and the wife, and they remove to another place where no such community exists, the rights of neither party are changed ; and the community applies in the same manner as in the original domicil.[3] And, on the other hand, if no such community exists in the matrimonial domicil, a transfer of domicil to a place where it does exist will not create it ; for a change of domicil would not add anything to the marriage rights in the case of an express contract, and therefore ought not to do so in that of a tacit contract.[4] This also is Dumoulin's opinion. He says that this is controverted by some authors ; but it is so unjustly and falsely. ‘ Sed controvertunt, si maritus postea cum uxore transtulerit domicilium, an debeat attendi illud, quod erat tempore contractus, an vero ultimum, quod invenitur tempore mortis ; et istud ultimum tenet Salicetus, et sequitur Alexander. Sed hoc non solum iniquum ; quia maritus de loco, in quo nihil lucratur, vel tantum quartam, posset transferre domicilium ad locum, in quo totam dotem lucraretur præmoriente uxore sine liberis. Et quod sit falsum, probo per testem dictæ legis, Exigere dotem.’[5] Bouhier makes no distinction whatsoever between movable property and immovable property.[6] Nor does he seem to recognize any distinction between property acquired before the change of domicil, and that acquired after the change of domicil.[7]

---

[1] Ante, s. 137–142; Id. 143–159; 1 Burge, Col. & For. Law, pt. 1, c. 7, s. 8, p. 609–640.

[2] Bouhier, Cout. de Bourg. c. 22, s. 63–72.   [3] Ibid.   [4] Ibid.

[5] Dig. 5, 1, 65, de Judiciis; ante, s. 147; Molin. Comm. ad Cod. lib. 1, tit. 1, l. 1; Molin Opera, tom. 3, p. 555.

[6] Bouhier, Cout. de Bourg. c. 22, s. 79, 80.   [7] Id. c. 22, per tot.

162. Le Brun supports the like opinion. He insists that, if there is no special contract of marriage, the law of the place where the marriage is celebrated and in which the parties are domiciled, governs as a tacit contract; and that no subsequent change of domicil can change the legal rights of the parties, even as to after-acquired property.[1] And he puts the case of a marriage in Paris, and a subsequent change of domicil of the parties to the province of Bar, where the survivor is by custom entitled to the whole property in movables by survivorship; and holds that if either die, the movables, whether acquired before the removal or after the removal, are governed by the law of community, and do not all remain to the survivor. 'Le raison est, que ce serait changer l'établissement de communauté fait par le contrat, ou par le coutume, selon lequel on a dû partager les meubles aussi bien que les conquêts.'[2]

163. Rodenburg puts the case of a marriage in a place where the law of community of property. between husband and wife prevails, and a subsequent removal to another place where it has no existence; and he asks if the community still subsists in the new domicil? He observes that most of the Dutch jurists are of opinion that it does; and in this opinion he concurs to this extent, that the community will continue until the parties have by some overt act discarded it, and then it will cease.[3] And he applies the same principle to cases of dowry by the customary law, holding that the matrimonial domicil ought to prevail.[4]

164. Hertius puts the following question: A marriage is contracted in a place where the civil law governs (i. e., where there is no community), and afterwards the couple remove to a place where the law of community exists; and to the inquiry whether in such a case there is a community in the acquisitions of the parties after the removal, he answers in the negative, adopting the doctrine of Rodenburg; and he gives this reason for his opinion, that it is not probable that the married couple, who did not agree to a community of goods in the beginning, intended to adopt it by a mere change of domicil. 'Nam probabile non est,

---

[1] Le Brun, Traité de la Communauté, liv. 1, c. 2, s. 55, 56, p. 20.
[2] Ibid. ; ante, s. 151.
[3] Rodenburg, de Div. Stat. pt. 2, tit. 2, c. 4, s. 3, 4; 2 Boullenois, Appx. p. 66, 67; Id. p. 85–87; Id. obs. 36, p. 173; ante, s. 154.
[4] Rodenburg, de Div. Stat. pt. 2, tit. 2, c. 4, s. 5; 2 Boullenois, Appx. p. 66, 67; Id. p. 87; ante, s. 154.

conjuges, qui pactis in societatem bonorum ab initio non con-
sensuerant, sola domicilii mutatione eam inducere voluisse.'[1] In
the more general form in which the question may be presented,
whether in the case of married persons removing from their matrimonial domicil where a community of property exists, to a place
where it does not, they are to be governed by the law of the
matrimonial domicil, he evidently adopts the affirmative, citing
Rodenburg.[2] And he applies his doctrine to immovable property,
as well as movable property, making an exception however of the
case where there is a prohibitory law of the country of the situs.[3]

165. Paul Voet appears to maintain the doctrine generally, that
a change of domicil does not change the effect of the marriage
contract, express or tacit. ' Quid, si maritus alio domicilium post-
modum transtulerit, eritne conveniendus, secundum loci statutum,
in quem postremum sese recepit. Non equidem. Quia non eo
ipso, qui domicilium transferat, censetur voluntatem circa facta
nuptialia mutasse. Nisi eadem solemnitas in actu contrario inter-
cesserit. Accedit, quod illa pacta solus mutare nequeat maritus,
id quod tamen posset, si per emigrationem in alium locum, ea
mutarentur.'[4] Merlin maintains the like opinion, saying that if
a couple are married at Paris, meaning at the time to live there,
and afterwards they remove to Lyons, in such a case the community formed at Paris will continue as to property acquired at
Lyons.[5]

166. Boullenois holds the opinion, as we have seen, that the
law regulating the community affects the state or condition of the
parties, and is therefore a personal law, and accompanies them
everywhere, and affects property wherever situate.[6] He accor-

---

[1] 2 Hertii Opera, de Collis. Leg. s. 49, p. 145, ed. 1737; Id. p. 205, ed.
1716.

[2] Id. s. 48, p. 145, ed. 1737; Id. p. 206, ed. 1716.

[3] Id. s. 47, 48, ed. 1737, p. 144, 145; Id. p. 205, ed. 1716.

[4] Voet, de Stat. s. 9, c. 2, n. 5, 6, 7, p. 264, 266, ed. 1716; Id. p. 319, 322,
ed. 1661; Id. s. 4, c. 2, n. 16, p. 127, ed. 1716; Id. p. 142, ed. 1661; Id. s. 4,
c. 3, n. 9, p. 134, 135, ed. 1716; Id. p. 151, 152, ed. 1661; post, s. 168. Paul
Voet holds all such contracts, whether express or tacit, to be real and not personal laws; and therefore not directly affecting property out of the territory,
but only indirectly. by a remedy to enforce the contract against extra-territorial
property. Voet, ad Statut. s. 4, c. 3, s. 9, p. 134, 135. ed. 1716; Id. p. 151,
152, ed. 1161; post, s. 168; Livermore, Dissert. s. 115–123, p. 87–92.

[5] Merlin, Répertoire, Communauté de Biens, s. 1, p. 111.

[6] Ante, s. 155; 1 Boullenois, obs. 29, p. 736, 741, 750–754; Id. p. 759–770;
2 Boullenois, obs. 38, p. 277; Saul v. His Creditors, 5 Mart. N.S. 607.

dingly insists that, if by the law of the matrimonial domicil a community of property exists, that community extends to all future acquisitions, whether movable or immovable, even in places to which the parties have afterwards removed, and where no such community exists.[1] Pothier has adopted the opinion of Boullenois, that the law of community is to be deemed a personal law and not a real law ; and he also adopts the doctrine of Dumoulin as to tacit contracts.[2] So that he has no hesitation in declaring, as we have seen, that the law of the matrimonial domicil governs the property everywhere.[3] But he has omitted to put the case of a change of domicil, and the effects which it would produce. In another place he has laid down as a general principle, that a change of domicil delivers all persons from the empire of the laws of their former domicil, and subjects them to the new.[4] What then ought to be the effect of a removal upon property acquired in the new domicil ?

167. Froland, after a good deal of hesitation, has given his own opinion on the subject to this effect. In cases where there is an express contract of community of property between the husband and the wife, he holds that a change of domicil does not alter the rights of the parties ; and that the community applies to property situate where the community is unknown as well as where it exists.[5] But where there is no express contract, he deems the law of community as purely real, and therefore as not extending beyond the matrimonial domicil.[6] He treats the notion of Dumoulin, of a tacit contract in such a case, as a mere imaginary thing ; words and nothing else ; a mere subtlety, phantom, and chimera. 'Ce ne sont là que des paroles, et rien au-delà. Mirificum illud Molinæi acumen : des subtilités d'esprit ; des idées ; des chimères ; enfin des moyens que la seule imagination échauffée produit. Hac grandiloquentia etiamsi Molinæus personat, tamen aperte non est verum, quod dicit.'[7] The conclusion to which he arrives is, that if two persons marry without any contract in a

[1] 2 Boullenois, obs. 38, p. 277, 278, 283–285; ante, s. 155.
[2] Pothier, Traité de la Communauté, art. Prélim. n. 10–13; ante, s. 156.
[3] Ibid. ; ante, s. 156.
[4] Pothier, Cout. d'Orléans, c. 1, n. 13; ante, s. 51 a, s. 156.
[5] 1 Froland, Mém. pt. 2, c. 1, s. 10, 11, p. 200–210; Id. p. 341; Id. p. 190.
[6] 1 Froland, Mém. pt. 2, c. 3, s. 9–11, p. 315–338; Id. p. 341; ante, s. 148, note, s. 149.
[7] 1 Froland, Mém. pt. 2, c. 3, s. 9, p. 316.

place where the law of community exists, and remove to another place where it does not exist, the change of domicil has no effect whatsoever; but the rights of each are the same as if they had remained in their matrimonial domicil; and the acquisitions of immovable property, situate in the new domicil, do not fall into community, but are governed by the law rei sitæ. As to movables, he holds that the law of the actual domicil ought to govern.[1]

168. There are many other jurists who maintain that the law of community among married persons is *real* and not personal; and among these the most distinguished are D'Argentré, Dumoulin, Paul Voet, and Vander Muelen.[2] According to them, the law rei sitæ will govern in all cases where there is no express or tacit contract. But then we must take this proposition with the accompanying qualification, that those of these jurists who admit of the doctrine of a tacit contract, adopting the law of the place of marriage, among whom are Dumoulin and Paul Voet, also hold, that although the law of the place of the marriage does not directly act upon the property in a foreign country, yet, through the means of this tacit contract, it acts indirectly, and enables the parties to enforce it against that property by a proper suit in rem.[3]

169. Huberus, as we have seen, does not hesitate to assert the doctrine that, in case of a change of domicil, future acquisitions of married persons are governed by the law of their actual domicil and not of their antecedent matrimonial domicil.[4] Thus, after asserting that in Holland there is a community of property,

[1] 1 Froland, Mém. pt. 2, c. 3, s. 9-11, p. 315-323; Id. p. 341. I confess myself under some difficulty in reconciling what is here said with what Froland seems to decide in the next chapter (4th), s. 3, p. 345, &c., where he appears to hold that a woman marrying in a place where the law of community does not exist, does not, by removing with her husband to a place where it does exist, acquire any right of community to his acquisitions or movables in the latter.

[2] 1 Boullenois, obs. 29, p. 758-761, 765; P. Voet, de Stat. s. 4, c. 3, p. 134, 135, s. 9, ed. 1716; Id. p. 151, 152, ed. 1661. See also J. Voet, ad Pand. 5, 1, n. 101; Merlin, Communauté de Biens, s. 1, art. 3, p. 104. 110; Bouhier, Cout. de Bourg. c. 33, s. 34. See Saul v. His Creditors, 5 Mart. N.S. (La.) 588, 593, 599; ante, s. 148, 149, note.

[3] P. Voet, de Statut. s. 9, c. 2, n. 5-7, p. 264-266, ed. 1716; Id. p. 319-323, ed. 1661; ante, s. 165, note; ante, s. 147; post, s. 169; 1 Burge, Col. & For. Law, pt. 1, c. 7, s. 8, p. 612-614.

[4] Ante, s. 145.

and in Friesland not, he says, if the married couple remove from the one province (Holland) to the other (Friesland) whatever property is afterwards acquired ceases to be common, and remains in distinct ownership (distinctis proprietatibus) ; and the property before held in community remains clothed with the same legal character that it previously possessed.[1]   And he applies this doctrine as well to immovable property as to movable property, relying upon the doctrine of tacit consent or tacit contract ;[2] and holding the opinion of Dumoulin: 'Quia pactio bene extenditur ubique, sed non statutum merum, hoc est, sola et mera vi statuti.'[3]

170. It would be endless to recount the diversities of opinion among foreign jurists on this subject, following out the almost infinitely varied cases which the customs and laws of different provinces and countries have brought before them. According to the opinion of the Supreme Court of Louisiana, already cited,[4] the greater number of foreign jurists are of opinion that, in settling the rights of husband and wife, on the dissolution of marriage, to the property acquired by them, the law of the domicil of the marriage, and not of the place where it is dissolved by death, is to be the guide.[5] It is probably so ; but there is more difficulty in affirming it where there has been a change of domicil than where there has been no such change. It may be inferred that the Scottish law has adopted the rule that, in cases of community, where there is no written contract, the law of the domicil of the parties at the death of either of them regulates the disposal of the property of the parties.[6]

[1] Ibid.   [2] Huberus, lib. 1, tit. 3, s. 9; ante, s. 145.
[3] Livermore. Diss. s. 89, p. 73, 74 ; 1 Froland, Mém. 63.
[4] Ante, s. 157.
[5] Mr. Justice Porter, in delivering the opinion of the court in Saul v. His Creditors, 5 Mart. N.S. (La.) 599; ante, s. 157.
[6] Fergusson on Mar. & Divorce, 346, 347; Id. 361. There are some remarks of Mr. Burge on this subject, which deserve to be cited in this place. ' In hoc igitur,' says he, ' conflictu quibus adstipulabimur? was the obvious question of one of the jurists after he had been reviewing these discordant opinions. The following considerations will perhaps justify a concurrence with him in the answer given by himself. "Mihi tutius videtur adhærere secundæ setentiæ (quæ negat prædia alibi sita communicari), quam non solum ratio validissima munit, sed et præstantes auctores, et consensus aliquot municiporum probant." 1st. The law which by its own force and operation, and independently of contract, gives an interest in immovable property, is a real law. 2d. Immovable property is not subject to the power of a real law, unless

17

171. *Law of England.*—No question appears to have arisen in the English courts upon the point which we have been discussing, that is, what rule is to govern in cases of matrimonial property where there is no express nuptial contract and there has been a change of domicil. But there is a case,[1] which Lord Eldon is reported to have said was founded in (a nuptial) contract, and

such law exists in the country where that property is situated. 3d. The joint interest which the husband and wife acquire under the community in the immovable property of each other, is conferred by the law alone, unless that law be controlled in its operation by a tacit agreement; such an interest, therefore, will not be acquired in immovable property situated in a country where the law of community does not exist. 4th. If a tacit agreement could be inferred for the purpose of giving to the law of community a more extensive operation than belongs to the quality of a real law, it might with equal propriety be inferred for a similar purpose in the case of other real laws, i. e. those which govern the succession to real property, &c. A preference of the law of the country in which a man has passed his life, to that of another country in which his real property may be situated, is as natural a presumption as that in favor of the law of the matrimonial domicil. 5th. It cannot be said that, because the title is conferred by the law, as the consequence of the marriage, there is a ground peculiar to marriage for admitting the presumption of a tacit agreement; because no such presumption is admitted in respect of other titles conferred by law as the consequence of marriage; e. g., the titles to douaire and droit de viduité. 6th. The laws which confer douaire, and le droit de viduité, are admitted by all jurists to be real laws; and consequently they attach on that property only which is situated in the country where they prevail, and they do not extend to that which is situated in another country, and no tacit agreement is presumed in order to control their powers. 7th. The law establishing a community in immovable property is not essentially distinguished from the laws of douaire and viduité, in any one of those particulars, which in the opinion of jurists, determine the reality or personality of laws, and consequently the extent of their power. There does not therefore appear to be any substantial reason for allowing the law of community to have the effect of a personal law, and to attach on immovable property in whatever country it may be situated. If this reasoning be admitted, the community, when it prevails in the matrimonial domicil, will be confined to such immovable property as is situated either there, or in a country in which a similar law exists; but it will not extend to such property situated in a country where a similar law does not exist. In the preceding observations the law of community has been considered only as it affected immovable property. Its effect on personal property is determined by other principles. According to a principle of international jurisprudence, the acquisition of movable or personal property by the operation of law, is, as will be presently shown, governed by the law of its owner's domicil. The community, if it prevailed in the matrimonial domicil, would therefore attach on the movable property of the husband and wife, in whatever place it was situated.' 1 Burge, Col. & For. Law, pt. 1, c. 7, s. 8, p. 617–619; and Lashley *v.* Hogg, cited id. p. 623–625.

[1] Lashley *v.* Hogg, cited in Robertson App. Cas. 4, and in 1 Burge, Col. & For. Law, pt. 1, c. 7, s. 8, p. 623–625; Feaubert *v.* Turst, Prec. Ch. 207.

that if there had been no such contract the law of England, notwithstanding the domicil of the parties at the time of their marriage was in France, would have regulated the rights of the husband and wife, who were domiciled in England at the dissolution of the marriage by death.[1] So that, according to this doctrine, the law of the actual domicil will govern as to all property, without any distinction, whether it is property acquired antecedently or subsequently to the removal.

171 a. In a more recent case, where the parties were inhabitants of Prussia, and domiciled there, a question arose in the Court of Exchequer upon the distribution of an intestate's estate under the administration of the court, whether the wife, being a distributee, was entitled in equity, upon a petition by her husband for the amount, to have any of the money settled on her, or whether the whole was to be paid to him. It appeared that, by the laws of Prussia, the whole of the personalty of the husband and wife is, during the coverture, at the absolute disposal of the husband ; but on the death of either it is divided between the survivor and the heirs of the deceased. The man made no application to the court, and the court ordered the whole money to be paid over to the husband.[2] Here, we see, the court adopted the law of their actual domicil to regulate the rights of the parties to the movable property. (a)

172. *Court of Louisiana.* — In America there has been a general silence in the states governed by the common law. But in Louisiana, whose jurisprudence is framed upon the general basis of the Spanish and French law, the point has several times come

---

[1] Ibid.

[2] Sawer v. Shute, 1 Anstr. 63. See also Anstruther v. Adair, 2 Mylne & K. 513.

(a) In Re Lett's Trusts, 7 L. R. Ir. 132, it was held that a married woman, who was domiciled with her husband in the state of New York, was entitled to receive payment of her distributive share of an intestate's estate in Ireland, it being proved that by the law of New York a married woman was entitled to receive a bequest or share of an intestate's estate as if she were unmarried. She and her husband at the time of their marriage were domiciled in Ireland, and had subsequently emigrated to New York and become domiciled there. See also Dues v. Smith, Jac. 544. Comp. Graham v. First National Bank, 84 N. Y. 393. It is there held that the effect of payment made to a husband of dividends of bank stock standing in his wife's name, the bank being located and the dividends paid in a state not the domicil of the payee, is to be governed by the law of the state in which the dividends were paid, not by the lex domicilii.

under judicial decision. The law of community exists in that state,[1] and from the frequency of removals from and to that state, it is scarcely possible that some of the doctrines which have so much perplexed foreign jurists should not be brought under review.

173. We have already had occasion to take notice of some of the views entertained by the Supreme Court of Louisiana upon this subject.[2] It has been very properly remarked by that court that questions upon the conflict of the laws of the different states are the most embarrassing and difficult of decision of any that can occupy the attention of courts of justice.[3] And it may be added, almost in their own language, that the vast mass of learning which the researches of counsel can furnish, leaves the subject as much enveloped in obscurity and doubt as it would be if one were called upon to decide without the knowledge of what others had thought and written upon it.[4]

174. It is manifest that the great body of foreign jurists who maintain the universality and ubiquity of the operation of the law of the matrimonial domicil, notwithstanding any subsequent change of domicil, found themselves upon the doctrine of a tacit contract, which, being once entered into, is of legal obligation everywhere.[5] The remarks of the Supreme Court of Louisiana on this point have been already cited, and certainly they have a great tendency to shake its foundation.[6] If the law of community be a real law and not a personal law, it would seem to follow that it ought to regulate all things which are situate within the limits of the country wherein it is in force, but not elsewhere.[7] The most strenuous advocate for the doctrine of tacit contract must admit that, if by the statute of any country community is prohibited as to property there, the law of the matrimonial domicil ought not to prevail in such country in contradiction to its own. And the learned court above referred to have said that they can perceive no solid distinction between the case of a real

[1] Civil Code of Louisiana (1809), 336, art. 2363; New Code (1825), art. 2369-2393.
[2] Ante, s. 157, 170.   [3] Ibid.
[4] Mr. Justice Porter in delivering the opinion of the court in Saul v. His Creditors, 5 Mart. N.S. (La.) 571, 572.
[5] Ante, s. 147-170.
[6] Saul v. His Creditors, 5 Mart. N.S. (La.) 599-608; ante, s. 157, 170.
[7] Mr. Justice Porter, in Saul v. His Creditors, 5 Mart. N.S. 601, 602.

statute and a prohibitory statute, as to property situate in that country.[1]

175. But if the law of community be personal, still there is strong ground to contend that the personal laws of one country cannot control the personal laws of another country, ipso facto, where they extend to and provide for property within the jurisdiction of the latter. No one can doubt that any country has a right to say that contracts for community made in another country shall have no operation within its own territory. The question then is reduced to the mere consideration, whether the law of the country does directly or indirectly provide for or repudiate the community as to property locally situate within it.[2]

176. Upon reasoning to this effect, after full consideration, the Supreme Court of Louisiana came to the conclusion that the law of community must, upon just principles of interpretation, be deemed a real law, since it relates to things more than to persons, and it has, in the language of D'Aguesseau, the destination of property to certain persons and its preservation in view.[3] The court therefore held that where a married couple had removed from Virginia (their matrimonial domicil), where community does not exist, into Louisiana, where community does exist, the acquests and gains acquired after their removal were to be governed by the law of community in Louisiana.[4]

177. This doctrine appears to be in full accordance with the laws of Spain. Those laws apply the same rule to cases of express contract, and to cases of tacit contract or customary law. Where there is an express contract, that governs as to all acquisitions and gains before the removal. Where there is no express contract, the customary law of the matrimonial domicil governs in like manner. But in both cases all acquisitions and gains made after the removal are governed by the law of the actual

[1] Ibid. See post, s. 449–454.

[2] Saul v. His Creditors, 5 Mart. N.S. (La.) 573, 574–588; 1 Hertii Opera, de Collis. Leg. s. 47, p. 143, 144, ed. 1737; Id. p. 294, ed. 1716; post, s. 449–454.

[3] Mr. Justice Porter, in Saul v. His Creditors, 5 Mart. N.S. (La.) 593–595, 606, 607; D'Aguesseau, Œuvres, tom. 4, pl. 54, p. 660, 4to ed.

[4] The law of community existed in Louisiana under the Spanish law, and now exists under the Civil Code of that State. Bruneau v. Bruneau, 9 Mart. 217; Code Civil of Louisiana (1809), 836, art. 63; Revised Code (1825), art. 2370; Saul v. His Creditors, 5 Mart. N.S. (La.) 573; 2 Kent Com. 183, note.

domicil.[1] The present revised Code of Louisiana adopts a like
rule, and declares that a marriage contracted out of the state
between persons who afterwards come to live within the state,
is subject to the community of acquests, with respect to such
property as is acquired after their removal.[2]

178. This code of course furnishes the rule for all future cases
in Louisiana ; but the discussions in that state have arisen upon
antecedent cases, and have involved a general examination of
the whole doctrine upon principle and authority.   The doctrine
which, with reference to public law, has been thus established in
that state, resolves itself into two fundamental propositions.
First, where there is an express nuptial contract that there shall
be a community of acquests and gains between the parties, even
though they should reside in countries where different laws prevail, that agreement will be held obligatory throughout, as a
matter of contract, in cases of the removal of the parties to another state ; with this restriction, however, which is applicable
to all contracts, that it is not to cause any prejudice to the citizens of the country to which they remove, and that its execution
is not incompatible with the laws of that country.[3] Secondly,
where there is no such express nuptial contract, the law of the
matrimonial domicil is to prevail as to the antecedent property,
but the property acquired after the removal is to be governed by
the law of the actual domicil.[4] This latter proposition has been
laid down in terms unusually strong by the Supreme Court of
that state. ' Though it was *once* a question (say the court), it
seems *now* to be a *settled* principle, that when a married couple
emigrate from the country where the marriage was contracted
into another, the laws of which are different, the property which
they acquire in the place to which they have removed is governed by the laws of that place.'[5] Upon these propositions the
court have accordingly decided that where a couple, who were
married in North Carolina, where community does not exist, had

---

[1] Saul *v.* His Creditors, 5 Mart. N.S. (La.) 576-581, 607, 608.

[2] Code Civil of Louisiana (1825), art. 2370.

[3] Mr. Justice Derbigny, in Murphy *v.* Murphy, 5 Mart. (La.) 83; Mr. Justice Porter, in Saul *v.* His Creditors, 5 Mart. N.S. (La.) 605, 606.

[4] Mr. Justice Derbigny in Gale *v.* Davis, 4 Mart. (La.) 645; Saul *v.* His
Creditors, 5 Mart. N.S. (La.) 605, 606; Le Breton *v.* Nouchet, 3 Mart. (La.)
60, 73.

[5] Mr. Justice Derbigny, in Gale *v.* Davis, 4 Mart. (La.) 645, 649.

removed to Louisiana, where it does exist, the property acquired after the removal was to be held in community.[1] And, in another case, where the marriage was in Cuba, and there was a special contract that there should be a community according to the custom of Paris, in whatever country the parties might reside, and the parties remove to South Carolina, where no community exists, the contract was held to govern the property acquired in the latter State.[2] The same doctrine has been maintained in New York, in the case of a marriage between French subjects, under a similar stipulation of community and of mutual donation in case of survivorship of either of the parties.[3]

179. An instance illustrative of the exception in cases of express contract may be drawn from other decisions in Louisiana. Upon a marriage celebrated in that state, the parties stipulated that the rights of the parties should be governed by the custom of Paris. The question was, whether the parties residing in the country were competent to enter into a nuptial contract, stipulating that the effect of it on their property should be governed by a foreign law. The court held that they had no such competency, and that the contract was void.[4]

180. A still more striking case occurred in the same state, upon some of the doctrines of which, as stated by the court, there may perhaps be reason to pause ; but the grounds are nevertheless stated with great force. A man ran away with a young lady of thirteen years of age, both of them being then domiciled in Louisiana, without the consent of her parents or guardian, and they went together to Natchez in Mississippi, and were there married, and soon after returned to New Orleans, the place of their original domicil. The wife afterwards died while they were living in Louisiana ; and after her death her mother demanded her property, as it would descend by the Louisiana law. The court sustained the demand.[5] From the elaborate opinion delivered for the court by Mr. Justice Derbigny, the following ex-

---

[1] Mr. Justice Derbigny, in Gale v. Davis, 4 Mart. (La.) 645.

[2] Mr. Justice Derbigny, in Murphy v. Murphy, 5 Mart. (La.) 83 ; Mr. Justice Porter, in Saul v.His Creditors, 5 Mart. N.S. (La.) 605 ; Mr. Justice Derbigny, in Bourcier v. Lanusse, 3 Mart. (La.) 581, 583.

[3] Decouche v. Savatier, 3 Johns. Ch. (N. Y.) 190, 211.

[4] Mr. Justice Derbigny, in Bourcier v. Lanusse, 3 Mart. (La.) 581. See Code Civil of France, art. 1390.

[5] Le Breton v. Nouchet, 3 Mart. (La.) 60, 73.

tract is made, as highly interesting : ' With respect,' say the court, ' to the law of nations, the principle recognized by most writers may be reduced to this : that although no power is bound to give effect within his own territory to the laws of a foreign country, yet, by the courtesy of nations and from a consideration of the inconveniences which would be the result of a contrary conduct, foreign laws are permitted to regulate contracts made in foreign countries. But in order that they may have such effect, it must first be ascertained that the parties really intended to be governed by those laws, and had not some other country in contemplation at the time of the contract. This being previously recognized, the government within the bounds of which such foreign laws claim admission, has next to consider whether the enforcing of these laws will cause no prejudice to its rights or to the rights of its citizens.

181. ' Let us take the first exception, and apply it to this case. Did the parties really intend to be governed by the laws of the Mississippi Territory, and had they not in contemplation at the time of contracting marriage their return to this country? If we were to judge from their acts alone, there could be no hesitation in saying that they went to Natchez for the purpose only of contracting marriage, and intended to come back as soon as it could conveniently be done. Their remaining at Natchez only a few weeks, and that in a tavern, their return to New Orleans not long after, and the continuation of their residence there until the death of the wife, would amount to an irresistible proof that they had this country in contemplation at the time of contracting their marriage. But it is alleged that, however evident their intention may appear from these facts, the appellant had really taken the resolution to settle at Natchez. Evidence has been furnished of his declarations to that purpose, both before his departure and after his arrival in the Mississippi Territory. One of his brothers has sworn that, previous to his leaving New Orleans, he told him and his other brothers that he intended to stay at Natchez. Other persons have deposed that letters expressive of the determination of the appellant to remain there were by them received from him shortly after their dates. Without questioning the propriety of the admission of such testimony, the court is satisfied that it is insufficient to counterbalance the weight of the facts which disclose the real intention of the parties.

182. 'But, should their intention still remain a subject of doubt, we have next to consider whether, by permitting the laws of the Mississippi Territory to regulate this case, this government would not injure its own rights or the rights of its citizens. For, a foreign law having no other force than that which it derives from the consent of the government within the bounds of which it claims to be admitted, that government must be supposed to retain the faculty of refusing such admission whenever the foreign law interferes with its own regulations. A party to this marriage was one of those individuals over whom our laws watch with particular care, and whom they have subjected to certain incapacities for their own safety. She was a minor. Has she by fleeing to another country removed those incapacities? Her mother is a citizen of this state; she herself was a girl of thirteen years, who had no other domicil than that of her mother. Did she not remain, notwithstanding her flight to Natchez, under the authority of this government? Did not the protection of this government follow her wherever she went? If so, this government cannot, without surrendering its rights, recognize the empire of laws the effect of which would be to render that protection inefficacious. But the laws of the Mississippi Territory, as stated by the parties, do not only interfere with our rights, but are at war with our regulations. By our laws, a minor who marries cannot give away any part of his property without the authorization of those whose consent is necessary for the validity of the marriage. By the laws of the Mississippi Territory all the personal estate of the wife (that would embrace in this case everything which she had) is the property of the husband. Again, according to our laws, we cannot give away more than a certain portion of our property when we have forced heirs. But what our laws thus forbid is permitted in the Mississippi Territory. And shall our citizens be deprived of their legitimate rights by the laws of another government, upon our own soil? Shall the mother of Alexandrine Dussuau lose the inheritance of her deceased child, secured to her by our laws, because her daughter married at Natchez? Shall our own laws be reduced to silence within our own precincts by the superior force of other laws? If such doctrine were maintainable it would be unnecessary for us to legislate. In vain should we endeavor to secure the persons and the property of our citizens. Nothing would be

more easy than to render our precautions useless and our laws a
dead letter.   But the municipal law of the Mississippi Territory,
which is relied upon by the appellant, is not the law which
would govern this case *even there.*   The law of nations is law at
Natchez as well as at New Orleans.   According to the principles
of that law, " Personal incapacities communicated by the laws of
any particular place accompany the person wherever he goes.
Thus he who is excused the consequences of contracts for want
of age in his country cannot make binding contracts in another."
Therefore even if this case were pending before a tribunal of the
Mississippi Territory, it is to be supposed that they would recognize the incapacity under which Alexandrine Dussuau was laboring when she contracted marriage, and decide that such marriage
could not have the effect of giving to her husband what she was
forbidden to give.   If that be sound doctrine in any case, how
much more so must it be in one of this nature, where the minor,
almost a child, has in all probability been seduced into an escape
from her mother's dwelling, and removed in haste out of her
reach?   We cannot here hesitate to believe that the courts of
our neighboring territory, far from lending their assistance to
this infraction of our laws, would have enforced them with becoming severity.   For if, when an appeal is made to those general principles of natural justice by which nations have tacitly
agreed to govern themselves in their intercourse with each
other, while nations entirely foreign to one another feel bound
to observe them, how much more sacred must they be between
governments, who, though independent of each other in matters
of internal regulation, are associated for the purposes of common
defence and common advantage, and are members of the same
great body politic.' [1] (a)

[1] Mr. Justice Derbigny in Le Breton v. Nouchet, 3 Mart. (La.) 60, 66, 71.

(a) It has been decided that a marriage settlement executed in one state,
where the parties at the time resided,
and where the property was situated,
if valid by the laws of the place where
made, cannot be affected by the subsequent removal of the parties to another state. Young v. Templeton, 4 La.
Ann. 254.   An analogous principle
was recently recognized in England
in the case of Duncan v. Cannan, 23
Eng. Law & Eq. 288; 18 Beav. 128.
There a Scotchman, whose domicil was
in Scotland, married an Englishwoman
in England, and a marriage settlement
was entered into according to the
Scotch form.   They went to reside in
Scotland, but subsequently returned
to England, where the husband engaged in trade and became bankrupt,
having received a large part of his
wife's property from a trustee under

183. In general, the doctrines thus maintained in Louisiana will most probably form the basis of the American jurisprudence on this subject. They have much to commend them in their intrinsic convenience and certainty, as well as in their equity; and they seem best to harmonize with the known principles of the common law in other cases. In concluding this topic, the following propositions may be laid down, as those which, although not universally established or recognized in America, have much of domestic authority for their support, and have none in opposition to them.

184. (1) *Summary.* — Where there is a marriage between parties in a foreign country, and an express contract respecting their rights and property, present and future, that, as a matter of contract, will be held equally valid everywhere, unless, under the circumstances, it stands prohibited by the laws of the country where it is sought to be enforced. It will act directly on movable property everywhere. But as to immovable property in a foreign territory, it will at most confer only a right of action, to be enforced according to the jurisprudence rei sitæ.[1] (a)

185. (2) Where such an express contract applies in terms or intent only to present property, and there is a change of domicil, the law of the actual domicil will govern the rights of the parties as to all future acquisitions.[2] (b)

186. (3) Where there is no express contract, the law of the matrimonial domicil will govern as to all the rights of the parties to their present property in that place, and as to all personal property everywhere, upon the principle that movables have no situs, or rather that they accompany the person

---

[1] See Henry on Foreign Law, 48, 49; Id. 95; ante, s. 143; Le Breton v. Miles, 8 Paige (N. Y.) 261.

[2] Ante, s. 171, 171 a.

her father's will. Upon a bill filed by the wife against the trustee, to have him make good to her the amount he had paid to the husband, it was held that the marriage settlement, though made in England, must be construed according to the law of Scotland, by the form of which law it was made; and that as, by the Scotch law, the joint receipt of the husband and wife would be a good discharge to the trustee, although not so in England, such receipt would be held a good defence in England, even for payments made after the parties had removed to England.

(a) Besse v. Pellochoux, 73 Ill. 285; Fuss v. Fuss, 24 Wis. 256.

(b) Besse v. Pellochoux, supra; Fuss v. Fuss, supra; Ordronaux v. Rey, 2 Sandf. Ch. (N. Y.) 45.

everywhere.[1]   As to immovable property the law rei sitæ will prevail.[2] (*a*)

187. (4) Where there is no change of domicil, the same rule will apply to future acquisitions as to present property. (5) But where there is a change of domicil, the law of the actual domicil, and not of the matrimonial domicil, will govern as to all future acquisitions of movable property ; and, as to all immovable property, the law rei sitæ.[3] (*b*)

[1] See Stein's Case, 1 Rose, Bank. Cases, Appx. 481; Selkrig *v.* Davis, 2 Rose, Bank. Cas. 99; S.C. 2 Dow, 230, 250; 1 Burge, Col. & For. Law, pt. 1, c. 7, s. 8, p. 619.

[2] See Henry on Foreign Law, 48, 49; 1 Burge, Col. & For. Law, pt. 1, c. 7, s. 8, p. 618, 619.

[3] How will it be as to personal or movable property antecedently acquired? See ante, s. 178; ante, s. 157, 158. Mr. Burge, adverting to the different opinions on this subject, has remarked: ' According to the general doctrine of jurists, the property of the husband and wife, whether it be acquired before or after the change of domicil, continues subject to the law of community, notwithstanding they have removed to another domicil, where that law does not exist. The change of the domicil neither divests them of any right which they had acquired under the law of their matrimonial domicil, nor confers on them any right which they could not acquire under that law. If the law of community existed in their matrimonial domicil, they will not cease to be in community, although they should have acquired another domicil in a country where no law of community was established ; and, on the other hand, if there was no law of community in their matrimonial domicil, they will not become subject to the law of community, because they have taken up their domicil in a country where that law does exist. The concurrence of jurists in this doctrine is so general that there are few who have dissented from it. This doctrine seems to result as a necessary and legitimate conclusion from the theory that the community exists by force of the tacit agreement of the parties, and which is considered of the same weight as if it had been an express agreement; because, if the rights of the parties, either in their present property or in their future acquisitions, had been conferred by an agreement, they could not be varied by a change of domicil. But if this theory be rejected, and the law of community has no greater operation than any other real law, it can never be necessary to consider the effect of a change of domicil on the interests of the husband and wife on their real property, because those interests in their present property, as well as in their future acquisitions, are determined by the lex loci rei sitæ. The application of this doctrine to the interests acquired by the husband and wife in the personal property of each other under the law of their matrimonial domicil, so far as it regards property acquired before their removal from their matrimonial domicil, might, it seems, be maintained without the aid of this theory. The matrimonial domicil of the parties may be supposed to be in a country where, as in England, the marriage is an absolute gift to the husband of the wife's whole personal estate; the subsequent domicil may be in a country

---

(*a*) Fuss *v.* Fuss, supra.   (*b*) Fuss *v.* Fuss, supra.

188. (6) And here also, as in cases of express contract, the
exception is to be understood, that the laws of the place where
the rights are sought to be enforced do not prohibit such arrangements.   For if they do, as every nation has a right to prescribe
rules for the government of all persons and property within its

where, as in British Guiana, the wife, by virtue of the communio bonorum,
retains an interest in her own, and acquires an interest in her husband's personal property; or the matrimonial domicil may have been in British Guiana,
and the subsequently acquired domicil in England.   In the one case, the whole
personal estate of the wife has become vested in the husband; the wife brings
no personal property of her own into British Guiana on which the law of community can attach.   In the other case the wife arrives in England, not only
retaining an interest in her own, but having acquired an interest in the property of her husband.   The law of the matrimonial domicil has, in this case,
already made a disposition of the property of the husband and wife at the
time when the parties and the property were subject to that law.   In neither
case could the law of the new domicil be admitted without divesting rights which
had been already legally acquired.   But, in the opinion of the greater number
of jurists, not only the property which had been acquired by the husband and
wife before their removal from their matrimonial domicil, but even that acquired
in their new domicil, is subject to the law of the matrimonial domicil; and their
opinion has been sanctioned even to this extent by the decisions in France.
A person was married and domiciled in L., where the civil law prevailed.
He afterwards removed to Paris, and established his domicil there.   On his
death his widow demanded a share of his movables, and of the acquêts made
since the marriage.   By an arrêt of the 29th of March, 1640, her demand was
rejected.   A similiar decision was given in the case of a person married and
domiciled in Normandy, who afterwards removed to and established his domicil in Paris.   A demand by his widow for a share of the acquêts, made since
the removal from Normandy, was rejected.   The application of this doctrine to
the acquisitions of personal property made by the husband and wife in their new
or actual domicil can only be sustained by means of the theory of a tacit agreement.   Even its advocates do not all concur in subjecting future acquisitions
after a change of domicil to the law of the matrimonial domicil.   Thus, Huber
was of opinion that they are governed by the law of the new or actual
domicil: " Cum primum vero conjuges migrant ex una provincia (where the
community prevailed) in aliam (where it does not prevail), bona quæ deinceps
alteri adveniunt, cessant esse communia, manentque distinctis proprietatibus ;
sicut res antea communes factæ, manent in eo statu juris, quem induerunt."
But if the law of community be a real law, its power as to personal property
cannot be more extensive than as to real property.   As it affects only such
real property as is actually situated in the country where it is established, so it
affects personal property only when its owner is actually domiciled in the
country where such law is established, because the place of his domicil is the
situs in fictione juris of his movable property.   The real law as to personal
property is that which prevails in the place of the owner's actual domicil.
He acquires and holds it according to the disposition of that law, and it
depends upon that law whether he and his wife acquire it for their joint
benefit or for his sole benefit.'   1 Burge, Col. & For. Law, pt. 1, c. 7, s. 8,
p. 619–622.   See also Lashley v. Hogg, cited Id. p. 623–625; Id. p. 626.

own territorial limits, its own law in a case of conflict ought to prevail.[1]

189. (7) Although, in a general sense, the law of the matrimonial domicil is to govern in relation to the incidents and effects of marriage, yet this doctrine must be received with many qualifications and exceptions. No other nation will recognize such incidents or effects, when they are incompatible with its own policy or injurious to its own interests. (a) A marriage in France or Prussia may be dissolved for incompatibility of temper; but no divorce would be granted from such a marriage, for such a cause, in England, Scotland, or America.[2] 'If,' said a learned Scottish judge, in a passage already cited, 'a man in this country were to confine his wife in an iron cage, or beat her with a rod of the thickness of the judge's finger, would it be any justification in any court to allege that these were powers which the law of England conferred on a husband, and that he was entitled to exercise them, because his marriage had been celebrated in that country.'[3] And he added, with great emphasis, 'Marriage is a contract sui generis; and the rights, duties, and obligations which arise out of it are matters of so much importance to the well-being of the state, that they are regulated not by the private contract, but by the public laws of the state, which are imperative upon all who are domiciled within its territory.'[4]

190. (8) The doctrine of tacit contract to regulate the rights and duties of matrimony, in cases where there is no express contract, according to the law of the place where the marriage has been celebrated, is questionable in itself; and, even if admitted, must be liable to many qualifications and restrictions.[5] We have seen that it has been much doubted in Louisiana;[6] and the Scottish courts have utterly refused (as we shall fully see hereafter) to allow the doctrine of such a tacit contract to regulate the right of divorce.[7]

[1] See Fergusson on Mar. & Div. 358-363; Id. 383, 392-422; Huberus, lib. 1, tit. 3, de Conflict. Leg. s. 2; ante, s. 111.

[2] Fergusson on Mar. & Div. 398.

[3] Per Lord Robertson. See Fergusson on Mar. & Div. 399; Id. 361.

[4] Id. 399; Id. 361.

[5] Ante, s. 147-170.

[6] Saul v. His Creditors, 5 Mart. N.S. (La.) 598-607; ante, s. 157.

[7] Fergusson on Mar. & Div. 358-363; Id. 382, 393-422.

(a) Comp. McVey v. Holden, 15 La. An. 317.

191. *Matrimonial Domicil considered.* — But a question may sometimes occur, What is to be deemed in the proper sense of the rule the true matrimonial domicil? Is it the place where the actual marriage is celebrated? or that where the contract of marriage is entered into? or that where the parties are domiciled, if the marriage is celebrated elsewhere? Or, if the husband and wife have different domicils, whose is to be regarded? These and many other perplexing inquiries may be raised; and foreign jurists have not passed them over without examination.[1]

192. Where the place of domicil of both the parties is the same with that of the contract and the celebration of the marriage, no difficulty can arise. The place of celebration is clearly then the matrimonial domicil. But, let us suppose that neither of the parties has a domicil in the place where the marriage is celebrated; but it is a marriage in transitu, or during a temporary residence, or on a journey made for that sole purpose, animo revertendi: what is then to be deemed the matrimonial domicil?

193. The principle maintained by foreign jurists in such cases is that, with reference to personal rights and rights of property, the actual or intended domicil of the parties is to be deemed the true matrimonial domicil; or, to express the doctrine in a still more general form, they hold that the law of the place where, at the time of marriage, the parties intend to fix their domicil, is to govern all the rights resulting from the marriage. Hence they would answer the question proposed, by stating that in such a case the law of the actual domicil of the parties is to govern, and not the place of the marriage in transitu.[2]

194. But suppose a man domiciled in Massachusetts should marry a lady domiciled in Louisiana, what is then to be deemed the matrimonial domicil? Foreign jurists would answer that it is the domicil of the husband, if the intention of the parties is to fix their residence there; and of the wife, if the intention is to fix their residence there; and if the residence is intended to be in some other place, as in New York, then the matrimonial domicil would be in New York. Rodenburg lays down the doctrine

---

[1] See on this subject 1 Burge, Col. & For. Law, pt. 1, c. 6, s. 2, p. 244–261.

[2] 2 Boullenois, obs. 36, p. 260; Pothier, Traité de la Communauté, art. Prélim. n. 14–16; Voet, de Statut. s. 9, c. 2, s. 5, 6, p. 264, ed. 1715; Id. p. 319, 320, ed. 1661; 1 Burge, Col. & For. Law, pt. 1, c. 6, s. 2, p. 244–261.

in explicit terms, and gives, as a reason, that the marriage is presumed to be contracted according to the laws of the place where
they intend to fix their domicil. 'Quia per destinationem in locis
illis domicilii matrimonium contractum esse intelligitur.'[1] Boullenois states the same doctrine, and says that, ordinarily, where the
domicil of the husband and that of the wife are not the same, the
law of the husband's domicil is to prevail, unless he means to establish himself in that of his wife.[2] Dumoulin is equally expressive.
'Hinc infertur,' says he, 'ad quæstionem quotidianam de contractu dotis et matrimonii, qui censetur fieri non in loco, in quo
contrahitur, sed in loco domicilii viri; et intelligitur, non de domicilio originis, sed de domicilio habitationis ipsius viri, de quo nemo
dubitat, sed omnes consentiunt.'[3] This appears also to be the
opinion of Mascardus, Bartholus, Bouhier, Pothier, Merlin, and
other distinguished jurists.[4]

195. *Foreign Jurists.* — Cujas affirms the same doctrine. 'Sed
ex eo contractu mulier migravit in alium locum, id est, talis est
contractus, ut ex eo mulier statim migret in alium locum. Ergo
non is locus spectatur, sed ille, in quem sit migratio. Hac ratione,
mulier non agit, ubi matrimonium contraxit; sed ubi ex matri-
monio migravit, divertit, aut aget.'[5] And in so doing he does
no more than affirm the very doctrine of the Pandects. 'Exigere
dotem mulier debet illic, ubi maritus domicilium habuit, non ubi
instrumentum dotale conscriptum est; nec enim id genus contractus est, ut eum locum spectari oporteat, in quo instrumentum
dotis factum est, quam eum, in cujus domicilium et ipsa mulier
per conditionem matrimonii erat reditura.'[6]

[1] Rodenburg, tit. 2, c. 5, s. 15; 2 Boullenois, Appx. p. 47; 1 Boullenois,
11, 682, 683; Id. obs. 29, p. 802; Voet, de Statut. s. 9, c. 2, s. 5; p. 264, ed.
1716; Id. p. 319, 320, ed. 1661; Le Brun, Traité de la Communauté, liv. 1,
c. 2, s. 42, 43, 46–48.

[2] 1 Boullenois, obs. 29, p. 802; 2 Boullenois, obs. 37, p. 259, 260, 265;
Voet, de Stat. s. 9, c. 2, s. 5, 6, p. 264, 265, ed. 1715; Id. p. 319, 320, ed. 1661.

[3] Molinæi, Com. ad Cod. lib. 1, tit. 1, l. 1, Conclus. de Statut. Molin.
Opera, tom. 3, p. 555; 2 Boullenois, obs. 37, p. 261.

[4] 2 Boullenois, obs. 37, p. 260–265; Pothier, Traité de la Communauté,
art. Prélim. n. 14–16; Bouhier, Cout. de Bourg. c. 22, s. 18–28; Merlin,
Répert. Autoris. Maritale, s. 10, art. 5 p. 244; Id. Communauté de Biens,
s. 1, p. 111; 1 Burge, Col. & For. Law, pt. 1, c. 6, s. 2, p. 244–261.

[5] Cujas, ad Legem, Exigere dotem, Dig. 5, 1, 65, Cujaccii Opera, tom. 7,
p. 164, ed. 1758. See also Ford *v.* Ford, 2 Mart. N.S. 577; Le Brun, Traité
de la Communauté, liv. 1, c. 2, s. 41 ; post, s. 198.

[6] Dig. 5, 1, 65; Pothier, Pand. 5, 1, n. 38.

196. Huberus holds very decisive language on the same subject. 'But,' says he, 'the place where a contract is made is not so exactly to be looked at, but that, if the parties have in contracting had reference to another place, that is rather to be regarded: Contraxisse unusquisque in eo loco intelligitur, in quo, ut solveret, se obligavit.[1] Therefore the place of the marriage contract is not so much to be deemed the place where the nuptial contract is made, as that in which the parties contracting matrimony intend to live. Thus, it daily happens that men in Friesland, natives or sojourners, marry wives in Holland, whom they immediately bring into Friesland. If this be their intention at the time of the contract, there is no community of property, although the marriage contract is silent, according to the law of Holland; but the law of Friesland in this case is the law of the place of contract.[2] Proinde et locus matrimonii contracti non tam is est, ubi contractus nuptialis initus est, quam in quo contrahentes matrimonium exercere voluerunt; ut omni die sit, homines in Frisia indigenas aut incolas, ducere uxores in Hollandia, quas inde statim in Frisiam deducunt; idque si in ipso contractu ineundo propositum habeant, non oritur communio bonorum, etsi pacta dotalia sileant, secundum jus Hollandiæ, sed jus Frisiæ in hoc casu est loco contractus.'[3]

197. Le Brun has discussed the question at considerable length, and has arrived at the same conclusion. And he puts the case of a person domiciled in Normandy, where the law of community does not exist, who marries in Paris without any contract, where the law of community does exist; and he holds that if he has not changed his domicil, but returns immediately to Normandy, the law of Normandy will govern, and no community of property will exist between himself and his wife.[4]

198. *Law of Louisiana.* — The same doctrine has been repeatedly acted on by the Supreme Court of Louisiana. In one case of a runaway marriage (already alluded to) in another state by parties domiciled in Louisiana, who immediately afterwards returned, the court held, as we have seen, that the law of Louisiana

---

[1] Id. 44, 7, 21; Pothier, Pand. 44, tit. 7, n. 21.
[2] Huberus, lib. 1, tit. 3, s. 10; Fergusson on Mar. & Div. 174; Voet, de Statut. s. 9, c. 2, s. 5, 6, p. 264, 265, ed. 1715; Id. p. 319, 320, ed. 1661.
[3] Huberus, lib. 1, tit. 3, s. 10.
[4] Le Brun, Traité de la Communauté, liv. 1, c. 2, s. 46–51, 55.

18

governed the marriage rights and property.[1] In another case
where the parties were married in one state, intending immediately to remove into another, which intention was consummated,
the court held that the marriage rights and property were governed by the law of the place of the intended residence. (a) On
this last occasion the court said: ' We think that it may be safely
laid down as a principle, that the matrimonial rights of a wife
who marries with the intention of an instant removal for residence into another state, are to be regulated by the laws of her
intended domicil, when no marriage contract is made, or one
without any provision in this respect.'[2] In the same case the
court also recognized the general rule that, where the husband
and wife have different domicils, the law of that of the husband
is to prevail ; because the wife is presumed to follow her husband's domicil.[3]

199. *Conclusion.* — Under these circumstances, where there is
such a general consent of foreign jurists to the doctrine thus
recognized in America, it is not perhaps too much to affirm that
a contrary doctrine will scarcely hereafter be established ; for in
England as well as in America, in the interpretation of other
contracts, the law of the place where they are to be performed
has been held to govern.[4] Treated therefore as a matter of tacit
matrimonial contract (if it can be so treated) there is the rule of
analogy to govern it. And treated as a matter to be governed by
the municipal law to which the parties were or meant to be subjected by their future domicil, the doctrine seems equally capable of a solid vindication.[5]

[1] Le Breton v. Nouchet, 3 Mart. 60; ante, s. 78, 180.
[2] Ford v. Ford, 2 Mart. N.S. (La.) 574, 578.   [3] Id. 577.
[4] Robinson v. Bland, 2 Burr. 1077; Lanusse v. Barker, 3 Wheaton, 101;
4 Cowen, 513, note; 2 Kent Com. 459 ; Fergusson on Mar. & Div. 341, 342,
395, 396, 416.
[5] See Fergusson on Mar. & Divorce, 339–346.

(a) See Mason v. Homer, 105
Mass. 116; Mason v. Fuller, 36 Conn.
160; State v. Barrow, 14 Tex. 187;
Arendell v. Arendell, 10 La. An. 567;
Hayden v. Nutt, 4 La. Ann. 66.

CHAPTER VII.

DIVORCES.

200. *Nature of Marriage.* — Having thus considered the operation of marriage upon the personal capacity and the property of the parties in the place of its celebration and in foreign countries, we next come to the consideration of the important subject of Divorce.[1] Marriage is not a mere contract between the parties, subject, as to its continuance, dissolution, and effects, to their mere pleasure and intentions. But it is treated as a civil institution, the most interesting and important in its nature of any in society. Upon it the sound morals, the domestic affections, and the delicate relations and duties of parents and of children, essentially depend. On this account it has in many nations the sanction and solemnity of religious obligation superadded to it.[2] And it may be truly said that Christianity, by giving to it a more affecting and sublime morality, has conferred upon mankind new blessings, and has elevated woman to the rank and dignity of an equal, instead of being a humble companion or a devoted slave of her husband.

201. *Divorce in Place of Domicil and Celebration.* — It is not my design to enter into any discussion as to the general right of the legislative power to authorize directly or indirectly a dissolution of the matrimonial state, and to release the parties from all the future obligation thereof. It is deemed by all modern nations to be within the competency of legislation to provide for such a dissolution and release in some form and for some causes. And there is no doubt that a divorce regularly obtained, according to the jurisprudence of the country where the marriage is celebrated and where the parties are domiciled, will be held a complete dis-

---

[1] See on this subject, 1 Burge, Col. & For. Law, pt. 1, c. 8, s. 1, p. 640–668; Id. s. 2, p. 668–694.

[2] See 1 Burge, Col. & For. Law, pt. 1, c. 8, s. 1, p. 642, 643; post, s. 209.

solution of the matrimonial contract in every other country.[1] I say, where the marriage is celebrated and where the parties are domiciled ; for both ingredients are, or may be, material ; and the presence of one and the absence of the other may change the legal predicament of the case according to the jurisprudence of different countries, when the subject comes under consideration therein.

202. *Marriage and Domicil in Different Places.* — The real difficulty is to lay down appropriate principles to govern cases where the marriage is celebrated in one place, and the parties are at the time domiciled in another ; where afterwards there is a change of domicil by one party without a similar change by the other ; where by the law of the place of celebration the marriage is indissoluble, or dissoluble only under peculiar circumstances, and where by the law of another place it is dissoluble for various other causes, and even at the pleasure of the parties. By the law of England marriage is indissoluble except by a special act of Parliament.[2] By the law of Scotland a divorce may be had through the instrumentality of a judicial process and a decree on account of adultery.[3] By the civil law an almost unbounded license was allowed to divorces, and wives were often dismissed by their husbands, not only for want of chastity and for intolerable temper, but for causes of the most trivial nature.[4] In France a divorce may be judicially obtained for the cause of adultery, excess, cruelty, or grievous injuries of either party ; and in certain cases by mutual and persevering consent.[5] In America an equal diversity of principle and practice exists. In some States, as in Massachusetts and New York, divorces are grantable by judicial tribunals for the cause of adultery.[6] In other States

---

[1] 2 Kent. Com. 107, 108.

[2] 1 Black. Com. 440, 441; 1 Burge, Col. & For. Law, pt. 1, c. 8, s. 1, p. 654–660.

[3] Fergusson on Mar. & Div. 1, 18; Erskine's Inst. b. 1, tit. 6, s. 38, 43; 1 Burge, Col. & For. Law, pt. 1, c. 8, s. 2, p. 670–680.

[4] 2 Kent Com. 102, 103; 1 Brown, Civ. Law, 89–92; 1 Black. Com. 441; Justin. Novellæ, 117, c. 8; Cod. 5, 17, 8; Merlin, Répert. Divorce, s. 2, p. 149, 150; Pothier, Traité de Mariage, art. 463; Van Leeuwen, Com. b. 1, c. 15, s. 1–3.

[5] Code Civil, art. 229–233; Id. 275, &c. See in Fergusson on Mar. & Div. Appx. 448, the Prussian Code on the subject of divorce; among others, incompatibility of temper, endangering life or health, is a good cause of divorce, art. 703.

[6] This also is the law in Holland, in Prussia, and in the Protestant states

divorces are grantable judicially for causes of far inferior grossness and enormity, approaching sometimes almost to frivolousness. In other states, divorces can be pronounced by the legislature only, and for such causes as in its wisdom it may choose from time to time to allow.[1]

203. *Embarrassing Questions.* — Some of the most embarrassing questions belonging to international jurisprudence arise under the head of marriage and divorce. Suppose, for instance, a marriage celebrated in England, where marriage is indissoluble, and a divorce obtained in Scotland a vinculo matrimonii, as it may be, for adultery under the laws thereof, will that divorce be operative in England, so as to authorize a new marriage there by either party? Suppose a marriage in Massachusetts, where a divorce may be had for adultery, will a divorce obtained in another state for a cause unknown to the laws of Massachusetts be held valid there? If, in each of these cases, the divorce would be held invalid in the country where the marriage is celebrated, but it would be held valid where the divorce is obtained, what rule is to govern in other countries as to such divorce? Is it to be deemed valid or invalid there? Will a new marriage contracted there by either party be good, or be not good? These and many other perplexing questions may be put; and it is difficult at the present moment to give any answer to them, which would receive the unqualified assent of all nations.

204. Other most perplexing inquiries may grow out of the consideration of the national character of the parties: whether they are both citizens or subjects, or both foreigners, or one a citizen and the other a foreigner; whether the marriage is celebrated at home, or celebrated abroad; whether the jurisdiction of any court to pronounce a decree of divorce is to be founded upon the national character of the parties, or upon the celebration of the marriage within the territorial jurisdiction, or upon the domicil of the parties within it, or upon the actual presence or temporary residence of one or both of them at the time when the process for divorce is instituted. And if, upon any of these grounds, the

of Germany, in Sweden, Denmark, and Russia. Fergusson on Mar. & Div. 202.

[1] See 2 Kent Com. 106–110, 117, 118. See also 1 Burge, Col. & For. Law, pt. 1, c. 8, s. 1, p. 640-668, where are brought together in a general review the laws of different nations on the subject of divorce.

jurisdiction is sustained, another not less important inquiry is, whether the law of divorce of the place of the marriage, or that of the place where the suit is instituted, is to be administered by the court before which the suit is pending.

205. It seems to have been thought that under the Scottish law it is not necessary, to found a jurisdiction for divorce in the courts of Scotland, that both the parties should at the time of the adultery committed, or at the time of the suit brought, have their actual domicil in Scotland. It seems to be sufficient that the defendant, against whom the suit is brought, is domiciled in that kingdom, so that a citation may be served upon him, and that a divorce under such circumstances may be granted, whether the adultery is committed at home or in a foreign country. Undoubtedly this doctrine is to be understood with the limitation that the domicil is real, and not pretended, and that it is bona fide, and not by collusion between the parties for the mere purpose of maintaining the suit and procuring the divorce.[1]

[1] Fergusson on Mar. & Div. Introd. p. 16–18; Id. p. 51; Id. p. 114, 115, note; St. Aubyn v. Obrien, Id. Appx. p. 276; Id. note B. p. 363–376; 1 Burge, Col. & For. Law, pt. 1. c. 8, s. 2, p. 672, 674–679, 688, 689. See McCarthy v. De Caix, cited in a note to 3 Hagg. 642, and in Warrender v. Warrender, 9 Bligh, 141, 142; Conway v. Beazley, 3 Hagg. Ecc. 639, 645, 646; 2 Russ. & Mylne, 614, 618–620; Tovey v. Lindsay, 1 Dow, 117, 131, 135–137; 2 Clark & Fin. 569, note; post, s. 216–218. See also Warrender v. Warrender, 9 Bligh, 89, 144; post, s. 226 a–226 c. Mr. Chief Justice Gibson, in delivering the opinion of the supreme court of Pennsylvania in a case of divorce, used the following language: ' In constructing our international law of divorce we naturally look for the materials of it in the jurisprudence of our ancestors, whose institutions are more congenial with our own than those of their continental neighbors, and whose process of forensic discussion is usually more exact. But we find an irreconcilable difference betwixt the decisions of the English and of the Scottish courts. The English judges acknowledge the legitimacy of no jurisdiction which is not founded in the law of divorce at the place of the marriage, if it be an English one; while the Scottish in the other extreme are willing to found theirs even on a temporary residence of the complainant in the country of the forum. Of the latter pretension I shall say little more than that it is in truth a usurpation of power to intermeddle in the domestic concerns of a neighbor. If a bona fide domicil in the strictest sense of the word were not essential to jurisdiction, there would be nothing to prevent the exhibition of a libel by a proctor, and without the presence even of the complainant. But the respondent's presence would be more essential still; for a sentence against one who was not subject to the jurisdiction would be void on the plainest principles of natural law. Moreover it is not perceived how the actual presence of both of them could confer jurisdiction of a cause of divorce which was not in its inception subject to the law of the forum. It seems to me the fallacy in the reasoning of the Scottish

206. A learned Scottish jurist, in remarking upon the embarrassments arising out of this state of the law of Scotland, has made the following powerful observations: ' These conclusions evidently demonstrate that unless the remedy in this judicature shall be limited either to that which the lex loci contractus affords, or to that which the lex domicilii, taken in the same fair sense as in questions of succession, might give, the public decrees of the only court of Scotland which is competent to pronounce one in such consistorial causes, become proclamations to invite all the married who incline to be free, not in the rest of the British

judges, plausible though it be, consists in their assumption that divorce is a penalty everywhere annexed to a breach of the marriage contract, which, like a civil cause of action attendant on the person, may be enforced anywhere; thus forgetting that whether it be a penalty at all depends not on the Scottish law as an interpreter or avenger, but on the law of the domicil, or else on the lex loci contractus, which exclusively furnishes the original conditions. The English doctrine on the other hand is not more reconcilable to our principle of finite allegiance; for notwithstanding the doubt and manifest inclination of Dr. Lushington in Conway v. Beazley, 3 Hagg. Ecc. 639, I take it to be settled by Lolley's Case, Russ. & Ry. 236, sanctioned in Tovey v. Lindsay, 1 Dow, 124, by the preponderating weight of Lord Eldon's name, that the dissolution of an English marriage for any cause whatever can be effected so as to be acknowledged in that country only by English authority. It was indeed intimated in Conway v. Beazley that the question of jurisdiction in Lolley's Case, perhaps turned on the difference between temporary and permanent residence; but the report certainly does not indicate it, and besides the conclusion attained was an unavoidable consequence of the British tenet of perpetual allegiance. Though an English subject acquire a foreign character from a foreign domicil, insomuch as to be treated as an alien for commercial purposes; though he formally renounce his primitive allegiance, and profess another, he is accounted but as a sojourner while abroad, and England by the dogma of her government is his home and his country still. Holding this dogma it would be strange did she tolerate foreign interference with her domestic relations within our pale. Insisting on jurisdiction of his person, absent or present, she necessarily regards an attempt to change any one of these as an invasion of her sovereignty; and in that aspect it cannot be denied that the matter is within her province and her power; for, though the status of marriage is juris gentium, the institution is undoubtedly a subject of municipal regulation. And it is this perpetual allegiance to the country, its institutions and its laws, — not an indissolubility of the marriage contract from the presumptive will and reservation of the parties, — which is the root of the English doctrine. It truly assumes that marriage is contracted on the basis of the laws, and that these forbid a British subject to dissolve it by the authority of any other country; but take away the law of perpetual allegiance, and you take away the foundation of the presumptive pledge not to submit the duration of it to foreign action.' Dorsey v. Dorsey 7 Watts (Penn.), 349; 1 (Boston) Law Reporter, p. 288, 289. (See Maguire v. Maguire, 7 Dana (Ky.) 181.)

empire alone, but in all countries where marriage is indissoluble by judicial sentence, to seek that object in this tribunal. Adultery and presence within our territory are the only requisites to found the jurisdiction by citation. What numbers of foreign parties may accept such an offer, and may even commit the crime here for the very purpose of affording ground for the action, it is impossible to conjecture. But it is manifest that, in exact proportion to their number, injury to the morals of this country must follow; and, by setting at nought the laws of other nations, reproach must be brought upon our own. For all foreign parties, while matters stand upon this footing, have it in their power, with the help of evidence as easily provided as it may be disgusting and impure, to oblige the Scotch Consistorial Court to entertain the whole mass of their foreign causes, although there is no fair interest to insist that the municipal law of Scotland shall decide these by its own peculiar rules. To what extent therefore the good order of society may eventually be disturbed by this compulsory abuse and pollution of its jurisdiction in consequence of the doubts and contests that must ensue as to rights of legitimacy and succession, no calculation can be made.' [1]

207. Upon the point, what is the rule of divorce, a learned Scottish judge has made the following remarks in a case depending before him in judgment: [2] 'With us the laws relative to divorce are founded on divine authority. How can a person withdraw himself from obedience to such laws? Are these laws relaxed as to a person domiciled in Scotland, because his marriage is contracted in a country where the law of divorce is different? If two natives of Scotland were married in France or Prussia according to the laws of those countries, the marriage would no doubt be valid here. But would they be entitled to come into the Commissary Court and insist for a dissolution a vinculo matrimonii, merely because their tempers were not suitable, which, in France, was a ground of divorce, or for any of the numberless reasons for dissolving a marriage which are allowed by the laws of Prussia? But if we would not listen to the lex loci when it facilitates divorce to a degree which our law considers as inconsistent with the best interests of society, and as

---

[1] Fergusson on Mar. & Div. Introd. p. 18, 19.

[2] Lord Robertson; The Cases of Edmonstone, of Levett, and of Forbes, in Fergusson, Appx. 383; Id. 398. See also Id. 415.

not warranted by the divine law, on what principle are we to give effect to the lex loci which prohibits divorce, even adulterii causa, though permitted in this country under the sanction of the divine law?'

208. These passages are sufficiently significant, as to the intrinsic difficulties of the subject, looking only to the law of divorce of a single country. But when we look at the almost endless diversities of foreign continental jurisprudence on the same subject, and the little regard which is habitually paid in that jurisprudence to the decrees of foreign courts, especially in matters which concern persons belonging to any other continental sovereignty, it ought not to surprise us that one nation should hold its own law of divorce of universal obligation and authority, and that another should yield it up in favor of the law of the domicil of the parties.

209. *Catholic and Protestant Countries.* — Upon the continent of Europe there has long existed a known distinction between the Catholics and the Protestants upon the subject of divorce. The former, according to the doctrine of the Romish Church, consider marriage as a sacrament, and in its effects to be governed by the divine law; and according to their interpretation of that law it was formerly held to be indissoluble.[1] The Protestants, on the contrary, have not generally considered it as a sacrament; but many, if not all of them, have considered it mainly as a civil institution, and subject to the legislative authority, as matter of public police and regulation.[2]

210. In Catholic France, we are informed that, until some time after the Revolution (until 1792), marriage was always treated as indissoluble.[3] 'Our church,' says Merlin, 'never approved of divorce, properly so called. It has always regarded it as contrary to the precept, Quod Deus conjunxit, homo non

---

[1] See Fergusson on Mar. & Div. Appx. note M. p. 443; Heinecc. Elem. Juris Germ. tit. 14, s. 328–332; Dalrymple v. Dalrymple, 2 Hagg. Cons. 63, 64, 67; 1 Burge, Col. & For. Law, pt. 1, c. 8, s. 1, p. 642, 643.

[2] 1 Black. Com. 433; 2 Hagg. Cons. 63, 67; 1 Burge, Col. & For. Law, pt. 1, c. 8, s. 1, p. 648, 649; Id. p. 650–653.

[3] We have already seen that, by the Code Civil of France, art. 229–233, divorce is allowed in a variety of cases. Upon the restoration of the Royal Family in 1816, it seems that the existing law of divorce was abolished. Merlin, Répert. Divorce, s. 4, p. 161. Whether, since the Revolution of 1830, it has been reinstated, I am not at this moment able to say. See Duranton, Cours de Droit Français, vol. 14, p. 535, note.

separet: What God hath joined together, let not man put asunder.[1] It is therefore a perpetual maxim among us, that marriage cannot be dissolved by means of a divorce.'[2] Pothier says: Marriage is not dissolved but by the natural death of one of the parties; while they live, it is indissoluble.[3] He adds that, though divorce was permitted by the Christian emperors, the church regarded it as prohibited by the gospel; and that it is not permitted by the French law for any cause whatsoever.[4]

211. Protestants have dealt differently by it.[5] In Scotland, which proposes on this subject to be governed exclusively by the scriptures, divorce is allowed for the scriptural causes, for adultery and for wilful desertion.[6] In many other Protestant countries it is not treated as indissoluble except for scriptural causes; but it may be dissolved for other causes. In England it is never dissolved except by an act of parliament, and for adultery.[7] In the Protestant continental nations of Europe, many other causes of divorce are known; and in America, as we have seen, it is generally treated as a matter of civil regulation.[8]

212. *Foreign Jurists.* — The conflict of laws on the subject of divorce does not seem to have undergone much discussion among the continental jurists; at least I have not been able to trace any systematic examination of the subject in those works which are within my reach, and in which almost all other topics of the conflict of laws are so amply treated. The silence of the French jurists may be accounted for, in a great measure, from the uniformity of operation of the Catholic religion and its canons over all the provinces of that kingdom; from the strong probability that few cases of foreign divorces between French subjects were ever judicially examined; and from the natural conclusion that, as in their view Christianity made the marriage union indissoluble, no earthly tribunal, either foreign or domestic, could rightfully pronounce a sentence of divorce. The silence of other

---

[1] Matthew, c. 19, v. 6.   [2] Merlin, Répert. Divorce, s. 3, p. 151.

[3] Pothier, Traité du Mariage, n. 462.

[4] Id. n. 464.   [5] Id. n. 465; ante, s. 209.

[6] Erskine's Instit. b. 1, tit. 6, s. 43, 44; Fergusson on Marr. and Div. Appx. note H. p. 423.

[7] Ante, s. 202.

[8] See 1 Black. Com. 441; Code Civil of France, art. 229–233; Fergusson on Mar. & Div. Appx. note N. p. 448; 2 Kent Com. 95–106; Van Leeuwen Com. b. 1, c. 15, s. 1–6.

Catholic countries may be accounted for in the same way. But it is not so easy to assign a satisfactory reason for the omission of the Protestant countries of the continent of Europe to discuss the subject at large. It is highly probable that, in those countries, the parties have been referred to their own matrimonial forum, either to furnish the true rule to expound the contract, or to administer the law of divorce, or for both purposes. This course has not been without example, even in our own country, upon cases bearing a close affinity.[1]

213. Merlin has treated the question purely as one arising under the French law, either with reference to the allowance of divorces under the legislation of 1792, or with reference to the prohibition of divorces after the restoration of the Bourbons in 1816.[2] He asks the question, whether in virtue of the new law of 1792, which introduced divorce, a marriage celebrated under the old law, which prohibited divorce, could be dissolved ; and vice versa, whether a marriage celebrated after the new law, which permitted divorce, could be dissolved after the promulgation of the law of 1816, which prohibited divorce.[3] He says that if divorce was, as the state of the parties (l'état des époux), the immediate effect and simple consequence of the marriage, the question might be easily answered.[4] Upon this hypothesis, as the state of the parties, the right of divorce would depend altogether upon the law at the time when the marriage was celebrated ; because then, in the first case put, the contract must be deemed one for an indissoluble union, and in the second case, a contract dissoluble for the proper causes of divorce.[5] But he goes on to state that divorce does not depend upon the intention of the parties, nor is it a consequence or interpretation of it. The legislature, in allowing or prohibiting divorce, has regard only to considerations of public order, and not to the mere contract of the parties. They are not permitted by private agreement to change the laws, or to make a marriage dissoluble or indissoluble in contravention of the policy of the state.[6] He, therefore comes to the conclusion that in a French court a di-

---

[1] 2 Kent Com. 108.   [2] Ante, s. 210, note.
[3] Merlin, Répert. Effet Rétroactif, s. 3, n. 2, art. 6.
[4] Id. s. 3, n. 2, art. 6, p. 19.
[5] Ibid.
[6] Merlin, Répert. Effet Rétroactif, s. 3, n. 3, art. 6, p. 19.

vorce in such case would be granted or denied according to the law of France at the time of the suit.[1]

214. *English and Scotch Decisions.* — The question how a marriage in a foreign country between French subjects, or between foreigners, would be affected by a naturalization or domicil in France, is not here touched. In another work however treating of moot questions, he has recently discussed the point. He asks whether French subjects, married in France since the repealing act of 1816, who have abandoned their country, and become naturalized in a country where divorce is allowed, could institute a suit there, and dissolve their marriage by a decree of divorce pronounced there by mutual consent. He supports the affirmative upon the general reasoning by which he has sustained the doctrine in the preceding paragraph.[2] It would seem however from his own statement that this is quite an open question in France.

215. It is to the decisions of the English and Scottish courts however that we must look for the most thorough and exact discussion of this subject. From the different nature of the respective laws of England and Scotland upon the subject of divorce, from their national union, and from their constant, easy, and familiar intercourse, the courts of both countries have been frequently called upon to pronounce very elaborate judgments respecting the jurisdiction and law of divorce in suits and contestations before them.

216. Several questions on this subject have been recently discussed in the courts of Scotland. One is whether a permanent domicil of the parties is indispensable to found a jurisdiction in cases of divorce in the Scottish tribunals, or whether a citation given formally to the party defendant, or left at his dwelling-place in Scotland after he has been forty days there, is sufficient to subject him to the jurisdiction of those courts in a suit for divorce. In the case in which this question was principally discussed the marriage was celebrated in England, the husband many years afterwards abandoned his wife and went to Scotland to reside, and the wife commenced a suit for divorce against her husband in the Scottish Consistorial Court. The court were of opinion that as the parties were English, and never cohabited as husband and wife in Scotland, and there was no proof that the husband had taken up a fixed and permanent residence in Scotland, the suit

---

[1] Ibid.   [2] Merlin, Questions de Droit, Divorce, s. 11, p. 350; ante, s. 213.

ought to be dismissed upon the ground of a want of jurisdiction. Upon appeal the decree was reversed by the superior tribunal, and a decree of divorce was ultimately pronounced.[1]

217. The leading grounds of the reversal were: 'That the relation of husband and wife is a relation acknowledged jure gentium; that the duties, obligations, and rights to redress wrongs incident to that relation, as recognized by the law of Scotland, attach on all married persons living within the territory and subject to that law, wheresoever their marriage may have been celebrated; that jurisdiction, or the right and duty of the courts of Scotland to administer justice in such matters over persons not natural-born subjects, arises from the person sued being resident within the territory at the time of their citation and appearance, or being duly domiciled, and being properly cited accordingly, at the instance of a person having a sufficient interest and title, and proceeding in due form of law.'[2] The result of this decision is, that permanent domicil, or the animus manendi, is not necessary to found the jurisdiction. In several other succeeding cases the court have followed up the same doctrine, affirming that a temporary residence is sufficient to found the jurisdiction, notwithstanding the permanent jurisdiction of the parties is in another country.[3]

218. *Lolley's Case.* — This doctrine has been maintained by the Scottish judges with great ability and learning, and no one can read their reasoning without admitting its force. It has not however been deemed satisfactory in England. In a very important case before the twelve judges (Lolley's Case), where English subjects were married in England, and afterwards the husband went to Scotland, and procured a divorce a vinculo there, and then returned to England and married another wife, it was decided that the second marriage was void, and the husband was guilty of bigamy.[4] It has been commonly supposed that this decision proceeded upon the broad and general ground, that an

[1] Utterton *v.* Tewsh, Fergusson on Mar. & Div. p. 1–67.
[2] Ibid.
[3] Duntze *v.* Levett, Fergusson on Mar. & Div. p. 68–167; Edmonstone *v.* Lockhart, Id. p. 168–208; Butler *v.* Forbes, Id. p. 209–225; Kibblewhite *v.* Rowland, Id. p. 226–248; Gordon *v.* Pye, Id. p. 276–362; Id. p. 383–422.
[4] Lolley's Case, Russ. & R. 237. See Warrender *v.* Warrender; 9 Bligh, 122, 123, 127–130, 139–143.

English marriage is incapable of being dissolved under any circumstances by a foreign divorce; and so it seems to have been
understood by Lord Eldon on a later occasion.[1] It has been sug-

[1] Tovey v. Lindsay, 1 Dow, 117, 131. See also M'Carthy r. Decaix, 1831,
cited 3 Hagg. Ecc. 642, note; 2 Russ. & M. 614, 620. Lord Eldon on this
occasion (1 Dow, 137) is reported to have used the following language: 'Here
then we have a case in which both parties were domiciled in England, and
then the husband went to Scotland, where it was said he had a domicil by
reason of origin and his being heir of entail of an estate there, and instituted
a suit against his wife, which she said did not affect her in England; and if
his domicil was at Durham, the answer would be sufficient, though the rule of
law should be admitted, that the domicil of the wife followed that of the husband. But if the jurisdiction by reason of the original domicil could be maintained, it would be attended with the most important consequences to the law
of marriage. The decision in the second case appeared rather singular, when
connected with the decision in the first. They stated, as a main ground of
the judgment in the second cause, that the respondent was *confessedly* domiciled in Scotland, and that therefore they had jurisdiction, which appeared to
imply a doubt whether they had jurisdiction in the first cause. If the first
cause could be supported, there was no occasion for the second. But, suppose
the respondent were domiciled in Scotland at the time of the alleged acts of
adultery there, the question still remained, whether in 1810 he could institute
a suit against her with effect, unless she had changed her forum likewise,
merely upon the ground of the fiction which had been stated. This was a
question of the very highest importance.' Lord Brougham, in delivering his
own judgment in M'Carthy v. Decaix, 2 Russ. & M. 614, 620, said: 'I find,
from the note of what fell from Lord Eldon on the present appeal, that his
Lordship labored under considerable misapprehension as to the facts in Lolley's
case; he is represented as saying he will not admit that it is the settled law,
and that therefore he will not decide whether the marriage was or not prema-
turely determined by the Danish divorce. His words are, " I will not without
other assistance take upon myself to do so." Now, if it has not validly and by
the highest authorities in Westminster Hall been holden that a foreign divorce
cannot dissolve an English marriage, then nothing whatever has been established. For what was Lolley's case? It was a case the strongest possible in
favor of the doctrine contended for. It was not a question of civil right, but
of felony. Lolley had bona fide, and in a confident belief, founded on the authority of the Scotch lawyers, that the Scotch divorce had effectually dissolved
his prior English marriage, intermarried in England, living his first wife. He
was tried at Lancaster for bigamy, and found guilty; but the point was reserved, and was afterwards argued before all the most learned judges of the
day, who, after hearing the case fully and thoroughly discussed, first at Westminster Hall, and then at Serjeant's Inn, gave a clear and unanimous opinion,
that no divorce or proceeding in the nature of divorce in any foreign country,
Scotland included, could dissolve a marriage contracted in England; and they
sentenced Lolley to seven years' transportation. And he was accordingly sent
to the hulks for one or two years; though in mercy the residue of his sentence
was ultimately remitted. I take leave to say he ought not to have gone to the
hulks at all, because he had acted bona fide, though this did not prevent his
conviction from being legal. But he was sent notwithstanding, as if to show

gested however that Lord Eldon was not prepared to carry the doctrine to such a length; and certainly there was room in that case for a distinction, founded upon the fact that neither of the parties at the time of the suit for the divorce in Scotland had a bona fide domicil there, but that they both at that very time in fact had their domicil in England, where the marriage was had.[1] (a)

219. It has been stated by another learned judge, in a very recent case, that Lolley's Case turned upon the very distinction in point of jurisdiction between a temporary and fugitive residence for the purpose of a divorce, and bona fide change of domicil by the husband and wife animo manendi. And upon the ground of that distinction, in a case where there was no change of domicil, and the parties were not at any time bona fide domiciled in Scotland, he declared a Scottish divorce from an English marriage utterly void.[2] The language of his opinion is so important that it deserves to be quoted at large. 'A case,' says he, 'in which all the parties are domiciled in England, and resort is had to Scotland (with which neither of them have any connection) for no other purpose than to obtain a divorce a vinculo,

clearly that the judges were confident of the law they had laid down; so that never was there a greater mistake than to suppose that the remission argued the least doubt in the judges. Even if the punishment had been entirely remitted, the remission would have been on the ground that there had been no criminal intent, though that had been done which the law declares to be felony. I hold it to be perfectly clear therefore that Lolley's case stands as the settled law of Westminster Hall at this day. It has been uniformly recognized since; and in particular it was repeatedly made the subject of discussion before Lord Eldon himself, in the two appeals of Tovey v. Lindsay (1 Dow, 117, 131), in the House of Lords, when I furnished his lordship with a note of Lolley's case, which he followed in disposing of both those appeals, so far as it affected them. That case then settled two points; first, that no foreign proceeding in the nature of a divorce in an ecclesiastical court could effectually dissolve an English marriage; and secondly, that a Scotch divorce is not such a proceeding in an ecclesiastical court as to bring the case within the exception in the Bigamy Act (1 Jac. 1, c. 11, s. 2) for which nothing less than the sentence of an English ecclesiastical court is sufficient.' See also 2 Clark & Fin. 567, note, and Warrender v. Warrender, 9 Bligh, 89, 121, 124, 127; Id. 141–143; post, s. 229 a.

[1] Lolley's Case, Russ. & R., 237; 2 Clark & Fin. 567, note.
[2] Dr. Lushington, in Conway v. Beazley, 3 Hagg. Ecc. 639, 645–647, 653.

(a) See Shaw v. Gould, L. R. 3 H. L. 55, in 1868, where the subject underwent elaborate examination. And see Dolphin v. Robins, 7 H. L. C. 390; Shaw v. Att'y-Gen., Law Rep. 2 P. & D. 156; post, s. 227 a.

may properly be decided on principles which would not altogether apply to a case differently circumstanced ; as where, prior to the cause arising on account of which a divorce was sought, the parties had been bona fide domiciled in Scotland.   Unless I am satisfied that every view of this question had been taken, the court cannot, from the case referred to (Lolley's Case), assume it to have been established as an universal rule, that a marriage had in England, and originally valid by the law of England, cannot, under any possible circumstances, be dissolved by the decree of a foreign court.   Before I could give my assent to such a doctrine (not meaning to deny that it may be true), I must have a decision after argument upon such a case as I will now suppose, viz., a marriage in England, the parties resorting to a foreign country, becoming actually bona fide domiciled in that country, and then separated by a sentence of divorce pronounced by the competent tribunal of that country.   If a case of that description had occurred and had received the decision of the twelve judges, or the other high authority (a) to which allusion has been made, then indeed it might have set this important matter at rest; but I am not aware that that point has ever been distinctly raised, and I think I may say with certainty that it has never received any express decision. . . . I believe the course of decision in Scotland up to the present hour has been to consider that the Scotch courts have a right to entertain jurisdiction with respect to marriages had in England, after the parties have been residents for a certain period in Scotland, though that period had been infinitely too short to constitute what we should call a legal domicil, and that those courts have proceeded in such cases to divorce a vinculo. . . . It is obvious that many most important differences may arise in cases of this description.   Two Scotch persons married in England may afterwards go to reside in Scotland.   Again, one of the contracting parties may be English, the other Scotch.   If the law of Scotland continue such as their courts have hitherto held it to be, and if the decision in Lolley's Case be of universal application, the issue of the second marriage may be legitimate in Scotland and illegitimate in England.   The son may take the real estate in Scotland and not the real estate in England.   He might possibly be a Scotch peer and lose his

(a) Lord Brougham in M'Carthy v. Decaix, 2 Russ. & M. 614.

English title, and with it the English estates, the only support of his Scotch peerage.'[1]

220. *Scotch Law.* — Independent of the point of general jurisdiction, founded upon the fact of the domicil of both the parties, or at least of the party defendant in the suit for a divorce, which for a series of years was most elaborately discussed, and remained in a state of distressing uncertainty, as well as to the effect of a permanent domicil as to that of a temporary domicil to found a sentence of divorce, the Scottish courts have been called on to decide other questions of a broader character and involving more extensive consequences. In the first place, the general question already hinted at, whether an English marriage between English subjects, being indissoluble by the law of England, can under any possible circumstances be dissolved by a decree of divorce in Scotland. In the next place, whether a marriage in Scotland by English subjects, domiciled at the time in England, is dissoluble under any circumstances by a decree of divorce in Scotland. In the next place, whether in case of a marriage in England, it will make any difference that the parties are both Scotch persons, domiciled in Scotland, or afterwards become bona fide and permanently domiciled there.

221. Upon these questions the highest tribunals in Scotland have come to the following conclusions : First, that a marriage between English subjects in England, and indissoluble there, may be lawfully dissolved by the proper Scottish court for a cause of divorce good by the law of Scotland, when the parties are within the process and jurisdiction of the court ; or, in other words, that it is not a valid defence against an action of divorce in Scotland for adultery committed there, that the marriage was celebrated in England. Secondly, that a Scotch marriage by persons domiciled at the time in England, is dissoluble in like manner by the proper Scottish court ; or, in other words, that it is not a valid defence that the parties were domiciled in England when the marriage was celebrated in Scotland. Thirdly, that, in case of a marriage in England, it will make no difference that the parties are Scottish persons domiciled in Scotland, or are afterwards bona fide and permanently domiciled there ; or, in other words, that it is not a valid defence that the parties are Scottish persons, happen-

---

[1] Conway *v.* Beazley, 3 Hagg. Ecc. 645-647, 653.

ing to be in England when their marriage was celebrated, but who afterwards returned to Scotland, and cohabited, and continued domiciled there. The result of these opinions, the unanimous opinions of the judges of the Court of Session, is, that the mere fact of the marriage having been celebrated in England, whether it is between English parties or Scottish parties, or both, is not per se a defence against a suit of divorce for adultery committed there.[1]

222. The reasoning by which these opinions are maintained, as it may be gathered from comparing the arguments of the different judges, is to the following effect. The relation of husband and wife, wherever it may have been originally constituted and the parties thereto been connected, is entitled to the same protection and redress from the courts of justice in Scotland, as to wrongs committed in Scotland, which belong of right to that relation by the law of Scotland.[2] By marrying in England the parties do not become bound to reside for ever in England, or to treat one another in every other country where they may afterwards reside according to the law of England. Their obligation is to fulfil the duties of husband and wife to each other in every country to which they may be called in the course of Providence; and they neither promise, nor have they power to engage, that they will carry the law of England along with them to regulate what the duties and powers shall be which they shall fulfil and exercise, or the redress which the violation of those duties or abuse of those powers may entitle them to in all other countries. All these functions belong to the law of the country where they may eventually reside, and to which they unquestionably contract the duties of obedience and subjection whenever they enter its territories. Even if it had been the will of the parties by any stipulation, however express, to make the lex loci the law of their marriage, it would derive no force from that circumstance. An action of divorce could not be dismissed because the parties, when intermarrying, had in the most formal manner renounced the benefit of divorce, and had become bound that their marriage should be indissoluble. It would be no objection to a divorce at the instance of a Roman Catholic, that his marriage was to him a

---

[1] Cases of Edmonstone, Levett, and Forbes, Fergusson on Mar. & Div. 383, 392, 393; Id. 414, 415.

[2] Fergusson on Mar. & Div. 358.

sacrament, and therefore by its own nature indissoluble. These are all facta privatorum, and cannot impede or embarrass the steady, uniform course of the jus publicum, which with regard to the rights and obligations of individuals, affected by the three great domestic relations, enacts them from motives of political expediency and public morality, and in no wise confers them as private benefits, resulting from agreements concerning meum et tuum, which are capable of being modified and renounced at pleasure.[1]

223. If this supposed obligation of indissolubility resulting from contract can derive no force from the will of the parties, it cannot derive any from the dictates of the municipal law where the relation of marriage originated, so as to give it efficacy ultra territorium ; for the general rule is, Extra-territorium jus dicenti impune non paretur.[2] In the fulfilment of ordinary contracts, as to meum et tuum, the lex loci contractus forms an implied condition of the contract, and is accordingly adopted as furnishing the means of construing it aright. But this is merely a proceeding in execution of the will of the parties, and not in the least a recognition of the authority of a foreign law. The case is therefore quite different where the will of the parties only constitutes, and does not modify, the relation or its rights, and where of course the municipal law, deriving nothing from stipulation or agreement, is merely the positive institution of the sovereign, and cannot direct the decisions of foreign courts or the circumstances occurring within their own jurisdiction. Matrimonial rights and obligations, so far as they are juris gentium, admit of no modification by the will of parties ; and foreign courts are therefore in no wise called upon to inquire after that will, or after any municipal law to which it may correspond.[3]

224. Foreigners, equally with natives, while residents, are subject to the law here, and of course are under the protection of the law. The relations in which they stand towards one another, and which have been duly constituted before they came here, if they are relations recognized by all civilized nations, must be observed ; and the obligations created by them must be fulfilled agreeably to the dictates of the law of Scotland. If the law re-

[1] Fergusson on Mar. & Div. 359, 360; Id. 398, 399, 402.
[2] Ante. s. 8; Dig. 2, 1, 20.
[3] Fergusson on Mar. & Div. 360, 361, 402, 410, 412, 414.

fused to apply its rules to the relation of husband and wife, parent and child, master and servant, among foreigners in this country, Scotland could not be deemed a civilized country; as thereby it would permit a numerous description of persons to traverse it, and violate with utter impunity all the obligations on which the principal comforts of human life depend. If it assumed jurisdiction, but applied not its own rules, but the rules of the law of a foreign country, the supremacy of the law of Scotland within its own territories would be compromised; its arrangements for domestic comfort would be violated, confounded, and perplexed; and the powers of foreign courts, unknown to its law and constitution, would be usurped and exercised.[1] In every country the laws relative to divorce are considered of the utmost importance, as positive laws affecting the domestic interests of society; and in some places they are treated as of divine authority.[2] A party domiciled here cannot be permitted to import into this country a law peculiar to his own case and in opposition to those great and important public laws which are held to be connected with the best interests of society.[3]

225. *English Law.* — That there is great force in this reasoning cannot well be denied. For a long time it did not obtain any positive sanction in England; but as far as judicial opinions went, they were against the doctrine that an English marriage is dissoluble by a Scottish divorce.[4] The reasoning by which this latter view was sustained, was to the following effect. The law of the place where the marriage is celebrated furnishes a just rule for the interpretation of its obligations and rights, as it does in the case of other contracts which are held obligatory according to the lex loci contractus.[5] It is not just that one party should be able at his option to dissolve a contract by a law different from that under which it was formed, and by which the other party understood it to be governed. If any other rule than the lex loci contractus is adopted, the law of marriage, on which the happiness of society so mainly depends, must be completely loose and

---

[1] Id. 57, 58, 414, 418.

[2] Id. 398, 402, 403; ante, s. 108, 210.

[3] Id. 399, 400, 412, 418.

[4] Lolley's Case, Russ. & R. p. 237; Tovey *v.* Lindsay, 1 Dow, 124; M'Carthy *v.* Decaix, 3 Hagg. Ecc. 642, note; 2 Russ. & M. 614, 620; 2 Kent Com. 116, 117.

[5] Fergusson on Mar. & Div. 283–285, 311–313, 318, 325, 335, 389.

unsettled ;[1] and the marriage state, whose indissolubility is so much favored by Christianity and by the best interests of society, will become subject to the mere will and almost to the caprice of the parties as to its duration.   The courts of the nations whose laws are most lax upon this subject will be constantly resorted to for the purpose of procuring divorces; and thus not only frauds will be encouraged, but the common cause of morality and religion be seriously injured, and conjugal virtue and parental affection become corrupted and debased.[2]   Thus, a dissatisfied party might resort to one foreign country, where incompatibility of temper is a ground of divorce, or to another which admits of divorce upon even more frivolous pretences, or upon the mere consent of both, or even of one of the parties.

226. In this manner a nation may find its own inhabitants throwing off all obedience to its own laws and institutions, and subverting, by the interposition of a foreign tribunal, its own fundamental policy.   Nay, a stronger case may be put of a marriage deemed as a sacrament, indissoluble by the public religion of a nation, which is yet dissolved at the will of a foreign nation, in violation of the highest of all human duties, a perfect obedience to the divine law.   There is no solid ground upon which any government can be held to yield up its own fundamental laws and policy as to its own subjects, in favor of the laws or acts of other countries.   Parties contracting in a country where marriage is indissoluble voluntarily submit to the jurisdiction and laws of that country, if they are foreigners domiciled there.   If they are natural subjects they are bound by the laws of the country in virtue of the general duty of allegiance.   Why then should England permit her subjects, by a foreign domicil, to escape from the indissolubility of a marriage contracted in England, and thus permit them to defeat a fundamental policy of the realm?[3]   Such is a summary of the reasoning on each side of this vexed question.

226 a. This whole subject however recently came before the House of Lords in England, upon an appeal from the Court of Session in Scotland, in which the direct question was, whether it

---

[1] Id. 283, 298, 312.   [2] Id. 103, 104, 283, 284, 318, 319, 353, 355, 356.

[3] Mr. Chancellor Kent has given an excellent summary of the reasoning on each side in his Commentaries, 2 Kent Com. 110–117. My own duty required me to follow out his doctrine by some additional sketches.

was competent for the Scottish courts to decree a divorce between parties domiciled in Scotland, who were married in England. The facts of the case in substance were these: A Scotchman domiciled in Scotland was married to an Englishwoman in England; and by their marriage contract a jointure was secured to her in his Scottish estates. After their marriage they went to Scotland, and resided there a short time, and then returned to England. They afterwards in England executed articles of separation, by which a separate maintenance was secured to the wife during her separation. Immediately afterwards the wife went abroad, and has ever since resided abroad. The husband continued to be domiciled in Scotland, where he brought a suit for a divorce against his wife, founded upon the charge of adultery. The preliminary question presented was, whether, even assuming the parties to be domiciled in Scotland, the suit could be maintained in Scotland for a divorce from an English marriage, which was by the law of England indissoluble. The Court of Session affirmed the jurisdiction to decree the divorce; and this decree was upon the appeal confirmed by the House of Lords.[1]

226 b. Very elaborate judgments were delivered by Lord Brougham and Lord Lyndhurst upon this occasion. The direct point decided was, that the courts of Scotland had by the laws of Scotland a clear jurisdiction to decree a divorce in such a case between parties actually domiciled in Scotland, notwithstanding the marriage was contracted in England; and that the House of Lords, sitting as a court of appeal in a case coming from Scotland, was bound to administer the law of Scotland. The court did not however decide what effect that divorce would have or ought to have in England, if it should be brought in question in an English court of justice.[2] Lolley's Case was a good deal discussed; and, without being overturned as to its professed general doctrine, must be now deemed to be greatly shaken, except as a decision upon its own peculiar circumstances.

226 c. But although the general question as to the indissolubility of an English marriage, so far at least as it could arise in England upon a litigation there, was left undecided, Lord Brougham in delivering his judgment went into an elaborate examination of the general principles of international law upon

[1] Warrender v. Warrender, 9 Bligh, 89; 2 Cl. & F. 488.
[2] Ibid.

this subject. It cannot therefore but be acceptable to the learned reader to have in the subjoined note a summary of the reasoning by which this distinguished judge maintained the opinion that, upon principles of public law, a divorce from an English marriage, made by a competent court of a foreign country where the parties are domiciled, ought to be deemed in England to dissolve the marriage, and to confer upon the parties all the rights arising from a lawful dissolution.[1]

[1] His lordship's reasoning was in substance to the following effect (9 Bligh, 110): ' The general principle is denied by no one, that the lex loci is to be the governing rule in deciding upon the validity or invalidity of all personal contracts. This is sometimes expressed, and I take leave to say inaccurately expressed, by saying that there is a comitas shown by the tribunals of one country towards the laws of the other country. Such a thing as comitas or courtesy may be said to exist in certain cases, as where the French courts inquire how our law would deal with a Frenchman in similar or parallel circumstances, and, upon proof of it, so deal with an Englishman in those circumstances. This is truly a comitas, and can be explained upon no other ground; and I must be permitted to say, with all respect for the usage, it is not easily reconcilable to any sound reason. But when the courts of one country consider the laws of another in which any contract has been made, or alleged to have been made, in construing its meaning or ascertaining its existence, they can hardly be said to act from courtesy, ex comitate, for it is of the essence of the subject-matter to ascertain the meaning of the parties, and that they did solemnly bind themselves; and it is clear that you must presume them to have intended what the law of the country sanctions or supposes, and equally clear that their adopting the forms and solemnities which that law prescribes, shows their intention to bind themselves, — nay more, it is the only safe criterion of their having entertained such an intention. Therefore the courts of the country where the question arises resort to the law of the country where the contract was made, not ex comitate, but ex debito justitiæ; and in order to explicate their own jurisdiction by discovering that which they are in quest of, and which alone they are in quest of, the meaning and intent of the parties. But whatever may be the foundation of the principle, its acceptance in all systems of jurisprudence is unquestionable. Thus, a marriage, good by the laws of one country, is held good in all others where the question of its validity may arise. For why? The question always must be, Did the parties intend to contract marriage? And if they did what in the place they were in is deemed a marriage, they cannot reasonably, or sensibly, or safely, be considered otherwise than as intending a marriage contract. The laws of each nation lay down the forms and solemnities, a compliance with which shall be deemed the only criterion of the intention to enter into the contract. If those laws annex certain qualifications to parties circumstanced in a particular way, or if they impose certain conditions precedent on certain parties, this falls exactly within the same rule; for the presumption of law is, in the one case, that the parties are absolutely incapable of the consent required to make the contract, and, in the other case, that they are incapable until they have complied with the conditions imposed. I shall only stop here to remark that the Eng-

227. *Questions raised.*—If in any nation the doctrine shall ever be established in regard to marriages, that the law of the place

lish jurisprudence, while it adopts this principle in words, would not perhaps, in certain cases which may be put, be found very willing to act upon it throughout. Thus, we should expect that the Spanish and Portuguese courts would hold an English marriage avoidable between uncle and niece, or brother and sister-in-law, though solemnized under papal dispensation, because it would clearly be avoidable in this country. But I strongly incline to think that our courts would refuse to sanction, and would avoid by sentence, a marriage between those relatives contracted in the Peninsula under dispensation, although beyond all doubt such a marriage would there be valid by the lex loci contractus, and incapable of being set aside by any proceedings in that country. But the rule extends, I apprehend, no further than to the ascertaining of the validity of the contract and the meaning of the parties, that is, the existence of the contract and its construction. If indeed there go two things under one and the same name in different countries, — if that which is called marriage is of a different nature in each, — there may be some room for holding that we are to consider the thing to which the parties have bound themselves, according to its legal acceptation in the country where the obligation was contracted. But marriage is one and the same thing substantially all the Christian world over. Our whole law of marriage assumes this; and it is important to observe that we regard it as a wholly different thing, a different status, from Turkish or other marriages among infidel nations, because we clearly never should recognize the plurality of wives, and consequent validity of second marriages, standing the first, which second marriages the laws of those countries authorize and validate. This cannot be put upon any rational ground, except our holding the infidel marriage to be something different from the Christian, and our also holding Christian marriage to be the same everywhere.' Therefore all that the courts of one country have to determine is, whether or not the thing called marriage, that known relation of persons, that relation which those courts are acquainted with, and know how to deal with, has been validly contracted in the other country where the parties professed to bind themselves. If the question is answered in the affirmative, a marriage has been had, the relation has been constituted; and those courts will deal with the rights of the parties under it according to the principles of the municipal law which they administer. But it is said that what is called the *essence* of the contract must also be judged of according to the lex loci; and as this is somewhat vague, and for its vagueness a somewhat suspicious proposition, it is rendered more certain by adding that dissolubility or indissolubility is of the essence of the contract. Now I take this to be really petitio principii. It is putting the very question under discussion into another form of words, and giving the answer in one way. There are many other things which may just as well be reckoned of the essence as this. If it is said that the parties marrying in England must be taken all the world over to have bound themselves to live until death or an act of parliament them "do part," why shall it not also be said that they have bound themselves to live together on such terms, and with such mutual personal rights and duties, as the English law recognizes and enforces? Those rights and duties are just as much of the essence as dissolubility or indissolubility; and yet all admit, all must admit, that persons married in England and settled in Scotland will be entitled only to the personal rights which the Scotch law sanctions,

of its actual celebration shall prevail, not only as to its original
validity, but also as to its mode of dissolution, some other inter-

and will only be liable to perform the duties which the Scotch law imposes. Indeed, if we are to regard the nature of the contract in this respect as defined by
the lex loci, it is difficult to see why we may not import from Turkey into England a marriage of such a nature as that it is capable of being followed by and
subsisting with another, polygamy being there of the essence of the contract. The
fallacy of the argument "that indissolubility is of the essence" appears plainly
to be this: it confounds incidents with essence; it makes the rights under a
contract, or flowing from and arising out of it, parcel of the contract; it makes
the mode in which judicatures deal with those rights and with the contract
itself part of the contract; instead of considering, as in all soundness of principle we ought, that the contract and all its incidents, and the rights of the
parties to it, and the wrongs committed by them respecting it, must be dealt
with by the courts of the country where the parties reside, and where the contract is to be carried into execution. But at all events this is clear, and it
seems decisive of the point that if on some such ground as this a marriage
indissoluble by the lex loci is held to be indissoluble everywhere, so, conversely, a marriage dissoluble by the lex loci must be held everywhere dissoluble. The one proposition is in truth identical with the other. Now it
would follow from hence, or rather it is the same proposition, that a marriage
contracted in Scotland, where it is dissoluble by reason of adultery or of non-
adherence, is dissoluble in England, and that at the suit of either party.
Therefore a wife married in Scotland might sue her husband in our courts
for adultery or for absenting himself four years, and ought to obtain a divorce
a vinculo matrimonii. Nay, if the marriage had been solemnized in Prussia,
either party might obtain a divorce on the ground of incompatibility of temper; and if it had been solemnized in France during the earlier period of the
Revolution, the mere consent of the parties ought to suffice for dissolving it
here. Indeed, another consequence would follow from this doctrine of confounding with the nature of the contract that which is only a matter touching
the jurisdiction of the courts, and their power of dealing with the rights and
duties to it. If there were a country in which marriage could be dissolved
without any judicial proceeding at all, merely by the parties agreeing in pais
to separate, every other country ought to sanction a separation had in pais
there, and uphold a second marriage contracted after such separation. It may
safely be asserted that so absurd a proposition never could for a moment
be entertained; and yet it is not like, but identical with, the proposition upon
which the main body of the appellant's argument rests, that the question of
indissoluble or dissoluble must be decided in all cases by the lex loci. Hitherto we have been considering the contract as to its nature and solemnities,
and examining how far, being English, and entered into with reference only
to England, it could be dissolved by a Scotch sentence of divorce. But the
circumstances of parties belonging to one country marrying in another (which
is the case at bar) presents the question in another light. In personal contracts much depends upon the parties having regard to the country where it is
to be acted under and to receive its execution — upon their making the contract
with a view to its execution in that country. The marriage contract is emphatically one which parties make with an immediate view to the usual place of
their residence. An Englishman marrying in Turkey contracts a marriage of

esting questions will still remain for decision.   In the first place, will any foreign court have a right to entertain jurisdiction to

an English kind, that is, excluding plurality of wives, because he is an Eng- lishman, and only residing in Turkey and under the Mahometan law acciden- tally and temporarily, and because he marries with a view of being a married man and having a wife in England and for English purposes; consequently the incidents and effects, nay, the very nature and essence (to use the lan- guage of the appellant's argument) must be ascertained by the English and not by the Turkish law.   So of an Englishman marrying in Prussia, where incompatible temper, that is, disagreement, may dissolve the contract.   As he marries with a view to English domicil his contract will be judged by English law, and he cannot apply for a divorce here upon the ground of incompatible tempers.   In like manner a domiciled Scotchman may be said to contract not an English but a Scotch marriage, though the consent wherein it consists may be testified by English solemnities.   The Scotch parties, looking to residence and rights in Scotland, may be held to regard the nature and incidents and consequences of the contract, according to the law of that country, their home ; a connection formed for cohabitation for mutual comfort, protection and en- dearment, appears to be a contract having a most peculiar reference to the con- templated residence of the wedded pair; the home where they are to fulfil their mutual promises, and peform those duties which were the objects of the union; in a word, their domicil; the place so beautifully described by the civilian, "'Locus, ubi quisque larem suum posuit sedemque fortunarum suarum, unde cum proficiscitur peregrinare videtur, quo cum revertitur redire domum." It certainly may well be urged, both with a view to the general question of lex loci, and especially in answering the argument of the alleged essential quality of indissolubility, that the parties to a contract like this must be held empha- tically to enter into it with a reference to their own domicil and its laws ; that the contract assumes as it were a local aspect, but that at any rate, if we infer the nature of any mutual obligation from the presumed intentions of the parties, and if we presume those intentions from supposing that the parties had a particular system of laws in their eye (the only foundation of the argu- ment for the appellant), there is fully more reason to suppose they had the law of their own home in their view, where they purposed to live, than the law of the stranger under which they happened for the moment to be.

' Suppose we take now another but a very obvious and intelligible view of the subject, and regard the divorce not as a remedy given to the injured party by freeing him from the chain that binds him to a guilty partner, but as a punishment inflicted upon crime for the purpose of preventing its repetition, and thus keeping public morals pure.   The language of the Scotch acts plainly countenances this view of the matter, and we may observe how strongly it bears upon the present question.   No one can doubt that every state has the right to visit offences with such penalties as to its legislative wisdom shall seem meet.   At one time adultery was punishable capitally in England; it is so in certain cases still by the letter of the Scotch law.   Whoever committed it must have suffered that punishment had the law been enforced, and without regard to the marriage of which he had violated the duties having been con- tracted abroad.   Indeed, in executing such statutes no one ever heard of a question being raised as to where the contract had been made.   Suppose again that the proposition frequently made in modern times were adopted,

decree a divorce for causes justified by the law of the matrimonial domicil? Will the like right exist where no divorce is grantable

and adultery were declared to be a misdemeanor, could any one, tried for it either here or in Scotland, set up in his defence, that to the law of the country where he was married there was no such offence known? In like manner if a disruption of the marriage tie is the punishment denounced against the adulterer for disregarding its duties, no one can pretend that the tie being declared indissoluble by the laws of the country where it was knit, could afford the least defence against the execution of the law declaring its dissolution to be the penalty of the crime. Whoever maintains that the Scotch courts are to take cognizance of the English law of indissolubility, when called upon to inflict the penalty of divorce, must likewise be prepared to hold that, in punishing any other offence, the same courts are to regard the laws of the state where the culprit was born, or where part of the transaction passed; that, for example, a forgery being committed on a foreign bill of exchange, the punishment awarded by the foreign law is to regulate the visitation of the offence under the law of Scotland. It may safely be asserted that no instance whatever can be given of the criminal law of any country being made to bend to that of any other in any part of its administration. When the Roman citizen carried abroad with him his rights of citizenship, and boasted that he could plead in all the courts of the world, "civis Romanus sum," his boast was founded not on any legal principle, but upon the fact that his barbarian countrymen had overrun the world with their arms, reduced all laws to silence, and annihilated the independence of foreign legislatures. Their orators regarded this very plea as the badge of universal slavery which their warriors had fixed upon mankind. But if any foreigner had come to Rome and committed a crime punishable with loss of civil rights, he would in vain have pleaded in bar of the capitis diminutio, that citizenship was indelible and indestructible in the country of his birth. The lex loci must needs govern all criminal jurisdiction from the nature of the thing and the purposes of that jurisdiction. How then can we say that, when the Scotch law pronounces the dissolution of a marriage to be the punishment of adultery, the Scotch courts can be justified in importing an exception in favor of those who had contracted an English marriage; an exception created by the English law, and to the Scotch law unknown? But it may be said that the offence being committed abroad, and not within the Scotch territory, prevents the application to it of the Scotch criminal law. To this it may however be answered that where a person has his domicil in a given country, the laws of that country to which he owes allegiance may visit even criminally offences committed by him out of his territory. Of this we have many instances in our own jurisprudence. Murder and treason committed by Englishmen abroad are triable in England and punishable here. Nay, by the bill which I introduced in 1811, and which is constantly acted upon, British subjects are liable to be convicted of felony for slave-trading in whatever part of the world committed by them. It would no doubt be going far to hold the wife criminally answerable to the law of Scotland in respect of her legal domicil being Scotch. But we are here not so much arguing to the merits of this case, which has abundant other ground to rest upon, as to the general principle; and at any rate the argument would apply to the case most frequently mooted, of English married parties living temporarily in Scotland, and adultery being there committed by one of them.

by the lex loci for a similar cause in case of a domestic marriage? For instance, could a Consistory Court of England entertain a

To such a state of facts the whole argument now adduced is applicable in its full force; and without admitting that application I do not well see how we can hold that the Scotch legislature ever possessed that supreme power which is absolutely essential to the very nature and existence of a legislature. If we deny this application, we truly admit that the Scottish parliament had no right to punish the offence of adultery by the penalty of divorce. Nay, we hold that English parties had a right to violate the Scotch criminal law with perfect impunity in one essential particular; for, suppose no other penalty had been provided by the Scotch law, except divorce, all English offenders against that law must go unpunished. Nay, worse still, all Scotch parties who chose to avoid the punishment had only to marry in England, and then the law, the criminal law of their own country, became inoperative. The gross absurdity of this strikes me as bearing directly upon the argument, and as greater than that of any consequences which I remember to have seen deduced from almost any disputed position. It may further be remarked that this argument applies equally to the case, if we admit that the Scotch divorce is invalid out of Scotland, and consequently that it stands well with even the principles of Lolley's Case. In order to dispose of the present question, it is not at all necessary on the one side to support, or on the other to impeach, the authority of Lolley's Case, or of any other which may have been determined in England upon that authority. This ought to be steadily borne in mind. The resolution in Lolley's Case was that an English marriage could not be dissolved by any proceeding in the courts of any other country for English purposes; in other words, that the courts of this country will not recognize the validity of the Scotch divorce, but will hold the divorced wife dowable of an English estate, the divorced husband tenant thereof by the curtesy, and either party guilty of felony by contracting a second marriage in England. Upon the force and effect of such a divorce in Scotland, and for Scotch purposes, the judges gave, and indeed could give, no opinion; and as there would be nothing legally impossible in a marriage being good in one country which was prohibited by the law of another, so, if the conflict of the Scotch and English law be complete and irreconcilable, there is nothing legally impossible in a divorce being valid in the one country which the courts of the other may hold to be a nullity. Lolley's Case therefore cannot be held to decide the present, perhaps not even to affect it in principle. In another point of view it is inapplicable; for, though the decision was not put upon any special circumstance, yet, in fairly considering its application, we cannot lay out of view that the parties were not only married, but really domiciled in England, and had resorted to Scotland for the manifest purpose of obtaining a temporary and fictitious domicil there, in order to give the Scotch courts jurisdiction over them, and enable them to dissolve their marriage; whereas here the domicil of the parties is Scotch, and the proceeding is bona fide taken by the husband in the courts of his own country, to which he is amenable and ought to have free access, and no fraud upon the law of any other country is practised by the suit. It must be added that, in Lolley's Case, the English marriage had been contracted by English parties, without any view to the execution of the contract at any time in Scotland; whereas the marriage now in question was had by a Scotchman and a woman whom the contract made Scotch, and therefore may be held to have

suit for a divorce a vinculo, for the cause of adultery, in case of
a Scottish marriage? Or in such cases is the remedy to be ex-

contemplated an execution and effects in Scotland. But although, for these
reasons, the support of my opinion does not require that I should dispute the
law in Lolley's Case, I should not be dealing fairly with this important question if I were to avoid touching upon that subject; and as no decision of this
house has ever adopted that rule, or assumed its principle for sound, and acted
upon it, I am entitled here to express the difficulty which I feel in acceding to
that doctrine, — a difficulty which much deliberation and frequent discussion
with the greatest lawyers of the age — I might say both of this and of the last
age — has not been able to remove from my mind. If no decision had ever
been pronounced in this country, recognizing the validity of Scotch marriages
between English parties going to Scotland with the purpose of escaping from the
authority of the English law, I should have felt it much easier to acquiesce in
the decision of which I am speaking. For then it might have been said consistently enough that whatever may be the Scotch marriage law among its
own subjects, and for the government of Scotch questions, ours is in an irreconcilable conflict with it, and we cannot permit the positive enactments of
our statute book, and the principles of our common law, to be violated or
eluded by merely crossing a river or an ideal boundary line. Nor could anything have been more obvious than the consistency of those who, holding that
no unmarried parties incapable of marrying here can, in fraud of our law, contract a valid marriage in Scotland by going there for an hour, should also hold
the cognate doctrine that no married parties can dissolve an English marriage
indissoluble here, by repairing thither for six weeks. But upon this firm
ground the decisions of all the English courts have long since prevented us
from taking our stand. They have held, both the Consistorial judges in
Compton v. Bearcroft and those of the common law in Ilderton v. Ilderton, the
doctrine uniformly recognized in all subsequent cases, and acted upon daily by
the English people, that a Scotch marriage, contracted by English parties in
the face and in fraud of the English law, is valid to all intents and purposes, and
carries all the real and all the personal rights of an English marriage, affecting
in its consequences land and honors and duties and privileges, precisely as it does
the most lawful and solemn matrimonial contract entered into among ourselves,
in our own churches, according to our ritual, and under our own statutes. It
is quite impossible after this to say that we can draw the line and hold a foreign
law, which we acknowledge all powerful for making the binding contract, to be
utterly impotent to dissolve it. Were the sentence of the Scotch court in a
declarator of marriage to be given in evidence here, it would be conclusive
that the parties were man and wife, and no exception could be taken to the
admissibility or the effect of the foreign evidence upon the ground of the parties having been English, and repaired to Scotland for the purpose of escaping
the provisions of the English law. A similar sentence of the same court
declaring the marriage to be dissolved by the same law of Scotland, is now
supposed to be given in evidence between parties who had married in England. Can it in any consistency of reason be objected to the reception or to
the force of this sentence that the contract had been made, and the parties
had resided here? In what other contract of a nature merely personal, in what
other transaction between men, is such a rule ever applied, such an arbitrary
and gratuitous distinction made, such an exception raised to the universal

clusively pursued in the domestic forum of the marriage? Whoever shall diligently consider these questions will not find them

position, that things are to be dissolved by the same process whereby they are
bound together; or rather, that the tie is to be loosened by reversing the operation which knit it, but reversing the operation according to the same rules?
What gave force to the ligament? If a contract for sale of a chattel is made,
or an obligation of debt is incurred, or a chattel is pledged in one country, the
sale may be annulled, the debt released, and the pledge redeemed by the law
and by the forms of another country in which the parties happen to reside,
and in whose courts their rights and obligations come in question, unless there
was an express stipulation in the contract itself against such voidance, release,
or redemption. But at any rate this is certain, that if the laws of one country
and its courts recognize and give effect to those of another, in respect of the
constitution of any contract, they must give the like recognition and effect to
those same foreign laws when they declare the same kind of contract dissolved.
Suppose a party forbidden to purchase from another by our equity as administered in the courts of this country (and we have some restraints upon certain
parties which come very near prohibition), and suppose a sale of chattels by
one to another party standing in this relation towards each other should be
effected in Scotland, and that our courts here should, whether right or wrong,
recognize such a rule because the Scotch law would affirm it, surely it would
follow that our courts must equally recognize a rescission of the contract of
sale in Scotland by any act which the Scotch law regards as valid to rescind it,
although our own law may not regard it as sufficient. Suppose a question to
arise in the courts of England respecting the execution of a contract thus
made in this country, and that the objection of its invalidity were waived for
some reason; if the party resisting its execution were to produce either a sentence of a Scotch court declaring it rescinded by a Scotch matter done in pais,
or were merely to produce evidence of the thing so done, and proof of its
amounting by the Scotch law to a rescission of the contract, I apprehend that
the party relying on the contract could never be heard to say, " The contract
is English, and the Scotch proceeding is impotent to dissolve it." The reply
would be, " Our English courts have, whether right or wrong, recognized the
validity of a Scotch proceeding to complete the obligation, and can no longer
deny the validity of a similar but reverse proceeding to dissolve it, — unumquodque dissolvitur eodem modo, quo colligatur." Suppose, for another
example (which is the case), that the law of this country precluded an infant,
or a married woman, from borrowing money in any way, or from binding
themselves by deed; and that in another country those obligations could be
validly incurred; it is probable that our law and our courts would recognize
the validity of such foreign obligations. But suppose a feme covert had
executed a power and conveyed an interest under it to another feme covert in
England, could it be endured that, where the donee of the power produced a
release under seal from the feme covert in the same foreign country, a distinction should be taken, and the court here should hold that party incapable of
releasing the obligation? Would it not be said that our courts, having
decided the contract of a feme covert to be binding when executed abroad,
must, by parity of reason, hold the discharge or release of the feme covert to
be valid, if it be valid in the same foreign country? Nor can any attempt
succeed, in this argument, which rests upon distinctions taken between mar-

without serious embarrassment.　They are incidentally treated in
the Scottish decisions already alluded to, and the reasoning on

riage and other contracts, on the ground that its effects govern the enjoyment
of real rights in England, and that the English law alone can regulate the
rights of landed property.　For, not to mention that a Scotch marriage between English parties gives English honors and estates to its issue, which
would have been bastard had the parties married or pretended to marry in
England, all personal obligations may in their consequences affect real rights
in England.　Nor does a Scotch divorce, by depriving a widow of dower, or
arrears of pin money charged on English property, more immediately affect
real estate here, than a bond or a judgment released in Scotland according to
Scotch forms discharges real estate of a lien, or than a bond executed, or indeed a simple contract debt incurred in Scotland, eventually and consequentially charges English real estate.　It appears to me quite certain that those
who decided Lolley's Case did not look sufficiently to the difficulty of following out the principle of the rule which they laid down.　At first sight, on a
cursory survey of the question, there seems no impediment in the way of a
judge who would keep the English marriage contract indissoluble in Scotland,
and yet allow a Scotch marriage to have validity in England; for it does not
immediately appear how the dissolution and the constitution of the contract
should come in conflict, though diametrically opposite principles are applied
to each.　But only mark how that conflict arises, and how, in fact and in
practice it must needs arise as long as the diversity of the rules applied is
maintained.　When English parties are divorced in Scotland it seems easy to
say, " We give no validity to this proceeding in England, leaving the Scotch
law to deal with it in that country; and with its awards we do not in any wise
interfere."　But the time speedily arrives when we can no longer refuse to
interfere, and then see the inextricable confusion that instantly arises and
involves the whole subject.　The English parties are divorced, — they return
to England, and one of them marries again; that party is met by Lolley's Case,
and treated as a felon.　So far all is smooth.　But what if the second marriage
is contracted in Scotland?　And what if the issue of that marriage claims an
English real estate by descent, or a widow demands her dower?　Lolley's Case
will no longer serve the purpose of deciding the rights of the parties; for Lolley's Case is confined to the effects of the Scotch divorce in England, and professes not to touch, as indeed they who decided it had no authority to touch,
the validity of that divorce in Scotland.　Then the marriage being Scotch, the
lex loci must prevail by the cases of Compton v. Bearcroft, and Ilderton v.
Ilderton.　All its consequences to the wife and issue must be dealt with by
the English courts, and the same judge who, sitting under a commission of
gaol delivery, has in the morning sent Mr. Lolley to the hulks for felony,
because he remarried in England, and the divorce was insufficient, sitting at
nisi prius in the afternoon, must give the issue of Mr. Lolley's second marriage an estate in Yorkshire, because he remarried in Scotland, and must
give it on the precise ground that the divorce was effectual.　Thus the
divorce is both valid and nugatory, not according to its own nature or
the law of any one state, but according to the accident, whether a transaction which follows upon it, and does not necessarily occur at all, chanced
to take place in one part of the island or in the other; and yet the
felony of the husband depended entirely upon his not having been divorced

each side is worthy of an exact perusal.[1]   The attempt to engraft
foreign remedial justice upon domestic institutions has always

validly in Scotland, and not at all upon his not being divorced validly in
England; and the title of the wife's issue to the succession, or of herself to
dower, depends wholly upon the same husband having been validly divorced
in that same country of Scotland.   Nor will it avail to contend that the parties
marrying in Scotland, after a Scotch divorce, is in fraud of the English rule
as laid down in that celebrated case.   It may be so; but it is not more in fraudem legis Anglicanæ than the marriage was in Compton v. Bearcroft (Bull.
N.P. 113), which yet has been held good in all our courts.   Neither will it
avail to argue that the indissoluble nature of the English marriage prevents
those parties from marrying again in Scotland as well as in England; for the
rule in Lolley's Case has no greater force in disqualifying parties from marrying in Scotland, where that is not the rule of law, than the English marriage
act has in disqualifying infants from marrying without banns published, and
yet these may, by the law of England, go and marry validly in Scotland.   Indeed, if there be any purely personal disqualification or incapacity caused by
the law, and which, more than any other, may be said to travel about with the
party, it is that which the law raises upon a natural status, as that of infancy,
and fixes on those who, by the order of nature itself, are in that condition,
and unable to shake it off, or by an hour to accelerate its termination.   If, in
a manner confessedly not clear, and very far from being unincumbered with
doubt and difficulty, we find that manifest and serious inconvenience is sure to
result from one view, and very little in comparison from adopting the opposite
course, nothing can be a stronger reason for taking the latter.   Now surely it
strikes every one, that the greatest hardships must occur to parties, the greatest embarrassment to their rights, and the utmost inconvenience to the courts
of justice in both countries, by the rule being maintained as laid down in
Lolley's Case: the greatest hardship to parties — for what can be a greater
grievance than that parties living bona fide in England, though temporarily,
should either not be allowed to marry at all during their residence here, or if
they do, and afterwards return to their own country, however great its distance,
that they must be deprived of all remedy in case of misconduct, however ag-
gravated, unless they undertake a voyage back to England, ay, and unless they
can comply with the parliamentary forms in serving notices? the greatest embarrassment to their rights — for what can be more embarrassing than that a
person's status should be involved in uncertainty, and should be subject to
change its nature, as he goes from place to place; that he should be married in
one country, and single, if not a felon, in another; bastard here, and legitimate
there? the utmost inconvenience to the courts — for what inconvenience can
be greater than that they should have to regard a person as married for one
purpose and not for another, single and a felon if he marries a few yards to
the southward, lawfully married if the ceremony be performed a few yards to
the north, a bastard when he claims land, legitimate when he sues for personal
succession, widow when she demands the chattels of her husband, his concu-
bine when she counts as dowable of his land?   It is in vain to remind us of
the opportunity which a strict adherence to the lex loci, with respect to dissolution of the contract, would give to violators of our English marriage law.

[1] See Fergusson on Mar. & Div. Appx. 383–422.

been found extremely difficult, and as we shall hereafter see has led to the conclusion, that the safest and best rule is to give

This objection comes too late. Before the validity of Scotch marriages had been supported by decisions too numerous and too old for any question, this argument ab inconvenienti might have been urged and set against those other reasons which I have adduced, drawn from the same consideration. But we have it now firmly established as the law of the land, and daily acted upon by persons of every condition, that, though the law of England incapacitates parties from contracting marriage here, they may go for a few minutes to the Scotch border, and be married as effectually as if they had no incapacity whatever in their own country, and then return, after eluding the law, to set its prohibitions at defiance without incurring any penalty, and to obtain its aid without any difficulty in securing the enjoyment of all the rights incident to the married state. Surely there is neither sense nor consistency in complaining of the risk, infraction, or evasion arising to the English law from supporting Scotch *divorces*, after having thus given to the Scotch *marriages* the power of eluding, and breaking, and defying that law for so many years.

' I have now been commenting upon Lolley's Case on its own principle, that is, regarding it as merely laying down a rule for England, and prescribing how a Scotch divorce shall be considered in this country, and dealt with by its courts. I have felt this the more necessary, because I do not see, for the reasons which have occasionally been adverted to in treating the other argument, how, consistently with any principle, the judges who decided the case could limit its application to England, and think that it did not decide also on the validity of the divorce in Scotland. They certainly could not hold the second English marriage invalid and felonious in England, without assuming that the Scotch divorce was void even in Scotland. In my view of the present question, therefore, it was fit to show that the Scotch courts have a good title to consider the principle of Lolley's Case erroneous even as an English decision. This, it is true, their lordships have not done ; and the judgment now under appeal is rested upon the ground of the Scotch divorce being sufficient to determine the marriage contract in Scotland only. I must now observe that, supposing (as may fairly be concluded) Lolley's Case to have decided that the divorce is void in Scotland, there can be no ground whatever for holding that it is binding upon the Scotch courts on a question of Scotch law. If the cases and the authorities of that law are against it, the learned persons who administer the system of jurisprudence are not bound to regard, nay, they are not entitled to regard, an English decision, framed by English judges upon an English case, and devoid of all authority beyond the Tweed. Now I have no doubt at all that the Scotch authorities are in favor of the jurisdiction and support the decision under appeal. But I must premise that, unless it could be shown that they were the other way, my mind is made up with respect to the principle, and I should be for affirming on that ground of principle alone, if precedent or dicta did not displace the argument. The principle I hold so clear, upon grounds of general law, that the proof is thrown, according to my view, upon those who would show the Scotch law to be the other way.'

I have given his lordship's reasoning at large, because it seemed difficult to admit particular passages which have been already cited, or will be cited hereafter in other connections, without impairing its true force. Ante, s. 115; post, s. 259 *b*.

20

remedies only to the extent and in the manner which the lex loci justifies and approves.[1]

228. In America questions respecting the nature and effect of foreign divorces upon domestic marriages, and vice versa, have, as might be expected, not unfrequently been under discussion in our courts. In Massachusetts, in some early cases, the Supreme Court refused to interfere and grant a divorce, where the parties lived in another state at the time the adultery was charged to have been committed, and the libellant had since that time removed into the state. These decisions seem mainly to have proceeded upon the construction of the local statutes, which conferred jurisdiction upon the court in matters of divorce; but it was admitted that the state to which the parties belonged had jursidiction, and could exercise it if it appeared expedient.[2] In a later case, where a marriage celebrated in Massachusetts had been dissolved in Vermont, upon a suit by the husband for a divorce, for the cause of extreme cruelty of his wife (a cause inadmissible by the laws of Massachusetts to dissolve a marriage), it appearing that the parties had not at the time any permanent domicil in Vermont, but that the husband had gone there for the purpose of obtaining a divorce, the divorce was held a mere nullity, upon the ground that there was no real change of domicil. 'If,' said the court, 'we were to give effect to this decree, we should permit another state to govern our citizens in direct contravention of our own statutes; and this can be required by no rule of comity.'[3]

229. In another case the general question came before the court, whether a marriage celebrated in Massachusetts could be dissolved by a decree of divorce of the proper state court of Vermont, both parties being at the time bona fide domiciled in that state, and the cause of divorce being such as would not authorize a divorce a vinculo in Massachusetts. The court decided in the affirmative, upon the ground that the law of the actual domicil must regulate the right. The reasoning of the court was to the following effect: 'Regulations on the subject of marriage and divorce are rather parts of the criminal than of the civil code, and

[1] See in (English) Law Magazine, vol. 6, p. 32, a review of the English law as to divorces. See on this very point the judgment of Lord Brougham in Warrender v. Warrender, 9 Bligh, 115–118, cited ante, s. 226 c, note.

[2] Hopkins v. Hopkins, 3 Mass. 158; Carter v. Carter, 6 Mass. 263.

[3] Hanover v. Turner, 14 Mass. 227, 231. See also Barber v. Root, 10 Mass. 265, 266.

apply not so much to the contract between the individuals as to the personal relation resulting from it, and to the relative duties of the parties, to their standing and conduct in the society of which they are members; and these are regulated with a principal view to the public order and economy, the promotion of good morals, and the happiness of the community. A divorce, for example, in a case of public scandal and reproach, is not a vindication of the contract of marriage, or a remedy to enforce it, but a species of punishment which the public have placed in the hands of the injured party to inflict, under the sanction and with the aid of the competent tribunal, operating as a redress of the injury, when, the contract having been violated, the relation of the parties and their continuance in the marriage state have become intolerable or vexatious to them, and of evil example to others. The lex loci therefore by which the conduct of married persons is to be regulated and their relative duties are to be determined, and by which the relation itself is to be in certain cases annulled, must be always referred, not to the place where the contract was entered into, but where it subsists for the time, where the parties have had their domicil, and have been protected in the rights resulting from the marriage contract, and especially where the parties are or have been amenable for any violation of the duties incumbent upon them in that relation.'[1]

229 a. In another case the question as to the jurisdiction to found a suit for a divorce also arose, and it was held that ordinarily such a suit cannot be entertained unless the parties are bona fide domiciled in the state in which the suit is brought; and that for this purpose the domicil of the husband must be treated as the domicil of his wife. Hence if a husband should bona fide

---

[1] Barber v. Root, 10 Mass. 265. By the Revised Statutes of Massachusetts, 1835, c. 76, s. 9–11, it is declared that no divorce shall be decreed for any cause, if the parties have never lived together as husband and wife in this state. No divorce shall be decreed for any cause which shall have occurred in any other state or country, unless the parties had, before such cause occurred, been living together as husband and wife in this state. No divorce shall be decreed for any cause which shall have occurred in any other state or country, unless one of the parties was then living in this state. It is also by another section (s. 39) of the same chapter provided that when an inhabitant of this state shall go into any other state or country in order to obtain a divorce for any cause which had occurred here, and whilst the parties resided here, or for any cause which would not authorize a divorce by the laws of this state, a divorce so obtained shall be of no force or effect in this state.

remove from Massachusetts to another state with his wife, and there a good cause for a divorce by law should occur, a suit could not be maintained therefor in the courts of Massachusetts.[1] But the court thought that cases might arise, in which the change of domicil of the husband might not deprive the wife of her right to sue for a divorce in the state where they originally lived together.[2] (*a*)

[1] Harteau *v.* Harteau, 14 Pick. (Mass.) 181.

[2] Ibid. On this occasion Mr. Chief Justice Shaw, in delivering the opinion of the court, said: ' Much obscurity has, we think, been thrown on the subject by confounding the two questions, which are essentially different, namely, (1) in what cases a party is entitled to claim a divorce, and (2) in what county the libel should be brought. As it is a right conferred by statute, the one question may sometimes depend on the other; for if by the terms of the statute no suit can be instituted, it is very clear that no divorce can be had. But I think there may be cases where the statute confers a right to have a divorce, in which the statute gives a general jurisdiction to this court, and yet where the parties do not *live*, that is, have their domicil, either at the time of the *act done* or at the time of the *suit commenced*, in any county in this commonwealth. If so, there are cases where the statute cannot be literally complied with, and must be construed 'cy près according to the intent. Suppose a husband commits adultery, and then purchases a house and actually takes up his domicil in another state, but before his wife has joined him, she is apprised of the fact, and immediately files a libel for a divorce, and obtains an order to protect her from the power of her husband, as by law she may. He is an inhabitant of another state, and can in no sense be said to *live* in any county in this state. And yet it would be difficult to say that she is not entitled to have a divorce here. Supposing, instead of the last case, he has actually purchased a house and changed his domicil to another state, and there commits adultery, and the wife, not having joined him, and not having left her residence in this state, becomes acquainted with the fact and libels, and obtains a similar order, could she not maintain it ? Yet, in the latter case, at the time of the *act done*, and in the other at the time of the *suit instituted*, the respondent, *one of the parties*, certainly did not live in any county of this commonwealth. This suggests another course of inquiry, that is, how far the maxim is applicable to this case, " that the domicil of the wife follows that of the husband." Can this maxim be true in its application to this subject, where the wife claims to act, and by law, to a certain extent and in certain cases, is allowed to act adversely to her husband? It would oust the court of its jurisdiction in all cases where the husband should change his domicil to another state before the suit is instituted. It is in the power of the husband to change and fix his domicil at his will. If the maxim could apply, a man might go from this county to Providence, take a house, live in open adultery, abandoning his wife altogether, and yet she could not libel for a divorce in this state, where till such change of domicil they had always lived. He clearly

(*a*) *Divorce Jurisdiction.* — In order to give validity *throughout the Union* to a decree of divorce, domicil of the parties within the state of the forum is held necessary by the courts of this country. Where neither party has even a residence within the state, the courts of the state resorted to will re-

230. In New York, as far as decisions have gone, they coincide with those of Massachusetts. Thus in a case where the marriage

lives in Rhode Island; her domicil, according to the maxim, follows his; she therefore, in contemplation of law, is domiciled there too; so that neither of *the parties* can be said to *live* in this commonwealth. It is probably a just view to consider that the maxim is founded upon a theoretic identity of person and of interest between husband and wife, as established by law, and the presumption that, from the nature of that relation, the home of the one is that of the other, and intended to promote, strengthen, and secure their interests in this relation, as it ordinarily exists where union and harmony prevail. But the law will recognize a wife as having a separate existence, and separate interests, and separate rights, in those cases where the express object of all proceedings is to show that the relation itself ought to be dissolved, or so modified as to establish separate interests, and especially a separate domicil and home, bed and board being put, a part for the whole, as expressive of the idea of *home*. Otherwise, the parties in this respect would stand upon very unequal grounds, it being in the power of the husband to change his domicil at will, but not in that of the wife. The husband might deprive the wife of the means of enforcing her rights, and, in effect, of the rights themselves, and of the protection of the laws of the commonwealth, at the same time that his own misconduct gives her a right to be rescued from his power on account of his own misconduct towards her. Dean *v.* Richmond, 5 Pick. (Mass.) 461; Barber *v.* Root, 10 Mass. 260. The place where the marriage was had seems to be of no importance. The law looks at the relation of husband and wife as it subsists and is regulated by our laws, without considering under what law or in what country the marriage was contracted. The good sense of the thing seems to be, if the statute will permit us to reach it, that where parties have bona fide taken up a domicil in this commonwealth, and have resided under the protection and subject to the control of our laws, and, during the continuance of such domicil, one does an act which may entitle the other to a divorce, such divorce shall be granted, and the suit for it entertained, although the act was done out of the jurisdiction, and whether the act be a crime, which would subject a party to punishment or not; that after such right has accrued, it cannot be defeated either by the actual absence of the other party, however long continued animo revertendi, or by a colorable change of domicil, or even by an actual change of domicil; and that it shall not be considered in law that the change of domicil of the husband draws after it the domicil of the wife to another state, so as to oust the courts of this state of their jurisdiction, and deprive the injured wife of the protection of the laws of this commonwealth and of her right to a divorce. But where the parties have bona fide renounced their domicil in this state, though married here, and taken up a domicil in another state, and there live as man and wife, and an act is done by one which, if done in this state, would entitle the other to a divorce, and one of the parties comes into this state, the courts of this commonwealth have not such jurisdiction of the parties, and of their relation as

---

fuse to entertain suit for divorce, unless authorized by statute. Blumenthal *v.* Tannenholz, 31 N. J. Eq. 194; Calef *v.* Calef, 54 Me. 365. See Van Fossen *v.* State, 37 Ohio St. 317; Lyon *v.* Lyon, 2 Gray, (Mass.) 367. And concerning the force of a decree in such a case when authorized by sta-

was in that state, and afterwards the wife went to Vermont and instituted a suit for divorce there for a cause not recognized

husband and wife, as to warrant them in saying that the marriage should be dissolved. The case of Barber v. Root is an authority for saying that such a divorce would not be valid in New York. It is of importance that such a question should be regulated, if possible, not by local law or local usage, under which the marriage relation should be deemed subsisting in one state and dissolved in another; but upon some general principle which can be recognized in all states and countries, so that parties who are deemed husband and wife in one shall be held so in all. So many interesting relations, so many collateral and derivative rights of property and of inheritance, so many correlative duties, depend upon the subsistence of this relation, that it is scarcely possible to overrate the importance of placing it upon some general and uniform principle which shall be recognized and adopted in all civilized states.'

---

tute, it is laid down that no effect will be allowed to it beyond the state in which it was made, even though the parties both submitted to the jurisdiction of the divorce court. Van Fossen v. State, supra.

It is very clear that this will be true where the plaintiff has gone from the state of the domicil into the state of the forum to avoid the laws of his or her own state, and obtain a divorce by the laws of the other state, though the defendant appeared. Smith v. Smith, 13 Gray (Mass.) 209; Lyon v. Lyon, 2 Gray (Mass.) 367; Chase v. Chase, 6 Gray (Mass.) 157; Shannon v. Shannon, 4 Allen (Mass.) 134; Sewall v. Sewall, 122 Mass. 156; Loud v. Loud, 129 Mass. 14, 18. And it may be shown that no bona fide residence had been acquired in the state of the divorce. Platt's Appeal, 80 Penn. St. 501; Kinnier v. Kinnier, 45 N. Y. 535; Lyon v. Lyon, 2 Gray (Mass.) 369; Leith v. Leith, 39 N. H. 20; Cox v. Cox, 19 Ohio, 502; Vischer v. Vischer, 12 Barb. 640; Thompson v. State, 28 Ala. 12; Kerr v. Kerr, 41 N. Y. 272; Reel v. Elder, 62 Penn. St. 308. Whether the decree would be invalid where there was no fraudulent purpose in the departure is not clear. See Loud v. Loud, supra. The Ohio court lay down the proposition broadly, and refuse to accord

validity to any foreign decree made between non-residents. Van Fossen v. State, supra. See Chase v. Chase, supra.

On the other hand it is often stated that husband and wife may, for the purposes of divorce, acquire separate domicils; and this view has actually been adopted in one or two cases. Harding v. Alden, 9 Greenl. (Me.) 140. As containing dicta to the same effect, see Cheever v. Wilson, 9 Wall. 108, 124. (The defendant appeared to the action.) Van Fossen v. State, 37 Ohio St. 317; Kline v. Kline, 57 Ia. 386; Irby v. Wilson, 1 Dev. & B. Eq. (N. C.) 568, 582; Ditson v. Ditson, 4 R. I. 87, 108; Harteau v. Harteau, 14 Pick. 181, 186. The effect of this doctrine in connection with the rule that the wife's domicil follows that of the husband, is that if the husband leave his wife and acquire a domicil in another state, she becomes thereby a citizen of the new state even against her will, and is of course bound, like other citizens, by its laws. Therefore a decree of divorce obtained by the husband, though without notice or appearance, would bind her, if authorized by the local law, not only in that state but everywhere else. Indeed it has been held that a divorce obtained by a *wife* who has acquired a residence in a state not that of the husband's domicil, will be valid

by the laws of New York, against her husband who remained domiciled in New York, the Supreme Court of the latter state

everywhere, regardless of notice or appearance. Harding v. Alden, 9 Greenl. (Me.) 140. And see Ditson v. Ditson, 4 R. I. 87. But that clearly is wrong. People v. Baker, 76 N. Y. 78; Prosser v. Warner, 47 Vt. 667; Lyon v. Lyon, 2 Gray, 367. And that it is extremely doubtful if the husband can go into another state or country, and there acquire a domicil such as will ipso facto draw the wife within the same jurisdiction, see the remarks of James, L.J. in Harvey v. Farnie, 6 P. D. 35, 47; of Lord Westbury in Pitt v. Pitt, 4 Macq. 640; and of the president of the court in Briggs v. Briggs, 5 P. D. 163, 165. And Borden v. Fitch, 15 Johns. (N. Y.) 121, is an express decision to the effect that the acquisition of a new domicil by the husband does not draw the wife into the same jurisdiction.

It is no doubt correct for most purposes to say that the wife's domicil follows the husband's. Thus if a Scotchman or a foreigner go to England and marry an Englishwoman there, her domicil becomes instantly changed to that of her husband. Harvey v. Farnie, 5 P. D. 153; 6 P. D. 35, 46. And then ' all the rights and consequences arising from the marriage are to be determined by the law of that country which . . . becomes the domicil of both parties exactly to the same extent as if they had both been originally of the foreign country.' Ib., James, L.J. But the husband cannot deprive the wife of the right to sue for a divorce by an abandonment of his late residence with intention to acquire a new domicil, or even by actually acquiring a new one. She may still sue in the courts of the state in which she was domiciled with her husband. Shaw v. Shaw, 98 Mass. 158; Harteau v. Harteau, 14 Pick. 181; Bell v. Kennedy, L. R. 1 H. L.

Sc. 307. And in the case of abandonment of residence the old domicil continues until the new one is acquired. It was accordingly held in Shaw v. Shaw, supra, that a wife who had gone from Massachusetts as far as Pennsylvania with her husband on the way to Colorado, where they intended to acquire a new domicil, might return to Massachusetts, and institute suit there for a divorce for a cause happening in Pennsylvania during a mere sojourn in that state.

Of course on the other hand the wife cannot by removal deprive the husband of the right to sue for divorce in the courts of his domicil; but no decree obtained by either against the other while a bona fide non-resident will have any extra-territorial force unless the defendant was served with process within the state, or appeared. To make divorce valid everywhere the court must have jurisdiction of both of the parties. People v. Baker, 76 N. Y. 78; Kinnier v. Kinnier, 45 N. Y. 535; Hunt v. Hunt, 72 N. Y. 217; Van Fossen v. State, 37 Ohio St. 317; Sewall v. Sewall, 122 Mass. 156; Hoffman v. Hoffman, 46 N. Y. 30; People v. Dawell, 25 Mich. 247; Lyon v. Lyon, 2 Gray, 367. The court in People v. Baker considered Kinnier v. Kinnier, and Hunt v. Hunt entirely within the rule. Of the last-named case it was said, ' That case was close. It went upon the ground, built up with elaboration, that both parties to the judgment were domiciled in Louisiana when the judicial proceedings were there begun and continued and the judgment was rendered, and were subject to its laws, including those of substituted service of process.' See also Pennoyer v. Neff, 95 U. S. 714; Collins v. Collins, 80 N. Y. 1.

It may be added that the English

refused to carry the decree into effect in regard to alimony,
notwithstanding the husband had appeared in the cause,[1] upon
the ground that, there being no bona fide change of the domicil
of the parties, it was an attempt fraudulently to evade the force
and operation of the laws of New York.[2] The court however
abstained from declaring what was the legal effect of the divorce
so obtained. In another case, where the marriage was in Connecticut, and the husband afterwards went to Vermont and instituted a suit there for a divorce against his wife, who never
resided there and never appeared in the suit, it was held that
the decree of divorce obtained in Vermont was invalid, being in
fraudem legis of the state where the parties were married and
had their domicil. It was further held that the courts of Vermont could not possess a proper jurisdiction over the case, both

[1] This does not appear in the statement of facts; but it is averred by counsel to appear upon the exemplification of the record of the decree of Vermont.
1 Johns. (N. Y.) 431.

[2] Jackson v. Jackson, 1 Johns. (N. Y.) 424.

---

rule in Lolley's Case is now treated
as resting on the ground that the domicil of the parties was fictitious; the
position being abandoned that a foreign court cannot dissolve an English marriage. Harvey v. Farnie,
6 P. D. 35, 44, 8 App. Cas. 43 (H. L.);
Conway v. Beasley, 3 Hagg. Eccl.
639. In Harvey v. Farnie, which has
just been affirmed by the House of
Lords, it was held that a Scotch decree dissolving marriage between a
Scotchman, domiciled in Scotland,
who had married an Englishwoman
in England, the parties both residing in
Scotland at the time of the suit, was
valid. M'Carthy v. Decaix, 2 Russ.
& M. 614, 2 Cl. & F. 568, was much
questioned.

Much question has been made in
England concerning the ground of
jurisdiction in cases of divorce instituted in England between parties,
one of whom is a non-resident. In
Niboyet v. Niboyet, 4 P. D. 1 (Ct. of
App.), reversing 3 P. D. 52, the court
entertained jurisdiction of a cause

of divorce against a Frenchman who
indeed appeared, but under protest,
and prayed to be dismissed. He had
lived in England for several years,
but only as consul for the French
government; his domicil therefore remaining in France. The decision is
criticised in 19 Alb. L. J. 146; and
see Westlake, p. 71-77 (ed. 1880);
Le Sueur v. Le Sueur, 1 P. D. 139,
where jurisdiction was declined;
Santo Teodoro v. Santo Teodoro,
5 P. D. 79, where jurisdiction was
entertained. And see further, on the
effect of mere residence, Brodie v.
Brodie, 2 Sw. & T. 259; Manning v.
Manning, 40 L. J. P. & M. 18. Questions of this sort are generally regulated by statute in this country;
concerning which it need only be
repeated that no state or country will
recognize the divorce laws of another
as applied to persons not within their
jurisdiction except to the extent of
conceding the right of every state to
exercise sovereignty over property
within its borders.

parties not being within the state, and the wife not having had any personal notice of the suit.[1] What would be the effect of a marriage in Connecticut, a subsequent bona fide change of domicil to New York, and then a divorce in Connecticut, both parties appearing in the suit, remains as yet undecided. (a)

230 a. Upon the whole the doctrine now firmly established in America upon the subject of divorce is, that the law of the place of the actual bona fide domicil of the parties gives jurisdiction to the proper courts to decree a divorce for any cause allowed by the local law, without any reference to the law of the place of the original marriage, or the place where the offence for which the divorce is allowed was committed.[2] (b) Perhaps the doctrine cannot be stated with more clearness than in the reasoning of Mr. Chief Justice Gibson in a recent case. 'The law of the place,' says he, 'is necessarily the law of the marriage for its primitive obligation; but, except on the principle of perpetual submission to its supremacy in all things, it is not the law of the contract for the determination of its dissolubility. Is then a rule thus founded adapted to the jurisprudence of a country whose law of allegiance is different, and whose asserted right of affiliation in respect to those whom it admits on that ground to its civil and political privileges, divorce among the rest, concedes the same right to every other country? Framed on the basis of this law, the contract implies no perpetuity of municipal regulation. While the parties remain subject to our jurisdiction, the marriage is dissoluble only by our law; when they are remitted to another, it is incidently remitted along with them. And that consequence must ensue as well when they are remitted to a jurisdiction entirely foreign, as when they are remitted to that of a sister state; for whatever ultra-territorial force a sentence of divorce by a court of competent jurisdiction may have been

---

[1] Borden v. Fitch, 15 Johns. (N. Y.) 121. See 2 Kent Com. 108–118. See also Bradshaw v. Heath, 13 Wend. (N. Y.) 407.

[2] Pawling v. Bird, 13 Johns. (N. Y.) 192, 208, 209.

(a) The question has recently been decided in Texas, the court entertaining jurisdiction to grant a divorce in just such a case. Shreck v. Shreck, 32 Tex. 578. But concerning the effect of a decree in such a case when called in question in another state, see note supra.

(b) Nor will alimony be granted when both parties are non-residents, though there be property in the state of the one against whom it is asked. Keerl v. Keerl, 34 Md. 21.

thought to gain from the constitutional precept, that the judgment of a state court is to receive the same faith and credit in every other state as in its own, nothing in the Federal constitution or laws has been thought to touch the question of jurisdiction ; and the members of the Union therefore stand towards each other in relation to it as strangers. With what consistency then would naturalized citizens be allowed our law of divorce, if the validity of a divorce by the law of the domicil in a sister state were disallowed because the marriage had not the same origin? Transfer of allegiance and domicil is a contingency which enters into the views of the parties, and of which the wife consents to bear the risk. By sanctioning this transfer beforehand, we consent to part with the municipal governance incident to it ; but with this limitation we part not with the remedy of past transgression.' [1]

230 b. The incidents to a foreign divorce are also naturally to be deduced from the law of the place where it is decreed. If valid there, the divorce will have, and ought in general to have, all the effects in every other country upon personal property locally situated there, which are properly attributable to it in the forum where it is decreed. In respect to real or immovable property, the same effects would in general be attributed to such divorce as would ordinarily belong to a divorce of the same sort by the lex loci rei sitæ. If a dissolution of the marriage would there be consequent upon such a divorce, and would there extinguish the right of dower, or of tenancy by the curtesy, according to such local law, then the like effects would be attributed to the foreign divorce which worked a like dissolution of the marriage.[2]

[1] Dorsey v. Dorsey, 7 Watts (Penn.) 349; 1 (Boston) Law Reporter, 287, 289.

[2] Warrender v. Warrender, 9 Bligh, 127; ante, s. 226 c, note.

CHAPTER VIII.

FOREIGN CONTRACTS.

231. *Subject of the Chapter.* — We next come to the consideration of the highly important branch of international jurisprudence arising from the conflict of laws in matters of contract generally.[1] This subject has been very much discussed, not only by foreign jurists and foreign courts, but in our own domestic tribunals. The general principles which regulate it have therefore acquired a high degree of certainty; although, upon so complex a topic, many intricate and difficult questions yet remain unsettled.

232. *Questions that arise.* — It is easy to see that in the common intercourse of different countries many circumstances may be required to be taken into consideration before it can be clearly ascertained what is the true rule by which the validity, obligation, and interpretation of contracts are to be governed. To make a contract valid, it is a universal principle, admitted by the whole world, that it should be made by parties capable to contract; that it should be voluntary; that it should be upon a sufficient consideration; that it should be lawful in its nature; and that it should be in its terms reasonably certain. But upon some of these points there is a diversity in the positive and customary laws of different nations. Persons capable in one country are incapable by the laws of another;[2] considerations good in one country are insufficient or invalid in another; the public policy of one country permits or favors certain agreements which are prohibited in another; the forms prescribed by the laws of one country, to insure validity and obligation of contracts, are unknown in another; and the rights acknowledged by one country

---

[1] See on the subject of this chapter, 1 Burge, Col. & For. Law, vol. 1, pt. 1, c. 1, p. 23, 24, 29; Id. vol. III. pt. 3, c. 20, p. 749–780; Foelix, Conflit des Lois, Revue Étrangère et Française, tom. 7, 1840, s. 39–51, p. 344–365.

[2] Ante, s. 51–90.

are not commensurate with those belonging to another. A person sometimes contracts in one country, and is domiciled in another; and is to pay in a third; and sometimes the property which is the subject of the contract is situate in a fourth; and each of these countries may have different and even opposite laws affecting the subject-matter. What then is to be done in this conflict of laws? What law is to regulate the contract, either to determine the rights, or the remedies, or the defences growing out of it, or the consequences flowing from it? What law is to interpret its terms, and ascertain the nature, character, and extent of its stipulations? Boullenois has very justly said that these are questions of great importance and embrace a wide extent of objects.[1]

233. *Two Texts of the Civil Law.* — There are two texts of the civil law which treat of this subject, which have been supposed by civilians and jurists to involve an apparent antinomy. One seems to require that the place where the contract is entered into should alone govern the contract. 'Si fundus venierit, ex consuetudine ejus regionis, in qua negotium gestum est, pro evictione caveri oportet;'[2] if land shall be sold, it is to be warranted against eviction, according to the law of the country in which the business is transacted. The other, on the contrary, seems to require that the place where the contract is to be executed should govern it. 'Contraxisse unusquisque in eo loco intelligitur, in quo, ut solveret, se obligavit;' every one is understood to have contracted in the place in which he has bound himself to perform the contract.[3]

234. *Foreign Jurists.* — Dumoulin has endeavored to reconcile these texts, by supposing that the former law, Si fundus, truly and fundamentally presupposes that the contracting parties have their domicil in the place of the contract, and that the contract is there to be executed; but that the latter law, Contraxisse, applies to the case where the party has bound himself to execute the contract throughout in another place than that in which the

---

[1] 2 Boullenois, obs. 46, p. 445.

[2] Dig. 21, 2, 6; Pothier, Pand. 21, 2, n. 7. See Everhardus, Concil. 178, p. 207; post, s. 300 b. See Bartolus's interpretation of this law. Bartolus, ad Cod. 1, 1, 1, n. 14–16; post, s. 301.

[3] Dig. 44, 7, 21; Pothier, Pand. 5, 1, n. 36. To the same effect is the text: 'Contractum autem non utique eo loco intelligitur, quo negotium gestum sit, sed quo solvenda est pecunia.' Dig. 42, 5, 3; Pothier, Paud. 42, 5, n. 24.

contract is made. 'Sed hic venditor eo ipso se obligat, solutionem et traditionem realem, per se vel per alium facere in loco in quo fundus situs est; ergo, ibi contraxisse, censetur. Et sic lex, Si fundus, ex viva et radicali ratione, praesupponit contrahentes habere domicilium in loco contractus.' [1] Le Brun says that when the doctors say, in commenting on the law, Si fundus, 'locus contractus regit in contractibus,' they mean in everything which concerns the manner of contracting, the exterior form of the contract. But that the law of the domicil is to govern in whatever respects the substance and effects of the acts done.[2] However the generality of French authors have reconciled these laws in a different manner, by considering that the place of a contract admits of a double meaning; namely, the place where the contract is entered into, ubi verba proferuntur, and that where the contract is to be executed, where payment is to be made, ubi solutio destinatur.[3] They think therefore that the law, Si fundus, is to be understood of the place where the contract is entered into, ubi verba prolata sunt; and that it properly applies to cases where it is necessary to decide upon the form, either of the proof, or the substance, or the constitution, or the mode of the contract, or of its extrinsic ceremonies or solemnities; and that the law, Contraxisse, applies to the case where the question is respecting the rights which spring from the contract of which the execution and performance are referred to another place.[4]

235. Boullenois holds both interpretations unsatisfactory, and insufficient for many occasions; for they suppose that two places only are to be examined in resolving all questions, the place of the making, and the place of performance of the contract; and in effect they put aside the law of the place of the situs of the thing (rei sitæ), and that of the domicil of the parties, which are often imperative, and on many occasions deserve a preference.[5] He adds that there is another difficulty which arises in these mixed questions, which is, that the laws in one place affix to certain clauses a certain sense and a certain effect, and the laws of an-

[1] Molin. Comment in Cod. 1, 1, 1; Conclusiones de Statutis Molin. Opera, tom. 3, p. 551; Everhardus, Consil. 178, p. 206, 207; 3 Burge, Col. & For. Law. pt. 2, c. 20, p. 851–853; 2 Boullenois, obs. 46, p. 445–447.
[2] Le Brun, de la Communauté, liv. 1, c. 2, s. 46.
[3] 2 Boullenois, obs. 46, p. 446, 447; post, s. 299–304.
[4] Ibid. See also Everhard. Consil. 78, n. 18, 19, p. 207.
[5] 2 Boullenois, obs. 46, p. 447.

other place give them a sense and an effect either more extensive or more restrained.[1] He also informs us that many foreign jurists have warned us against two errors, which constitute the quick-sands of the law on this subject, and which are necessary to be avoided.[2] One of these errors is the confounding of those things which belong to the solemnities of the acts, and the effects which result from the nature of the acts, on the one side, with those which belong to the charges or liens which spring up after the acts, purely as accidents, on the other side;[3] the other, the omission in a proper case to have a due regard or deference to the law of the situs or locality of the thing.[4]

236. Mævius has given us a warning in this matter against confounding the solemnities of acts and contracts, as well as the effects caused by them, with the charges thereof, and extrinsic accidents which follow the contracts, but are not in the contracts themselves. 'Cave, autem, in hac materia, confundas actuum et contractuum solennia, nec non effectus ac ipsis causatos cum eorum onere, et accidenti extrinseco, quod contractus subsequitur, sed ex non ipsis contractibus est. Id, dum multi ignorant, aut non discernunt, forenses maxime lædunt, et gravantur.'[5] So that, according to Mævius, the law of the place of the contract is to govern, first, as to the solemnities of the act or contract; and secondly, as to the effects caused thereby; but as to the charges (onus) and extrinsic accidents, that it is not to govern. 'Forenses servare teneri statuta et consuetudines loci, ubi aliquid agunt, et contrahunt ad validitatem actus et contractus. Statutum enim actus seu contractus semper attenditur, cui disponentes vel con-trahentes se alligare et conformare voluisse censetur.'[6] And speaking afterward upon the charges and extrinsic accidents of acts and contracts, he adds: 'In his enim, quia non spectant ad formam modumque contrahendi, contractum autem extrinsecus subsequuntur, non sectamur statuta loci contractus.'[7] In this system he is not generally followed; and Boullenois has observed that it is very difficult to say what ought to be deemed to belong to the solemnities of contracts, what are the effects caused by

[1] Post, s. 275. [2] 2 Boullenois, obs. 46, p. 447, 449.
[3] Id. p. 447–449. [4] Id. p. 449, 450.
[5] Mævius, ad Jus Lubecense, Quest. Prelim. 4, n. 18, p. 22.
[6] Id. 4, n. 11, 13, 14, p. 22.
[7] Id. 4, n. 18, p. 22; 2 Boullenois, obs. 46, p. 448–450.

them, and what are the charges and extrinsic accidents resulting from them.[1]

237. Burgundus has offered the following system. In relation to express contracts, two things are to be considered, the form and the matter of the contract. (' Omnis autem obligandi ratio habeat, necesse est, rem et verba, hoc est, formam et materiam.'[2]) But he adds that it is not indiscriminately permitted to contract in all times and places; but it is very often material with what persons we contract; and all these things will be unavailing, unless the contract is conformable to the laws. 'Sed nec omni loco et tempore contrahere licet; plurimum quoque refert, cum quibus stipulemur. Et sane hæc omnia supervacua sint, nisi et secundum leges paciscamur.'[3] These things being premised, Burgundus lays down the following rules: first, in everything which regards the form of contracts, and the perfecting of them, the law of the place where the contract is entered into is to be followed. 'Et quidem in scriptura instrumenti, in solemnitatibus et ceremoniis, et generaliter in omnibus, quæ ad formam, ejusque perfectionem pertinent, spectanda est consuetudo regionis, ubi fit negotiatio.'[4] These he deems the substantials of the contract (substantialia contractus); and among them he includes the necessity of giving a caution or security upon a sale against any eviction, according to the customary law.[5] So the laws which determine the place and time when and where contracts ought to be made belong to the perfection of the form. 'Conditio loci et temporis perfectionem formæ quoque respiciunt; et ideo regione contractus pariter diriguntur.'[6] In like manner, all special stipulations for a limited responsibility, as of particular heirs only, belong to the form.[7] And he concludes by observing that in all questions touching the obligation of the contract, or its interpretation, (as, for example, whom it binds, and to what extent, what is included, what is excluded from it, also in respect to all actions and all ambiguities arising out of the contract,) we are first to follow what has been done by the parties; or if it does not appear what has been done, the consequence will be that we are to

---

[1] 2 Boullenois, obs. 46, p. 447–449.
[2] Burgundus, tract. 4, n. 1, p. 100.
[3] Id. p. 100, 101: Boullenois, obs. 46, p. 450, 451; post, s. 300 a.
[4] Burgundus, tract. 4, n. 7, n. 29, p. 104, 105.
[5] Id. n. 7, p. 105.   [6] Ibid.   [7] Ibid.

follow what is usual in the country where the act took place.
For the law is the common instructor of the whole country,
whose voice all hear; and, therefore, every one who contracts in
another province is not supposed to be ignorant of its customs ;
but whatever he does not express plainly he refers to the interpretation of the law, and wills and intends that which the law
itself wills and intends.   And all these things may well be said
of the solemnities of contracts.   'Igitur ut paucis absolvam, quoties de vinculo obligationis vel de ejus interpretatione quæritur,
veluti, quos et in quantum obliget, quid sententiæ stipulationes
inesse, quid abesse credi oporteat : item in omnibus actionibus, et
ambiguitatibus, quæ inde oriuntur, primum quidem id sequemur,
quod inter partes actum erit; aut si non paret, quid actum est,
erit consequens, ut id sequamur, quod in regione in qua actum
est, frequentatur.   Imputandum enim ei est, qui dicit, vel agit,
quod apertius legem non dixerit, in cujus potestate erat cuncta
complecti, et voluntatem suam verbis exprimere.   Nec enim sti-
pulator ferendus est, si ejus inter sit aliter actum non esse, cum
scire debuerit, id quod a contrahentibus est omissum, suppleri
legibus, quæ haud aliter dirigunt humanas actiones, quam corpora
nostra luna alternat.   Lex enim communis est præceptrix civitatis,
cujus vocem cuncti exaudiunt.   Et ideo, qui in aliena provincia
paciscitur, non credendus est esse consuetudinis ignarus : sed id,
quod palam verbis non exprimit, ad interpretationem legum se
referre, atque idem velle, et intendere, quod lex ipsa velit.   Et
hæc quidem cuncta de solemnitate dicta sint.'[1]   He then passes
to the consideration of the matter of the contract, by which he
means the things of which it disposes ; and he affirms, in respect
to the matter, that the law of the situation of the property ought
to govern.   'Cæterum, ut sciamus, an contractus, ex parte materiæ utilis sit, vel inutilis, ad leges quæ, de quibus tractatur,
impressæ sunt, hoc est, ad consuetudinem situs respiciemus.'[2]
He applies the same rule to quasi contracts, as to express
contracts: 'Idem in quasi contractibus, quod in contractibus
obtinet.'[3]

[1] Burgundus, tract. 4, n. 8, p. 105, 106.   [2] Id. tract. 4, n. 8, 9.
[3] Id. tract. 5, n. 1.   See also 2 Boullenois, obs. 46, p. 450–454, where he
has given a summary of the doctrine of Burgundus.   Burgundus, in exempli-
fying what he means by the matter of the contract, where the law of the situs
governs, evidently confines himself to real estate or immovable property.   See
Everhardus, Consil. 78, n. 18, 19, p. 207; post, s. 299 c.

238. Hertius has laid down three general rules upon the subject of the operation of foreign law.[1] The first is, that, when the law respects the person, the law of the country to which the party is a subject is to be followed. 'Quando lex in personam dirigitur, respiciendum est ad leges civitatis, quæ personam habet subjectam.'[2] Secondly, when the law respects things, the law of the situs is to govern, wherever and by whomsoever the act may be celebrated. 'Si lex directo rei imponitur, ea locum habet, ubicunque etiam locorum et a quocunque actus celebretur.'[3] Thirdly, when the law imposes any form in the transaction of the business (actus), the law of the place where it is transacted is to govern, and not the law of the domicil of the parties, or of the place where the property is situate. 'Si lex actui formam dat, inspiciendus est locus actus, non domicilii, non rei sitæ.'[4] This last rule, in an especial manner, he applies to contracts, even when they regard property situated in a foreign country. 'Valet etiamsi, bona in alio territorio sunt sita.'[5]

239. Huberus lays down the following doctrine. All business and acts done in court and out of court (or, as we should say, in pais or judicial), whether testamentary or inter vivos, regularly executed in any place according to the law of that place, are valid everywhere, even in countries where a different law prevails, and where, if transacted in the like manner, they would have been invalid. On the other hand, business and acts executed in any place contrary to the law of that place where they are executed, as they are in their origin invalid, never can acquire any validity. And this rule applies not only to persons who are domiciled in the place of the contract, but to those who are commorant there. There is this exception, however, to be understood, that if the rulers of another people would be affected with any notable inconvenience thereby, they are not bound to give any effect to such business and transactions. 'Inde fluit hæc positio: cuncta negotia et acta, tam in judicio, quam extra judicium, seu mortis causa sive inter vivos, secundum jus certi loci rite celebrata, valent, etiam ubi diversa juris observatio viget, ac ubi

[1] Ante, s. 30.
[2] 1 Hertii Opera, de Collis. Leg. p. 123, s. 8; Id. p. 175, ed. 1716.
[3] Ibid. p. 125, s. 9; Id. p. 177, ed. 1716.
[4] Ibid. p. 126, s. 10; Id. p. 179, ed. 1716.
[5] 1 Hertii Opera, de Collis. Leg. s. 4, p. 126, s. 10, ed. 1737; Id. p. 179, 180, ed. 1716; post, 371 a.

sic inita, quemadmodum facta sunt, non valerent.　E contra, negotia et acta certo loco contra leges ejus loci celebrata, cum sint
ab initio invalida, nusquam valere possunt; idque non modo respectu hominum qui in loco contractus habent domicilium, sed
et illorum qui ad tempus ibidem commorantur.　Sub hac tamen
exceptione; si rectores alterius populi exinde notabili incommodo
afficerentur, ut hi talibus actis atque negotiis usum effectumque
dare non teneantur, secundum tertii axiomatis limitationem.'[1]
He applies the same doctrine indiscriminately to testamentary
acts, to acts inter vivos, and to contracts.　'Quod de testamentis
habuimus, locum etiam habet in actibus inter vivos.　Proinde
contractus celebrati secundum jus loci, in quo contrahuntur,
ubique tam in jure, quam extra judicium, etiam ubi hoc modo
celebrati non valerent, sustinentur: idque non tantum de forma,
sed etiam de materia contractus affirmandum est.'[2]　He adds
that the place where a contract is entered into is not to be so
precisely regarded that if the parties had another country in view
in making the contract, that ought not rather to be considered.
'Verum tamen non ita præcise respiciendus est locus, in quo contractus est initus, ut, si partes alium locum respexerint, ille non
potius sit considerandus.'[3]　But here the same restriction is to
apply, that no injury arise thereby to the citizens of the foreign
country in regard to their own rights.　'Datur et alia limitationis
sæpe dictæ applicatio in hoc articulo; effecta contractuum certo
loco initorum, pro jure loci illius alibi quoque observantur, si
nullum inde civibus alienis creetur præjudicium, in jure sibi
quæsito; ad quod potestas alterius loci non tenetur, neque potest
extendere jus diversi territorii.'[4]　And he deduces the following
general conclusion, that if the law of a foreign country is in conflict with the law of our own country, in which a contract is also
entered into, conflicting with another contract which is entered
into elsewhere, in such a case our own law ought to prevail, and
not the foreign law.　'Ampliamus hanc regulam tali extensione.
Si jus loci in alio imperio pugnet cum jure nostræ civitatis, in qua
contractus etiam initus est, confligens cum eo contractu, qui alibi
celebratus est, magis est, ut jus nostrum, quam jus alienum,
servemus.'[5]

[1] 2 Huberus, de Confl. Leg. lib. 1, tit. 3, s. 3.　　　[2] Ibid. s. 5–9.
[3] Ibid. s. 10; post, s. 281, 299.　　　[4] 2 Huberus, lib. 1, tit. 1, s. 11.
[5] Huberus, lib. 1, tit. 3, s. 11.

239 *a.* Bartolus, on the subject of contracts between foreigners
in another country, has expressed himself to the following effect:
That we are to distinguish whether the question is (1) as to the
law or custom which regulates the solemnities of the contract; or
(2) as to the institution of the remedy; or (3) as to those things
which belong to the jurisdiction in executing the contract. In the
first case, the law of the place of the contract is to govern; in the
second case, the law of the place where the suit is instituted. But
in the third case, as to those things which arise from the nature
of the contract at the time when it was made, or those which arise
afterwards on account of negligence or delay, the law of the place
of the contract is to govern. ' Et primo, quæro quid de contractibus? Pone contractum celebratum per aliquem forensem in hac
civitate; litigium ortum est, et agitatur lis in loco originis contrahentis; cujus loci statuta debent servari, vel spectari? Distingue,
aut loquimur de statuto, aut de consuetudine, quæ respiciunt
ipsius contractus solemnitatem, aut litis ordinationem, aut de his
quæ pertinent ad jurisdictionem ex ipso contractu evenientis executionis. Primo casu, inspicitur locus contractus. Secundo casu,
aut quæris de his, quæ pertinet ad litis ordinationem, et inspicitur
locus judicii. Aut de his quæ pertinent ad ipsius litis decisionem;
et tunc, aut de his, quæ oriuntur secundum ipsius contractus naturam tempore contractus, aut de his, quæ oriuntur ex post facto
propter negligentiam, vel moram. Primo casu, inspicitur locus
contractus.' [1]

240. Boullenois has discussed this subject in a most elaborate
manner; and has laid down a number of rules, which are entitled to great consideration.[2] *First:* The law of the place where
a contract is entered into is to govern as to everything which
concerns the proof and authenticity of the contract and the faith
which is due to it; that is to say, in all things which regard
its solemnities or formalities.[3] *Secondly:* The law of the place
of the contract is generally to govern in everything which forms
the obligation of the contract (le lien du contrat), or what is

[1] Bartol. Comment. ad Cod. 1, 1, n. 13, cited also 2 Boullenois, obs. 44, p.
455, 456.

[2] 2 Boullenois, obs. 46, p. 445–538. Mr. Henry has laid down the first eight
rules of Boullenois as clear law, without the slightest acknowledgment of the
source whence they are taken. In fact, his treatise is in substance taken from
Boullenois, whose name, however, occurs only once or twice in it.

[3] 2 Boullenois, obs. 46, p. 458.

called vinculum obligationis.[1] *Thirdly:* The law of the place of the contract is to govern as to the intrinsic and substantive form of the contract.[2] *Fourthly:* When the law has attached certain formalities to the things themselves which are the subject of the contract, the law of their situation is to govern.[3] This rule is aplicable to contracts respecting real estates. *Fifthly:* When the law of the place of the contract admits of dispositions or acts which do not spring properly from the nature of the contract, but have their foundation in the state and condition of the person, there the law which regulates the person, and upon which his state depends, is to govern.[4] *Sixthly:* In questions whether the rights which arise from the nature and time of the contract are lawful or not, the law of the place of the contract is to govern.[5] *Seventhly:* In questions concerning movable property, of which the delivery is to be instantly made, the law of the place of the contract is to govern.[6] *Eighthly:* If the rights which arise to the profit of one of the contracting parties in fact arise under a contract valid in itself, and not subject to rescission, but arise from a new cause purely accidental, and ex post facto; in this case the law of the place where these rights arise is to govern, unless the parties have otherwise stipulated.[7] *Ninthly:* These rules are to govern equally, whether the contestation be in a foreign tribunal or in a domestic tribunal having proper jurisdiction over the controversy.[8] *Tenthly:* In questions upon the true interpretation of any clauses in a contract or in a testament, the accompanying circumstances ought ordinarily to decide them.[9]

241. *Rules of the Common Law.* — Without entering further into the examination of the opinions and doctrines of foreign jurists [10] (a task which would be almost endless), we shall now proceed to the consideration of those doctrines touching contracts made in foreign countries, which appear to be recognized and settled in the jurisprudence of the common law. The law which is to govern in relation to the capacity of the parties to enter

---

[1] Ibid.   [2] Id. p. 467.   [3] Ibid.
[4] Ibid.; post, s. 437.   [5] Id. p. 472.   [6] Id. p. 475.
[7] Id. p. 477.   [8] Id. p. 489.

[9] 2 Boullenois, obs. 46, p. 489. See also Foelix, Conflit des Lois, Revue Étrang. et Franç. tom. 7, 1840, s. 39, p. 344–346.

[10] The learned reader who wishes for further instructions as to the opinions of foreign jurists on all these points will find many of them collected in 2 Boullenois, obs. 46, from p. 458–538.

into a contract has been already fully considered.[1] It has been shown that although foreign jurists generally hold that the law of the domicil ought to govern in regard to the capacity of persons to contract,[2] yet that the common law holds a different doctrine, namely, that the lex loci contractus is to govern.[3]

242. (1.) *Lex Loci Contractus.* — *Validity.* — Generally speaking, the validity of a contract is to be decided by the law of the place where it is made, unless it is to be performed in another country; for, as we shall presently see, in the latter case, the law of the place of performance is to govern.[4] If valid there, it is by the general law of nations, jure gentium, held valid everywhere, by the tacit or implied consent of the parties.[5] (a) The rule is founded,

[1] Ante, s. 51–79.

[2] Ibid. In addition to the foreign authorities already cited, we may add that of Cochin and D'Aguesseau. The former says that the subjects of the king of France are always subjects, and they cannot break the bonds which attach them to his authority; and parties contracting in a foreign country cannot possess any capacity to contract but according to the law of their own country. It is a personal law which follows them everywhere. Cochin, Œuvres, tom. 1, p. 153, 154; Id. 545, 4to ed.; Id. tom. 4, p. 555, 4to ed. 'When,' says D'Aguesseau, 'the question is as to an act purely personal, we consider only the law of the domicil. That alone commands all persons who are subject to it. Other laws cannot make those capable or incapable who do not live within their reach. And this is what Bartolus intended to remark when he said, statutum non potest habilitare personam sibi non subjectam.' D'Aguesseau, Œuvres, tom. 4, p. 639, 4th ed.

[3] See ante, s. 51–54, 100–106. See also Male v. Roberts, 3 Esp. 163; Thompson v. Ketcham, 8 Johns. (N. Y.) 189; Liverm. Dissert. p. 34, s. 21, p. 35; Id. s. 22–24, p. 38; Id. s. 26, 27, p. 40; Id. s. 31, p. 42; Id. s. 33, p. 43, s. 35; Andrews v. His Creditors, 11 La. 464, 476.

[4] Post, s. 280.

[5] Pearsall v. Dwight, 2 Mass. 88, 89. See Casaregis, Disc. 179, s. 1, 2; Willing v. Consequa, 1 Pet. C. C. 317; 2 Kent Com. 457, 458; De Sobry v. De Laistre, 2 Harr. & J. (Md.) 193, 221, 228; Smith v. Mead, 3 Conn. 253; Medbury v. Hopkins, 3 Id. 472; Houghton v. Page, 2 N. H. 42; Dyer v. Hunt, 5 Id. 401; Erskine's Inst. B. 3, tit. 2, s. 39–41, p. 514–516; Trimbey v. Vignier, 1 Bing. N. C. 151, 159; 4 Moore & Scott, 695; Andrews v. Pond, 13 Pet. 65; Andrews v. His Creditors, 11 La. 465; Fergusson v. Fyffe, 8 Cl. & Fin. 125; post, s. 316 a; Bayley on Bills, c. (A.) 5th ed. by F. Bayley, p. 78; Id.

(a) See White v. Hart, 13 Wall. 646; Black v. Zacharie, 3 How. 483; Musson v. Lake, 4 How. 262; Hoyt v. Thompson, 19 N. Y. 207, 1 Seld. 352; Eubanks v. Banks, 34 Ga. 407; Knowlton v. Erie Ry. Co., 19 Ohio St. 260; Flanagan v. Packard, 41 Vt. 561; Smith v. Godfrey, 28 N. H. 381; Smith v. McLean, 24 Iowa, 329; Bond v. Cummings, 70 Me. 125; and see post, s. 263, 279. If no place of payment is named, the law of the place where the contract is made is to govern. Cubbedge v. Napier, 62 Ala. 518; Merchants' Bank v. Griswold, 72 N. Y. 472; Benners v. Clemens, 58 Penn. St. 24.

not merely in the convenience, but in the necessities of nations;
for otherwise it would be impracticable for them to carry on an
extensive intercourse and commerce with each other.   The whole
system of agencies, of purchases and sales, of mutual credits,
and of transfers of negotiable instruments, rests on this foundation ; and the nation which should refuse to acknowledge the common principles would soon find its whole commercial intercourse
reduced to a state like that in which it now exists among savage
tribes, among the barbarous nations of Sumatra, and among
other portions of Asia washed by the Pacific. ' Jus autem gentium,' says the Institute of Justinian, ' omni humano generi commune est ; nam, usu exigente, et humanis necessitatibus, gentes
humanæ jura quædam sibi constituerunt.   Et ex hoc jure gentium, omnes pene contractus introducti sunt, ut emptio et ven-
ditio, locatio et conductio, societas, depositum, mutuum, et alii
innumerabiles.' [1] No more forcible application can be propounded
of this imperial doctrine, than to the subject of international
private contracts.[2] In this, as a general principle, there seems
a universal consent of all courts and jurists, foreign and domestic.[3]

242 a. Illustrations of this general doctrine may be derived
from cases which have actually occurred in judgment.   Thus, for

Amer. ed. Phillips and Sewell, 1836, p. 78–86; 1 Burge, Col. & For. Law, pt.
1, c. 1, p. 29, 30; Whiston v. Stodder, 8 Mart. (La.) 95; Bank of the United
States v. Donnally, 8 Pet. 361, 372; Wilcox v. Hunt, 13 Pet. 378, 379; French v.
Hall, 9 N. H. 137.

[1] 1 Inst. lib. 1, tit. 2, s. 2.

[2] 2 Kent Com. 454, 455, and note; 10 Toullier, art. 80, note; Pardessus,
Droit Com. vol. 5, art. 1482; Chartres v. Cairnes, 16 Mart. 1.

[3] The cases which support this doctrine are so numerous that it would be a
tedious task to enumerate them.   They may generally be found collected in the
Digests of the English and American Reports, under the head of Foreign Law or
Lex Loci.   The principal part of them are collected in 4 Cowen, 510, note, and
in 2 Kent Com. 457 et seq., in the notes.   See also Fonblanque Eq. B. 5, s. 6,
note (t), p. 443; Brackett v. Norton, 4 Conn. 517; Medbury v. Hopkins, 3 Id.
472; Smith v. Mead, 3 Id. 253; De Sobry v. De Laistre, 2 Harr. & J. (Md.)
193, 221, 228; Trasher v. Everhart, 3 Gill & J. (Md.) 234.   The foreign jurists
are equally full, as any one will find upon examining the most celebrated of
every nation.   They all follow the doctrine of Dumoulin. ' In concernentibus
contractibus, et emergentibus tempore contractus, inspici debet locus in quo
contrahitur.' Molin. Comment. ad Consuet. Paris, tit. 1, s. 12, gloss. n. 57,
tom. 1, 224; post, s. 260, 300 d. See Bouhier, c. 21, s. 190; 2 Boullenois,
obs. 46, p. 458. Lord Brougham, in Warrender v. Warrender, 9 Bligh, 110,
made some striking remarks on this subject, which have been already cited,
ante, s. 226 b, note.

example, where a bill of exchange was made and indorsed in blank in France, and the holder afterwards sued the maker in England, a question arose whether, upon such an indorsement in blank without following the formalities prescribed by the Civil Code of France, the indorsement passed the right of property to the holder; and it being found that it did not by the law of France, the court held that no recovery could be had by the holder upon the note in an English court. The court on that occasion said that the question as to the transfer was a question of the true interpretation of the contract, and was therefore to be governed by the law of France, where the contract and indorsement was made.[1] (a)

243. (2.) The same rule applies, *vice versa*, to the invalidity of contracts; if void or illegal by the law of the place of the contract, they are generally held void and illegal everywhere.[2] (b) This would seem to be a principle derived from the very elements of natural justice. The Code has expounded it in strong terms. 'Nullum enim pactum, nullam conventionem, nullum contractum, inter eos videri volumus subsecutum, qui contrahunt lege contrahere prohibente.'[3] If void in its origin, it seems difficult to find any principle upon which any subsequent validity can be given to it in any other country.

244. (3.) But there is an exception to the rule, as to the universal validity of contracts; which is, that no nation is bound to recognize or enforce any contracts which are injurious to its own interests, or to those of its own subjects.[4] (c)   Huberus has ex-

---

[1] Trimbey v. Vignier, 1 Bing. N.C. 151, 159; post, s. 267, 270.

[2] Huberus, lib. 1, tit. 3, De Confl. Leg. s. 3, 5; Van Reimsdyk v. Kane, 1 Gallison, 375; Pearsall v. Dwight, 2 Mass. 88, 89; Touro v. Cassin, 1 Nott & McC. (S. Car.) 173; De Sobry v. De Laistre, 2 Harr. & J. (Md.) 193, 221, 225; Houghton v. Paige, 2 N. H. 42; Dyer v. Hunt, 5 N. H. 401; Van Schaick r. Edwards, 2 Johns. Cas. (N. Y.) 355; Robinson v. Bland, 2 Burr. 1077; Burrows v. Jemine, 2 Str. 732; Alves v. Hodgson, 7 T. R. 241; 2 Kent Com. 457, 458; La Jeune Eugénie, 2 Mason, 459; Andrews v. Pond, 13 Pet. 65, 78.

[3] Code, 1, 14, 5.

[4] Greenwood v. Curtis, 6 Mass. 376, 379; Blanchard v. Russell, 13 Mass. 1, 6; Whiston v. Stodder, 8 Mart. (La.) 95; De Sobry v. De Laistre, 2 Harr. & J. (Md.) 193, 228; Trasher v. Everhart, 3 Gill & J. (Md.) 234; 3 Burge, Col.

(a) See note to s. 314.

(b) McDaniel v. Chicago & North Western R. Co., 24 Iowa, 417; Moore v. Clopton, 22 Ark. 125; Kennedy v. Cochrane, 65 Me. 594; Lindsay v. Hill, 66 Me. 212; Stevenson v. Payne, 109 Mass. 378.

(c) See Smith v. Godfrey, 8 Foster,

pressed it in the following terms: ' Quatenus nihil potestati aut juri alterius imperantis ejusque civium præjudicetur ; '[1] and Mr. Justice Martin still more clearly expresses it in saying that the exception applies to cases in which the contract is immoral or unjust, or in which the enforcing it in a state would be injurious to the rights, the interest, or the convenience of such state or its citizens.[2] This exception results from the consideration that the authority of the acts and contract done in other states, as well as the laws by which they are regulated, are not, proprio vigore, of any efficacy beyond the territories of that state ; and whatever effect is attributed to them elsewhere is from comity, and not of strict right.[3] And every independent community will and ought to judge for itself how far that comity ought to extend.[4] The reasonable limitation is, that it shall not suffer prejudice by its comity.[5] (a) This doctrine has been on many

& For. Law, pt. 2, c. 20, p. 779; post, s. 348–351; Andrews v. Pond, 13 Pet. 65, 78.

[1] Huberus, lib. 1, tit. 3, De Conflict. Leg. s. 2.

[2] Whiston v. Stodder, 8 Mart. (La.) 95, 97.

[3] Ante, s. 7, 8, 18, 20, 22, 23, 36.   [4] Ibid.

[5] Ante, s. 25, 27, 29; Huberus, lib. 1, tit. 3, De Conflict. Leg. s. 2, 3, 5; Trasher v. Everhart, 3 Gill & J. (Md.) 234 ; Greenwood v. Curtis, 6 Mass. 378; 2 Kent Com. 457 ; Pearsall v. Dwight, 2 Mass. 88, 89 ; Eunomus, Dial. 3, s. 67.

(N. H.) 382; Black v. Zacharie, 3 How. 483; Merchants' Bank v. Spalding, 9 N. Y. 53; Milnor v. New York R. Co., 53 N. Y. 363; Watkins v. Wallace, 19 Mich. 57; Liverpool Ins. Co. v. Massachusetts, 10 Wall. 566 (where an English joint-stock company was treated and taxed as a corporation); Eubanks v. Banks, 34 Ga. 407; Fuller v. Steiglitz, 27 Ohio St. 355; Lewis v. Woodfolk, 2 Baxter (Tenn.) 25 ; Union Locomotive Co. v. Erie Ry. Co., 37 N. J. 23; Donovan v. Pitcher, 53 Ala. 411; Wright v. Remington, 41 N. J. 48 (that the exception will not apply to a foreign statute empowering a married woman to become surety for her husband in a note); Receiver v. First National Bank, 34 N.J. Eq. 450; Paine v. France, 26 Md. 46; Simpson v. Fogo, 1 Hem. & M. 195.

(a) *Foreign Laws opposed to Domestic Policy.* — What will fall within the rule that a foreign law opposed to domestic policy will not be allowed to prevail in the domestic courts has never been strictly defined. Indeed the rule itself, as the language of the text shows, is stated in a variety of ways, often vague and indefinite. In the present note some observations will be made chiefly upon the application of the rule to corporations, concerning which the text is nearly silent.

It is clear that the mere fact of the non-existence of such a law of the forum as that of the foreign state is not to be treated as indicating that the foreign law is opposed to domestic policy, otherwise in no case would the domestic courts hear evidence of the law of another country. Thus in regard to the privileges of a foreign corporation, the mere fact that there

occasions recognized by the Supreme Court of Louisiana. On a recent occasion it was said by the court; 'By the comity of na-

exists no law of the forum authorizing the body to hold land within the state will not be sufficient to prevent such body from acquiring land there (if authorized by its charter to hold realty), and calling for the protection of the domestic courts over its interests if needed. Christian Union v. Yount, 101 U.S. 352. To prevent a foreign corporation from acquiring and holding realty, or in general from doing business, within the state of the forum, there must be some affirmative statutory prohibition, or some opposing 'public policy deduced from statutes and adjudications of the highest court' of the state in which the suit is brought. Ib., Harlan, J.; Cowell v. Springs Co., 100 U. S. 55; Williams v. Creswell, 51 Miss. 817; Mutual Benefit Ins. Co. v. Davis, 12 N. Y. 569. On the other hand, the claim of a foreign corporation of the right under its charter to hold in perpetuity real estate without limit for the purpose of selling and trading, if inconsistent with the powers of domestic corporations, 'and clearly against the general course of legislation from the organization of the state' of the forum, will not be sustained. Christian Union v. Yount, supra; Carroll v. East St. Louis, 67 Ill. 568. A fortiori, where the claim in question is opposed both to the law of the state in which the corporation was established and to that of the forum, the claim will be refused. Starkweather v. American Bible Soc., 72 Ill. 50.

It appears to be safe inference from these cases that a foreign corporation claiming rights consistent with the foreign law, and not inconsistent with the spirit of the domestic law concerning like corporations, will be entitled to the protection of the domestic courts, though having no statutory recognition by the state. And this principle will apply as well to the question of immunities as to that of active rights. Thus the immunity of the members of a foreign corporation from personal liability will be respected, within the limits above indicated. Merrick v. Van Santvoord, 34 N. Y. 208. See Second National Bank v. Hall, 35 Ohio St. 158; Bateman v. Service, 6 App. Cas. (P. C.) 386.

The author considers with much fulness the application to private persons of the rule under consideration, and later cases have furnished little to add. In England there has been some attempt apparently to deduce a general proposition upon the subject. In The Halley, L. R. 2 P. C. 193, Selwyn, L. J., said: 'The English court admits the proof of the foreign law as part of the circumstances attending the execution of the contract, or as one of the facts upon which the existence of the tort or the right to damages may depend, and it then applies and enforces its own law so far as it is applicable to the case thus established.' But no redress in damages will be given 'in respect of an act which according to its [the English court's] own principles imposes no liability on the person from whom the damages are claimed.' It seems doubtful however if the American courts have generally been inclined to narrow the application of foreign law to this extent. The doctrine thus laid down would (to refer to but one class of cases) cut off, as it seems, all right of action by the next of kin of a person killed by another's negligence except in those states in which statutes exist creating liability in such cases. Some of our courts have indeed refused redress in such cases on grounds perhaps according with the doctrine of Lord Justice Selwyn. Richardson v. New York Central R. Co., 98 Mass. 85;

tions a practice has been adopted by which courts of justice examine into and enforce contracts made in other states, and carry
them into effect according to the laws of the place where the
transaction took its rise. This practice has become so general
in modern times, that it may be almost stated to be now a rule
of international law, and it is subject only to the exception, that
the contract to which aid is required should not, either in itself
or in the means used to give it effect, work an injury to the inhabitants of the country where it is attempted to be enforced.'[1]
Mr. Justice Best, afterwards Lord Wynford, on another occasion
with great force said that, in cases turning upon the comity of
nations, comitas inter communitates, it is a maxim that the
comity cannot prevail in cases where it violates the law of our
own country, or the law of nature, or the law of God. Contracts therefore which are in evasion or fraud of the laws of a
country, or of the rights or duties of its subjects, contracts
against good morals, or against religion, or against public rights,
and contracts opposed to the national policy or national institutions, are deemed nullities in every country affected by such considerations, although they may be valid by the laws of the place
where they are made.[2] (a)

245. Indeed a broader principle might be adopted, and it is
to be regretted that it has not been universally adopted by all
nations in respect to foreign contracts, as it has been in respect
to domestic contracts, that no man ought to be heard in a court
of justice to enforce a contract founded in or arising out of moral
or political turpitude, or in fraud of the just rights of any foreign
nation whatsoever.[3] The Roman law contains an affirmation of

---

[1] Mr. Justice Porter, in Ohio Ins. Co. v. Edmondson, 5 La. 295, 299, 300.
[2] Forbes v. Cochrane, 2 B. & C. 448, 471.
[3] Armstrong v. Toler, 11 Wheat. 258, 260 ; Chitty on Bills (8th ed. 1833).
p. 143, note ; Boucher v. Lawson, Cas. temp. Hard. 84, 89, 194 ; Planché s.
Fletcher, Doug. 251 ; post, s. 255, 257.

Woodard v. Michigan Southern R. Co., 10 Ohio St. 121. But the weight of authority is in favor of the right of action in all states, if such right existed where the tort was committed. Dennick v. Railroad Co., 103 U. S. 11; Leonard v. Columbia Nav. Co., 84 N. Y. 48. See post, s. 625, note, for further consideration of these and other like cases.

(a) See Smith v. Godfrey, 8 Foster (N. H.) 382; Meservey v. Gray, 55 Me. 540; Milnor v. New York R. Co., 53 N. Y. 363, that the law of Connecticut as to a Connecticut corporation doing business in New York will not prevail over the law of New York in the latter state.

this wholesome doctrine. ' Pacta, quæ contra leges constitution-esque, vel contra bonos mores fiunt, nullam vim habere, indubi-tati juris est.[1] Pacta, quæ turpem causam continent, non sunt observanda.' [2] Unfortunately, from a very questionable subser-viency to mere commercial gains, it has become an established formulary of the jurisprudence of the common law, that no nation will regard or enforce the revenue laws of any other country, and that the contracts of its own subjects, made to evade or defraud the laws or just rights of foreign nations, may be enforced in its own tribunals.[3] Sound morals would seem to point to a very different conclusion. Pothier has, as we shall presently see, reprobated the doctrine in strong terms, as inconsistent with good faith and the just duties of nations to each other.[4]

246. A few cases may serve to illustrate the exceptions under each of the foregoing heads.[5] First, contracts which are in eva-sion or fraud of the laws of a particular country.[6] Thus if a contract is made in France to smuggle goods into America in violation of our laws, the contract will be treated by our courts as utterly void, as an intended fraud upon our laws.[7] And in such a case brought into controversy in our courts, it will be wholly immaterial whether the parties are citizens or are foreign-ers. So, if a collusive capture and condemnation are procured in our courts in fraud of our laws by foreigners, who are even enemies at the time, their contract for the distribution of the prize proceeds will be held utterly void by our courts, although the acts are a mere stratagem of war. And it will make no dif-ference that the laws have since been repealed, or that the war has since ceased; for the contract being clearly in fraud of the laws existing at the time, the execution of it ought not to be

---

[1] Cod. 2, 3, 6.

[2] Dig. 2, 14, 27, s. 4. See also 1 Chitty on Com. & Manuf. c. 4, p. 82, 83.

[3] See Boucher v. Lawson, Cas. temp. Hard. 85, 89, 194; post, s. 256, 257.

[4] Post, s. 257.

[5] Many of the cases upon this subject will be found referred to in the argu-ment of Armstrong v. Toler, 11 Wheat. 265, 266.

[6] See 1 Bell Com. s. 233-247, p. 232-240, 4th ed.; Id. p. 298-314, 5th ed.; Kames on Eq. B. 3, c. 8, s. 1.

[7] See Holman v. Johnson, Cowper, 341; Armstrong v. Toler, 11 Wheat. 258; Cambioso v. Maffet, 2 Wash. C. C. 98.

enforced by the courts of the country whose laws it was designed to evade.[1]

247. *Contracts connected with the Illegal Transaction.* — The same principle applies, not only to contracts growing immediately out of and connected with an illegal transaction, but also to new contracts, if they are in part connected with the illegal transaction and grow immediately out of it.[2] Thus, for example, a man who, under a contract made in a foreign country, imports goods for another by means of a violation of the laws of his own country, is disqualified from founding any action in the courts of that country, upon such illegal transaction, for the value or for the freight of the goods, or for other advances made on them. He is thus justly punished for the immorality of the act, and a powerful discouragement from the perpetration of the act thus provided.[3] And if the importation is the result of a scheme to consign the goods to a friend of the owner, with the security of the former that he may protect or defend them for the owner in case they should be brought into jeopardy, a promise afterwards made by the owner to such friend, to indemnify him for his advances and charges on account of any proceedings against the property, although it purports to be a new contract, will be held utterly void as constituting a part of the res gesta, or original transaction. It will clearly be a promise growing immediately out of and connected with the illegal transaction.[4]

248. *Independent Transactions* — But the principle stops here, and is not extended to new and independent transactions after the illegal act. If the new contract is wholly unconnected with the illegal act, and is founded on a new consideration, and is not a part of the original scheme, it is not tainted by the illegal act, although it may be known to the party with whom the contract is made.[5] Thus if, after the illegal act is accomplished, a new contract (not being unlawful in itself) is made by the importer for a sale of the goods to a retail merchant, and the merchant

[1] Hannay v. Eve, 3 Cranch, 242. See Jaques v. Withy, 1 H. Bl. 65; Springfield Bank v. Merrick, 14 Mass. 322.
[2] Armstrong v. Toler, 11 Wheat. 261, 262. See Cannan v. Bryce, 3 B. & A. 179.
[3] Ibid.   [4] Ibid.
[5] Armstrong v. Toler, 11 Wheat. 262, 268, 269. In this case the general principles applicable to the question of illegality as well as the authorities were fully discussed and considered by the court.

afterwards sells the same to a tailor or to a customer who had no participation whatsoever in the original illegal scheme, such new contract will be valid, although the illegality of the original importation was known to each of the vendees at the time when he entered into the new contract.[1]

249. *Independent Contract with the Contriver of the illegal Act.* —It will make no difference that such new and independent contract is made with the person who was the contriver and conductor of the original illegal act, if it is wholly disconnected therefrom; for a new contract founded on a new consideration, although in relation to property respecting which there have been prior unlawful transactions between the parties, is not in itself unlawful.[2] Thus, if A. should in a foreign country, during war, contrive a plan for importing goods from the country of the enemy on his own account, by means of smuggling or of a collusive capture, and goods should be sent in the same vessel by B., and A. should, upon the request of B., afterwards become surety for the payment of the duties, or should afterwards undertake to become answerable for the expenses on account of a prosecution for the illegal importation, or should afterwards advance money to B. to pay these expenses, any such act, if it constituted no part of the original scheme, and if A. was not concerned nor in any manner instrumental in promoting the illegal importation of B., but was merely engaged in a similar illegal transaction, devising the plan for himself, would be deemed a new contract upon a valid and legal consideration, unconnected with the original act, although remotely caused by it.[3] Hence such new contract would not be so contaminated by the turpitude of the offensive act, as to turn A. out of court when seeking to enforce the new contract in the courts of this country, although the illegal introduction of the goods into the country was the consequence of the scheme projected by himself in relation to his own goods.[4]

250. The same principle may be illustrated by another example. If A. should become answerable for expenses on account of a prosecution for the illegal importation, or should advance money to B. to enable him to pay those expenses, these acts would constitute a new contract, on which an action might be

---

[1] Armstrong v. Toler, 11 Wheat. 261.
[2] Id. 262, 268, 269.   [3] Ibid.   [4] Ibid.

maintained in our courts, if it constituted no part of the original scheme for the illegal importation, but was subsequent to and independent of it.[1]

251. The same general distinction has been asserted in many cases which have undergone a legal adjudication. Thus in a case where goods were sold in France by a Frenchman to an Englishman, for the known purpose of being smuggled into England, it was held that the Frenchman could maintain a suit in England for the price of the goods, upon the ground that the sale was complete in France and the party had no connection with the smuggling transaction. The contract, said the court, is complete, and nothing is left to be done. The seller, indeed, knows what the buyer is going to do with the goods, but he has no concern in the transaction itself.[2] But if it enters at all as an ingredient into the contract between the parties, that the goods shall be smuggled, or that the seller shall do some act to assist or facilitate the smuggling, such as packing them in a particular way, there the seller is deemed active, and the contract will not be enforced.[3] (a) The same doctrine has accordingly been held in other cases.[4]

252. Huberus puts a case illustrative of the same doctrine. In certain places, says he, particular merchandise is prohibited. If sold there, the contract is void. But if the same merchandise is sold in another place where there is no such prohibition, and a suit is brought upon the contract in the place where the prohibition exists, the buyer will be held liable (emptor condemnabitur), because the contract therefore was, in its origin, valid. But if the merchandise is sold to be delivered in the other place where it is prohibited, the buyer will not be held liable, because such a contract is repugnant to the law and interest of the country which made the prohibition.[5]

---

[1] Armstrong v. Toler, 11 Wheat. 258, 260, 268–271. But see Cannan v. Bryce, 3 B. & A. 179.

[2] Holman v. Johnson, Cowp. 341. But see Pellecat v. Angell, 2 C. M. & R. 311; post, s. 254, and note.

[3] Waymell v. Reed, 5 T. R. 599; 1 Esp. 91; Lightfoot v. Tenant, 1 B. & P. 551; Biggs v. Lawrence, 3 T. R. 454; Clugas v. Penaluna, 4 T. R. 466; Holman v. Johnson, Cowp. 341; post, s. 254, and note.   [4] Ibid.

[5] Huber. lib. 1, tit. 3, De Conflictu Legum, s. 5; Greenwood v. Curtis, 6 Mass. 378; Cambioso v. Maffet, 2 Wash. C. C. 98.

(a) Brown v. Duncan, 10 B. & C. 98.

253. The result of these decisions certainly is, that the mere knowledge of the illegal purpose for which goods are purchased will not affect the validity of the contract of sale of goods intended to be smuggled into a foreign country, even in the courts of that country, but that there must be some participation or interest of the seller in the act itself. (*a*)   It is difficult however to reconcile this doctrine with the strong and masculine reasoning of Lord Chief Justice Eyre in an important case upon the same subject, reasoning which has much to commend it in point of sound sense and sound morals. ‘Upon the principles of the common law,’ said he, ‘the consideration of every valid contract must be meritorious.   The sale and delivery of goods, nay, the agreement to sell and deliver goods, is, prima facie, a meritorious consideration to support a contract for the price.   But the man who sold arsenic to one who, he knew, intended to poison his wife with it, would not be allowed to maintain an action upon his contract.   The consideration of the contract, in itself good, is there tainted with turpitude, which destroys the whole merit of it.   I put this strong case, because the principle of it will be felt and acknowledged without further discussion.   Other cases where the means of transgressing a law are furnished, with the knowledge that they are intended to be used for that purpose, will differ in shade more or less from this strong case, but the body of the color is the same in all.   No man ought to furnish another with the means of transgressing the law, knowing that he intended to make that use of them.’[1]   The wholesome morality and enlarged policy of this passage make it almost irresistible to the judgment, and, indeed, the reasoning seems positively unanswerable.

254. The doctrine of the Lord Chief Justice Eyre has been expressly adopted in other cases.   Thus, on one occasion,[2] the Court of King’s Bench in England held that a person who sold drugs to a brewer, knowing that they were intended to be used in the brewing of beer contrary to an act of parliament, was not entitled to recover the money due upon the sale.   Lord Ellen-

---

[1] Lightfoot *v.* Tenant, 1 B. & P. 551, 556.
[2] Langton *v.* Hughes, 1 M. & S. 593.

(*a*) It is enough if the purchaser bought with intent to violate the law, though the seller was ignorant of the fact.   The latter cannot recover the price.   Meservey *v.* Gray, 55 Me. 540.

borough on that occasion said : ' A person who sells drugs with a knowledge that they are meant to be so mixed, may be said to cause or procure, quantum in illo, the drugs to be mixed. So, if a person sell goods with a knowledge and in furtherance of the buyer's intention to convey them upon a smuggling adventure, he is not permitted by the policy of the law to recover such a sale.'[1] And the other members of the court concurred in that opinion. Mr. Justice Bayley added : ' If a principal sell articles in order to enable the vendee to use them for illegal purposes, he cannot recover the price. The smuggling cases which were decided on that ground are very familiar.'[2] (a) There are other cases which adopt the same general principle of enlightened justice.[3] It has however been directly denied in some later decisions.[4] Whether these last decisions will be sustained remains a question for the determination of other tribunals. (b) It is difficult to perceive any just or solid ground upon which a contract is maintainable or ought to be enforced in the tribunals of a country, which is knowingly entered into in a foreign country with the subjects of the former country, for the sale of goods which are to be smuggled into it against its laws, for the sale thus made is the avowed means to accomplish the illegal end.[5]

[1] Ibid.   [2] Langton v. Hughes, 1 M. &. S. 593.
[3] Cannan v. Bryce, 3 B. & A. 179, 181; Catlin v. Bell, 4 Camp. 183.
[4] Hodgson v. Temple, 5 Taunt, 182; Pellecat v. Angell, 2 C. M. & R. 311. See also Johnson v. Hudson, 11 East, 180.
[5] In Pellecat v. Angell, 2 C. M. & R. 311, the case was of a bill of exchange accepted in France by the defendant, a British subject, payable to the plaintiff, a Frenchman, being for the price of goods sold by the plaintiff to the defendant in Paris for the avowed purpose of being smuggled into England. The bill was sued in the English Court of Exchequer. Lord Abinger on that occasion said: ' It is perfectly clear that, where parties enter into a contract to contravene the laws of their own country, such a contract is void; but it is

(a) See Ritchie v. Smith, 6 C. B. 462.
(b) The later English cases seem to hold that mere knowledge on the part of a vendor that the vendee bought the property to use for an illegal or immoral purpose vitiates the contract if the property be so used. See Pearce v. Brooks, L. R. 1 Ex. 213; Cowan v. Milbourn, 2 id. 230; Taylor v. Chester, Id. 4 Q. B. 309; Story on Sales, 4th ed. s. 506, and cases cited. Other authorities hold that *mere knowledge* of the intended illegal purpose is not sufficient, but that some participation in the design or purpose must also exist on the part of the vendor. See Tracy v. Talmage, 4 Kern. (N. Y.) 162; Kreiss v. Seligman, 8 Barb. (N. Y.) 439; Smith v. Godfrey, 8 Fost. (N. H.) 379; Dater v. Earl, 3 Gray (Mass.) 482; M'Intyre v. Parks, 3 Met. (Mass.) 207; Jameson v. Gregory, 4 Met. (Ky.) 370.

255. *Distinction in Contracts of a Subject and of a Foreigner.*— There seems at present a strong inclination in the courts of law to hold that if a contract is made in foreign parts by a citizen or subject of a country, for the sale of goods which he knows at the time are to be smuggled in violation of the laws of his own country, he shall not be permitted to enforce it in the courts of his own country, although the contract of sale is complete, and might be enforced in the like case of a foreigner.[1] The true doc-

equally clear from a long series of cases that the subject of a foreign country is not bound to pay allegiance or respect to the revenue laws of this; except indeed that where he comes within the act of breaking them himself, he cannot recover here the fruits of that illegal act. But there is nothing illegal in merely knowing that the goods he sells are to be disposed of in contravention of the fiscal laws of another country. It would have been most fortunate if it were so in this country, where, for many years, a most extensive foreign trade was carried on directly in contravention of the fiscal laws of several other States. The distinction is, where he takes an actual part in the illegal adventure, as in packing the goods in prohibited parcels or otherwise, there he must take the consequences of his own act. But it has never been said that merely selling to a party who means to violate the laws of his own country is a bad contract. If the position were true, which is contended for on the part of the defendant, that this appears upon the plea to have been a contract for the express purpose of smuggling the goods, it would follow that it would be a breach of the contract if the goods were not smuggled. But nothing of the kind appears upon the plea; it only states a transaction which occurs about once a week in Paris. The plaintiff sold the goods; the defendant might smuggle them if he liked, or he might change his mind the next day; it does not at all import a contract, of which the smuggling was an essential part.' It appears to me that this reasoning is wholly unsatisfactory. The question is not whether it is a part of the contract with the Frenchman that the goods shall be smuggled, but whether he does not knowingly co-operate by the very sale, as far as in him lies, to accomplish the illegal intention of a British subject to smuggle his goods contrary to the laws of his country. Can a British tribunal be called upon to enforce such a contract? Can it be called upon to aid a Frenchman to recover a debt contracted for the purpose of violating British laws? Could a Frenchman selling poison in France to an Englishman for the avowed purpose of poisoning the king or queen of England, recover on such a contract in England? In Wetherell v. Jones, 3 B. & Ad. 225, Lord Tenterden said: ' When a contract which a plaintiff seeks to enforce is expressly or by implication forbidden by the statute or common law, no court will lend its assistance to give it effect. And there are numerous cases in the books where an action on a contract has failed, because either the consideration for the promise or the act to be done was illegal, as being against the express provisions of the law, or contrary to justice, morality, or sound policy.' Can a contract be fit to be entertained in a British court whose very object is to aid in a violation of British laws and policy and morals?

[1] Biggs *v.* Lawrence, 3 T. R. 454; Clugas *v.* Penaluna, 4 T. R. 466; Weymell *v.* Reed, 5 T. R. 599; Eunomus, Dial. 3, s. 67; Cambioso *v.* Maffet, 5 Wash. C. C. 98.

trine would seem to be, to make no distinction whatsoever between the case of a sale between citizens or subjects, and the case of a sale between foreigners, but to hold the contract in each case to be utterly incapable of being enforced at least in the courts of a country whose laws are thus designedly sought to be violated. Sound morals and a due regard to international justice seem equally to approve such a conclusion.[1]

256. *Foreign Jurists.* — Pardessus has asked the question, whether, if Frenchmen have entered into a contract abroad forbidden by the laws of the place where it is made, they can insist upon its execution in France ; as, for example, a contract for contraband trade or smuggling, against the laws of that country. And he has answered that he rather thinks they may, since this offence is only a violation of the law of the foreign State, and governments in this respect exercise a sort of mutual hostility, and, without openly favoring enterprises of a contraband nature, they do not proscribe them.[2] But this doctrine of Pardessus is certainly a departure from the general principle that the validity of contracts depends upon the lex loci contractus, for, in the case supposed, the contract is clearly void by the laws of the country where it is made. Huberus holds a doctrine somewhat different, and approaching nearly to sound principles. If, says he, goods are secretly sold in a place where they are prohibited, the sale is void ab initio, and no action will lie thereon, in whatever country it may be brought, nay, not even to enforce the delivery thereof; for if there had been a delivery thereof, and the buyer should refuse to pay the price, he would be bound not so much by the contract as by the fact of having received the goods, and so far he would enrich himself at the expense and loss of another.[3]

257. *The Established Doctrine.* — It might be different, according to the received, although it should seem upon principle indefensible, doctrine of judicial tribunals, if the contract were made in some other country, or in the foreign country to which the parties belong ; for, as we have seen,[4] it has been long laid down as a settled principle that no nation is bound to protect or to regard the revenue laws of another country ; and therefore a contract made in one country, by subjects or residents there, to evade the revenue laws of another country, is not deemed illegal in the

---

[1] Ante, s. 244, 245.   [2] 5 Pardessus, art. 1492.
[3] Hub. de Conflict. c. 3, s. 5.   [4] Ante, s. 245.

country of its origin.[1] Against this principle Pothier argued
strongly, as being inconsistent with good faith and the moral
duties of nations.[2] Valin however supports it ; and Emerigon de-
fends it upon the unsatisfactory ground that smuggling is a vice
common to all nations.[3] An enlightened policy, founded upon
national justice as well as national interest, would seem to favor
the opinion of Pothier in all cases where positive legislation has
not adopted the principle as a retaliation upon the narrow and
exclusive revenue system of another nation.[4] The contrary doc-

[1] See Boucher v. Lawson, Cas. temp. Hard. 84, 89, 194; Holman v. Johnson, Cowp. 341; Biggs v. Lawrence, 3 T. R. 454; Clugas v. Penaluna, 4 T. R.
466; Ludlow v. Van Rensselaer, 1 Johns. (N. Y.) 94; Lightfoot v. Tenant, 1
B. & P. 551, 557; Planché v. Fletcher, Doug. 251; Lever v. Fletcher, 1 Marshall Ins. 58–61, 2d ed.

[2] Pothier, Assur. n. 58.

[3] 2 Valin Com. art. 49, p. 127; 1 Emerig. c. 8, s. 5, 212, 215 (p. 216–218,
édité par Boulay-Paty), and see note of Estrangin to Pothier, Assur. n. 58;
1 Marshall Ins. c. 3, s. 1, p. 59, 60, 2d ed.

[4] It is gratifying to find that Mr. Marshall and Mr. Chitty have both taken
side with Pothier on this point. The following passage from a work of the
latter expounds the reasoning with considerable force. ' There is something
in these decisions to which a liberal mind cannot readily assent, and the impropriety of them seems to have been hinted at by Lord Kenyon in the before-
mentioned case of Weymell v. Reed. It is impossible not to feel a greater
inclination towards the opinion of Pothier, who observes " that a man cannot
carry on a contraband trade in a foreign country without engaging the subjects
of that country to commit an offence against the laws which it is their duty to
obey; and it is a crime of moral turpitude to engage a man to commit a crime;
that a man carrying on commerce in any country is bound to conform to the
laws of that country; and therefore to carry on an illicit commerce there, and
to engage the subjects of that country to assist him in so doing, is against good
faith; and consequently a contract made to favor or protect this commerce is
peculiarly unlawful, and can raise no obligation." If our law be justifiable in
protecting these transgressions, it can be only on the plea of necessity. But
where is the necessity? Shall we be told that it is impossible to ascertain in
the English courts the complex provisions of another country's revenue law?
Surely this argument can avail but little when it is recollected that in all
cases where the argument is not convenient, the law of another country, however complex, is the rule by which contracts negotiated in that country are
tried and construed. It may be true that the rule of our law was adopted by
way of retaliation for the illiberal conduct of other states, and is continued
from a cautious policy. But a cautious policy in a great state is but too often
a narrow policy; and, after all, the best policy for a state, as well as for an individual, will perhaps be found to consist in honesty and honorable conduct.
Indeed the system is so directly opposite to the clear principles of right feeling
between man and man, that nothing could have withheld the states of Europe
from concurring for its total abrogation except the smallness of the gain or
loss that attends upon it.' 1 Chitty on Commerce and Manuf. p. 83, 84; 1

trine seems however firmly established in the actual practice of modern nations without any such discrimination, too firmly perhaps to be shaken except by some legislative act abolishing it. (a)

258. *Contracts opposed to Morality.* — The second class of excepted contracts comprehends those against good morals, or religion, or public rights.[1] Such are contracts made in a foreign country for future illicit cohabitation and prostitution;[2] contracts

Marshall Ins. 59–61, 2d ed. Mr. Chancellor Kent has also added his own high authority in favor of the rule of Pothier. He has observed: ' It is certainly matter of surprise and regret that in such countries as France, England, and the United States, distinguished for a correct and enlightened administration of justice, smuggling voyages, made on purpose to elude the laws and seduce the subjects of foreign states, should be countenanced and even encouraged by the courts of justice. The principle does no credit to the commercial jurisprudence of the age.' 3 Kent Com. 266, 267. See also La Jeune Eugénie, 2 Mason, 459, 461.

[1] 1 Bell, Com. s. 232, p. 232–242, 4th ed.; Id. p. 297–314, 5th ed.

[2] See 1 Selwyn's Nisi Prius, Assumpsit, p. 59, 60; Walker *v.* Perkins, 3 Burr. 1568; Greenwood *v.* Curtis, 6 Mass. 379; Binnington *v.* Wallis, 4 B. & A. 650; Lloyd *v.* Johnson, 1 B. & P. 340; Jones *v.* Randall, Cowp. 37; Appleton *v.* Campbell, 2 C. & P. 347; De Sobry *v.* De Laistre, 2 Harr. & J. (Md.) 193,

(a) See also The Renaisance, 5 La. Ann. 25. A contract which has for its object or which contemplates any act prohibited by express statute in the state where the act is done, or which incurs a penalty there, is as much illegal and void as if the statute in express terms so declared. Davidson *v.* Lanier, 4 Wall. 447. Hence a contract for the sale and delivery of spirituous liquors, to be sold without license in a state where license is required for such traffic, is void, and no recovery can be had thereon, or for the value of such spirits, although the sale is made in such state by a house situated in another state where the sale is legal, through their agent, and is forwarded by common carriers. Territt *v.* Bartlett, 21 Vt. 184; Spalding *v.* Preston, Id. 9. But if these transactions had occurred wholly out of the state, and the plaintiff's only agency in effecting a violation of the statute of the state consisted in delivering the liquors to common carriers at the place of his business in another state, with the knowledge that the purchaser intended to put them to an illegal use on their arrival at the place of destination, the casks being marked with his address by the seller, it would seem that this will not preclude a recovery. Ibid. See Kling *v.* Fries, 33 Mich. 275; Roethke *v.* Philip Best Brewing Co., Id. 340. So too in a late English case it was held, where an attorney entered into an agreement with a client on the terms that the attorney should be allowed to retain for his trouble half the sum recovered, the agreement being entered into in France, where by law it was not illegal, that, as the debt was to be recovered in England, the agreement was void as amounting to champerty, and that an officer of court could not shield himself in the violation of his official duty under a contract made abroad, where it was not against law, if it still had for its object the violation of the English law. Grell *v.* Levy, 10 Jur. N. s. 210; 16 C. B. (N.S.) 73.

for the printing or circulation of irreligious and obscene publications ; contracts to promote or reward the commission of crimes ; contracts to corrupt or evade the due administration of justice ; contracts to cheat public agents, or to defeat the public rights ; and, in short, all contracts which in their own nature are founded in moral turpitude and are inconsistent with the good order and solid interests of society.[1] (*a*)   All such contracts, even though they might be held valid in the country where they are made, would be held void elsewhere, or at least ought to be, if the dictates of Christian morality, or of even natural justice, are allowed to have their due force and influence in the administration of international jurisprudence. (*b*)

259. *Contracts opposed to National Policy.* — The next class of excepted contracts comprehends those which are opposed to the national policy and institutions. (*c*)   For example, contracts made in a foreign country to procure loans in our own country, in order to assist the subjects of a foreign State in the prosecution of war against a nation with which we are at

---

228. Lord Mansfield, in the case of Robinson *v.* Bland, 2 Burr. 1084, puts the very case. In many countries, says he, a contract may be maintained by a courtesan for the price of her prostitution ; and one may suppose an action to be brought here ; but that could never be allowed in this country. Therefore the lex loci cannot in all cases govern and direct.

[1] See Com. Dig., Assumpsit, F. 7 ; Smith *v.* Stotesbury, 1 W. Bl. 204 ; 2 Burr. 924 ; Fores *v.* Johnes, 4 Esp. 97 ; Willis *v.* Baldwin, Doug. 450 ; Walcot *v.* Walker, 7 Ves. 1 ; Southey *v.* Sherwood, 2 Meriv. 435, 441 ; Lawrence *v.* Smith, Jac. 471, 474, note ; Jones *v.* Randall, Cowp. 37.

(*a*) See Fenton *v.* Livingstone, 3 Macq. 497 ; Reg. *v.* Lesley, 6 Jur. N. S. 202, 1 Bell, C. C. 220, 8 Cox, C. C. 269 ; Bowry *v.* Bennet, 1 Camp. 348 ; Jennings *v.* Throgmorton, Ry. & M. 251 ; Appleton *v.* Campbell, 2 Car. & P. 347 ; Fergusson, Marr. & Div. 396, 397.

(*b*) But to come within this exception a contract must be clearly founded in moral turpitude and not simply contrary to the statutes of the country where it is sought to be enforced.   Thus in a case in New York, where the sale of lottery tickets is prohibited by law, an action was brought on a bond conditioned for the faithful performance of certain duties enjoined by a law of Kentucky, which authorized the obligees to sell lottery tickets for the benefit of a college in that state, and the bond was held valid, it being so at the place where the condition was to be performed ; and it was considered immaterial whether the bond was executed in New York or in Kentucky. Kentucky *v.* Bassford, 6 Hill (N. Y.) 526.

(*c*) See King *v.* Sarria, 69 N. Y. 24. But see Kling *v.* Fries, 33 Mich. 275 ; Roethke *v.* Philadelphia Brewing Co., Id. 340 ; Webber *v* Donnelly, Id. 469 ; that contracts made in other states for the shipment of goods of prohibited manufacture (intoxicating liquors) in Michigan will still be upheld in Michigan.

peace ; for such conduct is inconsistent with a just and impartial neutrality ;[1] contracts entered into with a foreign government or its agents, such as for a loan of money, such government being a new government, unacknowledged by our own government to which the party entering into the contract belongs,[2] for a like rule of public policy applies to such cases ; contracts entered into by our own citizens or others in violation of a monopoly granted by our own country to particular subjects thereof ;[3] contracts by our own citizens or others to carry on trade with the enemy, or to cover enemy property, or to transport goods contraband of war;[4] contracts to carry into effect the African slave-trade, or the rights of slavery, in countries which refuse to acknowledge its lawfulness, at least if entered into by subjects of or residents within such countries.[5]   In all such cases the contracts would or might be held utterly void, whatever might be their validity in the country where they are made, as being inconsistent with the duties, the policy, or the institutions of other countries where they are sought to be enforced.[6]

[1] De Wütz v. Hendricks, 9 Moore, 586; 2 Bing. 314.
[2] Thompson v. Powles, 2 Sim. 194.   See also Jones v. Garcia del Rio, 1 T. & R. 299.
[3] Pattison v. Mills, 1 Dow & Clark, 342.
[4] 1 Marshall, Ins. bk. 1, c. 3, s. 3, p. 78, s. 4, p. 85, 2d ed.; Griswold v. Waddington, 16 Johns. (N. Y.) 438; 2 Wheat. Appendix, 35; Richardson v. Maine Ins. Co., 6 Mass. 102, 110, 112, 113; Musson v. Fales, 16 Mass. 332; Coolidge v. Inglee, 13 Id. 26.
[5] See Somerset's Case, Lofft, 1; 20 Howell's State Trials, 79 ; Fergusson on Marr. & Div. 396, 397; Madrazo v. Willes, 3 B. & A. 353 ; Forbes v. Cochrane, 2 B. & C. 448; and especially the opinion of Best, J.   I am not unaware of the bearing of the case of Greenwood v. Curtis, 6 Mass. 358, on this point; and, without undertaking to examine its authority, it may be sufficient to say that it is not without difficulty in its principles and application, as will abundantly appear from the elaborate argument of Mr. Justice Sedgwick in the same case (Id. 362, n.), and the later reasoning of Mr. Justice Best, in Forbes v. Cochrane, 2 B. & C. 448.   I have given in the text what seems to me to be the just doctrine resulting from the modern cases, without meaning to assert that the authorities cited are fully in point.   Ante, s. 96 a.   Mr. Chief Justice Shaw, arguendo, in the case of Commonwealth v. Aves, 18 Pick. 193 (ante, s. 96 a, note), held that a suit brought here upon a note of hand given in a state where slavery was allowed, for the price of a slave, might be maintainable in our courts, and that the consideration would not be invalidated upon the ground of the consideration.   It may be so here ; but this doctrine, as one of universal application, may admit of question in other countries, where slavery may be denounced as inhuman and unjust, and against public policy.
[6] 1 Bell Com. s. 234–250, p. 232–240, 4th ed. ; Id. p. 298–314, 5th ed.

259 a. Andrews v. *His Creditors.* — A case illustrative of the same principle, but of far less repugnancy to the policy and interests of the particular country, where the rights under a contract are sought to be enforced, occurred in Louisiana. A debtor in another State made a contract, and transferred his property to certain creditors in preference to his general creditors, which was not deemed by the laws of that State fraudulent in regard to the latter creditors; he afterwards came to Louisiana and was arrested there; and he then by petition sought the benefit of the insolvent laws of Louisiana, by whose laws such a preference would be fraudulent, and would deprive the debtor of the benefit of a discharge under the insolvent acts of the State. The court held that, as the debtor sought the benefit of the Louisiana laws, he could entitle himself to it only by showing a compliance with all their provisions; and that, the preference so given being fraudulent by those laws, he was not entitled to the discharge. On that occasion the court said: ‘But it is said that if we put such a construction upon the act, we give an extra-territorial operation to our law, by treating as null contracts sanctioned by the lex loci, and regarding as fraudulent those transactions which were in fact not only legal but meritorious. To this it may be answered that we leave those contracts undisturbed, and take cognizance of them no further than as the voluntary disposition of property in reference to our own insolvent laws, when the insolvent seeks an extraordinary remedy to which he would not be entitled by the law of his domicil, that of being declared exonerated from the payment of his remaining debts, on the assignment of the remainder of his effects. We look at them only so far as they form a condition upon which depends his right to be discharged, and consequently as pertaining to the remedy sought for. It is further urged that the acts spoken of in the statute must be shown to have been done in contemplation of taking the benefit of the act, and that it cannot be supposed that Andrews had in view the bankrupt laws of Louisiana when he made these assignments in Alabama. Taken in their literal sense, it is certainly difficult, if not impossible, to give any legal effect to these expressions, without resorting to the extravagant supposition that the insolvent had procured his own arrest by colluding with some one creditor, and that he had done other acts which would tend to defeat his own project. But the discharge prayed for does not omit those expressions; and it is not now our duty to inquire in what sense they are to be understood, and whether by the general principles of our law all contracts of the kind spoken of, within three months preceding insolvency, between debtor and creditor, be not be presumed to be in fraud of other creditors.' [1]

259 b. *Case put by Lord Brougham.* — A case of a more difficult character, if indeed it be not of a more questionable character, is one put by Lord Brougham, arguendo, in the course of one of his judgments. Speaking upon the point that the lex loci contractus is the governing rule in deciding upon the validity or invalidity of all personal contracts, he said: ' Thus a marriage, good by the laws of one country, is held good in all others where the question of its validity may arise. For why ? The question always must be, Did the parties intend to contract marriage ? And if they did what in the place they were in is deemed a marriage, they cannot reasonably or sensibly or safely be considered otherwise than as intending a marriage contract. The laws of each nation lay down the forms and solemnities, a compliance with which shall be deemed the only criterion of the intention to enter into the contract. If those laws annex certain qualifications to parties circumstanced in a particular way, or if they impose certain conditions precedent on certain parties, this falls exactly within the same rule ; for the presumption of law is, in the one case, that the parties are absolutely incapable of the consent required to make the contract, and, in the other case, that they are incapable until they have complied with the conditions imposed. I shall only stop here to remark that the English jurisprudence, while it adopts this principle in words, would not perhaps, in certain cases which may be put, be found very willing to act upon it throughout. Thus we should expect that the Spanish and Portuguese courts would hold an English marriage avoidable between uncle and niece, or brother and sister-in-law, though solemnized under papal dispensation ; because it would clearly be avoidable in this country. But I strongly incline to think that our courts would refuse to sanction, and would avoid by sentence, a marriage between those relatives contracted in the Peninsula, under dispensation, although beyond all doubt such a marriage would there be valid by the lex loci contractus,

---

[1] Andrews *v.* His Creditors, 11 La. 464, 479.

and incapable of being set aside by any proceedings in that country.'[1]

260. (4.) *Formalities required by the Lex Loci.* — Another rule, naturally flowing from, or rather illustrative of, that already stated respecting the validity of contracts, is that all the formalities, proofs, or authentications of them, which are required by the lex loci, are indispensable to their validity everywhere else.[2] And this is in precise conformity to the rule laid down on the subject by Boullenois.[3] 'Il faut, par rapport à la forme intrinsèque et constitutive des actes, suivre encore la loi du contrat. Quand la loi exige certaines formalités, lesquelles sont attachées aux choses mêmes, il faut suivre la loi de la situation.'[4] Burgundus has expressed the same doctrine in very pointed terms. 'Et quidem in scriptura instrumenti, in solemnitatibus, et ceremoniis, et generaliter in omnibus, quæ ad formam ejusque perfectionem pertinent, spectanda est consuetudo regionis, ubi fit negotiatio.'[5] Dumoulin says: 'Aut statutum loquitur de his, quæ concernunt nudam ordinationem vel solemnitatem actus; et semper inspicitur statutum vel consuetudinem loci, ubi actus celebratur, sive in contractibus, sive in judiciis, sive in testamentis, sive in instrumentis, aut aliis conficiendis.'[6] And again: 'In concernentibus contractum, et emergentibus, spectatur locus, in quo contrahitur; et in concernentibus meram solemnitatem cujuscunque actus, locus, in quo ille celebratur.'[7] Casaregis says: 'Communissima

---

[1] Warrender v. Warrender, 9 Bligh, 111, 112; post, s. 226 c.

[2] See ante, s. 123; 1 Burge, Col. & For. Law, pt. 1, c. 1, p. 29, 30; 3 Id. pt. 2, c. 20, p. 752-764; Foelix, Confl. des Lois, Revue Étrang. et Franç. tom. 7, 1840, s. 40-51, p. 346-360; Warrender v. Warrender, 9 Bligh, 111; ante, s. 259 c.

[3] Erskine's Inst. bk. 3, tit. 2, s. 39-41, p. 514, 515; Boullenois, Quest. Mixt. p. 5; Bouhier, Cout. de Bourg. c. 21, s. 205; 2 Boullenois, obs. 46, p. 467; ante, s. 210; 1 Hertii Op. de Collis. Leg. s. 4, n. 59, ed. 1737; Id. p. 209, ed. 1716. See also Voet, ad Pand. 5, 1, s. 51; 1 Boullenois, obs. 23, p. 523; Id. p. 446-466; Henry on Foreign Law, 37, 38, 224; 5 Pardessus, Droit Com. art. 1485; Mr. Justice Martin, in Depau v. Humphreys, 8 Mart. N.S. (La.) 1, 22; ante, s. 122, 259 b; post, s. 299 a.

[4] 2 Boullenois, obs. 46, p. 467; ante, s. 240; 1 Boullenois, obs. 23, p. 491, 492.

[5] Burgundus, Tract. 4, n. 7, n. 29; post, s. 300 a; 2 Boullenois, obs. 46, p. 450, 451.

[6] Molin. Opera, Comment. Cod. lib. 1, tit. 4, l. 1, Conclus. de Statut. tom. 3, p. 554, ed. 1681; post, s. 441, 479 k.

[7] Molin. Opera, tit. 1, De Fiefs, s. 12, gloss. 7, n. 37, tom. 1, p. 224, ed. 1681.

enim est distinctio, quod aut disseritur de modo procedendi in judicio, aut de juribus contractus, cui robur et specialis forma tributa est a statuto, vel a contrahentibus. Et in primo casu attendendum sit statutum loci, in quo judicium agitatur; in secundo, vero, casu attendatur statutum loci, in quo fuit celebratus contractus.'[1] Hertius is still more direct. 'Si lex actui formam dat, inspiciendus est locus actus, non domicilii, non rei sitæ; id est, si de solemnibus quæratur, si de loco, de tempore, de modo actus, ejus loci habenda est ratio, ubi actus sive negotium celebratur.'[2] Christinæus, Everhardus, and other distinguished jurists, adopt the same doctrine.[3] And it seems fully established in the common law. Thus if by the laws of a country a contract is void unless it is written on stamped paper, it ought to be held void everywhere; for unless it be good there, it can have no obligation in any other country.[4] (a) It might be different if the contract

---

[1] Casaregis, Disc. Com. 179, n. 59.

[2] Hertii Opera, Collis. Leg. s. 4, n. 10, p. 126; Id. n. 59, p. 148, ed. 1737; Id. p. 179, 209, ed. 1716; ante, s. 3, 8, 10, 11. See also Cochin, Œuvres, tom. 1, p. 72, 4to ed.; Id. tom. 3, p. 26; Id. tom. 5, p. 697; D'Aguesseau, Œuvres, tom. 4, p. 637, 722, 4to ed.

[3] Everhard. Consil. 72, n. 11, p. 206; Id. n. 18, p. 207; Id. 27, p. 209; post, s. 300 b; Christin. Decis. 283, vol. 1, p. 355, n. 1, 4, 5, 8, 9–11; post, s. 300 c; Moliu. Comm. ad Consuet. Paris. tit. 1, s. 12, gloss. 7, n. 37, tom. 1, p. 224; post, s. 300 d; 2 Boullenois, obs. 46, p. 460, 461; ante, s. 122. Dumoulin pushes the doctrine further, and says: Et est omnium Doctorum sententia, ubicumque consuetudo, vel statutum locale, disponit de solemnitate, vel forma actus, ligari etiam exteros, ibi actum illum gerentes, et gestum esse validum, et efficacem ubique, etiam super bonis solis extra territorium consuetudinis. Molin. Consil. 53, s. 9; Molin. Oper. tom. 2, p. 965, ed. 1681; Burge, Col. & For. Law, pt. 2, c. 9, p. 865, 866; post, s. 441.

[4] Alves v. Hodgson, 7 T. R. 241; Clegg v. Levy, 3 Camp. 166. But see Chitty on Bills, 8th ed. 143, note, and Wynne v. Jackson, 2 Russ. 351; 3 Burge, Col. & For. Law, pt. 2, c. 20, p. 762. The case of Wynne v. Jackson, 2 Russ. 351, is certainly at variance with this doctrine. It was a bill brought to stay proceedings at law on a suit brought in England by the holder against the acceptor of bills of exchange made and accepted in France; and which, in an action brought in the French courts, had been held invalid for want of a proper French stamp. The vice-chancellor held 'that the circumstance of the bills being drawn in France, in such a form that the holder could not recover on them in France, was no objection to his recovering on them in an English court.' This doctrine is wholly irreconcilable with that in Alves v. Hodgson, 7 T. R. 241, and Clegg v. Levy, 3 Camp. 166; and if by the laws of France such contracts were void if not on stamped paper, it is equally un-

---

(a) See Satterwaithe v. Doughty, 1 Busb. (N. Car.) 314; Fant v. Miller, 17 Gratt. (Va.) 47.

had been made payable in another country; or if the objection were not to the validity of the contract, but merely to the admissibility of other proof of the contract in the foreign court [1] where a suit was brought to enforce it; or if the contract concerned real or immovable property situated in another country whose

supportable upon acknowledged principles. In the case of James *v.* Catherwood, 3 Dowl. & Ry. 190, where assumpsit was brought for money lent in France, and unstamped paper receipts were produced in proof of the loan, evidence was offered to show that by the laws of France such receipts required a stamp to render them valid; but it was rejected by the court, and the receipts were admitted in evidence upon the ground that the courts of England could not take notice of the revenue laws of a foreign country. But this is a very insufficient ground if the loan required such receipt and stamp to make it valid as a contract. And if the loan was good per se, but if the stamp was requisite to make the receipt good as evidence, then another question might arise, whether other proof than that required by the law of France was admissible of a written contract. This case also is inconsistent with the case in 3 Camp. 166. Can a contract be good in any country which is void by the law of the place where it is made because it wants the solemnities required by that law? Would a parol contract made in England, respecting an interest in lands against the statute of frauds, be held valid elsewhere? Would any court dispense with the written evidence required upon such a contract? On a motion for a new trial, the court refused it, Lord Chief Justice Abbott saying: ' The point is too plain for argument. It has been settled, or at least considered as settled, ever since the time of Lord Hardwicke, that in a British court we cannot take notice of the revenue laws of a foreign state. It would be productive of prodigious inconvenience if, in every case in which an instrument was executed in a foreign country, we were to receive in evidence what the law of that country was, in order to ascertain whether the instrument was or was not valid.' With great submission to his Lordship, this reasoning is wholly inadmissible. The law is as clearly settled as anything can be, that a contract, void by the law of the place where it is made, is void everywhere. Yet, in every such case, whatever may be the inconvenience, courts of law are bound to ascertain what the foreign law is. And it would be a perfect novelty in jurisprudence to hold that an instrument which, for want of due solemnities in the place where it was executed, was void, should yet be valid in other countries. We can arrive at such a conclusion only by overturning well-established principles. The case alluded to before Lord Hardwicke was probably Boucher *v.* Lawson (Cas. t. Hard. 85, Id. 194), which was the case of a contract between Englishmen, to be executed in England, to carry on a smuggling trade against the laws of Portugal. Lord Hardwicke said that such a trade was not only a lawful trade in England, but very much encouraged. The case is wholly distinguishable from the present case, and from that of any contract made in a country and to be executed there which is invalid by its laws. A contract made in Portugal by persons domiciled there, to carry on smuggling against its laws, would or ought to be held void everywhere. See also 3 Chitty on Comm. & Manuf. c. 2, p. 166.

[1] Ludlow *v.* Van Rensselaer, 1 Johns. (N. Y.) 94; James *v.* Catherwood, 3 Dowl. & Ry. 190. See Clarke *v.* Cochran, 3 Mart. (La.) 358, 360, 361; Brown *v.* Thornton, 6 A. & E. 185; Yates *v.* Thomson, 3 Cl. & F. 544.

laws are different, respecting which, as we shall presently see, there is a difference of opinion among foreign jurists, although in England and America the rule seems firmly established, that the law rei sitæ, and not that of the place of the contract, is to prevail.[1]

260 a. *Forms of Public Instruments.* — So where the forms of public instruments are regulated by the laws of a country, they must be strictly followed, to entitle them to be held valid elsewhere. As, for example, if a protest of a bill of exchange, made in another state, is required by the laws of that state to be under seal, a protest not under seal will not be regarded as evidence of the dishonor of the bill.[2]

261. *Ground of this Doctrine.* — The ground of this doctrine, as commonly stated, is that every person contracting in a country is understood to submit himself to the law of the place, and silently to assent to its action upon his contract. Paul Voet has expressed it in the following language: ' Quid si de contractibus proprie dictis, et quidem eorum solemnibus contentio ; quis locus spectabitur, an domicilii contrahentis, an loci ubi quis contrahit ? Respondeo, affirmanter, posterius. Quia censetur quis, semet contrahendo, legibus istius loci, ubi contrahit, etiam ratione solemnium subjicere voluisse. Ut quemadmodum loci consuetudo subintrat contractum, ejusque est declarativa ita etiam loci statutum.'[3] It would perhaps be more correct to say that the law

[1] Post, s. 363–373, 435–445; Foelix, Confl. des Lois, Revue Étrang. et Franç. tom. 7, 1840, s. 40–50, p. 346–359.

[2] Tickner *v.* Roberts, 11 La. 14; Bank of Rochester *v.* Gray, 2 Hill, (N. Y.) 227.

[3] P. Voet, de Stat. s. 9, c. 2, n. 9, p. 267; Id. p. 323, ed. 1661; Cochin, Œuvres, tom. 5, p. 697, 4to ed.; Fergusson on Mar. & Div. 397; 2 Boullenois, obs. 46, p. 475, 476; Id. 500–502; Casaregis, Disc. 179, s. 56; ante, s. 122. Boullenois and some other jurists contest the universality of this presumed assent to the law of the place of the contract, and assert that this principle generally and broadly taken, généralement et cruement (nuditer et indistincte), is not correct. But where no other place of performance is pointed out, it seems difficult to see what other law is to govern. See 2 Boullenois, obs. 46, p. 457–459; Id. 501–518; Bouhier, Cout. de Bourg. c. 21, s. 191, 192; Voet, de Stat. s. 9, c. 2, s. 10, p. 269; Id. p. 325, ed. 1661. Hertius even goes so far as to say that the law of the place of a contract does not govern where the party is a stranger, ignorant of its laws: ' Non valet, si exterus ignoravit statutum.' 1 Hertii Opera, de Collis. Leg. s. 4, p. 126, 127, s. 10, ed. 1737; Id. p. 179, ed. 1716. See also 2 Boullenois, obs. 46, p. 502. Can a stranger living in a country plead ignorance of the laws of that country in his defence? Is he not bound by them whether he knows them or not? Huberus, on the

of the place of the contract acts upon it, independently of any volition of the parties, in virtue of the general sovereignty possessed by every nation to regulate all persons and property and transactions within its own territory.[1] And in admitting the law of a foreign country to govern in regard to contracts made there, every nation merely recognizes, from a principle of comity, the same right to exist in other nations which it demands and exercises for itself.[2] Some foreign jurists make an exception from the general rule in cases of contract made in a foreign country by any persons for the purpose of evading the revenue system, or the local solemnities prescribed by the laws of their own country respecting such contracts.[3] Thus Paul Voet lays it down among his exceptions. ' Nisi quis, quo in loco domicilii evitaret molestam aliquam vel sumptuosam solemnitatem, adeoque in fraudem sui statuti nulla necessitate cogente alio proficiscatur, et mox ad locum domicilii, gesto alibi negotio, revertatur.[4] Nisi etiam extra locum domicilii velit uti statuto suæ patriæ favorabili, quoad solemnia ; tum forte contractus alibi ita gestus, ubi alia solemnia erant adhibenda, ex æquo et bono in patria sustineretur.'[5]

262. *Statute of Frauds.* — Illustrations of this rule might be easily multiplied. Thus by the English and American law, contracts which fall within the purview of what is called the statute of frauds are required to be in writing ; such are contracts respecting the sale of lands, contracts for the debts of third persons, and contracts for the sale of goods beyond a certain value. If such contracts made by parol (per verba) in a country by whose laws they are required to be in writing, are sought to be enforced in any other country, they will be held void, exactly as they are held void in the place where they are made. (a)   And the like

contrary, holds that the law of the place of the contract governs, not only in respect to those who are domiciled, but those who are commorant there. Huberus, lib. 1, tit. 3, De Conflict. Leg. s. 3.

[1] See the opinion of Mr. Chief Justice Marshall in Ogden *v.* Saunders, 12 Wheat. 332, 338–347.

[2] Blanchard *v.* Russell, 13 Mass. 1, 4.

[3] P. Voet, de Statut. s. 9, c. 2, n. 9, p. 268, excep. 3, 4; Id. p. 324, ed. 1661.

[4] Id. ex. 2, p. 268, ed. 1715; Id. p. 324, ed. 1661.   [5] Ibid.

(a) See Leroux *v.* Brown, 12 C. B. 801; Bristow *v.* Secqueville, 5 Ex. 275; Fant *v.* Miller, 17 Gratt. (Va.) 47. But if it be merely declared that the want

rule applies vice versa where parol contracts are good by the
law of the place where they are made; but they would be
void if originally made in another place where they are sought
to be enforced, for want of certain solemnities, or for want of
being in writing, as required by the local law.[1] (a) It is a
very different question, as we shall presently see, what rule is
to prevail where the contract respects real or immovable property, and the law of the place of the contract and that of the
situs rei require different forms and solemnities to give validity
to them.[2]

262 a. Safety of Goods to be delivered in a Foreign Country. —
But suppose goods are bargained for by a merchant in one country to be paid for on delivery by a merchant in another country,
who is domiciled there, and has given the order therefor ; and the
law of the country where the bargain is made does not require
that there should be any memorandum thereof in writing ; but the
law of the country where the delivery is to be made does require
such a memorandum in writing. By what law is the bargain to
be governed ; by the law of the place of the bargain, or by
that of the place of delivery? It seems to have been thought

---

[1] 2 Boullenois, obs. 33, p. 459–461; 1 Boullenois, obs. 46, p. 492–498; Id.
499; Id. 506; Id. 523; Erskine's Inst. bk. 3, tit. 5, s. 39, 40; Vidal v. Thompson,
11 Mart. (La.) 23; Casaregis, Disc. 179, n. 59, 60; 1 Hertii Opera, de Collis.
Leg. p. 148, s. 59, ed. 1737; Boullenois, Quest. de la Contrar. des Lois, p. 5;
Livermore, Dissert. p. 46, s. 41; 1 Burge, Col. & For. Law, pt. 1, c. 1, p. 29;
3 Id. pt. 2, c. 20, p. 758–762, 769; Alves v. Hodgson, 7 T. R. 241; Clegg v.
Levy, 3 Camp. 166. But see Wynne v. Jackson, 2 Russ. 351; and James v.
Catherwood, 3 Dowl. & R. 190; ante, s. 260, and note, p. 216; post, s. 362–
373. Hertius seems to think that, if foreigners in another country make a
contract according to the law of their own country (both belonging to the
same country), in such a case the contract will avail in their own country
even if not made according to the lex loci contractus. 1 Hertii Opera, de
Collis. Leg. s. 10, p. 126, 128, ed. 1737; Id. p. 179–181, ed. 1716. So is Voet,
de Statut. s. 9, c. 2, excep. 4, p. 268, ed. 1716; Id. p. 325, ed. 1661. But
Boullenois has observed that he does not find any authors who are of opinion
that such a contract made elsewhere, according to the law of their own country, ought to have place even beyond the country. 2 Boullenois, obs. 46,
p. 459.

[2] Post, s. 363–373, 435–445; 1 Boullenois, obs. 23, p. 448–472.

---

of a stamp shall make a note inadmissible evidence of debt, the note may
still be read in evidence in a state in
which stamps are not required. Fant

v. Miller, supra; Bristow v. Secqueville, supra.

(a) See Denny v. Williams, 5 Allen (Mass.) 1.

that in such a case the law of the place of delivery is to govern.[1] (a)

263. (5) *Nature, Obligation, and Interpretation of Contracts.* — Another rule illustrative of the same general principle is, that the law of the place of the contract is to govern as to the nature, the obligation, and the interpretation of the contract, locus contractus regit actum.[2] (b)   Again: 'Quod si de ipso contractu quæratur,' says Paul Voet, 'seu de natura ipsius, seu de iis, quæ ex natura contractus veniunt, puta fidejussione, etc., etiam spec-

---

[1] The case of Acebal v. Levy, 10 Bing. 376, seems to have involved this very question, although it does not appear to have attracted the attention either of the bar or of the court. The case went off upon a supposed variance between the counts and the evidence. The statement of the facts in the body of the report does not show whether the goods in the case which were sold and shipped at Gigon in Spain by order of an agent of the defendants, were to be sent to the defendants in England, were sold to be paid for in England after their arrival and delivery there, or were to be paid for on their shipment. But Lord Chief Justice Tindal in delivering the opinion of the court said that in point of fact the parol evidence at the trial established that the price of the goods was to be the current shipping price at Gigon, and to be paid for on the delivery thereof in England. The defendants refused to receive them, and the agent of the plaintiff then sold them for account of the plaintiff, and the action was brought for the difference between the price of the purchase and the sale thus made. One of the objections taken was that there was no memorandum in writing required by the English statute of frauds. The objection was not sustained because the court thought that there was a sufficient memorandum; but the memorandum varied from the counts in the declaration. But the court and bar seem to have supposed that the English statute of frauds did apply to the case; which is certainly a matter open to much discussion, and as we shall presently see, post, s. 285, 318, has been thought open to a very different conclusion. See Vidal v. Thompson, 11 Mart. (La.) 23-25.

[2] 1 Emer. Assur. c. 4, s. 8, p. 122, 125, 128. See Casaregis, Disc. 179, s. 60; Erskine's Inst. b. 3, tit. 2, s. 39, 40, p. 514, 515; Delvalle v. Plomer, 3 Camp. 47; Harrison v. Sterry, 5 Cranch, 289; Le Roy v. Crowninshield, 2 Mason, C. C. 151; Van Reimsdyk v. Kane, 1 Gallis. C. C. 371; 2 Kent Com. 394, 458-469; Fergusson v. Fyffe, 8 Cl. & F. 121, 140.

(a) See Green v. Lewis, 26 Q. B. Up. Can. 618.

(b) See Scudder v. Union Bank, 91 U. S. 406; Liverpool Credit Co. v. Hunter, L. R. 3 Ch. 479; Cobb v. Buswell, 37 Vt. 337; Cantu v. Bennett, 39 Tex. 303; Smith v. Chicago Ry. Co., 23 Wis. 267; Elliott Bank v. Western R. Co., 2 Lea (Tenn.) 676; Williams v. Carr, 80 N. Car. 294; Bliss v. Brainard, 41 N. H. 256; Frink v. Buss, 45 N. H. 325; Ivey v. Lalland, 42 Miss. 444; Drew v. Smith, 59 Me. 393; Stone v. Perry, 60 Me. 48; Wright v. Andrews, 70 Me. 86; Rabun v. Rabun, 15 La. An. 471; Harris v. Nasits, 23 La. An. 457; Archer v. National Ins. Co., 2 Bush (Ky.) 226; ante, s. 242; post, s. 279.

tandum est loci statutum, ubi contractus celebratur; quod ei
contrahentes semet accommodare præsumantur.'[1]   First, as to the

[1] P. Voet, de Stat. s. 9, c. 2, s. 10, p. 269, ed. 1737; Id. p. 253, ed. 1661.
J. Voet is still more full on the same point.   Voet, ad Pand. 4, 1, 29,
p. 240, 241. ' Si adversus contractum,' says he, ' aliudve negotium gestum
factumve restitutio desideretur, dum quis aut metu, aut dolo, aut errore
lapsus, damnum sensit contrahendo, trausigendo, solvendo, fidejubendo, hereditatem adeundo, aliove simili modo; recte interpretes statutisse arbitror,
leges regionis in qua contractum gestumve est id, contra quod restitutio petitur, locum sibi debere vindicare in terminenda ipsa restitutionis controversia,
sive res illæ, de quibus contractum est, et in quibus læsio contigit, eodem in
loco, sive alibi sitæ sint.   Nec intererit, utrum læsio circa res ipsas contigerit,
veluti pluris minorisve, quam æquum est, errore justo distractas, an vero propter neglecta solemnia in loco contractus desiderata.   Si tamen contractus implementum non in ipso contractus loco fieri debeat, sed ad locum alium sit
destinatum, non loci contractus, sed implimenti leges spectandas esse ratio
suadet: ut ita, secundum cujus loci jura implementum accipere debuit contractus, juxta ejus etiam leges resolvatur.'   Boullenois says that jurists distinguish four things in contracts.   (1.) Substantialia contractuum; (2.)
Naturalia contractuum; (3.) Accidentalia contractuum; (4.) Solemnia contractuum.   He says: ' Ils appellent substantialia contractuum, tout ce qui sert à la
composition intérieure des contrats; c'est-à-dire, tout ce qui est de l'essence
déterminant la nature de chaque acte, et sans quoi il ne serait pas un tel acte.
Substantialia sunt, quæ ita formam et essentiam uniuscujusque actus constituunt, ut sine iis talis actus esse non possit, cum forma dat unicuique esse id,
quod est.   Suivant cette définition, le consentement des parties dans tous les
contrats, la chose, et les prix de la chose dans un contrat de vente, pertinent
ad substantialia contractuum et ad speciem contractus constituendam; et elles
sont tellement nécessaires, intrinsèques et constitutives d'un contrat, que sine
iis actus qui geritur, non valeat.   Naturalia contractuum, ce sont les suites et
les engagements qui fluent et dérivent de la nature et de l'espèce des contrats,
dont il s'agit.   Naturalia contractuum dicuntur ea, quæ pendunt et manant a
natura et potestate cujusque actus; sed ejus formam non constituunt.   Telle
est la garantie dans la vente.   Mais par rapport à ces engagements qui dérivent des contrats, on en distingue de deux sortes.   Il y en a quæ sunt interna,
intrinseca, et inseparabilia; c'est-à-dire, qui sont liés et attachés à chaque
espèce de contrats, et qui sont propres à chacun de ces contrats, suivant la different nature, dont ils sont.   Quæ naturæ contractus cohærent, et sunt veluti
propriæ possessiones, propriæ affectiones ab essentialibus cujusque contractus principiis enatæ.   Telle est, dans un contrat de vente, la nécessité que le
domaine de la chose rendue soit transféré à l'acquéreur; et à cet égard on
ne peut se soustraire à ces choses; on ne pourrait pas en effet stipuler, que
le domaine de la chose rendue ne passerait pas à l'acquéreur; et il y en a qui ne
naissent que de l'usage ordinaire où on est d'en convenir, et qui, à raison de
ceci, sont toujours présumés être convenus par les parties.   Quæ ex consuetudine etiam insunt contractibus, quæ consuetudo in naturam quasi contractus
transiit; et on les appelle, externa et separabilia.   Telle est la garantie de fait
dans une cession, et à cet égard on peut y déroger, les parties peuvent stipuler
qu'il n'y aura d'autre garantie que celle que l'on appelle garantie de droit.
Accidentalia contractus, ce sont les choses, qui ne sont point de la substance

nature of the contract, by which is meant those qualities which properly belong to it, and by law or custom always accompany it or inhere in it.[1] Foreign jurists are accustomed to call such qualities naturalia contractus.[2] ' Ea enim, quæ auctoritate legis vel consuetudinis contractum comitantur, eidem adhærent, naturalia a doctoribus appellantur. Lex enim altera est quasi natura, et in naturam transit. Atque quoad naturalia contractuum etiam

constitutive de l'acte, qui ne fluent et ne dérivent point de sa nature et de son espèce, et ne tombent point en convention ordinaire; mais que ne se recontrent dans les contrats que parceque les parties en conviennent. Accidentalia contractus ea sunt, quæ neque substantiam contractuum constituunt, neque ex natura et potestate contractus dimanant, sed pro voluntate contrahentium, adjici contractibus solent, veluti varia pacta. Je voudrais ajouter, et encore celles, qui ne sont requises que par des dispositions légales, à la vérite, mais pures locales, comme la nécessité de donner caution pour la garantie d'un contrat, laquelle a lieu dans certains endroits. Enfin, il y a solemnia contractuum; et on en distingue de deux sortes, solemnia intrinseca, et solemnia extrinseca. Solemnia intrinseca sunt ea, quæ insunt in ipsa forma cujusque actus, neque separari ab ea possunt; telles sont les choses qui appartiennent à la preuve et à l'authenticité de l'acte, et qui comme telles sont partie de ce qui constitue l'être et l'existence de cet acte; aussi sont-elles appellées par quelques-uns substantialia contractuum. Solemnia extrinseca sunt ea, quæ actui per se formam habent et ultra conventionem contrahentium sed ad ipsam conventionem roborandam, extrinsecus accedunt, et ce sont les choses, qui n'appartenant en rien à la composition intrinsèque de l'acte, sont seulement requises, post actum originatum, pour lui procurer son exécution. La solemnité intrinsèque est tellement nécessaire, que si on l'omet, l'acte n'est pas acte, il n'a nul être, nulle existence ; l'omission vitiat et corrumpit actum; raison pour laquelle on la place volontiers inter substantialia contractuum. Mais à l'égard de la solemnité extrinsèque, il n'en est pas toujours de même, aliquando omissa impedit executionem ex omni parte.' 1 Boullenois, obs. 23, p. 446–448. See also 2 Burge, Col. & For. Law, pt. 2, c. 9, p. 848–850; 3 Id. pt. 2. c. 20, p. 758, 759, 762, 763; Don v. Lippmann, 5 C. & F. 1, 12, 13.

[1] Pothier, as well as other jurists, distinguish between the essence, the nature, and the accidents of contracts ; the former includes whatever is indispensable to the constitution of it; the next, whatever is included in it, without being expressly mentioned, by operation of law, but is capable of a severance without destroying it; and the last, those things which belong to it only by express agreement. Without meaning to contest the propriety of this division, I am content to include the two former in the single word nature as quite conformable to our English idiom. Cujas also adopts the same course. See Pothier, Oblig. n. 5. See also 2 Boullenois, obs. 46, p. 460, 461, 462; Bavon v. Vavasseur, 10 Mart. (La.) 61. Merlin, Répert. Convention, s. 2, n. 6, p. 357; Rodenburg, de Div. Stat. tit. 2, c. 5, s. 16; 2 Boullenois, Appx. 50; 1 Boullenois, 688; 3 Burge, Col. & For. Law, pt. 2, c. 20, p. 848–851.

[2] 1 Boullenois, obs. 23, p. 446; 2 Id. obs. 46, p. 460, 461; Voet, de Stat. s. 9, c. 10, s. 10, p. 287; Id. p. 325, ed. 1661; Hertius, de Collis. Leg. tom. 1, s. 10, p. 127; Id. p. 179, 180, ed. 1716; post, s. 301 f.

forenses statuta loci contractus observare debent.'[1] Thus whether
a contract be a personal obligation or a real obligation; whether
it be conditional or absolute; whether it be the principal or the
accessary; whether it be that of principal or surety; whether it
be of limited or of universal operation, — these are points properly
belonging to the nature of the contract, and are dependent upon
the law and custom of the place of the contract whenever there
are no express terms in the contract itself, which otherwise control them. By the law of some countries there are certain joint
contracts which bind each party for the whole, in solido; and
there are other joint contracts, where the parties are, under circumstances, bound only for several and distinct portions.[2] In
such case the law of the place of the contract regulates the
nature of the contract, in the absence of any express stipulations.[3] These may therefore be said to constitute the nature of
the contract.[4]

[1] Lauterback, Diss. 104, pt. 3, n. 58, cited 2 Boullenois, obs. 46, p. 460.

[2] 4 Burge, Col. & For. Law, pt. 2, c. 7, s. 2, p. 722-735: post, s. 322.

[3] Pothier on Oblig. n. 261-268; Van Leeuwen, Comment. b. 4, c. 4, s. 1;
Ferguson v. Flower, 4 Mart. N.S. (La.) 312; 2 Boullenois, obs. 46, p. 463;
Code Civil of France, art. 1197, 1202, 1220, 1222; Code de Com. art. 22, 140.
One may see how strangely learned men will reason on subjects of this nature
by consulting Boullenois. He puts the case of a contract made in a country
where all parties would be bound in solido, and by the law of their own domicil they would be entitled to the benefit of a division, and vice versa; and
asks, What law is to govern? In each case he decides that the law should
govern which is most favorable to the debtor. 'Ainsi les obligés solidaires
ont contracté sous une loi qui leur est favorable; j'embrasse cette loi; elle
leur est contraire, j'embrasse la loi de leur domicil.' 2 Boullenois, obs. 46,
p. 463, 464. See also Bouhier, c. 21, s. 198, 199.

[4] See Henry on Foreign Law, 39. Pothier on Obligations, n. 7, has explained the meaning of the words, the nature of the contract, in the following
manner: 'Things which are only of the nature of the contract are those which,
without being of the essence, form a part of it, though not expressly mentioned;
it being of the nature of the contract that they shall be included and understood. These things have an intermediate place between those which are of
the essence of the contract, and those which are merely accidental to it, and
differ from both of them. . They differ from those which are of the essence of
the contract, inasmuch as the contract may subsist without them, and they
may be excluded by the express agreement of the parties; and they differ from
things which are merely accidental to it, inasmuch as they form a part of it
without being particularly expressed, as may be illustrated by the following
examples. In the contract of sale the obligation of warranty which the seller
contracts with the purchaser is of the nature of the contract of sale; therefore
the seller, by the act of sale, contracts this obligation, though the parties do
not express it, and there is not a word respecting it in the contract; but as

264. *Nature.* — An illustration may be taken from a case often put by the civilians. By the law of some countries a warranty is implied in all cases of sale; by that of others it is not. Suppose a contract of sale is made in any of the former countries by parties domiciled in any of the latter countries. If the contract is to be executed in the country where it is made, a warranty will be implied, as an incident arising from the nature of the contract; if it is to be executed in the place of the domicil of the parties, for reasons which we shall presently see, no warranty will be implied.[1] By the civil law, there is an implied warranty as to the quality and soundness of goods sold; by the common law there is not.[2] A sale of goods in England would be governed by the common law; a sale in a foreign country, under the civil law,

the obligation is of the nature and not of the essence of the contract of sale, the contract of sale may subsist without it; and if it is agreed that the seller shall not be bound to warranty, such agreement will be valid, and the contract will continue a real contract of sale. It is also of the nature of the contract of sale, that as soon as the contract is completed by the consent of the parties, although before delivery, the thing sold is at the risk of the purchaser; and that, if it happens to perish without the fault of the seller, the loss falls upon the purchaser, who is, notwithstanding the misfortune, liable for the price; but as that is only of the nature and not of the essence of the contract, the contrary may be agreed upon. When a thing is lent to be specifically returned [commodatur], it is of the nature of the contract that the borrower shall be answerable for the slightest negligence in respect to the articles lent. He contracts this obligation to the lender by the very nature of the contract, and without anything being said about it. But as this obligation is of the nature and not of the essence of the contract, it may be excluded by an express agreement that the borrower shall only be bound to act with fidelity, and shall not be responsible for any accidents merely occasioned by his negligence. It is also of the nature of this contract, that the loss of the thing lent, when it arises from inevitable accident, falls upon the lender. But as that is of the nature and not of the essence of the contract, there may be an agreement to charge the borrower with every loss that may happen until the thing is restored. A great variety of other instances might be adduced from the different kinds of contracts. Those things which are accidental to a contract are such as, not being of the nature of the contract, are only included in it by express agreement. For instance, the allowance of a certain time for paying the money due, the liberty of paying it by instalments, that of paying another thing instead of it, of paying to some other person than the creditor, and the like, are accidental to the contract; because they are not included in it without being particularly expressed.'

[1] Pothier, Oblig. n. 7; 2 Boullenois, obs. 46, p. 475, 476; Id. 460-463; Code Civil of France, art. 1135; Voet, de Statut. s. 9, c. 2, s. 10, p. 296, ed. 1715; Id. p. 325, ed. 1661; 3 Burge, Col. & For. Law, pt. 2, c. 20, p. 769, 770.

[2] Pothier, Pand. 19, 1, 5, s. 48-51; 2 Black. Com. 451; 2 Kent, Com. 478-481.

would be governed by that law, as to this implied warranty.
Boullenois lays down this as one of his fundamental rules in the
interpretation of contracts. Whenever, says he, the controversy
respects movables of which an immediate delivery is made, the
law of the place of the contract is to govern ; adopting on this
point the doctrine, although not the reasoning, of Colerus. 'Consuetudo si quidem loci, ubi negotium geritur, ita subintrat ipsum
contractum, ut secundum leges loci intelligatur actus fuisse celebratus, quamvis ea de re nihil fuerit expressum.' [1]

265. *Illustration.* — Another illustration may be borrowed from
an actual decision under the common law. By the law of England an acceptance of a bill of exchange binds the acceptor to
payment at all events. By the law of Leghorn, if a bill is accepted, and the drawer fails, and the acceptor has not sufficient
effects of the drawer in his hands at the time of acceptance, the
acceptance becomes void. An acceptance in Leghorn is governed
by this latter law ; and under such circumstances it has been held
void, and not obligatory upon the acceptor.[2]

266. *Obligation.* — Secondly, the obligation of the contract,
which, though often confounded with, is distinguishable from, its
nature.[3] The obligation of a contract is the duty to perform it,
whatever may be its nature. It may be a moral obligation, or a
legal obligation, or both. But when we speak of obligation
generally, we mean legal obligation, that is, the right to performance which the law confers on one party, and the corresponding duty of performance to which it binds the other.[4] This
is what the French jurists calls le lien du contrat (the legal tie of
the contract), onus conventionis, and what the civilians generally
call vinculum juris, or vinculum obligationis.[5] The Institutes of
Justinian have thus defined it. 'Obligatio est juris vinculum,
quo necessitate adstringimur alicujus rei solvendæ, secundum
nostræ civitatis jura.'[6] A contract may in its nature be purely
voluntary, and possess no legal obligation. It may be a mere

[1] 2 Boullenois, obs. 46, p. 475, 476.

[2] Burrows v. Jemino, 2 Str. 733; 2 Eq. Abr. 526; Pardessus, tom. 5, art.
1495, p. 270, 271.

[3] See 2 Boullenois, obs. 46, p. 454, 460, 462, 463, 464 ; 3 Burge, Col. & For.
Law, pt. 2, c. 20, p. 764, 765.

[4] See 3 Story, Const. s. 1372–1379; Ogden v. Saunders, 12 Wheat. 213;
Pothier on Oblig. art. 1, n. 1, p. 173–175.

[5] 2 Boullenois, obs. 46, p. 458–460.

[6] Inst. 3, 14; Pothier, Pand. 44, 7, p. 1, art. 1, s. 1; Pothier, Oblig. n. 173, 174.

naked pact (nudum pactum). It may possess a legal obligation ;
but the laws may limit the extent and force of that obligation in
personam, or in rem. It may bind the party personally, but not
bind his estate; or it may bind his estate, and not bind his person.
The obligation may be limited in its operation or duration ; or it
may be revocable or dissoluble in certain future events, or under
peculiar circumstances.[1]

266 a. *Illustration.* — An illustration may be readily seen in
the common case of a Scotch heritable bond. It is well known
that by the common law of England a bond, which is also a charge
on land, as, for example, a bond accompanying a mortgage of
land as a security, is primarily, in a contest between the heir and
the administrator, a charge on the personal estate, and of course
the heir has a right in equity to be relieved therefrom, so far as
there are personal assets to discharge the bond.[2] In the Scotch
law the same rule prevails as to movable debts, which are primarily and properly chargeable upon the personal assets.[3] But,
as to heritable bonds, a different rule prevails ; and they are primarily a charge on the real estate of the debtor.[4] Now, suppose
a question should arise in England, as indeed it has arisen,
whether, in the case of a Scotch movable debt, the heir, upon
payment of it, was entitled to be exonerated therefrom, and to
receive the amount out of the personal assets in England. Upon
principle it should seem clear that he would be entitled to the
relief and exoneration ; for the heir, having by the law of the
country where the land lies, a right to such relief and exoneration, would have the same right in regard to the same debt in
every other country, since it properly belongs to the nature, obligation, and interpretation of the contract.[5] On the other hand a

[1] See 2 Boullenois, obs. 46, p. 452, 454; Code Civil of France, art. 1168–1196.
[2] 1 Story, Eq. Juris. s. 571, 574; Earl of Winchelsea v. Garetty, 2 Keen, 293, 309.
[3] Winchelsea v. Garetty, 2 Keen, 293, 309, 310; post, s. 487, 529.
[4] Post, s. 486–489, 529 ; Drummond v. Drummond, 6 Bro. P. C. by Tomlins, 601.
[5] Winchelsea v. Garetty, 2 Keen, 293, 308–310. Upon this occasion Lord
Langdale said: ' By the law of England, the personal estate is the primary
fund for the payment of all debts contracted by the deceased person, whose
estate it was. By the law of Scotland movable debts are primarily and properly chargeable upon the personal estate. The creditor may, indeed, enforce
payment against the real estate in the hands of the heir; but if he does so, the
heir is entitled to relief against the executors out of the personal estate; in

Scotch heir, paying a heritable bond, would be entitled to no such
relief or exoneration, because the debt is primarily by the local law

other words, according to the law of Scotland, the real estate, though subject
to the payment of movable debts, is only a subsidiary fund for the purpose of
payment. Payment by the heir does not extinguish the debt, but vests in him
the right to recover the amount against the personal estate, and constitutes
him a creditor against the personal estate; and whether he can enforce payment against the personal estate, which is to be distributed according to the
laws of another country, which makes the personal estate the primary fund for
the payment of debts, is the question. Prima facie there would seem to be no
difficulty; the heir, having by the law of the country in which the land lies a
right to relief or exoneration, would seem to be at liberty to make that right
available in a country where the personal estate is the primary fund for the
payment of all debts. But it is objected that, in all the opinions upon which
the finding of the master rests, it has been assumed that the law of domicil
makes no difference; whereas it is clear that the domicil determines the law
by which the personal estate is to be distributed; and that, although it be true
that in England the personal estate must be applied in exoneration of the English heir of real estate, yet that the right of the heir to be exonerated is founded
on the law peculiar to England, and that a foreign heir of foreign lands is not
entitled to the same relief as an English heir of English lands. The law of
England, it is said, affords no relief to foreign real estate out of English personal estate; and although the law of Scotland regulates the administration
of the real estate, and provides that the real estate, if applied in payment of
personal debts, shall be exonerated out of the personal estate, the proposition
must be limited to personal estate, of which the distribution is regulated according to the law of Scotland, and consequently to the personal estate of debtors
domiciled in Scotland. Several cases were cited. They sufficiently establish
the propositions, which are not disputed on either side; and Drummond v.
Drummond, 6 Bro. P. C. 601 (Tomlins' ed.), establishes that a Scotch heir is
ultimately liable to pay heritable debts which have in the first instance been
paid out of the personal estate distributable according to the law of England;
but no case has occurred in which it has been decided that the Scotch
heir, having paid movable debts, is entitled to be relieved out of the personal estate distributable according to the law of England; and that
is the question here. The personal estate is taken by the administrator,
according to the law of England, subject to the payment of all the debts
of the intestate. The real estate is taken by the heir, according to the law of
Scotland, subject to the payment of all movable debts, but with a right of
relief out of the personal estate, and subject to the payment of all heritable
debts without such right of relief. As to the heritable debts, in respect of
which there is no such right of relief, the heir is not entitled to the benefit of
the English law, which makes the personal estate subject to the payment of all
debts. The Scotch law, which makes the heir ultimately liable to the payment
of such debts, and which governs the distribution of the real estate, prevails in
favor of the persons entitled to the personal estate distributable according to
the laws of England. As to personal debts, in respect of which there is such
a right to relief, the English law subjects the personal estate to all debts; the
Scotch law relieves the real estate, as far as it can consistently with the claims
of the creditors. The heir, by paying, satisfies the creditor, but at the same

a charge on the real estate;[1] and if such heritable bond should be paid by an English administrator out of the personal assets, he would be entitled to reimbursement from the Scotch heir.[2]

267. *Illustrations.* — It would be easy to multiply illustrations under this head. Suppose a contract by the law of one country to involve no personal obligation (as was supposed to be the law of France in a particular case which came in judgment,[3]) but merely to confer a right to proceed in rem; such a contract would be held everywhere to involve no personal obligation whatsoever. Suppose, by the law of a particular country, a mortgage for money borrowed should, in the absence of any express contract to repay, be limited to a mere repayment thereof out of the land, a foreign court would refuse to entertain a suit giving to it a personal obligation. Suppose a contract for the payment of the debt of a third person, in a country where the law subjected such a contract to the tacit condition that pay-

time acquires for himself a right of demand against the executor; he may, if he pleases, take an assignation for the debt, and make it available; but that is not necessary, because, without any assignation, his own claim to relief subsists and constitutes him a creditor against the personal estate. Under these circumstances the question does not appear to me to be fully stated, when it is said to be, whether a foreign heir of foreign lands is entitled to the same relief as an English heir of English lands. The case is, that a foreign heir of foreign lands is, in respect of those lands, subsidiarily liable to pay debts, to which the personal estate, distributable according to the law of England, is primarily liable; and that, having paid the debt, he is, by the law of the country in which the land lies, constituted a creditor upon the personal estate distributable according to the law of that country. And it is under these circumstances, and without reference to English tenures, or the title to exoneration which an English heir may possess, that the question arises, whether the subsidiary debtor, or the person who, by the law of a foreign country, is constituted surety for the payment of debts primarily chargeable on another fund, and paying the debts by force of and according to the law which constitutes him a creditor upon that other fund, is or is not entitled to make his title as to creditors available in another country where the personal estate is distributable, and where the law makes the personal estate primarily liable to the payment of all debts. And, upon consideration of the case, I am of opinion that the right of relief or demand against the personal estate, which in the administration of the real estate by the law of Scotland is vested in the heir, who has paid movable debts, is capable of being made available in England, where the personal estate is the primary fund for the payment of all debts.'

[1] Drummond *v.* Drummond, 6 Bro. P. C. by Tomlins, 601; post, s. 486–489, 529; Elliott *v.* Lord Minto, 6 Madd. 16; Earl of Winchelsea *v.* Garetty, 2 Keen, 293, 308–310.

[2] Robertson on Personal Succession, 209–214.

[3] Melan *v.* Fitz James, 1 B. & P. 138.

ment must first be sought against the debtor and his estate; that would limit the obligation to a mere accessorial and secondary character; and it would not be enforced in any foreign country, except after a compliance with the requisitions of the local law. Sureties, indorsers, and guarantors are therefore liable everywhere, only according to the law of the place of their contract.[1] (a) Their obligation, if treated by such local law as an accessorial obligation, will not anywhere else be deemed a principal obligation.[2] So, if by the law of the place of a contract, its obligation is positively and ex directo extinguished after a certain period by the mere lapse of time, it cannot be revived by a suit in a foreign country whose laws provide no such rule, or apply it only to the remedy.[3] To use the expressive language of a learned judge, it must be shown, in all such cases, what the laws of the foreign country are, and that they create an obligation which our laws will enforce.[4] (b)

267 a. This doctrine was fully recognized in a recent case, where the question was as to the rights of parties, growing out of various bonds executed in a state which was governed by the common law, some of the bonds being designed as security or indemnity to a surety on the other bonds. The court said: 'These different bonds were entered into in states of the Union where the common law prevails, and consequently the rights and liabilities of the parties are to be measured by that system of jurisprudence; and whatever the plaintiff (the assignee of the surety) would be entitled to recover (upon the indemnity bond) in a court of law or equity in the state where the transaction originated, he is entitled to in this court, in the present form of action.'[5] (c)

268. *Another Case.* — Let us take another case which has actu-

---

[1] Aymar v. Sheldon, 12 Wend. (N. Y.) 439.

[2] See Pothier on Oblig. n. 407; Trimbey v. Vignier, 6 C. & P. 25; 1 Bing. N. C. 151, 159; 4 M. & Scott, 695; post, s. 314, 316 a; 3 Burge, Col. & For. Law, pt. 2, c. 20, p. 764–766.

[3] See Le Roy v. Crowninshield, 2 Mason, 151; Pothier, Oblig. n. 636–639; Voet, ad Pand. 4, 1, 29, ad finem.

[4] Lord Chief Justice Eyre, in Melan v. Fitz James, 1 B. & P. 141.

[5] Mr. Justice Bullard, in King v. Harman's Heirs, 6 La. 607, 617.

(a) As to indorsers, drawers, acceptors, and makers of bills and notes, see note to s. 314.

(b) See the note to s. 637, post.

(c) See Collins Iron Co. v. Burkam, 10 Mich. 283.

ally passed into judgment. By the common law, heirs are not bound by the simple contracts of their ancestor, but only by instruments under seal declaring them expressly bound. By the law of Louisiana, the heirs are ipso facto bound by such simple coutracts of their ancestors.[1] If a simple contract is made in a State governed by the common law, it cannot be enforced in Louisiana against the heirs of the debtor, although they are domiciled in Louisiana.[2] The remedy must be sought through the instrumentality of an administration of the assets there.[3]

268 a. *Dissolubility of Contracts.* — To this head of the obligation of contracts may also be appropriately referred the consideration of the nature and extent of the obligation of contracts, in respect to their dissolubility or indissolubility in point of duration. This topic has been already incidentally discussed in examining the nature and obligation of the contract of marriage, which indeed is truly a contract; but, properly speaking, it is something more, an institution of civil society.[4] It has been often urged, especially in regard to the contract of marriage, that indissolubility is of its very essence; and that what is of the essence of a contract must be judged of according to the lex loci contractus. It has been remarked by an eminent judge that this is somewhat a vague, and for its vagueness a somewhat suspicious, proposition, and that there are many other things which may just

---

[1] Brown v. Richardsons, 1 Mart. N. S. (La.) 202. Mr. Justice Porter, in delivering the opinion of the court in this case, said: ' We recognize the distinction made by the plaintiff's counsel between the right and the remedy, and agree with him that contracts should be expounded according to the laws of the country where they are made, and enforced according to the regulations which prevail where the debtor is found. It is that distinction which gives the defendants immunity in this case. For, in order to ascertain who is debtor, we must recur to the laws of the country where the contract was made; and if these laws do not make persons standing in the character of the appellants liable under the circumstances now in proof, they cannot be made so by a change of jurisdiction. It is true that, according to our jurisprudence, the heir is obliged to pay the debts of the ancestor, if he accepts the succession unconditionally; but it does not follow that the same rule exists in other countries. An embarrassment is created in considering the case, from a feeling which it is difficult to check, that there exists something like a natural obligation on the child to pay the parent's debts; particularly if he takes any of his property. But that obligation is, in fact, nothing but the creature of positive law, and is of course subject to all the modification which the policy of different states may induce them to adopt. Id. p. 208.

[2] Brown v. Richardsons, 1 Mart. N.S. (La.) 202.   [3] Ibid.

[4] Ante, s. 108 a ; s. 218–230, 226 c, note.

as well be reckoned of the essence of the contract as this. He afterwards added : ' The fallacy of the argument, " that indissolubility is of the essence," appears plainly to be this ; it confounds incidents with essence ; it makes the rights under a contract, or flowing from and arising out of it, parcel of the contract ; it makes the mode in which judicatures deal with those rights, and with the contract itself, part of the contract; instead of considering, as in all soundness of principle we ought, that the contract and all its incidents and the rights of the parties to it, and the wrongs committed by them respecting it, must be dealt with by the courts of the country where the parties reside, and where the contract is to be carried into execution.' [1] These considerations are certainly entitled to great weight ; but they only show the intrinsic difficulty of laying down any general rules, on such complicated subjects, which shall be of universal application. It will probably be found that the proposition that a contract cannot be dissolved, except in the manner and under the circumstances prescribed by the law of the place where it was made, if true at all, must be asserted with many qualifications and exceptions. Contracts of marriage, and other contracts of a peculiar nature, may perhaps require a different exposition in this respect from other ordinary pecuniary contracts. And even if a contract be indissoluble by the lex loci contractus, except in a special mode, it may nevertheless be thought reasonable that that rule should not prevail upon a change of domicil, as to an act of the parties done in the latter place, where another mode is prescribed or allowed for its dissolution.[2] But of this we shall speak hereafter.[3]

269. *Judgment founded on Mistake of Foreign Law.* — Cases sometimes occur in which the tribunals of a foreign country are called upon to decide upon the law of another country where the contract is made, and they by mistake misinterpret that law. In such a case, if they discharge the parties from the obligation of the contract, in consequence of such misinterpretation of the foreign law, that discharge will not be held obligatory upon the courts of the country where the contract was made.[4] A

---

[1] Lord Brougham, in Warrender v. Warrender, 9 Bligh, 114; ante, s. 226 c, note.

[2] Warrender v. Warrender, 9 Bligh, 114; ante, s. 226 c, note.

[3] See post, s. 351 a ; ante, s. 226 a, note.   [4] Novelli v. Rossi, 2 B. & Ad. 757.

recent case has occurred on this subject. A bill of exchange
drawn in France, and indorsed there, and accepted and payable
in England at a banker's, was passed by an indorsee in discharge
of an antecedent debt; and upon presentment for payment it
was dishonored, and the banker's clerk by mistake cancelled the
acceptance, and then wrote on it, ' cancelled by mistake.' Afterwards the indorser, who had so passed the bill in discharge of his
debt, cited all the parties, and, among others, the creditor and
holder of the bill, before the tribunals of France, who decreed
that the cancellation operated as a suspension of legal remedies
against the acceptor, and consequently discharged the other parties, the indorsers as well as the drawer. A suit was afterwards
brought by the creditor against the debtor-indorser in England;
and it was held that the courts of France had mistaken the law
of England as to the effect of the cancellation; and that the
plaintiff was entitled to recover against the defendant the full
amount of the debt, notwithstanding the decree in the French
courts.[1] (a)

270. *Interpretation.* — Thirdly. The interpretation of contracts.
Upon this subject there would scarcely seem to be any room for
doubt or disputation. There are certain general rules of interpretation recognized by all nations, which form the basis of all
reasoning on the subject of contracts. The object is to ascertain
the real intention of the parties in their stipulations; and when
the latter are silent or ambiguous, to ascertain what is the true
sense of the words used, and what ought to be implied in order
to give them their true and full effect.[2] The primary rule in all

[1] Ibid.

[2] See Lord Brougham's striking remarks on this subject already cited ante,
s. 226 c. In Prentiss v. Savage, 13 Mass. 23, Mr. Chief Justice Parker said:
' It seems to be an undisputed doctrine, with respect to personal contracts,
that the law of the place where they are made shall govern in their construction, except when made with a view to performance in some other country,
and then the law of such country is to prevail. This is nothing more than

(a) The difficulty in Novelli v. Rossi
was mainly one of jurisdiction in the
foreign court. That mere mistake of
the English law by a French court
would not affect the judgment when
brought before a court in England,
see Castrique v. Imrie, L. R. 4 H. L.
414; Castrique v. Behrens, 3 El. & E.
722; Doglioni v. Crispin, L. R. 1 H. L.
301. See Simpson v. Fogo, 1 Hem. &
M. 195, holding otherwise of a per-
verse disregard by the court of the law
that ought to govern. And see Liverpool Credit Co. v. Hunter, L. R. 3 Ch.
479, 484.

expositions of this sort is that of common sense so well expressed
in the Digest. ' In conventionibus contrahentium voluntas, potius
quam verba, spectari placuit.' [1] But in many cases the words
used in contracts have different meanings attached to them in
different places by law and by custom. And where the words
are in themselves obscure or ambiguous, custom and usage in a
particular place may give them an exact and appropriate meaning. Hence the rule has found admission into almost all, if not
into all, systems of jurisprudence, that if the full and entire
intention of the parties does not appear from the words of the
contract, and if it can be interpreted by any custom or usage of
the place where it is made, that course is to be adopted. Such
is the rule of the Digest. ' Semper in stipulationibus, et in cæteris
contractibus id sequimur, quod actum est, erit consequens, ut id
sequamur, quod in regione in qua actum est, frequentatur.' [2]
' Conservanda est consuetudo regionis et civitatis,' says J. Sande,
' ubi contractum est.   Omnes enim actiones nostræ (si non aliter
fuerit provisum inter contrahentes) interpretationem recipiunt a
consuetudine loci in quo contrahitur.' [3] Usage is indeed of so
much authority in the interpretation of contracts, that a contract

common sense and sound justice, adopting the probable intent of the parties
as the rule of construction. For when a citizen of this country enters into a
contract in another with a citizen or subject thereof, and the contract is intended
to be there performed, it is reasonable to presume that both parties had regard
to the law of the place where they were, and that the contract was shaped
accordingly.   And it is also to be presumed, when the contract is to be executed in any other country than that in which it is made, that the parties take
into their consideration the law of such foreign country. This latter branch
of the rule, if not so obviously founded upon the intention of the parties as the
former, is equally well settled as a principle in the law of contracts.' Mr.
Chancellor Walworth, in Chapman v. Robertson, 6 Paige (N. Y.), 627, 630, used
equally strong language. ' It is an established principle,' said he, ' that the
construction and validity of personal contracts, which are purely personal,
depend upon the laws of the place where the contract is made, unless it was
made with reference to the laws of some other place or country where such
contract in the contemplation of the parties thereto was to be carried into effect
and performed.' 2 Kent Com. 457, 458; 3 Burge, Col. & For. Law, pt. 2,
c. 20, p. 752-764.
   [1] Dig. 50, 16, 219. Many rules of interpretation are found in Pothier on
Obligations, n. 91-102; in Fonblanque on Equity, b. 1, c. 6, s. 11-20, and
notes; 1 Domat, Civil Law, b. 1, tit. 1, s. 2; 1 Powell on Contracts, 370 et
seq.; Merlin, Répertoire, Convention, s. 7, 366.
   [2] Dig. 50, 17, 34; 1 Domat, Civil Law, b. 1, tit. 1, s. 2, n. 9; 2 Boullenois, obs. 46, p. 490; 3 Burge, Col. & For. Law, pt. 2, c. 20, p. 775, 776.
   [3] J. Sande, Op. Comm. de Reg. Jur. l. 9, p. 17.

is understood to contain the customary clauses, although they are not expressed, according to the known rule, 'In contractibus tacite veniunt ea quæ sunt moris et consuetudinis.'[1]   Thus, if a tenant is by custom to have the outgoing crop, he will be entitled to it, although not expressed in the lease.[2]   And if a lease is entirely silent as to the time of the tenant's quitting, the custom of the country will fix it.[3]   By the law of England a month means ordinarily in common contracts, as in leases, a lunar month ; but in mercantile contracts it means a calendar month.[4] A contract therefore made in England for a lease of land for twelve months would mean a lease for forty-eight weeks only.[5] A promissory note to pay money in twelve months would mean in one year or in twelve calendar months.[6]   If a contract of either sort were required to be enforced in a foreign country, its true interpretation must be everywhere the same that it is according to the usage in the country where the contract was made.

271. *Illustrations.* — The same word, too, often has different significations in different countries.   Thus the term *usance*, which is common enough in negotiable instruments, means in some countries a month, in others two or more months, and in others half a month.   A note payable at one usance must be construed everywhere according to the meaning of the word in the country where the contract is made.[7]   There are many other cases illustrative of the same principle.   A note made in England for 100 pounds would mean 100 pounds sterling.   A like note made in America would mean 100 pounds in American currency, which is one-fourth less in value.   It would be monstrous to contend that on the English note, sued in America, the less sum only ought to be recovered ; and on the other hand, on the American

---

[1] Pothier, Oblig. n. 95; Merlin, Repertoire, Convention, s. 7; 2 Kent Com. 555.

[2] Wigglesworth *v.* Dallison, Doug. 201, 207.

[3] Webb *v.* Plummer, 2 B. & A. 746.

[4] 2 Black, Com. 141; Catesby's Case, 6 Rep. 62; Lacon *v.* Hooper, 6 T. R. 224; 3 Burge, Col. & For. Law, pt. 3, c. 20, p. 776, 777.

[5] Ibid.

[6] Chitty on Bills, 8th ed. 1833, p. 406; Lang *v.* Gale, 1 M. & S. 111; Cockell *v.* Gray, 3 Br. & B. 187; Leffingwell *v.* White, 1 Johns. Cas. (N. Y.) 99.

[7] Chitty on Bills, 8th ed. 1833, p. 404, 405.   See also 2 Boullenois, obs. 46, p. 447.

note sued in England, that one-third more ought to be recovered.[1]

271 a. Another illustration may easily be suggested which is not quite so simple in its circumstances. Suppose a contract is made in England between two Englishmen for the sale of lands situated in Jamaica ; and the vendee agreed to give £20,000 for the lands without specifying in what currency. The difference between Jamaica pounds currency and English sterling pounds currency, by the par of exchange, exclusive of any premium on bills of exchange on England, is forty per cent. Consequently £28,000 Jamaica currency would constitute only £20,000 sterling. The question might then arise, according to which currency the purchase-money is to be paid. In the absence of all expressions and circumstances from which a different intention may be inferred, the interpretation of the contract would be that it was payable in the currency of the country where the contract was made, and not in that of the situs of the property.[2] Another illustration may be in case of a sale of lands situated in one country, and the contract made in another, and the sale to be a certain number of acres for a gross price, or at a specific price per acre, the mode of measuring an acre, or the contents thereof, being different in different countries. The question might arise whether the acre was to be according to the measurement in the one country or in the other. Now upon this very point different opinions and judgments have been held by different jurists and tribunals on the continent of Europe ; some holding that the lex loci contractus ought to govern, and others that the lex situs ought to govern the admeasurement.[3] Choppin has reported a case where the highest tribunal of Orleans held that the laws of the place of the contract should determine the admeasurement of the acre. But he disapproves of it and says : ' Justior tamen est diversa opinio, venditi agri mensuram ex lege petendam situs prædiorum non loci pactæ venditionis.'[4] John Voet holds the

[1] See also Powell on Contracts, 876; 2 Boullenois, obs. 46, p. 498, 503; Henry on Foreign Law, Appendix, 233; Pardessus, Droit Com. art. 1492; 3 Burge, Col. & For. Law, pt. 3, c. 20, p. 772, 773; post, s. 272 a, s. 807, 808.

[2] 2 Burge, Col. & For. Law, pt. 2, c. 9, p. 860, 861.

[3] Id. 858, 859.

[4] Choppini Opera, de Feudis Andeg. tom. 2, lib. 2, tit. 3, n. 10, p. 132, 133, ed. 1611; 2 Boullenois, obs. 46, p. 497; 2 Burge, Col. & For. Law, pt. 2, c. 9, p. 858, 859.

same opinion : ' Si res immobiles ad certam mensuram debeantur, et ea pro locorum diversitate varia sit, in dubio solvi debent juxta mensuram loci in quo sitæ sunt.'[1] In respect to movables he holds the opposite opinion, that they are governed by the law of the place of the contract. Dumoulin holds the same opinion as to immovables, that they are governed by the lex situs. ' Unde stantibus mensuris diversis, si fundus venditur ad mensuram, vel affirmatur, vel mensuratur, non continuo debet inspici mensura, quæ viget in loco contractus, sed in dubio debet attendi mensura loci, in quo fundus debet metiri, et tradi, et executio fieri.'[2] He admits that other jurists differ from him, and that other circumstances may vary this interpretation. ' Et ita tenendum, nisi ex aliis circumstantiis constet, de qua mensura senserint.'[3] Indeed he denies that any universal rule can be established.[4] The same doctrine that the lex situs ought to govern in the like cases would seem to be favored, if not positively established, in the jurisprudence of England and America.[5]

272. *General Rule.* — The general rule then is that, in the interpretation of contracts, the law and custom of the place of the contract are to govern in all cases where the language is not directly expressive of the actual intention of the parties, but it is to be tacitly inferred from the nature and objects and occasion of the contract.[6] (*a*) The rule has been fully recognized in the courts of common law ; and it has been directly decided by those courts that the interpretation of the contract must be governed by the laws of the country where the contract is made.[7] (*b*) And

---

[1] J. Voet, 46, 3, n. 8, p. 949; 2 Burge, Col. & For. Law, pt. 2, c. 9, p. 859; 2 Boullenois, obs. 46, p. 497.

[2] Molin. Oper. Com. ad Cod. 1, 1, 1, tom. 3. Conclus. de Statut. p. 554.

[3] Ibid.   [4] Ibid.; post, s. 274 *a*.   [5] Ante, s. 270.

[6] See the opinion of the court delivered by Mr. Justice Martin in the case of Depau *v.* Humphreys, 8 Mart. N.S. (La.) 1, 8, 9, 13, 22–24; Mr. Justice Porter in the case of Morris *v.* Eves, 11 Mart. (La.) 730; Courtois *v.* Carpenteir, 1 Wash. C. C. 376.

[7] Trimby *v.* Vignier, 1 Bing. N. C. 151, 159; post, s. 316 *a;* De la Vega *v.* Vianna, 1 B. & Ad. 284 ; British Linen Co. *v.* Drummond, 10 B. & C. 903; Bank of the United States *v.* Donnally, 8 Pet. 368, 872; Pope *v.* Nickerson, 3 Story, 484; Harrison *v.* Sterry, 5 Cranch, 289; Wilcox *v.* Hunt, 13 Pet. 378, 379. We shall presently see that the same rule is adopted in the interpretation of wills. See Lansdowne *v.* Lansdowne, 2 Bligh, 60, 88, 89, 91, and cases there

(*a*) Bent *v.* Lauve, 3 La. An. 88.
(*b*) See ante, s. 242, 263 ; post, s. 314, and note.

the rule is founded in wisdom, sound policy, and general convenience. Especially in interpreting ambiguous contracts ought the domicil of the parties, the place of execution, the various provisions and expressions of the instrument, and other circumstances, implying a local reference, to be taken into consideration.[1] Thus Gothofredus says : ' Consuetudo regionis sequemur, et ideo conducere, concedere, contrahere, et quidvis agere pro modo regionis in dubio presumitur. Nam sicut natura non separatur a subjecto, ita nec a consueto. Quod est de consuetudine habetur pro pacto.'[2] Burgundus is more full and pointed to this point, as we have already seen.[3] John à Sande expresses the same doctrine in these words. ' Quando verba sunt dubia et ambigua, tunc inspicimus, quod verisimiliter a contrahentibus actum sit, aut quid testator senserit.'[4]

272 a. One of the simplest cases, to illustrate the rule, is the case of a promissory note made and dated in a particular country, payable in a currency which has the same name, but is of a different value in different countries. The question is, what currency is presumed to be intended by the parties? The answer would seem to be equally certain, the currency of the country where it is payable. Suppose then a promissory note dated in Dublin, and thereby the maker promises to pay to the payee, or order, one hundred pounds in forty days after date, and the note is afterwards sued in England ; the question would arise, whether the note meant a hundred pounds English currency, or Irish currency. This would depend upon another question, where the note was payable, as no place of payment was named, in England or in Ireland. Now, by the rules of law in the interpretation of all such contracts, when no other place of payment is named, the contract is treated as a contract made in and governed by the law of the place where it is made and dated, and therefore it would be interpreted to mean one hundred pounds Irish currency, because payable there, and indeed payable everywhere, where the

cited. Holmes v. Holmes, 1 Russ. & My. 660, 662; Chapman v. Robertson, 6 Paige (N. Y.) 627, 630; post, s. 479 a–479 n.

[1] Ante, s. 237. See Lansdowne v. Lansdowne, 2 Bligh, 60, 87 ; post, s. 479 a–479 n.

[2] Gothofred. ad Pand. 50, 17, 34; Le Brun, Traité de la Communauté, liv. 1, c. 2, s. 46.

[3] Ante, s. 237; 2 Boullenois, obs. 46, p. 451.

[4] J. à Sande, Op. Com. de Reg. Juris. l. 9, p. 17.

mus civem Tubingensem hic vendere vicino domum Genevæ, vel
Tiguri sitam, ubi sit statutum, quod venditor fundi tenetur de
duplo cavere, per duos idoneos cives, ne teneantur litigare extra
forum suum.   Iste est proprius casus et verus, intellectus, d. l. in
qua dicitur ; Venditorem teneri cavere secundum consuetudinem
loci contractus ; quod est intelligendum non de loco contractus
fortuiti, sed domicilii, prout crebrius usu venit, immobilia non
vendi peregre, sed in loco domicilii.   Lex autem debet adaptari
ad casus vel hypotheses, quæ solent frequenter accidere : nec
extendi ad casus raro accidentes.   Saltem quando contrarium
apparet de ratione diversitatis, vel quando sequeretur captio inge-
rentis.   Quia qua ratione dicta lex, excludit externum locum situs
rei, in quo contrahentes non habent domicilium ; multo fortius
excluditur locus fortuitus contractus, in quo partes peregre transeunt. Patet : Quia quis censetur potius contrahere in loco, in
quo debet solvere, quam in loco, ubi fortuito transiens contrahit.
Sed hic venditor eo ipso se obligat, solutionem et traditionem
realem, per se, vel per alium, facere in loco, in quo fundus situs
est : ergo ibi contraxisse censetur.   Et tamen in dubio non attenditur consuetudo loci contractus.   Quia venditor illi non subest,
nec ejus notitiam habere præsumitur, ergo multo minus consuetudo loci fortuiti, quam magis ignorat.'[1]

275. *Importance of the General Rule.* — Cases illustrative of the
importance of the general rule may be easily found in the jurisprudence of modern nations. 'In some countries,' says Boullenois, ' the laws give a certain sense and a certain effect to clauses
in an instrument, while the laws of another country give a sense
and effect more extensive or more restrained. For example, at
Toulouse, the clause, *si sine liberis,* added to a substitution, means
a gradual substitution ; and in other places it means only a condition, if other circumstances do not concur.'[2]   The full effect of

---

[1] Molin. Opera, Com. ad Cod. 1, 1, 1, Conclus. de Statut. tom. 3, p. 554;
3 Burge, Col. & For. Law, pt. 2, c. 20, p. 851, 852; Id. p. 858, 859.

[2] 2 Boullenois, obs. 46, p. 447, 518, 519. In the French law substitution is
either simple or gradual. It is called simple when one person only is substituted for another in a donation; as, a donation to A, and if he refuses or dies,
to B. It is called gradual when there are several substitutes in succession; as,
a donation to A, and if he refuses or dies, to B, and if B refuses or dies, to
C, and if C refuses or dies, to D, &c. Pothier, Traité des Substitutions,
art. prélim.; Id. s. 3, art. 1. See also 3 Burge, Col. & For. Law, pt. 2, c. 20,
p. 855–857.

this example may be felt only by a civilian.   But an analogous
one may be put from the common law.   A contract in England
for an estate there situate, or a conveyance of such an estate to
A and the heirs of his body begotten, would, before the statute
de donis, have been interpreted to mean a contract for or a conveyance of a conditional fee-simple; but since that statute it
would be construed to be a contract for or a conveyance of a fee-
tail.[1]   The rights growing out of these different interpretations
are, as every common lawyer knows, exceedingly different; and
to construe them otherwise than according to the common law
would defeat the intention of the parties, and uproot the solid
doctrines of law.   The sense of the terms and the legal effect of
the instrument ought, and it is to be presumed would be everywhere ascertained by the same mode of interpretation, wherever
the point should come, directly or indirectly, in judgment in any
foreign country.

276. *Marriage Contracts and Settlements.* — The language of
marriage contracts and settlements must, in like manner, be
interpreted according to the law of the place where they are
contracted. (*a*)   A moment's consideration would teach us the
inextricable confusion which would ensue from disregarding the
habitual construction put by courts of law upon instruments of
this sort, executed in England or in France, and brought into
controversy in any other country.   The whole system of interpretation of the clauses of marriage contracts and settlements in
England is in a high degree artificial; but it is built upon uniform
principles which could not now be swept away without leaving
innumerable difficulties behind.   What could a foreign court do
in interpreting the terms, *heirs of the body*, *children*, *issue*, connected with other words of limitation or description in a marriage
settlement or a will made in England?   The intricate branch of
English jurisprudence upon which the true exposition of such
clauses depends has tasked and exhausted the diligence and
learning of the highest professional minds, and requires almost
the study of a life to be thoroughly mastered.[2]   Probably the
system of interpretation in similar cases in France does not
involve fewer difficulties, dependent upon the nice shades of

[1] 2 Black. Com. 110–112.
[2] See Fearne on Contingent Remainders, passim.

(*a*) See McLeod *v.* Board, 30 Tex. 238.

meaning of words in different connections, and the necessary complexity of matrimonial rights and nuptial contracts and prospective successions.[1] The general rule is in no cases more firmly adhered to than in cases of nuptial contracts and settlements, that they are to be construed and enforced according to the lex loci contractus.[2]

276 a. *Case in England.* — The same doctrine was fully recognized in a recent case in England. In that case the parties were domiciled and married in Scotland, and executed a nuptial contract containing mutual provisions for the benefit of the parties and their offspring. Afterwards the wife, upon the death of her mother in England, became entitled to certain stock; and the husband filed a bill in chancery to have the stock conveyed to him by the trustee thereof, without a settlement being made upon his wife in regard thereto. The question was whether the wife was entitled to the common equity to a settlement out of the stock, according to the English law. It appeared that, by the law of Scotland, acting upon the interpretation and construction of the provisions of the nuptial contract, the wife was not entitled to any such equity to a settlement. The Lord Chancellor held that the court, in administering the rights of the parties under that nuptial contract, was bound to give the same construction and effect to it in England as the Scottish law would give to it; and he therefore awarded the stock to the husband without any settlement.[3] (a)

277. *Commercial Contracts.* — The same rule is also universally acknowledged in relation to commercial contracts.[4] Where the terms of an instrument executed by foreigners in a foreign country are free from obscurity, it will be construed according to the obvious import of those terms, unless there is some proof that, according to the law of the foreign country, the true interpretation of them would be different.[5] But where a particular interpreta-

---

[1] See 2 Boullenois, obs. 46, p. 489–494, 503, 504, 505, 513; Mosyn *v.* Fabrigas, Cowper, 174.

[2] Feaubert *v.* Turst, Prec. Ch. 207; De Couche *v.* Savatier, 3 Johns. Ch. (N. Y.) 190.

[3] Anstruther *v.* Adair, 2 My. & K. 513, 516. See also Breadalbane *v.* Chandos, cited in 4 Burge, Col. & For. Law, Appx. 749, 755.

[4] Pardessus, Droit Com. tom. 5, n. 1491, 1492; 2 Kent Com. 457, 458.

[5] King of Spain *v.* Machado, 4 Russ. 225; post, s. 286.

(a) See Thurburn *v.* Steward, L. R. 3 P.C. 504.

tion is established, that must be followed. Indeed the courts of every country must be presumed to be the best expositors of their own laws, and of the terms of contracts made with reference to them. And no court, professing to be governed by principle, would assume the power to declare that a foreign court misunderstood the laws of their own country, or the operation of them on contracts made there.[1]

278. The remarks already suggested upon this rule cannot be better enforced than by a quotation from an opinion of the late learned Mr. Chief Justice Parker: 'That the laws of any state cannot by any inherent authority be entitled to respect extraterritorially, or beyond the jurisdiction of the state which enacts them, is the necessary result of the independence of distinct sovereignties. But the courtesy, comity, or mutual convenience of nations, amongst which commerce has introduced so great an intercourse, has sanctioned the admission and operation of foreign laws relative to contracts. So that it is now a principle generally received, that contracts are to be construed and interpreted according to the laws of the state in which they are made, unless from their tenor it is perceived that they were entered into with a view to the laws of some other state. And nothing can be more just than this principle. For when a merchant of France, Holland, or England, enters into a contract in his own country, he must be presumed to be conusant of the laws of the place where he is, and to expect that his contract is to be judged of and carried into effect according to those laws; and the merchant with whom he deals, if a foreigner, must be supposed to submit himself to the same laws, unless he has taken care to stipulate for a performance in some other country, or has in some other way excepted his particular contract from the laws of the country where he is.'[2]

278 a. *Promissory Note.* — *Policy of Insurance.* — Hence it is adopted by the common law, as a general rule in the interpretation of contracts, that they are to be deemed contracts of the place where they are made, unless they are positively to be performed or paid elsewhere. Therefore a note made in France, and payable generally, will be treated as a French note, and go-

---

[1] Mr. Chief Justice Marshall, in Elmendorf *v.* Taylor, 10 Wheat. 159; Mr. Justice Porter, in Saul *v.* His Creditors, 5 Mart. N.S. (La.) 587.

[2] Blanchard *v.* Russell, 13 Mass. 1, 4, 5.

verned accordingly by the laws of France as to its obligation and
construction.   So a policy of insurance, executed in England on
a French ship for the French owner, on a voyage from one French
port to another, would be treated as an English contract, and in
case of loss the debt would be treated as an English debt.   Indeed all the rights and duties and obligations growing out of such
a policy would be governed by the law of England, and not by
the law of France, if the laws respecting insurance were different
in the two countries.[1]

279. *The Rule not affected by the Domicil.* — It has sometimes
been suggested, and especially by foreign jurists, that contracts
made between foreigners in a foreign country ought to be construed according to the law of their own country, whenever they
both belong to the same country.[2]   Where they belong to different countries, some controversy has arisen as to the point, whether the law of the domicil of the debtor or that of the creditor
ought to prevail.[3]   Where a contract is made in a country between a citizen and a foreigner, it seems admitted that the law
of the place where the contract is made ought to prevail, unless
the contract is to be performed elsewhere.[4]   In the common law
of England and America all these niceties are discarded.   Every
contract, whether made between foreigners or between foreigners
and citizens, is deemed to be governed by the law of the place
where it is made and is to be executed.[5]

---

[1] Donn v. Lippmann, 5 Cl. & F. 1, 18–20; post, s. 317.

[2] Ante, s. 273; 2 Boullenois, obs. 46, p. 455–458; Id. p. 495–593.   Hertius
seems to make the following distinction.   After having stated the general rule
to be: Si lex actui formam dat, inspiciendum est locus actus, non domicilii,
non rei sitæ; he adds: Nimirum valet hæc regula, etiam in extero, qui actum
celebrat, licet enim hic subjectus revera maneat patriæ suæ, tamen illud, de
acto primo est intelligendum, quoad actum vero secundum subditus illius loci
sit temporarius, ubi agit, vel contrahit, simulque ut forum ibi sortitur, ita statutis ligatur.   Non valet si exterus ignoravit statutum.   Hertii Opera, tom. 1,
de Collis. Leg. s. 4, n. 10, p. 126, 128; Id. ed. 1716, p. 179–181.

[3] See Foelix, Conflit des Lois, Revue Étrang. et Franç. 1840, tom. 7, s.
21–23, p. 200–209; Id. s. 40–50, p. 46–49; 3 Burge, Col. & For. Law, pt. 2,
c. 20, p. 775, 776.

[4] See Livermore, Dissert. s. 42, p. 46; 1 Hertii Opera, de Collis. Leg. s.
10, p. 126, 128; Id. p. 179–181, ed. 1716; Voet, de Statut. s. 9, c. 2, excep. 4;
Id. s. 10, p. 268, ed. 1715; Id. p. 325, ed. 1661.   But see contra, 2 Boullenois,
obs. 46, p. 459; ante, s. 263, 273, 274.

[5] Smith v. Mead, 3 Conn. 253; De Sobry v. De Laistre, 2 Harr. & J.
(Md.) 193, 228.

279 *a.* *Contract subject to a Condition to take place in another Country.* — Hertius has put a case where a contract made in a country is subject to ·a condition, and the performance of that condition takes place in another country, the laws of which are different; and the question is whether the laws of the one or those of the other ought to govern the contract. He answers that the laws of the country where the contract was made, because the condition, when fulfilled, refers back to the time of the contract. 'Quia conditio retrotrahitur ad tempus conventionis.'[1] J. à Sande adopts the same doctrine almost in the same words.[2]

280. *Place of Performance.* — The rules already considered suppose that the performance of the contract is to be in the place where it is made, either expressly or by tacit implication.[3] But where the contract is, either expressly or tacitly, to be performed in any other place, there the general rule is in conformity to the presumed intention of the parties that the contract, as to its validity, nature, obligation, and interpretation, is to be governed by the law of the place of performance.[4] This would seem to be a result of natural justice; and the Roman law has adopted it as a maxim: 'Contraxisse unusquisque in eo loco intelligitur, in quo ut solveret, se obligavit.'[5] And again, in the law, Aut ubi quisque contraxerit: 'Contractum autem non utique eo loco intelligitur, quo negotium gestum sit; sed quo solvenda est pecunia.'[6] The rule was fully recognized and acted on in a recent case by the Supreme Court of the United States, where the court said that the general principle in relation to contracts made in one place to be executed in another was well settled, that they are to be governed by the laws of the place of performance.[7] (*a*)

[1] 1 Hertii Opera, de Collis. Leg. s. 4, n. 54, p. 147, ed. 1737; Id. p. 207; ed. 1716.

[2] J. à Sande, Com. ad Reg. Jur. l. 9, p. 18; post, s. 287. [3] Ante, s. 242.

[4] 2 Kent Com. p. 393, 394, 459; Casaregis Disc. 179; 1 Emerigon, c. 4, s. 8; Voet, de Stat. s. 9, c. 2, s. 15, p. 270, ed. 1715; Id. p. 328, ed. 1661; Boullenois, Quest. Contr. des Lois, p. 339, &c ; 3 Burge, Col. & For. Law, pt. 2, c. 20, p. 771, 772; Don *v.* Lippman, 5 Cl. & F. 1, 13, 19; Fergusson *v.* Fyffe, 8 Cl. & F. 121.

[5] Dig. 44, 7, 21; ante, s. 233. [6] Dig. 42, 5, 3.

[7] Andrews *v.* Pond, 13 Pet. 65.

(*a*) *Place of Performance.* — Special rules prevail upon this subject with regard to the parties to bills and notes. See note to s. 314, post. The main rule itself is illustrated in cases without number. It may be of some ser-

281. *Foreign Jurists.* — *Common Law.* — Paul Voet has laid down the same rule. ' Hinc, ratione effectus et complimenti ipsius

vice to cite the body of the decisions in the order of the states, though many of them are elsewhere considered or cited. New Hampshire: Thayer *v.* Elliott, 16 N. H. 102; Little *v.* Riley, 43 N. H. 109; Chase *v.* Dow, 47 N. H. 405. Vermont: Peck *v.* Hibbard, 26 Vt. 698, 703; Peck *v.* Mayo, 14 Vt. 33. Massachusetts: Murphy *v.* Collins, 121 Mass. 6; Woodruff *v.* Hill, 116 Mass. 310; Stevenson *v.* Payne, 109 Mass. 378; Akers *v.* Demond, 103 Mass. 318. Connecticut: Richardson *v.* Rowland, 40 Conn. 565; Koster *v.* Merritt, 32 Conn. 246. New York: Wayne Bank *v.* Low, 81 N. Y. 566; Curtis *v.* Delaware R. Co., 74 N. Y. 116; Merchants' Bank *v.* Griswold, 72 N. Y. 472; King *v.* Sarria, 69 N. Y. 24; First National Bank *v.* Shaw, 61 N. Y. 283; Croninger *v.* Crocker, 62 N. Y. 151; Ockerman *v.* Cross, 54 N. Y. 29; Dike *v.* Erie Ry. Co., 45 N. Y. 113; Barry *v.* Equitable Soc., 59 N. Y. 587; Cutler *v.* Wright, 22 N. Y. 472; Bowen *v.* Newell, 13 N. Y. 290; Merchants' Bank *v.* Spalding, 9 N. Y. 53; Jacks *v.* Nichols, 5 N. Y. 178; Davis *v.* Garr, 6 N. Y. 124; Western *v.* Genesee Ins. Co., 12 N. Y. 258. Pennsylvania: Mills *v.* Wilson, 88 Penn. St. 118; Brown *v.* Camden R. Co., 83 Penn. St. 316; Benners *v.* Clemens, 58 Penn. St. 24; Townsend *v.* Maynard, 45 Penn. St. 198. Virginia: Freeman's Bank *v.* Ruckman, 16 Gratt. 126. North Carolina: Roberts *v.* McNeely, 7 Jones, 506. Georgia: Dunn *v.* Welsh, 62 Ga. 241; Goodrich *v.* Williams, 50 Ga. 425; Green *v.* East Tenn. R. Co., 37 Ga. 456. Alabama: Hunt *v.* Hall, 37 Ala. 702; Cowles *v.* Townsend, Id. 77. Mississippi: Allen *v.* Bratton, 47 Miss. 119; Frazier *v.* Warfield, 9 Sm. & M. 220. Louisiana: Galliano *v.* Pierre, 18 La. An. 10. Michigan: Roethke *v.* Philip Best Brewing Co., 33 Mich. 340; My-

ers *v.* Carr, 12 Mich. 63; Collins Iron Co. *v.* Burkam, 10 Mich. 283. Indiana: Butler *v.* Myer, 17 Ind. 77; Alford *v.* Baker, 53 Ind. 279. Illinois: Michigan Cent. R. Co. *v.* Boyd, 91 Ill. 268; Milwaukee R. Co. *v.* Smith, 74 Ill. 197; Evans *v.* Anderson, 78 Ill. 558; Pennsylvania Co. *v.* Fairchild, 69 Ill. 260; Adams *v.* Robertson, 37 Ill. 45; Lewis *v.* Headley, 36 Ill. 433; Mason *v.* Dousay, 35 Ill. 424. Kentucky: Tyler *v.* Trabue, 8 B. Mon. 306. Tennessee: Parham *v.* Pulliam, 5 Cold. 497; Senter *v.* Bowman, 5 Heisk. 14; Lewis *v.* Woodfolk, 2 Baxter, 25. Arkansas: White *v.* Friedlander, 35 Ark. 52; Bowles *v.* Eddy, 33 Ark. 645. Missouri: Golson *v.* Ebert, 52 Mo. 260; Garesché *v.* Chouteau, 37 Mo. 413; Bank of Louisville *v.* Young, Ib. 398. Iowa: Burrows *v.* Stryker, 47 Iowa, 477; McDaniel *v.* Chicago Ry. Co., 24 Iowa, 412; Arnold *v.* Potter, 22 Iowa, 194; Boyd *v.* Ellis, 11 Iowa, 97; Butters *v.* Olds, Id. 1. Nebraska: Kittle *v.* De Lamater, 3 Neb. 325; Sands *v.* Smith, 1 Neb. 108. United States: Railroad Co. *v.* Bank of Ashland, 12 Wall. 226; Miller *v.* Tiffany, 1 Wall. 298; Bell *v.* Bruen, 1 How. 169; Musson *v.* Lake, 4 How. 262; Tilden *v.* Blair, 21 Wall. 241.

Some of the cases indicate that the ' place of performance ' of a contract means the place where the engagement is to be completed, though begun in another jurisdiction, as where goods are delivered to a carrier in one state to be transported to another. Or perhaps it would state the effect of the cases as truly to say that where goods are entrusted to a carrier for transportation, the fact of the naming a place of delivery affords evidence that the law of that place was intended by the parties as the law which should govern their rights and duties. Cur-

contractus, spectatur ille locus, in quem destinata est solutio: id, quod ad modum, mensuram, usuras, etc., negligentiam, et moram

tis *v.* Delaware R. Co., 74 N. Y. 116; Brown *v.* Camden R. Co., 83 Penn. St. 316. Comp. Gay *v.* Rainey, 89 Ill. 221; Chatham Bank *v.* Allison, 15 Iowa, 357; Dickinson *v.* Edwards, 77 N. Y. 573; Tilden *v.* Blair, 21 Wall. 241. And see Dolan *v.* Green, 110 Mass. 322.

The courts however are not agreed upon this proposition. Thus it is sometimes held that where a carrier's contract is to be performed partly in the state in which the contract was executed, especially where such partial performance is considerable, the law of that state will govern the rights of the parties in the absence of evidence of a different intention. McDaniel *v.* Chicago R. Co., 24 Iowa, 412; Pennsylvania Co. *v.* Fairchild, 69 Ill. 260; Michigan Cent. R. Co. *v.* Boyd, 91 Ill. 268. And see the suggestion of Brett, L.J., in Cohen *v.* Southeastern Ry. Co., 2 Ex. D. 253. In the last-named case a contract had been made at Boulogne by an Englishwoman with an English railway for transportation of herself and luggage to England. Several of the judges inclined to the opinion that this was an English contract (see Brown *v.* Camden R. Co., supra, which seems to be to the same effect); but the case was decided on other grounds. Brett, L.J., suggested that if the contract had been to carry from Paris to England, the French law might govern in France during the transportation in French vehicles. And in Moore *v.* Harris, 1 App. Cas. 318, 331, it was laid down by the Privy Council that a bill of lading made in England by the master of an English ship, for transportation of goods to Canada, was an English contract. See, to the same effect, Peninsula Nav. Co. *v.* Shand, 3 Moore, P. C. N.S. 272. And see, as suggesting some qualification, at all

events, to the declared rule that the place of delivery may be treated as the place of performance, First National Bank *v.* Shaw, 61 N. Y. 283. Further, see Carpenter *v.* Grand Trunk Ry. Co., 72 Me. 388; Westlake, s. 207, 210 (ed. 1880).

It is difficult to escape the conviction that the courts, in applying the law of the place of delivery as the place of performance, have sometimes been actuated in part by a desire to impose liability on the carrier. It really seems idle in such cases to speak of any intention in the parties concerning the law to be applied in case of a failure of the carrier to transport successfully. In all probability they never thought of such a thing. The mere fact that delivery was to be made in a particular state can hardly be evidence of an intention that the law of that state should govern. The loss might occur before it reached such state; and why might it not be as reasonable to assume that the parties had in mind the law of the state in which the damage was done, as the law of a more distant state? And yet it is not denied that the law of the place of loss is not to govern in the absence of evidence of intention. Brown *v.* Camden R. Co., 83 Penn. St. 316; Curtis *v.* Delaware R. Co., 74 N. Y. 116; Dike *v.* Erie Ry. Co., 45 N. Y. 113. It seems doubtful then whether the rule concerning the place of performance has any proper application to this class of cases, unless there is better evidence of intention than is afforded by the fact of delivery. Where the parties live and contract in the same state, the presumption should be they have contracted with reference to a law which they are supposed to know; where they live in different states, a difficulty arises, to be overcome only by the special facts of the case. But the

post contractum initum accedentem referendum est.'[1] He puts
the question: 'Quid si in specie, de nummorum aut redituum

[1] P. Voet, de Stat. s. 9, c. 2, p. 270, s. 12, 14–16, p. 269–273, ed. 1715; Id.
p. 326–329, ed. 1661; post, s. 301 f.

intention, if ascertainable and lawful, should govern. The place where a contract is signed is not necessarily the place where the contract in contemplation of law is made, for it may not be the intention of the parties that it should go into effect there. Tilden v. Blair, 21 Wall. 241; Myers v. Carr, 12 Mich. 63; Campbell v. Nichols, 33 N. J. 81; Gay v. Rainey, 89 Ill. 221; Chatham Bank v. Allison, 15 Iowa, 357; Mills v. Wilson, 88 Penn. St. 118; Bullard v. Thompson, 35 Tex. 313; Lee v. Selleck, 33 N. Y. 615; Cook v. Litchfield, 9 N. Y. 279; Hyde v. Goodnow, 3 Comst. (N. Y.) 270; Dickinson v. Edwards, 77 N. Y. 573; Overton v. Bolton, 9 Heisk. (Tenn.) 762.

It may be too that both of the parties are but transiently in the place where the contract is executed; and it could hardly be supposed in such a case that it could have been their intention to be bound by a strange law, unless indeed the contract was expressed by a mercantile instrument, as a bill of exchange or a promissory note, due and payable there. The law of the country of the parties (excepting such a case as that just indicated) would doubtless be the law contemplated. See Peninsular Navigation Co. v. Shand, 3 Moore, P. C. N.S. 272. What law would govern if the parties were of different states or nationalities might be difficult to determine, in the absence of evidence of intention.

On the other hand, the fact that a contract is to be ratified in another state than that in which it is signed by an agent does not make the state of ratification the locus contractus. Golson v. Ebert, 52 Mo. 260; Findlay v. Hall, 12 Ohio St. 610; Pugh v.

Cameron, 11 W. Va. 523; post, s. 286 a. Nor is the fact that paper is payable in a particular state conclusive in all cases that the law of that state is to govern the case. Tilden v. Blair, 21 Wall. 241; Dickinson v. Edwards, 77 N. Y. 573; Wayne Bank v. Low, 81 N. Y. 566; Akers v. Demond, 103 Mass. 318. Further, what constitutes the place of making or performance, see Western Transp. Co. v. Kilderhouse, 87 N. Y. 430; Pine v. Smith, 11 Gray (Mass.) 38; Milliken v. Pratt, 125 Mass. 374; Dolan v. Green, 110 Mass. 322; French v. French, 126 Mass. 360; McIntyre v. Parks, 3 Met. (Mass.) 207; M'Carty v. Gordon, 16 Kans. 35; Worden v. Nourse, 36 Vt. 756; Broughton v. Bradley, 36 Ala. 689 (contract made in Alabama in substitution for one made in South Carolina treated as a South Carolina contract); Wayne Bank v. Low, 81 N. Y. 566 (to the same effect); Bowman v. Miller, 25 Gratt. (Va.) 331 (to the same effect). And see Jacks v. Nichols, 5 N. Y. 178; Cromwell v. Royal Ins. Co., 49 Md. 366; Read v. Edwards, 2 Nev. 262; Houston v. Potts, 64 N. Car. 33; Sharp v. Davis, 7 Baxter (Tenn.) 607; Garland v. Lane, 46 N. H. 245; Backhouse v. Selden, 29 Gratt. (Va.) 581; Lyon v. Ewings, 17 Wis. 61; Ex parte Holthausen, L. R. 9 Ch. 722; Hooper v. Gumm, L. R. 2 Ch. 282; Colliss v. Hector, L. R. 19 Eq. 334; post, s. 287–290.

Of course if the contract is contra bonos mores, it will not be enforced in another state, though it would be enforceable in the state in which it was to be performed. Kentucky v. Bassford, 6 Hill (N. Y.) 526; ante, s. 258.

A distinction has been taken between questions going to the legality of

solutione difficultas incidat, si forte valor sit immutatus, an spectabitur loci valor, ubi contractus erat celebratus, an loci, in quem
destinata erat solutio.   Respondeo; ex generali regula, spectandum esse loci statutum, in quem destinata erat solutio.' [1]   So that,
according to him, if a contract is for money or goods, the value
is to be ascertained at the place of performance, and not at the
place where the contract is made.[2]   And the same rule applies to
the weight or measure of things, if there be a diversity in different places.[3]   Everhardus adopts the same doctrine. ' Quod,
æstimatio rei debitæ consideratur secundum locum ubi destinata
est solutio, seu deliberatio, non obstante quod contractus alibi sit
celebratus.[4]   Ut videlicet inspiciatur valor monetæ, qui est in
loco destinatæ solutionis.' [5]   Huberus adopts the same exposition.
' Verum tamen non ita præcise respiciendus est locus, in quo contractus est initus, ut si partes alium in contrahendo locum respexerint, ille non potius sit considerandus.' [6]   Indeed, it has the
general consent of foreign jurists; [7] although to this, as to most
other doctrines, there are to be found exceptions in the opinions
of some distinguished names.   Thus, John à Sande maintains
that the law of the place where the contract is made is to govern,
although the payment is to be made in another place.   ' Denique
inspicitur locus contractus, etiamsi solutio in alium locum sit destinata.   Et proinde mensura usurpanda est non loci, ubi frumen-
tum vel vinum exigitur, sed ubi de eo conventum est.' [8]   The

[1] P. Voet, de Stat. s. 15, 16, p. 271, ed. 1715; Id. p. 328, ed. 1661; post,
s. 301 f.
[2] Ibid.   [3] Ibid.
[4] Everhard. Consil. 78, n. 9, p. 205; post, s. 300 b.   [5] Ibid.
[6] Huberus, lib. 1, tit. 3, s. 10; ante, s. 239; post, s. 299.
[7] 2 Boullenois, obs. 46, p. 475, 476; Id. p. 488; 1 Hertii Opera, de Collis.
Leg. s. 4, n. 53, p. 147, ed. 1737; Id. p. 207, ed. 1716; Voet, ad Pand. 4, 1,
s. 29; post, s. 300 a–300 f.
[8] J. à Sande, Opera, Com. de Reg. Jur. l. 9, p. 18. See also Colerus, de
Process. Exec. pt. 2, n. 79, cited 2 Boullenois, obs. 46, p. 475, 476.

a contract and questions incident to a
valid contract. The law of the place
of execution is deemed to govern the
former, while that of the place of payment governs the latter. Akers v.
Demond, 103 Mass. 318. Thus, if the
contract is declared absolutely void
where it was made, it will not be upheld elsewhere, though performable in
a state in which it would be valid.
Hyde v. Goodnow, 3 Comst. (N. Y.)
266; McDaniel v. Chicago Ry. Co.,
24 Iowa, 412. See Arnold v. Potter,
22 Iowa, 194; Butler v. Myer, 17 Ind.
77; Adams v. Robertson, 37 Ill. 45;
ante, s. 243; post, s. 314, note.

general rule has however been adopted both in England and
America. In one of the earliest cases Lord Mansfield stated the
doctrine with his usual clearness. 'The law of the place can
never be the rule where the transaction is entered into with an
express view to the law of another country as the rule by which
it is to be governed.'[1] And this has uniformly been recognized as
the correct exposition in the common law.[2]

282. *Difficulties in applying the Rule.* — But although the general rule is so well established, the application of it in many cases
is not unattended with difficulties; for it is often a matter of
serious question, in cases of a mixed nature, which rule ought to
prevail, the law of the place where the contract is made, or that
of the place where it is to be performed.[3] In general it may be
said that if no place of performance is stated, or the contract
may indifferently be performed anywhere, it ought to be referred
to the lex loci contractus.[4] (a) But there are many cases where
this rule will not be a sufficient guide; and, as the subject is important in its practical bearing, it may be well to illustrate it by
some cases.[5]

[1] Robinson v. Bland, 2 Burr. 1077, 1078; post, s. 308–314.
[2] Ludlow v. Van Rensselaer, 1 Johns. (N. Y.) 94; Thompson v. Ketcham,
8 Johns. (N. Y.) 189; Fanning v. Consequa, 17 Johns. (N. Y.) 511; Powers
v. Lynch, 3 Mass. 77; 4 Cowen, 510, note; Van Reimsdyk v. Kane, 1 Gall.
371; Cox v. United States, 6 Pet. 172, 203; 2 Fonbl. Eq. b. 5, c. 1, s. 6,
and note; Prentiss v. Savage, 13 Mass. 20, 23, 24; ante, s. 270, 280; 3 Burge,
Col. & For. Law, pt. 2, c. 20, p. 752–754; Id. 771–773; Don v. Lippman, 5 Cl.
& F. 1, 13, 19, 20.
[3] See 2 Kames, Eq. b. 3, c. 8, s. 4; Voet, de Statut. s. 9, c. 2, s. 10. Hertius puts some questions under this head. A condition is added to a contract
in Belgium, which is performed by the debtor in Germany; if the laws of the
countries are different, which are to prevail? Hertius says those of Belgium,
because the condition performed relates back to the time of making the contract. Again a contract made in one place is confirmed in another; what
laws are to govern? He answers, if the confirmation is to give greater credit
to the contract, as putting it in writing for the sake of proof, the law of the
place of the contract is to prevail. If to give validity to the contract, the law
of the place of the confirmation. 1 Hertii Opera, de Collis. Leg. p. 147, s. 54,
55; Id. p. 207, 208, ed. 1716.
[4] Don v. Lippman, 5 Cl. & F. 1, 13, 19, 20; post, s. 317.
[5] Mr. Burge has expressed the true sense of the general rule and its qualifications in the following terms: 'It may be stated generally that, with respect
to contracts of which movable property is the subject, the law of the place in
which the contract is made will in some respects exclusively prevail, although
the contract is to be performed in another; and that, in those respects in

(a) Benners v. Clemens, 58 Penn. St. 24.

283. *Mutual Accounts between Merchants.* — One of the most simple cases is where two merchants, doing business with each other, reside in different countries and have mutual accounts of debt and credit with each other for advances and sales. What rule is to be followed as to the balance of accounts existing from time to time between them? Is it the law of the one country or of the other, if there is a conflict between their laws on the subject? If the business transactions are all on one side, as in case of sales and advances made by a commission merchant in his own country for his principal abroad; there the contracts may well be referred to the country of the commission merchant, and the balance be deemed due to him according to its laws.[1] For, although it may be truly said that the debt is due from the principal, and he is generally expected to pay it where he dwells; yet it is equally true that the debt is due where the advances are made, and that payment may be insisted upon there.

284. *Illustrations.* — But suppose the advances have been made in the country of the principal, and the goods sold in the other country; is the same rule to prevail? Or are the advances to be governed by the law of the place where they are advanced, and the sales of the goods by that of the place where they are received by the commission merchant? Suppose both the merchants, in different countries, sell goods and make advances mutually for each other, and upon the accounts a balance is due from one to the other; by the law of what place is such balance to be ascertained and paid? In these and many other like mixed cases, the amount of the balance, the time, and the manner, and the place of payment, the true principle of the adjustment of the mutual accounts, may materially depend upon the operation of the lex loci, when the law of one country conflicts with that of the other. The habits of business and trade between the parties may sometimes decide these points; but if no such governing circumstances are established, the cases must be reasoned out upon principle. Upon principle, it may perhaps be found most easy to decide that each transaction is to be governed by the law of the place where

which it does not prevail, the law of the place where the contract is to be performed must be adopted. But this conclusion is subject to some qualifications and exceptions.'

[1] Coolidge *v.* Poor, 15 Mass. 427; Consequa *v.* Fanning, 3 Johns. Ch. (N. Y.) 587, 610. See also Bradford *v.* Farrand, 13 Mass. 18; Milne *v.* Moreton, 6 Binn. (Penn.) 353, 359, 365.

it originated ; advances by the law of the place where they are advanced ; and sales of goods by the law of the place where they are received.[1]   The importance of the true rule is peculiarly felt in all cases of interest to be paid on balances.

284 a. *Case.* — This subject was a good deal discussed in a recent case, where goods had been consigned for sale in Trieste by a merchant of Boston, and advances were made by the agent of the consignees in Boston to an amount exceeding the amount of the proceeds of the goods when sold.   A suit was brought by the consignees to recover the balance, and the question was, at what rate of exchange the balance was to be allowed ; and that depended upon another question, whether the balance was reimbursible at Boston, or in Trieste.   The court held that the balance was reimbursible at Boston where the advances were made ; but that, if the advances had been made at Trieste, the balance would have been reimbursible there.   The court consequently allowed the par of exchange at Boston upon the balance, it being payable there.[2] (a)

285. *Principal and Agent.* — Another case may serve to illustrate the same doctrine.   A merchant in America orders goods to be purchased for him in England.   In which country is the contract to be deemed complete, and by the laws of which is it to be

[1] See Consequa *v.* Fanning, 3 Johns. Ch. (N. Y.) 588, 610 ; 17 Johns. (N. Y.) 511 ; Casaregis, Disc. 179.

[2] Grant *v.* Healey, 3 Sum. 523.   See post, s. 311, a.

(a) On the other hand it has been determined in Louisiana that where an advance was obtained in that State from an agent residing there, of a foreign principal, on merchandise to be shipped to and sold by the latter abroad, the rate of interest on a balance due the foreign principal by reason of the proceeds of the sale falling short of the advances must be determined by the law of the domicil of the principal, where the merchandise was sold. Ballister *v.* Hamilton, 3 La. An. 401. Slidell, J., who delivered the judgment in this case, observed: ' We are aware that this view conflicts with the opinion of Judge Story in Grant *v.* Healey, 2 Law Rep. 113 ; 3 Sumner, 523 ; but we feel a strong conviction that the rule we have followed accords with the general mercantile opinion, which in a matter of this sort is entitled to great weight.' It would seem that questions of interest and exchange should depend not upon the place where the advances were made, but upon the place where it is presumable they were expected to have been paid; which, in such cases, will ordinarily be where the deficiency occurred. In both the cases named in the two preceding sections this was the place where the goods were sold and fell short of the advances.

governed?   Casaregis has affirmed that in such a case the law of
England ought to govern, for there the final assent is given
by the person who receives and executes the order of his correspondent.   'Pro hujus materiæ declaratione præmittenda est
regula ab omnibus recepta, quod contractus vel negotium inter
absentes gestum dicatur eo loci, quo ultimus in contrahendo assentitur, sive acceptat; quia tunc tantum uniuntur ambo consensus.[1]   Sic mandati contractus dicitur initus in loco, quo
diriguntur, literæ missivæ alicujus mercatoris, si alter ad quem
diriguntur, eas recipit, et acceptat mandatum.'[2]   He goes on to
illustrate the doctrine by putting the case of a merchant directing his correspondent in a foreign country to buy goods for him;
in which case he says, if the correspondent accepts the order, and
in the execution of it he buys the goods of a third person, two
contracts spring up; the first of mandate between the principal
and his agent, and the second of purchase and sale between the
vendor and the agent, as purchaser in the name of the principal;
and both are to be deemed contracts made in the place where the
agent resides.   His language is: 'Quando mercator alteri suo
corresponsori mandat, ut aliquas merces pro se emat, easque sibi
transmittat, quo casu si correspousor acceptet mandatum, et in
illius executionem ab aliqua tertia persona merces commissas emat,
duo perficiuntur contractus: Primus, mandati inter mandantem,
et mandatarium, et alter, emptionis, et respective venditionis inter
eundem mandatarium, uti emptorem nomine mandantis, et venditorem, et ambo perficiuntur in loco mandatarii: Nam, quoad mandati contractum, ratio est, quia consensus mandantis per literas
unitur cum ultimo consensu mandatarii in loco, quo mandatarius
reperitur, et acceptat mandatum, eoque magis quoad alterum
venditionis, et respective emptionis, quia mandatarius vere emit
in loco, in quo et ipse, et venditor existunt.'[3]   This doctrine, so
reasonable in itself, has been expressly affirmed by the Supreme
Court of Louisiana.[4]   It has also received a sanction in a recent
case in the House of Lords, where the Lord Chancellor said: 'If
I, residing in England, send down my agent to Scotland, and he

[1] Casaregis, Disc. 179, s. 1, 2.   See 1 Hertii Opera, de Collis. Leg. s. 56,
p. 147; Id. p. 208, ed. 1716; 3 Burge, Col. & For. Law, pt. 2, c. 20, p. 733.
[2] Ibid.   [3] Casaregis, Disc. 179, n. 10, p. 192.
[4] Mr. Justice Martin, in Whiston v. Stodder, 8 Mart. (La.) 95.   See also
Malpica v. McKown, 1 La. 251, 355.

makes contracts for me there, it is the same as if I myself went there and made them.'[1] The same rule has been held to apply even to an English corporation, contracting by its agent in Scotland; for the contract takes effect as a contract in Scotland.[2] (a)

286. *Ratification.* — And if a contract of purchase is made by an agent without orders, and the correspondent ratifies it, Casaregis says that the contract is not to be deemed a contract in the country of the ratification, but of the purchase, because the ratification has reference back to the time and place of the purchase. 'Ratio est, quia ille ratificationis consensus, licet emitatur in loco ratificantis, et ibi videatur se unire cum altero precedenti gerentis consensu qui venit a loco gerentis ad locum ratificantis, retrotrahitur ad tempus et ad locum, in quo fuit per gestorem initus contractus emptionis ; vel aliud negotium pro absente ; et ratio rationis est, quia consensus ratificantis non unitur in loco suo ad aliquem actum seu contractum perficiendum, sed acceptandum contractum vel negotium pro se in loco gestoris jam factum; ac si eodem tempore et loco, in quo fuit per gestorem negotium gestum, ipsemet ratificans esset præsens, ibique contraxisset.'[3] So a like rule applies, if a merchant in one country agrees to accept a bill drawn on him by a person in another country. It is deemed a contract in the place where the acceptance is to be made.[4] Paul Voet adopts the same conclusion. 'Quid si de literis cambii incidat

---

[1] Pattison v. Mills, 1 Dow & C. 342; Albion Ins. Co. v. Mills, 3 Wils. & Shaw, 218, 233. It is difficult to reconcile this doctrine with the views of the court and bar in Acebal v. Levy, 10 Bing. 376, 379, 380, 381 (ante, s. 262 a), where upon a sale of goods in Spain to be delivered in England, the purchase having been made by an agent of the purchasers by orders sent to Spain, the court and bar seem to have thought that the contract was governed by the English statute of frauds. See ante, s. 262 a; post, s. 318, and note. Did the place of the delivery and payment make any difference? See post, s. 318, and note.

[2] Albion Insur. Co. v. Mills, 3 Wils. & Shaw, 218, 233, 234. See also 3 Burge, Col. & For. Law, pt. 2, c. 20, p. 753.

[3] Casaregis, Disc. 179, s. 20, 64, 76–80, 83.

[4] Boyce v. Edwards, 4 Pet. 111.

(a) See Heebner v. Eagle Ins. Co., 10 Gray, 131. On the other hand it is held that if A in Georgia, having bought there of B, sell and deliver and send cotton to C in New York for value and without notice, the law of the latter state will prevail over the law of the former in respect of the rights of the first seller. Comer v. Cunningham, 77 N. Y. 397.

quæstio, Quis locus erit spectandus? Is spectandus est locus, ad quem sunt destinatæ, et ibidem acceptatæ.' [1]

286 *a. Hertius.* — Hertius takes a curious distinction on this subject. If, says he, a contract is made in one country and is ratified in another, it may be asked, if the laws of the different places vary, which is to govern? (*a*)   To which he answers: If the confirmation is made to add additional faith to the contract, as, for example, if the contract is reduced to writing for the sake of proof, then the law of the place where the contract is made is to be looked to.   But if to give validity to the contract itself, the law of the place of confirmation : ' Contractus in alio loco fit, in alio confirmatur ; quæritur, cujus loci leges, si discrepare eas usuveniat, intueri debeamus ?   Si confirmatio accedat ad conciliandam contractui majorem fidem, v. g. contractus probationis gratia in scripturam redigatur, arbitramur, spectandam loci, ubi contrahitur legem.   Sin, ut contractus sit validus, loci, ubi confirmatur, jura prævalebunt.' [2]   So that Hertius seems to put the solution of the case upon the point of the supposed intention of the parties to give validity to a defective contract, or only to impart a better proof of its original validity.

286 *b. Authority of Master of a Ship.* — A question of a somewhat analogous nature, growing out of agency, and of very familiar occurrence, deserves notice in this place.   It is well known that by the common law the master of a ship has a limited authority to take up money in a foreign port and give a bottomry bond, in cases of necessary repairs and other pressing emergencies.   But he is not at liberty to give such a bond for mere useful supplies or advances which are not strictly necessary. (*b*)   It is

[1] P. Voet, de Stat. s. 9, c. 2, s. 14, p. 271, ed. 1715; Id. p. 327, ed. 1661.

[2] 1 Hertii Opera, de Collis. Leg. s. 4, n. 55, p. 147, ed. 1737; Id. p. 208, ed. 1716; ante, s. 297.

(*a*) See Findlay *v.* Hall, 12 Ohio St. 610.   In this case the co-obligors of F in a promissory note made in New Mexico and bearing ten per cent interest, after a partial payment thereon, assumed in the absence of F to renew the same for the balance due; and accordingly they made a new note at Sante Fé, stipulating for ten per cent interest, and F afterwards, with knowledge of the facts, signed the new note in Missouri.   It was held that he had thereby ratified the acts of the co-obligors, and that the new note was to be treated as made in New Mexico, and governed by the laws of that territory.   See also Golson *v.* Ebert, 52 Mo. 260; Pugh *v.* Cameron, 11 W. Va. 523; note to s. 280, ante.

(*b*) The Gaetano, 7 P. D. 137, 144.

highly probable that in some maritime countries, the basis of whose jurisprudence is the civil law, a broader authority is allowed to the master, or at least a broader liability may attach upon the vessel and the owner.[1] In such a case the question might arise whether the liability of the ship or of the owner was to be decided by the authority of the master according to the law of the foreign place where the money was advanced, or by the law of the place of the domicil of the ship and owner. In England it would be held (at least such seems the course of the adjudications) that the master's authority to bind the ship or the owner in a foreign port would be governed by the law of the domicil of the owner; and that consequently the master of an English ship could not bind the owner for advances or supplies in a foreign port, which were not justifiable by the English law.[2] But it is

---

[1] See 2 Emerigon, Contrats à la Grosse, c. 4, s. 2–6, 8, p. 422–445.

[2] The Nelson, 1 Hagg. Adm. 169, 175, 176. In the case of The Nelson, Lord Stowell said: ' It is certainly the vital principle of this species of bonds that they shall have been taken where the owner was known to have no credit, no resources for obtaining necessary supplies. It is that state of unprovided necessity that alone supports these bonds. The absence of that necessity is their undoing. If the master takes up money from a person who knows that he has a general credit in the place, or at least an empowered consignee or agent willing to supply his wants, the giving a bottomry bond is a void transaction, — not affecting the property of the owner, — only fixing loss and shame on the fraudulent lender; but where honorably transacted under an honest ignorance of this fact, an ignorance that could not be removed by any reasonable inquiry, it is the disposition of this court to uphold such bonds, as necessary for the support of commerce in its extremities of distress, and as such recognized in the maritime codes of all commercial ages and nations. To the bond exhibited here some objections are taken respecting its form, but not affecting its validity. One objection is that it binds the owners personally as well as the ship and freight, which it cannot do. That is held in this court to be no objection to the efficacy of what it is admitted it can do. Here we do not take this bond in toto, as is done in other systems of law, and reject it as unsound in the whole if vicious in any part. But we separate the parts, reject the vicious, and respect the efficiency of those which are entitled to operate. The form of these bonds is different in different countries; so is their authority. In some countries they bind the owner or owners, in others not; and where they do not, though the form of the bond affects to bind the owners, that part is insignificant, but does not at all touch upon the efficiency of those parts which have an acknowledged operation. It is objected likewise that this bond does not express the obligation to be on the sea risk, and it does not expressly, or in exact terms; but it does in terms amounting to the same effect. The money is to be paid at such a time " after the ship arrives at her port." If the ship never arrives at her port, or is lost upon the voyage, that is a sufficient description of sea risk. I take no notice of the other objections

far from being certain that foreign courts, and especially the
courts of the country where the advances or supplies were fur

made to this bond. They are objections invariably paraded on these occasions, and as invariably overruled by the court.' Mr. Brodie, in his notes on
Lord Stair's Institutes (vol. 2, p. 955, 956), has gone into a full examination
of this subject, and said: ' It may be laid down as a general, though not absolute, principle, that people may be held to contract in reference to the law of
the country under whose protection they happen to be at the time. Grant
this however, and the conclusion follows that the lex loci contractus becomes
in reality a constituent quality of their agreements. Hence it may be argued
that if, on account of a vessel, a debt be contracted in a foreign country which
admits the principle of a tacit hypothecation for repairs, &c., such a jus in re
ought to be implied as the actual import and understanding of the transaction, and as therefore no less acquired ex lege loci, than if it had been constituted by a formal writing. But if in this way such a right do arise ex lege
loci, then ex justitia, and on principles of international law, it ought to be
rendered effectual with us; a point which will be manifest if we consider that
the validity of a written instrument must be tried by the law of the place in
which it was executed.   Still however must it be remembered that it is
merely as the presumed understanding and intention of parties that the jus in
re can so arise; as a right conceived in favor of the creditor, it can unquestionably be renounced by him; and then comes the question whether circumstances do not exclude the presumption quoad a mutual understanding founded on
the law of the place. When, not to speak of necessary advances, a foreign
ship is repaired here, the shipwright, who parts with the possession without
stipulating for and obtaining in due form a security over the thing, may be
supposed to have, according to the principle of the common law, relied exclusively on the personal credit of his debtor; did therefore the other party
even conceive that he had likewise bound the vessel, there would be wanting
the mutual understanding to infer an agreement. So far then does the lex
loci operate against the contraction of a jus in re for the debt; but it does not
thence follow that elsewhere the lex loci should operate in favor of a tacit
hypothecation.   A distinction is ever to be attended to between the case of a
party casually entering a foreign country and that of one who resides in it;
and the distinction is particularly strong in regard to an individual who, as
master, has the charge of a vessel in a foreign port. Well may such a person,
when he orders repairs on personal credit, be presumed to be ignorant of any
further condition which the law of his own country denies; and while, if the
other party leave that unexplained, it may be argued with great plausibility
that he has consented to waive the additional security, tacitly admitted in
ordinary cases, ex lege loci, it must be considered that there would at all
events be wanting the mutual assent which constitutes the basis of a contract.
But this is not all. The contract in such cases is made with the shipmaster,
who acts as the implied mandatory of the owners; and the effect of the transaction must greatly depend on the extent of his authority. Now it is true
that, as a person who has been appointed to an office must be presumed to be
invested with the usual powers, so restrictions upon the ordinary authority
will not be effectual against another party who has not been apprised of them;
yet it will be observed that, since it is the duty of those who deal with an
agent to make themselves acquainted with the extent of his powers, whether

nished, would adopt the same rules if the lender or supplier had acted with good faith, and in ignorance of the want of authority in the master.[1]

286 c. *Cases in Louisiana.* — In a recent case in Louisiana, where the question arose as to the liability of the owner for the property on board, belonging to a passenger who died on the voyage, the property being afterwards lost, the point was made whether, as the passenger and property were taken on board at a foreign port, the law of that port or the law of the place where the vessel and owner belonged ought to govern as to the owner's liability.   On that occasion the court said : ʻ We are of opinion that the law of the place of the contract, and not that of the owner's residence,

expressed or fairly implied from his office, so the presumed mandate here must be measured either by some general principle of maritime law, or by the law of the country to which the ship belongs.   Such a general principle of maritime law would of itself, though in a different way, tend, in my apprehension, to exclude the lex loci; but there is no such universally received principle, and the more positive exclusion of the principle of the lex loci is the consequence.   Thus the English law does not allow the master to hypothecate the vessel, at least expressly, unless in a foreign port, where personal credit is unattainable; but entitles him to pledge the absolute personal responsibility of his constituents for the amount of necessary repairs, furnishings, &c.; while, on the other hand, the French law authorizes him to hypothecate the vessel, &c., not bind his constituents personally, at least not beyond the eventual value of the ship and freight, &c., on her return.   And it is quite clear that the merchants and artisans of the respective countries must contract with the shipmasters of each other, according to the powers respectively inherent in those offices.   It would be to no purpose for the English artisan or merchant to plead in France the law of his own country in support of his action for absolute responsibility; and to allow the Frenchman to have the benefit of a privilege ex lege loci, while he has acquired the absolute personal liability of the owners, would, while an opposite measure of justice was awarded to the English, be to afford him a double advantage, the combined effect of the law of both countries, — would give him a right the opposite party never contracted for, nor himself could fairly anticipate.   The clear result then is, that the transactions must be held to have reference to the master's implied mandate, according to the law of his own country, — a mandate which it is the duty of those who deal with him as an agent to ascertain the extent of; and that, while they never can justly complain of having their right limited by such a principle, the shipmaster cannot be supposed to intend an abuse of his powers, — whence the very gist of all contracts, the understanding of parties, would be wanting to infer a right, ex lege loci contractus, which the scope of his authority did not import.   Thus much for the principle of the lex loci contractus.   We shall now proceed to inquire into the principles recognized in England.ʼ

[1] 2 Emerigon, Contrat à la Grosse, c. 4, s. 8, p. 441, 442; Malpica *v.* McKown, 1 La. 249, 254, 255.

must be the rule by which his obligations are to be ascertained.
The lex loci contractus governs all agreements unless expressly
excluded, or the performance is to be in another country where
different regulations prevail. What we do by another we do by
ourselves; and we are unable to distinguish between the responsibility created by the owner sending his agent to contract in another
country and that produced by going there and contracting himself.'[1] Perhaps the case itself did not require so broad an expression
of opinion, since the court seemed to have assumed that the law of
the owner's domicil coincided with the law of the place of the
contract, as to the owner's responsibility and the authority of the
master. But the same doctrine has been elaborately maintained
by the same court in another case. (a)

286 d. *Authority of Agent after Death of Principal.* — Another
case may readily be suggested as to the conflict of laws in cases
of agency. Let us suppose that A in Massachusetts should, by
a letter of attorney duly executed in Boston, authorize B, his
agent in New Orleans, to sell his ship, then lying in New Orleans, and to execute a bill of sale in his, A's, name to the purchaser, and B should accept the agency and sell the ship after
the death of A, but before he had received or could receive any
notice thereof, and should execute a bill of sale in A's name to

---

[1] Mr. Justice Porter in Malpica v. McKown, 1 La. 249, 254; ante, s. 258.

(a) The doctrine of the Louisiana
cases was disapproved in Pope v.
Nickerson, 3 Story, 465. In that case
it appeared that a vessel owned in
Massachusetts, being on a voyage
from Spain to Pennsylvania, was compelled by stress of weather to put into
Bermuda, where the master sold the
vessel and cargo. In an action by
the shippers against the owners to recover the amount of their consignment, in which the master's right to
sell the cargo was drawn in question,
it was held that the liability of the
owners was to be governed by the
law of Massachusetts. See also Lloyd
v. Guibert, L. R. 1 Q. B. 115 (Exch.
Ch.), which has sometimes been cited
in support of the same view. That
case however was deemed not an
authority in favor of the law of the
owner's domicil, and was distinguished in The Gaetano, 7 P. D. 137,
reversing 7 P. D. 1. The decision of
Dr. Lushington in The Hamburgh,
Brown & L. 253, which has also been
supposed to favor the rule of the owner's domicil, was explained and distinguished. It was laid down by the
Court of Appeal in The Gaetano that
he who ships goods on board a foreign
ship, ships them to be dealt with by
the master according to the law of the
country of the ship, unless there is
some special stipulation on the subject. Brett. L. J. It was also held
that it mattered not where the contract of affreightment was made. See
also King v. Sarria, 69 N. Y. 24, 33.
In regard to questions of collision between foreign vessels, see The Scotland,
105 U. S. 24; post, s. 423 g, and note.

the purchaser. In such a case the question might arise (especially if A died insolvent, or the money was invested, in pursuance of other orders of A, in goods which had perished by fire or other accident) whether the bill of sale was valid or not valid. By the law of Massachusetts a letter of attorney is revoked by the death of the principal, whether known or unknown, and all acts done after his death under it are mere nullities.[1] By the law of Louisiana, if any attorney, being ignorant of the death or of the cessation of the rights of his principal, should continue to act under his power of attorney, the transactions done by him during this state of ignorance would be valid.[2] Assuming that this provision covers all cases, not only when the transaction is executed in the name of the agent, but also when it is executed in the name of the principal, upon which some doubt may be entertained, as a dead man cannot act at all,[3] still the question would be, by what law the letter of attorney, with reference to its revocability, duration, and effect, is to be governed. The general rule certainly is that all the instruments made and executed in a country take effect and are to be construed, as to their nature, operation, and extent, according to the law of the country where they are made and executed. Locus regit actum.[4] But the question here would be, whether, as the execution of the power was to be in another country, the power should not be construed and executed, and its nature, operation, and extent ascertained, by the law of the latter, as an exception to the general rule. There is no doubt that, where an authority is given to an agent to transact business for his principal in a foreign country, it must be construed, in the absence of any counter-proofs, that it is to be executed according to the law of the place where the business is to be transacted.[5] But this may well be admitted to be the rule while the authority is in full force, without making the law of that place the rule by which to ascertain whether the original power of attorney is still subsisting or is revoked or dead by operation of law in the place of its origin. The point has never, as far as my researches extend, been directly decided either at home

[1] Story on Agency, s. 488, 489.
[2] Code Civil of Louisiana, art. 3001. The Civil Code of France contains a similar regulation. Code Civil of France, art. 2008; Pothier on Oblig. n. 81.
[3] See Story on Agency, s. 491-499.   [4] Ante, s. 263.
[5] Owings v. Hull, 9 Pet. 607, 627, 628.

or abroad; and therefore it is submitted to the learned reader for his consideration. Some of the cases already alluded to may be thought to furnish an analogy unfavorable to the validity of the sale.[1]

287. *Advances of Money.* — Another class of cases may be stated. A merchant in one country sends a letter to a merchant in another, requesting him to purchase goods, and to draw on him for the amount of the purchase-money by bills. In which country is the contract for the repayment of the advances, if the purchase is made, to be deemed to be made? Is it in the country where the letter is written, and on which the drafts are authorized to be drawn? Or where the goods are purchased? The decision has been that, when such advances are made, the undertaking is to replace the money at the same place at which the advances are made; and therefore the party advancing will be entitled to interest on the advances according to the law of the place of the advances.[2] (*a*) So if advances are made for a foreign merchant at his request, or security is given for a debt, the party paying or advancing is in like manner entitled to repayment in the place where the advances are made or the security is given, unless some other place is stipulated therefor.[3] (*b*)

287 *a. Loans secured by Mortgage.* — So where a loan is made in one state, and security is to be given therefor in another state by way of mortgage, it may be asked what law is to govern in re-

---

[1] Ante, s. 286 *b*, 286 *c*.

[2] Lanusse *v.* Barker, 3 Wheat. 101, 146; Grant *v.* Healey, 3 Sumner, 523; ante, s. 284 *a*. See also Hertii Opera, tom. 1, de Collis. Leg., s. 4, n. 55, p. 147, ed. 1737; Id. p. 208, ed. 1716.

[3] Boyle *v.* Zacharie, 6 Pet. 635, 643, 644; post, s. 320 *a*.

(*a*) See First National Bank *v.* Shaw, 61 N. Y. 283. But see Ballister *v.* Hamilton, 3 La. An. 401.

(*b*) So where a proposal to purchase goods is made by letter sent from one state to another state, and is there assented to, the contract of sale is made in the latter state. M'Intyre *v.* Parks, 3 Met. (Mass.) 207. Sales of personal property are generally held to be made in the state or country where the vendor resides and finally assents to the contract or delivers the article; and if valid by the law of that place they are held valid in the state or country where the vendee resides; although, if entirely made and completed in the latter place, they would have been contrary to the law thereof. See Kline *v.* Baker, 99 Mass. 254; Finch *v.* Mansfield, 97 Mass. 89; M'Intyre *v.* Parks, 3 Met. (Mass.) 207; Jameson *v.* Gregory, 4 Met. (Ky.) 370; Garland *v.* Lane, 46 N. H. 245; Marchant *v.* Chapman, 4 Allen (Mass.) 362; Hardy *v.* Potter, 10 Gray (Mass.) 89; Bligh *v.* James, 5 Allen (Mass.) 106.

lation to the contract and its incidents? The decision has been
that the law of the place where the loan is made is to govern; for
the mere taking of a foreign security does not, it is said, necessarily alter the locality of the contract. Taking such security
does not necessarily draw after it the consequence that the contract is to be fulfilled where the security is taken. The legal
fulfilment of a contract of loan on the part of the bondsman
is repayment of the money; and the security given is but the
means of securing what he has contracted for, which, in the eye
of the law, is to pay where he borrows, unless another place of
payment be expressly designated by the contract.[1] But if the
mortgage is actually to be executed in a foreign country, and the
money is to be paid there, the loan will be deemed to be there
completed, although the money may have been actually advanced
elsewhere.[2] (a)

288. *Portions charged on Lands.* — A case somewhat different
in its circumstances, but illustrative of the general principle,
occurred formerly in England. By a settlement made upon the
marriage of A in England, a term of five hundred years was
created upon estates in Ireland, in trust to raise £12,000 for
the portions of daughters. The parties to the settlement resided in England; and a question afterwards arose, whether the
£12,000, charged on the term of years, should be paid in England without any abatement or deduction for the exchange from
Ireland to England. It was decided that the portions ought to
be paid in England, where the contract was made and the parties
resided; and not in Ireland, where the lands lay which were
charged with the payment; for it was a sum in gross, and not a
rent issuing out of the land.[3]

---

[1] De Wolf v. Johnson, 10 Wheat. 367, 383. See also Ranelaugh v. Champante, 2 Vern. 395, and Raithby's note; Connor v. Bellamont, 2 Atk. 382; post,
s. 293. See Chapman v. Robertson, 6 Paige (N. Y.) 627, 630; post, s. 293 b.

[2] De Wolf v. Johnson, 10 Wheat. 367; Hosford v. Nichols, 1 Paige (N. Y.)
221; Lloyd v. Scott, 4 Pet. 211, 229. Whether a contract made in one State
for the sale of lands situate in another state on credit, reserving interest at
the legal rate of interest of the state where the lands lie, but more than that
of the state where the contract is made, would be usurious, has been much
discussed in the state of New York. In Van Schaick v. Edwards, 2 Johns.
Cas. (N Y.) 355, the judges were divided in opinion upon the question. See
also Hosford v. Nichols, 1 Paige (N. Y.) 220, and Dewar v. Span, 3 T. R.
425; ante, s. 279 a.

[3] Phipps v. Anglesea, cited 5 Vin. Ab. 209, pl. 8; 2 Eq. Ab. 220, pl. 1;

(a) See Cope v. Alden, 53 Barb. (N. Y.) 353.

289. *Bills of Exchange signed in Blank.* — Let us take another case. A merchant, resident in Ireland, sends to England certain bills of exchange, with blanks for the dates, the sums, the times of payment, and the names of the drawees. These bills are signed by the merchant in Ireland, indorsed with his own name, and dated from a place in Ireland, and are transmitted to a correspondent in England, with authority to him to fill up the remaining parts of the instrument. The correspondent in England accordingly fills them up, dated at a place in Ireland. Are the bills, when thus filled up and issued, to be deemed English or Irish contracts? It has been held that, under such circumstances, they are to be deemed Irish contracts, and of course to be governed, as to stamps and other legal requisitions, by the law of Ireland; and that, as soon as they are filled up, the whole transaction relates back to the time of the original signature of the drawer.[1] One of the learned judges on that occasion said, that if the drawer had died while the bills were on their passage, and afterwards the blanks had been filled up, and the bill negotiated to an innocent indorsee, the personal representatives of the drawer would have been bound.[2]

290. *Bonds of Government Officers.* — Bonds for the faithful discharge of the duties of office are often given with sureties, by public officers, to the government of the United States; and it sometimes happens that the bonds are executed by the principals in one state, and by the sureties in a different state, or in different states. What law is in such cases to regulate the contract? The rights and duties of sureties are known to be different in different states. In Louisiana one system prevails, deriving itself mainly from the civil law; in other states a different system prevails, founded on the common law. It has been decided that the bonds in such cases must be treated as made and delivered, and to be performed by all the parties, at the seat of the government of the Union, upon the ground that the principal is bound to account there; and therefore, by necessary implication, all the other parties look to that as the place of performance, by the law of which they are to be governed.[3]

Id. 754, pl. 3; 1 P. Wms. 696; 2 Bligh, 88, 89. See also Lansdowne *v.* Lansdowne, 2 Bligh, 60; Stapleton *v.* Conway, 3 Atk. 726; 1 Ves. 427.
[1] Snaith *v.* Mingay, 1 M. & S. 87. [2] Mr. Justice Bayley, id. p. 95.
[3] Cox *v.* United States, 6 Pet. 172, 202; Duncan *v.* United States, 7 Pet. 435.

291. *Interest.* — The question also often arises in cases respecting the payment of interest. The general rule is, that interest is to be paid on contracts according to the law of the place where they are to be performed, in all cases where interest is expressly or impliedly to be paid.[1] (a) ' Usurarum modus ex more regionis,

[1] Fergusson *v.* Fyffe, 8 Cl. & F. 121, 140; post, s. 292, 293, 293 a–293 e, 304; Connor *v.* Bellamont, 2 Atk. 382; Cash *v.* Kennion, 11 Ves. 314; Robinson *v.* Bland, 2 Burr. 1077; Ekins *v.* East India Company, 1 P. Wms. 395; Ranelaugh *v.* Champante, 2 Vern. 395, and note by Raithby; 1 Chitty on Com. & Manuf. c. 12, p. 650, 651; 3 Id. c. 1, p. 109; Eq. Ab. Interest, E.; Henry on Foreign Law, 43, note, 53; 2 Kames, Equity, b. 3, c. 8, s. 1; 2 Fonbl. Eq. b. 5, c. 1, s. 6, and note; Bridgman's Equity Digest, Interest, VII.; Fanning *v.* Consequa, 17 Johns. (N. Y.) 511; 3 Johns. Ch. (N. Y.) 610; Hosford *v.* Nichols, 1 Paige (N. Y.) 220; Houghton *v.* Page, 2 N. H. 42; Peacock *v.* Banks, 1 Minor (Ala.) 387; Lapice *v.* Smith, 13 La. 91, 92; Thompson *v.* Ketcham, 4 Johns. (N. Y.) 285; Stewart *v.* Ellice, 2 Paige (N. Y.) 604; Mullen *v.* Morris, 2 Barr (Pa.) 85; Healy *v.* Gorman, 3 Green (N. J.) 328; 2 Kent Com. 460, 461. A case illustrative of this principle recently occurred before the House of Lords. A widow in Scotland entered into an obligation to pay the whole of her deceased husband's debts. It was held by the court of session in Scotland that the English creditors on contracts made in England were entitled to recover interest in all cases where the law of England gave interest, and not where it did not. Therefore on bonds and bills of exchange interest was allowed, and on simple contracts not. And this decision was affirmed by the House of Lords. Montgomery *v.* Bridge, 2 Dow. & C. 297.

(a) See Miller *v.* Tiffany, 1 Wall. 298; Dickinson *v.* Edwards, 77 N. Y. 573 (following Jewell *v.* Wright, 30 N. Y. 259); Wayne Bank *v.* Low, 81 N. Y. 566; Tilden *v.* Blair, 21 Wall. 241; Bard *v.* Pool, 12 N. Y. 495; Jacks *v.* Nichols, 5 N. Y. 178; Faulkner *v.* Hart, 82 N. Y. 413 (that the decisions of a foreign court contrary to mercantile law which is to prevail in this particular case, will be disregarded; to the same effect, Franklin *v.* Twogood, 25 Iowa, 520); Mills *v.* Wilson, 88 Penn. St. 118; Bank of Louisville *v.* Young, 37 Mo. 398; Arnold *v.* Potter, 22 Iowa, 194; Sands *v.* Smith, 1 Neb. 108; Townsend *v.* Riley, 46 N. H. 300; Freese *v.* Brownell, 35 N. J. 285; Parham *v.* Pulliam, 5 Cold. (Tenn.) 497; Senter *v.* Bowman, 5 Heisk. (Tenn.) 14 (that a promissory note need not be payable on its face in a foreign state to make the law of such state govern); Bolton *v.* Street, 3 Cold. (Tenn.) 31; Cromwell *v.* Sac, 96 U. S. 51.

In Massachusetts, interest not stipulated for is awarded, when given, as damages, and is therefore governed by the lex fori. Ayer *v.* Tilden, 15 Gray, (Mass.) 178; Grimshaw *v.* Bender, 6 Mass. 157; Eaton *v.* Mellus, 7 Gray, (Mass.) 566; Barringer *v.* King, 5 Gray, (Mass.) 9. Contra if there was an agreement for interest. Ayer *v.* Tilden, supra; Von Hemert *v.* Porter, 11 Met. (Mass.) 210; Winthrop *v.* Carleton, 12 Mass. 4 (a doubted case); Lanusse *v.* Barker, 3 Wheat. 147; Railroad Co. *v.* Bank of Ashland, 12 Wall. 226; Hunt *v.* Hall, 37 Ala. 702; Cartwright *v.* Greene, 47 Barb. (N. Y.) 9. But the Massachusetts rule that non-stipulated interest is to be determined by the lex fori is repudiated in Ex parte Heidelback, 2 Lowell, 526.

ubi contractum est, constituitur," says the Digest.[1]   Thus a note made in Canada, where interest is six per cent, payable with interest in England, where it is five per cent, bears English interest only.[2]   Loans made in a place bear the interest of that place, unless they are payable elsewhere.[3]   And, if payable in a foreign country, they may bear any rate of interest not exceeding that which is lawful by the laws of that country.[4]   And, on this account, a contract for a loan made and payable .in a foreign country may stipulate for interest higher than that allowed at home.[5] (a)   If the contract for interest be illegal there, it will be

The case of Arnott v. Redfern, 2 C. & P. 88, may at the first view seem inconsistent with the general doctrine.   There the original contract was made in London between an Englishman and a Scotchman.   The latter agrees to go to Scotland as agent four times a year to sell goods, and collect debts for the other party, to remit the money, and to guarantee one fourth part of the sales; and he was to receive one per cent upon the amount of sales, &c.   The agent sued for the balance of his account in Scotland, and the Scotch court allowed him interest on it.   The judgment was afterwards sued in England; and the question was, whether interest ought to be allowed.   Lord Chief Justice Best said: ' Is this an English transaction?   For, if it is, it will be regulated by the rules of English law.   But if it is a Scotch transaction, then the case will be different.'   He afterwards added: ' This is the case of a Scotchman who comes into England and makes a contract.   As the contract was made in England, although it was to be executed in Scotland, I think it ought to be regulated according to the rules of the English law.   This is my present opinion.   These questions of international law do not often occur.'   And he refused interest, because it was not allowed by the law of England.   The court afterwards ordered interest to be given upon the ground that the balance of such an account would carry interest in England.   But Lord Chief Justice Best rightly expounded the contract as an English contract, though there is a slight inaccuracy in his language.   So far as the principal was concerned, the contract to pay the commission was to be paid in England.   The services of the agent were to be performed in Scotland.   But the whole contract was not to be executed exclusively there by both parties.   A contract made to pay money in England for services performed abroad is an English contract, and will carry English interest.

[1] Dig. 22, 1, 1; 2 Burge, Col. & For. Law, pt. 2, c. 9, p. 860-862.

[2] Scofield v. Day, 20 Johns. (N. Y.) 102.

[3] De Wolf v. Johnson, 10 Wheat. 367, 383; Consequa v. Willings, Pet. C. C. 225; 2 Boullenois, obs. 46, p. 477, 478; Andrews v. Pond, 13 Pet. 65, 78.

[4] Ibid.; 2 Kent Com. 460, 461; Thompson v. Ketcham, 4 Johns. (N. Y.) 285; Healy v. Gorman, 3 Green (N. J.) 328.

[5] 2 Kent Com. 460, 461; Hosford v. Nichols, 1 Paige (N. Y.) 220; Houghton v. Page, 2 N. H. 42; Thompson v. Powles, 2 Sim. 194.   In this last case

(a) Bard v. Pool, 12 N. Y. 495;   other hand, it has been recently held Davis v. Garr, 6 N. Y. 124.   On the   in Ohio that a contract made in that

illegal everywhere.[1] But if it be legal where it is made, it will
be of universal obligation, even in places where a lower interest
is prescribed by law.[2]

292. *Usury.* — The question therefore whether a contract is
usurious or not depends not upon the rate of the interest allowed,
but upon the validity of that interest in the country where the
contract is made and is to be executed.[3] (*a*)   A contract made in

the Vice-chancellor said: 'With respect to the question of usury, in order to
hold the contract to be usurious, it must appear that the contract was made
here, and that the consideration for it was to be paid here. It should appear
at least that the payment was not to be made abroad; for if it was to be
made abroad it would not be usurious.' See also Andrews *v.* Pond, 13 Pet. 65,
78; De Wolf *v.* Johnson, 10 Wheat. 383.

[1] 2 Kames, Equity, b. 3, c. 8, s. 1; Hosford *v.* Nichols, 1 Paige (N. Y.)
220; 2 Boullenois, obs. 46, p. 477. In the case of Thompson *v.* Powles, 2 Sim.
194, the Vice-chancellor said: 'In order to have the contract (for stock) usurious, it must appear that the contract was made here, and that the consideration
for it was to be paid here.' See also Yrisarri *v.* Clement, 2 C. & P. 223. In
Hosford *v.* Nichols, 1 Paige (N. Y.) 220, where a contract was made for the
sale of lands in New York by citizens then resident there, and the vendor
afterwards removed to Pennsylvania, where the contract was consummated,
and a mortgage given to secure the unpaid purchase-money with New York
interest, which was higher than that of Pennsylvania, the court thought the
mortgage not usurious, it being only a consummation of the original bargain
made in New York.

[2] Ibid.

[3] Harvey *v.* Archbold, 1 Ry. & M. 184; 3 B. & C. 626; Andrews *v.* Pond,
13 Peters, 65, 78; ante, s. 243.

state and payable in Pennsylvania may
stipulate for the payment of interest
according to Ohio law, though the
rate would be usurious in Pennsylvania. Kilgore *v.* Dempsey, 25 Ohio
St. 413; post, s. 298. In Pecks *v.*
Mayo, 14 Vt. 33, 38, the following
propositions are laid down: —

1. If a contract is entered into in
one country to be performed in another,
and the rate of interest differs in the
two countries, the parties may stipulate the rate of interest of either country, and thus, by their own express
contract, determine with reference to
the law of which country that incident
of the contract shall be decided.

2. If the contract so entered into
stipulate for interest generally, it shall

be the rate of interest of the place of
payment, unless it appear the parties
intended to contract with reference to
the law of some other place.

3. If the contract stipulate for the
payment of money at a time and place
named, and no interest be stipulated,
and payment be delayed, interest by
way of damages shall be allowed according to the rate at the place of payment, where the money may be supposed to be required by the creditor
for use, and where he might be supposed to have borrowed to supply the
deficiency caused by the default, and
to have paid the rate of interest of that
country. See Ex parte Heidelback,
2 Lowell, 526.

(*a*) See Railroad Co. *v.* Ashland,

England for advances to be made at Gibraltar, at a rate of interest beyond that of England, would nevertheless be valid in England; and so a contract to allow interest upon credits given in Gibraltar at such higher rate would be valid in favor of the English creditor.[1]

292 a. *Rodenburg and Burgundus.* — This too seems to be the doctrine propounded by Rodenburg, who says: 'Status quidem aut conditio personarum dirigitur a loco domicilii : cæterum tamen in vinculo cujusque obligationis, ut sciamus, quos obliget conventio, spectamus leges regionis, ubi illa celebratur. Quemadmodum et in illicita stipulatione, quæ legibus est interdicta, ut puta, si debitum modum usurarum excedit, traditum est valere pactum, quo foris secundum mores illius regionis stipulati sumus prohibitam domi usurarum quantitatem. Unde non longe abire videtur, quod nemini nuper apud nos responsum esse, si contracta sit eo loci obligatio, ubi sortem liceat exigere cum usuris, ut maxime jam earum aliquæ essent persolutæ, jure caput cum usuris et apud nos exigi, ubi usurarum solutione protinus via petitioni sortis præcluditur, locumque sibi vindicat decantata adeo parœmia.'[2] Burgundus is still more direct and positive.[3]

293. *Security.* — *New Contract.* — And in cases of this sort it will make no difference (as we have seen) that the due performance of the contract is secured by a mortgage or other security upon property situate in another country where the interest is lower.[4] (a) For it is collateral to such contract, and the interest reserved being according to the law of the place where the contract is made and to be executed, there does not seem to be any valid objection to giving collateral security elsewhere to enforce and secure the due performance of a legal contract.[5]

[1] Ibid.   [2] Rodenburg, Diversit. Stat. tit. 4, p. 2, c. 2, p. 92.
[3] Burgundus, Tract. 4, n. 10, p. 109; post, s. 293 e, 300 a ; 2 Burge, Col. & For. Law, pt. 2, c. 9, p. 860–862.
[4] Ante, s. 287.
[5] Connor v. Bellamont, 2 Atk. 382; Stapleton v. Conway, 3 Atk. 726; 1 Ves. 427; De Wolf v. Johnson, 10 Wheat. 367, 383.

12 Wall. 226; Bard v. Pool, 12 N. Y. 495; Mills v. Wilson, 88 Penn. St. 118; Phelps v. Kent, 4 Day (Conn.) 96; Pratt v. Adams, 7 Paige (N. Y.) 616; Greenwade v. Greenwade, 3 Dana (Ky.) 497; Cope v. Alden, 53 Barb. (N. Y.) 352; Newman v. Kershaw, 10 Wis. 333.
(a) See Cope v. Alden, 53 Barb. (N. Y.) 352; Mills v. Wilson, 88 Penn. St. 118; Chase v. Dow, 47 N. H. 405; Kavanaugh v. Day, 10 R. I. 393.

But suppose a debt is contracted in one country, and afterwards, in consideration of further delay, the debtor in another country enters into a new contract for the payment of interest upon the debt at a higher rate than that allowed by the country where the original debt was contracted, but not higher than that allowed by the law of the country where it is so stipulated ; it may be asked whether such stipulation is valid ? It has been decided that it is.[1] (a) On the other hand, suppose the interest so stipulated is according to the rate of interest allowed in the country where the debt was contracted, but higher than that in the country where the new contract is made, is the stipulation invalid? It has been decided that it is.[2] (b) In each of these cases the lex loci contractus was held to govern as to the proper rate of interest.

293 a. *Transactions intended to evade Usury Laws.* — In the cases hitherto stated the transaction is supposed to be bona fide between the parties. For if the transaction is a mere cover for usury, as if the transaction is in form a bill of exchange drawn upon and payable in a foreign country, but in reality the parties resort to that as a mere machinery to disguise usury in the transaction against the laws of the country where the contract is made, the form of the transaction will be treated as a mere nullity ; and the court will decide according to the real object of the parties. (c) Thus, for example, where a bill of exchange was drawn in New York payable in Alabama, and the bill was for an antecedent debt, and a large discount was made from the bill, greater than the interest in either state for the supposed difference of exchange, the court considered the real question to be as to the bona fides of the transaction. If a mere cover, it was usurious.[3]

[1] Connor v. Bellamont, 2 Atk. 382. See also Hosford v. Nichols, 1 Paige, (N. Y.) 220.

[2] Dewar v. Span, 8 T. R. 425. See also Stapleton v. Conway, 3 Atk. 726; 1 Ves. 427. See Chapman v. Robertson, 6 Paige (N. Y.) 627, 631.

[3] Andrews v. Pond, 13 Pet. 65, 77, 78. On this occasion Mr. Chief Justice Taney said: ' Another question presented by the exception, and much discussed here, is whether the validity of this contract depends upon the laws of New York or those of Alabama. So far as the mere question of usury is concerned this question is not very important. There is no stipulation for

(a) See Arnold v. Potter, 22 Iowa, 194.

(b) See Rose v. Phillips, 33 Conn. 570.

(c) See Miller v. Tiffany, 1 Wall. 298; Cutler v. Wright, 22 N. Y. 472; Parham v. Pulliam, 5 Cold. (Tenn.) 497; Bolton v. Street, 3 Cold. (Tenn.) 31.

293 b. Case in New York. — Indeed in all cases of this sort we are to look to the real intentions of the parties, and their acts are expressive of them. Thus, where a citizen of New York applied

interest apparent upon the paper. The ten per cent in controversy is charged as a difference in exchange only, and not for interest and exchange. And if it were otherwise, the interest allowed in New York is seven per cent and in Alabama eight; and this small difference of one per cent per annum, upon a forbearance of sixty days, could not materially affect the rate of exchange, and could hardly have any influence on the inquiry to be made by the jury. But there are other considerations which make it necessary to decide this question. The laws of New York make void the instrument when tainted with usury; and if this bill is to be governed by the laws of New York, and if the jury should find that it was given upon a usurious consideration, the plaintiff would not be entitled to recover, unless he was a bona fide holder without notice, and had given for it a valuable consideration; while by the laws of Alabama he would be entitled to recover the principal amount of the debt without any interest. The general principle in relation to contracts made in one place to be executed in another is well settled. They are to be governed by the law of the place of performance; and if the interest allowed by the laws of the place of performance is higher than that permitted at the place of the contract, the parties may stipulate for the higher interest, without incurring the penalties of usury. And in the case before us, if the defendants had given their note to H. M. Andrews & Co. for the debt then due to them, payable at Mobile in sixty days, with eight per cent interest, such a contract would undoubtedly have been valid, and would have been no violation of the laws of New York, although the lawful interest in that state is only seven per cent. And if, in the account adjusted at the time this bill of exchange was given, it had appeared that Alabama interest of eight per cent was taken for the forbearance of sixty days given by the contract, and the transaction was in other respects free from usury, such a reservation of interest would have been valid and obligatory upon the defendants, and would have been no violation of the laws of New York. But that is not the question which we are now called on to decide. The defendants allege that the contract was not made with reference to the laws of either state, and was not intended to conform to either. That a rate of interest forbidden by the laws of New York, where the contract was made, was reserved on the debt actually due, and that it was concealed under the name of exchange in order to evade the law. Now, if this defence is true, and shall be so found by the jury, the question is not which law is to govern in executing the contract, but which is to decide the fate of a security taken upon an usurious agreement, which neither will execute. Unquestionably, it must be the law of the state where the agreement was made, and the instrument taken to secure its performance. A contract of this kind cannot stand on the same principles with a bona fide agreement made in one place to be executed in another. In the last-mentioned cases the agreements were permitted by the lex loci contractus, and will even be enforced there if the party is found within its jurisdiction. But the same rule cannot be applied to contracts forbidden by its laws and designed to evade them. In such cases the legal consequences of such an agreement must be decided by the law of the place where the contract was made. If void there, it is void everywhere.' See Chapman *v.* Robertson, 6 Paige (N. Y.) 627, 630, 631.

in England to a British subject for a loan of money upon the security of a bond and mortgage upon land in New York at the legal rate of interest (seven per cent) of that state ; and it was agreed that the borrower should, upon his return to New York, execute the bond and mortgage, and duly record the same ; and upon the bond and mortgage being received in England, the lender agreed to deposit the money loaned at the bankers of the borrower in London for his use; and the bond and mortgage were executed and received, and the money paid accordingly to the bankers ; the question arose whether the transaction was usurious or not, and that depended upon the law of the place by which it was to be governed, whether by the law of England (where interest is only five per cent) or by the law of New York. It was held by the court that the contract was to be construed according to the laws of New York, and therefore that a bill to foreclose the mortgage, filed in New York, was maintainable, and that the law of usury of England was no defence to the suit. On that occasion the learned chancellor said that, as no place of payment was mentioned in the bond or mortgage, the legal construction of the contract was that the money was to be paid where the obligee resided or wherever he might be found ; that the residence of the obligee being in England at the time of the execution of the bond, that must be considered the place of payment for the purpose of determining the question where that part of the contract was to be performed, and that the execution of the bond in New York did not make it a personal contract there, because it was inoperative until received there and the money deposited with the bankers for the borrower. And he concluded by saying: ' Upon a full examination of all the cases to be found upon the subject, either in this country or in England, none of which however appear to have decided the precise question which arises in this cause, I have arrived at the conclusion that this mortgage, executed here, and upon property in this state, being valid by the lex situs, which is also the law of the domicil of the mortgagor, it is the duty of this court to give full effect to the security, without reference to the usury laws of England, which neither party intended to evade or violate by the execution of a mortgage upon the lands here.' [1]

---

[1] Chapman v. Robertson, 6 Paige (N. Y.) 627, 630, 638.

293 *c. Remarks on the Case.* — Whatever objections may be made to the reasoning of the learned chancellor, and it is certainly open to some observation, (*a*) the decision itself seems well supported in point of principle ; for the parties intended that the whole transaction should be in fact, as it was in form, a New York contract, governed by the laws thereof, and the payment of the debt was there to be made. It is easily reconcilable with other laws and principles, if viewed in this light ; if viewed as the chancellor interpreted the case, it is perhaps irreconcilable with other cases and with general principles.[1]

293 *d. Views of John Voet.* — John Voet, in his Commentaries on the Pandects, holds this very doctrine, which appears to me to

[1] Chapman *v.* Robertson, 6 Paige (N. Y.) 627–630, 633. It appears to me that the case was correctly decided; but, with the greatest deference for the learned chancellor, upon principles and expositions to which I cannot assent, and which appear to me inconsistent with the general reasoning of the authorities. It appears to me that there being no place of payment designated in the bond and mortgage, which was executed at New York, where the borrower was domiciled, that, although it was not operative until received by the lender, yet when received and adopted by him the transaction related back to its origin, and it was valid, not as a bond and mortgage executed in England for the payment of money there, but as a bond and mortgage for the payment of the money in New York, as having originated there, and having its whole validity and operation from the law of New York. If an order for goods were sent from New York to England, and the order were complied with, and the goods received in New York; after the receipt of the goods the debt would be treated as an English debt, since the contract of purchase would there be deemed to be negotiated and perfected. Ante, s. 285, 286. In truth, where no place of payment was mentioned, the law of the place where the contract is made fixes it in that place, wherever the parties may be domiciled. The bond and mortgage took effect as contracts of the borrower executed at New York. If a negotiable note is made in one state, and is negotiated to an indorsee in another state, the contract with the indorsee by the maker takes effect as a promise in the state where the note was made, and not where it was indorsed. The payment of the money to the bankers of the borrower in London was merely for his accommodation, and it by no means made the money repayable there. The case of Stapleton *v.* Conway, 3 Atk. 726; 1 Ves. 427, is, as far as it goes, in opposition to the decision in 6 Paige (N. Y.) 627. It is not however my design in this place to enter upon the reasons of my dissent from the doctrines stated by the learned chancellor in 6 Paige (N. Y.) 627. The principles stated from s. 280–321 sufficiently explain some of the grounds upon which that dissent may be maintained. See also 2 Kent Com. 460, 461, and Andrews *v.* Pond, 13 Pet. 65; ante, s. 291; post, s. 304.

(*a*) In Fisher *v.* Otis, 3 Chand. (Wis.) 83, 107, the case of Chapman *v.* Robertson was approved. See however Cope *v.* Alden, 53 Barb. 353. And see Curtis *v.* Leavitt, 15 N. Y. 88.

be entirely in harmony with the received principles of international law. He considers that the interest must be according to the law of the place where the contract is to be performed, whether that place be where the contract is made, or it be another place. If the interest is in either case stipulated for beyond that rate, he deems it usurious. 'Si alio in loco graviorum usurarum stipulatio permissa, in alio vetita sit, lex loci, in quo contractus celebratus est, spectanda videtur in quæstione, an moderatæ, an vero modum excedentes, usuræ per conventionem constitutæ sint. Dummodo meminerimus, illum proprie locum contractus in jure non intelligi, in quo negotium gestum est, sed in quo pecuniam ut solveret se quis obligavit. Modo etiam bona fide omnia gesta fuerint, nec consulto talis ad mutuum contrahendum locus electus sit, in quo graviores usuræ, quam in loco, in quo alias contrahendum fuisset, probatæ inveniuntur. Etiamsi de cætero hypotheca, in sortis et usurarum securitatem obligata, in alio loco sita sit, ubi solæ leviores usuræ permissæ; cum æquius sit contractum accessorium regi ex loco principalis negotii gesti, quam ex opposito contractum principalem regi lege loci, in quo accessorius contractus celebratus est.'[1]

293 e. *Burgundus.* — Burgundus adopts the same doctrine, and says: 'Licita vero sit, an illicita stipulatio, a forma quoque videtur, proficisci, et ideo ejusdem legibus dirigitur, quibus ipsa forma, et ad locum contractus collimare, oportet. Quare et usurarum modus is constituendus est, qui in regione in qua est, contractum legitime celebratur. Et cum reditus duodenarius, in Gallia stipulatus, in controversiam incidisset, patrocinante me judicatum est, in curia Flandriæ valere pactum: nec obesse, quod in Flandria, ubi reditus constitutus, sive hypothecæ impositus proponeretur, usuras semisse graviores stipulari non liceat; quia ratio hypothecæ non habetur, quæ hac in re nihil conferens ad substantiam obligationis, tantum extrinsecus accedit legitimæ stipulationi. Sed hoc intellige de usuris in stipulationem deductis, non autem de iis, quæ ex mora debentur, in quibus ad locum solutionis (ut docebimus postea) respicere oportet.'[2]

294. *Other Foreign Jurists.* — In cases of express contracts for interest, foreign jurists generally hold the same doctrine. Dumoulin, and after him, Boullenois, says: ' In concernentibus con-

---

[1] J. Voet, ad Pand. 22, 1, 6, p. 938; post, s. 304.
[2] Burgundus, tract. 4, s. 10, p. 108, 109; post, s. 302.

tractum, et emergentibus tempore contractus spectatur locus, in quo contrahitur.'[1] And hence the latter deduces the general conclusion that the validity of contracts for rates of interest depends upon the laws of the place where the contract is made and payable, whether it be in the domicil of the debtor, or in that of the creditor, or in that where the property hypothecated is situated, or elsewhere.[2] He holds this also to be a just inference from the language of the Digest. ' Cum judicio bonæ fidei disceptatur, arbitrio judicis usurarum modus ex more regionis, ubi contractum est constituitur;'[3] and that it applies where the parties have designedly contracted in the one place rather than in the other.[4] But, where there is no express contract, and interest is to be implied, foreign jurists are not so well agreed.[5] Some contend that, if the contract is between foreigners, the law of interest of the domicil of the creditor ought to prevail; and others, that that of the domicil of the debtor ought to prevail.[6]

295. *Same.* — Boullenois is of opinion that, where there is no express contract, the interest for which a delinquent debtor is tacitly liable, on account of his neglect to pay the debt, is the interest allowed by the law of the place where the debt is payable; because it is there that the interest has its origin.[7] And in this he follows the doctrine of Everhardus, who says: ' Quia, ubi certus locus solutionis faciendæ destinatus est, tunc non facta solutione in termino et loco præfixo, mora dicitur contrahi in loco destinatæ solutionis, non in loco celebrati contractus.'[8] Strykius holds the same opinion. ' Si lis oritur ex post facto propter negligentiam et moram, consideratur locus, ubi mora contracta est.'[9] Boullenois puts a distinction, which also deserves notice, between cases where the debt for money loaned is payable at a fixed day,

---

[1] Molin. Opera, Com. ad Consuet. Paris, tit. 1, s. 12, gloss. 7, n. 37, tom. 1, p. 224; 2 Boullenois, obs. 46, p. 472; Henry on Foreign Law, p. 53; Boullenois, Quest. de la Contr. des Lois, p. 330–338; ante, s. 82 a.

[2] 2 Boullenois, obs. 46, p. 472. [3] Dig. 22, 1, 1.

[4] Boullenois, obs. 46, p. 472. [5] Id. 472, 477–479, 496.

[6] Ibid.; Bouhier, Cout. de Bourg. c. 21, s. 194–199; Livermore, Dissert. s. 42, p. 46, 47.

[7] 2 Boullenois, obs. 46, p. 477. [8] Everhard. Consil. 78, n. 10, p. 205.

[9] 2 Boullenois, obs. 46, p. 477; Henry on Foreign Law, p. 53. For the citation from Strykius I have been obliged to rely on Boullenois; as I have not been able, after considerable research in the voluminous works of Strykius, to find the particular passage.

and where no day is fixed for payment, but it is at the pleasure of the creditor when it shall be paid, and no place of payment is mentioned.[1] In the former case he holds that the debtor is bound, in order to avoid default, to seek the creditor and pay him ; and therefore the neglect to make payment arises in the domicil of the creditor, and interest ought to be allowed according to the law of that place.[2] In the latter case the creditor is to demand payment of the debtor; and the neglect of payment is in the domicil of the debtor, and therefore interest ought to be allowed according to the law of his domicil.[3] And if, between the time of contracting the debt and the demand of the creditor, the debtor has changed his domicil, Boullenois is of opinion that, if the demand is in the new domicil, interest for neglect of payment should be according to the law of the latter; especially if the change of domicil is known to the creditor.[4] And he applies the same rule to a case where, by the law of the old domicil, a simple demand only is required, and, by the law of the new domicil, a demand by judicial process is necessary.[5] The distinction does not appear to have any foundation in our jurisprudence; for, whether the debt be payable at a fixed day or upon a demand of the creditor, if no place of payment is prescribed, the contract takes effect as a contract of the place where it is made ; and being payable generally, it is payable everywhere, and after a demand and refusal of payment, interest will be allowed according to the law of the place of the contract.[6]

296. *Rule of the Common Law.* — It may therefore be laid down as a general rule, that, by the common law, the lex loci contractus will, in all cases, govern as to the rule of interest, following out the doctrine of the civil law already cited : ' Cum judicio bona fidei disceptatur, arbitrio judicis usurarum modus, ex more regionis, ubi contractum constituitur ; ita tamen ut legi non offendat.' [7] But if the place of payment or of performance is different from that of the contract, then the interest may be validly contracted for at any rate not exceeding that which

---

[1] 2 Boullenois, obs. 46, p. 477, 478.

[2] Ibid.   [3] Ibid.   [4] Ibid.

[5] Id. p. 477–479.

[6] Ante, s. 272, 278 a ; post, s. 317, 329.

[7] Dig. 22, 1, 1, 37; ante, s. 294; 1 Eq. Abr. Interest, E.; Champant v. Renelagh, Prec. Ch. 128; De Sobry v. De Laistre, 2 Harr. & J. (Md.) 193, 228. See 1 Burge, Col. & For. Law, pt. 1, c. 1, p. 29, 30.

is allowed in the place of payment or performance. (*a*) And
in the absence of any express contract as to interest, the law
of the same place will silently furnish the rule, where interest
is to be implied or allowed for delay, ex mora, of payment or
performance.[1] (*b*)

297. *Difficulties in Application of the Rule. — Case in New York.*
— But clear as the general rule as to interest is, there are cases
in which its application has been found not without embarrassments. Thus where a consignor in China consigned goods for
sale in New York, and delivered them to the agent of the consignee in China, and the proceeds were to be remitted to the consignor in China, and there was a failure to remit, the question
arose, whether interest was to be computed according to the rate
in China or the rate in New York. Mr. Chancellor Kent held
that it should be according to the rate in China. But the appellate court reversed his decree, and decided in favor of the rate in
New York. Each court admitted the general rule that the interest should be according to the law of the place of performance,
where no express interest is stipulated. But the Court of Chan-

[1] Ante, s. 291; 2 Kent, Com. 460, 461; Robinson *v.* Bland, 2 Burr. 1077;
Ekins *v.* East India Company, 1 P. Wms. 396; Boyce *v.* Edwards, 4 Pet. 111;
2 Fonbl. Eq. b. 5, c. 1, s. 6; Fanning *v.* Consequa, 17 Johns. (N. Y.) 511;
De Sobry *v.* De Laistre, 2 Harr. & J. (Md.) 193, 228; Smith *v.* Mead, 3 Conn.
253; Winthrop *v.* Carleton, 12 Mass. 4; Foden *v.* Sharp, 4 Johns. (N. Y.)
183; Henry on Foreign Law, p. 53.

(*a*) See Lewis *v.* Ingersoll, 3 Abb.
App. Dec. (N. Y.) 55; Croninger *v.*
Crocker, 62 N. Y. 152.

(*b*) In the case of Ex parte Heidelback, 2 Lowell, 526, 530. Mr. Justice
Lowell says: ' In the case of a bill of
exchange the contracts of the various
parties are distinct, and the drawer is
bound, generally speaking, according
to the law of the place where the bill
is drawn, which is in most cases the
same as that in which it is to be paid
by him if he pays it. Still he is to a
certain extent involved in the same
law with the acceptor, because upon
due protest, demand, and notice, he is
bound to make good to the holder what
the acceptor ought to have paid at the
place where he was to pay, which

makes it necessary to ascertain what
that amount was by the law of that
place, and whether by the same law
due demand was made of the acceptor
and due protest upon the dishonor.
What the drawer should pay as interest ex mora, or as damages, does not
depend upon the law of the place where
the acceptor was to pay the bill, if that
is different from the place where the
drawer's contract is to be performed.'
In this case the Massachusetts rule
that the question of interest and damages in cases in which there is no
stipulation upon the subject is to be
determined by the lex fori as pertaining to the remedy (see ante, s. 291,
note) is repudiated. See also post,
s. 314, note.

cery thought that the delivery of the goods being in China, and the remittance being to be made there, the contract was not complete, until the remittance arrived, and was paid there. The appellate court thought that the delivery of the goods in China, to be sold at New York, was not distinguishable in principle from a delivery at New York; and that the remittance would be complete, in the sense of the contract, the moment the money was put on board the proper conveyance in New York for China; and it was then at the risk of the consignor. The duty of remittance was to be performed in New York, and the failure was there; and consequently the rate of interest of New York only was due.[1]

298. *Case in Louisiana. — Rule concerning Usury.* — Another case has arisen of a very different character. The circumstances of the case were somewhat complicated; but the only point for consideration there arose upon a note, of which the defendants were the indorsers, and with the amount thereof they had debited themselves in an account with the plaintiff; and which they sought now to avoid upon the ground of usury. The note was given in New Orleans, payable in New York, for a large sum of money, bearing an interest of ten per cent, being the legal interest of Louisiana, the New York legal interest being seven per cent only. The question was, whether the note was tainted with usury, and therefore void, as it would be if made in New York. The Supreme Court of Louisiana decided that it was not usurious; and that, although the note was made payable at New York, yet the interest might be stipulated for, either according to the law of Louisiana or according to that of New York. The court seems to have founded their judgment upon the ground that, in the sense of the general rule already stated,[2] there are, or there may be, two places of contract, that in which the contract is actually made, and that in which it is to be paid or performed; locus, ubi contractus celebratus est; locus, ubi destinata solutio est; and therefore, that if the law of both places is not violated in respect to the rate of interest, the contract for interest will be valid.[3] (a)

[1] Consequa v. Fanning, 3 Johns. Ch. (N. Y.) 587, 610; 17 Johns. (N. Y.) 511, 520, 521. See Grant v. Healey, 3 Sum. 523; ante, s. 284 a.

[2] Ante, s. 280.

[3] Depau v. Humphreys, 8 Mart. N.S. (La.) 1. Mr. Chancellor Walworth,

(a) See, to the same effect, Kilgore v. Dempsey, 25 Ohio St. 413; Bank of Louisville v. Young, 37 Mo. 398. And see Carnegie v. Morrison, 2 Met. (Mass.) 381; Pecks v. Mayo, 14 Vt. 33.

In support of their decision the court mainly relied upon the
doctrines supposed to be maintained by certain learned jurists of
continental Europe, whose language however does not appear to
me to justify any such interpretation, when properly considered,
and is perfectly compatible with the ordinary rule that the interest must be, or ought to be, according to the law of the place
where the contract is to be performed and the money is to be
paid. It may not be without use to review some of the more
important authorities thus cited, although it must necessarily involve the repetition of some which have been already cited.

299. *Place of Celebration and Place of Performance.* — There
is no doubt that the phrase, lex loci contractus, may have a
double meaning or aspect, and that it may indifferently indicate
the place where the contract is actually made, or that where it
is virtually made, according to the intent of the parties, that is,
the place of payment or performance.[1] We have seen that the
rule of the civil law clearly indicates this. ' Contractum autem
non utique eo loco intelligitur, quo negotium gestum sit; sed quo
solvenda est pecunia.' [2] Many distinguished jurists refer to this
distinction. Huberus, in the passage already cited, says: ' Verum
tamen non ita praecise respiciendus est locus, in quo contractus
est initus, ut si partes alium in contrahendo locum respexerint,
ille non potius sit considerandus.' [3] Everhardus, as we have seen,
says: ' Ubi certus locus solutioni faciendae destinatus est, tunc
non facta solutione in termino et loco praefixo mora dicitur contrahi in loco destinatae solutionis, et non in loco celebrati contractus. Nimirum, ergo, si inspiciatur valor rei debitae secundum
locum, ubi destinata est solutio. Tum etiam, quia locus contractus, conventio, sive obligatio, perficitur, seu verba proferuntur.
Secundo, ubi solutio seu deliberatio destinatur.' [4] And he adds:
' Quia dico, ut supra dixi; quod locus contractus dicitur duobus
modis; primo, ubi contractus celebratus est; secundo, ubi solutio
destinata est.' [5] And again: ' Duplex est locus contractus, ut

in Chapman *v.* Robertson, 6 Paige (N. Y.) 627, 634, has expressed his entire
concurrence in the decision in 8 Mart. N.S. (La.) 1. But see Van Schaick *v.*
Edwards, 2 Johns. Ch. (N. Y.) 355.

[1] 2 Boullenois, obs. 46, 446; ante, s. 235.
[2] Dig. 42, 5, 3; Pothier, Pand. 42, 5, n. 24; ante, s. 280.
[3] Ante, s. 239, 281; Huber, lib. 1, tit. 3, s. 10.
[4] Everhard. Consil. 78, n. 10, 11, p. 205; ante, s. 295.
[5] Everhard. Consil. 78, n. 18.

supra dixi, quo casu in tantum censetur contractus celebratus in
loco destinatæ solutionis, quod nullo modo censetur celebratus in
loco, ubi verba fuerunt prolata, quoad ea, quæ veniunt post contractum in esse productum.'[1]   Paul Voet places it in a strong
light. 'Ne tamen hic oriatur confusio, locum contractus dupli-
cem facio; alium, ubi fit, de quo jam dictum; alium, in quem
destinata solutio.   Illud locum verum, hunc fictum appellat Salicetus.[2] Uterque tamen recte locus dicitur contractus, etiam
secundum leges civiles, licet postremus aliquid fictionis con-
tineat.'[3]

299 *a. Language of Foreign Jurists.* — But for what purpose do
these foreign jurists refer to the distinction? Is it that the
validity of the same contract is to be at the same time ascertained in part by the law of one country, and in part by that of
another? By no means. They nowhere assert that the validity
of the contract is not to be judged of throughout by one and the
same law, that is, by the law of the place where it is made, or by
the law of the place where it is to be performed, according as, in
a just sense, with reference to the nature and objects of the particular contract, the one or the other is properly to be deemed
the place of the contract.   They nowhere assert that one and the
same rule is not to apply throughout to all the stipulations in the
contract.   That the contract is good, notwithstanding it does not
conform either to the law of the place where it is made, or to
that where it is to be performed.   That the contract is to be
treated not as a whole, but is to be distributed into parts, so
that, if in some of the stipulations it violates the law of each
place, it shall still be good throughout, if it does not violate in
the whole the law of both places.   In many of the passages cited
in support of the supposed mixed character and mixed interpretation and mixed operation of the contract, these learned jurists
were considering questions of a very different nature.   Some of
them were considering the question as to the rule which is to
govern generally in regard to the formalities, solemnities, and
modes of execution of contracts, where the place of execution is
the same place where it is made; others again were considering

---

[1] Id. n. 17; Id. n. 20.   [2] Cod. 1, 1, Summ. Trinit. n. 4.
[3] Voet, de Stat. s. 9, c. 2, s. 11, p. 270. ed. 1715; Id. p. 326, ed. 1661. See
also 2 Boullenois, obs. 46, p. 488; Boullenois, Quest. sur. Contr. des Lois,
p. 330–338.

the rule as to the interpretation and extent of the obligation of contracts generally, under the like circumstances ; and others again were considering the rule where the contract is made in one place and is to be executed in another. We are therefore to understand their language according to the particular occasion and the particular circumstances to which it is applied.

300. *Alexander.* — Let us examine then the particular language which is used by these jurists in the passages cited. Thus Alexander is said to use the following passage : [1] — ' In scriptura instrumenti, in ceremoniis, et solemnitatibus, et generaliter in omnibus, quæ ad formam et perfectionem contractus pertinent, spectanda est consuetudo regionis, ubi fit negotium. Debet enim servari statutum loci contractus, quoad hæc, quæ oriuntur secundum naturam ipsius contractus.' This language expresses only a general truth, and we have no means of knowing that the author intended to speak here of anything further than the general rule applicable to all contracts made and to be performed in the same place.[2]

. 300 a. *Burgundus.* — Burgundus says : ' Et quidem in scriptura instrumenti, in solemnitatibus, et ceremoniis, et generaliter in omnibus, quæ ad formam ejusque perfectionem pertinent, spectanda est consuetudo regionis, ubi fit negotiatio. Rationem assignant doctores quod consuetudo influat in contractus, et convenientes ad eam respicere, ac voluntatem suam accommodare videantur. Et recte.' [3] Now we know upon what occasion this

---

[1] I cite the passage from Alexander, Consil. 37, as I find it in 8 Mart. N.S. (La.) 22. 23, not having been able to obtain the works of Alexander. But I have some doubt whether the first part of the passage is not copied by mistake from Burgundus, who uses almost the identical language. Burgundus, tract. 4, n. 7, p. 104 ; post, s. 300 a. I now suspect that the citation is not, as I supposed it was, from Alexander al Alexandro, but by a mistake of the court in 8 Mart. N.S. (La.) 22, 23 (probably taking it at second hand from some other author), from Alexander Tartagni *Imolens*, or de Imola, who wrote a large work in 5 and 7 vols. folio, of Consilia, published Mediol. 1488, 1489. Lipenius in his Bibl. Jurid. vol. 1, p. 333, refers to this work. 1842. Everhardus in his Consil. 78, in several sections, refers to Alex. de Imola, Consil. 37, and Consil. 49.

[2] From other passages cited by Everhardus from Alexander de Imola, and Bartolus, and Baldus, it seems clear that they all consider the locus solutionis to be the proper locus contractus, except so far as regards the solemnities and creation of the contract. (Solemnitatem et subsistentiam contractus.) See Everhard. Consil. 78, n. 20, p. 207 ; Id. n. 24, p. 208.

[3] Burgundus, tract. 4, n. 7, p. 104 ; ante, s. 260.

language was used. Burgundus was here considering the question solely with reference to the point when a contract is to be deemed lawful or not, or, in other words, by what law its validity is to be governed. 'Illicita stipulatio est,' says he, 'quæ legibus est interdicta, ut puta, si debitum modum usurarum excedat. Nunc ergo considerandum, cujus loci ratio haberi debeat.'[1] He does not even allude to a case where the contract is made in one place and is to be performed in another place. He adds: 'Igitur, ut paucis absolvam, quoties de vinculo obligationis, vel de ejus interpretatione quæritur, veluti, quos et in quantum obliget, quid sententiæ, stipulationis inesse, quid abesse credi oporteat; item in omnibus actionibus, et ambiguitatibus, quæ inde oriuntur, primum quidem id sequemur, quod inter partes actum erit, aut si non apparet, quid actum est, erit consequens, ut id sequamur, quod in regione, in qua actum est, frequentatur.'[2] And he concludes by saying: 'Doctores toties ingerunt ea, quæ respiciunt solemnitatem actus, vel quæ tempore contractus ex natura ipsius adhibentur, orienturque, ex more regionis, ubi contractum est, legem accipere. Ea vero, quæ ad complementum vel executionem contractus spectant vel absoluto eo superveniunt, solere a statuto loci dirigi, in quo peragenda est solutio.'[3]

300 b. *Everhardus.* — Everhardus says: 'Quod quo ad perfectionem contractus seu ad solemnitatem ad esse seu substantiam ejus requisitam semper inspicitur statutum seu consuetudo loci celebrati contractus. Et est ratio, quia ex quo agitur de consuetudine contrahendi non mirum, si inspiciatur locus initæ conventionis, ubi contractus accepit perfectionem.'[4] But he immediately adds: 'Sed ubi agitur de consuetudine solvendi, ut in casu præsenti' (that is, where a contract made in one place was payable in another), 'vel de his, quæ veniunt implenda diu post contractum, et in alio loco impletioni destinato, tunc inspicitur locus destinatæ solutionis.' Now this latter passage would seem as strictly to apply to the case of payment of interest as to the case of payment of principal. If the parties have not stipulated for a particular rate of interest, the usage of the place of payment ought constantly to govern. If they have stipulated for a particular rate of interest, inconsistent with that of the lex loci solu-

---

[1] Id. n. 6, p. 104.   [2] Burgundus, tract. 4, n. 7, p. 105.
[3] Id. n. 29, p. 116. See also id. n. 10, p. 109; ante, s. 292 a, 293 e.
[4] Everhard. Consil. 78, n. 11, p. 206; Id. n. 18, p. 207; Id. n. 27, p. 209.

tionis, the question will still remain, whether it can lawfully be done. Everhardus has not here discussed it; far less has he decided it. And he cites Baldus in support of his opinion, as saying: 'Quod in expeditivis contractus non inspiciuntur ordinativi contractus, sed locus solutionis.' [1] He afterwards adds that this rule, in regard to the forms and solemnities required in order to create and perfect any contract, equally applies to cases where the performance is to be in the same place, and where it is to be in another place. 'Ubi vero in uno loco celebratus est contractus, et in alio loco destinata est solutio, tunc quoad ea, quæ concernunt solemnitatem actus, item ad esse et perfectionem contractus, inspicitur consuetudo loci celebrati contractus. Unde si ex statuto loci contractus requiratur certa solemnitas in ipso contractu, &c., tale statutum vel consuetudo debet observari, licet in loco destinatæ solutionis non sit simile statutum.' [2] How far this latter doctrine is correct and maintainable as a general rule we have already had occasion in some measure to consider.[3] It is not material to the present discussion, which turns upon another point, that is, whether the validity of a contract may depend partly upon the law of one place, and partly on the law of another place, some of its stipulations being contrary to the law of each place.

300 *c. Christinæus.* — Christinæus expressly professes to follow the doctrine of Everhardus on this subject. 'Consuetudo loci,' says he, 'ubi contrahitur spectanda est, scilicet quoad observantiam solemnitatum ipsius actus. Generaliter enim in omnibus, quæ ad formam ejusque perfectionem pertinent, spectanda est consuetudo regionis ubi fit negotiatio, quia consuetudo influit in contractus, et videtur ad eos respicere, et voluntatem suam eis accommodare. Itaque recte. Conditio quoque loci et temporis perfectionem formæ etiam respicit, et idcirco a regione contractus vicissim diriguntur.' [4] He adds: 'Sed quoad ejus executionem, utpote quoad solutionem faciendam, inspicienda venit consuetudo destinatæ solutionis.' [5] And again: 'Quoad ea, quæ celebrato contractu veniunt facienda, inspicitur consuetudo loci, ubi ea debent fieri, puta, tradi, solvi.' [6]

[1] Everhard. Consil. 78, n. 11, p. 206; Id. n. 17, p. 207; Id. n. 27, p. 209.
[2] Everhard. Consil. 78, n. 18, p. 207.   [3] Ante, s. 280.
[4] Christin. Decis. 283, vol. 1, n. 1, 4, 5, 9–11, p. 255.
[5] Id. n. 8, 9, p. 355.   [6] Id. n. 10, 11, 355.

300 *d. Gregorio Lopez. — Dumoulin.* — Gregorio Lopez states
only the general doctrine. 'Quando contractus celebratur in uno
loco, puta in Hispali, et destinata solutio in Corduba ; tunc non
inspicitur locus contractus, sed locus destinatæ solutionis; ut
habetur in ista lege ff. l. contraxisse.'[1] Dumoulin (Molinæus)
says : 'In concernentibus contractum, et emergentibus tempore
contractus, spectatur locus, in quo contrahitur, et in concernentibus meram solemnitatem, cujus actus, locus, in quo ille actus
celebratur.'[2] In another place he says : 'Aut statutum loquitur
de his, quæ concernunt nudam ordinationem et solemnitatem
actus ; et semper inspicitur statutum vel consuetudo loci, ubi
actus celebratur, sive in contractibus, sive in judiciis, sive in
testamentis, sive in instrumentis aut aliis conficiendis. Aut
statutum loquitur de his, quæ meritum scilicet causæ, vel decisionem concernunt ; et tunc, aut in his, quæ pendent a voluntate
partium, vel per eas immutari possunt, et tunc inspiciuntur
circumstantiæ, voluntatis, quarum una est statutum loci, in quo
contrahitur ; et domicilii contrahentium antiqui vel recentis, et
similes circumstantiæ.'[3] In another passage he finds fault with
those who exclusively look to the place where the contract is
made in all cases. 'Quia putant nuditer et indistincte quod
debeat ibi inspici locus et consuetudo, ubi fit contractus, et sic
jus in loco contractus.[4] Quod est falsum ; quinimo jus est in
tacita et verisimiliter mente contrahentium.' He adds : 'Quia
quis censetur potius contrahere in loco in quo debet solvere,
quam in loco ubi fortuito transiens contraxit.'[5] It is plain that
these passages do not justify the inference sought to be adduced
from them. They import no more than that the law which is
to govern contracts is not, in all cases, to be exclusively the
law of the place where they are made.

300 *e. Boullenois.* — Boullenois is also relied on in support of the
doctrine. In one of the passages cited he says : When the question is, whether, in contracts upon any subject, the rights which
spring from the nature and time of the contract (natura et tem-

---

[1] 8 Mart. N.S. (La.) 9, 17; ante, s. 233; Dig. 44, 7, 21.

[2] Dumoulin, cited in 8 Mart. N.S. (La.) 24; Molin. Com. ad Consuet.
Paris, tit. 1, s. 12, gloss. 7, n. 37, tom. 1, p. 224, ed. 1681; 2 Boullenois, obs.
46, p. 472.

[3] Molinæus, Com. in Cod. 1, 1, tom. 3, p. 554, ed. 1681.

[4] Ibid.   [5] Ibid.

pore contractus) are lawful or not, it is necessary to follow the law of the place where the contract is made.[1] And in another passage he says: When the question is to determine the lawfulness of a rate of rent or annuity (taux de rentes), and, in the place where the contract is made, the rate is different from that which is to be paid, either in the country of the domicil of the debtor or in that of the domicil of the creditor, or, finally, in the place where the property hypothecated is situated, — the rate will be adjudged lawful, if it conforms to the law of the place where the contract is made.[2] The context shows that Boullenois was only contemplating the case where the contract was made in the place of its intended performance. For he adds: This is the provision of the law of the Digest (De Usuris), where it is declared: Cum judicio bonæ fidei disceptatur, arbitrio judicis usurarum modus ex more regionis, ubi contractum est, constituitur; ita tamen, ut legi non offendat;[3] and I believe it takes place whenever the parties designedly contract in one place rather than another.[4] The true meaning of Boullenois, in this citation, may be gathered from his own interpretation of the law of the Digest in another page, where he cites with approbation the opinion of Gothofredus, that the words, ubi contractum, ought to be understood to mean the place where the payment ought to be made.[5] 'Hæc verba, "ubi contractum est," sic intellige, ubi actum est, ut solveret.'[6]

301. *Bartolus.* — Bartolus has discussed the question somewhat at large, how far the law of the place of the contract is obligatory upon foreigners, and what effects the laws of the place of the contract have beyond the territory. And first (he says) let us suppose a contract made by a foreigner in one place, and afterwards a suit is litigated thereon in another place, that of the origin of the contracting party; of which place ought the laws to be observed and followed in deciding it? He says we should make a distinction. Either we speak of the statute or custom which respects the solemnities of the contract, or of the process and proceedings in the suit, or of those things which appertain to the jurisdiction in the execution of the contract. In the first

---

[1] 2 Boullenois, obs. 46, p. 472.   [2] Ibid.

[3] Dig. 22, 1, 1; Pothier, Pand. 22, 1, n. 52; ante, s. 296.

[4] 2 Boullenois, obs. 46, p. 472; Id. p. 446.   [5] Id. p. 446.

[6] Gothofred. n. 10, ad Dig. 22, 1, 1.

case we are to look to the law of the place of the contract ; in the second case, as to the process and proceedings in the suit, to the place of judgment.[1] Or else we speak respecting those things which belong to the decision of the cause ; and then the question is as to those things which arise from the very nature of the contract itself in its origin, or as to those things which arise afterwards on account of negligence or delay. In the first case the law of the place of the contract is to be looked to, that is, the place where the contract is made, and not where it is performed. In the second case, either the payment is to be made in a fixed place, or alternately in several places, so that the plaintiff has his election ; or it is to be made in no particular place, because the promise is simply made. In the first case the custom of the place is to be looked to in which the payment is to be made. In the second and third cases the place is to be looked to where the suit is brought. His language is : ' Et primo, utrum statutum porrigatur extra territorium ad non subditos ; secundo, utrum effectus statuti porrigatur extra territorium statuentium. Et primo, quæro, quod de contractibus. Pone contractum celebratum per aliquem forensem in hac civitate ; litigium ortum est, et agitatur lis in loco originis contrahentis, cujus loci statuta debent servari et spectari. Distingue. Aut loquimur de statuto, aut de consuetudine, quæ respiciunt ipsius contractus solemnitatem, aut litis ordinationem, aut de his, quæ pertinent ad jurisdictionem ex ipso contractu evenientis executionis. Primo casu, inspicitur locus contractus. Secundo casu, aut quæris de his, quæ pertinent ad contractus solemnitatem, aut de his, quæ pertinent ad litis ordinationem ; et inspicitur locus judicii. Aut de his, quæ pertinent ad ipsius litis decisionem ; et tunc, aut de his, quæ oriuntur secundum ipsius contractus naturam tempore contractus, aut de his, quæ oriuntur ex post facto propter negligentiam, vel moram. Primo casu, inspicitur locus contractus, ubi est celebratus contractus ; et intelligo locum contractus, ubi est celebratus contractus, non de loco, in quem collata est solutio. Secundo casu, aut solutio est collata in locum certum, aut in pluribus locis alternative, ita quod electio sit actoris ; aut in nullum locum, quia promissio fuit facta simpliciter. · Primo casu inspicitur consue-

---

[1] Everhardus manifestly understands Bartolus to speak with reference to contracts, where payment is to be made in loco celebrati contractus. Everhard. Consil. 78, n. 26, 27, p. 208.

tudo, quæ est in illo loco, in quem est collata solutio ; secundo et
tertio casu, inspicitur locus, ubi petitur.   Ratio prædictorum est,
quia ibi est contracta negligentia vel mora.' [1]   Now taking this
whole passage together, it is difficult to misunderstand the meaning of Bartolus.   It is plain that he did not intend to repudiate
the common distinction as to the lex loci contractus and the
lex loci solutionis.   He gives full effect to the latter, where a
fixed place is prescribed for payment ; and whether he is right or
not, that where no place of payment is named the payment is to
be made according to the law of the place where it is demanded
by the promisee, he goes no further than to assert the general
proposition that the law of the place where the contract is made
is to govern in respect to its solemnities, and that the law of
the place of payment is to be regarded in cases of payment.[2]
He does not at all discuss the point which we have now under
consideration.

301 a. *Result of these Authorities.* — These are the principal
passages adduced from foreign jurists as authorities in support of
the doctrine that a contract is or may be valid, notwithstanding
it does not in its entirety conform either to the law of the place
where the contract is made or to that of the place where it is to
be performed.   Now in the first place it is manifest that many
of these jurists, in the passages cited, speak exclusively as to the
formalities and solemnities and modes of execution of contracts ;
and they hold that in these respects they must conform to the
law of the place where they are made.   Some of them make no
distinction, in the application of this rule, between cases of contracts to be performed in foreign places, and cases of contracts to
be performed in the place where they are made.   And perhaps
the generality of language used by most of them, even when they
do not refer to this distinction, may be fairly applied, indifferently
to both classes of cases.   But several, and indeed most of them,
do expressly and directly recognize the rule that where the contract is made in one place and is to be performed in another, not
only may the law of the latter be properly called the *locus contractus*, but that it ought in all respects, except as to the formalities and solemnities and modes of execution, to be deemed the
rule to govern such cases.

[1] Bartolus, ad Cod. 1, 1, 1, n. 14–16, tom. 7, p. 4, ed. 1602.
[2] Bartolus, ad Cod. 1, 1, n. 14–16, tom. 7, p. 4, ed. 1602. See Vidal *v.*
Thompson, 11 Mart. (La.) 23.

301 b. Same Rule applicable to Principal and Interest. — In the next place, when these foreign jurists speak of payment or performance, they all agree that the contract must be governed by the law of the place of payment or performance, and not by the law of the place where the contract is made. How then are we to distinguish between different parts of the payment? If principal and interest are both to be paid in a foreign place, how can the law of that place govern as to the one and not as to the other? As these jurists make no distinction in respect to the payment of principal and that of interest, but say generally that the payment must be according to the law of the place where the payment is to be made, it is certainly a reasonable inference that they did not intend to make any exception whatsoever, but deemed both the principal and the interest governed by the same rule. Indeed it will be found exceedingly difficult to maintain any distinction between them which is not purely artificial and arbitrary ; for interest is but an incident or accessory to principal.

301 c. Absence of any Exception. — But we need not rest entirely on the silence of foreign jurists in these passages ; for the subject of interest will be found to be expressly treated by some of them ; and therefore, if any exception was intended by them, there the exception would naturally have found its appropriate place. The omission of any exception becomes, under such circumstances, peculiarly significant. Let us therefore review, in this connection, some of the passages in which the subject of interest is expressly or impliedly discussed.

301 d. Foreign Jurists. — Everhardus says: ' Aut quærimus, quis locus inspiciatur, quoad accessoria, ut pute expensas et damna de jure canonico, et usuras de jure civili, si minores vel leviores sunt in uno loco, quam in alio, et similiter ; certum est, quod inspicitur locus destinatæ solutionis ; nedum quoad principalem obligationem, sed etiam quoad accessoria.'[1] And he insists that the leading jurists whom he quotes hold the same opinion. This language would seem to be as direct as possible to the present inquiry ; and it affirms that the *lex loci solutionis* must govern as well as to the interest as to the principal, the former being merely accessorial to the latter. It is no answer to sug-gest that he meant to speak of interest *ex mora*, or interest not

[1] Everhard. Consil. 78, n. 24, p. 208; Id. n. 27–29, p. 208, 209.

expressly provided for, because there is no such qualification in his language, and it is positive as well as general as to the accessorial rights, under all circumstances.

301 *e*. Christinæus avows the same doctrine : 'Sic etiam inspicitur statutum loci destinatæ solutionis, si agatur de extinctione actionis per præscriptionem statutariam vigentem in uno loco, et non in alio. Item si agatur de accessoriis, ut de expensis, damnis et interesse, aut denique usuris, si majores vel minores sint in uno loco, quam in alio.' [1]

301 *f*. Paul Voet may fairly be deemed to hold the same opinion. After having said in the passage already cited, that there may be a double place of the contract, one where it is made, and the other where it is to be paid or performed, he immediately adds ; 'Hinc ratione effectus, et complementi ipsius contractus, spectatur ille locus, in quem destinata est solutio, id, quod ad modum, mensuram, usuras, &c., negligentiam et moram post contractum dinitum accedentem referendum est ; '[2] and he then refers to several authorities in support of this opinion. It seems plain from this language, in this connection, that, as to interest, he deemed the true law by which the legality of the contract was to be adjudged was the law of the place of payment.

302. In one passage Burgundus says that interest is to be allowed according to the place of the contract; and that, if the question comes under consideration in a foreign court, the interest stipulated, though higher than what is lawful by the lex fori ought to be allowed. But where no interest is stipulated, there the interest is to be ex mora, according to the law of the place of payment.[3] His language is: 'Quare et usurarum modus is constituendus est, qui in regione, in qua est contractum, legitime celebratur. Et cum redditus duodenarius in Gallia stipulatus, in controversiam incidisset, patrocinante me, judicatum est, in curia Flandriæ, valere pactum ; nec obesse, quod in Flandria, ubi redditus constitutus, sive hypothecæ impositus proponeretur, usuras emisse graviores stipulari non liceat. Quia ratio hypothecæ non habetur, quæ hac in re nihil conferens ad substantiam obliga-

---

[1] Christin. Decis. 283, n. 12, 13, vol. 1, p. 355.

[2] P. Voet, de Statut. s. 9, c. 2, n. 12, p. 270, ed. 1715; Id. p. 326, ed. 1661; ante, s. 281.

[3] 8 Mart. N.S. (La.) 28; Burgundus, tract. 4, n. 10, p. 109. See also Vidal v. Thompson, 11 Mart. (La.) 23.

tionis, tantum extrinsecus accedit legitimæ stipulationi. Sed, hoc
intellige de usuris in stipulationem deductis, non autem de iis,
quæ ex mora debentur, in quibus ad locum solutionis (ut doce-
mus postea) respicere oportet.'[1] Now, if such be the rule where
the contract is made in France, and to be performed there, the
converse would seem equally to be correct, if the contract had
been made in France to be performed in Flanders, that the contract would be void for usury as against the law of the latter.
In another place he says : ' Idem ergo de solutionibus dicendum,
scilicet, ut in omnibus, quæ ex ea sunt, aut inde oriuntur, aut circa
illam consistunt, aut aliquo modo affinia sunt, consuetudines loci
spectemus ubi eamdem implere convenit.'[2] He adds : ' Itaque
ex solutione sunt solemnia, valor rei debitæ, pretium monetæ ;
ex solutione oriuntur præstatio apochæ, antigraphæ, similiaque ;
circa solutionem consistunt pondera, mensuræ bonitas expensæ,
mora, damna, interesse, usura ex mora debitæ, et ejusmodi.'[3]
And he concludes by stating the reason of the doctrine as given
by all jurists. ' Rationem mutuantur a juris consultis qui unumquemque vult in eo loco contraxisse intelligi, in quo ut solveret
se obligavit.'[4] So that, if this language is to be interpreted in
its broad sense, the interest must in all cases be according to the
law of the place of performance.[5] Burgundus's opinion may perhaps by some persons be thought of less value however, because
he applies the like rule to prescriptions. ' Affinia solutioni sunt
præscriptio, oblatio rei debitæ, consignatio, novatio, delegatio, et
ejusmodi.'[6]

303. Boullenois has nowhere, to my knowledge, directly and
positively treated the question, whether the interest may be stipulated for according to the place of the contract, when payment is
to be made in another place where it would be illegal. The citations already referred to,[7] which are supposed to countenance the
affirmative, put the case only of a rate of interest, or of an annuity, good by the law of the place of the contract (and for aught

---

[1] Burgundus, tract. 4, n. 10, p. 109.
[2] Burgundus, tract. 4, n. 25, 26, p. 114, 115; Id. n. 10, p. 109; 2 Boullenois, obs. 46, p. 488, 498; ante, s. 293 e.
[3] Burgundus, tract. 4, n. 27, p. 115.   [4] Id. n. 29, p. 116.
[5] Id. n. 10, p. 109; ante, s. 293 a.
[6] Burgundus, tract. 4, n. 28, p. 116; 2 Boullenois, obs. 46, p. 488, 498;
ante, s. 300 e.
[7] Ante, s. 300 e.

that appears, payable there), and hold that it will be good, although different from the law of the domicil of the creditor or debtor, or even from the law of the place where the property pledged for security is situate.[1]   There is however a passage which seems to indicate, although not directly, an opinion of Boullenois in the negative.   After referring to and approving the doctrine of Gothofredus, that interest is to be according to the law of the place of payment, he adds that it is in this sense that Gothofredus is to be understood in what he says of the Law 20, of the title of the Digest *de Jurisdictione*,[2] where he supposes a Parisian, who has contracted at Rome (Demus Romœ contractum essa) ; and inquires whether the Parisian, if sued at Paris, shall be condemned to pay the interest prescribed by the law of Rome for the delay ; and he answers in the affirmative, saying : ' Id videtur.   Contractus enim istius initium vitio caret.'   Boullenois says that this decision is very just in effect, if we suppose that the Parisian has not only made the contract at Rome, but also has promised to pay at Rome.[3]   The natural inference certainly would be, that if he expressly agreed to pay interest, that he should pay according to the rate of interest at the place of payment.

304.   It may then be affirmed with some confidence that the foreign jurists who have been relied on do not establish the asserted doctrine.   On the other hand there are other foreign jurists whose doctrines lead to an opposite conclusion.   Thus, John Voet says, if a stipulation for a high interest is allowed in one place, and in another it is prohibited, the law of the place where the contract is made is to decide whether it is good, or whether it exceeds that which is allowable.   Nevertheless we must remember that, in point of law, that is not properly to be deemed the place of the contract where the business is transacted, but where the money is by the contract to be paid.   But good faith must also be observed ; and the place of the contract, where higher interest is allowed, must not be sought for the purpose of evading the law.   He adds that an hypothecation of property, as security, situated in another place where the interest is lower, will not vary the rule, for the security will be treated as merely accessorial.   And it is more equitable that the accessorial contract should be governed by the law of the place where the principal

---

[1] 2 Boullenois, obs. 46, p. 472, 473.   [2] Dig. 2, 1, 20; Gothofred. n. 37.
[3] 2 Boullenois, obs. 46, p. 446.

contract is made, than, on the contrary, that the principal contract should be governed by the law of the place in which the accessorial contract is made.[1]

[1] Voet, ad Pand. 22, 1, s. 6, tom. 1, p. 938; Id. 4, 1, s. 29, tom. 1, p. 241; ante, s. 293 *d.* I have given the sense, although not a precisely literal translation of the passage. The words are: Si alio in loco graviorum usurarum stipulatio permissa, in alio vetita sit, lex loci in quo contractus celebratus est, spectanda videtur in quæstione, an moderatæ, an vero modum excedentes usuræ per conventionem constitutæ sint. Dummodo meminerimus, illum proprie locum contractus in jure non intelligi, in quo negotium gestum est, sed in quo pecuniam ut solveret, se quis obligavit. Modo etiam bona fide omnia gesta fuerint, nec consulto talis ad mutuum contrahendum locus electus sit, in quo graviores usuræ, quam in loco in quo alios contrahendum fuisset, probatæ convenientur. Etiamsi de cætero hypotheca in sortis et usurarum securitatem obligata, in alio loco sita sit, ubi solæ leviores usuræ permissæ; cum æquius sit, contractum accessorium regi ex loco principalis negotii gesti, quam ex opposito contractum principalem regi lege loci, in quo accessorius contractus celebratur. It appears to me that the first part of the passage has been misunderstood, or at least mistranslated, in Depau v. Humphreys, 8 Mart. N.S. (La.) 32. The reasoning of the court upon the passage will here be given in justice to that learned tribunal: ' The authority of the passage,' says Martin, J., in delivering the opinion of the court, ' from Voet remains to be examined. This author says: Si alio in loco graviorum usurarum stipulatio permissa, in alio vetita sit, lex loci, ubi contractus celebratus est, spectanda videtur, an moderatæ, an vero modum excedentes usuræ, per conventionem stipulatæ sint. If in a place the stipulation of higher interest be permitted, in another forbidden, the law of the place in which the contract was celebrated is to be resorted to, in order to ascertain whether the lesser or the greater rate of interest be stipulated by the contract. Thus far Voet teaches what we have seen Alexander, Bartolus, Burgundus, Everhard, Strykius, and Boullenois teach, and the contrary of which no other commentator positively asserts, what in our opinion every sound principle of law dictates. But the appellant's counsel urges that Voet unsays in the succeeding paragraph what he appears to have so emphatically expressed. The words of the second paragraph are: Dummodo meminerimus illum proprie locum contractus, in jure non intelligi, in quo negotium gestum est, sed in quo ut pecuniam solveret se obligavit. In the argument which the appellee's counsel draws in this respect, he is fully supported by what is said, arguendo, by Lord Mansfield, in Robinson v. Bland, and in some degree by Judge Kent in the same manner, in the case of Van Schaick v. Edwards, already cited. In endeavoring to ascertain the character of the rate of interest stipulated in a note given in Massachusetts, Judge Kent says: " Had the money, for instance, in this case been made payable at Albany, or elsewhere in this state (New York), then perhaps the decision in Robinson v. Bland would have applied." If, in the second paragraph, Voet meant to introduce an exception to the rule laid down in the first; if he meant to teach that the legality of a rate of conventional interest, arising not ex mora, but tempore contractus, is exclusively to be tested by the law loci solutionis, even when it is different from the law loci celebrati contractus, then we cannot consider him as affording to us a legitimate rule of decision in the present case; because the weight of his authority is borne down by that of a crowd of the most respectable com-

304 a. True Test of Validity as regards Usury. — If to this doctrine, thus maintained by John Voet (himself an author of distinguished weight and ability) we add the concurrent testimony of Huberus, Everhardus, Christinæus, and Paul Voet, already cited,[1] on the same side, and the entire absence of any direct and absolute authority to the contrary, it is not perhaps too much to affirm that the decision, already alluded to, of the Supreme Court of Louisiana[2] is not supported by the reasoning or the principles of foreign jurists. (a) It is certainly also at variance with the doctrine maintained by Lord Mansfield and the judges of the King's Bench, in a highly interesting case (although not positively necessary to the judgment then pronounced), that the law of the place of payment or performance constitutes the true test by which to ascertain the validity or invalidity of contracts.[3] And finally, in a very recent case, the Supreme Court of the United States have adopted the doctrine that where a contract is made in one place, to be executed in another, it is to be governed as to usury by the law of the place of performance, and not by the law of the place where it is made. So that, if the transaction is bona fide, and not with intent to evade the law against usury, and the law of the place of performance allows a

mentators of the law he cites. Perhaps he must be understood, in the second paragraph, to convey to the student a warning that, by what he teaches in the first, he must not be understood to impugn the proposition that, in a great degree, the law loci solutionis influences the obligation of the party who bound himself, ut solveret pecuniam. Upon the whole we must conclude, as we did in Norris v. Eves, and Vidal v. Thompson, that contracts are governed by the law of the country in which they were made, in everything which relates to the mode of construing them, the meaning to be attached to the expressions by which the parties bound themselves, and the nature and validity of the engagement. But that, wherever the obligation be contracted, the performance must be according to the law of the place where it is to take place. In other words, that in a note executed here, on a loan of money made here, the creditor may stipulate for the legal rate of conventional interest authorized by our law, although such a rate be disallowed in the place in which payment is to be made.' If I am right in the remarks in the text, it will be found that the authorities cited by the learned judge by no means justify the judgment. See Bouhier, Cout. de Bourgogne, vol. 1, c. 21, p. 313; 3 Burge, Col. & For. Law, pt. 2, c. 20, p. 773–775.

[1] Ante, s. 299, 300 *b*, 300 *c*.

[2] Depau v. Humphreys, 8 Mart. N.S. (La.) 1.

[3] Robinson v. Bland, 2 Burr. 1077. See also Van Schaick v. Edwards, 2 Johns. Cas. (N. Y.) 355.

(a) See Ex parte Heidelback, 2 Lowell, 526.

higher rate of interest than that permitted at the place of the
contract, the parties may lawfully stipulate for the higher interest.[1]
But then the transactions must be bona fide, and not intended as
a mere cover of usury.[2] Bouhier indeed thinks that every contract of this sort would almost from its very terms and nature
import a design to evade the laws and to cover usury. But he
manifestly presses the presumption far beyond its legitimate application ; for the circumstances of the case may often establish that
the contract is perfectly innocent and praiseworthy.

305. *Application of the Principle.* — It has been said that if the
principle be that a contract, valid in the place where the contract
is celebrated, is void if it is contrary to the law of the place of
payment, it must establish the converse proposition, that a contract void by the law of the place where it is made is valid
if good by the law of the place of payment.[3] This would
seem to be reasonable; and the doctrine is supported by the
modern cases, notwithstanding the old cases have been supposed
to lead to a contrary conclusion. In one case,[4] a bond was executed in Ireland for a debt contracted in England ; and because
it constituted a security on lands in Ireland, Lord Chancellor
Hardwicke held that it was valid, although it bore the Irish interest of seven per cent. But he thought it would have been
otherwise if it had been a simple contract debt, or if the bond
had been executed in England.[5] Mr. Chancellor Kent has correctly laid down the modern doctrine; and he is fully borne
out by the authorities. ' The law of the place,' says he, ' where
the contract is made is to determine the rate of interest when
the contract specifically gives interest; and this will be the case
though the loan be secured by a mortgage on lands in another
state, unless there be circumstances to show that the parties had
in view the law of the latter place in respect to interest. When
that is the case, the rate of interest of the place of payment is to
govern.' [6] (a)

[1] Andrews v. Pond, 13 Pet. 65, 77, 78.
[2] Bouhier, Cout. de Bourg. vol. 1, c. 21, p. 413.
[3] Depau v. Humphreys, 8 Mart. N.S. (La.) 1, 30.
[4] Connor v. Bellamont, 2 Atk. 382.
[5] Stapleton v. Conway, 3 Atk. 726; 1 Ves. 427. See Dewar v. Span, 3 T.
R. 425.
[6] 2 Kent Com. 460, 461; DeWolf v. Johnson, 10 Wheat. 367; Scofield v.

(a) See Pine v. Smith, 11 Gray, 38.

424CONFLICT OF LAWS.[s. 306–308.

306. *Limits of the Operation of Foreign Laws.* — But it has been asked, if this be the established doctrine, of what use is it for any legislature to pass a law for the protection of the weak and necessitous?[1] And the case of minors has been mentioned, as exhibiting the inconvenience of the principle. But we have already seen that minors in one country may lawfully contract in another in which they are deemed of age.[2] The true answer to all such suggestions is, that no country can give to its own laws any extra-territorial authority, so as to bind other nations. If it undertakes to legislate in regard to acts done or contracts performed elsewhere, it can claim for its own laws no other validity than such as the comity of other nations may choose to allow towards them. It may, if it chooses, deem all such acts and contracts valid or invalid, according to its own laws; but it cannot impose a like obligation on other nations so to treat them. The repose and common interest of all nations therefore require each to observe towards all others the principles of reciprocal justice and comity; and these, as we have seen, are best subserved by the adoption of the general rule, that the law of the place of the contract and payment shall govern.[3]

307. *Damages.* — Analogous to the rule respecting interest would seem to be the rule of damages in cases of contract, where damages are to be recovered for a breach thereof ex mora, or where the right to damages arises ex delicto, from some wrong or injury done to personal property. Thus if a ship should be illegally or tortiously converted in the East Indies by a party, the interest there will be allowed by way of damages in a suit against him.[4] (a) So the rate of damages on a dishonored bill of exchange will be according to the lex loci contractus of the particular party.[5] So if a bill of exchange be made in one state and

Day, 20 Johns. (N. Y.) 102; Thompson v. Powles, 2 Sim. 194; Robinson v. Bland, 2 Burr. 1077; Boyce v. Edwards, 4 Pet. 111. But see Chapman v. Robertson, 6 Paige (N.Y.) 627, 630.

[1] Depau v. Humphreys, 8 Mart. N.S. (La.) 1, 30.
[2] Saul v. His Creditors, 5 Mart. N.S. (La.) 596, 597; ante, s. 82.
[3] Ante, s. 242, 280.
[4] Ekins v. East India Company, 1 P.Wms. 395, 396; Consequa v. Willings, Pet. C. C. 225, 303.
[5] Slacum v. Pomery, 6 Cranch, 221; Hazelhurst v. Kean, 4 Yeates (Penn.) 19; Pothier on Oblig. n. 171.

(a) See Holmes v. Barclay, 4 La. Ann. 64.

indorsed in another state, and again indorsed by a second indorser in a third state, the rate of damages upon the dishonor of the bill will be against each party according to the law of the place where his own contract had its origin, either by making or by indorsing the bill.[1] So if a note made in a foreign country is for the payment of a certain sum in sugar, and by the custom of that place the like notes are payable in sugar at a valuation, the law of the place is to govern in assessing the damages for a breach thereof.[2] (a)

808. *Exchange.* — Where a contract is made in one country, and is payable in the currency of that country, and a suit is afterwards brought in another country to recover for a breach of the contract, a question often arises as to the manner in which the amount of the debt is to be ascertained, whether at the nominal or established par value of the currencies of the two countries, or according to the rate of exchange at the particular time existing between them. In all cases of this sort, the place where the money is payable, as well as the currency in which it is promised to be paid, are, as we shall presently see, material ingredients.[3] (b) For instance, a debt of £100 sterling is contracted in England, and is payable there ; and afterwards a suit is brought in America for the recovery of the amount. The present par fixed by law between the two countries is to estimate the pound sterling at four dollars and forty-four cents.[4] But the rate of exchange on bills drawn in America on England is generally at from eight to ten per cent advance on the same amount. In a recent case, it was held by the King's Bench, in an action for a debt payable in Jamaica and sued in England, that the amount should be ascertained by adding the rate of exchange to the par

---

[1] Post, s. 314, 317.   [2] Courtois v. Carpentier, 1 Wash. C. C. 376.
[3] Post, s. 310.
[4] This is the par for ordinary commercial purposes. But by the Act of Congress of 1832, c. 224, s. 16, the par for the purpose of estimating the value of goods, paying an ad valorem duty, and for that purpose only, is declared to be to estimate a pound sterling at four dollars and eighty cents. The still more recent Act of 22d July, 1842, c. 66, makes the par for estimating duties, in like cases, at four dollars and eighty-four cents for the pound sterling.

(a) See further In re State Ins. Co., 9 Jur. N.S. 298; Suse v. Pompe, 8 C. B. N.S. 538.   (b) See Marburg v. Marburg. 26 Md. 8; Capron v. Adams, 28 Md. 529.

value, if above it; and so vice versa, by deducting it, when the exchange is below the par.[1] Perhaps it is difficult to reconcile this case with the doctrine of some other cases.[2] In a late American case, where the payment was to be in Turkish piastres, but it does not appear, from the report, where the contract was made or was made payable, it was held to be the settled rule 'where money is the object of the suit, to fix the value according to the rate of exchange at the time of the trial.'[3] It is impossible to say that a rule laid down in such general terms ought to be deemed of universal application; and cases may easily be imagined which may justly form exceptions.

809. *The Proper Rule.* — The proper rule would seem to be, in all cases, to allow that sum in the currency of the country where the suit is brought, which should approximate most nearly to the amount to which the party is entitled in the country where the debt is payable, calculated by the real par, and not by the nominal par, of exchange.[4] (*a*) This would seem to be the rule also which is adopted by foreign jurists.[5] In some countries there is an established par of exchange by law, as in the United States, where the pound sterling of England is now valued at four dollars and forty-four cents for all purposes, except the estimation of the duties on goods paying an ad valorem duty.[6] In other countries the original par has, by the depreciation of the

[1] Scott *v.* Bevan, 2 B. & Ad. 78. Lord Tenterden in delivering the opinion of the court in favor of the rule, said: ' Speaking for myself personally, I must say that I still hesitate as to the propriety of the conclusion.' See Delegal *v.* Naylor, 7 Bing. 460; Ekins *v.* East India Company, 1 P. Wms. 396.

[2] See Cockerell *v.* Barber, 16 Ves. 461; post, s. 312.

[3] Lee *v.* Wilcocks, 5 Serg. & R. (Pa.) 48. It is probable that in this case the money was payable in Turkey.

[4] In Cash *v.* Kennion, 11 Ves. 314, Lord Eldon held that, if a man in a foreign country agrees to pay £100 in London upon a given day, he ought to have that sum there on that day. And if he fails in that contract, wherever the creditor sues him, the law of that country ought to give him just as much as he would have had if the contract had been performed. J. Voet says: ' Si major, alibi minor, eorundem nummorum valor sit, in solutione facienda; non tam spectanda potestas pecuniæ, quæ est in loco, in quo contractus celebratus est, quam potius quæ obtinet in regione illa, in qua contractus implementum faciendum est.' Voet, ad Pand. 12, 1, s. 25; Henry on Foreign Law, 43, note. See also ante, s. 281; 3 Burge, Col. & For. Law, pt. 2, c. 20, p. 771–773.

[5] Ante, s. 281.　　　　　[6] Ante, s. 308, n. 2.

(*a*) See Benners *v.* Clemens, 58 Penn. St. 24.

currency, become merely nominal; and there we should resort to the real par. Where there is no established par from any depreciation of the currency, there the rate of exchange may justly furnish a standard, as the nearest approximation of the relative value of the currencies. And where the debt is payable in a particular known coin, as in Sicca rupees or in Turkish piastres, there the mint value of the coin, and not the mere bullion value in the country where the coin is issued, would seem to furnish the proper standard, since it is referred to by the parties in their contract by its descriptive name as coin.

310. *Place of Performance to be regarded.* — But in all these cases we are to take into consideration the place where the money is, by the original contract, payable; for wheresoever the creditor may sue for it, he is entitled to have an amount equal to what he must pay, in order to remit it to that country.[1] Thus if a note were made in England for £100 sterling, payable in Boston, Mass., if a suit were brought in Massachusetts, the party would be entitled to recover four hundred and forty-four dollars and forty-four cents, that being the established par of exchange by our laws. But if our currency had become depreciated by a debasement of our coinage, then the depreciation ought to be allowed for, so as to bring the sum to a real par, instead of the nominal par.[2] But if a like note were given in England for £100 payable in England, or payable generally, which in legal effect would be the same thing there, in a suit in Massachusetts, the party would be entitled to recover, in addition to the four hundred and forty-four dollars and forty-four cents, the rate of exchange between Massachusetts and England, which is ordinarily from eight to ten per cent above par. And if the exchange were below par, a proportionate deduction should be made; so that the party would have his money replaced in England at exactly the same amount which he would be entitled to recover in a suit there.

[1] See 1 Chitty on Com. & Manuf. c. 12, p. 650, 651. See ante, s. 281, 308.
[2] Paul Voet has expressed an opinion upon this subject in general terms: 'Quid, si in specie de nummorum aut redituum solutione difficultas incidat, si forte valor sit immutatus; an spectabitur loci valor, ubi contractus erat celebratus, an loci, in quem destinata erat solutio? Respondeo, ex generali regula, spectandum esse loci statutum, in quem destinata erat solutio.' P. Voet, de Stat. s. 9, c. 2, s. 15, p. 271; Id. p. 328, ed. 1661. And he applies the same rule where contracts are for specific articles, the measures whereof are different in different countries. Id. s. 16, p. 271; Id. p. 328, ed. 1661.

311. *Reconciliation of some Cases.* — This distinction may perhaps reconcile some of the cases between which there might seem, at first view, to be an apparent contrariety. It was evidently acted on in an old case, where money, payable in Ireland, was sued for in England; and the court allowed Irish interest, but directed an allowance to the debtor for the payment of it in England, and not in Ireland.[1] It is presumable that the money was of less value in Ireland than in England. A like rule was adopted in a later case, where money payable in India was recovered in England; and the charge of remitting it from India was directed to be deducted.[2]

311 a. *Difference in some of the Cases.* — There is however an irreconcilable difference in some of the authorities on this subject. Thus it has been held in New York that, where a debt is contracted in a foreign country and is payable there, if the creditor afterwards sues the debtor here for the debt, he is entitled to recover only for the debt according to the par of exchange, and not according to the rate of exchange necessary to remit the amount to the foreign country. On that occasion the court said: ' The debt is to be paid according to the par, and not the rate of exchange. It is recoverable and payable here to the plaintiffs or their agent, and the courts are not to inquire into the disposition of the debt after it reaches the hands of the agent. He may remit the debt to his principal abroad in bills of exchange, or he may invest it here on his behalf, or transmit it to some other part of the United States, or to other countries on the same account. We cannot trace the disposition which is to take place subsequent to the recovery, nor award special damages upon such uncertain calculations.[3] The same doctrine has been adhered to in subsequent decisions.[4] It has also been adopted by the Supreme Court of Massachusetts, as the proper rule in all cases, except bills of exchange.[5] (a) On the contrary, in the Circuit

---

[1] Dungannon v. Hackett, 1 Eq. Cas. Abr. 288, 289.

[2] Ekins v. The East India Company, 1 P. Wms. 396; s. c. 2 Bro. P. C. 382, ed. Tomlins.

[3] Martin v. Franklin, 4 Johns. (N. Y.) 124, 125.

[4] Scofield v. Day, 20 Johns. (N. Y.) 102.

[5] Adams v. Cordis, 8 Pick. (Mass.) 260, 266, 267.

(a) See Alcock v. Hopkins, 6 Cush. (Mass.) 484; Lodge v. Spooner, 8 Gray (Mass.) 166; Hussey v. Farlow, 9 Allen (Mass.) 263; Burgess v. Alliance Ins. Co., 10 Allen (Mass.) 226.

Courts of the United States the opposite doctrine has been maintained.[1]

[1] Smith *v.* Shaw, 2 Wash. C. C. 167, 168; Grant *v.* Healey, 3 Sumner, 523; ante, s. 284 *a.* In this last case the subject was considered at great length, and the following remarks were made by the judge in delivering the opinion of the court: ' I take the general doctrine to be clear that whenever a debt is made payable in one country, and is afterwards sued for in another country, the creditor is entitled to receive the full sum necessary to replace the money in the country where it ought to have been paid, with interest for the delay; for then, and then only, is he fully indemnified for the violation of the contract. In every such case the plaintiff is therefore entitled to have the debt due to him first ascertained at the par of exchange between the two countries, and then to have the rate of exchange between those countries added to or subtracted from the amount, as the case may require, in order to replace the money in the country where it ought to be paid. It seems to me that this doctrine is founded on the true principles of reciprocal justice. The question therefore, in all cases of this sort, where there is not a known and settled commercial usage to govern them, seems to me to be rather a question of fact than of law. In cases of accounts and advances the object is to ascertain where, according to the intention of the parties, the balance is to be repaid. In the country of the creditor or of the debtor? In Lanusse *v.* Barker, 3 Wheat. 101, 147, the Supreme Court of the United States seem to have thought that where money is advanced for a person in another state, the implied understanding is to replace it in the country where it is advanced, unless that conclusion is repelled by the agreement of the parties, or by other controlling circumstances. Governed by this rule, the money being advanced in Boston, so far as it was not reimbursed out of the proceeds of the sales at Trieste, would seem to be proper to be repaid in Boston. In relation to mere balances of account between a foreign factor and a home merchant, there may be more difficulty in ascertaining where the balance is reimbursable, whether where the creditor resides, or where the debtor resides. Perhaps it will be found, in the absence of all controlling circumstances, the truest rule and the easiest in its application, that advances ought to be deemed reimbursable at the place where they are made, and sales of goods accounted for at the place where they are made or authorized to be made. Thus, if a consignment is made in one country for sales in another country, where the consignee resides, the true rule would seem to be to hold the consignee bound to pay the balance there, if due from him; and if due to him on advances there made, to receive the balance from the consignor there. The case of Consequa *v.* Fanning, 3 Johns. Ch. (N. Y.) 587, 610, which was reversed in 17 Johns. (N. Y.) 511, proceeded upon this intelligible ground both in the court of chancery and in the court of errors and appeals; the difference between these learned tribunals not being so much in the rule as in its application to the circumstances of that particular case. I am aware that a different rule in respect to balances of account and debts due and payable in a foreign country, was laid down in Martin *v.* Franklin, 4 Johns. (N. Y.) 125, and Scofield *v.* Day, 20 Johns. (N. Y.) 102; and that it has been followed by the supreme court of Massachusetts in Adams *v.* Cordis, 8 Pick. (Mass.) 260. It is with unaffected diffidence that I venture to express a doubt as to the correctness of the decisions of these learned courts upon this point. It appears to me that the reasoning in 4 Johns. 125, which

312. *Cockerell* v. *Barber.* — In one case where, by a will made
in India, a legacy was given of 30,000 Sicca rupees, and the

constitutes the basis of the other decisions, is far from being satisfactory. It
states very properly that the court have nothing to do with inquiries into the
disposition which the creditor may make of his debt after the money has
reached his hands; and the court are not to award damages upon such uncertain calculations as to the future disposition of it. But that is not, it is
respectfully submitted, the point in controversy. The question is, whether if
a man has undertaken to pay a debt in one country, and the creditor is compelled to sue him for it in another country, where the money is of less value,
the loss is to be borne by the creditor, who is in no fault, or by the debtor,
who by the breach of this contract has occasioned the loss. The loss of which
we here speak is not a future contingent loss. It is positive, direct, immediate. The very rate of exchange shows that the very same sum of money paid
in the one country is not an indemnity or equivalent for it when paid in another country, to which by the default of the debtor the creditor is bound to
resort. Suppose a man undertakes to pay another $10,000 in China, and vio-
lates his contract; and then he is sued therefor in Boston, when the money, if
duly paid in China, would be worth at the very moment twenty per cent more
than it is in Boston; what compensation is it to the creditor to pay him the
$10,000 at the par in Boston? Indeed, I do not perceive any just foundation
for the rule that interest is payable according to the law of the place where
the contract is to be performed, except it be the very same on which a like
claim may be made as to the principal, viz., that the debtor undertakes to pay
there, and therefore is bound to put the creditor in the same situation as if he
had punctually complied with his contract there. It is suggested that the case
of bills of exchange stands upon a distinct ground, that of usage, and is an
exception from the general doctrine. I think otherwise. The usage has done
nothing more than ascertain what should be the rate of damages for a violation of the contract generally, as a matter of convenience and daily occurrence
in business, rather than to have a fluctuating standard dependent upon the
daily rates of exchange; exactly for the same reason that the rule of deducting
one third new for old is applied to the cases of repairs of ships, and the deduction of one third from the gross freight is applied in cases of general average.
It cuts off all minute calculations and inquiries into evidence. But in cases of
bills of exchange drawn between countries where no such fixed rate of damages
exists, the doctrine of damages applied to the contract is precisely that which
is sought to be applied to the case of a common debt due and payable in another country; that is to say, to pay the creditor the exact sum which he ought
to have received in that country. That is sufficiently clear from the case of
Mellish *v.* Simeon, 2 H. Black. 378, and the whole theory of re-exchange.
My brother, the late Mr. Justice Washington, in the case of Smith *v.* Shaw,
2 Wash. C. C. 167, 168, in 1808, which was a suit brought by an English
merchant on an account for goods shipped to the defendant's testator, where
the money was doubtless to be paid in England, and a question was made,
whether, it being a sterling debt, it should be turned into currency at the par of
exchange, or at the then rate of exchange, held that the debt was payable at
the then rate of exchange. To which Mr. Ingersoll, at that time one of the
ablest and most experienced lawyers at the Philadelphia bar, of counsel for
the defendant, assented. It is said that the point was not started at the argu-

testator afterwards died in England, leaving personal property both in England and in India, upon a suit in chancery for the legacy, the master, to whom it was referred, estimated the Sicca rupees at 2s. 6d. per Sicca rupee, being the East India Company's rate of exchange between India and Great Britain, i. e., on bills drawn in India on Great Britain, at the time the legacy became due. At the same time, the par or sterling value of the Sicca rupees in India and England was 2s. 1d. per Sicca rupee; and the East India Company's rate of exchange between Great Britain and India, i. e. on bills drawn in England on India, was 2s. 3d. Upon exceptions taken to the report, it was contended that either the par of exchange, or the rate of exchange between Great Britain and India, ought to have been adopted.[1] Lord Eldon on that occasion said: ' In all the cases reported upon the wills of persons in Ireland or Jamaica, and dying there, and vice versa in this country, some legacies being expressed in sterling money, others in sums, without reference to the nature of the coin in which they are to be paid, the legacies are directed here to be computed according to the real value of the currency of the country to which the testator belonged, or where the property was; and I apprehend no more was done in such cases than ascertaining the value of so many pounds in the current coin of the country, and paying that amount out of the funds in

ment, and was settled by the court suddenly without advancing any reasons in support of it. I cannot but view the case in a very different light. The point was certainly made directly to the court, and attracted its full attention. The learned judge was not a judge accustomed to come to sudden conclusions, or to decide any point which he had not most scrupulously and deliberately considered. The point was probably not at all new to him; for it must frequently have come under his notice in the vast variety of cases of debts due on account by Virginia debtors to British creditors, which were sued for during the period in which he possessed a most extensive practice at the Richmond bar. The circumstance that so distinguished a lawyer as Mr. Ingersoll assented to the decision is a further proof to me that it had been well understood in Pennsylvania to be the proper rule. If, indeed, I were disposed to indulge in any criticism I might say that the cases in 4 Johns. 125, and 20 Johns. 101, 102, do not appear to have been much argued or considered; for no general reasoning is to be found in either of them upon principle, and no authorities were cited. The arguments and the opinion contained little more than a dry statement and decision of the point. The first and only case in which the question seems to have been considered upon a thorough argument, is that in 8 Pick. 260. I regret that I am not able to follow its authority with a satisfied assent of mind.'

[1] Cockerell v. Barber, 16 Ves. 461, 465.

court. On the other hand, I do not believe the court have ever said they would not look at the value of the current coin of the country, but would take it as bullion. At the time of Wood's halfpence in Ireland, whatever was their actual worth, yet payment in England must have been according to their nominal current value, not the actual value. So whatever was the current value of the rupee at the time when this legacy ought to be paid, is the ratio according to which payment must be made here in pounds sterling. If twelve of Wood's halfpence were worth sixpence in this court, sixpence must have been the sum paid. And in a payment in this court the cost of remittance has nothing to do with it. So if the value of 30,000 rupees, at the time the payment ought to have been made in India, was £10,000, that is the sum to be paid here, without any consideration as to the expense of remittance.' And he accordingly directed the master to review his report, and the legacies to be paid according to the current value of the Sicca rupee in Calcutta.[1] (a)

313. *Consideration of this Case.* — In considering this decision it is material to observe that the will was made in India, and of course the legacy payable there; and the testator died in England, leaving personal assets in both countries. Under these circumstances the legatee was not compellable to resort to England for payment of the legacy; but he elected of his own mere choice to receive it there. He might have resorted to India if he had pleased;[2] and if so, he would have been entitled to the exact amount of 30,000 Sicca rupees, according to their current value there. He ought not then, by resorting to a court in England, to oblige the estate to bear the charge of the remittance of the amount to England, with which it was charged by the master's report. Nor ought the estate, upon his mere election to receive the amount in England, to pay for the remittance of the same from England to India. The decree of the court was, therefore manifestly right and consistent with the principles above stated. The language of the court however

---

[1] Ibid.

[2] See Bourke *v.* Ricketts, 10 Ves. 332, and Raithby's notes to Ranelaugh *v.* Champante, 2 Vern. 395; Saunders *v.* Drake, 2 Atk. 466; Stapleton *v.* Conway, 1 Ves. 427.

(a) See Bowditch *v.* Soltyk, 99 Mass. 136.

not liberate himself by paying the nominal amount of his debt in
the debased money, that is, he may pay in the debased money,
being the current coin, but he must pay so much more as would
make it equal to the sum he borrowed.   But he says if the
nominal value of the currency, leaving it unadulterated, were to
be increased, as if they were to make the guinea pass for 30s.,
the debtor may liberate himself from a debt of 1l. 10s, by paying
a guinea, although he had borrowed the guinea when it was but
worth 21s.   I have said it is unnecessary to consider whether the
conclusion drawn by Vinnius or the decision in Davies's Reports
be the correct one ; for we think this has no analogy to the case
of creditor and debtor.   There is a wrong act done by the French
government ; then they are to undo that wrong act, and to put
the party in the same situation as if they never had done it.   It
is assumed to be a wrong act, not only in the treaty, but in the
repealing decree.   They justify it only with reference to that
which as to this country has a false foundation ; namely, on the
ground of what other governments had done towards them, they
having confiscated the property of French subjects ; therefore
they say we thought ourselves justified at the time in retaliating
upon the subjects of this country.   That being destitute of
foundation as to this country, the republic themselves in effect
confess that no such decree ought to have been made, as it
affected the subjects of this country.   Therefore it is not merely
the case of a debtor paying a debt at the day it falls due, but it
is the case of a wrong-doer, who must undo, and completely
undo, the wrongful act he has done ; and if he has received the
assignats at the value of 50d. he does not make compensation by
returning an assignat which is only worth 20d. : he must make
up the difference between the value of the assignat at different
periods.   And that is the case stated by Sir John Davies, where
restitutio in integrum is stated.   He says, two cases were put by
the judges who were called to the assistance of the Privy Council,
although they were not positively and formally resolved.   He
says, it is said if a man upon marriage receive 1,000l. as a portion
with his wife, paid in silver money, and the marriage is dissolved
causa præcontractus, so that the portion is to be restored, it must
be restored in equal good silver money, though the state shall
have depreciated the currency in the mean time.   So if a man
recover 100l. damages, and he levies that in good silver money,

and that judgment is afterwards reversed by which the party
is put to restore back all he has received, the judgment creditor
cannot liberate himself by merely restoring 100*l.* in the debased
currency of the time; but he must give the very same currency
that he had received. That proceeds upon the principle that if
the act is to be undone it must be completely undone, and the
party is to be restored to the situation in which he was at the
time the act to be undone took place. Upon that principle therefore undoubtedly the French government, by restoring assignats
at the end of thirteen months, did not put the party in the
same situation in which he was when they took from him assignats that were of a very different value. We have said that, as
this point is not directly or immediately before us, it can make
no part of our decree. At the same time it may not perhaps
have been without some utility to have given an opinion upon it,
inasmuch as it was argued and discussed at the bar. And we
think therefore the commissioners have proceeded on a perfectly
right principle in those cases in which we understand they have
made an allowance for the depreciation of paper-money; and,
considering that this case does not differ from those in which
they have made that allowance, we are of opinion that the
claimants ought to have the same equity administered to them in
remunerating them for the loss they have sustained.'[1]

313 *b. Foreign Jurists.* — The opinions of Vinnius and Pothier,
alluded to in the opinion of Sir William Grant, fully confirm his
statements. Vinnius is of opinion that the value of the money
at the time when it ought to be paid is the value which is to be
allowed to the creditor. Of the same opinion, he adds, are Bartolus and Baldus and De Castro, and indeed jurists generally,
with the exception of Dumoulin and Hotomannus and Donellus,
who think the value at the time of making the contract ought to
govern. Hence, after having discussed the principle, Vinnius
says, in conformity with the opinions of the former jurists:
' Hoc autem fundamento posito, siquidem neutri contrahentium
injuriam fieri volumus, ita definiendum videtur, ut si bonitas
monetæ intrinseca mutata sit, tempus contractus, si extrinseca,
id est valor imposititius, tempus solutionis in solutione facienda,
spectari debeat.'[2] Pothier holds the opposite opinion, and says:

[1] Pilkington *v.* Commissioners for Claims, 2 Knapp, 17–21.
[2] Vinnius, ad Instit. lib. 3, tit. 15, Textus, De Mutuo, Com. n. 12, p. 599, ed.

'It remains to be observed, in regard to the price, that it may be rendered in a money different from that in which it is paid.

1726; Id. p. 664, ed. 1777, Lugduni. The whole passage deserves to be cited. 'Atque hinc pendet decisio nobilissimæ quæstionis, si post contractum æstimatio nummorum creverit aut decreverit, utrum in solutione facienda spectare oporteat valorem, quem habebant tempore contractus, an qui nunc est tempore solutionis: intellige si nihil, de ea re expresse dictum sit, neque mora intervenerit. Molinæus, Hotomannus, Donellus contendunt, tempus contractus inspiciendum esse, id est, ea æstimatione nummos reddendos, non quæ nunc est, sed quæ initio fuit, cum dabantur. Nimirum nihil illi in pecunia numerata præter æstimationem considerandum putant, totamque nummi bonitatem in hac ipsa æstimatione consistere: ac proinde creditori non facere injuriam, qui eandem æstimationem, quam accepit, reddit: tantum enim reddere eum, quantum accepit, quod ad solutionem mutui sit satis. Itaque secundum horum sententiam, si 100 aurei mutuo dati sint, cum aureus valebat asses 50 reddantur autem, cum singuli valent asses 55 debitor reddens creditori aureos 90 aut in singulos aureos 50 asses reddit, quantum accepit, et liberatur: et vicissim si imminuta sit ad eundem modum accepit, et liberatur: et vicissim si imminuta sit ad eundem modum aureorum æstimatio, non liberatur, nisi reddat aureos 110, aut in singulos aureos asses 55. Bartolus vero (in l. Paulus. 101 de solut.) Baldus (in l. res in dotem, 24 de jur. dot.) Castro (in lib. 3, de reb. cred.) et DD. comm. ut videre est apud Boer. decis. 327, contra censent, spectandum esse in proposito tempus solutionis, id est, aucto vel diminuto nummorum valore, ea æstimatione reddi eos oportere, non quæ tunc fuit, cum dabantur, sed quæ nunc est, cum solvuntur; neque aliud statui posse sine creditoris aut debitoris injuria. Quæ sententia, ut mihi videtur, et verior et æquior est. Nam quod contrariæ sententiæ auctores unicum urgent, in nummis non materiæ, sed solius æstimationis impositæ atque externæ, quam ob id vulgo extrinsecam nummi bonitatem vocant, rationem duci, nummumque nihil aliud esse, quam quod publice valet, vereor, ut simpliciter verum sit. Utique enim materia numismatis fundamentum est et causa valoris: quippe qui variatur pro diversitate materiæ: oportetque valorem hunc justa aliqua proportione materiæ respondere: neque in bene constituta repub. nummo ea æstimatio imponi debet, quæ pretium materiæ, ex qua cuditur, superat, aut superet ultra modum expensarum, quæ in signanda pecunia fiunt; quod ad singularum specierum valorum parum addere potest. Sed hoc ad actus et præstationes privatorum non pertinet. Illud pertinet, quod si dicimus, creditis nummis nihil præter æstimationem eorum creditum intelligi, necessario sequitur, creditorem teneri in alia forma aut materia nummos accipere contra definitionem Pauli in d. l. 99 de solut. etiamsi damnum ex eo passurus sit: nam, qui recipit, quod credidit, nihil habet, quod conqueratur. Sequitur et hoc, si contingat mutari nummorum bonitatem intrinsecam, id est, si valore veteri retentio percutiantur novi nummi ex deteriore materia. quam ex qua cusi, qui dati sunt, puta, si qui dati sunt, cusi fuerint ex puro auro, postea alii feriantur ex auro minus puro et mixto ex ære, debitorem restituendo tot mixtos et contaminatos, quot ille puros accepit, liberari cum insigni injuria creditoris: et contra interpp. pene omnium doctrinam, qui hoc casu solutionem faciendam esse statuunt ad valorem intrinsecum monetæ, qui currebat tempore contractus, testibus Gail. 2, obs. 73, n. 6 and 7. Borcholt. de feud. ad cap. un. quæ sunt regal. num. 62. Illud enim maxime

If it is paid to the seller in gold, the seller may repay it in pieces of silver, or vice versa. In like manner, though, subsequent to the payment of the price, the pieces in which it is paid are increased or diminished in value, though they are discredited, and at the time of their redemption their place is supplied with new ones of better or worse alloy, the seller, who exercises the redemption, ought to repay, in money which is current at the time he redeems, the same sum or quantity which he received in payment, and nothing more nor less. The reason is that in money we do not regard the coins which constitute it, but only the value which the sovereign has been pleased that they shall signify: "Eaque materia forma publica percussa, usum dominiumque non tam ex substantia præbet, quam ex quantitate." D. 18, 1, 1. When the price is paid, the seller is not considered to receive the particular pieces, so much as the sum or value which they signify; and, consequently, he ought to repay, and it is sufficient for him to repay, the same sum or value in pieces which are current, and which have the signs authorized by the prince to signify that value. This principle being well established in our French practice, it is sufficient merely to state it. It cuts off all the questions made by the doctors concerning the changes of money.' [1]

314. *Bills of Exchange.* — Negotiable instruments often present questions of a like mixed nature.[2] Thus suppose a negotiable bill of exchange is drawn in Massachusetts on England, and is indorsed in New York, and again by the first indorsee in Pennsylvania, and by the second in Maryland, and the bill is

in hac disputatione considerandum est, quoniam hic finis nummi principalis est, ut serviat rebus necessariis comparandis, auctore Aristotele, 1 Polit. 6, quod mutata monetæ bonitate sive extrinseca, sive intrinseca, pretia rerum omnium mutentur, et pro modo auctæ aut imminutæ bonitatis nummorum crescant aut decrescant: quod ipsa docet experientia: eoque facit l. 2 C. de vet. num. pot. lib. 11. Crescunt rerum pretia, si deterior materia electa, aut manente eadem materia valor auctus sit: decrescunt electu materiæ melioris, aut si eadem bonitate materiæ manente valor imminutis fuerit. Fallitur enim imperitum vulgus, dum sibi persuadet, ex augmento valoris aurei aliquid sibi lucri accedere. Hoc autem fundamento posito, siquidem neutri contrahentium injuriam fieri volumus, ita definiendum videtur, ut si bonitas monetæ intrinseca mutata sit, tempus contractus si extrinseca, id est, valor imposititius tempus solutionis in solutione facienda spectari debeat. Atque ita sæpissime judicatum est.'

[1] Pothier, Traité du Contrat de Vente, n. 416. I quote from Mr. Cushing's excellent translation, n. 419, p. 264, 265. See Pardessus, tom. 5, art. 1495, p. 269–271.   [2] See post, s. 344, 353–361.

dishonored ; what damages will the holder be entitled to ? The law as to damages in these States is different. In Massachusetts it is ten per cent, in New York and Pennsylvania twenty per cent, and in Maryland fifteen per cent.[1] What rule then is to govern ? The answer is that, in each case, the lex loci contractus. The drawer is liable on the bill according to the law of the place where the bill was drawn ; and the successive indorsers are liable on the bill according to the law of the place of their indorsement, every indorsement being treated as a new and substantive contract.[2] The consequence is, that the indorser may render himself liable, upon a dishonor of the bill, for a much higher rate of damages than he can recover from the drawer. But this results from his own voluntary contract ; and not from any collision of rights arising from the nature of the original contract.[3] (a)

[1] 3 Kent Com. 116–120.

[2] Ante, s. 307; post, s. 316; Powers v. Lynch, 3 Mass. 77; Prentiss v. Savage, 13 Mass. 20, 23, 24; Slacum v. Pomery, 6 Cranch, 221; Depau v. Humphreys, 8 Mart. N.S. (La.) 1, 14, 15; Hicks v. Brown, 12 Johns. (N. Y.) 142; Bayley on Bills, c. A, p. 28; Phillips & Sewall's edition; Trimbey v. Vignier, 1 Bing. N. C. 151, 159, 160; ante, s. 267; post, s. 316 a, 353–361; 3 Burge, Col. & For. Law, pt. 2, c. 20, p. 771–774.

[3] Pardessus has discussed this matter at large. He adopts the general doctrine here stated, that the law of the place of each indorsement is to govern. as each indorsement constitutes a new contract between the immediate parties. And he applies the same rule to damages, and says that if the law of the place where a bill of exchange is drawn admits of the accumulation of costs and charges on account of re-exchanges, as is the law of some countries, in such a case each successive indorser may become liable to the payment of such successive accumulations, if allowed by the law of the place where they made their indorsement. He seems indeed to press his doctrine further, and to hold that if the law of the place of such indorsement does not allow such accumulation of re-exchanges, but the law of the place where the bill is drawn does, the indorsers will be liable to pay, as the drawer would. But his reasoning does not seem satisfactory; and it is certainly inconsistent with the acknowledged doctrines of the common law. Pardessus, Droit Com. art. 1500. See also Henry on Foreign Law, 53, Appx. 239-242; 3 Kent Com. 115. See Rothschild v. Currie, 1 Q. B. 43.

(a) *Bills and Notes.* — The question of the rights and the liabilities of parties to bills of exchange and promissory notes, growing out of the fact of execution or indorsement in a foreign country, as determined in England, may be thus stated : —

1. In regard to the liability of the maker of a note or the acceptor of a bill. If the paper is made or accepted abroad and also indorsed there, the question whether a title has been conveyed to the plaintiff indorsee will depend upon the law of the foreign country; the acceptor's engagement in that case being to pay to any indorsee

315. *Contract of Drawer and Indorser.* — It has sometimes been suggested that this doctrine is a departure from the rule that the

who acquires a title by the law of the acceptor's domicil. If by that law the plaintiff has not acquired a title, he cannot recover in England though his title would have been good had the indorsement been made in England. Trimbey *v.* Vignier, 1 Bing. N. C. 151. (Long after the decision in this case, in which it was held that no title had passed by the foreign and governing law to the plaintiff, it was discovered that the court had mistaken the law of the foreign country; but the principle of law declared was not affected. Bradlaugh, *v.* De Rin, L. R. 5 C. P. 473.)

But if the paper — e. g. a note — was *made* in England and payable there, and indorsed abroad, so as to pass a title by the English law, though not by the foreign law, then the indorsee may sue in England. Lebel *v.* Tucker, L. R. 3 Q. B. 77. For as Lush, J., says in the case just cited, it would be anomalous that a contract made in England could be affected by the negotiation and circulation in another country of the instrument by which it was constituted. "The original contract cannot be varied by the law of any foreign country through which the instrument passes." See also Woodruff *v.* Hill, 116 Mass. 310.

Shortly after the decision of this case it was however held by the Common Pleas, with Lebel *v.* Tucker before the court, that in the case of a bill *drawn* in France and accepted in England, and then indorsed in France, effectively according to English law but not so according to French law, the indorsee could not sue the acceptor in England. Bradlaugh *v.* De Rin, L. R. 3 C. P. 538, Montague Smith, J., dissenting. The case was reversed by the Exchequer Chamber, but simply on the ground that the lower court

had mistaken the law of France. 5 C. P. 473. See supra. Whether this case is consistent with the clearly correct decision in Lebel *v.* Tucker may deserve consideration; for though the bill was drawn in France, it was accepted and payable in England. Could the acceptor's contract be "varied by the law of any foreign country"?

2. In regard to the liability of an indorser or the drawer of a bill. When presentment and demand should be made to charge such party is to be determined by the law of the country in which the paper is payable. Rouquette *v.* Overmann, L. R. 10 Q. B. 525. See Rothschild *v.* Currie, 1 Q. B. 43; Hirschfield *v.* Smith, L. R. 1 C. P. 340. In Rouquette *v.* Overmann, Cockburn, C.J., lays down the proposition that the drawer or indorser "engages as surety for the due performance by the acceptor of the obligations which the latter takes upon himself by the acceptance. His liability therefore is to be measured by that of the acceptor, whose surety he is; and as the obligations of the acceptor are to be determined by the lex loci of performance, so also must those of the surety," that is, with regard to presentment and demand. In a word, the indorser cannot on the one hand become liable before the maturity of the contract of the acceptor or the maker; and on the other, when the liability of the acceptor or the maker does accrue by force of law, then the liability of the indorser may be fixed.

The question when notice of dishonor (on a demand good by the law of the place of payment) should be given is governed by the law of the country where the indorsement is made. Horne *v.* Rouquette, 3 Q. B. D. 514 (Court of App.), doubting Rothschild *v.* Currie, 1 Q. B. 43, 49.

law of the place of payment is to govern.[1] But, correctly considered, it is entirely in conformity to the rule. The drawer and

[1] 2 Kent Com. 459, 460; Chitty on Bills, p. 191–194, 8th ed.; ante, s. 313 a, et seq.

In Hirschfield v. Smith, L. R. 1 C. P. 340, the place of payment was thought, on authority of Rothschild v. Currie, to give the law of the time of notice; but it was laid down that if this view was doubtful, and the law of the place of indorsement was to govern, then the "reasonable notice" of the law (which is in reality the rule, though what constitutes such notice in common cases is strictly defined) would ordinarily permit notice by the law of the place where the demand of payment was to be made. In this view only, it may be remarked, is Rothschild v. Currie deemed good law; that case appears to be overruled so far as it declares against the law of the place of indorsement in the particular of time of notice. The importance of the rule (notwithstanding the fact that notice by the law of the country of payment is ordinarily to be regarded as reasonable notice) may be seen by supposing that by the law of the domicil of the drawee of a bill no notice of non-acceptance is required, as is the case in Spain and in Pennsylvania. Horne v. Rouquette, supra; Read v. Adams, 6 Serg. & R. 356. Now if an indorsement of the bill had been made in England, or in any of our States where notice of non-acceptance is required, failure to give notice would discharge the indorser; some reasonable notice, according to the situation, would be necessary, notwithstanding the state of the foreign law. Horne v. Rouquette, supra.

On the other hand, speaking in the language substantially of judicial authority, the indorser's contract with reference to notice is that if his own or a later indorsee is compelled by law to pay, he, the indorser, will indemnify him on receiving due notice of dishonor. Hence where there is a foreign indorsee who has been compelled to pay by the law of his country in regard to notice, though he would not have been bound by the law of the country of the indemnifying indorser, the latter will be bound to reimburse him if notified according to the law of his own country. Horne v. Rouquette, Brett, J.

Turning to the American cases, it has sometimes been broadly said that the drawer's and indorser's contract is governed by the law of the state where it was made. Aymar v. Sheldon, 12 Wend. (N. Y.) 439, 443; Holbrook v. Vibbard, 2 Scam. (Ill.) 465; and other cases. But none of the actual decisions go to this extent; indeed there is little divergence from the doctrines above laid down as the rule of the English courts. All that was held in Aymar v. Sheldon was that an indorsee of a bill indorsed in New York could sue the drawer in that state upon notice of non-acceptance, though he could not have done so had the indorsement been made where the bill was drawn. And all that the court decided in Holbrook v. Vibbard was that a New York indorser was discharged by failure of the holder in Illinois to make demand at the place of payment (in Illinois). Again, in Hibernia Bank v. Lacombe, 84 N. Y. 367, 378, it was said in general terms that the contracts of parties to bills and notes were to be construed according to the laws of each place at which the doing of anything is contemplated by any of the parties. But this was said of a bill drawn in Louisiana upon a party in New York, by whom it was dishonored, the court well deciding that

indorsers do not contract to pay the money in the foreign place
on which the bill is drawn ; but only to guarantee its acceptance

the holder might give notice of the
dishonor at the place thereof.

Few of the peculiar questions of
title against a maker or an acceptor
upon an indorsement under a law different from that of the forum, such
as the English courts have had to consider, appear to have arisen in this
country. A question somewhat similar in principle to that in Lebel v.
Tucker, supra, arose in Woodruff v.
Hill, 116 Mass. 310, and a similar
conclusion was reached; the title of
indorsees suing in Massachusetts on a
note payable in that State, but indorsed to them in New York, being
held to depend on Massachusetts law.
Still more like Lebel v. Tucker was
Everett v. Vendryes, 19 N. Y. 436,
with the same result. The liability
of the maker or acceptor has more
often been considered with reference
to questions of interest, usury, and
damages; and it has been generally
held that the law of the place of payment must govern. Railroad Co. v.
Ashland,12 Wall. 226; Lee v. Selleck,
33 N. Y. 615; Dickinson v. Edwards,
77 N. Y. 573; Hibernia Bank v. Lacombe, 84 N. Y. 367, 377; Roberts v.
McNeely, 7 Jones (N. C.) 506; Hunt
v. Hall, 37 Ala. 702; Howard v. Bran-
ner, 23 La. An. 369; White v. Friedlander, 35 Ark. 52; Short v. Trabue,
4 Met. (Ky.) 299; Trabue v. Short,
18 La. An. 257; Trabue v. Short, 5
Coldw. (Tenn.) 293; Ex parte Heidelback, 2 Lowell, 526; ante, s. 296. See
also Suse v. Pompe, 8 C. B. N.S. 538;
In re State Ins. Co., 9 Jur. N.S. 298.
As to the rule in Massachusetts concerning interest, see note (a) to s. 291,
ante; Ex parte Heidelback, supra.

If however all contracts affected
with usury are declared absolutely
void, then it seems they will be held
void everywhere, regardless of the
place of performance. Akers v. De-

mond, 103 Mass. 318; Hyde v. Goodnow, 3 Comst. (N. Y.) 266; Andrews v.
Pond, 13 Peters, 65; McDaniel v. Chicago Ry. Co., 24 Iowa, 412. See ante,
s. 243, 280, note. So if the place of
performance be inserted for the mere
purpose of evading the local law, that
law, it is said, will still be applied.
Railroad Co. v. Ashland, 12 Wall. 226;
Miller v. Tiffany, 1 Wall. 298. On
the other hand it is held that a note
made in good faith at a rate of interest allowable in the state in which it
was executed, but payable in a state
in which such rate would be usurious,
will be governed by the law of the state
of the making. Miller v. Tiffany, supra; Arnold v. Potter, 22 Iowa, 194,
198; Butters v. Olds, 11 Iowa, 1. See
Chapman v. Robertson, 6 Paige (N. Y.)
627.

There is want of harmony among
the American cases upon the question
of the right of an indorser or the
drawer of a bill to raise the defence
of usury in the contract of the maker
or acceptor, where that contract was
made in another state by the laws of
which usury is a defence. In some of
the cases it is laid down on the authority of English decisions that the law
of the place of indorsement or drawing
must govern concerning the question
of interest and of usury. The English
cases referred to are Gibbs v. Fremont,
9 Ex. 25, Allen v. Kemble, 6 Moore,
P. C. 314, 321, and Cooper v. Waldegrave, 2 Beav. 282, 285 (concerning
which see the observations of Cockburn, C.J., in Rouquette v. Overmann,
L. R. 10 Q. B. 525). The cases in apparent accord with these are the following : Bank of Georgia v. Lewin, 45 Barb.
(N. Y.) 340; Balme v. Wombough, 38
Barb. 352; Bowen v. Bradley, 9 Abb.
Pr. N.S. (N. Y.) 395; Wayne Bank v.
Low, 6 Abb. N. C. (N. Y.) 76; Opdyke
v. Merwin, 13 Hun (N. Y.) 401; Aymar

and payment in that place by the drawee; and in default of such payment they agree upon due notice to reimburse the holder in

v. Sheldon, 12 Wend. (N. Y.) 439; Short *v.* Trabue, 4 Met. (Ky.) 299, 304; Dundas *v.* Bowler, 3 McLean, 397, 400. None of these cases however were decided by courts of final resort except Short *v.* Trabue, and that contains only a dictum on the subject.

The law of the place of payment was on the other hand held to be the governing law in Jewell *v.* Wright, 30 N. Y. 259, and in Dickinson *v.* Edwards, 77 N. Y. 573; unless an intention were shown that it was contemplated that the paper, before the liability of the drawer or indorser attached, should be negotiated in some state other than the one whose law was set up in defence. Upon this ground the court in Dickinson *v.* Edwards distinguished Tilden *v.* Blair, 21 Wall. 241, where a bill, though payable in New York, was returned by the New York acceptors to the drawer in Illinois, that it might be there negotiated by him. 'The ruling consideration in that case,' said Folger, J. in Dickinson *v.* Edwards, 'was the intention of the acceptors that the draft should be used in Illinois as a contract of that state, in accordance with its laws.' See Wayne Bank *v.* Low, 81 N. Y. 566, 570. On the same ground the court in Dickinson *v.* Edwards distinguished Bank of Georgia *v.* Lewin, 45 Barb. (N. Y.) 340, and National Bank *r.* Morris, 1 Hun (N. Y.) 680, and considered that Kentucky *v.* Bassford, 6 Hill (N. Y.) 526, Hyde *v.* Goodnow, 3 Comst. (N. Y.) 266, and Merchants' Bank *v.* Spalding, 9 N. Y. 53, were not inconsistent with the decision laid down in Jewell *v.* Wright, supra, and now reaffirmed. The following cases were overruled: Bowen *r.* Bradley, 9 Abb. N.S. (N. Y.) 395; Wayne Bank *v.* Low, 6 Abb. N. C. (N. Y.) 76. But see Wayne Bank *v.* Low, 81 N. Y. 566. See

also, as declaring Jewell *v.* Wright to be the law, Hildreth *v.* Shepard, 65 Barb. (N. Y.) 269. Other cases were also reviewed in Dickinson *v.* Edwards; and that case may be considered as having settled the law of New York. See Hibernia Bank *v.* Lacombe, 84 N. Y. 367, 377.

In the absence of evidence to indicate some other intention by the parties, the rule in Dickinson *v.* Edwards, and Jewell *v.* Wright, must be correct if it is true (and there can be no doubt on that point) that the drawer or indorser, for the purpose in question, stands as surety to the acceptor. The liability of the principal and surety, in the absence of fraud upon the latter, must be commensurate. If the principal debtor must pay a certain sum, how can the surety escape liability to the creditor for any part of that sum when nothing has been done by the creditor to affect his liability? And on the other hand if by the law of the place of payment the principal debtor has a defence in whole or in part, or if the rate of interest there is lower than where the indorsement or the drawing was effected, how can the indorser or drawer be compelled to pay the whole, or to pay at the rate fixed by the lex loci contractus?

The question of the time for presentment and demand in relation to the liability of drawers and indorsers, as well as of acceptors and makers, must, according to the same principles, be governed by the law of the place of payment; and so our courts hold, with the English. Aymar *v.* Sheldon, 12 Wend. 439; Chatham Bank *v.* Allison, 15 Iowa, 357; Thorp *v.* Craig, 10 Iowa, 461. But see Hatcher *v.* McMorine, 4 Dev. 122, 124.

Whether notice of dishonor should be given, and whether, on demand good at the place of payment, such

principal and damages at the place where they respectively entered into the contract.[1]

316. *Time of Payment.* — Nor is it any departure from the rule to hold that the time when the payment of such a bill is to accrue is to be according to the law of the place where the bill is payable; so that the days of grace (if any) are to be allowed according to the law or custom where the bill is to be accepted and paid; [2] for such is the appropriate construction of the con-

---

[1] Potter v. Brown, 5 East, 124, 130; Hicks v. Brown, 12 Johns. (N. Y.) 142; Powers v. Lynch, 3 Mass. 77; Prentiss v. Savage, 13 Mass. 20, 24; Pardessus, Droit Com. art. 1497.

[2] See 2 Kent Com. 459, 460; Chitty on Bills, p. 191, 8th ed ; Pothier, Contrat de Change, n. 15, 155; 5 Pardessus, s. 1495; post, s. 347, 361.

---

notice will be effective, are to be determined by the law of the place of indorsement. The matter of notice (unlike presentment and demand) has nothing to do with the liability of the maker or acceptor; it concerns the party notified alone. Aymar v. Sheldon, 12 Wend. (N. Y.) 439; Thorp v. Craig, 10 Iowa, 461; Allen v. Merchants' Bank, 22 Wend. (N. Y.) 215; Short v. Trabue, 4 Met. (Ky.) 299; Holbrook v. Vibbard, 2 Scam. (Ill.) 465; Hatcher v. McMorine, 4 Dev. (N. C.) 122; Lowry v. Western Bank, 7 Ala. 120; Hunt v. Standart, 15 Ind. 33 (overruling Shanklin v. Cooper, 8 Blackf. (Ind.) 41); Huse v. Hamblin, 29 Iowa, 501. Whether protest is necessary is said to depend on the law of the place of payment. Dunn v. Adams, 1 Ala. 527. Sed quære, because protest (like notice) has nothing to do with the liability of the payor. But.if protest is required by the law of the indorser's contract, it may be made according to the practice in the country of the demand; any other requirement would be unreasonable. Aymar v. Sheldon, 12 Wend. (N. Y.) 439; Bank of Rochester v. Gray, 2 Hill (N. Y.) 227; Tickner v. Roberts, 11 La. 14. The law of the place of indorsement, limiting the liability of an indorser in a way unknown to the law merchant, will also

govern in an action against the indorser. Williams v. Wade, 1 Met. (Mass.) 82; Short v. Trabue, 4 Met. (Ky.) 299; Trabue v. Short, 18 La. An. 257; Trabue v. Short, 5 Coldw. (Tenn.) 293; Carlisle v. Chambers, 4 Bush (Ky.) 268; Hyatt v. Bank of Kentucky, 8 Bush (Ky.) 193; Mix v. State Bank, 13 Ind. 521; Nichols v. Porter, 2 W. Va. 13; Dunn v. Adams, 1 Ala. 527; Cox v. Adams, 2 Kelly (Ga.) 158; Dundas v. Bowler, 3 McLean, 397, 400. But see Coffman v. Bank of Kentucky, 41 Miss. 212, which appears to have been wrongly decided. (Whether, in an action against the maker of a note, the paper is negotiable, will depend upon the law of the place where it is made, unless payable elsewhere. Dow v. Rowell, 12 N. H. 49).

Indorsement however is not necessarily effected in contemplation of law in the place where the signature is written. Where an indorsement is written in one state, but is not to become effective until negotiation and delivery of the paper in another, the indorsement is deemed to be made in the state of delivery. Lee v. Selleck, 33 N. Y. 615; Cook v. Litchfield, 9 N. Y. 279; Hyde v. Goodnow, 3 Comst. (N. Y.) 270; Gay v. Rainey, 89 Ill. 221; Chatham Bank v. Allison, 15 Iowa, 357; Freese v. Brownell, 35 N. J. 285.

tract according to the rules of law and the presumed intention of the parties.[1]

316 *a. Indorsement.*—Another illustration of the general doctrine may be derived from the case of negotiable paper, as to the binding obligation and effect of a blank indorsement. It seems that by the law of France an indorsement in blank of a promissory note does not transfer the property to the holder unless certain prescribed formalities are observed in the indorsement, such as the date, the consideration, and the name of the party to whose order it is passed; otherwise it is treated as a mere procuration.[2] Now let us suppose a note made at Paris, payable to the order of the payee, and he should there indorse the same in blank without the prescribed formalities, and afterwards the holder should sue the maker of the note in another country, as, for example, in England, where no such formalities are prescribed; the question would arise, whether the holder could recover in such a suit in an English court upon such an indorsement. It has been held that he cannot; and this decision seems to be founded in the true principles of international jurisprudence; for it relates not to the form of the remedy, but to the interpretation and obligation of the contract created by the indorsement, which ought to be governed by the law of the place of indorsement.[3]

316 *b. Contract of Indorser.* — Another illustration may be derived from the different obligations which an indorsement creates in different States. By the general commercial law, in order to entitle the indorsee to recover against any antecedent indorser upon a negotiable note, it is only necessary that due demand should be made upon the maker of the note at its maturity, and due notice of the dishonor to the indorser. But by the laws of some of the American States it is required, in order to charge an antecedent indorser, that not only due demand should be made and due notice given, but that a suit shall be previously commenced against the maker, and prosecuted with effect in the country where he resides; and then, if payment cannot be obtained from him under the judgment, the indorsee may have recourse to the indorser. In such a case it is clear, upon prin-

---

[1] Mr. Justice Martin, in Vidal *v.* Thompson, 11 Mart. (La.) 23, 24.

[2] Code de Commerce, art. 137, 138; Trimbey *v.* Vignier, 1 Bing. N. C. 151, 158–160.

[3] Trimbey *v.* Vignier, 1 Bing. N. C. 151, 158–160; ante, s. 272.

ciple, that the indorsement, as to its legal effect and obligation and the duties of the holder, must be governed by the law of the place where the indorsement is made. This very point has been recently decided in a case where a note was made and indorsed in the state of Illinois. On that occasion Mr. Chief Justice Shaw, in delivering the opinion of the court, said : ' The note declared on, being made in Illinois, both parties residing there at the time, and it also being indorsed in Illinois, we think that the contract created by that indorsement must be governed by the law of that state. The law in question does not affect the remedy, but goes to create, limit, and modify the contract effected by the fact of indorsement. In that which gives force and effect to the contract, and imposes restrictions and modifications upon it, the law of the place of contract must prevail when another is not looked to as a place of performance. Suppose it were shown that, by the law of Illinois, the indorsement of a note by the payee merely transferred the legal interest in the note to the indorsee so as to enable him to sue in his own name, but imposed no conditional obligation on the indorser to pay ; it would hardly be contended that an action could be brought here upon such an indorsement if the indorser should happen to be found here, because by our law such an indorsement, if made here, would render the indorser conditionally liable to pay the note. By the law of Illinois the indorser is liable only after a judgment obtained against the maker ; and as no such judgment appears to have been obtained on this note, the condition upon which alone the plaintiff may sue is not complied with, and therefore the action cannot be maintained.' [1]

317. *Defences to Negotiable Securities.* — But suppose a negotiable note is made in one country and is payable there, and it is afterwards indorsed in another country, and by the law of the former country equitable defences are let in in favor of the maker, and by the latter such defences excluded ; what rule is to govern, in regard to the holder, in a suit against the maker to recover the amount upon the indorsement to him ? The answer is, the law of the place where the note was made ; for there the maker undertook to pay ; and the subsequent negotiation of the note did not change his original obligation, duty, or rights.[2]

[1] Williams *v.* Wade, 1 Met. (Mass.) 82, 83.
[2] Ory *v.* Winter, 4 Mart. N.S. (La.) 277; post, s. 332, 343, 344.

Acceptances of bills are governed by the same principles. They are deemed contracts of acceptance in the place where they are made and where they are to be performed.[1] So Paul Voet lays down the doctrine.[2] ' Quid si de literis cambii incidat quæstio; quis locus erit spectandus? Is spectandus est locus, ad quem sunt destinatæ, et ibidem acceptatæ.' But suppose a negotiable acceptance, or a negotiable note, made payable generally without any specification of place ; what law is to govern in case of a negotiation of it by one holder to another in a foreign country in regard to the acceptor or to the maker? Is it a contract by them to pay in any place where it is negotiated, so as to be deemed a contract of that particular place and governed by its laws ? The Supreme Court of Massachusetts have held that it creates a debt payable anywhere, by the very nature of the contract ; and it is a promise to whosoever shall be the holder of the bill or note.[3] Assuming this to be true, still it does not follow that the law of the place of the negotiation is to govern ; for the transfer is not, as to the acceptor or the maker, a new contract ; but it is under and a part of the original contract, and springs up from the law of the place where that contract was made. A contract to pay generally is governed by the law of the place where it is made ; for the debt is payable there as well as in every other place.[4] (a)   To bring a contract within the general

---

[1] Lewis v. Owen, 4 B. & A. 654; ante, s. 307; post, s. 333–345. If made in one place and accepted there, payable in another place, the law of the place where the bill is payable governs. Cooper v. Earl of Waldegrave, 2 Beav. 282. What bills are deemed foreign? Bills drawn in one state, payable in another state, are deemed foreign. Buckner v. Finley, 2 Pet. 586; Halliday v. McDougal, 22 Wend. (N. Y.) 264, 272; Wells v. Whitehead, 15 Wend. (N. Y.) 527; Rothschild v. Currie, 1 Q. B. 43.

[2] P. Voet, de Statut. s. 9, c. 2, n. 14, p. 270, ed. 1713; Id. p. 327, ed. 1661; post, s. 346, note.

[3] Braynard v. Marshall, 8 Pick. (Mass.) 194. And see Savoye v. Marsh, 10 Met. (Mass.) 594; post, s. 341, 343–346.

[4] See Kearney v. King, 2 B. & A. 301; Sprowle v. Legge, 1 B. & C. 16; ante, s. 272 a ; post, s. 329; Don v. Lippmann, 5 Cl. & F. 1, 12, 13. In this last case a bill of exchange was drawn and accepted in Paris by a Scotchman domiciled in Scotland, and it was payable generally. It seems that, by the law of Scotland, an acceptance is deemed payable at the place of the domicil of the acceptor at the time when it becomes due. Lord Brougham on this occasion said: ' It appears that in Scotland, — and it is rather singular that it should be so, — where a bill is accepted generally, without any particular place being named, it shall be deemed payable at the place at which the ac-

(a) See Peck v. Hibbard, 26 Vt. 702.

rule of the lex loci, it is not necessary that it should be payable exclusively in the place of its origin. If payable everywhere, then it is governed by the law of the place where it is made; for the plain reason that it cannot be said to have the law of any other place in contemplation to govern its validity, its obligation, or its interpretation. All debts between the original parties are payable everywhere unless some special provision to the contrary is made; and therefore the rule is that debts have no situs, but accompany the creditor everywhere.[1] The holder then takes the contract of the acceptor or maker, as it was originally made, and as it was in the place where it was made. It is there that the promise is made to him to pay everywhere.[2]

318. *Formalities required by the Lex Solutionis.* — A case a little more difficult in its texture is when a contract is made in one country for payment of money in another country, and, by the laws of the latter, a stamp is required to make the contract valid, and it is not by those of the former; whether it is governed by the lex solutionis, or by the lex loci contractus, as to the stamp. It has been held that a stamp is not required in such a case to give validity to the contract, upon the ground that an instrument, as to its form and solemnities, is to be governed by the lex loci contractus, and not by the law of the place of payment; and that therefore a stamp is not required by the principal.[3] On that occasion the court said: 'An instrument, as to its form and the formalities attending its execution, must be tested

ceptor is domiciled when it becomes due. It becomes of some importance to know where the bills were payable, because this principle, which has been adopted of late years in many of the Scotch decisions, and towards which I admit the great leaning of the Scotch profession is, renders it material to consider whether this is a Scotch or a foreign debt. Yet sometimes this expression is used in the cases without affording any accuracy of description; for sometimes the debt is called English, or French, in respect of the place where the contract was made; sometimes it is the place of the origin, sometimes of the payment of the contract, and sometimes of the domicil of one of the parties. But at all events it becomes important to consider whether this was a foreign or a Scotch debt. In the present case it was held most properly to be a foreign debt. That is a fact admitted; it is out of all controversy. This therefore must now be taken to be a French debt; and then the general law is that where the acceptance is general, naming no place of payment, the place of payment shall be taken to be the place of the contracting of the debt. I shall therefore deal with this bill as if it was accepted payable in Paris.'

[1] Blanchard v. Russell, 13 Mass. 1, 6; Slacum v. Pomery, 6 Cranch, 221; post, s. 329, 362, 399, 400.   [2] Post, s. 343, 344.

[3] Mr. Justice Martin, in Vidal v. Thompson, 11 Mart. (La.) 23-25. But

by the laws of the place where it is made; but the laws and usages of the place where the obligation of which it is evidence is to be fulfilled must regulate the performance. A bill drawn out of London must be paid at the expiration of the days of grace which the laws and usages of that place recognize, but need not have those stamps which are by law required on a bill drawn there.' [1]

319. *Case as to Place of Contract.* — But a case more difficult to reconcile with established principles in its actual adjudication has occurred in Massachusetts. A bill of exchange was drawn in Manchester, in England, upon a firm established at Boston, in Massachusetts, payable in London, and was accepted at Manchester by one of the firm then there. The bill was therefore drawn in England, accepted in England, and payable in England. But upon its dishonor it was held that it was to be deemed a bill accepted in Boston, because the domicil of the firm was there, and that damages were recoverable of ten per cent, as they would be upon a like bill accepted in Boston.[2] There was nothing upon the face of the bill that alluded to an acceptance in Boston, and nothing in the circumstances that pointed in that direction. It was certainly competent for the firm to contract in England, and to accept in England; and, beyond all question, if the bill had been drawn solely on the person who accepted it, the acceptance must have been deemed to be made in England, notwithstanding his domicil was in Boston. Is there any difference between an acceptance by a firm and an acceptance by a single person? Is not the general principle of law that which is affirmed by Casaregis, that a contract or acceptance is to be deemed made where the contract or acceptance is perfected; ' eo loci, quo ultimus in contrahendo assentitur?' [3] It has certainly been put

---

see ante, s. 260 and note, 262, 262 *a*; Wynne *v.* Jackson, 2 Russ. 351; Clegg *v.* Levy, 3 Camp. 166; James *v.* Catherwood, 3 Dowl. & Ry. 190.

[1] Ibid.

[2] Grimshaw *v.* Bender, 6 Mass. 157. The case of Acebal *v.* Levy, 10 Bing. 376, 379, seems to have involved a question very nearly the same, arising under the statute of frauds of England, the contract having been made in Gijon, in Spain, for the delivery of the goods purchased in England. The court and bar seem to have thought that the contract was to be governed by the English statute of frauds, although made in Spain. See ante, s. 262 *a*, and note. See also Cooper *v.* Earl Waldegrave, 2 Beav. 282. (*a*)

[3] Casaregis, Disc. 179, n. 1; ante, s. 285.

(*a*) Leroux *v.* Brown, 12 C. B. 801, is an express decision to that effect.

upon that ground in many modern authorities.[1]   And therefore, if the acceptor be an accommodation acceptor in one country, payments made by him of the bills drawn by the drawer in a foreign country will be deemed payments under a contract made with the drawer in the place of acceptance and payment.[2]

320. *Case in New York.* — The doctrine maintained in Massachusetts in this last case is directly in conflict with that maintained under similar circumstances by the Supreme Court of New York.   The latter court has held that the bill, having been drawn in England, and made payable there, and accepted there, it was to be treated as an English contract; and that the English interest of five per cent only was to be allowed for the delay of payment.[3]   This decision, being in entire harmony with the general principles on this subject, will probably obtain general credit in the commercial world.[4]

320 a. *Limited Partnerships.* — Many other cases might easily be put to illustrate the law in relation to the conflict of the laws of different countries in cases of contract.   In some countries there are limited or special partnerships, called in France partnerships en commandité.   In these partnerships the contract is between one or more partners who are jointly and severally responsible for the whole contracts and orders of the partnership, and one or more partners who merely furnish a particular amount of funds, and are responsible only to the amount of such funds, and who are called commandataires, or partners en commandité.[5]   Similar limited partnerships are also authorized in some of the American states.   Now let us suppose an order given by the general partner in such a firm in one of such states, upon a house in England, for the purchase of goods there; and they were accordingly purchased in England on the credit of the firm. If the partnership became insolvent, the question might then arise, whether the partner en commandité was liable to pay for the goods beyond the amount of the funds which he had contributed or was bound to contribute for the partnership. That question might essentially depend upon another, whether the contract

---

[1] Boyce v. Edwards, 4 Pet. 111; P. Voet, de Statut. s. 9, c. 2, s. 14. See also M'Candlish v. Cruger, 2 Bay (S. C.) 377; Bain v. Ackworth, 1 Mill (S. C.) 107; Lewis v. Owen, 4 B. & A. 654.

[2] Lewis v. Owen, 4 B. & A. 654.   [3] Foden v. Sharp, 4 Johns. (N. Y.) 183.

[4] See Bayley on Bills (5th ed.), c. A, p. 72–86, Phillips & Sewall's ed.

[5] Code of Commerce of France, art. 23–37.

is to be treated as made in the American states, where the partnership was established, or in England, where the contract was consummated. And it might also be important in the case, whether the seller knew that the partnership was so limited or not. No point of this sort has as yet arisen for decision; and therefore it is left for the more full consideration of those who may be called upon to examine it in the case of a judicial controversy.[1] (a)

321. *Effects of Contracts.* — In stating the foregoing rules we have been necessarily led to the consideration of many of what are properly deemed the effects of contracts, which, like the validity of contracts, are dependent upon, and are to be governed by, the lex loci contractus. These effects are: the right conferred on the party for whose benefit the contract is made; the correspondent duty of the other party to fulfil it; the right of action which arises from the non-fulfilment of it; and the consequential right to interest or damages, for the injury done by such non-fulfilment, belonging to the injured party.[2] The manner in which remedies are to be administered will fall under another and distinct head.[3]

322. *Other Incidents of Contracts.* — But there are some other effects which may be deemed accompaniments, effects, or incidents of contracts which may here deserve a passing notice. They are properly collateral to them, and arise by operation of law or by the act of the parties. Among these may be placed the liability of partners and part owners for partnership debts. If, by the law of the place where the contract is made, they would be liable in solido, although, by the law of the domicil of the partnership, they might be liable only for a proportionate share, the law of the former will follow the debt everywhere; or, in other words, the effect of the lex loci of the contract upon the liability of the partners and part owners will be of universal obligation.[4] By the law of some countries the acceptor of a bill of ex-

[1] Ante, s. 285–287.

[2] See Pothier, Oblig. n. 141–172; P. Voet, de Statut. s. 9, c. 2, s. 12; Boullenois, Quest. de la Contr. des Lois, p. 830–338.

[3] Post, s. 556–575.

[4] Ferguson r. Flower, 4 Mart. N.S. (La.) 312. See also Carroll v. Waters, 9 Mart. (La.) 500; Pardessus, Droit Com. art. 1495.

(a) See Lawrence v. Batcheller, 131 Mass. 504, 509; King v. Sarria, 69 N. Y. 24; Barrows v. Downs, 9 R. I. 446, showing that the local law will be recognized in other jurisdictions.

change is discharged from his acceptance, if, when he accepted, the drawer was bankrupt; and this effect of the acceptance regularly accompanies it everywhere as an incident.[1]

322 a. *Illustration.* — Another illustration may be found in the law of some countries, as in Alost in Flanders, which allows to a debtor, who has assigned or transferred a debt, the right of redemption of it upon payment back of the price. In such a case, according to Burgundus, the right of redemption will exist, notwithstanding the debt has been contracted in another country ; for, in such a case, the right is for the benefit of the debtor, and the debts and the rights of action are judged of by the law of his domicil, without any consideration of the place where the debts were contracted. 'Unde recte dici potest, consuetudinem Alostensem, quæ indulget debitori redemptionis cessi nominis, eo pretio, quod actionis auctori solutum est, etiam locum habere in ære alieno extra territorium Alostense contracto. Cum enim ejusmodi redemptio in favorem debitoris introducta, situm nominum, et actionum ex domicilio ejus metitur, sine consideratione qua regione contracta fuerint.'[2] A more unexceptionable illustration is the incidental right of warranty, conferred by the civil law in cases of sales of merchandise, not merely as to title, but as to quality.[3]

322 b. *Other Cases.* — Of the like nature is the benefit of the right of discussion as it is called. By the Roman law sureties were not primarily liable to pay the debt for which they became bound as sureties, but were liable only after the creditor had sought payment from the principal debtor, and he was unable to pay. This was called the benefit or right of discussion.[4] Under those systems of jurisprudence which adopt the Roman law, and under the present law of France, the rule is similar ; and the obligation contracted by the surety with the creditor is, that the latter shall not proceed against him until he has first discussed the principal debtor, if he is solvent. This right the surety enjoys, as the beneficium ordinis vel excussionis.[5] And again: if other persons are joined with him in the obligation as sureties, he

---

[1] Pardessus, Droit Com. art. 1495.   [2] Burgundus, tract. 2, n. 24, 25.
[3] Ante, s. 264; Henry on Foreign Law, 51, 52; 2 Boullenois, obs. 46, p. 475, 476; P. Voet, de Statut. s. 9, c. 2, s. 10.
[4] 1 Domat, b. 3. tit. 4, s. 2, art. 1; Dig. 46, 1, 68; Novell. tit. 4, cap. 1.
[5] Pothier on Oblig. n. 407–414; Code Civil of France, art. 2021–2026.

is not in the first instance to be proceeded against for the whole
debt, but only for his share of it, if his co-sureties and co-obligees
are solvent.[1] This is commonly known as the benefit of division,
or beneficium divisionis. If the suit should be brought in a
different country from that where the contract or obligation is
made, the right of discussion or division would still belong to the
surety as an incident to his contract, although it did not exist by
the law of the place where the suit was brought (lex fori).[2] The
converse proposition would be equally true.[3] Such, also, is the lien
of a vendor upon a real estate sold for the payment of the purchase-money, according to the law of England ; the lien given for
the purchase-money, upon goods or merchandise sold, by the civil
law and by the law of some modern countries ;[4] the right of stop-
page in transitu of the vendor of goods in case of the insolvency
of the purchaser in the course of the transit ;[5] the lien of a bottomry bond on the thing pledged ; the lien of mariners on the ship
for their wages ; the priority of payment in rem, which the law
sometimes attaches to peculiar debts, or to particular persons. In
these, and like cases, where the lien or privilege is created by
the lex loci contractus, it will generally, although not universally, be respected and enforced in all places where the property
is found, or where the right can be beneficially enforced by the
lex fori.[6] And on the other hand, where the lien or privilege

[1] Pothier on Oblig. n. 415–427; Code Civil of France, art. 2026.
[2] 3 Burge, Col. & For. Law, pt. 2, c. 20, p. 765, 766; Carroll v. Waters,
9 Mart. (La.) 500.
[3] Ibid; ante, 316 b.
[4] 1 Domat, Civil Law, b. 4, s. 2, n. 3; 3 Burge, Col. & For. Law, pt. 2,
c. 20, p. 770, 771. See, as to lien of vendor on real estate, Gilman v. Brown,
1 Mason, 219–221; Warrender v. Warrender, 9 Bligh, 127. It seems that a
lien created by the lex loci contractus may be dissolved and extinguished not
only according to the law of that place, but also by any act done in a foreign
country which, according to the law of that country, would work such dissolution or extinguishment. See post, s. 351 a–351 d.
[5] Post, s. 401.
[6] See 3 Burge, Col. & For. Law, pt. 2, c. 20, p. 770, 771, 779; post, s. 401;
Foelix, Confl. des Lois, Revue Étrang. et Franç. 1840, tom. 7, s. 33, p. 227,
228. The latter says: ' Nous avons vu que la règle suivant laquelle les
meubles sont régis par la loi du domicile de celui à qui ils appartiennent,
repose sur le rapport intime entre les meubles et la personne du propriétaire,
sur une fiction légale qui les répute exister au lieu du domicile de ce dernier.
De là il suit que cette règle ne peut s'appliquer qu'aux circonstances ou actes
dans lesquels les meubles n'apparaissent que comme un accessoire de la personne; par exemple: en cas de succession ab intestato, de dispositions de der-

does not exist in the place of the contract, it will not be allowed in another country, although the local law where the suit is brought would otherwise sustain it.[1] Thus, if goods are purchased in England by a citizen of Louisiana, no lien or privilege will exist for the unpaid price, in case of his insolvency, although the law of Louisiana allows it in common cases ; because it is not given by the law of the place of the contract (England).[2] (*a*) Nor would there seem to be any just ground of doubt that a bottomry bond would generally be held valid in rem in all commercial countries, if the lien is good by the law of the place of the contract.[3]

322 *c. Liens* — We have said that such liens will be generally, although not universally, respected ; for, although the foreign jurists generally assert the doctrine, they do not universally agree in it as to all kinds of property, or under all circumstances. Some of them take a distinction between personal or movable property and real or immovable property ; giving effect to the former according to the law of the place of the contract, and insisting, as to the latter, that no lien can exist, except it is founded in the law of the place where the property is situated (rei sitæ). Others make no distinction whatsoever in respect to such lien or privilege between movable property and immovable property ;

---

nière volonté ou entre-vifs (telles que les contrats de mariage exprès ou tacites). La règle est sans application à tous les cas où les meubles n'ont pas un rapport intime avec la personne du propriétaire : par exemple, lorsque la propriété de meubles est réclamée et contestée, lorsqu'on invoque la maxime qu'en fait de meubles possession vaut titre ; lorsqu'il s'agit d'exercer des priviléges ou des voies d'exécution sur les meubles, d'en prohiber l'aliénation, d'en prononcer la confiscation, ou de déclarer une succession mobilière en déspérence au profit du fisc, ou enfin d'interdire l'exportation des meubles. Dans tous ces cas, il faut appliquer la loi du lieu où les meubles se trouvent effectivement: car la dite fiction cesse par le fait. Par rapport aux priviléges sur les meubles, Hert soutient l'opinion contraire, en faisant observer que toutes les questions de privilége sur les meubles doivent être décidées dans le lieu du domicile du débiteur, par suite de la connexité des causes. Cette opinion revient à celle qui attribue à la loi du domicile son effet sur l'universalité des biens d'un individu: nous réfuterons cette opinion au n°, 37 ci-après. Ce que nous venons de dire des meubles s'applique non seulement aux meubles corporels, mais aussi aux meubles incorporels; il y a identité de raison.' See post, s. 401–403.

   [1] Ibid.   [2] Whiston *v.* Stodder, 8 Mart. (La.) 95, 134, 135.
   [3] Post, s. 323, note 3.

     (*a*) See Tyree *v.* Sands, 24 La. An. 363.

some holding that, in both cases, the lex loci contractus is equally
to govern; and some, that in both cases the lex rei sitæ is equally
to govern.[1]

322 d. *Rodenburg.* — Rodenburg notices these distinctions;
and says that although, by the laws of some countries where a
marriage is had, the wife has an hypothecation upon all the property of her husband for her dotal portion (pro restitutione dotis),
yet a question may arise whether this hypothecation can reach
the property of the husband situate in another country, where no
such law exists, or the law is to the contrary. He remarks also
that Christinæus has stated that the affirmative has been maintained in many decisions. But Rodenburg adds that he dares not
affirm that they have been rightly made. ' Quæ tamen an recte
se habeant, affirmare non ausim.' And he thinks, that the hypothecation does not extend to the real property of the husband
situate in a foreign country, because the statute is real and cannot have an extra-territorial authority. ' Consequenter non tacita seu legalis hypotheca adstringit bona alia, quam quibus lex
poterit imperare; ea nimirum, quæ legislatoris territorio sunt
supposita, cujus solius loci legis est, tanquam statuti realis, realem
in rebus effectum producere, cum ulterius judicis auctoritas non
efficiat hypothecam." [2]

323. *Priority of Liens.* — But the recognition of the existence
and validity of such liens by foreign countries is not to be confounded with the giving them a superiority or priority over all
others liens and rights justly acquired in such foreign countries
under their own laws, merely because the former liens in the
countries where they first attached had there, by law or by custom
such a superiority or priority. Such a case would present a very
different question, arising from a conflict of rights equally well
founded in the respective countries.[3] This very distinction was

---

[1] See some of these opinions cited in Rodenburg, de Divers. Statut. tit. 2,
c. 5, s. 16; 2 Boullenois, Appx. p. 49–51; Matthæus, de Auctionibus, lib. 1,
c. 21, n. 35–41, p. 294–299; 1 Boullenois, obs. 30, p. 833, 834, 838; Foelix,
Conflit des Lois, Revue Étrang. et Franç. 1840, tom. 7, s. 32–34, p. 222–
228.

[2] Rodenburg, de Divers. Stat. tit. 2, c. 5, s. 16; 2 Boullenois, Appx. p. 47.
See also Rodenburg, tit. 2, c. 5, s. 5–7; 2 Boullenois, Appx. p. 37, 38. See
also post, s. 324, 325; 1 Boullenois, 684, 685.

[3] Post, s. 324, 327, 524–527, 582; Foelix, Conflit des Lois, Revue Étrang.
et Franç. tom. 7, 1840, s. 33, p. 227, 228. This question might arise even in
relation to a bottomry bond, which by the law of most maritime countries

pointed out by Mr. Chief Justice Marshall in delivering the opinion of the court in an important case. His language was: 'The law of the place where a contract is made is, generally speaking, the law of the contract; i.e., it is the law by which the contract is expounded. But the right of priority forms no part of the contract. It is extrinsic, and rather a personal privilege, dependent on the place where the property lies, and where the court sits which is to decide the cause.'[1] And the doctrine was on that occasion expressly applied to the case of a contract made in a foreign country with a person resident abroad.[2] (a)

324. *Foreign Jurists.* —Huberus has also laid down the same qualifying doctrine: Foreign contracts are to have their full effect here, provided they do not prejudice the rights of our own country, or its citizens. 'Quatenus nihil potestati aut juri alterius imperantes ejusque civium præjudicetur.'[3] Or, as he has more fully expressed it in another place: 'Effecta contractuum certo loco initorum, pro jure loci illius alibi quoque observantur, si nullum inde civibus alienis creatur præjudicium in jure sibi quæsito; ad quod potestas alterius loci non tenetur, neque potest extendere jus diversi territorii.'[4] Hence he adds that the general rule should be thus far enlarged. If the law of another country is in conflict with that of our own state, in which also a contract is made, conflicting with a contract made elsewhere, we should in such a case, rather observe our own law than the foreign law.[5] 'Ampliamus hanc regulam tali extensione. Si jus loci in alio imperio pugnet cum jure nostræ civitatis, in qua contractus etiam initus est, confligens cum eo contractu, qui alibi celebratus fuit; magis est, ut jus nostrum, quam jus alienum,

has a priority or preference over most other claims in case of a deficiency of the proceeds to satisfy all claims. In such a case if the local law of the country where the bond was sought to be enforced differed, as to such priority or preference from that of the place where the bond was made and executed, it might be a very nice question which ought to prevail, and would therefore probably be disposed of upon considerations of local and municipal policy. But upon this subject we shall have occasion to speak hereafter. See post, s. 401–403.

[1] Harrison *v.* Sterry, 5 Cranch, 289, 298. See Ogden *v.* Saunders, 12 Wheat. 361, 362.

[2] Ibid.   [3] Huberus, de Confl. Leg. tom. 2, lib. 1, tit. 3, s. 2.

[4] Huberus, tom. 2, lib. 1, tit. 3, de Confl. Leg. s. 11; post, s. 525.

[5] Huberus, tom. 2, lib. 1. tit. 3, s. 11; post, s. 525.

(a) See also Ex parte Melbourn, L. R. 6 Ch. 67.

servemus.'[1] And he puts several cases to illustrate the rule. By the Roman law and the law of Friesland, an express hypothecation of movable property, oldest in date, is entitled to a preference or priority, even against a third possessor. But it is not so among the Batavians. And therefore, if upon such an hypothecation the party brings a suit in Holland against such third possessor, his suit will be rejected ; because the right of such third possessor cannot be taken away by the law of a foreign country.[2] (a)

325. He also puts another case. In Holland if a marriage contract is privately or secretly made, stipulating that the wife shall not be liable for debts contracted solely by the husband, it is valid, notwithstanding it is to the prejudice of subsequent creditors. But in Friesland such a contract is not valid, unless published ; nor would the ignorance of the parties be any excuse according to the Roman law and equity. If the husband should contract debts in Friesland, on a suit there, the wife would be held liable for a moiety thereof to the Frisian creditors, and could not defend herself under her private dotal contract ; for the creditors might reply that such a private dotal contract had no effect in Friesland, because it was not published. But the Batavian creditors contracting in Holland, although suing in Friesland, would not be entitled to a similar remedy ; for in such a case the law of the place of their contract alone, and not the law of both countries, would come under consideration.[3] The author was probably here treating of a case where the debts were contracted in Friesland after the husband and wife had removed their domicil there ; or at least, if there was no change of domicil, where the property of the parties to be affected by

---

[1] Ibid.; ante, s. 239.

[2] Huberus, tom. 2, lib. 1, tit, 3, s. 11; post, s. 525; ante, s. 239. See also Rodenburg, de Divers. Stat. tit. 2, c. 5 ; 2 Boullenois, Appx. p. 47; 1 Boullenois, p. 683, 684.

[3] Huberus, lib. 1, tit. 3, de Confl. Leg. s. 11. Huberus adds: Et hoc prevalet apud nos, in contractibus heic celebratis, ut nuperrime consultus respondi. The sense of this passage in Huberus is mistranslated in the note to 3 Dallas, 375. The translator has translated the words in contractibus heic celebratis, 'where the marriage was contracted here,' and jus loci contractus, 'the law of the place where the marriage was contracted;' whereas the author in this clause is manifestly referring to the contracts (debts) of the respective creditors.

(a) See Thurburn v. Steward, L. R. 3 P. C. 507.

the marriage contract was situated in Friesland. Under any
other aspect it would be difficult to maintain the doctrine.

325 *a*. Huberus in another place asserts a similar doctrine.
A creditor, says he, on account of a bill of exchange, exercising
his right in due time, has a preference in Holland to all other
creditors against the movable property of his debtor. The
debtor has property of the same kind in Friesland, where no such
law obtains. The question is whether such a creditor will be
preferred there to all other creditors? Certainly not, since by
the law there the right of the creditor is established. 'Creditor
ex causa cambii, jus suum in tempore exercens, præfertur apud
Batavos omnibus aliis creditoribus in bona mobilia debitoris.
Hic habet ejusmodi res in Frisia, ubi hoc jus non obtinet. An
ibi creditor etiam præferetur aliis creditoribus? Nullo modo;
quoniam his creditoribus vi legum hic receptarum jus pridem
quæsitum est.'[1]

325 *b*. The same doctrine is adopted by Hertius. After remarking that, in this matter of preferences and privileges of
creditors, the statute laws of particular countries have changed
the common (the civil) law; in answer to the question, what
law ought to govern in such cases, he says: If the controversy
respects immovables, the law of the country of the situs rei is,
without doubt, to govern. But in respect to movables, if the
question arises in cases of contract or of quasi contract, the law
of the place of the contract is to be examined. But inasmuch as
the preference arises from some peculiar law or privilege, it
ought not to be extended to the prejudice of the state where the
debtor resides and his movables are deemed to be collected. In
the conflict (concursus) of creditors, the law of the place of
domicil of the debtor ought to be observed. 'Enimvero, quia
antelatio ex jure singulari vel privilegio competit, non debet in
præjudicium illius civitatis, sub qua debitor degit, et res ejus
mobiles contineri consentiuntur, extendi. Ad juraigitur domicilii
debitoris, ubi fit concursus creditorum, et quo omnes cujuscunque
generis lites adversus illum debitorem propter connexitatem
causæ traduntur, regulariter respiciendum erit.'[2]

---

[1] D. Hub. lib. 3, J. P. Univer. cap. 10, s. 44, cited 1 Hertii Opera, de
Collis. Leg. s. 4, n. 64, p. 150, ed. 1737; Id. p. 511, ed. 1716; post, s. 627.

[2] 1 Hertii Opera, de Collis. Leg. s. 4, n. 64, p. 150, ed. 1737; Id. p. 211,
ed. 1716.

325 *c*. Rodenburg has discussed this subject at large in relation to the liens, the privileges, and the priorities of creditors in
cases of insolvency, and in other cases where their property, movable or immovable, is situated in different countries, and is not
sufficient to satisfy all their debts. This is commonly known by
the name of concursus creditorum, and the privilege or priority
itself by the name of the jus prælationis. It may be useful
to present a brief sketch of the substance of his remarks and
his conclusions on the subject. In respect to the property of
debtors in different countries, he says that jurists have distinguished between those things which concern the form and order
of the suit, and those which concern the decision or matter of
the suit. The suit is to be according to the law of the place
where it is instituted. As, for example, if the debtor's property
is to be taken in satisfaction of a judgment, the execution and
sale thereof are to be according to the law of the place where the
goods are situated or where they are taken upon the judgment.
But if the debtor has become bankrupt or notoriously insolvent,
so that there is no further opportunity for the seizure of his
movables, or for execution thereon, all the creditors being in the
same condition, the question as to their rights and privileges
should be discussed or litigated in the place of his domicil; for
it is properly a question as to the proceedings in the suit, de litis
ordinatione.[1] But a different rule prevails as to the decision and
merits of a suit; and the rights of the creditors, in respect to the
priority of their debts upon the property of the debtor, ought to
be measured according to the law of the place where it is really
situated, or is presumed to be situated.[2]

325 *d*. In respect to movable property, as it is always supposed to be in the place of the domicil of the debtor (for all
effects not having a fixed location are presumed to adhere to his
person), it is the law of his domicil which ought to decide the
rights of creditors as to such movables. This rule will prevail
where the goods are in his possession, unless indeed a creditor
has by his diligence, according to the laws of the place, acquired
a superior right by an execution over them; for he will then

---

[1] Rodenburg, de Div. Stat. tit. 2, c. 5, s. 16; 2 Boullenois, Appx. p. 47,
48; 1 Boullenois, 684, 685.
[2] Rodenburg, ibid.; 2 Boullenois, Appx. p. 48; 1 Boullenois, 685; post,
s. 524–527, 582.

retain that privilege, since it is not so much founded in the quality of the debt as that the creditor has by his diligence gained a priority; so that this privilege being attached to the formalities regulating the execution, it ought therefore to be regulated by the law of the place of execution. And besides, the judge who puts the creditor judicially in possession of property seized within his jurisdiction is regarded as acting in the name of the debtor; so that it may be deemed affected by the same reasoning as if the debtor himself had given it in pledge to the creditor in the place where the property is seized.[1]

325 *e*. Rodenburg afterwards puts the case of a merchant having different shops of trade in different places; and he says that the question has been put whether in such a case the creditors in each place are entitled to be paid out of the property there in trade, or the whole property is to be divided among all the creditors. Some jurists maintain the affirmative. But others, with whom Rodenburg agrees, hold that the whole should be distributed among the creditors generally in cases of insolvency.[2]

325 *f*. Rodenburg then puts the case of a contract made in a foreign country, not being the domicil of the debtor, by whose laws a preference is granted to creditors by promissory notes of hand; and he says that it might seem in such a case that the law of the place where the contract is made ought to govern; for that is the law by which the obligation of contracts is ordinarily expounded and governed;[3] 'Eo quod obligationes dirigi soleant a loco, ubi contrahuntur.'[4] (*a*) But after stating that Mascardus has expressed a similar opinion, following Decianus, he adds: That it is a nearer approach to the truth to say, that the law of the place of the contract ought not to govern; because that law can determine only the greater or less extent of the engagements of the debtor, and concerns only the contracting parties who, having contracted in another place than that of their domicil, are presumed to have referred to the laws of that place the form,

---

[1] Rodenburg, ibid.; 2 Boullenois, Appx. p. 48; 1 Boullenois, 685.
[2] Rodenburg, ibid.; 2 Boullenois, Appx. p. 49, 50; 1 Boullenois, 687, 688.
[3] Rodenburg, ibid.; 2 Boullenois, Appx. p. 50; 1 Boullenois, 688.
[4] Ibid.

(*a*) See also Ex parte Melbourn, L. R. 6 Ch. 67.

the obligation, the mode, the condition and whole nature of the contract. 'Verum non esse respiciendum locum contractus vero proprius est; utpote, qui eo duntaxat pertineat quo vel arctius, vel remissius ex contractu suo teneatur ipse debitor, adeoque spectatur, quoad ipsos contrahentes, quod eo ipso, quod alio in loco contractum celebrant, ad ejusdem léges, formam, vinculum, modum, conditionem, totam denique negotii naturam, sui respectu, componunt.'[1]   He proceeds to render the reasons of his opinion that this preference of creditors constitutes no part of the law of the contract, obligatory in other countries, and says: Moreover what does not arise from the act of man, but simply from the authority of the law, of which sort all privileges of preference among creditors are, it should be said that the authority of the legislator has no effect upon property not subjected to him, when the controversy respects the interest of third persons or of other creditors who have not contracted in that place, and who consequently have submitted themselves to the laws of that place. Besides it is manifest that we do not exercise these sorts of privileges upon the persons of debtors, because, being directed upon the property, they have their place properly among all the creditors. 'Cæterum, si quid non ab actu hominis, sed a potestate legis proficiscitur, cujusmodi sunt prælationis privilegia omnia, dicendum est vim legislatoris nullam esse in bona sibi non subjecta tertii respectu, seu creditorum aliorum, qui inibi nullum gesserint negotium, nec legibus loci istius se submiserint. Ad hæc constat privilegiis istis non agi in debitoris personam, utpote quæ in res directa, locum habeant inter creditores.'[2]

325 g. Rodenburg further insists that the same rule applies when the debtor has changed his domicil to another country. If in the country of his original domicil where the contract is made, there would be a privilege thereby created upon the movables of the debtor, and he afterwards removes to another country where no such privilege exists, Rodenburg says that, although it might seem that the privilege ought still to continue on his movables in his old domicil, yet the true rule is that the law of the new domicil is to prevail; for movables are governed by the law of the domicil. 'Nec aliud de eo debitore dicendum est, qui in

[1] Ibid.
[2] Ibid.; 3 Burge, Col. & For. Law, pt. 2, c. 20, p. 770, 771.

loco illo privilegii domicilium foverit tempore celebrati contractus ; quamvis enim videri possit jus illud prælationis creditori per leges loci domicilii in rebus mobilibus legitime quæsitum, subsecuta domicilii mutatione non debere amitti ; mobilia tamen, in quibus prioris domicilii lege tenuit prælationis privilegium, traductis alio domesticis laribus, traducuntur quoque in leges novi domicilii, eaque lege administrantur; mutatione enim domicilii mutatur et mobilium conditio eorum, quæ in manum aliis tradita non sunt, etiam dispendio tertii.' [1] (*a*)

325 *h.* *His Doctrine as to Immovables.* — In regard to immovables, Rodenburg holds that if there is either an express or tacit hypothecation or lien by the law of the domicil of the debtor, which is not equally allowed by the law of the situs thereof, the law of the situs or situation is to govern ; and that the creditor will in vain seek to assert any right of priority or privilege ; for as no man has authority expressly to create such a charge under a foreign law by a judicial proceeding, so neither can the foreign law itself exert such an authority ; since real statutes have no operation beyond the territory where they are enacted. 'Tandem ut ad immobilia transeam. Fac, jus tacitæ seu legalis hypothecæ non obtinere idem in loco rei sitæ, quod obtinet in loco domicilii debitoris, dicendum frustra est esse creditorem, qui hujusmodi hypothecæ obtentu prioritatem sibi asseruerit ; cum æque atque expressim facto hominis, coram uno judicio, hypothecæ nexu devinciri nequeunt alterius territorii bona, ita nec legis ullius potestas est afficere prædia extera ; quod statuta realia territorium non egrediantur.' [2] The result, therefore of the doctrine of Rodenburg seems to be that the proper

---

[1] Rodenburg, de Div. Stat. tit. 2, c. 5, s. 16; 2 Boullenois, Appx. p. 50; 1 Boullenois, 688, 689; 3 Burge, Col. & For. Law, pt. 2, c. 20, p. 770, 771.

[2] Rodenburg, ibid. ; 2 Boullenois, Appx. p. 50, 51; 1 Boullenois, 689, 690; Id. obs. 30, p. 818–875.

(*a*) See Donald *v.* Hewitt, 33 Ala. 546; Goodsill *v.* Brig St. Louis, 16 Ohio, 178; McMahan *v.* Green, 12 Ala. 71; Merrick *v.* Avery, 14 Ark. 370; Marsh *v.* Elsworth, 37 Ala. 85; note to s. 383, post.

In Pardo *v.* Bingham, L. R. 6 Eq. 485, it was held that if an Englishman contracts a debt in a foreign country, and there gives an instrument to secure payment, which by the laws of that country entitles the creditor to a priority out of the general assets of the debtor, it will not have that effect in England, as to equitable assets existing there, which by the laws of England are to be distributed equally to all creditors.

forum to decide upon all questions of the priorities and preferences of creditors is the place of the domicil of the debtor; and that the law of that place, and not the law of the place of the contract, is to govern in all cases of such priorities and preferences, in respect to movables situated in his place of domicil. But as to movables situate elsewhere, as well as to immovables, the law rei sitæ is to govern; although to prevent confusion and inconvenience, the administration and adjudication thereof in all cases is to be by the forum or tribunal of the debtor's domicil.[1]

[1] 1 Boullenois, obs. 30, p. 818–820. As the work of Rodenburg is rarely found in our libraries, and the subject here discussed is of great practical consequence, it may be useful to subjoin the whole passage in this note. 'Pergamus quærere ulterius, creditoribus de prælatione contendentibus, quod jus cujusque loci oporteat inspicere. Primum utamur vulgata DD. distinctione, qua separantur ea, quæ litis formam concernunt ac ordinationem, ab iis, quæ decisionem aut materiam. Lis ordinanda secundum morem loci, in quo ventilatur. Ut, si judicati exequendi causa bona debitoris distrahantur, qui solvendo sit, executio peragatur eo loci, ubi bona sita sunt, aut in causam judicati capiuntur. Sin cesserit foro debitor, aut propalam desierit esse solvendo, ut isti mobilium captioni, aut ulli omnino executioni non sit ultra locus, facta jam omnium creditorum conditione pari, disputatio de privilegiis, aut concursu creditorum veniat instituenda, ubi debitor habuerit domicilium. Unde cum apud nos relictis fortunis solum vertisset debitor obæratus, ac res ejus sitas in Hollandia venum proscriberet curator, creditores Hollandi, apud Provinciæ suæ curiam venditioni intercedentes, causa ibidem ventilata tulerunt repulsam: audito in et curatore, quod apud nos super universis debitoris facultatibus, adeoque et pretio ex venditione illa redigendo, ab uno eodemque judice peragenda decidendaque sit creditorum contentio: ex communi scribentium placito. Ob manifestam quoque causæ continentiam, ne super creditorum jure a diversis judicibus dissonæ sententiæ pronuntientur. Hæc de litis ordinatoriis. Aliud fere a præcedentibus obtinere dixeris in ejusdem decisoriis: jus enim creditorum super prioritate in bonis debitoris demeteri oportet a loco ubi distracta bona sita sunt, vel esse, intelliguntur. Et quidem de mobilibus si quæratur, cum semper ibi esse existimentur, ubi creditor [debitor] fovet domicilium, cujus ossibus vagæ hæ res intelligentur adhærere, utique ex lege ejusdem domicilii discutienda causa creditorum est. Hæc ita nisi forsan executio directa sit in ejus debitoris mobilia, qui adhuc in possessione suorum bonorum sit, feret enim tum creditor diligentiæ ac vigilantiæ suæ præmium, si quod eo nomine loci mores, ubi in causam judicati ceperit mobilia, præ aliis creditoribus ipsi indulserint; quod privilegium illud non tam proficiscatur ex credito, quam ex actu ipso executionis, qua alios creditor prævertit, adeoque hæc res tanquam concernens exequendi ordinem, legem accipiat a loco, ubi illa peragitur, ac præterea pignus illud judiciale ita constituens judex in bonis, apud se in causam judicati captis, dicitur supplere vicem debitoris; ut perinde res habeatur, ac si ipse debitor bona illa eo loci pignori tradidisset. Hæc ita si in uno loco debitoris sit domicilium.' Again: 'Fac foris contractum celebratum, ubi per mores ejusdem loci jus prælationis inter chiro-

325 *i*. Boullenois, in commenting upon Rodenburg, says that
every hypothecation or privilege upon property is to be deemed a

grapharios competit, locus videri posset attendendus esse contractæ obligationis: eo quod obligationes dirigi soleant a loco ubi contrahuntur. Verum
non esse respiciendum locum contractus vero proprius est: utpote qui eo duntaxat pertineat, quo vel arctius, vel remissius ex contractu suo teneatur ipse
debitor, adeoque spectetur quoad ipsos contrahentes, quod eo ipso, quod alio
in loco contractum celebrent, ad ejusdem leges, formam, vinculum, modum,
conditionem, totam denique negotii naturam, sui respectu, componunt. Cæterum si qui non ab actu hominis, sed a potestate legis proficiscitur, cujusmodi
sunt prælationis privilegia omnia, dicendum est vim legislatoris nullam esse in
bona sibi non subjecta tertii respectu, seu creditorum aliorum, qui inibi nullum
gesserint negotium, nec legibus loci istius se submiserint. Ad hæc constat
privilegiis istis non agri in debitoris personam, utpote quæ in res directa,
locum habeant inter creditores. Ecquid autem juris est alieno judici circa res
sibi non suppositas, dispendio tertii, qui apud se non contraxit ? Nec est,
quod retorserit creditor suum non minus spectari oportere, atque debitoris
domicilium. Constat quippe, qui cum alio contrahit, non esse vel debere esse
conditionis ejus ignarum. Ut nihil imputetur ei, qui in mobilibus a loci domicilii debitoris sua mensus est privilegia, ad quem locum palam est mobilia
pertinere: cum culpa non vacent alii, qui privilegium sibi assumpserint a
potestate legislatoris alieni, cui de mobilibus disponendi nullum jus est. Nec
aliud de eo debitore dicendum est, qui in loco illo privilegii domicilium foverit
tempore celebrati contractus: quamvis enim videri possit jus illud prælationis,
creditori per leges loci domicilii in rebus mobilibus legitime quæsitum, subsecuta domicilii mutatione non debere amitti; mobilia tamen, in quibus prioris
domicilii lege tenuit prælationis privilegium, traductis alio domesticis laribus,
traducuntur quoque in leges novi domicilii, eaque lege administrantur: mutatione enim domicilii mutatur et mobilium conditio eorum, quæ in manum aliis
tradita non sunt, etiam dispendio tertii: quo argumento, alia quanquam in
specie, usus est Senatus Parisiensis, apud Chopin. Et huc spectat quod Bar-
gundus tradit, mobilia sequi personam, hoc est (inquit) in domicilio ejus
existere, et non aliter quam cum domicilio transferri. Tandem ut ad immobilia transeam. Fac jus tacitæ, seu legalis hypothecæ non obtinere idem in
loco rei sitæ, quod obtinet in loco domicilii debitoris, dicendum frustra esse
creditorem, qui hujusmodi hypothecæ obtentu prioritatem sibi asseruerit: cum
æque atque expressim facto hominis, coram uno judicio, hypothecæ nexu
devinciri nequeunt alterius territorii bona, ita nec legis ullius potestas est afficere prædia extera; quod statuta realia territorium non egrediantur, ut supra
tractatum est. Ita si Hollandus, cui generaliter bona debitoris coram quocunque Hollandiæ judicio, hypothecæ data sunt, apud nos cum reliquis creditoribus experiatur de prælatione, profutura erit ei hypotheca in bonis, in quacunque Hollandiæ parte, extra districtum Amstelodamensem, sitis; non autem
in bonis suppositis territorio nostratium, quibus nulla subsistit hypothecæ
datio, nisi pacta coram judice rei sitæ. Contra cum apud Hollandos hypotheca generalis extinguatur alienatione, non juvabitur creditor moribus nostris,
quibus res ita obligata ad emptores transit cum suo onere. Consimiliter, si
teneat alibi consuetudo, ut in bonis debitoris concurrant creditores, nulla
habita ratione hypothecarum quale statutum profert florentium straccha. Ex
lege loci rei sitæ dirimenda creditorum contentio.' Rodenburg, de Div. Stat.
tit. 2, c. 5, s. 16; 2 Boullenois, Appx. p. 47–51.

real right (jus ad rem, or, jus in re). An action without any
hypothecation or privilege is purely personal. The existence of
a real right must depend either upon local ordinances, or upon
the law of the situs of the property; and if the law of the situs
differs from the ordinances of the place where the parties create
the hypothecation or privilege in allowing or disallowing such an
hypothecation or privilege, the law of the situs must govern.
In regard to movables, they are presumed to have their situs in
the place of the domicil of the owner; and if the law of that
domicil gives a privilege upon them, that privilege ought to be
regarded in every other place in which those movables may be
found.[1] Boullenois in this respect adopts the language of Lau-
tenburg. ‘In rebus mobilibus observari debent jura illius loci,
in quo illorum dominus vel creditor habet domicilium, etiam
quando agitur de concursu et prælatione creditorum.’[2] In regard to immovables Boullenois adopts the doctrine that all preferences and privileges thereon are real, and are therefore
governed by the law rei sitæ.[3]

325 k. John Voet has treated this question with great fulness.
In respect to priority and privileges in cases of hypothecations, he
insists that, as to movable property, the law of the domicil of the
debtor ought to govern the order thereof, as well because all
movables are understood to be in the place where the owner
lives, and are to be governed by the law of that place, as because
all creditors who ought to bring their suit in the tribunal where
the property is (forum rei), are deemed in their contracts to have
had reference to the place of domicil of the debtor, since in that
place the debtor, as the principal forum, ought to be sued; and
also because if the laws of the place where the contract is made,
or of the forum in which is the controversy respecting the conflict of rights and preferences between creditors, are to be observed, inexplicable difficulties will arise, or notorious absurdities
will be fallen into; of which he proceeds to give some illustrations. But in respect to immovables he holds that the law of
the place of the situs ought to govern in all questions of priority
and privileges. ‘Immobilia regenda esse jure loci, in quo sita
sunt.’[4]

[1] 1 Boullenois, obs. 30, p. 832-834.　　[2] Id. p. 834.　　[3] Ibid.
[4] J. Voet, ad Pand. 20, 4, 38, p. 904. The whole passage deserves to be
cited. ‘In quæstione, cujus loci statuta in prælatione tum hypothecariorum
30

325 *l*. Matthæus holds in a great measure the same opinion, and has discussed the subject at large. The whole passage is too long for insertion in this place; but a moderate extract will present his views in a very clear manner. Speaking of movables, he says: ' Quantum igitur ad res mobiles attinet, tametsi omnes sint ejusdem generis atque naturæ, motu tamen et quiete discriminari possunt. Earum enim aliæ nullo certo loco dispositæ, huc illuc

tum chirographariorum privilegio munitorum spectari debeant, dicendum videtur secundum fundamenta generalia in tit. de constitut. Princip. parte altera, de statutis proposita. In mobilibus debitoris bonis illum observari oportere prælationis ordinem, qui in loco domicilii debitoris probatus est; tum quia mobilia omnia, ubicunque existentia, illic domino suo præsentia esse intelliguntur, ac propterea isto quoque jure regenda sunt; tum quia creditores omnes, qui sequi in agendo debent forum rei, etiam maxime locum domicilii in contrahendo respexisse videntur, quippe in quo præcipue debitor, velut in foro præprimis competente, conveniendus est; tum denique, quia, si leges vel loci in quo contractum est, vel fori in quo de creditorum prælatione ac concursu disputatur, observandas censueris, aut inexplicabilibus et difficultatibus implicaturus es, aut ad notabiles delapsurus absurditates. Etenim, si contractuum singulorum loca spectari debere contendas, explicari non poterit, quid fieri debeut, si in Hollandia, Frisia, Anglia, Italia, Hispania diversi per eundem debitorem contractus initi sint, quarum regionum unaquæque diversis ex parte. quin et subinde contrariis de protopraxia legibus utitur, dum in Anglia aut Hollandia contrahens ex legibus Anglicanis aut Hollandicis præferri desiderabit ei, qui in Frisia contraxit; hic vero ex Frisiæ legibus contrariis potior esse velit eo, qui in Hollandia vel Anglia effecit sibi devinctum debitorem. Quod si locum, ubi mobilia proscribuntur, et judicium concursus inter creditores agitatur, spectandum existimes quasi distributio pecuniarum inter creditores pars et sequela executionis sit (posito, quod alibi, quam in loco domicilii postremi debitoris obærati mobilia vendi et lis de protopraxia agitari possit, cujus contrarium apud nos nunc obtinere, supra x. t. num. 12 dictum est), absurdum illud inde sequeretur, quod tunc non mobilium tantum sed et immobilium intuitu leges loci, in quo judicium de protopraxia agitur, observandæ forent; cum non minus distributio pecuniæ ex immobilibus, quam ex mobilibus, redactæ dici deberet executionis sequela aut pars; atque ita fieret, immobilia non ex lege situs regi, sed incerti juris subesse dispositioni, prout in hoc vel illo loco. diversis juribus utente, contentio fuerit inter creditores instituta de prælatione. Quinimo, posito illo jure, quod judicium universale concursus creditorum in eo loco ventilari debeat, in quo debitor, cum moraretur aut foro cederet, domicilium habuit, esse in arbitrio debitoris positum, ut migrando de loco in locum creditores non privilegiatos, efficeret privilegiatos, hypothecam legalem faceret aliis nasci, aliis interire, prout aliud atque contrarium domicilii prioris aut rei sitæ legibus jus in novissimi domicilii loco viguerit; quod in immobilibus loco certo alligatis, nec arbitrio domini situm mutantibus, ferendum non est; sed potius (cum jam ad immobilia nos deduxerit ratiocinium) in immobilium pretio inter creditores secundum cujusque privilegium distribuendo servandæ erunt leges locorum illorum, in quibus immobilia singula existunt, idque, convenienter regulæ in tit. de constit. princip. parte altera de statutis num. 12 firmatæ, ac dictanti, immobilia regenda esse jure loci, in quo sita sunt.'

feruntur trahunturve ; veluti merces in itinere deprehensæ, et ut
hodie fieri solet, arresto retentæ : aliæ vero certo loco dispositæ
quiescunt; veluti instrumentum et supellex, quam paterfamilias,
prædiorum instruendorum gratia, in provinciam misit : item feræ
bestiæ, et pisces, et reliqua animalia, quæ in fundis habentur fœ-
turæ et propagationis gratia. Quæcunque ejus generis deprehend-
untur, ut certo loco prædiove affixæ non sint, in iis haud dubie
superior definitio observanda est. Cum enim maxime in motu
sint, ac incertis quasi sedibus vagentur, nihil proprius est, quam
ut in disputatione de prærogativa creditorum spectemus domicilium debitoris. Quæ vero loco affixæ, aut certis possessionibus
attributæ sunt, eæ naturam prædiorum sequuntur ejusque provinciæ esse censentur, in qua prædia sita sunt. Unde dicendum
videbatur, in his rebus spectandas esse leges loci, ubi prædia sita
sunt, non ubi domicilium debitor habet.'[1] Again referring to objections which might be made, he says : ' Illud etiam objici poterat definitioni nostræ : In contractibus spectandas esse leges ejus
loci, ubi contractum est, vel in quem solutio destinata est : his
enim legibus contrahentes ultro subjecisse se intelliguntur. Igitur
in creditorum quoque contentione, non semper leges domicilii,
sed si alibi contractum sit, loci contractus sunt observandæ. Respondeo ; Si ex contractu agatur, spectari quidem leges ejus loci
ubi contractum est, non tamen in omnibus controversiis. Etenim,
si de solemnibus quæratur, si de loco, de tempore, et modo obligationis, tum quidem locum contractus observamus : sin de materia obligationis, seu de rebus, quæ in eam deducuntur, ejus loci
habenda ratio est, ubi res sitæ sunt. Situm autem cum dicimus,
prædia denotamus : hæc enim proprie sita dicuntur, non etiam
res mobiles. In disputatione vero creditorum de prærogativa,
quo minus locum contractus spectemus, ipsa quodammodo rerum
natura impedimento est. Quid enim si obæratus cum multis contraxerit, et variis quidem in locis, vario ac diverso jure utentibus :
veluti Romæ, Lugduni, Antuerpiæ, Amstelodami, Dantisci, Ge-
nuæ, etc., qui poterit spectari locus contractus, et cujus potissimum loci leges spectabis citra manifestam aliorum creditorum injuriam ? At locum domicilii debitoris possis observare citra cujusquam injuriam, dum omnes cujuscunque gentis aut nationis
cum aliquo debitore contrahentes, domicilium ejus spectasse, ac

---

[1] Matthæus, de Auctionibus, lib. 1. c. 21, n. 35, 36, p. 295.

fortunam judiciorum ibidem experiri voluisse videantur.　Postremo, opponi poterat, non tam domicilium debitoris spectandum esse, quam eum locum ubi bona proscribuntur.　Executionis enim seu pars, seu appendix, et sequela, videtur esse illa distributio pecuniarum inter creditores.　Communi autem calculo doctorum traditur, in executione facienda spectandum eum locum ubi executio sit.　Verum hunc obicem ita facile removebimus, si cogitaverimus communem illam sententiam de ordine et solemnibus executionis duntaxat loqui, non etiam de ipsa creditorum contentione et causa, quæ inter eos vertitur : hæc enim incidit quidem in executionem, ab ordine tamen executionis separata est.　In iis autem, quæ ad causæ decisionem pertinent, non illico locum judicii, sed antiquiorem aliquem, puta domicilii, interdum contractus, aliquando situm rei spectamus.　Instari poterat : Si ad decisionem causæ pertinet disputatio illa creditorum, jam sententia hæc premetur alio argumento : Nempe, quod in decisoriis litis observandæ sint leges ejus loci, ubi contractum est.　Sed respondetur, hoc tum procedere, cum inter creditorem et debitorem lis vertitur : cum vero plures creditores ejusdem debitoris de prærogativa disputant, locum domicilii debitoris spectamus ; quia locum contractus citra injuriam aliorum spectare per rerum naturam non possumus : nullo certe modo, cum idem debitor, qui variis in locis negotiari solet, habuerit variarum gentium atque locorum creditores : puta Italos, Gallos, Belgas, Germanos, Hispanos, etc. Hic enim constituere non possis, cujus potissimum loci leges sint spectandæ : ut autem omnium simul locorum leges atque mores spectentur, rerum natura non patitur.' [1]

325 *m*.　And then, referring to immovables, he says : ' Quantum ad res immobiles attinet, videndum, an recte separaverimus hypothecam a privilegio : ita ut in æstimandis viribus hypothecæ spectemus eum locum, ubi prædium situm est ; in privilegio inter hypothecarios exercendo, domicilium debitoris ?　Argumentum enim, quo usi sumus, infirmius videtur : Privilegium concernit personam : igitur domicilium debitoris in eo spectandum.　Quasi vero non sit duplex privilegiorum ratio : ita ut alia quidem personæ, alia rei seu causæ data sint.　Deinde, non videtur illa necessaria consecutio : privilegia personam concernunt ; igitur personam comitantur, quocunque locorum commigraverit.　Etenim

---

[1] Matthæus, de Auctionibus, lib. 1. c. 21, n. 37–40, p. 296-298.

illo duntaxat jura quæ personæ qualitatem aliquam imprimunt, comitari personam solent: veluti si quis minor, fatuus, prodigus, infamis, declaretur: Vitium enim hoc perdurat, et quocunque locorum te contuleris, circumferes tecum notam illam et qualitatem in loco domicilii tibi impressam. At privilegium, quod personæ conceditur, nullam qualitatem personæ imprimit, nullam notam inurit: comitari ergo personam non poterit in eam provinciam, in qua forte privilegium cessat. Sed imprimis illud obstat, quod privilegium detur quidem personæ, tamen in bonis debitoris exercendum. Ut autem in prædiis debitoris in alia provincia sitis exerceam privilegium, non possunt mihi tribuere ii, qui in loco domicilii debitoris jura condunt: quippe quorum jurisdictioni ager alterius territorii subjectus non sit. Mobilia duntaxat, quia personam comitantur, jurisdictioni eorum subjecta videntur, quocunque in loco reperiantur. Itaque si mulier nupserit in Frisia, ubi dotes sunt, dotiumque privilegia: distrahantur mariti prædia in Gelria, Hollandia, Trajecti, ubi ne dotes quidem veræ sunt, nedum dotium privilegia: non videtur mulier inter hypothecarios habitura privilegium, quod haberet, si in Frisia sita prædia distraherentur. Valde enim absurdum sit, velle hypothecariis eam præferri, quam ne numerant quidem Gelri inter hypothecarios. His de causis generalius concludendum, sive de viribus hypothecæ, sive de privilegio inter hypothecarios exercendo loquamur, in prædiis spectandas esse leges ejus loci ubi prædia sita sunt.'[1]

325 n. Mævius adheres to the same rule in cases of movables, that is to say that the law of the domicil of the debtor is to govern in all cases of preferences and privileges.[2] D'Argentré adopts the same opinion: 'Quare statutum de bonis mobilibus vere personale est, et loco domicilii judicium sumit; et quodcumque judex domicilii de eo statuit, ubique locum obtinet.'[3] Burgundus may also fairly be presumed to hold the like opinion. 'De cætero mobilia ibi esse dicemus, ubi quis instruxit domicilium; et ideo quodcumque judex domicilii de iis statuerit, ubique locorum obtinet, sive, quod persona ibi est, aut esse, semper intelligitur, sive quod ibi rerum suarum summam collocavit. Et sic intelligendum est, quod dicimus mobilia sequi personam, hoc est, in domicilio ejus existere, et non aliter quam cum domicilio trans-

---

[1] Matthæus, de Auctionibus, lib. 1, c. 21, n. 41, p. 298, 299.
[2] Mævius, ad Jus. Lubesense, lib. 3. tit. 1, art. 11, n. 23–35.
[3] D'Argentré, de Briton. Leg. art. 218, gloss. 6, n. 30, p. 654.

ferri. Nec refert, eadem bona in loco domicilii reperiantur, an
non.'[1] Many other jurists assert the same doctrine.[2] Still however (as has been already intimated) all foreign jurists are not
agreed in this doctrine, at least not without many modifications
thereof.[3]

325 o. *Creditors' Rights against Immovables.* — But whatever
may be the differences of opinion among them as to the operation
of the rights of preference or privilege of creditors upon movable
property, situate in fact in a foreign country, there seems to be a
great preponderance of authority, although certainly not an universal agreement in respect to immovable property in favor of
the doctrine that the law of the place rei sitæ ought to prevail,
as to the denial or allowance of such preferences and privileges.[4]
Paul Voet expressed the general sense when he said: ' Vero immobilia reguntur locorum statutis, ubi sita; etiam quoad ea, si de
æstimanda hypotheca, aut de privilegiis inter hypothecarios agatur, non inspiciendus erit locus domicilii, vel debitoris, vel creditoris, verum locus statuti, ubi jacent.'[5] An easy example may
illustrate the importance of the distinction. Suppose a contract
made in Massachusetts for the sale of lands lying in New York,
by whose laws the vendor has a lien for the unpaid purchase-
money, and by the laws of Massachusetts there would in such a
case be no lien, if the land were in Massachusetts; the question
would then arise, whether any lien attached on such a contract
on the land. According to the opinions of the foreign jurists already referred to, the law rei sitæ and not the law of the place of
the contract would attach upon the contract; and consequently
a lien for the unpaid purchase-money would exist on the lands in
New York, although no such lien would exist in Massachusetts
under or in virtue of the contract.[6] (a)

326. *Lord Ellenborough.* — *Supreme Court of Louisiana.* — Lord
Ellenborough has laid down a doctrine essentially agreeing with
that of Huberus. ' We always import,' says he, ' together with
their persons, the existing relations of foreigners, as between

---

[1] Burgundus, tract. 2, n. 21, p. 113.
[2] 1 Boullenois, obs. 30. p. 834, 835, 840.   [3] Ante, s 322 b, 322 c.
[4] Ante, s. 322–325 m, post s. 362–373.
[5] P. Voet, de Stat. s. 9, c. 2, n. 8, p. 267, ed. 1715; Id. p. 322, ed. 1661.
[6] See Gilman v. Brown, 1 Mason, 219–221; 4 Wheat. 255.

(a) See note to s. 383, post.

themselves, according to the laws of their own countries ; except indeed where those laws clash with the rights of our own subjects here, and one or other of the laws must necessarily give way ; in which case our own is entitled to the preference. This having been long settled in principle, and laid up among our acknowledged rules of jurisprudence, it is needless to discuss it further.'[1] The Supreme Court of Louisiana have adopted a little more modified doctrine coinciding exactly with that of Huberus : ' That, in a conflict of laws, it must oftener be a matter of doubt which should prevail ; and that, whenever that doubt does exist, the court which decides will prefer the law of its own country to that of a stranger.[2] And if the positive laws of a state prohibit particular contracts from having effect according to the rules of the country where they are made, the former must prevail.'[3]

327. *Kent. — Burge.* — Mr. Chancellor Kent has laid down the same rule in his Commentaries, as stated by Huberus and Lord Ellenborough, and has said : ' But on this subject of conflicting laws, it may be generally observed that there is a stubborn principle of jurisprudence that will often intervene and act with controlling efficacy. This principle is, that when the lex loci contractus and the lex fori, as to conflicting rights acquired in each, come in direct collision, the comity of nations must yield to the positive law of the land. In tali conflictu magis est, ut jus nostrum, quam jus alienum, servemus.'[4] Mr. Burge has expressed his own exposition of the same doctrine in the following terms : ' It may be stated generally that with respect to contracts of which movable property is the subject, the law of the place in which the contract is made will in some respects exclusively prevail, although the contract is to be performed in another ; and that in those respects in which it does not prevail, the law of the place where the contract is to be performed must be adopted. But this conclusion is subject to some qualifications and exceptions. If a right which is claimed as resulting from the contract, or if an act or disposition, affect the interest of third parties, as the creditors of the owner, resort must be had to the law of his domicil to determine whether that right exists, and whether he was compe-

---

[1] Potter *v.* Brown, 5 East, 124.

[2] Mr. Justice Porter, in the case of Saul *v.* His Creditors, 5 Mart. N.S. (La.) 596.

[3] Id. p. 586, 587.   [4] 2 Kent Com. 461.

tent to do the act or make the disposition. A preference claimed
by a creditor on the estate of his debtor by virtue of the contract,
and a disposition made by a debtor which might be void against
his creditors, are instances of this exception. The law of a foreign country is admitted in order that the contract may receive
the effect which the parties to it intended. No state however is
bound to admit a foreign law, even for this purpose, when that
law would contravene its own positive laws, institutions, or
policy, which prohibit such a contract, or when it would prejudice the rights of its own subjects.' [1]

327 a. *Case of Bottomry in Louisiana.* — A question involving
considerations of this nature came recently before the Supreme
Court of Louisiana. It was a suit brought in Louisiana upon a
bottomry bond of a peculiar character given by the owner of a
steamboat in Cincinnati (Ohio), and pledging the vessel for the
repayment of a sum of money and interest, lent to the owner for
a year. The steamboat had in the intermediate time been sold in
Kentucky to a purchaser with notice of the lien, and she was at
New Orleans at the time of the suit brought; and the object
thereof was to enforce the hypothecation or lien created by the
bond. Various objections were taken in the defence; and among
them was the objection that no lien was created in such a case by
the laws of Louisiana, where the suit was brought. Mr. Justice
Porter, in delivering the opinion of the court on this occasion,
said: ' But a more formidable objection has been raised against
the regularity of the proceedings. The statutes and jurisprudence
of Louisiana, it is contended, only confer the privilege of sequestration to enforce liens given by its laws; and that, in aid of
which this remedy was extended here, was not one that had any
force or conferred any privilege in our state, though it might
have that effect in the country where it was made. The objection now taken raises a distinction in cases so circumstanced, between remedies before and after judgment; and we confess we
are unable to see any solid grounds on which it can rest. If it
be true, as we apprehend it is, that the court can and should enforce the personal obligation which a party, not a citizen of the
state, may have entered into in another country, and that, on the

---

[1] 3 Burge, Col. & For. Law, pt. 2, c. 20, p. 778, 779; Id. p. 770. See
also Foelix, Confl. des Lois, Revue Étrang. et Franç. tom. 7, 1840, s. 33,
p. 227, 228.

judgment so rendered, the foreign creditor could obtain the benefit of all writs of execution which an inhabitant of Louisiana might
resort to against a domestic debtor, then we can see no good ground
for refusing the auxiliary process in the first instance ; whether
it be an order to arrest the person of the debtor and hold him to
bail, or a writ to seize the property brought within the jurisdiction of a court, if it be the subject of contest. Both seem to rest
on the same principles. And a familiar illustration of the commonly received opinion on this subject may be given in the case
of attachments, which are almost every day resorted to in aid of
the foreign creditor against the foreign debtor ; and yet there is
nothing in our law more expressly giving that remedy to the
stranger than there is in the case of sequestration.' After taking
notice that, by the laws of Ohio, it had been found that the bond
created a lien on the steamboat, the learned judge proceeded to
say : 'If the steamboat then had remained within the state of
Ohio, the evidence satisfies us the plaintiffs could have had a lien
on her. But the main difficulty in the cause still remains. She
was sold in the state of Kentucky under a decree of one of the
courts of that state, and purchased by the defendant at the sale.
It is admitted on all hands that this sale was legal and regularly
made, and the question is not what was the effect of the lien in
the country where the contract was made, nor in that where it is
sought to be enforced, but what effect it had in the state where
the defendant acquired title to the property.' He then examined
the laws of Kentucky on the subject ; and concluded in the
following words : ' The state of Kentucky we presume gives effect to liens existing on property brought there from another
country, on the principle of comity, which we have already noticed, and we must also presume, until the contrary be shown,
that she admits them with the same limitation which other states
do, namely, that they shall not work an injury to her own citizens. To ascertain whether they do or not, recurrence must be
had to her laws and policy in relation to contracts made within
her limits ; for we take the true principle in such cases to be,
that the foreign creditor who has a lien should have no greater or
no less privilege than the domestic creditor. If, for example, the
laws of Kentucky required no record to be made of liens given on
personal property within the state, she would not require registry
on the part of the stranger who came there to enforce a mortgage

on property on which he had a lien in another country; for if she did, she would neither carry the contract into effect according to the law of the country where it was made, nor according to her own. If this be true, whatever time is given to the domestic creditor to record his lien should be given to him who comes from another state with one, if his lien be recognized as valid when enregistered, and his prayer to enforce it be admitted, as we are told by the testimony it could be.' The court accordingly enforced the lien against the steamboat.[1]

327 b. *Priorities and Contributions between Underwriters.* — Another case, which may serve to illustrate the difficulty of laying down any universal rule on the subject of contracts, as the incidents and rights which may attach to or against third persons, residing in different countries, may readily be stated, as it is one which may not infrequently occur in practice. By the law of England, if two policies are underwritten on the same ship or cargo for the same voyage, to the full amount of the property at risk, it is treated as a double insurance, and each policy is valid, without any reference to the respective dates thereof. And in case of a loss the insured may recover the whole loss from the underwriters on either policy, at his own election; and they are then entitled to contribution pro rata from the underwriters on the other policy.[2] Now in France, no such rule of contribution exists; but the policy prior in date is, in case of a double insurance, to be first exhausted, and if that is sufficient to pay the whole loss, there is no right to recover the loss, or to exact contribution from the underwriters on the policy of a later date.[3] This also seems to be the general rule among most of the maritime nations of continental Europe.[4] Now let us suppose that two policies of different dates are underwritten on the same ship or cargo, the one in France and the other in England, for an American owner, on the same voyage, each policy being for a sum equal to the full value of the property at risk, and

---

[1] Ohio Ins. Co. v. Edmondson. 5 La. 295–305; ante, s. 244.

[2] Park on Insur. c. 15, p. 280, 281, 5th ed.; 3 Kent Com. 280, 281; 1 Marsh. on Insur. c. 4, s. 4, p. 146, 2d ed.; 2 Phillips on Insur. p. 59, 60, 2d ed.

[3] 3 Kent Com. 280, 281; Code de Commerce, art. 359, Ordin. of Louis XIV. tit. ; 2 Valin. Com. lib. 3, tit. 6, art. 23–25, p. 72, 73.

[4] 1 Emerigon, Assur. c. 1, s. 7, p. 23; 1 Marsh. on Insur. c. 4, s. 4, p. 146, 2d ed. note a.

there should be a total loss on the voyage; the question might arise whether the English underwriters were liable at all if the French policy was prior in date; and also whether, if liable, they could claim contribution from the French underwriters; and conversely, the question might arise whether, if the English policy was prior in date, the French underwriters were liable at all; and if liable, whether they could claim contribution from the English underwriters. No such case seems as yet to have undergone any judicial decision. But probably it would be held that each contract was to be exclusively construed according to the obligations and rights created by the lex loci contractus between the parties themselves, without any regard to the collateral rights and obligations which might arise between the underwriters, if both contracts were made in the same country. If a different rule were adopted, there might be an entire want of reciprocity in its operation. Thus if the French policy were prior in date, and a recovery were had thereon against the French underwriters, they might have contribution from the English underwriters; and yet, if a recovery were had against the English underwriters, they could not have contribution from the French underwriters. On the other hand, if the English policy were prior in date, the French underwriters might be exempted from all liability for the loss, or, if liable, might recover a contribution from the English underwriters; at the same time that, if a recovery were had against the English underwriters, they would not be entitled to any contribution against the French underwriters. However this case is merely propounded as one on which the author professes to have no fixed opinion, and is designed rather to awaken inquiry than to satisfy doubts.[1]

328. *Lord Robertson.* — This subject will be resumed hereafter under other heads.[2] But the remarks of a learned Scottish judge [3] may here be properly introduced as exceedingly pertinent to the present discussion. ‘The application of the lex loci to

[1] In some of the present American policies there is now what is commonly called a priority clause, similar in effect to the French law. The very question therefore may arise in the case of a double insurance by different policies in England and in a state using the priority clause, or in the latter state and a state which uses the common English policy, and is governed by its laws.

[2] Post, s. 401, 402, 423 a, 524–527.

[3] Lord Robertson, in the case of Mrs. Levett, in Fergusson on Mar. & Div. 385, 397.

contracts, although general, is not universal. It does not take place where the parties at the time of entering into the contract had the law of another kingdom in view ; or where the lex loci is in itself unjust, or contra bonos mores, or contrary to the public law of the state, as regarding the interests of religion or morality, or the general well-being of society.'

329. *Where Debts are payable.* — It may also be stated, although the proposition has been already incidentally considered, that when a debt is contracted in a foreign country, it is not to be deemed exclusively payable there, unless there is in the contract itself some stipulation to that effect.[1] On the contrary, a debt contracted in a particular country, and not limited to a particular place of payment, is by operation of law payable everywhere, and may be enforced wherever the debtor or his property can be found.[2]

330. *Discharge of Contracts.* — Having considered the principles applicable to the nature, validity, interpretation, and incidents and effects of contracts we are next led to the consideration of the manner in which they may be discharged, and what matters upon the merits will constitute a good defence to them. I say upon the merits ; for the objections arising from the law of the state where the suit is brought (lex fori), such as the limitations of remedies, and the form and modes of suit, will constitute a separate head of inquiry.[3]

331. *General Rule.* — *Foreign Jurists.* — And here the general rule is, that a defence or discharge, good by the law of the place where the contract is made or is to be performed, is to be held of equal validity in every other place where the question may come to be litigated.[4] John Voet has laid down this doctrine in the broadest terms. ' Si adversus contractum aliudve negotium gestum factumve restitutio desideretur, dum quis aut metu, aut dolo, aut errore lapsus, damnum sensit contrahendo, transigendo, solvendo, fidejubendo, hereditatem adeundo, aliove simili modo;

---

[1] Ante, s. 272 a, 278 a, 295, 317 ; Don v. Lippmann, 5 Cl. & F. 1, 12, 13.

[2] See Blake v. Williams, 6 Pick. (Mass.) 286, 315 ; ante, s. 272 a, s. 317; Don v. Lippmann, 5 Cl. & F. 1, 12, 13.

[3] Post, s. 524–527.

[4] 2 Bell Comm. b. 8, c. 3, s. 1267, p. 692, 4th ed ; Id. p. 688, 5th ed.; 3 Burge, Col. & For. Law, pt. 2, c. 21, s. 7, p. 874–886 ; Id. c. 22, p. 924–929. As to what will constitute a discharge in foreign countries, and especially by novation, by confusion, by set-off or compensation, by payment or consignation, and by relapse, see 3 Burge, Col. & For. Law, pt. 2, c. 21, s. 1–6, p. 781–880. See also Bartsch v. Atwater, 1 Conn. 409.

recte interpretes statuisse arbitror, leges regionis in qua contractum gestumve est, id, contra quod restitutio petitur, locum sibi
debere vindicare in terminanda ipsa restitutionis controversia ;
sive res illæ, de quibus contractum est, et in quibus læsio contigit, eodem in loco, sive alibi sitæ sint. Nec intererit utrum læsio
circa res ipsas contigerit, veluti pluris minorisve, quam æquum est,
errore justo distractas, an vero propter neglecta solennia in loci
contractus desiderata. Si tamen contractus implementum non in
ipso contractus loco fieri debeat, sed ad locum alium sit destinatum, non loci contractus, sed implementi, leges spectandas esse
ratio suadet ; ut ita secundum cujus loci jura implementum accipere debuit contractus, juxta ejus etiam leges resolvatur.'[1] Casaregis in substance lays down the same doctrine ;[2] and Huberus
throughout implies it,[3] as indeed does Dumoulin.[4]

331 a. Burgundus says : ' Idem ergo de solutionibus dicendum ;
scilicet, ut in omnibus quæ ex ea sunt, aut inde oriuntur, aut circa
illam consistunt, aut aliquo modo affinia sunt, consuetudinem loci
spectemus, ubi eandem implendam convenit. Itaque ex solutione
sunt solemniæ valor rei debitæ, pretium monetæ ; ex solutione oriuntur præstatio apochæ, antigraphi, similiaque. Affinia solutioni
sunt, præscriptio, oblatio rei debitæ, consignatio, novatio, delegatio, et ejusmodi.[5] Ea, vero, quæ ad complementum vel executionem
contractus spectant, vel absoluto eo superveniunt, sola a statuto
loci dirigi, in quo peragenda est solutio.'[6] Many other foreign
jurists maintain the same doctrine.[7]

332. *Rule of England and America.* — In England and America the same rule has been adopted, and acted on with a most
liberal justice.[8] Thus infancy, if a valid defence by the lex loci
contractus, will be a valid defence everywhere.[9] A tender and
refusal, good by the same law either as a full discharge or as a

---

[1] J. Voet ad Pand. 4, 1, s. 29, p. 240.

[2] See Casaregis, Disc. 179, s. 60, 61.

[3] Huberus, lib. 1, tit. 3, s. 3, 7 ; J. Voet, de Statut. s. 9, c. 2, s. 20, p. 275,
ed. 1715; Id. p. 332, 333, ed. 1661.

[4] 2 Boullenois, obs. 46, p. 462; Molin. Com. ad Cod. 1, 1, 1 ; Conclus. de Stat.
tom. 3, p. 554, ed. 1681.

[5] Burgundus, tract. 4, n. 27, 28, p. 114–116   [6] Id. n. 29, p. 116.

[7] 3 Burge, Col. & For. Law, pt. 2, c. 21, s. 7, p. 874–876.

[8] 2 Kent Com. 459; Potter *v.* Brown, 5 East, 124; Dwarris on Stat. pt. 2,
p. 650, 651 ; 2 Bell Com. s. 1267, p. 691, 692, 4th ed. ; Id. p. 688, 5th ed.

[9] Thompson *v.* Ketcham, 8 Johns. (N. Y.) 189; Male *v.* Roberts, 3 Esp.
163.

present fulfilment of the contract, will be respected everywhere.[1] Payment in paper money bills or in other things, if good by the same law, will be deemed a sufficient payment everywhere.[2] And, on the other hand, where a payment by negotiable bills or notes is, by the lex loci, held to be conditional payment only, it will be so held, even in states where such payment under the domestic law would be held absolute.[3] (a)   So if by the law of the place of a contract (even although negotiable), equitable defences are allowed in favor of the maker, any subsequent indorsement will not change his rights in regard to the holder.[4] The latter must take it cum onere.[5]

333. *Acceptance of a Bill of Exchange.* — The case of an acceptance of a bill of exchange in a foreign country affords another illustration. Although by our law it is absolute and binding in every event; yet if by that of the foreign country it is merely a qualified contract, it is governed by that law in all its consequences.[6] Acceptances are deemed contracts in the country where they are made; and the payments are regulated by the law thereof.[7]

334. *Exceptions.* — But although the general rule is clear, as above stated, that a discharge by the law of the place where a contract is made is a discharge everywhere, yet there are exceptions to the rule, which every country will enforce or not according to its own discretion and sense of justice.[8]   Thus where a contract was made in England between two Danish subjects, one of whom was domiciled in England; and afterwards, during a war between England and Denmark, the Danish government confiscated the debt and required it to be paid by the debtor, who was then in Denmark, and he paid it accordingly; the English Court of

[1] Warder v. Arell, 2 Wash. (Va.) 282, 293, &c.

[2] Warder v. Arell, 2 Wash. Va.). 282, 293; 1 Brown, Ch. 376; Searight v. Calbreath, 4 Dall. 325; Bartsch v. Atwater, 1 Conn. 409.

[3] Bartsch v. Atwater, 1 Conn. 409.   See other cases cited, 3 Burge, Col. & For. Law, pt. 2, c. 21, s. 7, p. 876–878.

[4] Ante, s. 317.

[5] Ory v. Winter, 4 Mart. N.S. (La.) 277.   See also Evans v. Gray, 12 Mart. (La.) 475; Chartres v. Cairnes, 4 Mart. N.S. (La.) 1.

[6] Burrows v. Jemino, 2 Str. 733; 2 Eq. Abr. 525.   See Van Cleef v. Therasson, 3 Pick. (Mass.) 12.

[7] Lewis v. Owen, 4 B. & A. 654; 5 Pardessus, s. 1492; ante, s. 307, 317; Cooper v. Waldegrave, 2 Beav. 282.

[8] Post, s. 887.

(a) See Descadillas v. Harris, 8 Greenl. (Me.) 298.

King's Bench, on a suit brought in England, after the peace, by the creditor against the debtor, held that the payment to the Danish government was no discharge, although it would have been so by the laws of Denmark, upon the ground that such a confiscation was not justified by the law of nations.[1]

335. *Discharge in Bankruptcy.* — The most important, or at least most frequent, cases of discharges of contracts occurring in practice, are those of discharges arising from matters ex post facto ; such as a discharge from the contract upon the subsequent insolvency of bankruptcy or the contracting party. And here the general rule is that a discharge from the contract according to the law of the place where it is made, or where it is to be performed, is good everywhere and extinguishes the contract.[2] This doctrine was fully recognized in the English law by Lord Mansfield (and it doubtless had a much earlier existence) in a formulary of language which has been since often quoted as a general axiom of jurisprudence. 'It is a general principle,' said he, 'that where there is a discharge by the law of one country it will be a discharge in another.'[3] The expression is too broad and should have the qualification annexed which the case before him required, and which has been uniformly understood, viz., that it is a discharge in the country where the contract was made or was to be performed. And so it was interpreted by Lord Ellenborough in a much later case. 'The rule,' said he, 'was well laid down by Lord Mansfield, in Ballantine v. Golding, that what is a discharge of a debt in the country where it was contracted is a discharge of it everywhere.'[4] This doctrine is also firmly established and generally recognized in America.[5] By some judges

[1] Wolff v. Oxholm, 6 M. & S. 92. See post, s. 348-351. It is wholly unnecessary here to consider whether the confiscation of debts by an enemy is conformable or not to the law of nations. That is a point belonging to the public law of nations, and underwent very grave discussions in England, in the case in 6 M. & S. 92, as well as in the American courts during the late war with Great Britain. See The Emulous, 1 Gall. 563 ; s.c. on appeal, Brown v. United States, 8 Cranch, 110.

[2] 2 Kent Com. 392, 393 ; 2 Bell Com. s. 1267, p. 691-695, 4th ed.; Id. p. 688, 5th ed. ; 1 Chitty on Com. & Manuf. c. 12, p. 654.

[3] Ballantine v. Golding, 1 Cooke Bank. Laws, p. 347, 5th ed. p. 515, 4th ed.; p. 487, 8th ed.; Blanchard v. Russell, 13 Mass. 7 ; 2 Bell Com. s. 1267, p. 691, 692, 4th ed.; Id. p. 688, 5th ed.

[4] Potter v. Brown, 5 East, 124, 130. See Hunter v. Potts, 4 T. R. 182; Quin v. Keefe, 2 H. Bl. 553.

[5] See on this point, Smith v. Smith, 2 Johns. (N. Y.) 235 ; Hicks v. Brown,

the doctrine has been put upon the implied consent of the parties in making the contract, that they would be governed as to all its effects by the lex loci contractus.[1] By others it has been put upon the more firm and solid basis of the sovereign operation of the local law, upon all contracts made within its sovereignty; and the indispensable comity which all other nations are accustomed to exercise towards such laws whenever they are brought into question, either as to contracts, or to rights, or to property.[2]

336. The doctrine has been stated in a more general form by a late learned American judge, who said : ' It may be assumed as a rule affecting all personal contracts, that they are subject to all the consequences attached to contracts of a similar nature by the laws of the country where they are made, if the contracting party is a subject of or resident in that country where it is entered into, and no provision is introduced to refer to the laws of another country.'[3] This is not perhaps, in strictness of language, entirely correct. There are many consequences flowing from contracts in the place where they are made, which do not accompany them everywhere, and are not of universal obligation.[4] Remedies are a consequence of contracts when broken ; but, as we shall hereafter see, they are governed by different rules from rights.[5] And the rights given by the law of the place of the contract are not always deemed of universal obligation or validity. Marriage for instance is admitted to be a valid contract everywhere when it is valid by the law of the place where it is celebrated.[6] But as we have seen, all the consequences attached to marriage in one

12 Johns. (N. Y.) 142; Van Reimsdyk v. Kane, 1 Gall. 371; Blanchard v. Russell, 13 Mass. 1; Baker v. Wheaton, 5 Mass. 511; Watson v. Bourne, 10 Mass. 337; 4 Cowen (N. Y.) note, p. 515; Green v. Sarmiento, Pet. C. C. 74; M'Menomy v. Murray, 3 Johns. Ch. (N. Y.) 435, 440, 441; Walsh v. Nourse, 5 Binn. (Pa.) 381; Sturges v. Crowninshield, 4 Wheat. 122; Ogden v. Saunders, 12 Wheat. 213, 358; 2 Kent Com. 392, 393, 459; Atwater v. Townsend, 4 Conn. 47; Hempstead v. Reed, 6 Conn. 480; Houghton v. Page, 2 N. H. 42; Dyer v. Hunt, 5 N. H. 401; 2 Bell Com. s. 1267, p. 691–693, 4th ed.; Id. p. 688, 5th ed.

[1] See ante, s. 261; Blanchard v. Russell, 13 Mass. 1, 4, 5; Prentiss v. Savage, 13 Mass. 20, 23.

[2] Potter v. Brown, 5 East, 124; ante, s. 261.

[3] Mr. Chief Justice Parker, in delivering the opinion of the court in the case of Blanchard v. Russell, 13 Mass. 1, 5.

[4] Ante, s. 325–327.   [5] Post, s. 556–575.

[6] Ante, s. 111, 113, 121–125.

country do not follow it into other countries.[1] In Scotland a subsequent marriage legitimates children antecedently born ; but this consequence has not yet been (as we have seen) finally adjudged in England to the extent of making such antenuptial children legitimate, so as to be entitled to inherit lands of their parents situate in England. ' Adhuc sub judice lis est.'[2] So, the indissolubility of marriage by the law of one country will not attach to it everywhere.[3]

337. *Qualifications of the Rule.* — And even in regard to common contracts of a different nature, the general rule as to the consequences of them must receive many qualifications and limitations resulting from the public policy or the domestic laws of other states where they are sought to be enforced, and the right and duty of self-protection against unjust foreign legislation.[4] If, for example, a country where a contract was made should, under the pretence of a general bankrupt act, authorize a discharge from all contracts made with foreigners, and should at the same time exclude the latter from all participation with domestic creditors in the assets, it cannot be presumed that such an act would be held a valid discharge in the countries to which such foreigners belonged.[5] And certainly the priorities and privileges annexed by the laws of particular states to certain classes of debts contracted therein are not generally admitted to have the same pre-eminence over debts contracted in another country which is called upon to enforce them.[6] Nor are the courts of any state under any obligation to give effect to a discharge of a foreign debtor, where, under its own laws, the creditor has previously acquired a right to proceed against his property within its own territory.[7] (a)

---

[1] See ante, s. 145-190; Fergusson on Marr. & Div. 359-361, 397-399, 402, 414; Conway *v.* Beazley, 3 Hagg. Ecc. 639.

[2] Birtwhistle *v.* Vardill, 5 B. & C. 438; 9 Bligh, 468; ante, s. 87, 93-93 *v.*; 1 Hertii Opera, de Collis. Leg. s. 4, 15, p. 129, ed. 1737; Id. p. 183, 184, ed. 1716.

[3] Ante, s. 215-230.   [4] Ante, s. 325-327, 334.

[5] Blanchard *v.* Russell, 13 Mass. 1, 6; Huberus, de Conflict. Leg. lib. 1. tit. 3, s. 11.

[6] See ante, s. 322-327; Huberus, de Conflict. Leg. lib. 1, tit. 3, s. 11.

[7] Tappan *v.* Poor, 15 Mass. 419; Le Chevalier *v.* Lynch, Doug. 170. But see Hunter *v.* Potts, 4 T. R. 182; s. p. 2 H. Bl. 402; ante, s. 325-327.

(a) Hall *v.* Winchell, 38 Vt. 590.

338. *Distinction between Discharge from the Debt, and Exemptions. — Some of the Remedies.* — When we speak of the discharge of a debt in the country where it is contracted being a discharge thereof everywhere, care must be taken to distinguish between cases where by the lex loci contractus there is a virtual or direct extinguishment of the debt itself, and where there is only a partial extinguishment of the remedy thereon. (*a*) By the bankrupt laws of England, and by the corresponding insolvent laws of some of the United States, an absolute discharge from all rights and remedies of the creditors is provided for, as part of the system ; and therefore the whole obligation of the contract is deemed, ipso facto, extinguished.[1] (*b*) But there are insolvent laws, and other special systems, both in Europe and America, which fall short of this extent and operation. In some cases the person only is liberated from future imprisonment and responsibility ; in others, particular portions of property only are exempted ; and in others again a mixed system, embracing some postponed or modified liabilities both of the person and property, prevails.[2]

339. *Exemption from Imprisonment.* — Now in all these cases where there is not any positive extinguishment, or any virtual extinguishment, of all rights and remedies of the creditors, the contract is not deemed to be extinguished ; and therefore it may be enforced, as we shall hereafter more fully see, in other countries.[3] (*c*) By the Roman law a cessio bonorum of the debtor was not a discharge of the debt, unless the property ceded was to the full sufficient for that purpose. It otherwise operated only as a discharge pro tanto, and exonerated the debtor from imprisonment. 'Qui bonis cesserint,' says the Code, ' nisi solidum

[1] See 2 Kent Com. 389–402; 3 Burge, Col. & For. Law, pt. 2, c. 22, p. 886–929.

[2] See 1 Domat, Civ. Law, b. 4, tit. 5, s. 1; Morris *v.* Eves, 11 Mart. (La.) 730. See Mather *v.* Bush, 16 Johns. (N. Y.) 233; 2 Bell Com. c. 5, s. 1162–1164, p. 563–567, 4th ed. ; Id. 580–997, 5th ed. ; Phillips *v.* Allan, 8 B. & C. 477 ; 2 Kent Com. 389–404; 2 Burge, Col. & For. Law, pt. 2, c. 22, p. 886–904.

[3] Post, s. 340–352.

(*a*) See Carver *v.* Adams, 38 Vt. 501.

(*b*) See Einer *v.* Beste, 32 Mo. 240; In re Coates, 3 Abb. App. Dec. (N. Y.) 231.

(*c*) Judd *v.* Porter, 7 Greenl. (Me.) 337; Boston Type Foundry *v.* Wallack, 8 Pick. (Mass.) 186; Coffin *v.* Coffin, 16 Pick. (Mass.) 323.

creditor reciperit, non sunt liberati.   In eo enim tantum'modo hoc
beneficium eis prodest, ne judicati detrahantur in carcerem.'[1]
Huberus informs us that in Holland a cessio bonorum does not
even exempt from imprisonment unless the creditors assent.
'Secundum jus nostrum cessio bonorum, invitis creditoribus,
debitorem a carcere publico non liberat;[2] and Heineccius pro-
claims the same as the law of some parts of Germany.[3] The
Scottish law conforms to the Roman Code in its leading out-
lines;[4] and the modern Code of France adopts the same system.[5]
An insolvent act, or bankrupt act, or cessio bonorum, which only
absolves the person of the debtor from imprisonment, but not his
future property, or which only suspends remedies against either
the one or the other for a limited period, is not to be deemed a
discharge from the contract, and its operation is, as we shall presently see, purely intra-territorial.[6]

[1] Cod. 7, 71, 1; 1 Domat, Civ. Law, b. 4, tit. 5, s. 1, n. 1, 2. See Mather
v. Bush, 16 Johns. (N. Y.) 233; 2 Bell Com. c. 5, s. 1162–1164, p. 563–567,
4th ed.; Id. p. 580–598, 5th ed.

[2] Huberus, tom. 3, lib. 42, tit. 3, s. 1, 3, note; Ex parte Burton, 1 Atk. 255;
M'Menomy v. Murray, 3 Johns. Ch. (N. Y.) 442; Voet, ad Pand. lib. 42, tit. 3,
s. 8; Le Roy v. Crowninshield, 2 Mason, 160.   Lord Mansfield is reported to
have said, in Ballantyne v. Golding, 1 Cooke, Bankrupt Laws, p. 347, 5th ed.,
p. 515, 4th ed.: 'That he remembered a case in chancery, of a cessio bonorum
in Holland, which is held a discharge in that country, and it had the same
effect here.' The case alluded to is most probably Ex parte Burton, 1 Atk. 255.
The law of Holland is the reverse of what his lordship is here supposed to
affirm, as the case in 1 Atk. 255, and the citations from Huberus and Voet,
establish.   Whether the error is in the reporter, or in Lord Mansfield himself,
may well be questioned.   Mr. Henry has given a sketch of the present law of
France, as to the cessio bonorum in cases of foreign contracts, which certainly
has some peculiarities, not conforming to the general principles of international law adopted in other nations.   Henry on Foreign Law, Appx. p. 250.
See Pardessus, art. 1324–1328.   The cessio bonorum of Scotland is, it seems,
a mere discharge of the person. See 2 Bell Com. c. 5, p. 563, &c., 4th ed.;
Id. p. 580, &c., 5th ed.; Phillips v. Allan, 8 B. & C. 479.

[3] Heinecc. Elem. Jur. Civ. ad Pand. 42, 3, s. 252, 254, p. 6; M'Menomy v. Murray, 3 Johns. Ch. (N. Y.) 441, 442.

[4] Erskine, Inst. b. 4, tit. 3, s. 26, 27; 2 Bell Com. c. 5, s. 1162–1164,
p. 563–567, 4th ed.; Id. p. 580, 5th ed.

[5] Code Civil of France, art. 1265–1270; Merlin, Répert. Cession de Biens.

[6] Tappan v. Poor, 15 Mass. 419; Morris v. Eves, 11 Mart. (La.) 730; Boston
Type Foundry v. Wallack, 8 Pick. (Mass.) 186; Judd v. Porter, 7 Greenl.
(Me.) 337; Hinckley v. Marean, 3 Mason, 88; Titus v. Hobart, 5 Mason,
378; 1 Kent Com. 420, 422; 2 Bell Com. s. 1162–1164, p. 562, 567,
594, 4th ed.; Id. p. 580–598, 5th ed.; Mason v. Haile, 12 Wheat. 370; 2
Kent Com. 394–401; Phillips v. Allan, 8 B. & C. 479; Ex parte Burton, 1

340. *Parties upon whom Discharge is binding.* — The general
form in which the doctrine is expressed, that a discharge of a
contract by the law of the place where it is made is a discharge
everywhere, seems to preclude any consideration of the question
between what parties it is made; whether between citizens, or
between a citizen and a foreigner, or between foreigners. The continental jurists recognize no distinction in the cases. The English decisions are understood to maintain the universality of the
doctrine, whatever may be the allegiance of the country of
the creditor.[1] And a like doctrine would seem generally to be
maintained in America.[2] (a) There are however some cases in
which a more limited doctrine would seem to be laid down; and
which appear to confine it to cases of a discharge from contracts
between citizens of the same state. Thus in one case it was
laid down by the Supreme Court of Massachusetts, that if, when
the contract was made, the promisee was not a citizen of the
state where it was made, he would not be bound by the laws of
such state in any other state; and therefore that a discharge there
would not bind him or his rights.[3] In another case, the same
learned court said that a discharge of the contract can only operate where the law is made by an authority common to the creditor and the debtor in all respects; where both are citizens and
subjects.[4] But this qualification of the doctrine (which was
only incidentally argued in those cases) was afterwards deliberately overruled by the same court; and the general doctrine was
established in its universality.[5] The qualification seems however
again to have been asserted in a more recent decision of the same
court; upon grounds not very clearly defined, or perhaps not

Atk. 255; Huberus, lib. 42, tit. 3, s. 5; Heineccii Elem. ad Pand. tom. 3, pt.
6, lib. 42, tit. 3, s. 253; 3 Burge, Col. & For. Law, pt. 2, c. 22, p. 924-929;
White v. Canfield, 7 Johns. (N. Y.) 117; James v. Allen, 1 Dall. 188; Quin
v. Keefe, 2 H. Bl. 553; Le Roy v. Crowninshield, 2 Mason, 160; Wright v.
Paton, 10 Johns. (N. Y.) 300; Peck v. Hozier, 14 Johns. (N. Y.) 346; Walsh
v. Nourse, 5 Binn. (Penn.) 381.
 [1] See Mason v. Haile, 12 Wheat. 370; Potter v. Brown, 5 East, 124.
 [2] See Robinson v. Bland, 1 W. Bl. 258; Blanchard v. Russell, 13 Mass. 1;
Smith v. Smith, 2 Johns. (N. Y.) 235; 2 Kent Com. 392, 393; Ory v. Winter,
4 Mart. N.S. (La.) 277; Sherrill v. Hopkins, 1 Cowen (N. Y.) 103, 107.
 [3] Baker v. Wheaton, 5 Mass. 511.   [4] Watson v. Bourne, 10 Mass. 337, 340.
 [5] Blanchard v. Russell, 13 Mass. 1, 10-12.

    (a) See Peck v. Hibbard, 26 Vt. 703, infra, s. 341, note.

entirely satisfactory, unless the case is to be governed by decisions of the Supreme Court of the United states upon the subject of discharges under insolvent laws, with reference to the
constitution of the United States.[1] It has been expressly denied

[1] Braynard v. Marshall, 8 Pick. (Mass. 194). The case was a negotiable
promissory note made by A., in New York, to B., or order; the note was afterwards indorsed to C. in Massachusetts, who sued A., the maker, there, and he
pleaded his discharge under the insolvent laws of New York. On that occasion, Mr. Chief Justice Parker, in delivering the opinion of the court, declaring the discharge no bar to the suit, said: ' The questions which arise out of
the subject of state insolvent laws, and the effect of discharges under them,
have been so long unsettled in this commonwealth, owing to the unsatisfactory
character of the decisions of the Supreme Court of the United States, which ought
to govern cases of this nature, that we have waited with anxiety for a revision
of all the cases by that high court, and a final adjudication upon a subject so
universally interesting and hitherto involved in so much perplexity. The case
of Ogden v. Saunders seemed in its progress to promise such a result, but un-
happily, on some of the points which the case presented, the law is left as
uncertain as it was before. One thing however we understand to have been
clearly decided by a majority of the justices of that court, and virtually by all
(as those who admit no validity at all to such laws may be considered as unit-
ing with those who give them only a limited operation), which is, that discharges under such laws have no effect without or beyond the territory of the
state where they are obtained, or against a party not a citizen of that state, or
where the suit shall be brought in a court of the United States, or of any state
other than that in which the proceedings took place, notwithstanding the contract on which the discharge was intended to operate was entered into and was
to be performed in the state in which the discharge was granted. Now this
law, thus settled, is binding upon this court as well on account of the nature
of the question, which is peculiarly proper for the decision of the highest court
of the nation, as because the case itself, unless restrained by the smallness of
the sum in controversy, may be carried to that court by a writ of error, and
our judgment be reversed; it being a question of which, by s. 25 of the judiciary act of the United States of Sept. 24, 1789, that court has jurisdiction.
But even if we were not inclined to repose on the decision in Ogden v. Saunders,
but considered ourselves at liberty to resort to general principles, we are disposed to think that the defence set up under the certificate in this case could
not prevail. It does not come within the case of Blanchard v. Russell, 13
Mass. 1, in which the contract was made in New York by a citizen of that
state, and was to be performed there, it not being transferable in its nature,
being matter of account. A negotiable instrument made in New York, and
indorsed for a valuable consideration to a citizen of Massachusetts before an
application for the benefit of the insolvent law, ought not to be discharged
under the process provided by that law. It is a debt payable anywhere by the
very nature of the contract, and it is a promise to whosoever shall be the holder
of the note. At the time of the defendant's application for a discharge, his
creditor upon this note was a Massachusetts man, and according to the case of
Baker v. Wheaton, 5 Mass. 509, the certificate would be no bar to the action.
The principle of this case was fully recognized and adopted in the case of

by other learned state courts.[1] (a)   In commenting upon some of
the cases in which, upon questions of discharge, considerable im-

Watson v. Bourne, 10 Mass. 337.   Nor is there anything in the case of Blanchard v. Russell to controvert these decisions, whatever may have been said,
arguendo, by the judge who delivered the opinion.   The contract in that case
was in its nature to be performed in New York, and so was to be governed entirely by the laws of that state.   The case before us is that of a negotiable
promissory note, given in the first place by a citizen of New York to a person
resident there, by whom it was immediately indorsed to a citizen of Massachusetts.   The promisor became, immediately upon the indorsement, the
debtor to the indorsee, who was not amenable to the laws of New York, where
the application was made for relief under the insolvent law.'   See Ogden v.
Saunders, 12 Wheat. 213, 358; post, s. 341, 343, 344.

   [1] Sherrill v. Hopkins, 1 Cowen (N. Y.) 103, 107.

   (a) See Ory v. Winter, 16 Mart. (La.) 277; Peck v. Hibbard, 26 Vt. 702; infra, s. 341.   And the doctrine of these cases is now settled law in Mas-sachusetts also.   May v. Breed, 7 Cush. (Mass.) 15; Marsh v. Putnam, 3 Gray (Mass.) 551.

   In Peck v. Hibbard, supra, Isham, J. said: 'We are satisfied, upon principle as well as authority, that, at common law, when a note is executed and pay-able in a foreign country, and a regu-lar discharge in bankruptcy has been obtained by the debtor resident there, the discharge will constitute a valid defence to the note, wherever the cre-ditor may be domiciled, or wherever the note may be prosecuted.   The cases in this country in which this subject has been considered to any great ex-tent have arisen under the insolvent laws of the different states.   Under those laws the question has arisen to what extent such discharges are valid against creditors who were citizens of other states, and who by no act of their own have waived their extra-territorial immunity, and submitted themselves or their claim to the laws of that state.   Since the cases of Sturges v. Crowninshield, 4 Wheat. 122; M'-Millan v. M'Niell, 4 Wheat. 209, and Ogden v. Saunders, 12 Wheat. 358, the rule has been generally adopted, that a discharge under the insolvent laws of a state where the contract was made will not be considered a valid discharge of a debt, if the creditor was a resident of another state.   Such laws are considered as impairing the obliga-tion of contracts, when they affect contracts made out of the state, or a citizen not a resident of the state where the discharge is granted.   Jus-tice Story, Conflict of Laws, s. 341, observes " that those cases have arisen under the peculiar structure of the Constitution of the United States, pro-hibiting the states from passing laws impairing the obligation of contracts."   But in relation to the doctrine of all those cases, he says it " is wholly in-applicable to contracts and discharges in foreign countries, which must therefore be decided upon general principles of international law."   This difference between the two cases is apparent; for the legality of those acts of the provincial parliament, and their universality, are not affected or limi-ted by that or any other provision of our constitution.   Their binding and universal obligation rests upon those principles of comity which convenience and commercial relations have intro-duced and established.   Upon those principles, we think the discharge granted in the country where the note was executed and payable is a valid defence in this suit.   We are satisfied

portance has been attached to the circumstance that one or both
of the parties were inhabitants of and domiciled in the state or
country where the contract was made, the supreme court of
New York have said: ' All these cases stand upon a principle
entirely independent of that circumstance. It is that of the lex
loci contractus, that the place where the contract is made must
govern the construction of the contract; and that, whether the
parties to the contract are inhabitants of that place or not. The
rule is not founded upon the allegiance due from citizens or subjects to their respective governments, but upon the presumption
of law that the parties to a contract are conusant of the laws of
the country where the contract is made.' [1]

341. *Effect of the Constitution on Discharges under State Laws.* —
Under the peculiar structure of the constitution of the United
States, prohibiting the states from passing laws impairing the
obligation of contracts, it has been decided that a discharge
under the insolvent laws of the state where the contract was
made will not operate as a discharge of the contract, unless it
was made between citizens of the same state. It cannot therefore discharge a contract made with a citizen of another state.[2] (*a*)

[1] Sherrill *v.* Hopkins, 1 Cowen (N. Y.) 103, 108.

[2] Ogden *v.* Saunders, 12 Wheat. 358–369; Boyle *v.* Zacharie, 6 Pet. 348;
2 Kent Com. 392, 393; 3 Story Const. s. 1834; 1 Kent Com. 418, 422; Hicks
v. Hotchkiss, 7 John. Ch. (N. Y.) 197; Van Hook *v.* Whitlock, 26 Wend.
(N. Y.) 43.

also that the result would be the same
if we were to apply to this case the
rule adopted in this country, in relation to discharges under state insolvent
laws. In the case of Braynard *v.* Marshall, 8 Pick. (Mass.) 194, the insolvent's
discharge was held inoperative on the
ground that the note was indorsed to
the plaintiff, a citizen of Massachusetts, before the defendant's application was made for his discharge under
the insolvent law of New York. The
plaintiff's right as a creditor in that
case was perfected before the application was made for the debtor's discharge. Parker, C.J., observed, "that
at the time of the defendant's application for a discharge his creditor was a
Massachusetts man, and according to
the case of Baker *v.* Wheaton, 5 Mass.

509, the certificate would be no bar
to the action." He further observed,
"that a note made in New York, and
indorsed to a citizen of Massachusetts,
before an application for the benefit
of the insolvent law, ought not to be
discharged under the process provided
by that law." It is apparent from the
language of the court that the discharge would have been operative, if
the indorsement had been made after
the debtor's application for his discharge under that law.'

(*a*) See Poe *v.* Duck, 5 Md. 1; Donnelly *v.* Corbett, 3 Seld. (N. Y.) 500;
Agnew *v.* Platt, 15 Pick. (Mass.) 417;
Savoye *v.* Marsh, 10 Met. (Mass.)
594; Producers' Bank *v.* Farnum, 5
Allen (Mass.) 10; Pierce *v.* O'Brien,
129 Mass. 314; Guernsey *v.* Wood,

But this doctrine is wholly inapplicable to contracts and discharges in foreign countries, which must therefore be decided upon the general principles of international law. (*a*)

342. *Contract not affected by Discharge.* — The converse doctrine is equally well established, viz., that a discharge of a contract by the law of a place where the contract was not made, or to be performed, will not be a discharge of it in any other country.[1] Thus it has been held in England that a discharge of contract, made there, under an insolvent act of the state of Maryland, is no bar to a suit upon the contract in the courts of England.[2] On that occasion Lord Kenyon said : ' It is impossible to say that a contract made in one country is to be governed by the laws of another. It might as well be contended that if the state of Maryland had enacted that no debts due from its own subjects to the subjects of England should be paid, the plaintiff would have been bound by it. This is the case of a contract lawfully made by a subject in this country, which he

---

[1] See 2 Bell Com. s. 1267, p. 691–695, 4th ed.; Id. p. 688–692, 5th ed.; Phillips *v.* Allan, 8 B. & C. 479; Lewis *v.* Owen, 4 B. & A. 654; 3 Burge, Col. & For. Law, pt. 2, c. 22, p. 924–929; Quelin *v.* Moisson, 1 Knapp, 265, note. Rose *v.* McLeod, 4 S. & D. 311, cited 3 Burge, ubi supra, p. 927, 928.

[2] Smith *v.* Buchanan, 1 East, 6, 11.

130 Mass. 503; Soule *v.* Chase, 39 N. Y. 342; Pratt *v.* Chase, 44 N. Y. 597; Baldwin *v.* Hale, 1 Wall. 223; Felch *v.* Bugbee, 48 Me. 9; Dunlap *v.* Rogers, 47 N. H. 281; Gilman *v.* Lockwood, 4 Wall. 409.

A distinction in the case of a contract made with a citizen of another state, but to be performed in the state of the former, was laid down in Scribner *v.* Fisher, 2 Gray (Mass.) 43, the court (Metcalf, J., dissenting) holding a discharge in the latter state a bar against the foreign creditor. But this case and others similar have been overruled. Baldwin *v.* Hale, 1 Wall. 223; Stoddard *v.* Harrington, 100 Mass. 88; Kelley *v.* Drury, 9 Allen (Mass.) 28; Pratt *v.* Chase, 44 N. Y. 597; Newmarket Bank *v.* Butler, 45 N. H. 236 (overruling previous cases); Gilman *v.* Lockwood, 4 Wall. 409; Felch *v.* Bugbee, 48 Me. 9; Chase *v.* Flagg, Ib. 182. See post, s. 383, note.

In Stoddard *v.* Harrington, *supra*, it was decided that if a contract is made between citizens of the same state within the state, and one of them afterwards removes and becomes a citizen of another state, and the other then obtains a discharge in insolvency in the state of the contract, under a law of the state existing when the contract was made, the discharge will bind the non-resident; following Brigham *r.* Henderson, 1 Cush. (Mass.) 430; Converse *v.* Bradley, Ib. 434, note. See Brown *v.* Bridge, 106 Mass. 563, 566; May *v.* Wannamacher, 111 Mass. 202.

Of course if a citizen of another state be made a party by service of process within the state of the former or intervene in the cause, he will be bound by the judgment. Gilman *v.* Lockwood, *supra*.

(*a*) See Peck *v.* Hibbard, 26 Vt. 703, *supra*.

resorts to a court of justice to enforce; and the only answer given is that a law has been made in a foreign country to discharge these defendants from their debts on condition of their having relinquished all their property to their creditors. But how is that an answer to a subject of this country, suing on a lawful contract made here? How can it be pretended that he is bound by a condition to which he has given no assent either express or implied?'[1] In America the same doctrine has obtained the fullest sanction.[2] It is also clearly established in Scotland.[3]

843. *Operation of Discharge as to Negotiable Securities.* — The subject of negotiable paper is generally governed by the same principles. Wherever the contract between the particular parties is made, the law of the place will operate, as well in respect to the discharge as to the obligation thereof. A nice question however has recently arisen on this subject, in a case already mentioned.[4] A negotiable note was made at New York between persons resident there, and was payable generally; and the payee subsequently indorsed the note to a citizen of Massachusetts, by whom a suit was brought in the state court of the latter state against the maker.[5] One point of argument was, whether a discharge of the maker, under the insolvent laws of New York, operated as a bar to the suit? The case was decided upon another ground. But the court expressed a clear opinion that it did not, and said: 'It is a debt payable anywhere by the very nature of the contract; and it is a promise to whoever shall be the holder of the note.' 'The promisor became, immediately upon the indorsement, the debtor to the indorsee, who was not amenable to the laws of New York, where the discharge was obtained.'[6] (a)

---

[1] Smith *v.* Buchanan, 1 East, 6, 11; Lewis *v.* Owen, 4 B. & A. 654; Phillips *v.* Allan, 8 B. & C. 477.

[2] Van Raugh *v.* Van Arsdaln, 3 Caines (N. Y.) 154; Frey *v.* Kirk, 4 Gill & J. (Md.) 509; Green *v.* Sarmiento, Pet. C. C. 74; Le Roy *v.* Crowninshield, 2 Mason, 151; Smith *v.* Smith, 2 Johns. (N. Y.) 235; Ellicott *v.* Early, 3 Gill (Md.) 439; Bradford *v.* Farrand, 13 Mass. 18; 2 Kent Com. 392, 393, 458, 459; 2 Bell Com. s. 1267, p. 692, 693, 4th ed.; Id. p. 688-692, 5th ed.; 3 Burge, Col. & For. Law, pt. 2, c. 22, p. 924-929; Rose *v.* McLeod, 4 S. & D. 311, cited in 3 Burge, 928, 929.

[3] 2 Bell Com. s. 1267, p. 692, 693, 4th ed.; Id. p. 688-692, 5th ed.

[4] See Aymer *v.* Sheldon, 12 Wend. (N. Y.) 439. [5] Ante, s. 317, 340.

[6] Braynard *v.* Marshall, 8 Pick. (Mass.) 194. See Ogden *v.* Saunders, 12 Wheat. 358, 362-364.

(a) See Newmarket Bank *v.* Butler, 45 N. H. 236 (overruling Brown *v.*

344. It is difficult, as has been already intimated, to perceive the ground upon which this doctrine can be maintained as a doctrine of public law.[1] The court admit that a debt contracted in New York, and not negotiable, would be extinguished by such a discharge; although such a debt is by its very nature payable everywhere, as debts have no locality. As between the original parties (the maker and the payee,) the same result would follow. How then can the indorsement vary it? It does not create a new contract between the maker and the indorsee in the place of the indorsement. The rights of the indorsee spring from and under the original contract, and are a component part of it. The original contract promises to pay the indorsee as much as the payee, and from the first of its existence. The indorsement is but a substitution of the indorsee for the payee; and it transfers over the old liability, and creates no new liability of the maker.[2] If the indorsement created a new contract in the place where it was made, between the maker and the indorsee, then the validity, obligation, and interpretation of the contract would be governed by the law of the place of the indorsement, and not by that of the place where the note was originally made. It would not then amount to a transfer of the old contract, but to the creation of a new one, which from a conflict of laws, not unusual in different states, would or might involve obligations and duties wholly different from, and even incompatible with, the original contract. Nay, the maker might, upon the same instrument, incur the most opposite responsibilities to different holders, according to the law of the different places where the indorsement might be made.[3]

345. Such a doctrine has never been propounded in any common-law authority, nor ever been supported by the opinion of any foreign jurist. The same principle would apply to general negotiable acceptances as to negotiable notes; for the maker stands in the same predicament as the acceptor. Yet no one ever supposed that an indorsement after an acceptance ever varied the rights or obligations of the acceptor. It is as to all

---

[1] Ante, s. 340.   [2] Pothier, de Change, art. 22; ante, s. 317.
[3] Ante, s. 314, 316, 317.

Collins, 41 N. H. 405, and Smith v. Brown, 43 N. H. 44); Felch v. Bugbee, 48 Me. 9; Chase v. Flagg, Id. 182; Vanzant v. Arnold, 31 Ga. 210; Northern Bank v. Squires, 8 La. An. 318; ante, s. 317.

persons who become holders, in whatever country, treated as a
contract made by the acceptor in the country where such acceptance is made.[1] Yet the acceptance being general, payment may
be required in any place where the holder shall demand it. The
other point, that the indorsement was to a citizen of another
state, is equally inadmissible. The question is not whether he
is bound by the laws of New York generally; but whether he
can, in opposition to them, avail himself of a contract made under the sovereignty of that state, and vary its validity, obligation, interpretation, and negotiability, as governed by those laws.
If the payee had been a citizen of Massachusetts, and the note
had been made by the maker in New York, there could be no
doubt that the contract would still be governed by the laws of
New York in regard to the payee. What difference then can it
make, that the indorsee is a citizen of another state, if he cannot
show that his contract has its origin there? In short, the doctrine of this case is wholly repugnant to that maintained by the
same court in another case, which was most maturely considered,
and in which the argument in its favor was repelled. The court
there declared their opinion to be that full effect ought to be
given to such discharges, as to all contracts made within the
state where they are authorized, although the creditor should be
a citizen of another state.[2]

346. The Supreme Court of Louisiana have adopted the same
reasoning, and held that where a negotiable promissory note was
made in one state, and was indorsed in another state to a citizen
of the latter, the contract was governed by the law of the place
where the note was made, and not by that of the place where
the indorsement was made. 'We see nothing,' said the court, 'in
the circumstance of the rights of one of the parties being transferred to the citizens of another state, which can take the case
out of the general principle. It is a demand made under an
agreement, (a note) entered into in a foreign state; and consequently the party claiming rights under it must take it with all
the limitations to which it was subject in the place where it was
made; and that although he be one of our citizens.'[3] This is cer-

[1] Ante, s. 314, 317.
[2] Blanchard v. Russell, 13 Mass. 1, 11, 12. See also Prentiss v. Savage,
13 Mass. 20, 23, 24; ante, s. 317, 340.
[3] Ory v. Winter, 4 Mart. N.S. (La.) 277; Sherrill v. Hopkins, 1 Cowen
(N. Y.) 103; ante, s. 317, 340.

tainly in conformity to what is deemed settled doctrine in England as well as in some other states in America.[1] It was taken for granted by the Supreme Court of the United States to be the true doctrine in the case of a negotiable bill of exchange, in which the drawer's responsibility was supposed to be governed by the law of the place where the bill was drawn, notwithstanding an indorsement in another country;[2] and also by the Court of King's Bench in England, in a case in which a right to a Bank of England note was supposed to be governed by the law of England, notwithstanding a transfer of the same had been subsequently made in France.[3] (a)

347. *Pardessus.* — Pardessus has laid down a doctrine equally broad. He says that it is by the law of the place where a bill of exchange is payable that we are to ascertain when it falls due, the days of grace belonging to it, the character of these delays, whether for the benefit of the holder or of the debtor; in one word, everything which relates to the right of requiring payment of a debt, or the performance of any other engagement, when the parties have not made any stipulation to the contrary.[4] (b) And it is of little consequence whether the person who demands payment is the creditor who made the contract, or an assignee of his right, such as the holder of a bill of exchange by indorsement. This circumstance makes no change in regard to the debtor. The indorsee cannot require payment in any other manner than the original creditor could.[5] And he applies this doctrine to the case of successive indorsements of bills of exchange, made in different countries, stating that the rights of each holder are the same as those of the original payee against the acceptor.[6]

---

[1] See Blanchard *v.* Russell, 13 Mass. 12; Ogden *v.* Saunders, 12 Wheat. 360; Potter *v.* Brown, 5 East, 123, 130.

[2] Slacum *v.* Pomeroy, 6 Cranch, 221.

[3] De la Chaumette *v.* Bank of England, 9 B. & C. 208; 2 B. & Ad. 385; post, s. 353. See also 2 Bell Com. s. 1267, p. 692, 693, 4th ed.; Id. p. 688–692, 5th ed. 'Quid si de literis cambii incidat quæstio,' says Paul Voet, 'quis locus spectandus? Is locus, ad quem sunt destinatæ et ibidem acceptatæ.' P. Voet, de Stat, s. 9, c. 2, s. 14, p. 271, ed. 1715; Id. p. 327, ed. 1661; ante, s. 317.

[4] Pardessus, Droit Com. art. 1495, 1498–1500: ante, s. 316; post, s. 361.

[5] Ibid.   [6] Ibid.

(a) See ante, s. 314, note.   dale, 36 Mo. 563; Todd *v.* Neal, 49
(b) See Commercial Bank *v.* Barks- Ala. 266.

He adds also that the effects of an acceptance are to be determined by the law of the place where it has been made;[1] that every indorsement subjects the indorser to the law of the place where it has been made; and that it governs his responsibility accordingly.[2] (a)

348. *Discharges not Operative out of the State.* — Notwithstanding the principle that a discharge by the lex loci contractus is valid everywhere, and vice versa, is generally admitted as a part of private international law, yet it cannot be denied that any nation may by its own peculiar jurisprudence refuse to recognize it, and may act within its own tribunals upon an opposite doctrine.[3] But then, under such circumstances, its acts and decisions will be deemed of no force or validity beyond its own territorial limits. Thus if a state should by its own laws provide that a discharge of an insolvent debtor under its own laws should be a discharge of all the contracts, even of those made in a foreign country, its own courts would be bound by such provisions.[4] (b) But they would or might be held mere nullities in every other country.[5] (c)

349. *Laws manifestly Unjust.* — And even in relation to a discharge according to the laws of the place where the contract is made, there are (as we have seen) some necessary limitations and exceptions ingrafted upon the general doctrine, which every country will enforce, whenever those laws are manifestly unjust, or are injurious to the fair rights of its own citizens.[6] It has been said by a learned judge with great force: ' As the laws of foreign countries are not admitted ex proprio vigore, but merely ex comitate, the judicial power will exercise a discretion with

---

[1] Ibid. See Rothschild v. Currie, 1 Q. B. 43; ante, s. 314, 316; post, s. 361.

[2] Pardessus, Droit Com. art. 1499.

[3] Ante, s. 334; post, s. 349-351.

[4] See Penniman v. Meigs, 9 Johns. (N. Y.) 325; Babcock v. Weston, 1 Gallison, 168; Murray v. De Rottenham, 6 Johns. Ch. (N. Y.) 52; Holmes v. Remsen, 4 Johns. Ch. (N. Y.) 471.

[5] See Blanchard v. Russell, 13 Mass. 6; post, s. 349; Van Raugh v. Van Arsdaln, 3 Caines (N. Y.) 154; Smith v. Buchanan, 1 East, 6; Smith v. Smith, 2 Johns. (N. Y.) 235; Green v. Sarmiento, Pet. C. C. 74; McMenomy v. Murray, 3 Johns. Ch. (N. Y.) 435; Wolff v. Oxholm, 6 M. & S. 92; ante, s. 338.

[6] Ante, s. 339; post, s. 350, 351.

(a) See ante, s. 314, note.

(b) See Soule v. Chase, 39 N.Y. 342. 208.

(c) See Very v. McHenry, 29 Me.

respect to the laws which they may be called upon to sanction; for if they should be manifestly unjust, or calculated to injure their own citizens, they ought to be rejected. Thus if any state should enact that its citizens should be discharged from all debts due to creditors living without the state, such a provision would be so contrary to the common principles of justice, that the most liberal spirit of comity would not require its adoption in any other state. So if a state, under the pretence of establishing a general bankrupt law, should authorize such proceedings as would deprive all creditors living out of the state of an opportunity to share in the distribution of the effects of the debtor, such a law would have no effect beyond the territory of the state in which it was passed.'[1]

350. The same reasoning was again asserted by the same learned judge in another case, calling for an exposition of the limitations of the doctrine. 'This rule,' said he, 'must however from its very nature, be qualified and restrained; for it cannot be admitted as a principle of law or justice, that when a valid personal contract is made, which follows the person of the creditor and may be enforced in any foreign jurisdiction, a mode of discharge, manifestly partial or unjust, and tending to deprive a foreign creditor of his debt, while he is excluded from a participation with the domestic creditors in the effects of the debtor, should have force in any country, to the prejudice of their own citizens. The comity of nations does not require it, and the fair principles of a contract would be violated by it.'[2]

351. 'Thus if a citizen of this state, being in a foreign country, should, for a valuable consideration, receive a promise to pay money, or to perform any other valuable engagement, from a subject of that country; and the law should provide for a discharge from all debts upon a surrender of his effects, without any notice which could by possibility reach creditors out of the country where such a law should exist; we apprehend that the contract ought to be enforced here, notwithstanding a discharge obtained under such law. For although the creditor is to be presumed to know the laws of the place where he obtains his contract, yet that presumption is founded upon another, which is, that those laws are not palpably partial and unjust, and calculated to protect the creditors at home at the expense of those who are abroad. Such

[1] Mr. Chief Justice Parker, in Blanchard v. Russell, 13 Mass. 6.
[2] Mr. Chief Justice Parker, in Blanchard v. Russell, 13 Mass. 6.

laws would come within the well-known exception to the rules of
comity, viz., that the laws which are to be admitted in the tribunals of a country where they are not made, are not to be injurious to the state, or the citizens of the state, where they are so
received.[1](a)

351 a. *Discharges not governed by Lex Loci Contractus.* — But
although the general rule, that a contract, as to its dissolution
and discharge, is to be governed by the law of the place where it
is made, is thus, with few exceptions and limitations, admitted
to be well established; yet we are not to understand that it
thence follows, as a necessary consequence, that in no cases
whatever can a contract be discharged or dissolved, except in
the mode, and by the process and formalities, prescribed by the
same law: or, in other words, that it must be discharged and
dissolved eo ligamine quo ligatur, or rather by reversing the
operation which knit it under the local law.[2] On the contrary,
there are, or may be, circumstances under which an opposite rule
may be maintainable; and the law of another country, prescribing different modes of proceeding, or different formalities, or
different acts, which shall establish a dissolution thereof, may also
well prevail to annul or discharge the contract. A change of
domicil of the parties to the latter country, or an act done in that
country, which would there operate to dissolve or discharge the
contract, may well produce the fullest effect, although the same
act might not be recognized by the law of the place of the origin
of the contract. Thus, for example, as we well know, the obligation of a bond, or other sealed instrument, after a breach of the
contract created thereby, cannot in England be discharged, or
released, except by a sealed instrument, or a release under seal,
according to the known maxim of the common law: Eodem
modo, quo quid constituitur, eodem modo dissolvitur. And yet
by the law of most, if not of all, of the continental countries
whose jurisprudence is founded on the Roman law, a simple
receipt or discharge, not under seal, would, if executed in such
countries, be held to discharge the bond or other sealed instru-

[1] Mr. Chief Justice Parker, in Prentiss *v.* Savage, 13 Mass. 23, 24. See
also Fergusson on Marr. & Div. 396, 397; Wolff *v.* Oxholm, 6 M. & S. 92;
ante, s. 244.

[2] See Warrender *v.* Warrender, 9 Bligh, 124, 125; ante, s. 226 c, note.

(a) See Very *v.* McHenry, 29 Me. 208.

ment. Let us then suppose a bond executed in England for the
payment of money, and when it became due there should be a
default in payment, and afterwards the creditor should receive
payment of the debtor in France, or otherwise should discharge
him by a written unsealed instrument in France; such a discharge would in France be held valid and conclusive, if good by
the law of France, notwithstanding it might be held invalid in
an English court of common law. In short, any act done, after
such an obligation was created, in a foreign country, by whose
laws the act would operate as a dissolution thereof, would be
treated, in that country at least, as a complete extinguishment
thereof.

351 *b. Principles applicable to such Discharge.* — It is not easy
therefore upon principle to say why such an extinguishment of a
contract, according to the lex loci, ought not everywhere else to
have the same operation, even in the country of the origin of the
contract. For, if the contract derives its whole original obligatory force from the law of the place where it is made, it is but
following out the same principle to hold that any act subsequently done, touching the same contract by the parties, should
have the same obligatory force and operation upon it, which the
law of the place where it is done attributes to it. And in this
respect there certainly is, or at least may be, a clear distinction
between acts done by the parties in a foreign country, and which
derive their operation from their voluntary consent and intention,
and acts in invitum, deriving their whole authority and effect
from the operation of the local law, independent of any such
consent.[1]

351 *c. Lord Brougham's Remarks on the Subject.* — Indeed the
reasonable interpretation of the general rule would seem to be,
that while contracts made in one country are properly held to be
dissoluble and extinguishable according to the laws of that country, as natural incidents to the original concoction of such contracts, they are and may at the same time also be equally
dissoluble and extinguishable by any other acts done or contracts
made subsequently in another country by the parties, which acts
or contracts, according to the law of the latter country, are sufficient to work such a dissolution or extinguishment. It is to this
double posture of a case that Lord Brougham referred in one of

[1] Post, s. 411.

his judgments. 'If a contract,' said he, 'for sale of a chattel is made, or an obligation of debt is incurred, or a chattel is pledged in one country, the sale may be annulled, the debt released, and the pledge redeemed, by the law and by the forms of another country in which the parties happen to reside, and in whose courts their rights and obligations come in question, unless there was an express stipulation in the contract itself against such avoidance, release, or redemption. But, at any rate, this is certain, that if the laws of one country and its courts recognize and give effect to those of another in respect of the constitution of any contract, they must give the like recognition and effect to those same foreign laws when they declare the same kind of contract dissolved. Suppose a party forbidden to purchase from another by our equity, as administered in the courts of this country (and we have some restraints upon certain parties which come very near prohibition), and suppose a sale of chattels by one to another party standing in this relation towards each other should be effected in Scotland, and that our courts here should (whether right or wrong) recognize such a rule because the Scotch law would affirm it; surely it would follow that our courts must equally recognize a rescission of the contract of sale in Scotland by any act which the Scotch law regards as valid to rescind it, although our own law may not regard it as sufficient. Suppose a question to arise in the courts of England respecting the execution of a contract thus made in this country, and that the objection of its invalidity were waived for some reason; if the party resisting its execution were to produce either a sentence of a Scotch court declaring it rescinded by a Scotch matter done in pais, or were merely to produce evidence of the thing so done, and proof of its amounting by the Scotch law to a rescission of the contract; I apprehend that the party relying on the contract could never be heard to say: "The contract is English, and the Scotch proceeding is impotent to dissolve it." The reply would be, "Our English courts have (whether right or wrong) recognized the validity of a Scotch proceeding to complete the obligation, and can no longer deny the validity of a similar but reverse proceeding to dissolve it, — unumquodque dissolvitur eodem modo, quo colligatur." Suppose, for another example (which is the case), that the law of this country precluded an infant or a married woman from borrowing money in any way, or from binding themselves

32

by deed ; and that in another country those obligations could be validly incurred ; it is probable that our law and our courts would recognize the validity of such foreign obligations. But suppose a feme covert had executed a power, and conveyed an interest under it to another feme covert in England ; could it be endured that where the donee of the power produced a release under seal from the feme covert in the same foreign country, a distinction should be taken, and the court here should hold that party incapable of releasing the obligation ? Would it not be said that our courts, having decided the contract of a feme covert to be binding, when executed abroad, must, by parity of reason, hold the discharge or release of the feme covert to be valid, if it be valid in the same foreign country ?'[1]

351 d. *Application of the Principle to Immovables.* — Nor does there seem to be in this respect any acknowledged distinction between contracts which are purely personal, and contracts which impose or may impose any charge on real estate ; for although in respect to immovable property the law of the situs should be admitted (as certainly is the case at the common law) to regulate all the rights to immovable property, yet it does not thence follow that an act which would operate as a dissolution or extinguishment of the contract creating such charge, according to the law of a foreign country where it is subsequently done, may not incidentally and indirectly work such a dissolution or extinguishment thereof, although it does not conform to the lex rei sitæ. Lord Brougham on the same occasion, referring to this topic, said: 'All personal obligations may in their consequences affect real rights in England. Nor does a Scotch divorce, by depriving a widow of dower or arrears of pin-money charged on English property, more immediately affect real estate here, than a bond or a judgment released in Scotland according to Scotch forms discharges real estate of a lien, or than a bond executed, or indeed a simple contract debt incurred, in Scotland, eventually and consequently charges English real estate.'[2]

352. *Principles applicable to Negotiable Instruments.* — Before we quit this head of contracts, it may be well to bring together some principles applicable to negotiable instruments, which have not been brought as distinctly under review in the preceding dis-

[1] Warrender v. Warrender, 9 Bligh, 125–127 ; ante s. 226 c, note.
[2] Warrender v. Warrender, 9 Bligh, 127; ante, s. 226 c, note.

cussions as they deserve to be, and which afford important illustrations of the operation of foreign law upon contracts and their
incidents. The subject of the assignments of debts and other
choses in action not negotiable by the general law merchant or
the laws of particular countries, will more properly find a place
in our subsequent inquiries.[1]

353. Questions have arisen whether negotiable notes and bills
made in one country are transferable in other countries, so as to
found a right of action in the holder against the other parties.
Thus a question occurred in England in a case where a negotiable note made in Scotland, and there negotiable, was indorsed,
and a suit brought in England by the indorsee against the maker,
whether the action was maintainable. It was contended that
the note, being a foreign note, was not within the statute of
Anne (3 & 4 Anne, c. 9), which made promissory notes payable to
order assignable and negotiable ; for that statute applied only to
inland promissory notes. But the court overruled the objection,
and held the note suable in England by the indorsee, as the statute embraced foreign as well as domestic notes.[2] In another
case, a promissory note made in England and payable to the
bearer was transferred in France ; and the question was made
whether the French holder could maintain an action thereon in
England, such notes not being by the law of France negotiable ;
and it was held that he might.[3] But in each of these cases the
decision was expressly put upon the provisions of the statute of
Anne respecting promissory notes, leaving wholly untouched the
general doctrine of international law.

353 a. In a more recent case, which has been already cited,[4] a
negotiable note was made in France and indorsed in France, and
afterwards a suit was brought thereon by the indorsee against the
maker in England. One question in the case was, whether a
blank indorsement in France was by the law of France sufficient

[1] Post, s. 355, 395–400, 566; 3 Burge, Col. & For. Law, pt. 2, c. 20,
p. 777, 778.
[2] Milne v. Graham, 2 B. & C. 192. It does not distinctly appear upon the
report, whether the indorsement was made in Scotland or in England. But it
was probably in England. But see Carr v. Shaw, Bayley on Bills, p. 16, note,
5th ed. ; Id. p. 22, Amer. ed., by Phillips & Sewall, 1836.
[3] De la Chaumette v. Bank of England, 2 B. & Ad. 385; 9 B. & C. 208; and
see Chitty on Bills, p. 551, 552, 8th ed. ; ante, s. 346.
[4] Ante, s. 316 a.

to transfer the property in the note without any other formalities. It was held that it was not sufficient. But it seems to have been taken for granted that if the note was well negotiated by the indorsement, a suit might be maintained thereon in England by the indorsee in his own name. On that occasion the court said: ' The rule which applies to the case of contracts made in one country, and put in suit in the courts of law of another country, appears to be this: that the interpretation of the contract must be governed by the law of the country where the contract was made (lex loci contractus); the mode of suing, and the time within which the action must be brought, must be governed by the law of the country where the action is brought (in ordinandis judiciis, loci consuetudo, ubi agitur). This distinction has been clearly laid down and adopted in the late case of De la Vega v. Vianna. See also the case of the British Linen Company v. Drummond, where the different authorities are brought together. The question therefore is, whether the law of France, by which the indorsement in blank does not operate as a transfer of the note, is a rule which governs and regulates the interpretation of the contract, or only relates to the mode of instituting and conducting the suit: for in the former case it must be adopted by our courts; in the latter it may be altogether disregarded, and the suit commenced in the name of the present plaintiff. And we think the French law on the point above mentioned is the law by which the contract is governed, and not the law which regulates the mode of suing. If the indorsement has not operated as a transfer, that goes directly to the point that there is no contract upon which the plaintiff can sue. Indeed, the difference in the consequences that would follow if the plaintiff sues in his own name, or is compelled to use the name of the former indorser, as the plaintiff by procuration, would be very great in many respects, particularly in its bearing on the law of set-off; and with reference to those consequences, we think the law of France falls in with the distinction above laid down, that it is a law which governs the contract itself, not merely the mode of suing. We therefore think that our courts of law must take notice that the plaintiff could have no right to sue in his own name upon the contract in the courts of the country where such contract was made; and that such being the case there, we must hold in our courts that he can have no right of suing here.' [1]

---

[1] Trimbey v. Vignier, 1 Bing. N. C. 151, 159, 160; post, s. 565, 566.

354. Several other cases may be put upon this subject. In the first place suppose a note, negotiable by the law of the place where it is made, is there transferred by indorsement; can the indorsee maintain an action in his own name against the maker in a foreign country (where both are found) in which there is no positive law on the subject of negotiable notes applicable to the case? If he can, it must be upon the ground that the foreign tribunal would recognize the validity of transfer by the indorsement according to the law of the place where it is made. According to the doctrine maintained in England, as choses in action are by the common law (independent of statute) incapable of being transferred over, it might be argued that he could not maintain an action, notwithstanding the instrument was well negotiated, and transferred by the law of the place of the contract.[1] So far as this principle of non-assignability of choses in action would affect transfers in England, it would seem reasonable to follow it. But the difficulty is in applying it to transfers made in a foreign country, by whose laws the instrument is negotiable and capable of being transferred, so as to vest the property and right in the assignee. In such a case it would seem that the more correct rule would be, that the lex loci contractus ought to govern; because the holder under the indorsement has an immediate and absolute right in the contract vested in him, as much as he would have in goods transferred to him. Under such circumstances, to deny the legal effect of the indorsement is to construe the obligation, force, and effect of a contract, made in one place, by the law of another place. The indorsement in the place where it is made creates a direct contract between the maker and the first indorsee; and, if so. that contract ought to be enforced between them everywhere. It is not a question as to the form of the remedy, but as to the right.[2] (a)

355. *Assignee of Irish Judgment.* — The same view of the doctrine seems to have been taken in another case in England, much stronger in its circumstances than the case of a foreign negotiable note, which may be thought to stand in some measure upon the

---

[1] See 2 Black. Com. 442; Jeffrey v. McTaggart, 6 M. & S. 126; Inne v. Dunlop, 8 T. R. 595; post, s. 565. 566.

[2] See Trimbey v. Vignier, 1 Bing. N. C. 159–161; ante, s. 353 a, where the same reasoning seems to have applied; post, s. 565, 566.

(a) See Levy v. Levy, 78 Penn. St. 507.

custom of merchants. A suit was brought by the assignee of an Irish judgment against the judgment debtor in England, the judgment being made expressly assignable by Irish statutes; and the objection was taken that no action could be maintained by the assignee, because it would contravene the general principle of the English law, that choses in action were not assignable. But the court intimated a strong opinion against this ground of argument; and the cause finally was disposed of upon another point, but in such a manner as left the opinion in full force.[1] It is matter of surprise that in some of the more recent discussions in England upon the negotiations of notes in foreign countries, this doctrine has not been distinctly insisted on. For, even in England, negotiable notes are not treated as mere choses in action; but they are deemed to have a closer resemblance to personal chattels on account of their transferability; so that the legal property in them passes upon the transfer, as it does in the case of chattels.[2] If so, no one could doubt that a title of transfer of personal property, in a foreign country, good by the laws of the country where it is made, ought to be held equally good everywhere.[3]

356. *Transfer where Transfer is not allowed.* — In the next place let us suppose the case of a negotiable note, made in a country by whose laws it is negotiable, is actually indorsed in another by whose laws a transfer of notes by indorsement is not allowed. Could an action be maintained by the indorsee against the maker, in the courts of either country? If it could be maintained in the country whose laws do not allow such a transfer, it must be upon the ground that the original negotiability by the lex loci contractus is permitted to avail in contradiction to the lex fori. On the other hand, if the suit should be brought in the country where the note was originally made, the same objection might arise, that the transfer was not allowed by the law of the place where the indorsement took place. But at the same time it may be truly said that the transfer is entirely in conformity to the intent of the parties, and to the law of the original contract.[4]

[1] O'Callaghan v. Thomond, 3 Taunt. 82; post, s. 565, 566.
[2] McNeilage v. Holloway, 1 B. & A. 218.   [3] Ante, s. 353 a.
[4] See Chitty on Bills, c. 6, p. 218, 219, 8th ed. See Kames Eq. b. 3, c. 8, s. 4; ante, s. 353, 354. In the cases of Milne v. Graham, 1 B. & C. 192; De la Chaumette v. Bank of England, 2 B. & Ad. 385, and Trimbey v. Vignier, 1 Bing. N. C. 151, the promissory notes were negotiable in both countries, as well where the note was made, as where it was transferred.

357. *Transfer of Note not Negotiable by the Lex Loci Contractus.*
— In the next place let us suppose the case of a note, not negotiable by the law of the place where it is made, but negotiable
by the law of the place where it is indorsed ; could an action be
maintained, in either country, by the indorsee against the maker?
It would seem that in the country where the note was made, it
could not ; because it would be inconsistent with its own laws.
But the same difficulty would not arise in the country where the
indorsement was made ; and therefore if the maker used terms of
negotiability in his contract, capable of binding him to the indorsee, there would not seem to be any solid objection to giving the
contract its full effect there.   And so it has been accordingly
adjudged in the case of a note made in Connecticut, payable to
A. or order, but by the laws of that state not negotiable there,
and indorsed in New York, where it was negotiable.   In a suit
in New York by the indorsee against the maker, the exception
was taken and overruled.   The court on that occasion said,
' That personal contracts, just in themselves and lawful in the
place where they are made, are to be fully enforced, according
to the law of the place and the intent of the parties, is a principle which ought to be universally received and supported.   But
this admission of the lex loci contractus can have reference only
to the nature and construction of the contract, and its legal
effect, and not to the mode of enforcing it.'   And the court ultimately put the case expressly upon the ground that the note
was payable to the payee or order ; and therefore the remedy
might well be pursued according to the law of New York
against a party who had contracted to pay to the indorsee.[1] (a)
But if the words ' or order' had been omitted in the note, so
that it had not appeared that the contract between the parties
originally contemplated negotiability as annexed to it, a different question might have arisen, which would more properly come
under discussion in another place ; since it seems to concern the
interpretation and obligation of contracts, although it has sometimes been treated as belonging to remedies.[2]

[1] Lodge *v.* Phelps, 1 Johns. Cas. (N. Y.) 139; 2 Caines Cas. (N. Y.) 321.
See Kames Eq. b. 8, c. 8, s. 4.
[2] See Chitty on Bills, c. 6. p. 218, 219, 8th ed.; 3 Kent Com. 77; ante,
s. 253 *a.*

(a) See also Warren *v.* Copelin, 4 Met. 594; Foss *v.* Nutting, 14 Gray, 484.

358. *Transfer by Foreign Executor.* — Another case may be
put, which has actually passed into judgment. A negotiable
note was given by a debtor, resident in Maine, to his creditor,
resident in Massachusetts. After the death of the creditor, his
executrix, appointed in Massachusetts, indorsed the same note
in that state to an indorsee, who brought a suit, as indorsee,
against the maker in the state court of Maine. The question
was, whether the note was, under the circumstances, suable by
the indorsee; and the court held that it was not; for the court
said that the executrix could not herself have sued upon the
note without taking out letters of administration in Maine; and
therefore she could not, by her indorsement, transfer the right
to her indorsee.[1] (a)

359. It does not appear by the report, (b) whether the note
was made in Massachusetts or in Maine. It is not perhaps in
the particular case material, as according to the law of both
states the note was negotiable by indorsement, whether made in
the one or in the other state. If it had been different, it might
have given rise to a different inquiry. But in either state, the
creditor might certainly in his lifetime, by his indorsement, have
transferred the property in the note to the indorsee; and as
clearly his executrix could do the same; for it is entirely well
settled that an executor or administrator can so transfer any negotiable security by his indorsement thereof.[2] If then, by the
transfer in Massachusetts, the property passed to the indorsee,
it is difficult to perceive why that transfer was not as effectual
in Maine as in Massachusetts; and by the law of both states, an
indorsee may sue on negotiable instruments in his own name. (c)
In truth, such instruments are treated, not as mere choses in
action, but rather as chattels personal.[3] Choses in action are

[1] Stearns v. Burnham, 5 Greenl. (Me.) 261; Thompson v. Wilson, 2 N. H.
291. But see Huthwaite v. Phaire, 1 Man. & Gr. 159, 164; and Rand v.
Hubbard, 4 Met. (Mass.) 252, 258, 259; post, s. 516, 517.

[2] See Rawlinson v. Stone, 3 Wilson, 1; 2 Str. 1260.

[3] McNeilage v. Holloway, 1 B. & A. 218. But see Richards v. Richards, 2
B. & Ad. 447, 452, 453; ante, s. 355.

(a) See Levy v. Levy, 78 Penn. St. 507; Dixon v. Ramsay, 3 Cranch, 319; Pond v. Makepeace, 2 Met. (Mass.) 114; Harper v. Butler, 2 Pet. 239.

(b) In the second edition of Green-leaf's Reports, by Bennett, in 1852, it appears that this note was made and indorsed in Massachusetts.

(c) See Barrett v. Barrett, 8 Greenl. (Me.) 353; Riddick v. Moore, 65 N. Car. 382; Levy v. Levy, supra.

not assignable by law, and actions must be brought thereon in
the name of the original parties.   But negotiable notes are transferable by indorsement, and when transferred, the indorsee
may sue in his own name.   Upon the reasoning in the above
case, the note would cease to be negotiable after the death of
the payee ; which is certainly not an admissible doctrine.[1]   The
decision in a recent case in the Supreme Court of the United
States is founded upon the doctrine that an assignment by an
executor of a chose in action in the state where he is appointed,
and which is good by its laws, will enable the assignee to sue in
his own name in any other state, by whose laws the instrument
would be assignable, so as to pass the note to the assignee, and
enable him to sue thereon.[2] (a)

360. *Presentment, Protest and Notice.* — As to bills of exchange
it is generally required, in order to fix the responsibility of other
parties, that upon their dishonor they should be duly protested by
the holder, and due notice thereof given to such parties.   And the
first question which naturally arises is, whether the protest and
notice should·be in the manner and according to the forms of the
place in which the bill is drawn, or according to the forms of
the place in which it is payable.   By the common law the protest
is to be made at the time, in the manner, and by the persons prescribed in the place where the bill is payable.[3] (b)   But as to the
necessity of making a demand and protest, and the circumstances
under which notice may be required or dispensed with, these are
incidents of the original contract, which are governed by the law

[1] Rawlinson v. Stone, 3 Wilson, 1 ; 2 Str. 1260; Bayley on Bills, c. 5, p. 78,
5th ed.   The effect of assignments of debts and other personal property will
come more fully under review in the succeeding chapter, when we enter upon
the subject of the law which regulates the transfer of personal property.
Post, s. 395-400.

[2] 3 Kent Com. 88; Rand v. Hubbard. 4 Met. (Mass.) 252, 258, 259; Harper v. Butler, 2 Pet. 239.   The case of Trimbey v. Vignier, 1 Bing. N. C. 151
(ante, s. 353 a), seems to inculcate the doctrine as general, that a transfer of
property, good by the lex loci of the transfer, will, at least in cases of negotiable instruments, be held good everywhere, so as to enable the indorsee to sue
in his own name.

[3] Chitty on Bills, p. 193, 490, 506-508, 8th ed. ; post, s. 631.   See Rothschild
r. Currie. 1 Q. B. 43 ; Pothier, de Change. n. 155; Pardessus, Droit Com. tom.
6, art. 1497, 1489, n. 155, states the same point.

(a) Trecothick v. Austin, 4 Mason, 16.   (b) See ante, s. 314, note.

of the place where the bill is drawn.[1] They constitute implied
conditions, upon which the liability of the drawer is to attach,
according to the lex loci contractus ; and if the bill is negotiated,
the like responsibility attaches upon each successive indorser, according to the law of the place of his indorsement ; for each indorser is treated as a new drawer.[2] The same doctrine, according
to Pardessus, prevails in France.[3]

361. *Days of Grace.* — Upon negotiable instruments it is the
custom of most commercial nations to allow some time for payment beyond the period fixed by the terms of the instrument.
This period is different in different nations ; in some it is limited
to three days, in others it extends as far as eleven days.[4] The
period of indulgence is commonly call the days of grace ; as to
which, the rule is, that the usage of the place on which the bill
is drawn, and where payment of a bill or note is to be made,
governs as to the number of the days of grace to be allowed
thereon.[5] (*a*)

[1] Ibid. See Aymar *v.* Sheldon, 12 Wend. (N. Y.) 439; Chitty on Bills,
p. 490, 506–508, 8th ed.; 1 Boullenois, obs. 23, p. 531, 532; Pardessus, tom.
5, art. 1489, 1498; Savary, Le Parfait Négotiant, tom. 1, pt. 3, lib. 1, c. 14,
p. 851.

[2] See Rothschild *v.* Currie, 1 Q. B. 43; Pothier, de Change, n. 155; Bayley
on Bills, c. A, p. 78–86, 5th ed. by Phillips & Sewall; Chitty on Bills, c. 6,
p. 266, 267, 370, 8th ed.; Ballingalls *v.* Gloster, 3 East, 481; ante, s. 314–317.

[3] Pardessus, Droit Com. art. 1485, 1495, 1496–1499; Henry on Foreign
Law, 53, Appx. p. 239–248. Ante, s. 314–347. Boullenois admits that the
protest ought to be according to the law of the place where the bill is payable.
But in case of a foreign bill indorsed by several indorsements in different countries, he contends that the time within which notice or recourse is to be had,
upon the dishonor, is to be governed by a different rule. Thus, he supposes a
bill drawn in England on Paris in favor of a French payee, who indorses it to
a Spaniard in Spain, and he to a Portuguese in Portugal, and he to the holder;
and then says that the holder is entitled to have recourse against the Portu- .
guese within the time prescribed by the law of France, because the holder is
there to receive payment; the Portuguese is to give notice to the Spaniard
within the time prescribed by the law of Portugal, because that is the only law
with which he is presumed to be acquainted, &c.; and so in regard to every
other indorser, he is to have recourse within the period prescribed by the
law of the place where the indorsement was made, and not of the domicil
of the party indorsing. 1 Boullenois, obs. 20, p. 370–372; Id. obs. 23, p.
531, 532.

[4] Bayley on Bills, 5th Am. ed. by Phillips & Sewall, p. 234, 235; Chitty on
Bills. p. 407, 8th ed.; Id. p. 193.

[5] Ibid.; Bank of Washington *v.* Triplett, 2 Pet. 30, 34; ante, s. 316–347;

(*a*) See Commercial Bank *v.* Barksdale, 36 Mo. 563; ante, s. 314, note.

362. *Situs of Debts.* — This head respecting contracts in general may be concluded by remarking that contracts respecting personal property and debts are now universally treated as having no situs or locality; and they follow the person of the owner in point of right (mobilia inhærent ossibus domini);[1] although the remedy on them must be according to the law of the place where they are sought to be enforced. The common language is: 'Mobilia non habent sequelam; mobilia ossibus inhærent; actor sequitur forum rei; debita sequuntur personam debitoris.'[2] (a) That is to say: they are deemed to be in the place, and are disposed of by the law, of the domicil of the owner, wherever in point of fact they may be situate. 'Quin tamen ratione mobilium,' says Paul Voet, a strenuous opposer of the general doctrine of the extra-territorial operation of statutes, 'ubicunque sitorum, domicilium seu personam domini sequamur.'[3] Burgundus says: 'Sed tamen, ut existimem, bona moventia, et mobilia, ita comitari personam, ut extra domicilium ejus censeantur existere; adduci sane non possum.'[4] Rodenburg says the same. 'Diximus, mobilia situm habere intelligi, ubi dominus instruxerit domicilium, nec aliter mutare eundem, quam una cum domicilio.'[5] He goes on to assign the reasons, founded upon the perpetually

Pardessus, tom. 6; Chitty on Bills, p. 407, 8th ed.; Id. p. 193; 2 Boullenois, obs. 23, p. 531, 532, and Mascard. Conclus. 7, n. 72, there cited.

[1] Thorne v. Watkins, 2 Ves. 35; 1 Boullenois, obs. 20, p. 348; Livermore, Dissert. s. 251, p. 162, 163; P. Voet, de Statut. c. 2, s. 4, n. 8, p. 126, ed. 1715; Id. p. 139, ed. 1661; post, s. 377, 378.

[2] Kames Eq. b. 3, c. 8, s. 3, 4; Dwarris on Statutes, pt 2, p. 650; Livermore, Dissert. s. 251, 252, 254, p. 162, 163, 167; Foelix, Confl. des Lois, Revue Étrang. et Franç. tom. 7, 1840, s. 32, p. 221–226; Id. s. 33, p. 227, 228; Christinæus, ad Cod. 1, 1, decis. 5, n. 1–3, p. 7; 3 Burge, Col. & For. Law, pt. 2, c. 20, p. 777; post, s. 376–385, 395–400.

[3] P. Voet, de Statut. s. 4, c. 2, n. 8, p. 126; Id. p. 139, 140, ed. 1661.

[4] Burgundus, tract. 2, n. 20, p. 71.

[5] Rodenburg, de Diver. Statut. tit. 2, c. 1, n. 1; 2 Boullenois, Appx. p. 14, 15.

(a) *Creditoris?* — Whether "debitoris" or "creditoris" would doubtless depend upon circumstances. In a question of distribution of the estate of the debtor, the law of the debtor's domicil would ordinarily apply; while in a question of distribution of the creditor's estate the law of *his* domicil would probably prevail, at least if domicil and forum were the same. In a contest between several creditors the lex situs of the debtor's property would govern. Again, in a contest between the creditor and the debtor, the place of the contract would govern the validity of the transaction. See note to s. 383, post.

changeable location of movables. Pothier is equally expressive
on the same point.[1] Indeed, the doctrine is so firmly established
that it would be a waste of time to go over the authorities ;[2] and

[1] Post, s. 381.

[2] See Bouhier, Coutum. de Bourg. c. 21, s. 172, p. 408; Id. c. 22, s. 79, p. 429;
Id. c. 25, s. 5, 6, p. 490; Pothier, des Choses, tom. 8, pt. 2, s. 3, p. 109, 110;
Id. Coutum. d'Orléans, tom. 10, n. 24, p. 7; 2 Bell Com. 684, 685, 4th ed.;
Bruce v. Bruce, 2 B. & P. 230; Sill v. Worswick, 1 H. Bl. 690, 691; In re
Ewing, 1 Tyrw. 91; Thorne v. Watkins, 2 Ves. 35; 4 Cowen (N. Y.) 517, note;
Blanchard v. Russell, 13 Mass. 6; Livermore, Dissert. 163–171; Foelix, Conf.
des Lois, Revue Étrang. et Franç. tom. 7, 1840, s. 31, p. 220, s. 32, p. 221,
s. 36, p. 229. There are some few jurists who seem to dissent from the doctrine, either in a qualified or absolute manner, who are cited by M. Foelix.
He enumerates Tittman, Muhlenbruch, and Eichhorn. Id. p. 223, 224. John
Voet has expounded this whole doctrine very fully. 'Atque ita,' says he,
'evictus hactenus existimo, in omnibus statutis, realibus, personalibus, mixtis,
aut quacunque alia sive denominatione sive divisione concipiendis, verissimam
esse regulam, perdere omnino officium suum statuta extra territorium statuentis;
neque judicem alterius regionis, quantum ad res in suo territorio sitas ex necessitate quadam juris obstrictum esse, ut sequatur probetve leges non suas. In
eo tamen forte scrupulus hæserit; si scilicet hæc ita sint, qui ergo fiat, quod
vulgo reperitur traditum, in successionibus, testandi facultate, contractibus,
aliisque, mobilia ubicunque sita regi debere domicilii jure, non vero legibus
loci illius in quo naturaliter sunt constituta; videri enim hac saltem ratione
jurisdictionem judicis domicilii non raro ultra statuentis fines operari in res
dispersas per varia aliorum magistratuum, etiam remotissimis ad orientem
occiduumque solem regionibus imperitantium, territoria. Sed considerandum,
quadam fictione juris, seu malis, præsumptione, hanc de mobilibus determina-
tionem conceptam niti: cum enim certo stabilique hæc situ careant, nec certo sint
alligata loco; sed ad arbitrium domini undiquaque in domicilii locum revocari
facile ac reduci possint, et maximum domino plerumque commodum adferre
soleant, cum ei sunt præsentia; visum fuit, hanc inde conjecturam surgere,
quod dominus velle censeatur, ut illic omnia sua sint mobilia, aut saltem esse
intelligantur, ubi fortunarum suarum larem summamque constituit, id est, in
loco domicilii. Proinde si quid domicilii judex constituerit, id ad mobilia
ubicunque sita non alia pertinebit ratione, quam quia illa in ipso domicilii loco
esse concipiuntur. Si tamen has juris fictiones quis a ratione naturali, in
hisce solum consideranda, alienas putet, quippe desiderantes unum communem
legislatorem, lege sua fictiones tales introducentem ac stabilientem; non equidem repugnaverim, atque adeo tunc hoc ipsum comitati, quam gens genti
præstat, magis, quam rigori juris, et summæ potestati, quam quisque magistratus in mobilia, suo in territorio constituta, habet, adscribendum putem.
Præsertim cum considero, subinde per magistratus loci, in quo mobilia vere
existunt, de illis ea constitui sancirique, quæ domicilii judici displicere possent. Quid enim, si domicilii judex frumenta importari jubeat, penuria
frugum vexata regione; incola spe lucri majoris frumenta sua in alia regione horreis recondita inferre desiderit; regioni vero isti imperans omnem
vetuerit frugum exportationem, jure suo in sui territorii frumentis usus?
Quis hic obsecro negare sustineat, mobilia regi lege loci, in quo vere
sunt, non in quo ob domicilium domini esse finguntur. Nec minus id in

especially as the same subject will occur in a more general form in the succeeding chapter.[1]

362 *a*. *Debts*. — Debts in the vocabulary of the civil law are often known by the title of nomina debitorum ;[2] and they also follow the person of the owner, or as Jason says : ' Nomina infixa sunt ejus ossibus.'[3] Burgundus also says : ' Nomina et actiones loco non circumscribuntur, quia sunt incorporales ; tamen et ibi per fictionem esse intelliguntur, ubi creditor habet domicilium. Nam, quod quidam ossibus creditoris, esse affixa putant, non magis movet, quam si dicamus, dominium fundi esse in proprietario ; cum alioquin, si quis strictius interpretetur, aliud est fundus, aliud dominium ; sicuti aliud est obligatio, aliud creditum.'[4] Dumoulin is equally explicit. ' Nomina et jura, et quæcumque incorporalia, non circumscribantur loco ; et sic non opus est accedere ad certum locum. Tum si hæc jura alicubi esse censerentur, non reputarentur esse in re pro illis hypothecata, nec in debitoris personâ, sed magis in persona creditoris, in quo active resident, et ejus ossibus inhærent.'[5]

362 *b*. The language of Hertius is : ' Mobilibus interdum etiam κατ᾽ ἀναλογίαν (nam proprie neque mobiles sunt, nec immobiles) accensentur res incorporales.'[6] Huberus holds them to fall under the class of movables.[7] Paul Voet says : ' Verum, quid de

rerum publicationibus ex delicto apparet, in quantum fisco loci in quo reus condemnatus est, non sunt cessura bona omnia mobilia ubicunque sita, sed ea sola, quæ in loco condemnantis inveniuntur; nisi aliud ex comitate alicubi servetur. Nec dicam, variare de rebus quibusdam locorum plurimorum statuta, utrum mobilibus illæ, an immobilibus accensendæ sint; nec novum esse, ut quæ una in regione mobilia habentur, immobilium catalogo alibi adscripta inveniantur; annui, verbi gratia, reditus a Provincia debiti, in Hollandia mobiles, immobiles Trajecti: arbores grandiores solo hærentes passim immobiles, mobiles tamen in Flandria habitæ. Quo posito, necesse fuerit, ut, quæ in domicilii loco mobilia habentur, immobilia vero illic ubi sunt, regantur lege loci in quo vere sunt, magistratu ne ex comitate quidem permissuro, ut quasi mobilia domicilii dominici sequerentur jura.' J. Voet, ad Paud. 1, 4, 2, s. 11, p. 44, 45; post, s. 481, 482.

[1] Post, s. 374–401.

[2] Ersk. Inst. b. 3, tit. 9, s. 4; Cujaccii Opera, tom. 7, p. 491, ed. 1758; Dig. 10, 2, 2, 6; Vicat. Vocab. Voce, Nomen.

[3] 1 Boullenois, obs. 20, p. 348. [4] Burgundus, tract. 2, n. 33, p. 73.

[5] Dumoulin, de Consuetud. Paris. tom. 1, de Fiefs, tit. 1, gloss. 4, n. 9, p. 56, 57; Livermore Dissert. s. 251, p. 162, 163; 3 Burge, Col. & For. Law, pt. 2, c. 20, p. 777; post, s. 392–400.

[6] Hertii Opera, de Collis. Leg. s. 4, n. 6, p. 122, 123, ed. 1737; Id. p. 174, ed. 1716. [7] Ibid.

nominibus et actionibus statuendum erit? Respondeo, quia proprie loquendo, nec mobilium nec immobilium veniunt appellatione; etiam vere non sunt in loco, quia incorporalia. Ideo non sine distinctione res temperari poterit. Aut igitur realis erit actio, tendens ad immobilia, et spectabitur statutum loci situs immobilium. Aut erit actio realis spectans mobilia, et idem servandum erit, quod de mobilibus dictum est. Aut erit actio personalis sive ad mobilia sive ad immobilia pertinens, quæ cum inhæreat ossibus personæ statutum loci creditorum æstimari debebit.' [1]

363. *Contracts concerning Immovables.* — But a question of a very different character may arise as to executory contracts respecting real estate or immovables. Are they governed by the law of the place where the contract is made, or by the law of the place where the property is situate? Take for instance the case of a contract for the purchase or sale of lands in England or America, arising under the statute of frauds, by which all contracts respecting real estate, or any interest therein, are required to be in writing; and otherwise they are void. If such a contract is made in France by parol or otherwise, in a manner not conformable to the law rei sitæ, for the purchase or sale of lands situate in England or in America, and the contract is conformable to the law of France on the same subject; is the contract valid in both countries? Is it valid in the country where the land lies, so as to be enforced there? If not, is it valid in the country where the contract was made? [2]

364. *Statute of Frauds.* — If this question were to be decided exclusively by the law of England, it might be stated that by the law of England such a contract would be utterly void; and it would be so held in a suit brought to enforce it in that realm, upon the ground that all real contracts must be governed by the lex rei sitæ.[3] (a) Lord Mansfield took occasion in a celebrated case to examine and state the principle. ' There is a distinction,' said he. ' between local and personal statutes. Local ones regard such things as are really upon the spot in England, as the statute of frauds, which respects land situate in this kingdom. So

[1] P. Voet, de Statut. s. 9, c. 1, n. 11, p. 256, ed. 1715, p. 312, 313. ed. 1661.

[2] Ante, s. 262; post, s. 435, 436–445. See 2 Burge, Col. & For. Law, pt. 2, c. 9, p. 840–871; 4 Id. pt. 2, c. 5, s. 11, p. 217.

[3] See 2 Dwarris on Statut. 648; Warrender v. Warrender, 9 Bligh, 127, 128; ante, s. 351 d.

(a) See Siegel v. Robinson, 56 Penn. St. 19.

stock-jobbing contracts, and the statutes thereupon, have a reference to our local funds. And so the statutes for restraining
insurances upon the exportation of wool respect our own ports
and shores. Personal statutes respect transitory contracts as
common loans and insurances.'[1] And in another report of the
same case, after a second argument, he said: 'In every disposition or contract where the subject-matter, relates locally to
England, the law of England must govern, and must have been
intended to govern. Thus a conveyance or will of land, a mortgage, a contract concerning stocks, must all be sued upon in England; and the local nature of the thing requires them to be
carried into execution according to the law here.'[2]

[1] Robinson v. Bland, 1 W. Bl. 334, 346; post, s. 383, and note.

[2] Robinson v. Bland, 2 Burr. 1079; 1 W. Bl. 259. See also Ersk. Inst. b.
3, tit. 9, s. 4; Henry on For. Law, p. 12–15; Scott v. Alnutt, 2 Dow & Cl. 404.
See also Selkrig v. Davis, 2 Dow, 230, 250; post, s. 383, 435. Mr. Burge,
speaking on this subject, says: 'There is an entire concurrence amongst
them (jurists) in considering that the title to movables, or the validity of any
disposition of them, is not governed by the law of their actual situs. This,
which may be regarded as a general rule, is subject to this qualification, that
the law of the country in which the movable may be actually situated has
not prescribed some particular mode by which alone the movable can be transferred. Thus property in the public funds or stocks, shares in companies,
joint stocks, &c., is a species of personal property, which as it is created, so
it is regulated by the law of the country in which it exists. Certain forms are
prescribed, by which alone the holder of any share or interest can transfer it.
Here the transfer is so far subject to the law of the place where the property
is situated, that the legal title to it is not acquired unless those forms are observed. But although the contract may, in consequence of a non-compliance
with those forms, fail in conferring the legal title on the disponee, yet it will
give him a right to compel the disponer, by action or suit, to make a transfer
in the manner required by the local law. To this limited extent the lex loci rei
sitæ affects and controls the transfer by acts inter vivos of certain movables.
But unless the local law gives to them the quality of immovable or real, as it
may do, and has done in many instances, they still, as subjects of succession,
are governed by the law of the owner's domicil. The rule is, that the title to
movable property is governed by the law of the place of the owner's domicil;
and this rule is uniformly applied in deciding on the title to movable property
as a subject of succession. The law of the owner's domicil is not that which
exclusively decides on the title to movable property as a subject of transfer
and acquisition by acts inter vivos. When contracts of purchase and sale,
mortgage or pledge, are complete in a place which is not the domicil of the
owner, the validity of such contracts and the rights and obligations which they
confer are governed by the law of the country in which they are completed.
" Semper in stipulationibus, et in cæteris contractibus id sequimur, quod actum est; aut si non pareat, quid actum est, erit consequens, ut id sequamur,
quod in regione in qua actum est frequentatur." "Generaliter enim in

865. *Doctrine of Scotch Courts.* — The same doctrine has been laid down in equally emphatic terms in the Scottish courts. Lord Robertson in a highly interesting case said: ‘Although the rule as to the lex loci contractus is of very general application, particularly as to the constitution and validity of personal contracts and obligations, it is not universal. In the first place, it does not apply to contracts or obligations relative to real estates.’[1] Lord Bannatyne, on the same occasion, affirmed the like principle.[2] And it has received an unequivocal sanction in America, where it has been broadly declared to be a well-settled rule, that any title or interest in land or in other real estate can only be acquired or lost agreeably to the law of the place where the same is situate.[3] (a)

865 a. *Paul Voet.* — Paul Voet has expressed the same opinion. ‘ Quid si itaque contentio de aliquo jure in re, seu ex ipsa se descendente? Vel ex contractu, vel actione personali, sed in rem scripta? An spectabitur loci statutum, ubi dominus habet domicilium, an statutum rei sitæ? Respondeo, statutum rei sitæ. Ut tamen actio etiam intentari possit, ubi reus habet domicilium. Idque obtinet, sive forensis sit ille, de cujus re controversia est, sive incola loci, ubi res est sita.’[4]

omnibus, quæ ad formam ejusque perfectionem pertinent, spectanda est consuetudo regionis, ubi sit negotiatio, quia consuetudo influit in contractus, et videtur ad eos respicere, et voluntatem suam eis accommodare.” ’ 3 Burge, Col. & For. Law, pt. 2, c. 20, p. 751, 752; 2 Id. pt. 2, c. 9, p. 863–870. See post, s. 434.

[1] Fergusson on Marr. & Div. p. 395, 397. See Ersk. Inst. b. 3, tit. 2, s. 40, p. 515; post, s. 436, and note.

[2] Fergusson on Marr. & Div. p. 401; 2 Kames on Equity, b. 3, c. 2, s. 2. Erskine, in his Institutes, seems to assert a more modified doctrine. He says: ‘All personal obligations or contracts entered into according to the law of the place where they are signed, or as it is expressed in the Roman law, secundum legem domicilii, vel loci contractus, are deemed effectual when they come to receive execution in Scotland, as if they had been perfected in the Scotch form. And this holds even in such obligations as bind the grantor to convey subjects within Scotland; for where one becomes bound by a lawful obligation he cannot cease to be bound by changing places.’ Yet Erskine afterwards adds that if an actual conveyance of the property had been made, not according to the Scotch forms, the courts of Scotland would not compel the party to convey, nor treat it as an obligation of the grantor to execute a more perfect conveyance. Ersk. Inst. b. 3, tit. 3, s. 40, 41, p. 515. See post, s. 436.

[3] Cutter v. Davenport, 1 Pick. (Mass.) 81; Hosford v. Nichols, 1 Paige (N.Y.) 220; Wills v. Cowper, 2 Hamm. 124; post, s. 424, 427, 435.

[4] P. Voet, de Statut. s. 9, c. 1, n. 2, p. 250, ed. 1715; Id. p. 305, ed. 1661; post, s. 426, 442.

(a) See Doyle v. McGuire, 38 Iowa, 410; Thurston v. Rosenfield, 42 Mo. 474.

366. *Scotch Heritable Bonds.* — This doctrine may be further illustrated by the case of Scotch heritable bonds. By heritable bonds in that law are meant bonds for the payment of money, which are secured by a conveyance or charge upon real estate. Such bonds usually contain not only a charge upon real estate, but a personal obligation to pay the debt. In general, by the Scotch law, mere personal bonds and other debts, on the decease of the creditor, pass to his personal representative; but heritable bonds belong to the heir; because the charge on the real estate, being jus nobilius, draws to it the personal right to the debt. According to the Scotch law, no contract or other act, disposing of an heritable bond, will be good unless it is according to the law of Scotland; and no contract, intended to create such a heritable bond, will be valid as such, unless it be made with the solemnities of the Scotch law.[1] There are other collateral consequences growing out of the same doctrine. Thus if a Scotch heir should seek to be exonerated from a heritable bond by the application of the personal assets in England, his right would depend upon the law of Scotland, that is, the law of the place where the real estate was situate; and would not depend upon the law of the place where the personal estate happened locally to be.[2]

367. *Money to be invested in Land.* — The same reasoning seems to have governed in the House of Lords in a recent case, where certain entailed estates in Scotland were sold for the redemption of the land-tax, and the surplus money of the proceeds of the sale was vested, according to a statute on the subject, in trustees, who were required to pay the interest of it to the heir of entail in possession, until the money should be reinvested in land. The heir of entail next entitled sold his reversionary and contingent right to the interest of this fund by a deed in the English form and executed in England, where the parties were domiciled, but without the solemnities required by the law of

[1] Ersk. Inst. b. 2, c. 2, s. 9–20, p. 198–204; Id. b. 3, tit. 2, s. 39–41, p. 514, 515; Jerningham *v.* Herbert, 1 Tamlyn, 103; 2 Bell Com. s. 608, p. 7, 8; s. 1266, p. 690, 4th ed.; Id. p. 687, 5th ed.; post, s. 485–489. Yet Mr. Erskine in his Institutes, seems to admit that obligations to convey things in Scotland, although not perfected in the Scottish form, yet if perfected according to the lex domicilii of the parties, are binding in Scotland, not as conveyances, but as contracts, under some circumstances. Ante, s. 365, note 2.

[2] Elliott *v.* Lord Minto, 6 Madd. 16; Winchelsea *v.* Garetty, 2 Keen, 293, 309, 310; ante, s. 266 a. See also 4 Burge, Col. & For. Law, c. 15, s. 4, p. 722 *et seq.*

Scotland. It was admitted that the fund was to go to the heirs in entail, and that the principal thereof was consequently herita-ble, and could only be passed according to the solemnities of the law of Scotland. But the House of Lords adjudged the inter-mediate interest of the surplus, before the investment in lands, to be movable property, and alienable by the proprietor as such; and therefore they held the assignment of it according to the English law good.[1]

868. *Views of Foreign Jurists.* — From what has been already stated in the preceding discussions, it will be seen that foreign jurists are by no means agreed in admitting the general doctrine.[2] On the contrary some of them maintain that the validity of a contract is, in all cases, to be governed by the law of the place where it is made, whether it regards movables or immovables.[3] Thus, in respect to the capacity of persons to contract, their doc-trine is, that if they are of age to contract in the place of their domicil, but are not in the place where their immovable property is situate, the contract to sell or alienate the latter will be valid everywhere; and so, vice versa.[4] Others hold a different opi-nion, and insist that, whatever may be the law of the domicil as to capacity, and although it governs the person universally, yet it does not apply to immovable property in another country.[5]

---

[1] Scott *v.* Alnutt, 2 Dow & Cl. 404, 412.

[2] Ante, s. 260–263. See also ante, s. 82, 325–327; post, s. 369–373, 474–479. See 2 Burge, Col. & For. Law, pt. 2, c. 9, p. 840–871.

[3] Ante, s. 52, 53, 60–62; post, s. 435–445. See also Foelix, Confl. des Lois, Revue Étrang. et Franç. tom. 7, 1840, s. 37, p. 307–311; Id. p. 352–360; post, s. 371 *f*, note. Mr. Burge has made a large collection of the various opinions of foreign jurists on this subject. 2 Burge, Col. & For. Law, pt. 2, c. 9, p. 840–871.

[4] Ante, s. 51–54, 58–63; post, s. 430–435; Rodenburg, tit. 1, c. 3; Id. tit. 2, c. 3; Livermore, Dissert. s. 44–46, p. 48, 49; Id. s. 55, 56, p. 56; Id. s. 58, 59, p. 58; 1 Boullenois, obs. 2, p. 27; Id. p. 145; Id. obs. 9, p. 152–154; Id. obs. 12. p. 175–177; Id. obs. 23, p. 456–460; 1 Froland, Mém. 156, 160. See on this point Foelix, Confl. des Lois, Revue Étrang. et Franç. tom. 7, 1840, s. 27–33, p. 216–228; 2 Burge, Col. & For. Law, pt. 2, c. 9, p. 840–870.

[5] Ante, s. 54–62; post, s. 430–432, 435–445; Livermore, Dissert. s. 44, p. 48, 49; Id. s. 46–53, p. 49–53; Id. s. 59, p. 58. See 1 Boullenois, obs. 6, p. 127–130, 135; Id. obs. 9, p. 150–156; J. Voet, ad Pand. 1, 4, s. 7, p. 40; 2 Fro-land, Mém. des Stat. 821. There are some nice distinctions put by different au-thors upon this subject, which are stated with great clearness and force by Mr. Livermore (Dissert. s. 58, p. 58–62), and upon which we may have occasion to comment more fully hereafter. At present it is only necessary to say that Boullenois, Bouhier, and others hold that, while the law of the domicil, as to

369. *Nuptial Contracts.* — So in respect to express nuptial contracts we have seen that many foreign jurists hold them obli-

general capacity, governs as to contracts and property everywhere, the law of the situs of immovable property governs as to the quantity which the party, having full capacity, may sell, convey, or dispose of. See Livermore, Dissert. s. 58-63, p. 58; 1 Boullenois, Prin. Gén. 8, p. 7; Id. obs. 6, p. 127-133; Id. obs. 12, p. 172, 175-178; Id. obs. 13, p. 177, 183, 184, 188, 189; Bouhier, Cout. de Bourg. c. 21, s. 68-70; Id. s. 81-84. See also 1 Boullenois, obs. 5, p. 101, 102, 107, 111, 112; 2 Henry, Œuvres, lib. 4, c. 6, quest. 105. Rodenburg seems to admit that a contract respecting real property, which is entered into according to the forms of the lex loci contractus, may be good to bind the party personally, although it is not according to the forms prescribed by the lex rei sitæ. Rodenburg, tit. 2, c. 3; 1 Boullenois, 414-416; 2 Boullenois, Appx. p. 19. Mr. Foelix has enumerated many of the jurists on each side of this question in his dissertation on the Conflict of Law, Foelix, Confl. des Lois, Revue Étrang. et Franç. 1840, tom. 7, s. 27-32, p. 216-221; 2 Burge, Col. & For. Law, pt. 2, c. 9, p. 840-870. Muhlenbruch, who is a very modern author, and is cited by Mr. Foelix, has a single passage on the subject, which, from its generality, may serve to show how difficult it is to obtain any certainty as to the exact opinion of foreign jurists on the various questions which may arise from the conflict of laws as to personal capacity, contracts, and rights to property. He lays down the following rules on the subject: '1. Jura atque officia ejusmodi, quæ hominum personis inhærent, et quasi sunt infixa, ex hisque apte pendentia, tum etiam ea, quæ ad universitatem patrimonii pertinent, ex legibus judicanda sunt, quæ in civitate valent, ubi is, de quo quæritur, larem rerumque ac fortunarum suarum summam constituit, scilicet non adversante exterarum civitatum jure publico. Enimvero mutato domicilio jura quoque hujusmodi mutantur, sic tamen, ut ne cui jus ex pristina ratione quæsitum, certisque suis terminis jam definitum eripiatur. 2. Jura, quæ proxime rebus sunt scripta, velut quæ ad dominii causam spectant, vel ad vectigalium tributorumque onus, vel ad pignorum in judicati executionem et capiendorum, et distrahendorum, tum etiam rerum apud judicem petendarum persequendarumve rationem, et quæ sunt reliqua ex hoc genere, æstimantur ex legibus ejus civitatis, ubi sitæ sunt res, de quibus agitur, atque collocatæ, nullo rerum immobilium atque mobilium habito discrimine. 3. Negotiorum rationem quod attinet, de forma quidem, quatenus non nisi ad fidem auctoritatemque negotio conciliandam valeat, nec in aliarum legum fraudem actum sit non est quod dubitemus, quin accommodate ad ejus loci instituta, ubi geritur res, dirigenda sit atque æstimanda. Nec est, quod non idem statuamus aut de personis, scilicet possintne omnino jure suo et velut arbitrio negotia instituere? Aut de negotiorum materia, atque vi et potestate quæ iis cum per se insit, tum vero quoad agendi excipiendique facultatem, hac tamen itidem adscripta exceptione, ut ne quid in aliena civitate fiat contra ejusdem civitatis mores, leges, instituta, ad quæ immutanda prorsus, nihil valet privatorum arbitrium. Quid? quod omnino sese, qui negotium aliquod instituerunt, tacite accommodasse videri possunt ad ejus regionis leges consuetudinesve, in qua ut exitum, habeat res, de qua agitur, aut legum decreto, aut privatorum auctoritate certo constitutum est. 4. Judex igitur, qui rem apud exteros natam judicabit, ea certe, quæ ad formam modumque litium instituendarum pertinent, ad jurium normas institutaque, quibus ipse paret, dirigat necesse est. In reliquis vero, quatenus aut idem illud ser-

gatory upon all property, whether movable or immovable, belonging to the parties in other countries, if they are valid by the
law of the place of the nuptial contract.[1]   And in respect to implied nuptial contracts, all those jurists who maintain that the
law of the domicil furnishes, in the absence of any express contract, the rule to ascertain the rights and intentions of the parties,
by way of tacit contract, necessarily give to the doctrine the same
universal operation.[2]

369 a. *Dumoulin.* — Dumoulin is most emphatic upon this matter. ' Primo, in sano intellectu,' says he, ' nullum habet dubium,
quin societas' (he is speaking of cases of marriage), ' semel contracta, complectatur bona ubicunque sita, sine ulla differentia
territorii, quam ad modum quilibet contractus, sive tacitus, sive
expressus, ligat personam, et res disponentis ubique.   Non obstat, quod hujusmodi societas non est expressa, sed tacita, nec
oritur ex contractu expresso partium sed ex tacito, vel præsumpto
contractu a consuetudine locali introducto.'[3]

370. *Merlin.* — Merlin seems to think that, although in general the French law must govern in all cases of immovables in
France, even when the owners are foreigners; yet that there are
exceptions to the rule. As, for instance, if the foreign law, in
the country where a contract is made respecting immovables, has
been adopted by the contracting parties, and converted by them
into an express contract; in such a case, he holds that the contract is binding, because the foreign law, as such, does not act

vet jus domesticum, aut jus exteris scriptum, tamquam privatorum voluntate
constitutum, in judicando sequatur, id ex principiis modo propositis quisque
qui facile intelliget.   Quibus etiam hæc esse consentanea videntur, ut præscriptio quidem acquisitiva, quam vocant, ex juribus rei sitæ, extinctiva vero
ex judicii accepti legibus æstimanda sit, præterquam quod nihil hac quoque
ratione juris detrahatur actori, si forte ingratiis suis loco haud condicto conve-
nire reum cogatur; ut actiones, quæ vel ad rescindenda negotia, vel ad damna
resarcienda comparatæ sunt, secundum legis loci, ubi res acta est, judicentur,
nisi si ut alio loco fiat solutio, inter partes convenerit.   Cæterum quæ de
negotiorum alibi contractorum in alieno territorio vi diximus atque potestate,
eadem sententiis quoque decretisque a judice prolatis aut convenient.   Muhlenbruch, Doctrina Pandectarum, tom. 1, p. 166-170.   See also P. Voet, de
Statut. s. 4, c. 2, n. 15, p. 127; Id. p. 142, ed. 1661.

[1] Ante, s. 143-160.

[2] Ante, s. 57, 143-171; Boullenois, obs. 5, p. 120, 121; Id. p. 673, 674; Id.
obs. 29, p. 757-767.

[3] Dumoulin, Consil. 53, tom. 2, s. 2, p. 964, ed. 1681; 2 Burge, Col. &
For. Law, pt. 2, c. 9, p. 864, 865; ante, s. 260.

upon the immovables in France, but it acts solely by way of contract.[1]   And he applies the same principle to cases where there is no express adoption of the foreign law, but where it arises by way of tacit contract from the place of the contract.[2]

371. *Pothier.* — On the other hand, Pothier treats as real property, not only lands and houses and inheritable property, but also all rights in them and growing out of them, such as ground-rents or other rents annexed to land and inheritances, which fall under the denomination of jus in re, and also all rights to inheritances which fall under the denomination of jus ad rem, such as contracts or debts (créances), respecting the sale and delivery of immovable property, which are deemed to have the same situation as the things which are the object of them. ' Les choses, qui ont une situation véritable, sont les héritages, c'est-à-dire, les fonds de terre, les maisons, et tout ce qui en fait partie. Les droits réels, que nous avons dans un hèritage, qu'on appelle jus in re, tels qu'un droit de rente foncière, de champart, &c., sont censés avoir la même situation que cet héritage. Pareillement, les droits que nous avons à un héritage, qu'on appelle jus ad rem, c'est-à-dire, les créances, que nous avons contre quelqu'un qui s'est obligé à nous donner un certain héritage, sont censés avoir la même situation que l'héritage qui en est l'objet.'[3] And he asserts the general principle that all things which have a real or fictitious situation are subject to the law of the place where they are situate or are supposed to be situate. ' Toutes ces choses qui ont une situation réelle, ou feinte, sont sujettes à la loi ou coutume du lieu où elles sont situées, ou censées d'être.'[4] This also is the doctrine maintained by Rodenburg and Boullenois.[5]

---

[1] Merlin, Répert. Lois, s. 6, n. 2, 3.   [2] Ibid.

[3] Pothier, Coutum. d'Orléans, c. 1, s. 2, n. 23, 24; Id. c. 3, n. 51; Id. Traité des Choses, s. 3; post, s. 382.

[4] Pothier, Coutum. d'Orléans, c. 1, s. 2, n. 24; Id. c. 3, n. 51; Id. Traité des Choses, s. 3.

[5] 1 Boullenois, Prin. Gén. 34–36, p. 8, 9; Id. obs. 5, p. 121, 129; Id. p. 223–225; Id. obs. 20, p. 374, 381, 488; 2 Boullenois, obs. 46, p. 472; Rodenburg, de Div. Stat. tit. 2, c. 2, n. 2, p. 15; Henry on Foreign Law, 14, note; Id. 15.   Cochin lays down the following doctrine: ' Les formalités, dont un acte doit être revêtu, se réglent par la loi, qui exerce son empire dans le lieu où l'acte a été passé; mais quand il s'agit d'appliquer les clauses qu'il renferme, aux biens des parties contractantes, c'est le lieu de la situation de ses biens, qui doit seul être consulté.'   And he illustrates by reference to a donation in Paris of property situate in places where donations inter vivos are pro-

Merlin, in a general view, assents to it.[1] Pothier further states
in relation to debts, which are but jus ad rem, that they follow the nature of the thing which is the object of the contract,
according to the maxim, 'Actio mobilis est mobilis; actio ad im-
mobile est immobilis.' Hence a debt due for money, or for any
movable thing, belongs to the class of movable property. So
also does a contract to do or not to do any particular thing. He
admits that the same rule applies, even when it is accompanied
by an hypothecation of immovable property therefor. So that,
when a debt is executed, and an hypothecation is made of immovable property as collateral security, the debt is still to be
deemed a movable debt, although the hypothecation might per
se, be an immovable debt; because the debt is the principal, and
the hypothecation the accessory; and accessorium sequitur naturam principalis.[2] But he insists that contracts which have for
their objects any inheritable property, or other immovable, are to
be deemed immovable property; such as, for instance, in the
case of a contract for the purchase of real estate, the right of the
vendee against the vendor for the delivery of the same.[3]

371 a. *D'Argentré.* — D'Argentré says: Whenever the question respects immovables or inheritances situate in different
places, where there are different modes of acquiring, transferring, and asserting ownership, and the question is, by what law
they are to be governed, the most certain rule in use is, that the
law of the place where the property is situate is for the most part
to be observed, and its laws, statutes, and customs to be observed.
He adds that this rule prevails in contracts, in testaments, and in
commercial matters. 'Cum de rebus soli, id est immobilibus,
agitur (qu'ils appellent d'héritage), et diversa diversarum posses-
sionum loca et situs proponuntur, in acquirendis, transferendis,
aut asserendis dominiis, et in controversia est, quo jure regantur,
certissima usu observatio est, id jus de pluribus spectari, quod loci

hibited, holding that such donations, although clothed with all the proper
Parisian formalities, are nullities. He then adds, 'Ce n'est donc pas la loi du
lieu où l'acte a été passé, qui en détermine l'effet.' Cochin, Œuvres, tom. 5,
p. 697. See also 1 Boullenois, Prin. Gén. 31, p. 8.

[1] Merlin, Répertoire, Meubles, s. 5; Id. Biens, s. 2, n. 2; Id. Loi, s. 6, n. 3.
[2] Pothier, Coutum. d'Orléans, c. 1, s. 2, n. 24; Id. n. 50.
[3] Pothier, Coutum. d'Orléans, c. 3, art. 2, n. 50, 51; Id. Traité des Choses,
s. 2. See Merlin, Répertoire, Biens, s. 1, n. 13, s. 2, n. 1; Id. Meubles, s. 2,
3; Livermore, Dissert. p. 162, 163.

est, et suas, cuique loco leges, statuta, et consuetudines servandas, et qui cuique mores de rebus, territorio, ét potestatis finibus sint recepti, sic ut de talibus nulla cujusquam potestas sit præter territorii legem.   Sic in contractibus, sic in testamentis, sic in commerciis omnibus, et locis conveniendi constitutum ; ne contra situs legem in immobilibus, quidquam decerni privato consensu, et par est sic judiciari.' [1]

371 *b. Christinæus.* — Christinæus adopts the very language of D'Argentré with seeming approbation ; [2] although there are other passages in which he seems to admit that a different rule prevails in respect to the acts which are done by a party, which are to be governed by the lex loci actus.   At least he cites without disapprobation the doctrine of Baldus (who certainly contradicts himself in the passages cited) that, in the solemnities of testaments, the law of the place where the testament is made, is to govern, even although the property is situate elsewhere. [3]   However, he admits that in Belgium, by an express edict, the law of the situs in such cases prevails. [4]

371 *c. John Voet.* — John Voet has expressed a very different opinion.   He holds that it is sufficient in all cases, whether the contract respects movable property or immovable property, to follow the law of the place where the contract is made and the act done, whether it be a contract or a will. 'Neque minus de statutis mixtis, actus cujusque solemnia respicientibus, percrebuit, insuper habitis de summo cujusque jure ac potestate ratiociniis, ad validitatem actus cujusque adhibitionem solemnitatum, quas lex loci, in quo actus geritur, præscripserit observandas; sic ut quod ita gestum fuerit, sese porrigat ad bona mobilia et immobilia, ubicunque sita aliis in territoriis, quorum leges longe alium, longeque pleniorem requirunt solemnium interventum.' [5]   He assigns as the principal reason, that otherwise, from ignorance or want of skill, it would be almost impossible for a man who possessed real property, to make a valid disposition thereof by an act inter vivos, or by testament. [6]   He adds that this rule prevails in Belgium, in Spain, in Germany, and in France. [7]

[1] D'Argent. ad Boit. Leg. de Donat. art. 218, gloss. 6, n. 3, vol. 1, p. 637; post, s. 438.

[2] Christinæus, tom. 2, decis. 3, n. 1, 2; Id. decis. 4, n. 1, 4–6, p. 4–6.

[3] Id. decis. n. 7.   [4] Id. decis. 4, n. 1–3, p. 6.

[5] J. Voet, ad Pand. 1, 4, 2, s. 13, p. 45.   [6] Ibid.

[7] Ibid., citing authorities. His language is: 'Quod ita placuisse videtur,

371 *d*. *Paul Voet.* — Paul Voet holds a similar opinion, and puts several cases to illustrate it. If a testator in the place of his domicil makes a will according to the law of the place rei sitæ, but not according to the law of the place of his domicil, he asks the question, whether such a will is good as to property situate elsewhere; and he answers in the negative. He next puts the case of a testator, who makes his will according to the law of his place of domicil, as for example, before a notary and two witnesses; and asks whether the will has effect upon property situate in another country where more and other solemnities are required; and he answers in the affirmative. He then asks, if a foreigner makes his will according to the law of the place where he is merely lodging or commorant, whether the will is valid elsewhere, where he either has immovable property, or he has his domicil; and he answers in the affirmative. The only exception he makes is, where the testator, in order to evade the law, or in fraud of the law of his own domicil, goes into another country, and there makes his will.[1]

tum, ne in infinitum prope multiplicarentur et testamenta et contractus, pro numero regionum diverso jure circa solemnia utentium; atque ita summis implicarentur molestiis, ambagibus, ac difficultatibus, quotquot actum, res plures pluribus in locis sitas concernentem, expedire voluerint: tum etiam, ne plurima bona fide gesta nimis facile ac prope sine culpa gerentis conturbarentur. Tum quia ne ipsis quidem in juris praxi versatissimis, multoque minus aliis simplicitate desidiaque laborantibus, ac juris scientiam haud professis, satis compertum est, ac vix per industriam exquisitissimam esse potest, quæ in unoquoque loco requisita sint actuum solennia, quid indies in hac vel illa regione novis legibus circa solennium observantiam mutetur: ut proinde, quæ ratio de militari testamento obtinuit Quiritium jure, milites nempe solennibus paganorum non fuisse adstringendos, dum in castris et expeditione occupati erant, quia et juris imperiti erant, et peritiores consulere in castris non poterant, etiam nunc suadeat, illum, qui actum gerit, ad alterius loci, quam in quo gerit, solennia non esse obligandum; quia et probabiliter aliorum locorum solennia ignorare potest, et in loco, in quo actum gerit, peritiores morum alienæ regionis non satis consulere; dum ita fere comparatum est, ut pragmatici, quibus auctoribus contractus celebrantur, aut conduntur testamenta, versati quidem plerumque satis sint in jure patrio, non item locorum omnium et universi orbis jure; atque insuper non raro moræ ad inquisitionem anxiam adhibendam impatiens est, quod geritur negotium. Quamvis ergo in Frisia septem testes in testamento requiri constet, alibi fere tabellionis testiumque duorum præsentia ac fides sufficiat, aut saltem in universum longe minor solennitas desideretur; tamen æquitate rei motus Frisiæ senatus ratam habuit de bonis Frisicis dispositionem, Sylvæducis coram parocho duobusque testibus declaratum, juxta Sylvæducensis regionis usum. Et ita in praxi hæc Belgis, Germanis, Hispanis, Gallis, aliisque, placuisse, auctores cujusque gentis testantur.'

[1] P. Voet, de Statut. s. 9, c. 2, n. 1–4, p. 261, 262, ed. 1715; Id. p. 317–319, ed. 1661.

371 *e. Hertius.* — Hertius, as we have seen,[1] lays down the rule, that, as to the forms and solemnities of acts and contracts, they are to be governed altogether by the law of the place where the acts are done, and contracts made, and not by the law of the domicil of the party, or the law of the situs rei. 'Si lex actui formam dat, inspiciendum est locus actus, non domicilii, non rei sitæ; id est, si de solennibus quæratur, si de loco, de tempore, de modo actus, ejus loci habenda est ratio, ubi actus vel negotium celebratur.'[2]   He adds: 'Regula hæc apud omnes, quantum quidem sciam, est indubitata;' and then says: 'Valet etiamsi bona in alio territorio sint sita.'[3]

372. *Burgundus.* — Burgundus apparently admits that generally the law of the place of the contract ought in all cases to prevail, so far as respects its form, its ceremonies, and its obligation.   The passage already cited[4] is to this effect. 'In scriptura instrumenti, in solemnitatibus, et ceremoniis, et generaliter in omnibus, quæ ad formam ejusque perfectionem pertinent, spectanda est consuetudo regionis, ubi fit negotiatio. Igitur, ut paucis absolvam, quoties de vinculo obligationis vel de ejus interpretatione vel interpretatione quæritur, veluti quos, et in quantum obliget, quid sententiæ stipulationem inesse, quid abesse credi oporteat, etc., ut id sequamur, quod in regione, in qua actum est, frequentatur.'[5]   But he immediately adds that, if we would know whether the contract was valid or not in respect to the subject-matter thereof, we must look to the law of the situs. 'Cæterum, ut sciamus, contractus ex parte materiæ utilis sit vel inutilis, ad leges, quæ rebus, de quibus tractatur, impressæ sunt, hoc est, ad consuetudinem situs, respiciemus.'[6]   He also expresses surprise, that authors, in considering contracts, should have excluded altogether the nature of the thing contracted for, and generally have interpreted contracts according to the law of the place where they are made; for in sales, and also in letting to hire, and in other contracts, it becomes us to look to the usage touching the subject-matter. 'Quippe non solum in emptione obtinet,

[1] Ante, s. 260.
[2] Hertii Opera, de Collis. Leg. s. 4, n. 10, p. 126, ed. 1737; Id. p. 179, 180; ante, s. 238.
[3] Ibid.   [4] Ante, s. 300 a.
[5] Burgundus, tract. 4, n. 7, 8, p. 104.
[6] Burgundus, tract. 4, n. 8, 9, p. 107, 108; 2 Boullenois, obs. 46, p. 450–454. See J. Voet, ad Pand. 1, 4, 2, s. 12, 13, p. 45; post, s. 433.

ut ad consuetudinem rei spectare deceat, sed in locatione præterea, in conductione, ceterisque contractibus.'[1]   It must be confessed that, on this subject, the distinctions and doctrines of
Burgundus are open to much question.

372 a. *Dumoulin. — Gaill.* — Dumoulin says that it is the general opinion of jurists that, wherever the custom or law of a place
prescribes the solemnities or form of an act, it binds foreigners
who there do the act ; and the act is valid and efficacious even in
respect to immovable property, beyond the territory of the custom
or law.   'Et est omnium doctorum sententia, ubicunque consuetudo, vel statutum locale, disponet de solemnitate, vel forma actus,
ligari etiam exteros, ibi actum illum gerentes, et gestum esse
validum, et efficacem, ubique etiam super bonis solis extra territorium consuetudinis vel statuti.'[2]   Gaill adopts an equally broad
conclusion.   'Contractus enim, celebratus cum solemnitate requisita in loco contractus, extendit se ad omnia bona, licet in loco
bonorum major solemnibus requiretur.'[3]

372 b. *Rodenburg.* — Rodenburg, as we shall presently see,
goes the full length of this doctrine, and applies it even to the
cases of wills and testaments, which, he says, if made according
to the law of the place where they are executed, are valid even
upon property situate elsewhere.[4]   There are many other jurists
who maintain the same opinion both as to contracts and other
instruments, and to wills and testaments.[5]

---

[1] Burgundus, tract. 4, n. 9; Id. n. 7; ante, s. 302; post, s. 433–438.
[2] Dumoulin, Consil. 53, tom. 2, s. 9, p. 965; post, s. 441.
[3] Gaill, Prac. obs. 123, n. 2, p. 548.
[4] Rodenburg, de Div. Statut. tit. 2, c. 3, n. 1; 2 Boullenois, Appx. p. 19;
post, s. 475.
[5] Many of them are enumerated in 1 Boullenois, obs. 23, p. 491–516; ante,
s. 301.   M. Foelix has also given us a long list of jurists who hold the doctrine.   Indeed, he thinks the doctrine firmly and generally established. His
language is : 'Un principe aujourd'hui généralement adopté par l'usage des
nations, c'est que " la forme des actes est réglée par les lois du lieu dans lequel
ils sont faits ou passés." C'est-à-dire que, pour la validité de tout acte, il
suffit d'observer les formalités prescrites par la loi du lieu où cet acte a été
dressé ou rédigé: l'acte ainsi passé exerce ses effets sur les biens meubles
et immeubles situés dans un autre territoire, dont les lois établissent des
formalités différentes et plus étendues (locus regit actum).   En d'autres termes,
les lois qui règlent la forme des actes étendent leur autorité tant sur les
nationaux que sur les étrangers qui contractent ou disposent dans le pays, et
elles participent ainsi de la nature des lois réelles.   Le droit romain ne conti-
ent aucune disposition qui consacrât le principe, locus regit actum.   Les lois
dans lesquelles on a pretendu trouver cette règle, ne parlent point de la forme,

372 c. *Boullenois.* — Boullenois seems to have labored under
no small embarrassment as to the question, whether a contract

mais de la matière des contrats. Dès le temps des glossateurs, la question
s'est présentée par rapport aux testaments. Bartole a adopté l'affirmative:
Albert de Rosate s'est prononcé pour la négative, sur le motif que la loi
n'oblige que les sujets, et que ceux-ci seuls ont le droit d'employer une forme
prescrite. Plus tard, Cujas a soutenu, qu'il faut suivre la loi du domicile du
testateur; Fachinée exigeait l'accomplissement des formalités prescrites dans
le lieu de la situation des biens: Burgundus, tout en admettant la règle rela-
tivement aux contrats, la rejette quant aux testaments; il regarde comme
affectant la chose et comme lois réelles les solennités prescrites pour les testaments en invoquant l'édit de 1611 (pour les Pays-Bas), art. 12. Choppin, au
contraire, soutient que le testament fait en pays étranger, d'après les formes
prescrites dans le lieu de la confection, doit sortir ses effets, même à l'égard
des immeubles situés dans un autre lieu, et il rapporte un arrêt du parlement
de Paris, rendu en ce sens. Dumoulin, Mynsinger et Gail, professent la même
doctrine. Ces deux derniers auteurs attestent la jurisprudence constante de
la chambre impériale (Reichskammergericht) en ce sens. Mevius, en admettant aussi la règle générale, fait remarquer que la coutume de Lubeck ne la
reconnait que sous les trois conditions suivantes: 1°, maladie qui met le testateur en danger de mort; 2°, decès réel en pays étranger; 3°, absence de toute
intention de préjudicier aux héritiers naturels. Rodenburg et Voet, en adoptant
la règle par rapport aux contrats comme aux testaments, la motivent sur les
raisons suivantes: 1°, nécessité d'éviter aux individus possédant des biens
dans différents pays, l'embarras et la difficulté de rédiger autant de testaments
ou de contrats qu'il y a d'immeubles situés sous l'empire de lois différentes,
ou de remplir dans un même testament ou contrat toutes les solennités prescrites dans les divers lieux de la situation des biens; 2°, impossibilité dans
laquelle l'individu surpris à l'étranger par une maladie mortelle peut se trouver
de remplir les solennités prescrites dans le pays de son domicile ou de la
situation de ses biens; 3°, nécessité d'empêcher que les actes faits de bonne foi
soient annullés trop facilement sans la faute de la partie; 4°, impossibilité
pour la majeure partie des hommes de connaître les formes prescrites dans
chaque localité; 5°, enfin, Voet ajoute qu'il faut appliquer ici les motifs qui,
chez les Romains, ont fait introduire la forme simple du testament militaire.
En terminant, cet auteur cite presque tous ses devanciers indiqués ci-dessus, en
déclarant que l'opinion professée par lui a été reconnue par la jurisprudence dans
les Pays-Bas, en Allemagne, en Espagne, et en France. Tel est aussi le sentiment
de Zoesius, Grotius, Christin, Paul Voet, Vinnius, Jean de Sande, Vander Kessel, Vasquez, Perez, Cochin, Boullenois, Menochius, Carpzov, Huber, Hert, Hommel,
mel, Glück, Thibaut, Danz, Weber, Mansord, Muhlenbruch, Mittermaier,
Tittman, Merlin, Meier, Pardessus, Story, Rocco, Hattogh, et Burge." Foelix,
Conflit des Lois, Revue Étrang. et Franç. 1840, tom. 7, s. 40, 41, p. 346–350.
M. Foelix has however subsequently qualified the general doctrine here
stated by the following exceptions: ' L'acte fait d'après les formes prescrites
par la loi du lieu de sa rédaction est valable, non seulement par rapport aux
biens meubles appartenant à l'individu et qui se trouvent au lieu de son domicile, mais encore par rapport aux immeubles, en quelque endroit qu'ils fussent
situés. Cette dernière proposition, selon la nature des choses, admet une exception, dans le cas ou la loi du lieu de la situation prescrit, à l'égard des actes

was obligatory or not, merely by pursuing forms or solemnities prescribed by the law of the place where it is made. He puts

translatifs de la propriété des immeubles, ou qui y affectent des charges réelles, des formes particulières, qui ne peuvent être remplies ailleurs que dans ce même lieu ; telles sont le rédaction des actes par un notaire du même territoire, la transcription ou l'inscription aux registres tenus dans ce territoire des actes d'aliénation, d'hypothèque, etc. L'acte fait dans un pays étranger suivant les formes qui y sont prescrites, ne perd pas sa force, quant à sa forme, par le retour de l'individu au lieu de son domicile: aucune raison de droit ne milite en faveur de l'opinion contraire. La règle, locus regit actum, ne doit pas être étendue au delà des limites que nous lui avons tracées au n° 40 ; elle ne s'applique qu'à la forme extérieure, et non pas à la matière ou substance des actes, ainsi que nous l'expliquerons encore au s. suivant. Ainsi, dans un testa- ment, la capacité de la personne et la disponibilité des biens ne se règlent point par la loi du lieu de la rédaction. Dans les dispositions entre-vifs, soit à titre onéreux, soit à titre gratuit, la loi du lieu de la rédaction peut avoir influé, soit sur l'ensemble de l'acte, soit sur les termes employés par les parties ; et, sous ce double titre, cette loi peut être consultée par les juges comme moyen d'interprétation ; mais elle ne forme pas la loi décisive, à moins que les parties ne s'y soient soumises expressément.' He afterwards adds: ' La règle d'après laquelle la loi du lieu de la rédaction régit la forme de l'acte, admet différentes exceptions, dont voici les principales: 1°, Lorsque les con- tractants ou l'individu dont émane une disposition se sont rendus en pays étranger dans l'intention d'éluder une prohibition portée par la loi de leur domicile ; car la fraude fait exception à toutes les règles ; 2°, Lorsque la loi de la patrie défend expressément de contracter ou de disposer hors du territoire et avec des formes autres que celles prescrites par cette même loi ; car alors l'idée d'un consentement tacite de cette nation se trouve formellement exclue. Cette exception est la même que celle indiquée par M. Eichhorn, sous le n° 2 ; 3°, En cas d'opposition expresse du statut réel (voy. supra, n° 43) ; 4°, Lorsque la loi lieu la de la rédaction attache à la forme qu'elle prescrit un effet qui se trouve en opposition avec le droit public du pays où l'acte est destiné à recevoir son exécution ; 5°, Par rapport aux ambassadeurs ou ministres publics et à leur suite. Ces personnes ne sont pas soumises aux lois de la nation près de laquelle elles exercent leur mission diplomatique.' And he finally sums up thus: ' Une autre question est celle de savoir si le contractant ou disposant qui se trouve en pays étranger, peut se borner à employer les formes prescrites par la loi du lieu de la situation de ses immeubles, au lieu de suivre celle du lieu de la rédaction. Nous tenons pour l'affirmative, par une raison analogue à celle donnée sur la question précédente. Le statut réel régit les immeubles ; c'est un principe résultant de la nature des choses ; la permission d'user des formes établies par la loi du lieu de la rédaction de l'acte n'est qu'une exception introduite en faveur du propriétaire, et à laquelle il lui est loisible de renoncer. Tel est aussi le sentiment de Rodenburg, de Jean Voet, et de Vander Kessel ; Cocceji soutient même que la forme des actes entre-vifs ou testamentaires est régie exclusivement par la loi de la situation des biens. Fachinée et Burgundus (v. supra, n° 41) parta- geaient cet avis, mais par rapport aux testaments seulement. En Belgique, l'édit perpétuel de 1611, art. 13, ordonnait qu'en cas de diversité de coutumes au lieu de la résidence du testateur et au lieu de la situation de ses biens, on suivrait par rapport à la forme, et à la solennité, la coutume de la situation. Paul Voet, Huber,

the case of two persons contracting, who are domiciled in one place, and contract in another, and the thing, respecting which

Hert, Hommel, et l'auteur de l'ancien Répertoire de jurisprudence, se prononcent pour la nullité; ce dernier invoque l'autorité de Paul de Castres, au passage rapporté au n° précédent, et le principe que la loi lie tous les individus qui vivent dans son ressort, ne fût-ce que momentanément. Nous renvoyons à ce sujet aux observations présentées sur la question précédente. Mevius distingue entre le citoyen faisant partie de la nation dans le territoire de laquelle les biens sont situés, et l'étranger; il n'accorde qu'au premier la faculté de tester ou de contracter partout d'après les formes prescrites au lieu de la situation. L'auteur ne donne pas de motif de cette distinction, et nous ne pouvons la trouver fondée.' Foelix, Conflit des Lois, Revue Étrang. et Franç. 1840, tom. 7, s. 43-45, 48, 50, p. 352-360. See also the opinions of foreign jurists on the subject, 2 Burge, Col. & For. Law, pt. 2, c. 9, p. 840-871. In respect to some of these he has certainly been led into an error; and some speak so indeterminately that it is difficult to gather what their opinion is. It is certain that M. Foelix has misunderstood the opinion of Mr. Story in his Conflict of Laws (see s. 364); and also the opinion of Mr. Burge. See 1 Burge, Col. & For. Law, pt. 1, c. 1, p. 21-24. His language is : ' In examining all contracts, instruments, or dispositions, whether they are made inter vivos, or are testamentary, our attention may be directed to four subjects: the first is, the capacity of him who makes it; the second is, the property which is the subject or occasion of the contract or instrument; the third regards the formalities or ceremonies with which it is made; and the fourth is the judicial process by which the rights which it confers are to be enforced. The capacity of the party to make the instrument is ascertained by consulting the law of the place of his domicil; because it is that law, and that law alone, which affects the person, and which gives or denies him the capacity or power to make the instrument. With respect to the property, the subject of the contract, disposition, instrument, or testament, recourse is had to the real law, being that which prevails in the place in which the property, if immovable, is actually situated; or in which, if it be movable or personal, it is presumed to be situated; that is, in the place of the possessor's domicil. When however it is necessary to ascertain whether the contract be valid, what is its true construction and effect, and whether the instrument in which it is expressed, or whether a testament, be duly and formally made, recourse is had to the law of the place in which the contract is entered into, or the instrument or testament was made; because if it be made according to the forms prescribed by that law, it is valid everywhere. " Aut statutum loquitur de his, quæ concernunt nudam ordinationem vel solemnitatem actus, et semper inspicitur statutum, vel consuetudo loci, ubi actus celebratur, sive in contractibus, sive in judiciis, sive in testamentis, sive in instrumentis aut aliis conficiendis, ita quod, testamentum, factum coram duobus testibus in locis, ubi non requiritur major solemnitas, valet ubique." A distinction however must be observed between such solemnities as are purely formal, and those which are of the substance and essence of the disposition or instrument. There are some solemnities which intrinsically affect the disposition itself, so as to render their observance essential to its validity, whilst there are others which only extrinsically regard them. An example of the former description of solemnities is given by Stockman, in the case of a law which prohibits the husband and wife from

the contract is made, being situate in another, and asks what
ought to be the form and solemnities necessary to make it valid,
if in each place they are different. If it is clear that the forms
appertain to the solemnities of the act, he thinks that there is
no difficulty in affirming that the law of the place of the contract ought to govern. If the forms relate to the capacity of the
person, then the law of the place of his domicil ought to govern.
But if, on the contrary, they appertain either to the substantials of
the contract, or its nature, or its accidents, or its fulfilment (sive
ad substantialia contractus, sive ad naturalia, sive ad accidentalia,
aut complementaria), there is great difficulty ; and if any general
rule is established, either to follow the law of the place of the
contract, or that of the situs of the thing, or that of the domicil
of the contracting parties, a false principle will be introduced ;
for sometimes the formalities belong to the quality of the person,
sometimes to the contract, and sometimes to other things. He
therefore arrives at the conclusion that no universal rule can be
laid down applicable to all classes of cases.[1] In another place
Boullenois remarks that the French authors (nos auteurs) are

instituting the one the heir of the other, unless by a will executed before
two notaries. If the party made a will in the common form in a place where
no such law prevailed, it would be invalid in respect of property situated in
the place where it did prevail. Similar examples are afforded by the English
statute of frauds, which denies the capacity to devise real property, otherwise
than by a will attested by three or more credible witnesses ; and by the law of
Jamaica, which enables a married woman to convey her real estate, and a
tenant in tail to bar the remainder and acquire the fee by a simple conveyance ; but it requires, at the same time, that the married woman should be
examined apart from her husband, and that the conveyance should be acknowledged and recorded. The following example of that species of solemnity
which is extrinsic to the disposition is given by Stockman, in the case which
has been cited : " Si quis incola ditionis regiæ testetur in urbe Leodiensi, ubi
testatoris subscriptio in testamentis necessaria non est, sed sufficit communis
ritus, qui in aliis publicis instrumentis requiritur." There may be said to be
three species of solemnities : first, those which are requisite to enable the person ; as, for instance, the authority from the husband to the wife, essential by
the law of some countries to the validity of her act. These are derived from
and must be examined with reference to the law of the domicil, or the lex loci
rei sitæ. Secondly, those which form a part of and are essential to the act, such
as the delivery of the subject-matter of a gift. The third species of solemnities consists of those which are designed to establish the truth or authenticity of
the instrument, such as the proof by two or more notaries, or one notary and
two witnesses, or the number, age, and quality of witnesses required for the
validity of a will.'

[1] 1 Boullenois, obs. 23, p. 464–466 ; 2 Boullenois, obs. 46, p. 445.

generally of opinion that the law of the place of the contract is to govern. Locus contractus regit actum.[1] And he then proceeds to lay down certain rules on the subject, which have been already cited as the guiding principles.[2] And among them is the very important rule, applicable to the subject before us, that where the law requires certain formalities which are attached to the things themselves, the law of the situs or situation is to govern.[3]

372 d. *Distinction between Transfers of Immovables and Contracts to transfer. — Burge's Opinion.* — Mr. Burge, after suggesting that there are three species of solemnities, which he enumerates, adds : ' A further distinction may be made between those solemnities which relate to contracts and instruments for the transfer of real property, and those by which it is actually transferred. With respect to the first, those are to be followed which prevail in the place where those contracts are made, or those instruments executed ; but with regard to the actual transfer of such property, those are to be observed which are prescribed by the law of the place where it is situated. Thus a contract to sell or mortgage real property will be valid if the solemnities are observed which are required by the law of the place where the contract is made, and will be the foundation of a personal action against the party to that contract to compel the transport or mortgage of such property ; but no transport or mortgage will be complete, nor will the dominium in the property have been transferred or acquired, unless those solemnities are observed which are required by the law of the place where it is situated.'[4] Again he adds in another place : ' In considering the law by which the transfer of immovable property is governed, a distinction should be made between the contract to transfer and the actual transfer of the dominium. There may be cases in which the law of the domicil or that of the place of the contract will prevail, notwithstanding it may be opposed to that of the situs, whilst in other cases the law of the situs will prevent the contract taking effect. Thus instances are cited by jurists where the law of the domicil incapacitates the party from contracting, but the law of the situs authorizes the alienation of his

---

[1] 2 Boullenois, obs. 46, p. 456.   [2] Ante, s. 240.
[3] 2 Boullenois, obs. 46, p. 467; ante, s. 240.
[4] 1 Burge, Col. & For. Law, pt. 1, c. 1, p. 24; 2 Id. pt. 2, c. 9, p. 844, 845.

immovables. Thus by the law of Ghent, persons were minors
until they had attained the age of twenty-five years; but in
Hainault a person of the age of twenty might alienate his fief
situated in that country. An inhabitant of Ghent contracts to
sell a fief in Hainault of which he was the owner. The contract,
in the opinion of Burgundus, would create no obligation on him
to complete this alienation. " Ut puta, civis Gandensis ætate
minor, tamen vigesimum egressus annum, Hannonica feuda sine
auctoritate tutoris vendidit; procul dubio in ejusmodi actu nihil
agi existimandum est, et inutilem omnino contrahi obligationem;
quia Gandavi, qui aliter emancipati non sunt, ante vigesimum
quintum annum rebus suis intervenire prohibentur." But if
the alienation were actually made, the same jurist considers that
it would be valid: "Si tamen ejusmodi feudi mancipationem
fecerit venditor, tutum esse emptorem, et quod actum erit valere
quotidiana accipimus experientia, quando hæc sit ætas et compe-
tens, quæ in Hannonicorum feudorum alienatione requiritur.
Nec enim consuetudo Gandensis potest tollere libertatem manci-
pationis, quia res alienas legibus suis alligare non potest; hoc
enim jus dicere extra territorium." A decision is reported by
Stockman in which the same doctrine was held. T., being of
the age of twenty and married, was according to the law of his
domicil so far emancipated as to be capable of administering but
not of alienating his estate. He alienated a property situated
in Louvain, where the effect of his marriage gave him the full
capacity of majority. An action was brought by his heir to recover back the purchase-money, on the ground that T. was
incompetent by the law of his domicil to alienate his property,
and that this law extended to and prevented the disposition by
him of his property in Louvain. But the purchaser insisted,
and the court held, that the validity of the alienation must be
decided according to the law of Louvain, and dismissed the action. It follows from this doctrine that if the person competent
by the law of his domicil should contract to make an alienation
of property situated in a country where he was incompetent to
make it, his contract could not be enforced, although he might
be answerable in damages to the person with whom he had contracted. On the other hand, if he were incompetent by the law
of his domicil to contract, but competent to alienate by the lex
loci rei sitæ, and an alienation was actually made by him, it

would not be rescinded on the ground that he was incompetent by the law of his domicil to contract. In the cases put by Burgundus, and reported by Stockman, it will be perceived that the alienation was complete. It does not follow that if the vendor had refused to perform his contract, the forum of the rei sitæ would have enforced it. The doctrine of Rodenburg is, that the contract is a nullity, and that effect cannot be given to it in any court to compel its performance by the delivery of the property. Wesel, who concurs with Rodenburg, treats the delivery or mancipatio as the simplex implementum of the contract; and as it is required for the validity of a sale that there should have been a preceding contract, he urges: " Cum ergo totus venditionis contractus ob defectum ætatis sit irritus, nec sit quod mancipatione solemni impleri possit, utique nuda simplexque fundi mancipatio omnino nihil operatur, cessante causa ad mancipandum idonea." ' [1]

372 *e. Same continued.* — And again he says: 'So if those solemnities which the lex loci contractus requires have been observed, and the contract according to that law is valid and obligatory, it will be valid everywhere else. But the latter proposition is subject to the qualification that it does not affect immovable property subject to a law in the country of its situs which annuls a contract, because it has not been entered into with the solemnities which it requires. If the disposition of the law does not annul the contract on account of its non-observance of the solemnities which are prescribed, but gives to it a degree of authenticity or credit which it will want if they are not observed, or if, in other words, its effect is either to dispense with a more formal proof of the instrument, if it bears on it evidence of their observance, or if in consequence of the non-observance it attaches a presumption against the execution of the instrument, and therefore requires from the parties a greater burden of proof, such solemnities are to be classed amongst the proofs in the cause which are governed neither by the lex loci contractus, nor by that of the situs, but by that of the forum. This question, in the opinion of Paul Voet, regards " non tam de solemnibus, quam probandi efficacia ; quæ licet in uno loco sufficiens, non tamen ubique locorum; quod judex unius territorii

[1] 3 Burge, Col. & For. Law, pt. 2, c. 20, p. 844–846; Id. p. 867–870.

nequeat vires tribuere instrumento, ut alibi quid operetur.'"[1]
There are other jurists who maintain the same distinction.[2]

372 f. *Rule of the Common Law.* — That there may be some
ground for such a distinction as is above stated may well be
admitted. But that the rule generally prevails in all nations
may well be doubted. Thus, it seems very clear that a contract,
made in a foreign country, for the sale of lands situate in England, Scotland, or America, would not be held a binding contract

---

[1] 2 Id. pt. 2, c. 9, p. 867, 868. See also 3 Id. pt. 2, c. 20, p. 751, 752.

[2] P. Voet, ad Statut. s. 4, c. 2, n. 15, 16, p. 142, ed. 1661; Ersk. Inst. b.
3, tit. 2, s. 40. Mr. Burge adds on this point: 'When the question regards
the property which the law allows to be alienated, or the persons to whom, or
the purposes for which, its alienation may be made, it can be determined only
by the law of the situs. The statutes of mortmain, the law of death-bed, the
restriction of gifts inter conjuges, are strictly real laws to which the parties to
the contract must conform, although no such laws exist in the place of their
domicil, or in that of the contract. In these instances the law of the situs is
prohibitory, and impresses on the property a quality excluding it from the
alienation. A contract therefore to make such an alienation as would in any
of these respects contravene the law of. the situs would be wholly ineffectual.
But when the contract does not expressly, nor by necessary implication, contravene it, but, on the contrary, may be carried into effect consistently with
or by means of its provisions, although the contract itself may not give a title,
yet it will be the foundation of an action by the one to compel the other to
complete it in that manner which the law of the situs requires in order to give
him that title. The observation of Du Moulin, in commenting on an article
of the Coutume of Auvergne, illustrates this distinction. By that article all
contracts or conventions respecting the succession had the effect of vesting the
seisin in the person in whose favor they were made. This great jurist, while
he thus limits its operation, de prædiis sitis sub hac consuetudine, et non extra
ejus territorium, at the same time adds, Valet quidem pactio ubique, sed
translatio possessionis, quæ sit in vim consuetudinis, non valet nisi intra ejus
territorium. The deed by which parties in England convey an estate in British
Guiana has no effect as a transport of it, but it operates as a contract of transport, and enables the purchaser to compel the vendor to complete the transport
in the manner prescribed by the law of that settlement. Erskine has thus
stated the doctrine of the law of Scotland on this subject. All personal obligations or contracts entered into according to the law of the place where they
are signed, or secundum legem domicilii, vel loci contractus, are deemed as
effectual, when they come to receive execution in Scotland, as if they had been
perfected in the Scottish form. And this holds even in such obligations as
bind the grantor to convey subjects within Scotland; for where one becomes
bound by a lawful obligation, he cannot cease to be bound by changing places.
An English deed, if so executed in point of form as validly to carry a Scotch
heritage, will be given effect to in regard to such heritage, agreeably to the
law of Scotland, notwithstanding the same deed would by the English law,
under similar circumstances, be unavailable in respect of a heritage situate in
England.' 2 Burge, Col. & For. Law, pt. 2, c. 9, p. 845–848; Id. p. 864, 865.

in either of those countries, to be enforced in their courts in personam or in rem, unless the contract was in conformity to the forms prescribed by those countries.[1] At the same time it is quite possible that the same contract might be enforced in the country where it was made, if it should conform to the law of that country touching real property.[2] But after all, looking to the great diversity of views of foreign jurists, there is much reason to be satisfied with the general rule of the common law on this whole subject; that is to say, that in respect to movables the law of the place where the contract is made will, with few exceptions, be allowed to govern the forms and solemnities thereof;[3] but as to immovables, no contract is obligatory or binding unless the contract is made with the forms and solemnities required by the local law where they are contracted (lex situs).[4]

373. *Prohibitions of the Lex Situs.* — But whatever may be the true rule in cases where the law of the situs does not prohibit the contract, as, for instance, a contract for the sale of land, it is very clear that, if prohibited there, it is everywhere invalid to all intents and purposes. So the doctrine is laid down by Rodenburg. After remarking that, if a contract is made that the dotal rights shall be according to the custom of another place than that of the domicil of the husband, it will be good if there is no local law of either place which prohibits it; he adds that the contrary, if the contract is opposed to the local law, is true rei sitæ. 'Contra, si per leges loci, ubi bona constituta sunt, limitetur illud rerum immobilium doarium, &c.; eo quod nemini liceat privata cautione refragari legi publicæ negativæ aut prohibitoriæ.'[5] Boullenois also lays down the same rule among his general maxims: 'Une convention, toute légitime qu'elle soit en elle-même, n'a pas son exécution sur les biens, lorsqu'ils sont situés en coutumes prohibitives de la convention.'[6] Mr. Burge also lays down among his general principles the following rule. 'In a conflict between a personal law of the domicil and a real law, either of the domicil or of any other place, the real law prevails over the personal law. Thus, a per-

---

[1] Ante, s. 363–365.　　　　　　　　　　[2] Ante, s. 76.

[3] Ante, s. 362, 364; post, s. 379, 383, 384.

[4] Ante, s. 364–367, s. 382, 383.

[5] Rodenburg, de Div. Stat. tit. 3, c. 4, n. 1, 2; 2 Boullenois, obs. 42, p. 401, 402; Id. Appx. p. 79, 80.

[6] 1 Boullenois, Princ. Gén. 41, p. 9, 10; ante, s. 262.

son who has attained his majority has, as an incident to that status, the power of disposing by donation inter vivos of everything he possessed, and may, by the real statute of the place in which his property is situated, be restrained from giving the whole, or from giving it, except to particular persons.'[1]

[1] 1 Burge, Col. & For. Law, pt. 1, c. 1, p. 28, s. 20; Id. p. 26, s. 8, 9. It may be remarked that some of the general principles laid down by Mr. Burge in the chapter here cited, which he says 'may be adopted,' admit of grave question, and are not supported by the common law.